PENGUIN CLASSICS

THOMAS PAINE READER

THOMAS PAINE was born in Thetford, England, in 1737, the son of a staymaker. He had little schooling and worked at a number of jobs, including tax collector, a position he lost for agitating for an increase in excisemen's pay. Persuaded by Benjamin Franklin he emigrated to America in 1774. In 1776 he began his *American Crisis* series of thirteen pamphlets, and also published the incalculably influential *Common Sense*, which established Paine not only as a truly revolutionary thinker, but as the American Revolution's fiercest political theorist. In 1787 Paine returned to Europe, where he became involved in revolutionary politics. In England his books were burned by the public hangman. Escaping to France, Paine took part in drafting the French constitution and voted against the king's execution. He was imprisoned for a year and narrowly missed execution himself. In 1802 he returned to America and lived in New York State, poor, ill, unfairly attacked and largely despised for his extremism and so-called atheism (he was in fact a deist). Thomas Paine died in 1809. His body was exhumed by William Cobbett, and the remains were taken to England for a memorial burial. Unfortunately, the remains were subsequently lost.

MICHAEL FOOT was born in 1913 and was educated in Reading and at Oxford, where he read Philosophy, Politics and Economics. He became Editor of the *Evening Standard* in 1942 and subsequently of *Tribune*. He first entered Parliament as Labour Member for Devonport in 1945, and after a series of increasingly important political posts became Deputy Leader of the Labour Party in 1976 and Leader in 1980, until his resignation in 1983. He is Labour Member for Blaenau Gwent. Michael Foot is also the author of *The Pen and the Sword* (1957), *Anuerin Bevan, Vol. 1, 1897–1945* (1962), and *Vol. 2, 1945–1960* (1973), *Debts of Honour* (1980) and *Another Heart and Other Pulses* (1984).

ISAAC KRAMNICK was born in 1938 and educated at Harvard University, where he received a BA degree in 1959 and a PhD in 1965, and at Peterhouse. He has taught at Harvard, Brandeis, Yale and Cornell, where he is now Professor of Government. He is married to Miriam Brody and lives in Ithaca, New York. Among his publications are *Bolingbroke and His Circle*, *The Rage of Edmund Burke*; and numerous articles on eighteenth-century topics. He has edited William Godwin's *Enquiry Concerning Political Justice* and Thomas Paine's *Common Sense* for Penguin Classics.

THOMAS PAINE
READER

EDITED BY MICHAEL FOOT
AND ISAAC KRAMNICK

PENGUIN BOOKS

Penguin Books Ltd, Harmondsworth, Middlesex, England
Viking Penguin Inc., 40 West 23rd Street, New York, New York 10010, U.S.A.
Penguin Books Australia Ltd, Ringwood, Victoria, Australia
Penguin Books Canada Ltd, 2801 John Street, Markham, Ontario, Canada L3R 1B4
Penguin Books (N.Z.) Ltd, 182–190 Wairau Road, Auckland 10, New Zealand

This collection first published 1987

Made and printed in Great Britain by
Richard Clay Ltd, Bungay, Suffolk
Typeset in 10 on 12 pt. Monophoto Bembo

CONTENTS

EDITORS' INTRODUCTION:
THE LIFE, IDEOLOGY AND LEGACY
OF THOMAS PAINE

In Number VII of his *American Crisis*, addressed in 1778 'To the People of England', Thomas Paine described his feelings on arriving in America four years earlier. An unknown Englishman of thirty-seven undistinguished years, he was plunged into tumultuous Philadelphia:

I happened to come to America a few months before the breaking out of hostilities . . . The world could not then have persuaded me that I should be either a soldier or an author . . . But when the country, into which I had just set my foot, was set on fire about my ears, it was time to stir. It was time for every man to stir.

Few men have 'stirred' as much as Paine would in the last quarter of the eighteenth century.

PAINE'S LIFE

Thomas Paine was born in the country town of Thetford, Norfolk, on 29 January 1737. His father, Joseph Paine, was a respected Quaker staymaker, his mother the daughter of an attorney. Tom was raised a Quaker and schooled in the village from his sixth to his thirteenth year. In 1750 he was apprenticed to his father's shop, where he learned the trade of making women's corsets and inserting their steel or whalebone ribs. He ran away from home at the age of sixteen and went to sea on a merchant ship only to be brought back by his father. Three years later he left Thetford for good.

Staymaking was his trade. In 1757 he turned up in London as a journeyman staymaker and a year later in Dover. He then moved on to the small village of Sandwich on the coast, where he opened a shop of his own. There he met and married, in 1759, Mary Lambert, a maid in service to the local woollen draper's wife. It was a short-lived marriage, for she died the next year. Two years later Paine abandoned staymaking and started a new career as exciseman, a customs official assigned to collect the internal duties levied on beverages, tobacco and other household items. For the next few years he was assigned to Lincolnshire. In 1765 he lost his job because he had stamped goods that he had not, in fact, examined. A one-year return to staymaking in the village of Diss in Norfolk was followed by some months teaching English in London and several more as tutor and itinerant preacher. Paine was reinstated in the Excise Service in 1768 and assigned to Lewes in Sussex, where he remained for the next six years.

Throughout these itinerant years Paine pursued a disciplined regimen of self-education. He bought books and scientific equipment from his meagre earnings and attended lectures whenever possible. Having settled down in Lewes at the age of thirty-one, he turned to politics, business and family. He became a regular at the White Hart social club where national and parish politics were the constant topics of conversation. Contemporaries later noted what a joy it was to hear young Tom Paine take on the town officers in debate after a few beers. It was a reputation that would haunt Paine all his life. In addition to politics and drink Paine devoted a good deal of the time left over from his official excise duties to a snuff, tobacco and grocery business. He had little head for business and the shop fared poorly. He also remarried in Lewes. His second wife was the daughter, ten years his junior, of the former owner of his shop. In April 1774 the business failed. The marriage did no better; he and his second wife were permanently separated.

There was one important and enduring achievement in those six years in Lewes, however. Paine found his first cause and he threw himself into it with the same zeal that he would later bring to the American and French revolutions. Excise officers throughout Britain were seeking higher salaries in the 1770s and in 1772 Paine drafted a pamphlet, *The Case of the Officers of Excise*, to make their case. He went so far as to spend a winter in London distributing copies to Members of Parliament. The cause failed, too, but Paine was in print, and his appetite for social reform had been whetted. The six months in London lost him his job in the excise service, however; he was dismissed in 1774 for having left his post.

Bankrupt, separated and jobless, Paine left Lewes in 1774 and headed for London. He had not done much with his life in his thirty-seven years. He had failed in business, in marriage and in vocation. America tempted him. It offered a fresh start far from the drudgery of collecting taxes or making ladies' stays. Through connections made in the unsuccessful excise campaign Paine was introduced in London to Benjamin Franklin, then acting as agent for Pennsylvania. Franklin agreed to give Paine some letters of introduction to take to America. Franklin's note indicates how little he or any one expected from Paine. He wrote to his son-in-law, a Philadelphia merchant:

The bearer Mr Thomas Paine is very well recommended to me, as an ingenious, worthy young man. He goes to Pennsylvania with a view of settling there. I request you give to him your best advice and countenance, as he is quite a stranger there. If you can put him in a way of obtaining employment as a clerk, or assistant tutor in a school, or assistant surveyor (of all which I think him very capable) so that he may procure a subsistence at least, till he can make acquaintance and obtain a knowledge of the country, you will do well, and much oblige your affectionate father.[1]

In Philadelphia, Paine tried his hand first at teaching. But he was soon persuaded to write, by the printer of the *Pennsylvania Magazine*, himself a recently arrived Scotsman. Throughout 1775 Paine wrote short miscellaneous pieces for Philadelphia newspapers and magazines. One was an outspoken attack on slavery. In the *Pennsylvania Magazine*, which Paine edited, he wrote scientific articles as well as political ones. His interests were wide-ranging and instinctively progressive.

In November 1775 Paine began writing his anonymous essay *Common Sense*. Ever since 1763 Britain and the American colonies had been at odds over the British government's newly levied taxes and customs duties, which were intended to make the colonists pay for some of the huge expenses of the recently concluded French and Indian wars (the Seven Years' War, in its European phase). Only in 1773 and 1774, however, with the Boston Tea Party and Britain's harsh reprisals, did tensions rise to the point where armed clashes developed and talk of independence could be heard. It was by no means certain even as late as 1775 that reconciliation was not possible – that is, until Paine published *Common Sense*, with its simple and dramatic call for America to declare its independence.

The plea for independence boldly urged in *Common Sense* caught the public imagination. The pamphlet 'struck a string which required but a touch to make it vibrate', a contemporary noted. 'The country was ripe for independence, and only needed somebody to tell the

1 Cited in David Freeman Hawke, *Paine* (New York, 1974), p. 20.

people so, with decision, boldness and plausibility.' Edmund Ran-
dolph of Virginia later noted that 'the public sentiment which a few
weeks before [the publication of *Common Sense*] had shuddered at the
tremendous obstacles, with which independence was environed,
overleaped every barrier'. General Washington commented that increased hostilities, 'added to the sound doctrine and unanswerable
reasoning contained in the pamphlet *Common Sense*, will not leave
numbers at a loss to decide upon the propriety of a separation'. In
Massachusetts a citizen noted that he believed 'no pages was ever
more eagerly read, nor more generally approved. People speak of it
in rapturous praise.' In Philadelphia the book made numerous converts. In sending the pamphlet to a friend in London a contemporary
of Paine's noted that '*Common Sense* which I herewith send you is
read to all ranks; and as many as read, so many became converted;
though perhaps the hour before were most violent against the least
idea of independence'.[2]

George Trevelyan in his *History of the American Revolution* has
summarized the impact of this pamphlet, which by February everyone knew was from the pen of Tom Paine:

It would be difficult to name any human composition which has had an
effect at once so instant, so extended and so lasting ... It was pirated,
parodied and imitated, and translated into the language of every country
where the new republic had well-wishers. It worked nothing short of miracles
and turned Tories into Whigs.

It is estimated that almost one hundred thousand copies of *Common
Sense* were sold in 1776. Translated immediately into French, with
the anti-monarchical passages deleted, it became an instant success in
Paris. Silas Deane, the American emissary in France, noted that
Common Sense 'has a greater run, if possible, here than in America'.[3]

Paine's pamphlet had influential opponents as well. John Adams, for
example, who shared Paine's views on independence, feared the
radicalism of the pamphlet and the effect 'so popular a pamphlet
might have among the people'. He replied to Paine in the draft of his
Thoughts on Government which he circulated among influential
patriots in the spring of 1776. Adams, a much more conservative
thinker than Paine, agreed with his call for separation, but he
trembled at its popular tone and its prescription of a simple political

2 Ibid., pp. 47–8.
3 'The Deane Papers', *New York Historical Society Collections*, I, p. 214.

system for independent America without the complex balancing and separation of powers inherent in the older British model. Paine's ideal sketched in *Common Sense*, Adams wrote, was 'so democratical, without any restraint or even an attempt at any equilibrium or counter poise, that it must produce confusion and every evil work'.[4]

John Adams notwithstanding, far fewer criticized Paine's pamphlet than praised it. Instant fame came to Paine when it became known that he was the author of *Common Sense*. But he was not a man to sit idly in his newly acquired literary and political glory. In July 1776 he enlisted in the American army, soon becoming aide-de-camp to General Greene. For the next seven years, while the war with Britain dragged on, Paine combined his military role with journalism and produced a series of remarkable pamphlets designed to maintain American morale as well as to make the case for America in England and Europe. The first of these papers, later to be published together as *The American Crisis*, appeared on 23 December 1776. Addressed to all Americans as much as to Washington and his troops huddled in the New Jersey cold, its opening lines have remained to this day the most frequently quoted of all that Paine wrote. All America must persevere, must suffer, he wrote, for all history awaited the battle's outcome:

These are the times that try men's souls: The summer soldier and the sunshine patriot will, in this crisis, shrink from the service of his country; but he that stands it now, deserves the love and thanks of man and woman. Tyranny, like hell, is not easily conquered; yet we have this consolation with us, that the harder the conflict, the more glorious the triumph. What we obtain too cheap, we esteem too lightly.

In addition to his military experience and his inspirational journalism, Paine played an active role in the politics of the war period. In 1777 he was appointed Secretary to the Committee of Foreign Affairs by the Congress and in this capacity worked tirelessly to obtain supplies, loans and military assistance from France. In the course of arranging this aid Paine found himself embroiled in a bitter controversy with Silas Deane. Paine contended that the supplies which America received from France through the offices of Caron de Beaumarchais, the adventurer and playwright author of *The Marriage of Figaro*,

4 John Adams, *Diary and Autobiography*, C. F. Adams (ed.) (Boston, 1850–6), II, p. 330.

were a gift and not a loan. Deane claimed they were a loan and demanded a commission. Never one to hide his anger, Paine rushed into print with a public attack on Deane, which led ultimately to Paine's dismissal from his congressional position by a coalition of those who supported Deane and those who had felt all along that the appointment of such a radical was a mistake. Gouverneur Morris, one of the latter, insisted that it was inappropriate for such a delicate position to be held by 'a mere adventurer from England, without fortune, without family or connections, ignorant even of grammar'.[5]

Paine was also active during these years in the local politics of Pennsylvania. He was an ardent supporter of its constitution of 1776, the most radically democratic of all the thirteen state constitutions. By 1780 Paine had, in fact, been appointed Clerk of the Pennsylvania Assembly. One of his acts as Clerk was to draft the legislation that provided for the gradual emancipation of slaves in that state, the first such legislation passed in the United States. During this Pennsylvania period Paine also helped found the Bank of Pennsylvania with several well-to-do merchants and bankers. For Paine this seemed the only way to allow Pennsylvania to answer Washington's call for money to pay and provisions to feed his troops. Paine's defence of this bank against farmer and radical attack in 1786 was taken by some as a sign that he had moved to a more conservative position. However, Paine himself argued that the bank was essential for commercial growth and would ultimately contribute to the well-being of all. He contended that the people had no right to revoke economic contracts entered into by the Legislature of Pennsylvania.

Throughout this period when America was governed by the states-centred Articles of Confederation, Paine was a self-proclaimed advocate for a stronger central government, the cause which would triumph in the Constitution of 1787. He opposed Virginia's claim to land in the West, for example, insisting that such land belonged to the nation and not to individual states. He also urged the individual states to approve amendments to the Articles that would have granted Congress the power to levy national tariff duties to support the war.

Paine's writings on the Bank of Pennsylvania as well as his opposition to unlimited state sovereignty may well have fuelled spe-

5 Cited in 'Introduction', *The Complete Writings of Thomas Paine*, Philip S. Foner (ed.) (New York, 1945), p. xviii.

culation that he had been bought off by the merchants of Philadelphia or by the élites calling for constitutional reform. But this was not the case. His views were shaped by his vision of America as a powerful and flourishing nation, the better to represent the democratic ideal; and he was virtually penniless throughout this period of his life. Most of his earnings from *Common Sense* and his political appointments had been contributed over the years to the revolutionary army or to facilitate the printing and distribution of his writings. In 1783 Paine was forced to ask Congress for financial assistance. He received nothing from the central government. Pennsylvania, however, gave him $500 in cash, and New York gave him a farm in New Rochelle, confiscated from a loyalist.

Like many of his contemporaries in England and America – Priestley, Price, Jefferson and Franklin among others – Paine combined political liberalism with the dream of technological and scientific progress. The ease with which political arguments could use scientific and technical principles is illustrated beautifully in *Common Sense* with its discussions of weights and forces. In terms of his career, the project to which Paine devoted most of his energy in the 1780s was the construction of an iron bridge. His efforts to develop and finance his bridge led Paine in April 1787 to leave America and return to Europe. France was where engineering was most understood, Paine felt, and he went there hoping to find backers for the single-arch bridge he contemplated building across the Schuylkill River in Philadelphia. This innocent quest brought about the third development of Paine's meteoric career. First a failure, then an American revolutionary, Paine was destined next to emerge not as a great inventor but as an English revolutionary.

English radicalism had persisted from its first explosion with Wilkes in the 1760s, gathering momentum with the American Revolution in the 1770s and the growth of the County Association movement in the 1780s. The French Revolution brought to a head middle-class discontent with the archaic and unreformed constitution. A new and progressive order had come with such apparent ease to the French that English reformers assumed that change in English institutions would follow quickly and painlessly. A heady faith in progress and the dawning of a new era swept through English intellectual and radical circles. Paine was in France furthering his bridge-building interests in the winter of 1789. The hero of America,

he was toasted in the circles of Lafayette and Jefferson, then serving
as American ambassador to France. From Lafayette Paine received
the key to the Bastille to bring back to Washington. He was present
during the early stages of the French Revolution and was pleased by
what he saw.

One Englishman much less pleased than Paine was Edmund Burke,
whose *Reflections on the Revolution in France* appeared in 1790 while
Paine was in England ostensibly still *en route* to America. Burke's
was a vicious attack on the French Jacobins and their English sym-
pathizers. They had no reverence for the past, no respect for institutions like the Church and the aristocracy, he insisted. They tore
down the entire political and social edifice and built completely
anew with no effort to repair damaged parts. Government and
society, Burke wrote, were fragile and complex entities, the product
of generations of slow and imperceptible growth. No reformer's
plans or blueprints could substitute for the experience of the ages.
Burke's message was clear. English radicals should not copy their
French counterparts; the aristocratic and hierarchical English past and
present must be defended from its enemies. The intellectual spokes-
men and -women for that subversive enemy replied in legions to
Burke. Godwin rose to the occasion with his *Inquiry Concerning
Political Justice*, Wollstonecraft with her *Vindication of the Rights of
Woman*; but none would be so powerful and so popular an answer
as Paine's *The Rights of Man* which appeared in 1791.

Once again the uncomplicated, unscholarly and unsophisticated
rhetoric of Paine brought him unprecedented popular success. Paine
was an instant hero in England, not only to the intellectual radicals
among whom he moved, such as Blake, Holcroft, Horne Tooke,
Godwin and Wollstonecraft, but to hundreds of thousands of artisans
and journeymen who bought *Rights of Man* for sixpence or read it
reprinted by their provincial radical association. Paine's book was
more than a simple defence of the French from the obloquy heaped
upon them by Burke; it was also a call to the British to replace the
aristocratic institutions so praised by Burke with new liberal institutions, to replace the principle of privilege and heredity with the new
ideals of talent and merit. The monarchy and the aristocracy were
relics of a feudal past. Republican government rested with the people
and was designed to serve their interests alone. Far from the past and
its institutions weighing heavy on modern man, Paine's message was

that every age and every generation acted for itself, set up its own political and social order to meet its own needs. 'The vanity and presumption of governing beyond the grave', he wrote, 'is the most ridiculous and insolent of all tyrannies. Man has no property in man; neither has any generation a property in the generations which are to follow.' Paine champions the rights of the living, not the hoary rights of privileged classes from time immemorial.

Paine was no hero to George III's Prime Minister, William Pitt the younger. Burke wrote to dissuade people from entering the radical camp; Reeves and his mob in the Church and King Society literally burned down the insurgents' camps; while the role of Pitt and his agents in the repressive atmosphere of the early and middle 1790s was to arrest radicals, try them and throw them in gaol. In 1792 charges of seditious writings were lodged against Paine, and a trial was scheduled. Pitt would not allow a writer, especially one so widely read, to state freely as Paine had done in the introduction to *The Rights of Man*: 'If universal peace, civilization and commerce are ever to be the happy lot of man, it cannot be accomplished but by a revolution in the system of governments.'

The mood of England had shifted dramatically in the two years since Wordsworth felt such bliss to be alive in the reflected glory of the French Revolution. On the night of 22 November 1792 a patriotic mob burned Paine's effigy at Chelmsford, Essex. According to a newspaper account:

On Wednesday last, the Effigy of that Infamous Incendiary, Tom Paine, was exhibited in this town, seated in a chair, and borne on four men's shoulders; – in one hand he held the 'Rights of Man' and under the other arm he bore a pair of stays; upon his head a mock resemblance of the Cap of Liberty, and a halter round his neck.

On a banner carried before him, was written,
'Behold a Traitor!
Who, for the base purposes of Envy, Interest and Ambition,
Would have deluged this Happy Country in BLOOD!'[6]

All they had was Paine's effigy, for, sensing the justice he would receive in an England enflamed by Pitt, Burke and Reeves, Paine had fled to France two months earlier. The trial nevertheless took place in December. Paine was found guilty *in absentia* of seditious libel, and outlawed from ever returning to Britain.

6 Cited in Audrey Williamson, *Thomas Paine* (New York, 1973), pp. 160–61.

Remaining in France for the next ten years, Paine now entered the historical stage as French revolutionary. He was chosen delegate to the National Convention by a constituency that included Calais and Oise, and threw himself into the chaotic politics of the revolution in the critical year of internecine fighting between Girondin and Jacobin. Once again Paine was no mere bystander. In October 1792 he was appointed to the Committee of Nine to frame the new French Constitution. But all was not easy for Paine in the suspicious atmosphere of Paris. He became entangled in the labyrinth of revolutionary personalities and politics. His associations with the moderate Girondin would anger the more radical Jacobins when they came to power. Most particularly he alienated Robespierre and Marat by pleading in the Convention that Louis XVI's life be spared. No one was criminal enough, he argued, for the barbarity of the death penalty. In addition, he pleaded, whatever were Louis Capet's manifest faults he had after all 'aided my much-loved America to break its chains'. The English-speaking Paine became further suspect when war broke out in 1793 between France and England. In October his allies the Girondins were tried and condemned. In December foreigners in the Convention were denounced. Paine was arrested and imprisoned.

For ten months of his imprisonment Paine busied himself working on *The Age of Reason*, a penetrating attack on theistic Christianity and defence of a natural deistic religion free from supernatural trappings. In it he examined the Bible and regaled his readers with its contradictions, its false chronology and its tales of barbarism, slaughter and inhumanity. This was not, he argued, the work of God who presided over the natural universe. In an age of reason, he insisted, men and women would replace such superstition with science and nature. In place of a mysterious and brutal God, they would have God the first cause, the Supreme Being. While he wrote on religion, Paine also worked on his release from prison through the good offices of the new American minister, James Monroe. After some confusion about his status as American or British, Paine was released in the autumn of 1794.

One of Paine's first works after his release from prison was a stinging attack on George Washington, whom he held responsible for the length of his imprisonment. In fact, the much more likely culprit was Paine's old conservative nemesis Gouverneur Morris, who was the American minister to France before Monroe. It was he, not Washington, who apparently saw no reason to speed Paine's release. Nevertheless, Paine lashed out at Washington in rage-filled pages that denounced the President's military skills as well as his Federalist politics. Once again, Paine voiced his deepest feelings in print.

The Jacobins had fallen in the meantime, and Robespierre himself had been guillotined. Paine was re-elected to the Assembly in December 1794 and sat through the following year, but he had contracted a malignant fever in prison and for the most part could summon energy enough only to write. His last years in Paris, therefore, were less political than polemical. He produced a second part of *The Age of Reason*, a political essay, *Dissertation on First Principles of Government*, and a major piece of social and economic criticism, *Agrarian Justice*.

In 1802 Paine returned to America for the final and tragic chapter in his career. The America he found was very different from the Philadelphia he had known in 1774 or even in 1783. The social ferment of those years had been stilled by a federal constitution and a federalist ideology which seemed to throw the balance of political and social power into the hands of the powerful and well-to-do. *Common Sense* was a thing of the distant past. Paine was no longer the celebrated author of the pamphlet so influential in its day. He was now the notorious author of the godless *Age of Reason* with its assault on Christianity. Jefferson was man enough to renew his old ties with Paine, but to most Americans Paine was evil personified. The federalist press wrote of him as a 'lilly-livered sinical [sic] rogue', a 'loathsome reptile', a 'demi-human archbeast', an 'object of disgust, of abhorrence, of absolute loathing to every decent man except the President of the United States'. A Boston newspaper summed up the feelings of polite and privileged America; Paine was a 'lying, drunken, brutal infidel'.[7]

The ageing Paine, with no family and few close friends, became cantankerous and argumentative, turning more and more to the solace of drink and to bitter reflections on having been forgotten or ignored. He had come full circle. From an unknown self-educated parvenu arriving in America in 1774 he had climbed the heights of world fame. Now he was once again ignored or mocked. It was a

7 Cited in Foner (ed.), op. cit., p. xlii.

difficult fate for a man like Paine whose arrogance and conceit knew no bounds. His was a colossal ego. Had he not claimed that the success of *Common Sense* 'was beyond anything since the invention of printing'? Had he not told a friend that his '*Rights of Man* could take the place of all the books in the world', and that 'if it were in his power to demolish all the libraries in existence he would do it, so as to destroy all the errors of which they are the depository – and with the *Rights of Man* begin a new chain of ideas and principles'? Paine seemed to Morris 'to become every hour more drunk with self-conceit'.[8]

The aristocratic Morris had always held Paine in contempt as an outsider, an arriviste. He described him, as already noted, as an adventurer, lacking wealth, family and connections, 'ignorant even of grammar'. In an 'age of gentlemen' Paine stood out not only because of his less than perfect speech; to a French observer 'he was coarse and uncouth in his manners, loathsome in his appearance, and a disgusting egoist, rejoicing mostly in talking of himself and read-ing the effusions of his own mind'.[9]

Parvenus often seem uncouth to the established; in turn, it is not unusual for angry newcomers to cultivate vulgarity. Paine was con-vinced that his was a superior talent and he lashed out at the aristo-cratic belief that rewards were due only to those born to privilege, to the nobility, whom he called men of 'no-ability'. Paine's writings are filled with defiance of and disrespect towards kings, ambassadors, nobility, presidents and pious priests. How better to subvert these untalented superiors in a world of polished privilege than by re-pudiating the pattern of civility they dictated?

Paine's last years were spent in New York City, in what is now Greenwich Village, or on his farm in New Rochelle outside the city. He died on 8 June 1809. Few people saw the coffin from the city to the farm in New Rochelle. At the burial site there were even fewer present, merely a handful of New Rochelle neighbours and friends. There were no dignitaries, no eulogies, no official notices of his death. The staymaker from Thetford who had shaped the world as few have ever done, who had known and been known by many great men of America, France and England, was laid to rest in a quiet

8 Cited in David Powell, *Tom Paine: The Greatest Exile* (London, 1985), pp. 197, 206.
9 Ibid., p. 123.

pasture with no ceremony, no fanfare, no appreciation. The irony of such a funeral for such a man was too much for Madame de Bonneville, who had acted for several years as Paine's housekeeper, and who was one of the few present. She later wrote:

This interment was a scene to affect and to wound any sensible heart. Contemplating who it was, what man it was, that we were committing to an obscure grave on an open and disregarded bit of land, I could not help feeling most acutely. Before the earth was thrown down upon the coffin, I, placing myself at the east end of the grave, said to my son Benjamin, 'stand you there, at the other end, as a witness for grateful America'. Looking round me, and beholding the small group of spectators, I exclaimed, as the earth was tumbled into the grave, 'Oh! Mr Paine! My son stands here as testimony of the gratitude of America, and I, for France!' This was the funeral ceremony of this great politician and philosopher![10]

PAINE'S IDEOLOGY

No democrat so enthusiastically rejected the aristocratic world as did Thomas Paine. Burke wrote of him that he sought 'to destroy in six or seven days' the feudal and chivalric past that 'all the boasted wisdom of our ancestors has laboured to bring to perfection for six or seven centuries'.[11] Paine's every reflex was egalitarian, bent on undermining what he considered the 'quixotic age of chivalric nonsense'. Kings were the first nonsense to go. Doing nothing more than make war and give away positions, they were paid 'eight hundred thousand sterling a year and worshipped into the bargain'. They were useless and unproductive: 'of more worth is one honest man to society . . . than all the crowned ruffians that ever lived'.[12]

After kings, the nonsense of aristocracy was next to go. Is there anything more absurd than the hereditary principle, Paine asked in *The Rights of Man*, 'as absurd as an hereditary mathematician, or an hereditary wiseman, and as ridiculous as an hereditary poet laureate'? What mattered was not a man's pedigree but his productivity. Society should be led by men of 'talents and abilities', yet its offices of privilege and power were filled by a nobility that, according to

10 Cited in Williamson, op. cit., p. 275.
11 Edmund Burke, 'Letters on a Regicide Peace', in *Burke's Works*, Bohn (ed.) (London, 1855), V, p. 395.
12 *The Rights of Man; Common Sense*.

Paine, really meant 'no-ability'. Paine, like Wat Tyler, could scan 'all the vocabulary of Adam' and find there 'not such an animal as a duke or a count'. The great of the world could shout leveller at such Jacobin sentiments, and proud citizen Tom Paine would reply, 'France has not levelled, it has exalted. It has put down the dwarf, to set up the man.' Monarchs and aristocrats were unproductive idlers, parasites and 'drones . . . who neither collect the honey, nor form the hive, but exist only for lazy enjoyment'.

Behind the power of these drones lay the deception that government and society were mysterious and arcane realms where secrets possessed only by some enabled the few to lead, to govern, to oppress. For Paine, 'the age of fiction and political superstition, and of craft, and mystery is passing away'. The 'craft of courts' is banished from popular government. 'There is no place for mystery, no where for it to begin' when the people govern themselves.[13] Such a government was simple and uncomplicated. Defenders of balanced or separated powers, like John Adams, were criticized for their glo- rification of complexity – which Paine insisted was merely a return to the fiction, crafts and mystery of the pre-democratic age.

In the age of mystery and 'chivalric nonsense', the poor fared worst of all. To their defence, in moving and bitter language, sprang Paine, the former staymaker, in terms no less meaningful two centuries later. 'The present state of civilization', he wrote in *Agrarian Justice*,

is as odious as it is unjust. It is absolutely the opposite of what it should be, and it is necessary that a revolution should be made in it. The contrast of affluence and wretchedness continually meeting and offending the eye is like dead and living bodies chained together.

There is nothing wrong with riches, he adds, 'provided that none be miserable in consequence of it'. In Part Two of *The Rights of Man*, he laments that nations are 'governed like animals, for the pleasure of their riders'. 'When . . . we see age going to the workhouse and youth to the gallows' in a civilized country, he adds, 'something must be wrong in the system of government'. Why is it 'that scarcely any are executed but the poor'? Youth should be instructed, and the aged supported; instead, Paine fumes, 'the resources of a country are lavished upon kings, upon courts, upon hirelings'. What pathetic

13 *Letter Addressed to the Addressers on the Late Proclamation; The Rights of Man.*

irony that the poor themselves 'are compelled to support the fraud that oppresses them'. Paine calculated that

the millions that are superfluously wasted upon government are more than sufficient to reform those evils . . . were an estimation to be made of the charge of aristocracy to a nation, it will be found nearly equal to that of supporting the poor. The Duke of Richmond alone (and there are cases similar to this) takes away as much for himself as would maintain two thousand poor and aged persons.

Paine's solution was for the authorities to grant the poor four pounds a year for children under fourteen, and to require that the children be schooled. For the elderly there would be, at age fifty, six pounds per year, and ten pounds after sixty. 'It is painful', Paine writes, 'to see old age working itself to death, in what are called civilized countries, for daily bread.' He calculated how much the poor pay in taxes over a lifetime, and notes, in anticipation of modern social security, 'the money he shall receive after fifty years, is but little more than the legal interest of the net money he has paid'. Is it more civilized, he asks, to render comfortable the old age of 140,000 people, 'or that a million a year of public money be expended on any one individual, and him often of the most worthless or insignificant character'?

Public education could be provided for all, according to Paine, at the cost of ten shillings a year for 400,000 children. Women would receive twenty shillings immediately after the birth of a child, and couples twenty shillings upon marriage. Paine insisted that this was not the Christian philanthropy of traditional paternalist attitudes to the poor. In striking anticipation of a doctrine that even two hundred years later is unacceptable to many, he is certain in *The Rights of Man* that 'this support, as already remarked, is not of the nature of a charity, but of a right'. No one else in that age of revolution, none of the 'sober and cautious' democrats who were America's founders, proclaimed as Paine did:

When it shall be said in any country in the world, my poor are happy, neither ignorance nor distress is to be found among them; my jails are empty of prisoners, my streets of beggars; the aged are not in want, the taxes are not oppressive . . . when these things can be said, then may that country boast its constitution and its government.

Such sentiments endeared Paine to democratic working men. He was applauded by the artisans of Philadelphia and by the members of the London Corresponding Society in the 1790s. His writings would be quoted by the Chartists and the early trade unionists in the nineteenth century. But it is a mistake to read Paine's radicalism as proto-socialism, as some have. His merciless indictment of an aristocratic polity and society did serve the interests of the workers and touched their souls, but Paine's radical egalitarianism also served, and was bound up with, the interests of bourgeois liberalism, the principal architect and beneficiary of the destruction of 'chivalric nonsense'.

It detracts in no way from Paine's radicalism and his egalitarianism to note their liberal sources. Such, indeed, were the terms a progressive and humanitarian assault on the old order had to take in his age. The limitations liberalism placed on his radicalism would become clearer in a later age. In his day there was no incompatibility between his democratic ideals and his defence of individualism, property and business enterprise. Bourgeois ideals in his mind were intimately linked to an egalitarian vision of society. The stratified society of privilege and rank would be levelled in a bourgeois world of competitive individualism – a world in which political and social place would be determined by talent, merit and hard work.

His political theory was vintage liberalism. Like Adam Smith and James Madison, and like liberal apologists to this day, Paine assumed that co-operation and fellowship were strangers to the political arena, a place of conflict and competition constituted by atomistic individualism. A nation, he wrote, 'is composed of distinct, unconnected individuals, following various trades, employments and pursuits; continually meeting, crossing, uniting, opposing and separating from each other, as accident, interest, and circumstances shall direct'.[14]

Government had no positive agency to promote justice or virtue for these clashing individuals and interests. It was merely to preside as umpire over a world where individualism was the central value. Its sole justification was providing a stable and secure setting for the operation of a commercial society:

Every man wishes to pursue his occupation and to enjoy the fruits of his labour and the produce of his property in peace and safety and with it the least possible expense. When these things are accomplished, all the objects for which government ought to be established are answered.[15]

14 *Dissertations on Government, the Affairs of the Bank, and Paper Money.*
15 *The Rights of Man.*

Paine was read by the artisans and the poor, but his natural friends were also the manufacturers, who were fast destroying traditional society. Paine the entrepreneur, the salesman forever hawking his iron bridge, had great respect for the Wedgwoods, the Arkwrights, the Watts, and their counterparts in America who chartered the Bank of Pennsylvania. These enterprising individuals stood outside government; indeed, their achievements occurred in spite of government:

It is from the enterprise and industry of the individuals and their numerous associations, in which, tritely speaking, government is neither pillow nor bolster, that these improvements have proceeded. No man thought about the government, or who was in, or who was out, when he was planning or executing those things; and all he had to hope with respect to government, was that it would let him alone.[16]

Paine's entrepreneurial friends were engaged in the same egalitarian crusade as he was. Like him, they sought a redistribution of wealth and power that would be based on equality of opportunity and that would enable individuals of real ability to replace those of 'no-ability'. Paine's most progressive writings, his *Agrarian Justice* and the justly celebrated Part Two of *The Rights of Man*, while advocating the redistribution of much wealth to the poor, still served the greater interest of individuals of 'enterprise and industry', relieving them of that most burdensome of weights, the poor rates. Relief would come to both the middle and lower classes; indeed in greater measure to the former. Equal conditions, equal results, were not his goal nor theirs. The end of 'chivalric nonsense' would bring not levelling but equal opportunity in a competitive individualistic society. 'That property will ever be unequal is certain', he wrote in 1795. This was neither unjust nor unfair, but simply a result of 'industry, superiority of talents, dexterity of management, extreme frugality and fortunate opportunities'. His political creed was a simple one – pure liberalism at its most radical and progressive historical moment: 'Establish the Rights of Man; enthrone equality . . . let there be no privileges, no distinctions of birth, no monopolies; make safe the liberty of industry and trade, the equal distribution of family inheritances.'[17]

'Society in every state is a blessing, but government even in its best

16 Ibid.
17 *Dissertation on First Principles of Government; Anti-Monarchical Essay.*

state is but a necessary evil', wrote Paine in *Common Sense*. With this formula Paine distils the essence of liberal social theory and in turn reveals the flaw that limits his and any radical vision operating within the confines of liberalism. From Locke through Paine and even unto Milton Friedman, the liberal sees civil society as peopled by self-reliant individuals. Such a society is benignly innocent, self-regulating and harmonious. Government is pernicious, the source of threats to individual freedom; it, along with its ally the established Church, is in essence tyrannical. Coercion and abuse are the fruits only of government, never of the social and economic institutions of civil society.

Poverty, for example, according to Paine, is a direct result of governmental interference with 'the great laws of society', the 'laws of nature and reciprocal interest'. 'How often is the natural propensity to society disturbed or destroyed by the operations of government?' he asks. Instead of 'consolidating society, it divided it; it deprived it of its natural cohesion, and engendered discontents and disorders, which otherwise would not have existed'. The 'excess and inequality of taxation' has but one effect: 'A great mass of the community are thrown thereby into poverty and discontent.' Governments thus create the poor; the economic institutions of civil society do not. In America there is little or no government, according to Paine. Society performs there quite naturally, with 'order and decorum'. It follows, according to Paine, that poverty is unknown in America.[18]

Paine's preoccupation with government as the source of all coercion, his conviction that civil society is the realm of true freedom, is nowhere better revealed than in his obsession with taxation. The real threat to individual freedom, for Paine, is governmental taxation. Taxation is the symbol of tyranny and corruption. His self-appointed mission was to defend 'the cause of the poor, of the manufacturers, of the tradesmen, of the farmer, and of all those on whom the real burden of taxes fall'. Monarchy, aristocracy and taxes were all of a piece in Paine's mind. In his anti-monarchical essay of 1792 he insisted that 'whoever demands a king, demands an aristocracy, and thirty millions of taxes'. Royalty 'has been invented only to obtain from man excessive taxes'. The turmoil of his revolutionary age was produced, he said, by taxpayers who had had enough. He wrote in 1792: 'There are two distinct classes of men in the nation [England].

18 *The Rights of Man.*

Those who pay taxes and those who receive and live upon the taxes. . . . When taxation is carried to excess, it cannot fail to disunite these two, and something of this is now beginning to appear.'[19]

America represented for Paine 'a revolution in the principles and practice of governments'. He meant by this its repudiation of monarchy and the hereditary principle and its commitment to representative government. In addition, America represented liberal Utopia, the triumph of civil society over government. Like Locke, who had claimed that 'in the beginning all the world was America', Paine contended that 'the case and circumstances of America present themselves as in the beginning of a world'. Paine was struck with how well revolutionary America performed with little central direction: 'A little more than what society naturally performed was all the government that was necessary.' American government was also cheap. Extending over a country ten times as large as England, Paine calculated its costs as 'a fortieth part of the expense which government costs in England'. No vast patronage network here; no costly system of jobs. The civil list for the support of one man, the King of England, Paine noted, is 'eight times greater than the whole expense of the federal government in America'. What little government there was in America was simple, local and understandable. The Americans put into practice Paine's maxim that the 'sum of necessary government is much less than is generally thought'. In America, 'the poor are not oppressed, the rich are not privileged. Industry is not mortified by the splendid extravagance of a court rioting at its expense. There taxes are few.' In England, men were envious of America, and calls for change were coming fast, Paine wrote in 1792, because 'the enormous expense of government has provoked men to think'.[20]

The triumph of civil society over government, of cheap and simple self-regulation over expensive and tyrannical taxation, is seen in a fascinating and repeated preference Paine acknowledges for local over centralized government. England, he suggests, really governs itself, with constables, assizes, magistrates and juries. This is done at virtually no expense, at no great intrusion of taxation on individual freedom. Central government, on the contrary, or 'court government', while useless, is a leviathan, an overblown monster spewing forth jobs and wars. It is the 'most productive machine of

19 *Letter Addressed to the Addressers on the Late Proclamation.*
20 *The Rights of Man; Letter Addressed to the Addressers on the Late Proclamation.*

taxation that was ever invented'.[21] The latter, centralized monarchical government, is unnecessary and a constant threat to individual liberty. The former, self-regulation by local society, is natural, cheap and really not government at all. It is thus no threat to individual rights or to the self-realization of talented individuals.

For the liberal Paine there is but one villain: government. Merchants, manufacturers and bankers, even magistrates and justices of the peace, are part of benign and wholesome civil society. Traditional republican doctrine is turned on its head; self-serving individuals further the common good, and public government serves its own selfish and corrupt interest. 'The greedy hand of government' is thrust 'into every corner and crevice of industry', to grasp 'the spoil of the multitude'. Governments are evil incarnate. They engage in wars abroad and practise 'oppression and usurpation' at home. They 'exhaust the property of the world'. Reversing the conventional identification of courts and the great with civility, and provincial manufacturers and artisans with vulgarity, Paine holds that governments work for the forces of barbarism, society for the forces of civilization. 'Governments ... pervert the abundance which civilized life produces to carry on the uncivilized part.' Paine pushes aside what most take to be the political issues that divide people and finds not class war but a heroic and quintessentially liberal struggle between individuals and governments:

It is not whether this or that party shall be in or not, or Whig or Tory, or high or low shall prevail; but whether man shall inherit his rights, and universal civilization take place? Whether the fruits of his labours shall be enjoyed by himself, or consumed by the profligacy of government? Whether robbery shall be banished from courts, and wretchedness from countries?[22]

It was inconceivable to Paine and other liberals that civil society and its institutions, economic, familial or cultural, could be a source of coercion, of 'oppression' and 'usurpation'. That concentrations of power and wealth in non-governmental institutions could be the source of inequality and poverty was incompatible with the liberal urge to indict political institutions and to seek progressive change through political reform. Threats to freedom come from the state,

21 *The Rights of Man.*
22 Ibid.

from churches and tyrants in the liberal world, not from factory owners, corporate power or financial manipulators.

Nowhere is this limitation of Paine's vision more apparent than in his strident defence of the Bank of Pennsylvania, a defence that alienated him from many of his Jeffersonian friends in 1786. Paine rejected the fears of the bank's radical critics, who charged that its directors would wield great economic power even to the point of controlling the state and the government. On the contrary, Paine answered, the bank illustrates the superiority of civil institutions over state institutions. Men in society have little need for government; they can supply their internal wants and needs by private co-operative activity. Non-governmental institutions like the bank by definition could not be oppressive; only taxing governments could. The bank came into being, he wrote, because government was inadequately financing the war: 'A public spirit awakened itself with energy out of doors.' The bank 'facilitates the commerce of the country'. More significantly,

If merchants by this means or farmers by similar means among themselves can mutually aid and support each other, what has the government to do with it? What right has it to expect emolument from associated industry, more than from individual industry? It would be a strange sort of government that should make it illegal for people to assist each other, or pay a tribute for doing so.

The real threat to individual freedom here was not from any potential or real economic power of the bank and its directors, according to Paine. The enemy is government. Corporate groups must be free of government, Paine writes of the bank. They must not be dependent on government each year for renewal of their charters: 'The citizens who compose those corporations are not free; the government holds an authority and influence over them in a manner different from what it does over other citizens, and by this means destroys that equality of freedom which is the bulwark of the republic.[23]

When he wanted to, Tom Paine could summon citizens to collective action with stirring phrases. In *The American Crisis* he had written that 'these are the times that try men's souls; the summer soldier and the sunshine patriot will, in this crisis, shrink from the service of his country'. But common action and fraternity, for Paine,

23 *Dissertations on Government, the affairs of the Bank and Paper Money.*

are found only in the angry response of a basically individualistic society to public oppression and injustice. When the stimulus of rebellion and war against tyrants and aristocrats is removed, equal individuals will pursue their own livelihoods, and seldom will they be moved to co-operate with one another for common purposes. Among equal citizens there is little or no sense of community; self-regulating society, yes, but no consciousness of solidarity, nor any real emotional feelings of unity. In society, there is little need for popular power; there are, after all, no collective goals.

Democratic egalitarian citizens for Paine are free, not powerful. Power was something governments had, and with it they taxed, coerced worship and gave jobs to incompetent second sons of elderly peers. Its abusive association with government permanently tainted 'power' for the individualist Paine and for liberals like him. America was the beacon of light in an otherwise dark world because its equal citizens were free, not because its people had power. Americans did not tax, establish churches or give away public jobs. That power might serve less abusive ends could not occur to individualistic liberals like Paine, for a free people were not united in pursuing communal ends, nor were they even interested in community itself. Such a linkage of power, community and freedom could come only with democratic theorists like Rousseau, less wedded to an individualistic vision of society. For such democrats, it was not power itself that corrupted, but the wielders who corrupted power.

Trapped as he was by the limitations of liberal social theory from seeing non-governmental threats to freedom, equality and democracy, confined as he was to seeing society only in terms of competitive individualism, it still bears repeating that there have been precious few in the liberal camp who so passionately assaulted privilege as Paine did. Few liberals were so fervently committed to democracy and egalitarianism. Lest we forget the democrat Paine, we need remember only how he was hated by the conservatives of his day. John Adams could not bear him. In 1805 Adams wrote of Paine, who was for him the symbol of mischievous radicalism:

I know not whether any man in the world has had more influence on its inhabitants or affairs for the last thirty years than Tom Paine. There can be no severer satyr on the age. For such a mongrel between pig and puppy, begotten by a wild boar on a bitch wolf, never before in any age of the world was suffered by the poltroonery of mankind, to run through such a career of mischief. Call it the Age of Paine.[24]

PAINE'S LEGACY

When William Cobbett set sail from New York for England on 30 October 1819, he carried with him in his baggage the bones of Thomas Paine. The precise moment in English history and the strange, elaborate tribute devised by one English radical leader and writer to another combined to make the event memorable. Just a few weeks before, Manchester had witnessed on its streets the Peterloo massacre, and the nation was still gripped by the political debate which followed. Cobbett had chosen to cross the Atlantic months earlier to escape the clutches of the same persecuting, panic-stricken government. The memory of Thomas Paine figured prominently in his thoughts. No such intrusion could normally displace his own claims and pretensions; he had a reputation for being preposterously vain. But on this occasion, most notably, he wished the world to know what was his own considered verdict on his great forebear and exemplar. (Sadly, the body never had the memorial over it that Cobbett intended. It was washed overboard at sea.)

No small part of Cobbett's energies during the whole of his stay in America was devoted to tasks associated with Paine. He cited Paine's views in several of his own writings and took the trouble to engage in controversy about his alleged blasphemies and irreligion. He made the acquaintance of Madame de Bonneville and others who had known Paine in his last days before his death a decade earlier. He proposed to himself and others the idea of writing Paine's life and publishing a full edition of his works. In an article written in February 1819 he declared: 'I hope to see an Act of Parliament to cause his bones to be conveyed to England and deposited in the stead of those of Pitt, whose system he opposed, the ruin attending whose schemes he foretold, and for which foretelling he was persecuted.' Six months later he returned to the subject:

Paine lies in a little hole under the grass and weeds of an obscure farm in America. There, however, *he shall not lie, unnoticed, much longer.* He belongs

24 Cited in Hawke, op. cit., p. 7.

to England. His fame is the property of the English; and if no other people will show they value that fame, the people of England will.

A few weeks later he went and fetched the bones himself. 'Let this be considered', he said,

the act of the reformers of England, Scotland, and Ireland. In their name we opened the grave and in their name will the tomb be raised. We do not look upon ourselves as adopting *all* Paine's opinions upon *all* subjects. He was *a great man, an Englishman*, a friend of freedom and the *first and greatest enemy of the Borough and Paper system*. This is enough for us.[25]

Back in England, the mood was not so respectful and euphoric, even among all the various groups of reformers. The very week before Cobbett's return, Richard Carlile had been found guilty of blasphemy and sentenced to two years' imprisonment for publishing *The Age of Reason*. Some ridicule was lavished by the caricaturists and political satirists of the day on Cobbett's bag of bones, about which, as he said, 'the hypocrites were in alarm lest they might injure the cause of religion'. He was variously denounced as a 'grave robber', a 'bone grabber' and a 'resurrection man'. But Cobbett was only fortified in his most estimable display of magnanimity. At a Crown Anchor reformers' dinner in December, he defended his action more belligerently than ever. He had no wish to engage in religious controversy; that was to be left to individual consciences, but he felt it necessary to atone for the injustices he had done to Paine in many of his previous writings – 'and, if he lived another year, he intended to erect a colossal statue in bronze, in honour of his memory'. Here, alas, Cobbett was not as good as his word. No statue to Paine's memory was erected on English soil until nearly 150 years later when, to the alarm of some Conservative ratepayers and councillors in Thetford who could match the post-Peterloo excitement, the awful deed was done in the town of his birth. Cobbett had shown a truer sense of history than his assailants. 'At his expiring flambeau', he said, 'I lighted my taper.'[26]

Paine and Cobbett were men of quite differing temperaments; they drew their inspiration from very different sources. Cobbett looked back to a medieval golden age; Paine looked forward to

---

25 Cited in George Pater, *William Cobbett: The Poor Man's Friend* (Cambridge, 1983), II, pp. 377–8.
26 Ibid., p. 387.

a Utopia, to the perfectibility of man. Each helped to weld English radicalism into the same egalitarian tradition.

A momentary diversion from the mainspring of the great *democratic* Paineite appeal – before, indeed, that word had gained any of its modern currency – might seem to be offered by the theological disputes, such as those which led to Richard Carlile's trial, but it would be churlish and misleading to draw too fine a distinction. Richard Carlile was sentenced to imprisonment for publishing *The Age of Reason* in 1819, but he was sentenced again in 1823 for publishing *The Rights of Man*. His own memoir put many of Paine's writings in a proper perspective. He recognized the force of *Common Sense* and the courage of *The Age of Reason*, and eagerly asserted that *The Rights of Man* 'will finally form the basis of the English Government'. He never ceased to marvel at the power of Paine's writing, how he could destroy all rivals: 'His pen continued an overmatch for the whole brood.' Richard Carlile, a real publisher who loved his trade, knew how authors should be respected. 'Mr Paine', he wrote in that same memoir, 'would not allow any man to make the least alteration or even correction in his writings.'[27] His fastidiousness in this respect shows with what care he wrote and how well he knew what he was attempting. His sharpness, his clarity, his potency were all deliberate acquisitions at a time when a very different style was considered more appropriate for those engaged in political controversy.

It is indeed Paine's own writings which have made his name survive while the forgotten historians were busy expurgating it from the records. Almost every great democratic statesman and writer has found his way back to these source books. Yet, even on this reckoning, as a writer, Paine has seldom had his due. American Tories who disliked his arguments found fault with his grammar. Hazlitt was scoffed at for calling him a great writer. More often than not since then, any reference to his literary claims is compressed into a few patronizing paragraphs. While he lived his pamphlets had phenomenal sales, and since his death they have been reprinted and reprinted again, in almost every language. Momentary best-sellers can be dismissed; but how can the critics deride the verdict of so mammoth an electorate?

Paine's pamphlets may sometimes seem ill-constructed and uneven.

27 *The Age of Reason by Thomas Paine*, Richard Carlile (ed.), preceded with a 'Life of Paine' by Carlile (London, n.d.), pp. 13, 14.

There is none of the smooth perfection of Swift – although, like Hazlitt and Cobbett, Paine had obviously soaked himself in Swift. There is indeed a grating, metallic flavour in some of his writing. All the mysteries of the universe are quickly made to fit into his mechanical symmetrical system. The lack of subtlety and colour can begin to pall. But then, suddenly, the whole surrounding landscape is lit up by another streak of lightning. These are the real riches of Paine's prose, the abundance of his aphorisms, sharp, hard and glittering, like diamonds. How the gorgeous eloquence of Edmund Burke on the tragedy of Marie Antoinette withers before Paine's most famous epigram: 'He pities the plumage, but forgets the dying bird.' More perhaps than all the others who revolted against the English prose style of the eighteenth century, Paine changed the fashion.

He also changed the language of politics. He wrote in the plain style of common speech, avoiding references to classical authors and learned philosophers. The stylized conventions of the humanist essay written for gentlemen and the cultural élite were replaced by Paine with the language of ordinary life used by the common men to whom he addressed his writings. Paine developed and was the first master of democratic prose, which is as important in explaining his appeal to a mass readership as is the content of his arguments. Jefferson, himself a master of political prose, saw the unique strength of Paine's, writing in 1821 that 'No writer has exceeded Paine in ease and familiarity of style, in perspicuity of expression, happiness of elucidation, and in simple and unassuming language.'[28]

Paine is still read, because he is still modern; he is a foremost figure in the history of English literature. Hazlitt developed the modern colloquial style, breaking out of Dr Johnson's restrictive rules more deliberately. But Paine knew what he was doing. 'I never quote; I am always thinking for myself,' Carlile quoted him as saying.[29] The cocksure clarity had more virtues than vices.

Another of his later free-thinking disciples, and a very good one, the nineteenth-century American Robert G. Ingersoll, delivered an oration in Paine's honour in which, at first hearing, the claim for his writing was pushed too high:

In my judgement, Thomas Paine was the best political writer that ever lived.

28 Cited in Foner (ed.), op. cit., p. xlvi.
29 Carlile (ed.), op. cit., p. 15.

What he wrote was pure nature, and his soul and his pen went together. Ceremony, pageantry, and all the paraphernalia of power had no effect upon him. He examined into the why and wherefore of things. He was perfectly radical in his mode of thought. Nothing short of the bedrock satisfied him.

Naturally enough he became, for ever afterwards, the patron hero of all the free-thinking sects in the fields where he had delivered his most frontal challenge. 'Paine', wrote Ingersoll, 'had denied the authority of bibles and creeds; this was his crime, and for this the world shut the door in his face, and emptied its slops upon him from the windows.'[30] But this, the Paine of *The Age of Reason*, was only one strand in his theme; it merged with something larger and deeper. Throughout the century he never lost his hold on a vast, active politically minded readership. The English rebels who raised the ferment which led to the Reform Bill pored over his forbidden pages. 'Government is for the living, not the dead,' had been Paine's reply to Burke in 1791; forty years later England marched on, in company with France and America, along the road which Paine, not Burke, had mapped out for it.

When the East London Democratic Association was formed in 1837 by Julian Harney and other Chartist leaders, their manifesto declared that its object would be to promote the moral and political condition of the working class 'by disseminating the principles propagated by that great philosopher and redeemer of mankind, the Immortal Thomas Paine'.[31] When Bronterre O'Brien raised afresh with others the need for an attack on the landed monopoly, it was often to Paine's *Agrarian Justice* they would turn. But more potent and comprehensive still was Paine's claim for democracy when that word, in its modern sense, had barely been invented. His *Rights of Man*, wrote A. J. P. Taylor, just two hundred years after the Declaration of Independence, is 'the best statement of democratic belief in any language'. The historians, or at least the very greatest of them, return to Paine to renew their own insights. Edward Thompson, in his *The Making of the English Working Class* (1963), constantly quotes Paine in his double role, as a guiding active hand and inspired recorder of the events he witnessed.

In America Paine's legacy inspired the leaders of Jeffersonian

30 Robert G. Ingersoll, *An Oration on Thomas Paine* (New York, 1976), pp. 21, 25.
31 Cited in A. R. Schoyen, *The Chartist Challenge* (London, 1980), p. 14.

democracy in the early years of the nineteenth century. At meetings of their societies copies of *The Rights of Man* were distributed and toasts were drunk to Paine. In the 1830s the first stirrings of the American labour movement saw dinners held by workingmen's parties to commemorate Paine's birthday. American land reformers at mid-century drew on Paine's *Agrarian Justice*. The great radical poet Walt Whitman gave testimony to Paine's influence at the end of the nineteenth century, and in the twentieth the socialist and trade-union activist Eugene V. Debs saluted Paine as a founder of the American radical tradition. The French, too, have recognized their debt to Paine; according to Napoleon, Paine deserved a statue in gold in every town.

Enough of achievement for one man, surely: to understand the three great revolutions of his age before they happened, to bring politics home to the common people, to build a bridge of common idealism across the Atlantic and the English Channel (as firm as the iron bridge to which Paine devoted so much of his time and energy). Yet this was not all. Scattered through Paine's writings we can find hints, often much more than hints, of the other ideas which have given vitality to progressive movements for the past two hundred years.

Almost a century before Lincoln, Paine sought to write into the American Constitution a clause against slavery. He was among the very first of English writers to espouse the cause of Indian freedom. Well ahead of social reformers on both sides of the Atlantic, he had a good plan for old-age pensions. And how men and women in all our modern parties might tremble at his proposals for land nationalization. He wanted new laws for marriage and divorce. International arbitration, family allowances, maternity benefits, free education, prison reform, full employment; much of the future later offered by the British Labour Party was previously on offer, in better English, from Thomas Paine. Note how true these single syllables ring with the triumphant organ note of the last final word: 'It is wrong to say God made *rich* and *poor*; He made only *male* and *female*; and He gave them the earth for their inheritance.'

Despite, or perhaps because of, much of this legacy, Paine has had more than his fair share of troubles at the hand of later generations. He proved too radical for the bourgeoisie of the Anglo-American world as that class triumphed and took the reigns of power. The egalitarianism of his message and its assault on privilege and rank seemed subversive when the middle class itself assumed the posture of a privileged class against challenges from the left. Another element was the reaction against freethinking that characterized post-Enlightenment England and America; Paine was doubly cursed, for he was also the Antichrist of *The Age of Reason*.

Paine has begun slowly to receive his due in the twentieth century. His books have been republished, and his reputation has been rehabilitated. After 120 years of biographies emphasizing subversion, atheism and drunkenness, one finds biographies detailing his amazingly productive life, and monographs dealing with the intricacies of his thought.

Nowadays, Paine societies abound in America and England. The statue of Paine was erected in Thetford in 1964, and, according to the *Guardian*, the Tory deputy mayor 'failed in an attempt to have details of Paine's trial and conviction as a traitor engraved under the statue'. Political passion runs long and deep for sons of Thetford. On the other hand, a pub called the Rights of Man was built on the Thetford motorway in 1968, complete with a Tom Paine Lounge, its walls decorated with posters of early Paine editions. Paine might have liked this tribute. In America his face was put on a postage stamp in 1968 (he might have liked the symbolism of that, too), and his farmhouse in New Rochelle has been restored for the edification of tourists and schoolchildren.

Somehow Paine rarely loses his topicality, and when his reputation in this respect is in peril other figures on the political stage, small and large, come to the rescue. During a recent debate (12 May 1986) on televising the House of Lords, Lord Thomas of Swynnerton opposed the proposition on the grounds that the inquisitive cameras threatened the blend of intimacy, ceremony and mystery 'which made the Lords what it was'. Paine would have been eager to reply. Apart from favouring the full-scale abolition of the Lords, he held extremely strong views on those who sought to present politics in general as something the common people could not be expected to understand: 'In all cases', he wrote in *The Rights of Man*,

the people's enemies take care to represent government as a thing made up of mysteries, which only themselves understood; and they hid from the understanding of the nation, the only thing that was beneficial to know, namely, that government is nothing more than a national association acting on the principles of society.

Again, in his *Dissertation on First Principles of Government*, Paine wrote:

Notwithstanding the mystery with which the science of government has been enveloped, for the purpose of enslaving, plundering and imposing upon mankind, it is of all things the least mysterious and most easy to be understood. The meanest capacity cannot be at a loss, if it begins its inquiries at the right point.

Lord Thomas might not have known how he was inviting Paine's eloquence on his head. President Reagan – or his speech writers – should have known better. 'We have in our power', the President said, quoting Paine's words soon after his first arrival in America, 'to begin the world over again'. But he was referring to the SDI (Star Wars) programme, and he must have forgotten, or never knew, that Paine, one of the first opponents of imperial power, insisted that no nation, not even the United States, had the right to impose its will on another, that the supreme cause of peace would require *international* action on an imaginative scale which national states could scarcely conceive. Both English peers and American Presidents should have learned to treat Thomas Paine with greater care. He had long since taken the measure of both.

PAINE'S WRITINGS

[1] THE CASE OF THE OFFICERS OF EXCISE

(1772)

Paine was asked by his fellow collectors of excise in 1772 to make their case to Parliament on how overworked and underpaid they were. Paine's effort produced his first important writing, and as with so much he was to write its basic approach was a plea for social justice. Some four thousand copies of the pamphlet were printed in 1773. Paine's moving case for higher wages and his personal efforts lobbying Members of Parliament were rewarded by his dismissal from HM Excise Service.

THE INTRODUCTION

As a design among the excise officers throughout the kingdom is on foot for a humble application to Parliament next session, to have the state of their salaries taken into consideration; it has been judged not only expedient, but highly necessary, to present a state of their case, previous to the presentation of their petition.

There are some cases so singularly reasonable, that the more they are considered, the more weight they obtain. It is a strong evidence both of simplicity and honest confidence, when petitioners in any case ground their hopes of relief on having their case fully and perfectly known and understood.

Simple as this subject may appear at first, it is a matter, in my humble opinion, not unworthy of Parliamentary attention. 'Tis a subject interwoven with a variety of reasons from different causes. New matter will arise on every thought. *If the poverty of the officers of excise, if the temptations arising from their poverty, if the qualifications of persons to be admitted into employment, if the security of the revenue itself,* are matters of any weight, then I am conscious that my voluntary services in this business, will produce some good effect or other, either to the better security of the revenue, the relief of the officers, or both.

THE STATE OF THE SALARY OF THE OFFICERS OF EXCISE

When a year's salary is mentioned in the gross, it acquires a degree of consequence from its *sound,* which it would not have if separated into daily payments, and if the charges attending the receiving and other unavoidable expenses were considered with it. Fifty pounds a year, and one shilling and ninepence farthing a day, carry as different degrees of significancy with them, as My Lord's steward, and the steward's labourer; and yet an outride officer in the excise, under the name of fifty pounds a year, receives for himself no more than one shilling and ninepence farthing a day.

After tax, charity and sitting expenses are deducted there remains very little more than forty-six pounds; and the expenses of horse-keeping in many places cannot be brought under fourteen pounds a year, beside the purchase at first, and the hazard of life, which reduces it to thirty-two pounds *per annum,* or one shilling and ninepence farthing per day.

I have spoken more particularly of the outrides, as they are by far the most numerous, being in proportion to the footwalks as eight is to five throughout the kingdom. Yet in the latter the same misfortunes exist; the channel of them only is altered. The excessive dearness of house-rent, the great burden of rates and taxes, and the excessive price of all necessaries of life, in cities and large trading towns, nearly counterbalance the expenses of horsekeeping. Every office has its stages of promotions, but the pecuniary advantages arising from a footwalk are so inconsiderable, and the loss of disposing of effects, or the charges of removing them to any considerable distance so great, that many outride officers with a family remain as they are, from an inability to bear the loss, or support the expense.

The officers resident in the cities of *London* and *Westminster,* are exempt from the particular disadvantages of removals. This seems to be the only circumstance which they enjoy superior to their country brethren. In every other respect they lay under the same hardships, and suffer the same distresses.

There are no perquisites or advantages in the least annexed to the employment. A few officers who are stationed along the coast, may sometimes have the good fortune to fall in with a seizure of contraband goods, and yet, that frequently at the hazard of their lives:

but the inland officers can have no such opportunities. Besides, the surveying duty in the excise is so continual that without remissness from the real business itself there is no time to seek after them. With the officers of the customs it is quite otherwise; their whole time and care is appropriated to that service, and their profits are in proportion to their vigilance.

If the increase of money in the kingdom is one cause of the high price of provisions, the case of the excise officers is peculiarly pitiable. No increase comes to them – they are shut out from the general blessing – they behold it like a map of *Peru*. The answer of Abraham to Dives is somewhat applicable to them, '*There is a great gulf fixed.*'

To the wealthy and humane it is a matter worthy of concern that their affluence should become the misfortune of others. Were the money in the kingdom to be increased double the salary would in value be reduced one-half. Every step upward is a step downward with them. Not to be partakers of the increase would be a little hard, but to be sufferers by it exceedingly so. The mechanic and the labourer may in a great measure ward off the distress by raising the price of their manufactures or their work, but the situation of the officers admits of no such relief.

Another consideration in their behalf (and which is peculiar to the excise) is that, as the law of their office removes them far from all their natural friends and relations, it consequently prevents those occasional assistance from them, which are serviceably felt in a family, and which even the poorest among the poor enjoys. Most poor mechanics, or even common labourers, have some relations or friends, who, either out of benevolence or pride, keep their children from nakedness, supply them occasionally with perhaps half a hog, a load of wood, a chaldron of coals, or something or other which abates the severity of their distress; and yet those men thus relieved will frequently earn more than the daily pay of an excise officer.

Perhaps an officer will appear more reputable with the same pay than a mechanic or labourer. The difference arises from sentiment, not circumstances. A something like reputable pride makes all the distinction, and the thinking part of mankind well knows that none suffers so much as they who endeavour to conceal their necessities.

The frequent removals which unavoidably happen in the excise are attended with such an expense, especially where there is a family, as few officers are able to support. About two years ago, an officer with a family, under orders for removing, and in rather embarrassed circumstances, made his application to me, and from a conviction of his distress I advanced a small sum to enable him to proceed. He ingenuously declared, that without the assistance of some friend, he should be driven to do injustice to his creditors, and compelled to desert the duty of his office. He has since honestly paid me, and does as well as the narrowness of such circumstances can admit of.

There is one general allowed truth which will always operate in their favour, which is, that no set of men under His Majesty earn their salary with any comparison of labour and fatigue with that of the officers of excise. The station may rather be called a seat of constant work than either a place or an employment. Even in the different departments of the general revenue they are unequalled in the burden of business; a riding officer's place in the customs, whose salary is sixty pounds a year, is *ease* to theirs; and the work in the window-light duty, compared with the excise, is lightness itself; yet their salary is subject to no tax, they receive forty-nine pounds twelve shillings and sixpence, without deduction.

The inconveniences which affect an excise officer are almost endless; even the land-tax assessment upon their salaries, which though the Government pays, falls often with hardship upon them. The place of their residence, on account of the land tax, has in many instances, created frequent contentions between parishes, in which the officer, though the innocent and unconcerned cause of the quarrel, has been the greater sufferer.

To point out particularly the impossibility of an excise officer supporting himself and family, with any proper degree of credit and reputation, on so scanty a pittance, is altogether unnecessary. The times, the voice of general want, is proof itself. Where facts are sufficient, arguments are useless; and the hints which I have produced are such as affect the officers of excise *differently* to any other set of men. A single man may barely live; but as it is not the design of the Legislature or the honourable Board of Excise, to impose a state of celibacy on them, the condition of much the greater part is truly wretched and pitiable.

Perhaps it may be said, why do the excise officers complain; they are not pressed into the service, and may relinquish it when they please; if they can mend themselves, why don't they? Alas! what a mockery of pity would it be to give such an answer to an honest, faithful old officer in the excise, who had spent the prime of his life in the service, and was become unfit for anything else. The time limited for an admission into an excise employment, is between twenty-one and thirty years of age – the very flower of life. Every other hope and consideration is then given up, and the chance of establishing themselves in any other business becomes in a few years not only lost to them, but they become lost to it. 'There is a tide in the affairs of men,' which if embraced, leads on to fortune – *that neglected,* all beyond is misery or want.

When we consider how few in the excise arrive at any comfortable eminence, and the date of life when such promotions only can happen, the great hazard there is of ill rather than good fortune in the attempt, and that all the years antecedent to that is a state of mere existence, wherein they are shut out from the common chance of success in any other way: a reply like that can be only a derision of their wants. 'Tis almost impossible after any longer continuance in the excise that they *can* live any other way. Such as are of trades would have their trade to learn over again; and people would have but little opinion of their abilities in any calling who had been ten, fifteen, or twenty years absent from it. Every year's experience gained in the excise is a year's experience lost in trade; and by the time they become wise officers they become foolish workmen.

Were the reasons for augmenting the salary grounded only on the charitableness of so doing, they would have great weight with the compassionate. But there are auxiliaries of such a powerful cast that in the opinion of policy they obtain the rank of originals. The first is truly the case of the officers, but this is rather the case of the revenue.

The distresses in the excise are so generally known that numbers of gentlemen, and other inhabitants in places where officers are resident, have generously and humanely recommended their case to the members of the Honourable House of Commons: and numbers of traders of opulence and reputation, well knowing that the poverty of an officer may subject him to the fraudulent designs of some selfish persons under his survey, to the great injury of the fair trader, and trade in general, have, from principles both of generosity and justice, joined in the same recommendation.

THOUGHTS ON THE CORRUPTION OF PRINCIPLES,
AND ON THE NUMEROUS EVILS ARISING
TO THE REVENUE , FROM THE TOO GREAT POVERTY
OF THE OFFICERS OF EXCISE

It has always been the wisdom of Government to consider the situation and circumstances of persons in trust. Why are large salaries given in many instances, but to proportion it to the trust, to set men above temptation, and to make it even literally worth their while to be honest? The salaries of the judges have been augmented, and their places made independent even of the Crown itself, for the above wise purposes.

Certainly there can be nothing unreasonable in supposing there is such an instinct as frailty among the officers of excise, in common with the rest of mankind; and that the most effectual method to keep men honest is to enable them to live so. The tenderness of conscience is too often overmatched by the sharpness of want; and principle, like chastity, yields with just reluctance enough to excuse itself.

There is a powerful rhetoric in necessity, which exceeds even a *Dunning* or a *Wedderbrune*. No argument can satisfy the feelings of hunger, or abate the edge of appetite. Nothing tends to a greater corruption of manners and principles than a too great distress of circumstances; and the corruption is of that kind that it spreads a plaster for itself: like a viper it carries a cure, though a false one, for its own poison. *Agur,* without any alternative, has made dishonesty the immediate consequence of poverty. 'Lest I be poor and steal.' A very little degree of that dangerous kind of philosophy, which is the almost certain effect of involuntary poverty, will teach men to believe that to starve is more criminal than to steal, by as much as every species of self-murder exceeds every other crime; that true honesty is sentimental, and the practice of it dependent upon circumstances.

If the gay find it difficult to resist the allurements of pleasure, the great temptation of ambition, or the miser the acquisition of wealth, how much stronger are the provocations of want and poverty? The excitements to pleasure, grandeur or riches, are mere 'shadows of a shade' compared to the irresistible necessities of nature. Not to be led into temptation is the prayer of Divinity itself; and to guard against, or rather to prevent, such ensnaring situations is one of the greatest heights of human prudence: in private life it is partly religious; and in a revenue sense it is truly political.

The rich, in ease and affluence, may think I have drawn an unnatural portrait; but could they descend to the cold regions of want, the circle of polar poverty, they would find their opinions changing with the climate. There are habits of thinking peculiar to different conditions, and to find them out is truly to study mankind.

That the situation of an excise officer is of this dangerous kind, must be allowed by every one who will consider the trust unavoidably reposed in him, and compare the narrowness of his circumstances with the hardship of the times. If the salary was judged competent a hundred years ago, it cannot be so now. Should it be advanced that if the present set of officers are dissatisfied with the salary enough may be procured not only for the present salary, but for less, the answer is extremely easy. The question needs only be put; it destroys itself. Were two or three thousand men to offer to execute the office without any salary, would the Government accept them? No. Were the same number to offer the same service for a salary less than can possibly support them, would the Government accept them? Certainly no; for while nature, in spite of law or religion, makes it a ruling principle not to starve, the event would be this, that if they could not live on the salary they would discretionarily live out of the duty.

Query, whether poverty has not too great an influence now? Were the employment a place of direct labour, and not of trust, then frugality in the salary would be sound policy: but when it is considered that the greatest single branch of the revenue, a duty amounting to near five millions sterling, is annually charged by a set of men, most of whom are wanting even the common necessaries of life, the thought must, to every friend to honesty, to every person concerned in the management of the public money, be strong and striking. Poor and in power are powerful temptations; I call it power, because they have it in their power to defraud. The trust unavoidably reposed in an excise officer is so great that it would be an act of wisdom, and perhaps of interest, to secure him from the temptations of downright poverty. To relieve their wants would be charity, but to secure the revenue by so doing would be prudence.

Scarce a week passes at the office but some detections are made of fraudulent and collusive proceedings. The poverty of the officers is the fairest bait for a designing trader that can possibly be; such introduce themselves to the officer under the common plea of the insufficiency of the salary. Every considerate mind must allow that poverty and opportunity corrupt many an honest man. I am not at all surprised that so many opulent and reputable traders have recommended the case of the officers to the good favour of their representatives. They are sensible of the pinching circumstances of the officers, and of the injury to trade in general, from the advantages which are taken of them.

The welfare of the fair trader and the security of the revenue are so inseparably one, that their interest or injuries are alike. It is the opinion of such whose situation gives them a perfect knowledge in the matter that the revenue suffers more by the corruption of a few officers in a country than would make a handsome addition to the salary of the whole number in the same place.

I very lately knew an instance where it is evident, on comparison of the duty charged since, that the revenue suffered by one trader (and he not a very considerable one) upward of one hundred and sixty pounds *per annum* for several years; and yet the benefit to the officer was a mere trifle, in consideration of the trader's. Without doubt the officer would have thought himself much happier to have received the same addition another way. The bread of deceit is a bread of bitterness; but alas! how few in times of want and hardship are capable of thinking so: objects appear under new colours and in shapes not naturally their own; hunger sucks in the deception and necessity reconciles it to conscience.

The commissioners of excise strongly enjoin that no officer accept any treaty, gratuity or, in short, lay himself under any kind of obligation to the traders under their survey: the wisdom of such an injunction is evident; but the practice of it, to a person surrounded with children and poverty, is scarcely possible; and such obligations, wherever they exist, must operate, directly or indirectly, to the injury of the revenue. Favours will naturally beget their likenesses, especially where the return is not at our own expense.

I have heard it remarked by a gentleman whose knowledge in excise business is indisputable that there are numbers of officers who are even afraid to look into an unentered room, lest they should give offence. Poverty and obligation tie up the hands of office and give a prejudicial bias to the mind.

There is another kind of evil, which, though it may never amount to what may be deemed criminality in law, yet it may amount to what is much worse in effect, and that is, *a constant and perpetual leakage in the revenue*: a sort of gratitude in the dark, a distant requital for such civilities as only the lowest poverty would accept, and which are a thousand *per cent* above the value of the civility received. Yet there is no immediate collusion; the trader and officer are both safe; the design, if discovered, passes for error.

These, with numberless other evils, have all their origin in the poverty of the officers. Poverty, in defiance of principle, begets a degree of meanness that will stoop to almost anything. A thousand refinements of argument may be brought to prove that the practice of honesty will be still the same, in the most trying and necessitous circumstances. He who never was an hungered may argue finely on the subjection of his appetite; and he who never was distressed may harangue as beautifully on the power of principle. But poverty, like grief, has an incurable deafness, which never hears; the oration loses all its edge; and '*To be, or not to be*' becomes the only question.

There is a striking difference between dishonesty arising from want of food, and want of principle. The first is worthy of compassion, the other of punishment. Nature never produced a man who would starve in a well-stored larder, because the provisions were not his own: but he who robs it from luxury of appetite deserves a gibbet.

There is another evil which the poverty of the salary produces, and which nothing but an augmentation of it can remove; and that is negligence and indifference. These may not appear of such dark complexion as fraud and collusion, but their injuries to the revenue are the same. It is impossible that any office or business can be regarded as it ought, where this ruinous disposition exists. It requires no sort of argument to prove that the value set upon any place or employment will be in proportion to the value of it; and that diligence or negligence will arise from the same cause. The continual number of relinquishments and discharges always happening in the excise are evident proofs of it.

Persons first coming into the excise form very different notions of it, to what they have afterwards. The gay ideas of promotion soon expire. The continuance of work, the strictness of the duty, and the poverty of the salary, soon beget negligence and indifference: the course continues for a while, the revenue suffers, and the officer is discharged: the vacancy is soon filled up, new ones arise to produce the same mischief and share the same fate.

What adds still more to the weight of this grievance is that this destructive disposition reigns most among such as are otherwise the most proper and qualified for the employment; such as are neither fit for the excise, or anything else, are glad to hold it by any means; but the revenue lies at as much hazard from their want of judgement, as from the others' want of diligence.

In private life, no man would trust the execution of any important concern to a servant who was careless whether he did it or not, and the same rule must hold good in a revenue sense. The commissioners may continue discharging every day, and the example will have no weight while the salary is an object so inconsiderable, and this disposition has such a general existence. Should it be advanced that if men will be careless of such bread as is in their possession they will still be the same were it better, I answer that, as the disposition I am speaking of is not the effect of natural idleness, but of dissatisfaction in point of profit, they would *not* continue the same.

A good servant will be careful of a good place, though very indifferent about a bad one. Besides, this spirit of indifference, should it procure a discharge, is no ways affecting to their circumstances. The easy transition of a qualified officer to a counting-house, or at least to a school master, at any time, as it naturally supports and backs his indifference about the excise, so it takes off all punishment from the order whenever it happens.

I have known numbers discharged from the excise who would have been a credit to their patrons and the employment, could they have found it worth their while to have attended to it. No man enters into excise with any higher expectations than a competent maintenance; but not to find even that, can produce nothing but *Corruption, Collusion and Neglect*.

REMARKS ON THE QUALIFICATIONS OF OFFICERS

In employments where direct labour only is wanted, and trust quite out of the question, the service is merely animal or mechanical. In cutting a river, or forming a road, as there is no possibility of fraud, the merit of honesty is but of little weight. Health, strength and hardiness are the labourer's virtues. But where property depends on the trust, and lies at the discretion of the servant, the judgement of the master takes a different channel, both in the choice and the wages. The honest and the dissolute have here no comparison of merit. A known thief may be trusted to gather stones; but a steward ought to be proof against the temptations of uncounted gold.

The excise is so far from being of the nature of the first that it is all and more than can commonly be put together in the last: 'Tis a place of *poverty, of trust, of opportunity, and temptation*. A compound of discords, where the more they harmonize the more they offend. Ruin and reconcilement are produced at once.

To be properly qualified for the employment it is not only necessary that the person should be honest, but that he be sober, diligent and skilful: sober, that he may be always capable of business; diligent, that he may be always in his business; and skilful, that he may be able to prevent or detect frauds against the revenue. The want of any of these qualifications is a capital offence in the excise. A complaint of drunkenness, negligence or ignorance, is certain death by the laws of the board.

It cannot then be all sorts of persons who are proper for the office. The very notion of procuring a sufficient number for even less than the present salary is so destitute of every degree of sound reason that it needs no reply. The employment, from the insufficiency of the salary, is *already* become so inconsiderable in the general opinion that persons of any capacity or reputation will keep out of it; for where is the mechanic, or even the labourer, who cannot earn at least 1s. 9¼d. per day? It certainly cannot be proper to take the dregs of every calling, and to make the excise the common receptacle for the indigent, the ignorant and the calamitous.

A truly worthy commissioner, lately dead, made a public offer a few years ago, of putting any of his neighbours' sons into the excise; but though the offer amounted almost to an invitation, one only, whom seven years' apprenticeship could not make a tailor, accepted it; who, after a twelve-months' instruction, was ordered off, but in a few days finding the employment beyond his abilities, he prudently deserted it and returned home, where he now remains in the character of a husbandman.

There are very few instances of rejection even of persons who can scarce write their own names legibly; for as there is neither law to compel, nor encouragement to incite, no other can be had than such as offer, and none will offer who can see any other prospect of living. Everyone knows that the excise is a place of labour, not of ease; of hazard, not of certainty; and that downright poverty finishes the character.

It must strike every considerate mind to hear a man with a large family faithful enough to declare that he cannot support himself on the salary with that honest independence he could wish. There is a great degree of affecting honesty in an ingenuous confession. Eloquence may strike the ear, but the language of poverty strikes the heart; the first may charm like music, but the second alarms like a knell.

Of late years there has been such an admission of improper and ill-qualified persons into the excise that the office is not only become contemptible, but the revenue insecure. Collectors whose long services and qualifications have advanced them to that station are disgraced by the wretchedness of new supers continually. Certainly some regard ought to be had to decency, as well as merit.

These are some of the capital evils which arise from the wretched poverty of the salary. Evils they certainly are; for what can be more destructive in a revenue office, than CORRUPTION, COLLUSION, NEGLECT AND ILL QUALIFICATIONS?

Should it be questioned whether an augmentation of salary would remove them, I answer there is scarce a doubt to be made of it. Human wisdom may possibly be deceived in its wisest designs; but here every thought and circumstance establish the hope. They are evils of such a ruinous tendency that they must, by some means or other, be removed. Rigour and severity have been tried in vain; for punishment loses all its force where men expect and disregard it.

Of late years the Board of Excise has shown an extraordinary tenderness in such instances as might otherwise have affected the circumstances of their officers. Their compassion has greatly tended to lessen the distresses of the employment: but as it cannot amount to a total removal of them, the officers of excise throughout the kingdom have (as the voice of one man) prepared petitions to be laid before the Honourable House of Commons on the ensuing Parliament.

An augmentation of salary sufficient to enable them to live honestly and competently would produce more good effect than all the laws of the land can enforce. The generality of such frauds as the officers have been detected in have appeared of a nature as remote from inherent dishonesty as a temporary illness is from an incurable disease. Surrounded with *want, children* and *despair,* what can the *husband* or the *father* do? No laws compel like nature – no connections bind like blood.

With an addition of salary the excise would wear a new aspect, and recover its former constitution. Languor and neglect would give place to care and cheerfulness. Men of reputation and abilities would seek after it, and finding a comfortable maintenance, would stick to it. The unworthy and the incapable would be rejected; the power of superiors be re-established, and laws and instructions receive new force. The officers would be secured from the temptations of poverty, and the revenue from the evils of it; the cure would be as extensive as the complaint, and new health out-root the present corruptions.

[2] AFRICAN SLAVERY
IN AMERICA

(1775)

In Philadelphia, Paine busied himself with reform politics. One of his principal concerns was the abolition of slavery. To this end he joined in 1775 the first anti-slavery society created in America. In this essay published that same year Paine asks his new country to 'discontinue and renounce' slavery.

To Americans: That some desperate wretches should be willing to steal and enslave men by violence and murder for gain, is rather lamentable than strange. But that many civilized, nay, Christianized people should approve, and be concerned in the savage practice, is surprising; and still persist, though it has been so often proved contrary to the light of nature, to every principle of justice and humanity, and even good policy, by a succession of eminent men,[1] and several late publications.

Our traders in MEN (*an unnatural commodity!*) must know the wickedness of that SLAVE-TRADE, if they attend to reasoning, or the dictates of their own hearts; and such as shun and stiffle all these, wilfully sacrifice conscience, and the character of integrity to that golden idol.

The managers of that trade themselves, and others, testify, that many of these African nations inhabit fertile countries, are industrious farmers, enjoy plenty, and lived quietly, averse to war, before the Europeans debauched them with liquors, and bribing them against one another; and that these inoffensive people are brought into slavery, by stealing them, tempting kings to sell subjects, which they can have no right to do, and hiring one tribe to war against another, in order to catch prisoners. By such wicked and inhuman ways the English are said to enslave towards one hundred thousand yearly; of which thirty thousand are supposed to die by barbarous treatment in the first year; besides all that are slain in the unnatural wars excited to take them. So much innocent blood have the managers and sup-

1 Dr Ames, Baxter, Durham, Locke, Carmichael, Hutcheson, Montesquieu, and Blackstone, Wallace, etc., etc. Bishop of Gloucester. – Paine.

porters of this inhuman trade to answer for to the common Lord of all!

Many of these were not prisoners of war, and redeemed from savage conquerors, as some plead; and they who were such prisoners, the English, who promote the war for that very end, are the guilty authors of their being so; and if they were redeemed, as is alleged, they would owe nothing to the redeemer but what he paid for them.

They show as little reason as conscience who put the matter by with saying – 'Men, in some cases, are lawfully made slaves, and why may not these?' So men, in some cases, are lawfully put to death, deprived of their goods, without their consent; may any man, therefore, be treated so, without any conviction of desert? Nor is this plea mended by adding – 'They are set forth to us as slaves, and we buy them without farther inquiry, let the sellers see to it.' Such men may as well join with a known band of robbers, buy their ill-got goods, and help on the trade; ignorance is no more pleadable in one case than the other; the sellers plainly own how they obtain them. But none can lawfully buy without evidence that they are not concurring with men-stealers; and as the true owner has a right to reclaim his goods that were stolen, and sold; so the slave, who is proper owner of his freedom, has a right to reclaim it, however often sold.

Most shocking of all is alleging the sacred scriptures to favour this wicked practice. One would have thought none but infidel cavillers would endeavour to make them appear contrary to the plain dictates of natural light, and conscience, in a matter of common justice and humanity; which they cannot be. Such worthy men, as referred to before, judged otherways; Mr Baxter declared, *the slave-traders should be called devils, rather than Christians; and that it is a heinous crime to buy them*. But some say, 'the practice was permitted to the Jews'. To which may be replied.

1. The example of the Jews, in many things, may not be imitated by us; they had not only orders to cut off several nations altogether, but if they were obliged to war with others, and conquered them, to cut off every male; they were suffered to use polygamy and divorces, and other things utterly unlawful to us under clearer light.

2. The plea is, in a great measure, false; they had no permission to catch and enslave people who never injured them.

3 Such arguments ill become us, *since the time of reformation came,* under gospel light. All distinctions of nations, and privileges of one

above others, are ceased; Christians are taught to *account all men their neighbours; and love their neighbours as themselves; and do to all men as they would be done by; to do good to all men; and man-stealing is ranked with enormous crimes*. Is the barbarous enslaving our inoffensive neighbours, and treating them like wild beasts subdued by force, reconcilable with all these *divine precepts*? Is this doing to them as we would desire they should do to us? If they could carry off and enslave some thousands of us, would we think it just? – One would almost wish they could for once; it might convince more than reason, or the Bible.

As much in vain, perhaps, will they search ancient history for examples of the modern slave-trade. Too many nations enslaved the prisoners they took in war. But to go to nations with whom there is no war, who have no way provoked, without farther design of conquest, purely to catch inoffensive people, like wild beasts, for slaves, is an height of outrage against humanity and justice, that seems left by heathen nations to be practised by pretended Christians. How shameful are all attempts to colour and excuse it!

As these people are not convicted of forfeiting freedom, they have still a natural, perfect right to it; and the governments whenever they come should, in justice set them free, and punish those who hold them in slavery.

So monstrous is the making and keeping them slaves at all, abstracted from the barbarous usage they suffer, and the many evils attending the practice; as selling husbands away from wives, children from parents, and from each other, in violation of sacred and natural ties; and opening the way for adulteries, incests, and many shocking consequences, for all of which the guilty masters must answer to the final Judge.

If the slavery of the parents be unjust, much more is their children's; if the parents were justly slaves, yet the children are born free; this is the natural, perfect right of all mankind; they are nothing but a just recompense to those who bring them up: And as much less is commonly spent on them than others, they have a right, in justice, to be proportionably sooner free.

Certainly one may, with as much reason and decency, plead for murder, robbery, lewdness, and barbarity, as for this practice. They are not more contrary to the natural dictates of conscience, and feelings of humanity; nay, they are all comprehended in it.

But the chief design of this paper is not to disprove it, which many have sufficiently done; but to entreat Americans to consider.

1. With that consistency, or decency they complain so loudly of attempts to enslave them, while they hold so many hundred thousands in slavery; and annually enslave many thousands more, without any pretence of authority, or claim upon them?

2. How just, how suitable to our crime is the punishment with which providence threatens us? We have enslaved multitudes, and shed much innocent blood in doing it; and now are threatened with the same. And while others' evils are confessed, and bewailed, why not this especially, and publicly; than which no other vice, if all others, has brought so much guilt on the land?

3. Whether, then, all ought not immediately to discontinue and renounce it, with grief and abhorrence? Should not every society bear testimony against it, and account obstinate persisters in it bad men, enemies to their country, and exclude them from fellowship; as they often do for much lesser faults?

4. The great question may be – What should be done with those who are enslaved already? To turn the old and infirm free, would be injustice and cruelty; they who enjoyed the labours of their better days should keep, and treat them humanely. As to the rest, let prudent men, with the assistance of legislatures, determine what is practicable for masters, and best for them. Perhaps some could give them lands upon reasonable rent, some, employing them in their labour still, might give them some reasonable allowances for it; so as all may have some property, and fruits of their labours at their own disposal, and be encouraged to industry; the family may live together, and enjoy the natural satisfaction of exercising relative affections and duties, with civil protection, and other advantages, like fellow men. Perhaps they might sometime form useful barrier settlements on the frontiers. Thus they may become interested in the public welfare, and assist in promoting it; instead of being dangerous, as now they are, should any enemy promise them a better condition.

5. The past treatment of Africans must naturally fill them with abhorrence of Christians; lead them to think our religion would make them more inhuman savages, if they embraced it; thus the gain of that trade has been pursued in opposition to the Redeemer's cause, and the happiness of men. Are we not, therefore, bound in duty to him and to them to repair these injuries, as far as possible, by taking

some proper measures to instruct, not only the slaves here, but the Africans in their own countries? Primitive Christians laboured always to spread their *divine religion*; and this is equally our duty while there is an heathen nation. But what singular obligations are we under to these injured people!

These are the sentiments of

JUSTICE AND HUMANITY.

[3] REFLECTIONS ON THE LIFE
AND DEATH OF LORD CLIVE

(1775)

Even as he contemplated America's independence from the British, Paine thought of other peoples only then losing their freedom to the expanding colonial empire. In this early concern for the plight of an India ravaged by the British, Paine was at one with Burke, his future antagonist. Burke, too, would indict the inhumanity of Britain's imperial conquest in the East.

Ah! The tale is told – The scene is ended – and the curtain falls. As an emblem of the vanity of all earthly pomp, let his monument be a globe, but be that globe a bubble; let his effigy be a man walking round it in his sleep; and let fame, in the character of a shadow, inscribe his honours on the air.

I view him but as yesterday on the burning plains of Plassey,[1] doubtful of life, health, or victory. I see him in the instant when '*To be or not to be,*' were equal chances to a human eye. To be a lord or a slave, to return loaded with the spoils, or remain mingled with the dust of India. Did necessity always justify the severity of a conqueror, the rude tongue of censure would be silent, and however painfully he might look back on scenes of horror, the pensive reflection would not alarm him. Though his feelings suffered, his conscience would be acquitted. The sad remembrance would move serenely, and leave the mind without a wound. But oh India! thou loud proclaimer of European cruelties, thou bloody monument of unnecessary deaths, be tender in the day of inquiry, and show a Christian world thou canst suffer and forgive.

Departed from India, and loaded with plunder, I see him doubling the Cape and looking wistfully to Europe. I see him contemplating on years of pleasure, and gratifying his ambition with expected honours. I see his arrival pompously announced in every newspaper, his eager eye rambling through the crowd in quest of homage, and his ear listening lest an applause should escape him. Happily for him

1 Battle of Plassey, in the East Indies, where Lord Clive, at that time Colonel Clive, acquired an immense fortune, and from which place his title is taken. – Paine.

he arrived before his *fame*, and the short interval was a time of rest. From the crowd I follow him to the court, I see him enveloped in the sunshine of sovereign favour, rivalling the great in honours, the proud in splendour, and the rich in wealth. From the court I trace him to the country, his equipage moves like a camp; every village bell proclaims his coming; the wondering peasants admire his pomp, and his heart runs over with joy.

But, alas! not satisfied with uncountable thousands, I accompany him *again* to India. I mark the variety of countenances which appear at his landing. Confusion spreads the news. Every passion seems alarmed. The wailing widow, the crying orphan, and the childless parent remember and lament; the rival nabobs court his favour; the rich dread his power, and the poor his severity. Fear and terror march like pioneers before his camp, murder and rapine accompany it, famine and wretchedness follow in the rear.

Resolved on accumulating an unbounded fortune, he enters into all the schemes of war, treaty, and intrigue. The British sword is set up for sale; the heads of contending nabobs are offered at a price, and the bribe taken from both sides. Thousands of men or money are trifles in an India bargain. The field is an empire, and the treasure almost without end. The wretched inhabitants are glad to compound for offences never committed, and to purchase at any other rate the privilege to breathe; while he, the sole lord of their lives and fortunes, disposes of either as he pleases, and prepares for Europe.[2]

2 In April, 1773, a Committee of the House of Commons, under the name of the Select Committee, were appointed to inquire into the state of the East India affairs, and the conduct of the several Governors of Bengal. The Committee having gone through the examinations, General Burgoyne, the chairman, prefaced their report to the House, informing them, 'that the reports contained accounts shocking to human nature, that the most infamous designs had been carried into execution by perfidy and murder.' He recapitulated the wretched situation of the East-Indian princes, who held their dignities on the precarious condition of being the highest bribers. No claim, however just on their part, he said, could be admitted without being introduced with enormous sums of rupees, nor any prince suffered to reign long, who did not quadrate with this idea; and that Lord Clive, over and above the enormous sums he might with some appearance of justice lay claim to, had obtained others to which he could have no title. He (General Burgoyne) therefore moved, 'That it appears to this house, that Robert Lord Clive, Baron of Plassey, about the time of deposing Surajah Dowla, nabob of Bengal, and establishing Meer Jaffier in his room, did, through the influence of the power with which he was intrusted, as member of the Select Committee in India, and Commander-in-Chief of the British forces there, obtain and possess himself of two lacks of rupees, as member of the Select Committee; a further sum of two lacks and 80,000 rupees, as member of the Select Committee; a further sum of two lacks of

Uncommon fortunes require an uncommon date of life to enjoy them in. The usual period is spent in preparing to live: And unless nature prolongs the time, fortune bestows her excess of favours in vain.

The conqueror of the east having nothing more to expect from the one, has all his court to make to the other. Anxiety for wealth gives place to anxiety for life; and wisely recollecting that the sea is no respecter of persons, resolves on taking his route to Europe by land. Little beings move unseen, or unobserved, but he engrosses whole kingdoms in his march, and is gazed at like a comet. The burning desert, the pathless mountains, and the fertile valleys, are in their turns explored and passed over. No material accident distresses his progress, and England once more receives the spoiler.

How sweet is rest to the weary traveller; the retrospect heightens the enjoyment; and if the future prospect be serene, the days of ease and happiness are arrived. An uninquiring observer might have been inclined to consider Lord Clive, under all these agreeable circumstances, one whose every care was over, and who had nothing to do but sit down and say, *Soul, take thine ease, thou hast goods laid up in store for many years.*

The reception which he met with on his second arrival, was in every instance equal to, and in many exceeded, the honours of the first. 'Tis the peculiar temper of the English to applaud before they think. Generous of their praise, they frequently bestow it unworthily: but when once the truth arrives, the torrent stops, and rushes back again with the same violence.[3] Scarcely had the echo of the applause

---

rupees, as Commander-in-Chief; a further sum of 16 lacks of rupees, or more, under the denomination of *private donations*; which sums, amounting together to 20 lacks and 80,000 rupees, were of the value, in English money, of £234,000, (equal to £340,000 Pennsylvania currency), and that in so doing, the said Robert Lord Clive abused the powers with which he was intrusted, to the evil example of the servants of the public.' – Paine.

3 Lord Clive, in the defence which he made in the House of Commons, against the charges mentioned in the preceding note, very positively insists on his innocence, and very pathetically laments his situation; and after informing the House of the thanks which he had some years before received, for the same actions which they are now endeavouring to censure him for, he says,

'After such certificates as these, Sir, am I to be brought here like a criminal, and the very best part of my conduct construed into crimes against the State? Is this the reward that is now held out to persons who have performed such important services to their country? If it is, Sir, the future consequences that will attend the execution of any important trust, committed to the persons who have the care of it, will be fatal indeed;

ceased upon the ear, then the rude tongue of censure took up the tale. The newspapers, fatal enemies to ill-gotten wealth! began to buzz a general suspicion of his conduct, and the inquisitive public soon refined it into particulars. Every post gave a stab to his fame – a wound to his peace – and a nail to his coffin. Like spectres from the grave they haunted him in every company, and whispered murder in his ear. A life chequered with uncommon varieties is seldom a long one. Action and care will in time wear down the strongest frame, but guilt and melancholy are poisons of quick dispatch.

Say, cool deliberate reflection was the prize, though abstracted from the guilt, worthy of the pains? Ah no! Fatigued with victory he sat down to rest, and while he was recovering breath he lost it. A conqueror more fatal than himself beset him, and revenged the injuries done to India.

As a cure for avarice and ambition let us take a view of him in his latter years. Ha! what gloomy being wanders yonder? How visibly is the melancholy heart delineated on his countenance. He mourns no common care – his very steps are timed to sorrow – he trembles with a kind of mental palsy. Perhaps 'tis some broken hearted parent, some David mourning for his Absalom, or some Heraclitus weeping for the world. I hear him mutter something about wealth. Perhaps he is poor, and has not wherewithal to hide his head. Some debtor

---

and I am sure the noble Lord upon the treasury bench, whose great humanity and abilities I revere, would never have consented to the resolutions that passed the other night, if he had thought on the dreadful consequences that would attend them. Sir, I cannot say that I either sit or rest easy, when I find that all I have in the world is likely to be confiscated, and that no one will take my security for a shilling. These, Sir, are dreadful apprehensions to remain under, and I cannot but look upon myself as a bankrupt. I have not anything left which I can call my own, except my paternal fortune of £500 per annum, and which has been in the family for ages past. But upon this I am contented to live, and perhaps I shall find more real content of mind and happiness than in the trembling affluence of an unsettled fortune. But, Sir, I must make one more observation, that, if the definition of the Hon. Gentleman, [General Burgoyne,] and of this House, is that the *State,* as expressed in these resolutions is, *quoad hoc,* the company, then, Sir, every farthing that I enjoy is granted to me. But to be called, after sixteen years have elapsed, to account for my conduct in this manner, and after an uninterrupted enjoyment of my property, to be questioned and considered as obtaining it unwarrantably, is hard indeed! and a treatment I should not think the British Senate capable of. But if it should be the case, I have a conscious innocence within me, that tells me my conduct is irreproachable. *Frangas, non flectes.* They may take from me what I have; they may, as they think, make me poor, *but I will be happy!* I mean not this as my defence. My defence will be made at the bar; and before I sit down, I have one request to make to the House, *that when they come to decide upon my honour, they will not forget their own.'* – Paine.

started from his sleepless pillow, to ruminate on poverty and ponder on the horrors of a jail. Poor man! I'll to him and relieve him. Ha! 'tis Lord Clive himself! Bless me, what a change! He makes, I see, for yonder cypress shade – fit scene for melancholy hearts! I'll watch him there and listen to his story.

LORD CLIVE. 'Can I but suffer when a beggar pities me. Erewhile I heard a ragged wretch, who every mark of poverty had on, say to a sooty sweep, Ah, poor Lord Clive! while he the Negro-coloured vagrant, more mercifully cruel, cursed me in my hearing.

'There was a time when fortune, like a yielding mistress, courted me with smiles – She never waited to be told my wishes, but studied to discover them, and seemed not happy to herself, but when she had some favour to bestow. Ah! little did I think the fair enchantress would desert me thus; and after lavishing her smiles upon me, turn my reproacher, and publish me in folio to the world. Volumes of morality are dull and spiritless compared to me. Lord Clive is himself a treatise upon vanity, printed in a golden type. The most unlettered clown writes explanatory notes thereon, and reads them to his children. Yet I could bear these insults could I but bear myself. A strange unwelcome something hangs about me. In company I seem no company at all. The festive board appears to me a stage, the crimson coloured port resembles blood. Each glass is strangely metamorphosed to a man in armour, and every bowl appears a nabob. The joyous toast is like the sound of murder, and the loud laughs are groans of dying men. The scenes of India are all rehearsed, and no one sees the tragedy but myself. Ah! I discover things which are not, and hear unuttered sounds —

'O peace, thou sweet companion of the calm and innocent! Whither art thou fled? Here take my gold, and all the world calls mine, and come thou in exchange. Or thou, thou noisy sweep, who mix thy food with soot and relish it, who canst descend from lofty heights and walk the humble earth again, without repining at the change, come teach that *mystery* to me. Or thou, thou ragged wandering beggar, who, when thou canst not beg successfully, will pilfer from the hound, and eat the dirty morsel sweetly; be thou Lord Clive, and I will beg, so I may laugh like thee.

'Could I unlearn what I've already learned – unact what I've already acted – or would some sacred power convey me back to youth and innocence, I'd act another part – I'd keep within the value of humble life, nor wish for what the world calls pomp.

'But since this cannot be,
And only a few days and sad remain for me,
I'll haste to quit the scene; for what is life
When every passion of the soul's at strife?'[4]

---

4 Some time before his death he became very melancholy – subject to strange
imaginations – and was found dead at last. – Paine.

[4] LIBERTY TREE

(1775)

Throughout his life Paine tried his hand at poetry. One poem, written in 1775, has stood the test of time. The 'liberty tree' would become an important symbol of radical politics for late eighteenth- and nineteenth-century democratic movements.

A SONG, WRITTEN EARLY IN THE AMERICAN REVOLUTION
Tune – The Gods of Greece.

In a chariot of light, from the regions of day,
    The Goddess of Liberty came,
Ten thousand celestials directed her way,
    And hither conducted the dame.
A fair budding branch from the gardens above,
    Where millions with millions agree,
She brought in her hand as a pledge of her love,
    And the plant she named Liberty Tree.

The celestial exotic stuck deep in the ground,
    Like a native it flourished and bore;
The fame of its fruit drew the nations around
    To seek out this peaceable shore.
Unmindful of names or distinctions they came,
    For freemen like brothers agree;
With one spirit endued, they one friendship pursued,
    And their temple was Liberty Tree.

Beneath this fair tree, like the patriarchs of old,
    Their bread in contentment they ate,
Unvexed with the troubles of silver or gold,
    The cares of the grand and the great.
With timber and tar they Old England supplied,
    And supported her power on the sea:
Her battles they fought, without getting a groat,
    For the honour of Liberty Tree.

But hear, O ye swains ('tis a tale most profane),
   How all the tyrannical powers,
Kings, Commons, and Lords, are uniting amain
   To cut down this guardian of ours.
From the East to the West blow the trumpet to arms,
   Thro' the land let the sound of it flee:
Let the far and the near all unite with a cheer,
   In defence of our Liberty Tree.

[5] COMMON SENSE

(1776)

Published anonymously, Common Sense *appeared on Philadelphia streets in January 1776. It was an instant success, and copies of the pamphlet were soon available in all the thirteen colonies. Paine's was an unequivocal call for independence, and many Americans wavering between reconciliation with and independence from Britain were won over to separation by Paine's powerful polemic against monarchy, in general, and the British, in particular. General Washington, writing to a friend in Massachusetts, noted that 'by private letters which I have lately received from Virginia, I find that* Common Sense *is working a powerful change there in the minds of many men'. Few pamphlets have had so dramatic an effect on political events.*

INTRODUCTION

Perhaps the sentiments contained in the following pages, are not yet sufficiently fashionable to procure them general favour; a long habit of not thinking a thing *wrong*, gives it a superficial appearance of being *right*, and raises at first a formidable outcry in defence of custom. But the tumult soon subsides. Time makes more converts than reason.

As a long and violent abuse of power, is generally the Means of calling the right of it in question (and in matters too which might never have been thought of, had not the Sufferers been aggravated into the inquiry) and as the K— of England had undertaken in his *own Right*, to support the Parliament in what he calls *Theirs*, and as the good people of this country are grievously oppressed by the combination, they have an undoubted privilege to inquire into the pretensions of both, and equally to reject the usurpation of either.

In the following sheets, the author hath studiously avoided every thing which is personal among ourselves. Compliments as well as censure to individuals make no part thereof. The wise, and the worthy, need not the triumph of a pamphlet; and those whose sentiments are injudicious, or unfriendly, will cease of themselves unless too much pains are bestowed upon their conversion.

The cause of America is in a great measure the cause of all mankind.

Many circumstances hath, and will arise, which are not local, but universal, and through which the principles of all Lovers of Mankind are affected, and in the Event of which, their Affections are interested. The laying a Country desolate with Fire and Sword, declaring War against the natural rights of all Mankind, and extirpating the Defenders thereof from the Face of the Earth, is the concern of every Man to whom Nature hath given the Power of feeling; of which Class, regardless of Party Censure, is the

AUTHOR.

PS. The Publication of this new Edition hath been delayed, with a View of taking notice (had it been necessary) of any Attempt to refute the Doctrine of Independence: As no Answer hath yet appeared, it is now presumed that none will, the Time needful for getting such a Performance ready for the Public being considerably past.

Who the Author of this Production is, is wholly unnecessary to the Public, as the Object for Attention is the *Doctrine itself,* not the *Man.* Yet it may not be unnecessary to say, That he is unconnected with any Party, and under no sort of Influence public or private, but the influence of reason and principle.

OF THE ORIGIN AND DESIGN OF GOVERNMENT IN GENERAL. WITH CONCISE REMARKS ON THE ENGLISH CONSTITUTION

Some writers have so confounded society with government, as to leave little or no distinction between them; whereas they are not only different, but have different origins. Society is produced by our wants, and government by our wickedness; the former promotes our happiness *positively* by uniting our affections, the latter *negatively* by restraining our vices. The one encourages intercourse, the other creates distinctions. The first is a patron, the last a punisher.

Society in every state is a blessing, but government even in its best state is but a necessary evil; in its worst state an intolerable one; for when we suffer, or are exposed to the same miseries *by a government,* which we might expect in a country *without government,* our calamities are heightened by reflecting that we furnish the means by which we suffer. Government, like dress, is the badge of lost innocence; the palaces of kings are built on the ruins of the bowers of paradise. For were the impulses of conscience clear, uniform, and irresistibly obeyed, man would need no other lawgiver; but that not being the case, he finds it necessary to surrender up a part of his property to furnish means for the protection of the rest; and this he is induced to do by the same prudence which in every other case advises him out of two evils to choose the least. *Wherefore*, security being the true design and end of government, it unanswerably follows that whatever *form* thereof appears most likely to ensure it to us, with the least expense and greatest benefit, is preferable to all others.

In order to gain a clear and just idea of the design and end of government, let us suppose a small number of persons settled in some sequestered part of the earth, unconnected with the rest, they will then represent the first peopling of any country, or of the world. In this state of natural liberty, society will be their first thought. A thousand motives will excite them thereto, the strength of one man is so unequal to his wants, and his mind so unfitted for perpetual solitude, that he is soon obliged to seek assistance and relief of another, who in his turn requires the same. Four or five united would be able to raise a tolerable dwelling in the midst of a wilderness, but *one* man might labour out the common period of life without accomplishing any thing; when he had felled his timber he could not remove it, nor erect it after it was removed; hunger in the mean time would urge him from his work, and every different want call him a different way. Disease, nay even misfortune would be death, for though neither might be mortal, yet either would disable him from living, and reduce him to a state in which he might rather be said to perish than to die.

Thus necessity, like a gravitating power, would soon form our newly arrived emigrants into society, the reciprocal blessings of which, would supersede, and render the obligations of law and government unnecessary while they remained perfectly just to each other; but as nothing but heaven is impregnable to vice, it will unavoidably happen, that in proportion as they surmount the first difficulties of emigration, which bound them together in a common cause, they will begin to relax in their duty and attachment to each other; and this remissness, will point out the necessity, of establishing some form of government to supply the defect of moral virtue.

Some convenient tree will afford them a State-House, under the branches of which, the whole colony may assemble to deliberate on public matters. It is more than probable that their first laws will have the title only of REGULATIONS, and be enforced by no other penalty than public disesteem. In this first parliament every man, by natural right will have a seat.

But as the colony increases, the public concerns will increase likewise, and the distance at which the members may be separated, will render it too inconvenient for all of them to meet on every occasion as at first, when their number was small, their habitations near, and the public concerns few and trifling. This will point out the convenience of their consenting to leave the legislative part to be managed by a select number chosen from the whole body, who are supposed to have the same concerns at stake which those have who appointed them, and who will act in the same manner as the whole body would act were they present. If the colony continue increasing, it will become necessary to augment the number of the representatives, and that the interest of every part of the colony may be attended to, it will be found best to divide the whole into convenient parts, each part sending its proper number; and that the *elected* might never form to themselves an interest separate from the *electors*, prudence will point out the propriety of having elections often; because as the *elected* might by that means return and mix again with the general body of the *electors* in a few months, their fidelity to the public will be secured by the prudent reflection of not making a rod for themselves. And as this frequent interchange will establish a common interest with every part of the community, they will mutually and naturally support each other, and on this (not on the unmeaning name of king) depends the *strength of government, and the happiness of the governed.*

Here then is the origin and rise of government; namely, a mode rendered necessary by the inability of moral virtue to govern the world; here too is the design and end of government, viz. freedom and security. And however our eyes may be dazzled with snow, or our ears deceived by sound; however prejudice may warp our wills, or interest darken our understanding, the simple voice of nature and of reason will say, it is right.

I draw my idea of the form of government from a principle in nature, which no art can overturn, viz. that the more simple any thing is, the less liable it is to be disordered, and the easier repaired when disordered; and with this maxim in view, I offer a few remarks on the so much boasted constitution of England. That it was noble for the dark and slavish times in which it was erected is granted. When the world was overrun with tyranny the least remove therefrom was a glorious rescue. But that it is imperfect, subject to convulsions, and incapable of producing what it seems to promise, is easily demonstrated.

Absolute governments (tho' the disgrace of human nature) have this advantage with them, that they are simple; if the people suffer, they know the head from which their suffering springs, know likewise the remedy, and are not bewildered by a variety of causes and cures. But the constitution of England is so exceedingly complex, that the nation may suffer for years together without being able to discover in which part the fault lies, some will say in one and some in another, and every political physician will advise a different medicine.

I know it is difficult to get over local or long standing prejudices, yet if we will suffer ourselves to examine the component parts of the English constitution, we shall find them to be the base remains of two ancient tyrannies, compounded with some new republican materials.

First. – The remains of monarchical tyranny in the person of the king.

Secondly. – The remains of aristocratical tyranny in the persons of the peers.

Thirdly. – The new republican materials, in the persons of the commons, on whose virtue depends the freedom of England.

The two first, by being hereditary, are independent of the people; wherefore in a *constitutional sense* they contribute nothing towards the freedom of the state.

To say that the constitution of England is a *union* of three powers reciprocally *checking* each other, is farcical, either the words have no meaning, or they are flat contradictions.

To say that the commons is a check upon the king, presupposes two things.

First. – That the king is not to be trusted without being looked after, or in other words, that a thirst for absolute power is the natural disease of monarchy.

Secondly. – That the commons, by being appointed for that

purpose, are either wiser or more worthy of confidence than the crown.

But as the same constitution which gives the commons a power to check the king by withholding the supplies, gives afterwards the king a power to check the commons, by empowering him to reject their other bills; it again supposes that the king is wiser than those whom it has already supposed to be wiser than him. A mere absurdity!

There is something exceedingly ridiculous in the composition of monarchy; it first excludes a man from the means of information, yet empowers him to act in cases where the highest judgement is required. The state of a king shuts him from the world, yet the business of a king requires him to know it thoroughly; wherefore the different parts, unnaturally opposing and destroying each other, prove the whole character to be absurd and useless.

Some writers have explained the English constitution thus; the king, say they, is one, the people another; the peers are an house in behalf of the king; the commons in behalf of the people; but this hath all the distinctions of an house divided against itself; and though the expressions be pleasantly arranged, yet when examined they appear idle and ambiguous; and it will always happen, that the nicest construction that words are capable of, when applied to the description of some thing which either cannot exist, or is too incomprehensible to be within the compass of description, will be words of sound only, and though they may amuse the ear, they cannot inform the mind, for this explanation includes a previous question, viz. *How came the king by a power which the people are afraid to trust, and always obliged to check?* Such a power could not be the gift of a wise people, neither can any power, *which needs checking,* be from God; yet the provision, which the constitution makes, supposes such a power to exist.

But the provision is unequal to the task; the means either cannot or will not accomplish the end, and the whole affair is a *felo de se*; for as the greater weight will always carry up the less, and as all the wheels of a machine are put in motion by one, it only remains to know which power in the constitution has the most weight, for that will govern; and though the others, or a part of them, may clog, or, as the phrase is, check the rapidity of its motion, yet so long as they cannot stop it, their endeavours will be ineffectual; the first moving power will at last have its way, and what it wants in speed is supplied by time.

That the crown is this overbearing part in the English constitution needs not be mentioned, and that it derives its whole consequence merely from being the giver of places and pensions is self-evident, wherefore, though we have been wise enough to shut and lock a door against absolute monarchy, we at the same time have been foolish enough to put the crown in possession of the key.

The prejudice of Englishmen, in favour of their own government by king, lords, and commons, arises as much or more from national pride than reason. Individuals are undoubtedly safer in England than in some other countries, but the *will* of the king is as much the *law* of the land in Britain as in France, with this difference, that instead of proceeding directly from his mouth, it is handed to the people under the most formidable shape of an act of parliament. For the fate of Charles the First, hath only made kings more subtle – not more just.

Wherefore, laying aside all national pride and prejudice in favour of modes and forms, the plain truth is, that *it is wholly owing to the constitution of the people, and not to the constitution of the government* that the crown is not as oppressive in England as in Turkey.

An inquiry into the *constitutional errors* in the English form of government is at this time highly necessary; for as we are never in a proper condition of doing justice to others, while we continue under the influence of some leading partiality, so neither are we capable of doing it to ourselves while we remain fettered by any obstinate prejudice. And as a man, who is attached to a prostitute, is unfitted to choose or judge of a wife, so any prepossession in favour of a rotten constitution of government will disable us from discerning a good one.

OF MONARCHY AND HEREDITARY SUCCESSION

Mankind being originally equals in the order of creation, the equality could only be destroyed by some subsequent circumstance; the distinctions of rich, and poor, may in a great measure be accounted for, and that without having recourse to the harsh, ill-sounding names of oppression and avarice. Oppression is often the *consequence,* but seldom or never the *means* of riches; and though avarice will preserve a man from being necessitously poor, it generally makes him too timorous to be wealthy.

But there is another and greater distinction for which no truly natural or religious reason can be assigned, and that is, the distinction of men into KINGS and SUBJECTS. Male and female are the distinctions of nature, good and bad the distinctions of heaven; but how a race of men came into the world so exalted above the rest, and distinguished like some new species, is worth inquiring into, and whether they are the means of happiness or of misery to mankind.

In the early ages of the world, according to the scripture chronology, there were no kings; the consequence of which was there were no wars; it is the pride of kings which throw mankind into confusion. Holland without a king hath enjoyed more peace for this last century than any of the monarchial governments in Europe. Antiquity favours the same remark; for the quiet and rural lives of the first patriarchs hath a happy something in them, which vanishes away when we come to the history of Jewish royalty.

Government by kings was first introduced into the world by the Heathens, from whom the children of Israel copied the custom. It was the most prosperous invention the Devil ever set on foot for the promotion of idolatry. The Heathens paid divine honours to their deceased kings, and the Christian world hath improved on the plan by doing the same to their living ones. How impious is the title of *sacred majesty* applied to a worm, who in the midst of his splendour is crumbling into dust.

As the exalting one man so greatly above the rest cannot be justified on the equal rights of nature, so neither can it be defended on the authority of scripture; for the will of the Almighty, as declared by Gideon and the prophet Samuel, expressly disapproves of government by kings. All anti-monarchial parts of scripture have been very smoothly glossed over in monarchial governments, but they undoubtedly merit the attention of countries which have their governments yet to form. 'Render unto Caesar the things which are Caesar's' is the scriptural doctrine of courts, yet it is no support of monarchial government, for the Jews at that time were without a king, and in a state of vassalage to the Romans.

Near three thousand years passed away from the Mosaic account of the creation, till the Jews under a national delusion requested a king. Till then their form of government (except in extraordinary cases, where the Almighty interposed) was a kind of republic administered by a judge and the elders of the tribes. Kings they had none, and it was held sinful to acknowledge any being under that title but the Lord of Hosts. And when a man seriously reflects on the idolatrous homage which is paid to the persons of kings, he need not wonder, that the Almighty, ever jealous of his honour, should disapprove of a form of government which so impiously invades the prerogative of heaven.

Monarchy is ranked in scripture as one of the sins of the Jews, for which a curse in reserve is denounced against them. The history of that transaction is worth attending to.

The children of Israel being oppressed by the Midianites, Gideon marched against them with a small army, and victory, thro' the divine interposition, decided in his favour. The Jews, elate with success, and attributing it to the generalship of Gideon, proposed making him a king, saying, *Rule thou over us, thou and thy son and thy son's son.* Here was temptation in its fullest extent; not a kingdom only, but an hereditary one, but Gideon in the piety of his soul replied, *I will not rule over you, neither shall my son rule over you,* THE LORD SHALL RULE OVER YOU. Words need not be more explicit; Gideon doth not *decline* the honour but denieth their right to give it; neither doth he compliment them with invented declarations of his thanks, but in the positive style of a prophet charges them with disaffection to their proper sovereign, the King of Heaven.

About one hundred and thirty years after this, they fell again into the same error. The hankering which the Jews had for the idolatrous customs of the Heathens, is something exceedingly unaccountable; but so it was, that laying hold of the misconduct of Samuel's two sons, who were entrusted with some secular concerns, they came in an abrupt and clamorous manner to Samuel, saying, *Behold thou art old, and thy sons walk not in thy ways, now make us a king to judge us like all the other nations.* And here we cannot but observe that their motives were bad, viz. that they might be *like* unto other nations, i.e. the Heathens, whereas their true glory laid in being as much *unlike* them as possible. *But the thing displeased Samuel when they said, give us a king to judge us; and Samuel prayed unto the Lord, and the Lord said unto Samuel, Hearken unto the voice of the people in all that they say unto thee, for they have not rejected thee, but they have rejected me,* THAT I SHOULD NOT REIGN OVER THEM. *According to all the works which they have done since the day that I brought them up out of Egypt, even unto this day; wherewith they have forsaken me and served other Gods; so do they also unto thee. Now therefore hearken unto their voice, howbeit, protest solemnly unto them and shew them the manner of the king that shall reign over them,* i.e. not of any particular king, but the general manner of the kings of the earth, whom Israel was so eagerly copying after. And notwithstanding the great distance of time and difference of manners, the character is still in fashion, *And Samuel told all the words of the Lord unto the people, that asked of him a king. And he said, This shall be the manner of the king that shall reign over you; he will take your sons and appoint them for himself for his chariots, and to be his horsemen, and some shall run before his chariots* (this description agrees with the present mode of impressing men) *and he will appoint him captains over thousands and captains over fifties, and will set them to ear his ground and to reap his harvest, and to make his instruments of war, and instruments of his chariots; and he will take your daughters to be confectionaries and to be cooks and to be bakers* (this describes the expense and luxury as well as the oppression of kings) *and he will take your fields and your olive yards, even the best of them, and give them to his servants; and he will take the tenth of your seed, and of your vineyards, and give them to his officers and to his servants* (by which we see that bribery, corruption, and favouritism are the standing vices of kings) *and he will take the tenth of your men servants, and your maid servants, and your goodliest young men and your asses, and put them to his work; and he will take the tenth of your sheep, and ye shall be his servants, and ye shall cry out in that day because of your king which ye shall have chosen,* AND THE LORD WILL NOT HEAR YOU IN THAT DAY. This accounts for the continuation of monarchy; neither do the characters of the few good kings which have lived since, either sanctify the title, or blot out the sinfulness of the origin; the high encomium given of David takes no notice of him *officially as a king,* but only as a *man* after God's own heart. *Nevertheless the People refused to obey the voice of Samuel, and they said, Nay, but we will have a king over us, that we may be like all the nations, and that our king may judge us, and go out before us and fight our battles.* Samuel continued to reason with them, but to no purpose; he set before them their ingratitude, but all would not avail; and seeing them fully bent on their folly, he cried out, *I will call unto the Lord, and he shall send thunder and rain* (which then was a punishment, being the time of wheat harvest) *that ye may perceive and see that your wickedness is great which ye have done in the sight of the Lord,* IN ASKING YOU A KING. *So Samuel called unto the Lord, and the Lord sent thunder and rain that day, and all the people greatly feared the Lord and Samuel. And all the people said unto Samuel, Pray for thy servants unto the Lord thy God that we die not, for* WE HAVE ADDED UNTO OUR SINS THIS EVIL, TO ASK A KING. These portions of scripture are direct and positive. They admit of no equivocal construction. That the Almighty hath here entered his protest against monarchial government is true, or the scripture is false. And a man hath good reason to believe that there is as much of king-craft, as priest-craft in withholding the scripture from the public in Popish countries. For monarchy in every instance is the Popery of government.

To the evil of monarchy we have added that of hereditary succession; and as the first is a degradation and lessening of ourselves, so the second, claimed as a matter of right, is an insult and an imposition on posterity. For all men being originally equals, no *one* by *birth* could have a right to set up his own family in perpetual preference to all others for ever, and though himself might deserve *some* decent degree of honours of his contemporaries, yet his descendants might be far too unworthy to inherit them. One of the strongest *natural* proofs of the folly of hereditary right in kings, is, that nature disapproves it, otherwise she would not so frequently turn it into ridicule by giving mankind an *ass for a lion.*

Secondly, as no man at first could possess any other public honours than were bestowed upon him, so the givers of those honours could have no power to give away the right of posterity, and though they might say 'We choose you for *our* head', they could not, without manifest injustice to their children, say 'that your children and your children's children shall reign over *ours* for ever'. Because such an unwise, unjust, unnatural compact might (perhaps) in the next succession put them under the government of a rogue or a fool. Most wise men, in their private sentiments, have ever treated hereditary right with contempt; yet it is one of those evils, which when once established is not easily removed; many submit from fear, others from superstition, and the more powerful part shares with the king the plunder of the rest.

This is supposing the present race of the kings in the world to have had an honourable origin; whereas it is more than probable, that could we take off the dark covering of antiquity, and trace them to their first rise, that we should find the first of them nothing better than the principal ruffian of some restless gang, whose savage manners or pre-eminence in subtlety obtained him the title of chief among plunderers; and who by increasing in power, and extending his depredations, over-awed the quiet and defenceless to purchase their safety by frequent contributions. Yet his electors could have no idea of giving hereditary right to his descendants, because such a perpetual exclusion of themselves was incompatible with the free and unrestrained principles they professed to live by. Wherefore, hereditary succession in the early ages of monarchy could not take place as a matter of claim, but as something casual or complimental; but as few or no records were extant in those days, and traditionary history stuffed with fables, it was very easy, after the lapse of a few generations, to trump up some superstitious tale, conveniently timed, Mahomet like, to cram hereditary right down the throats of the vulgar. Perhaps the disorders which threatened, or seemed to threaten on the decease of a leader and the choice of a new one (for elections among ruffians could not be very orderly) induced many at first to favour hereditary pretensions; by which means it happened, as it hath happened since, that what at first was submitted to as a convenience, was afterwards claimed as a right.

England, since the conquest, hath known some few good monarchs, but groaned beneath a much larger number of bad ones, yet no man in his senses can say that their claim under William the Conqueror is a very honourable one. A French bastard landing with an armed banditti, and establishing himself king of England against the consent of the natives, is in plain terms a very paltry rascally original. – It certainly hath no divinity in it. However, it is needless to spend much time in exposing the folly of hereditary right, if there are any so weak as to believe it, let them promiscuously worship the ass and lion, and welcome. I shall neither copy their humility, nor disturb their devotion.

Yet I should be glad to ask how they suppose kings came at first? The question admits but of three answers, viz. either by lot, by election, or by usurpation. If the first king was taken by lot, it establishes a precedent for the next, which excludes hereditary succession. Saul was by lot yet the succession was not hereditary, neither does it appear from that transaction there was any intention it ever should. If the first king of any country was by election, that likewise establishes a precedent for the next; for to say, that the *right* of all future generations is taken away, by the act of the first electors, in their choice not only of a king, but of a family of kings for ever, hath no parallel in or out of scripture but the doctrine of original sin, which supposes the free will of all men lost in Adam; and from such comparison, and it will admit of no other, hereditary succession can derive no glory. For as in Adam all sinned, and as in the first electors all men obeyed; as in the one all mankind were subjected to Satan, and in the other to Sovereignty; as our innocence was lost in the first, and our authority in the last; and as both disable us from re-assuming some former state and privilege, it unanswerably follows that original sin and hereditary succession are parallels. Dishonourable rank! Inglorious connection! Yet the most subtle sophist cannot produce a juster simile.

As to usurpation, no man will be so hardy as to defend it; and that William the Conqueror was an usurper is a fact not to be contradicted. The plain truth is, that the antiquity of English monarchy will not bear looking into.

But it is not so much the absurdity as the evil of hereditary succession which concerns mankind. Did it ensure a race of good and wise men it would have the seal of divine authority, but as it opens a door to the *foolish*, the *wicked*, and the *improper*, it hath in it the nature of oppression. Men who look upon themselves born to reign, and others to obey, soon grow insolent; selected from the rest of mankind their minds are early poisoned by importance; and the world they act in differs so materially from the world at large, that they have but little opportunity of knowing its true interests, and when they succeed to the government are frequently the most ignorant and unfit of any throughout the dominions.

Another evil which attends hereditary succession is, that the throne is subject to be possessed by a minor at any age; all which time the regency, acting under the cover of a king, have every opportunity and inducement to betray their trust. The same national misfortune happens, when a king worn out with age and infirmity, enters the last stage of human weakness. In both these cases the public becomes a prey to every miscreant, who can tamper successfully with the follies either of age or infancy.

The most plausible plea, which hath ever been offered in favour of hereditary succession, is, that it preserves a nation from civil wars; and were this true, it would be weighty; whereas, it is the most barefaced falsity ever imposed upon mankind. The whole history of England disowns the fact. Thirty kings and two minors have reigned in that distracted kingdom since the conquest, in which time there have been (including the Revolution) no less than eight civil wars and nineteen rebellions. Wherefore instead of making for peace, it makes against it, and destroys the very foundation it seems to stand on.

The contest for monarchy and succession, between the houses of York and Lancaster, laid England in a scene of blood for many years. Twelve pitched battles, besides skirmishes and sieges, were fought between Henry and Edward. Twice was Henry prisoner to Edward, who in his turn was prisoner to Henry. And so uncertain is the fate of war and the temper of a nation, when nothing but personal matters are the ground of a quarrel, that Henry was taken in triumph from a prison to a palace, and Edward obliged to fly from a palace to a foreign land; yet, as sudden transitions of temper are seldom lasting, Henry in his turn was driven from the throne, and Edward recalled to succeed him. The parliament always following the strongest side.

This contest began in the reign of Henry the Sixth, and was not entirely extinguished till Henry the Seventh, in whom the families were united. Including a period of 67 years, viz. from 1422 to 1489.

In short, monarchy and succession have laid (not this or that kingdom only) but the world in blood and ashes. 'Tis a form of government which the word of God bears testimony against, and blood will attend it.

If we inquire into the business of a king, we shall find that in some countries they have none; and after sauntering away their lives without pleasure to themselves or advantage to the nation, withdraw from the scene, and leave their successors to tread the same idle round. In absolute monarchies the whole weight of business civil and military, lies on the king; the children of Israel in their request for a king, urged this plea 'that he may judge us, and go out before us and fight our battles'. But in countries where he is neither a judge nor a general, as in E—d, a man would be puzzled to know what *is* his business.

The nearer any government approaches to a republic the less business there is for a king. It is somewhat difficult to find a proper name for the government of E——. Sir William Meredith calls it a republic;

but in its present state it is unworthy of the name, because the corrupt influence of the crown, by having all the places in its disposal, hath so effectually swallowed up the power, and eaten out the virtue of the house of commons (the republican part in the constitution) that the government of England is nearly as monarchical as that of France or Spain. Men fall out with names without understanding them. For it is the republican and not the monarchical part of the constitution of England which Englishmen glory in, viz. the liberty of choosing an house of commons from out of their own body – and it is easy to see that when the republican virtue fails, slavery ensues. Why is the constitution of E—d sickly, but because monarchy hath poisoned the republic, the crown hath engrossed the commons?

In England a k— hath little more to do than to make war and give away places; which in plain terms, is to impoverish the nation and set it together by the ears. A pretty business indeed for a man to be allowed eight hundred thousand sterling a year for, and worshipped into the bargain! Of more worth is one honest man to society, and in the sight of God, than all the crowned ruffians that ever lived.

THOUGHTS ON THE PRESENT STATE OF
AMERICAN AFFAIRS

In the following pages I offer nothing more than simple facts, plain arguments, and common sense; and have no other preliminaries to settle with the reader, than that he will divest himself of prejudice and prepossession, and suffer his reason and his feelings to determine for themselves; that he will put *on*, or rather that he will not put *off*, the true character of a man, and generously enlarge his views beyond the present day.

Volumes have been written on the subject of the struggle between England and America. Men of all ranks have embarked in the controversy, from different motives, and with various designs; but all have been ineffectual, and the period of debate is closed. Arms, as the last resource, decide the contest; the appeal was the choice of the king, and the continent hath accepted the challenge.

It hath been reported of the late Mr Pelham (who tho' an able minister was not without his faults) that on his being attacked in the house of commons, on the score, that his measures were only of a temporary kind, replied, '*They will last my time.*' Should a thought so fatal and unmanly possess the colonies in the present contest, the name of ancestors will be remembered by future generations with detestation.

The sun never shined on a cause of greater worth. 'Tis not the affair of a city, a country, a province, or a kingdom, but of a continent – of at least one eighth part of the habitable globe. 'Tis not the concern of a day, a year, or an age; posterity are virtually involved in the contest, and will be more or less affected, even to the end of time, by the proceedings now. Now is the seed time of continental union, faith and honour. The least fracture now will be like a name engraved with the point of a pin on the tender rind of a young oak; the wound will enlarge with the tree, and posterity read it in full grown characters.

By referring the matter from argument to arms, a new era for politics is struck; a new method of thinking hath arisen. All plans, proposals, &c. prior to the nineteenth of April, i.e. to the commencement of hostilities, are like the almanacs of the last year; which, though proper then, are superseded and useless now. Whatever was advanced by the advocates on either side of the question then, terminated in one and the same point, viz. a union with Great Britain; the only difference between the parties was the method of effecting it; the one proposing force, the other friendship; but it hath so far happened that the first hath failed, and the second hath withdrawn her influence.

As much hath been said of the advantages of reconciliation, which, like an agreeable dream, hath passed away and left us as we were, it is but right, that we should examine the contrary side of the argument, and inquire into some of the many material injuries which these colonies sustain, and always will sustain, by being connected with, and dependent on Great Britain. To examine that connection and dependence, on the principles of nature and common sense, to see what we have to trust to, if separated, and what we are to expect, if dependent.

I have heard it asserted by some, that as America hath flourished under her former connection with Great Britain, that the same connection is necessary towards her future happiness, and will always have the same effect. Nothing can be more fallacious than this kind of argument. We may as well assert, that because a child has thrived upon milk, that it is never to have meat; or that the first twenty years of our lives is to become a precedent for the next twenty. But even this is admitting more than is true, for I answer roundly, that America would have flourished as much, and probably much more, had no European power had any thing to do with her. The commerce by which she hath enriched herself are the necessaries of life, and will always have a market while eating is the custom of Europe.

But she has protected us, say some. That she hath engrossed us is true, and defended the continent at our expense as well as her own is admitted, and she would have defended Turkey from the same motive, viz. the sake of trade and dominion.

Alas, we have been long led away by ancient prejudices, and made large sacrifices to superstition. We have boasted the protection of Great Britain, without considering, that her motive was *interest* not *attachment*; that she did not protect us from *our enemies* on *our account*, but from *her enemies* on *her own account*, from those who had no quarrel with us on any *other account*, and who will always be our enemies on the *same account*. Let Britain wave her pretensions to the continent, or the continent throw off the dependence, and we should be at peace with France and Spain were they at war with Britain. The miseries of Hanover last war ought to warn us against connections.

It hath lately been asserted in parliament, that the colonies have no relation to each other but through the parent country, *i.e.* that Pennsylvania and the Jerseys, and so on for the rest, are sister colonies by the way of England; this is certainly a very round-about way of proving relationship, but it is the nearest and only true way of proving enemyship, if I may so call it. France and Spain never were, nor perhaps ever will be our enemies as *Americans*, but as our being the *subjects of Great Britain*.

But Britain is the parent country, say some. Then the more shame upon her conduct. Even brutes do not devour their young, nor savages make war upon their families; wherefore the assertion, if true, turns to her reproach; but it happens not to be true, or only partly so, and the phrase *parent* or *mother country* hath been Jesuitically adopted by the — and his parasites, with a low papistical design of gaining an unfair bias on the credulous weakness of our minds. Europe, and not England, is the parent country of America. This new world hath been the asylum for the persecuted lovers of civil and religious liberty from *every part* of Europe. Hither have they fled, not from the tender embraces of the mother, but from the cruelty of the monster; and it is so far true of England, that the same tyranny which drove the first emigrants from home, pursues their descendants still.

In this extensive quarter of the globe, we forget the narrow limits of three hundred and sixty miles (the extent of England) and carry our friendship on a larger scale; we claim brotherhood with every European Christian, and triumph in the generosity of the sentiment.

It is pleasant to observe by what regular gradations we surmount the force of local prejudice, as we enlarge our acquaintance with the world. A man born in any town in England divided into parishes, will naturally associate most with his fellow parishioners (because their interests in many cases will be common) and distinguish him by the name of *neighbour*; if he meet him but a few miles from home, he drops the narrow idea of a street, and salutes him by the name of *townsman*; if he travels out of the county, and meet him in any other, he forgets the minor divisions of street and town, and calls him *countryman, i.e. countyman*; but if in their foreign excursions they should associate in France or any other part of *Europe*, their local remembrance would be enlarged into that of *Englishmen*. And by a just parity of reasoning, all Europeans meeting in America, or any other quarter of the globe, are *countrymen*; for England, Holland, Germany, or Sweden, when compared with the whole, stand in the same places on the larger scale, which the divisions of street, town, and county do on the smaller ones; distinctions too limited for continental minds. Not one third of the inhabitants, even of this province, are of English descent. Wherefore I reprobate the phrase of parent or mother country applied to England only, as being false, selfish, narrow and ungenerous.

But admitting that we were all of English descent, what does it amount to? Nothing. Britain, being now an open enemy, extinguishes every other name and title: And to say that reconciliation is our duty, is truly farcical. The first king of England, of the present line (William the Conqueror) was a Frenchman, and half the peers of England are descendants from the same country; wherefore by the same method of reasoning, England ought to be governed by France.

Much hath been said of the united strength of Britain and the colonies, that in conjunction they might bid defiance to the world.

But this is mere presumption; the fate of war is uncertain, neither do the expressions mean any thing; for this continent would never suffer itself to be drained of inhabitants to support the British arms in either Asia, Africa, or Europe.

Besides, what have we to do with setting the world at defiance? Our plan is commerce, and that, well attended to, will secure us the peace and friendship of all Europe; because it is the interest of all Europe to have America a *free port*. Her trade will always be a protection, and her barrenness of gold and silver secure her from invaders.

I challenge the warmest advocate for reconciliation, to shew, a single advantage that this continent can reap, by being connected with Great Britain. I repeat the challenge, not a single advantage is derived. Our corn will fetch its price in any market in Europe, and our imported goods must be paid for buy them where we will.

But the injuries and disadvantages we sustain by that connection, are without number; and our duty to mankind at large, as well as to ourselves, instruct us to renounce the alliance: Because, any submission to, or dependence on Great Britain, tends directly to involve this continent in European wars and quarrels; and sets us at variance with nations, who would otherwise seek our friendship, and against whom, we have neither anger nor complaint. As Europe is our market for trade, we ought to form no partial connection with any part of it. It is the true interest of America to steer clear of European contentions, which she never can do, while by her dependence on Britain, she is made the make-weight in the scale of British politics.

Europe is too thickly planted with kingdoms to be long at peace, and whenever a war breaks out between England and any foreign power, the trade of America goes to ruin, *because of her connection with Britain*. The next war may not turn out like the last, and should it not, the advocates for reconciliation now will be wishing for separation then, because, neutrality in that case, would be a safer convoy than a man of war. Every thing that is right or natural pleads for separation. The blood of the slain, the weeping voice of nature cries, 'TIS TIME TO PART. Even the distance at which the Almighty hath placed England and America, is a strong and natural proof, that the authority of the one, over the other, was never the design of Heaven. The time likewise at which the continent was discovered, adds weight to the argument, and the manner in which it was peopled encreases the force of it. The reformation was preceded by the discovery of America, as if the Almighty graciously meant to open a sanctuary to the persecuted in future years, when home should afford neither friendship nor safety.

The authority of Great Britain over this continent, is a form of government, which sooner or later must have an end: And a serious mind can draw no true pleasure by looking forward, under the painful and positive conviction, that what he calls 'the present constitution' is merely temporary. As parents, we can have no joy, knowing that *this government* is not sufficiently lasting to ensure any thing which we may bequeath to posterity: And by a plain method of argument, as we are running the next generation into debt, we ought to do the work of it, otherwise we use them meanly and pitifully. In order to discover the line of our duty rightly, we should take our children in our hand, and fix our station a few years farther into life; that eminence will present a prospect, which a few present fears and prejudices conceal from our sight.

Though I would carefully avoid giving unnecessary offence, yet I am inclined to believe, that all those who espouse the doctrine of reconciliation, may be included within the following descriptions. Interested men, who are not to be trusted; weak men who *cannot* see; prejudiced men who *will not* see; and a certain set of moderate men, who think better of the European world than it deserves; and this last class by an ill-judged deliberation, will be the cause of more calamities to this continent than all the other three.

It is the good fortune of many to live distant from the scene of sorrow; the evil is not sufficiently brought to *their* doors to make *them* feel the precariousness with which all American property is possessed. But let our imaginations transport us for a few moments to Boston, that seat of wretchedness will teach us wisdom, and instruct us for ever to renounce a power in whom we can have no trust. The inhabitants of that unfortunate city, who but a few months ago were in ease and affluence, have now no other alternative than to stay and starve, or turn out to beg. Endangered by the fire of their friends if they continue within the city, and plundered by the soldiery if they leave it. In their present condition they are prisoners without the hope of redemption, and in a general attack for their relief, they would be exposed to the fury of both armies.

Men of passive tempers look somewhat lightly over the offences of Britain, and, still hoping for the best, are apt to call out, '*Come we shall be friends again for all this.*' But examine the passions and feelings of mankind. Bring the doctrine of reconciliation to the touchstone of nature, and then tell me, whether you can hereafter love, honour, and faithfully serve the power that hath carried fire and sword into your land? If you cannot do all these, then are you only deceiving yourselves, and by your delay bringing ruin upon posterity. Your future connection with Britain, whom you can neither love nor honour, will be forced and unnatural, and being formed only on the plan of present convenience, will in a little time fall into a relapse more wretched than the first. But if you say, you can still pass the violations over, then I ask, Hath your house been burnt? Hath your property been destroyed before your face? Are your wife and children destitute of a bed to lie on, or bread to live on? Have you lost a parent or a child by their hands, and yourself the ruined and wretched survivor? If you have not, then are you not a judge of those who have. But if you have, and can still shake hands with the murderers, then are you unworthy the name of husband, father, friend, or lover, and whatever may be your rank or title in life, you have the heart of a coward, and the spirit of a sycophant.

This is not inflaming or exaggerating matters, but trying them by those feelings and affections which nature justifies, and without which, we should be incapable of discharging the social duties of life, or enjoying the felicities of it. I mean not to exhibit horror for the purpose of provoking revenge, but to awaken us from fatal and unmanly slumbers, that we may pursue determinately some fixed object. It is not in the power of Britain or of Europe to conquer America, if she did not conquer herself by *delay* and *timidity*. The present winter is worth an age if rightly employed, but if lost or neglected, the whole continent will partake of the misfortune; and there is no punishment which that man will not deserve, be he who, or what, or where he will, that may be the means of sacrificing a season so precious and useful.

It is repugnant to reason, to the universal order of things, to all examples from the former ages, to suppose, that this continent can longer remain subject to any external power. The most sanguine in Britain does not think so. The utmost stretch of human wisdom cannot, at this time compass a plan short of separation, which can promise the continent even a year's security. Reconciliation is and was a falacious dream. Nature hath deserted the connection, and Art cannot supply her place. For, as Milton wisely expressed, 'Never can true reconcilement grow where wounds of deadly hate have pierced so deep.'

Every quiet method for peace hath been ineffectual. Our prayers have been rejected with disdain; and only tended to convince us, that nothing flatters vanity, or confirms obstinacy in kings more than repeated petitioning – and nothing hath contributed more than that very measure to make the kings of Europe absolute: Witness Denmark and Sweden. Wherefore since nothing but blows will do, for God's sake, let us come to a final separation, and not leave the next generation to be cutting throats, under the violated unmeaning names of parent and child.

To say, they will never attempt it again is idle and visionary, we thought so at the repeal of the Stamp Act, yet a year or two undeceived us; as well may we suppose that nations, which have been once defeated, will never renew the quarrel.

As to government matters, it is not in the power of Britain to do this continent justice: The business of it will soon be too weighty, and intricate, to be managed with any tolerable degree of convenience, by a power, so distant from us, and so very ignorant of us; for if they cannot conquer us, they cannot govern us. To be always running three or four thousand miles with a tale or a petition, waiting four or five months for an answer, which when obtained requires five or six more to explain it in, will in a few years be looked upon as folly and childishness – There was a time when it was proper, and there is a proper time for it to cease.

Small islands not capable of protecting themselves, are the proper objects for kingdoms to take under their care; but there is something very absurd, in supposing a continent to be perpetually governed by an island. In no instance hath nature made the satellite larger than its primary planet, and as England and America, with respect to each other, reverses the common order of nature, it is evident they belong to different systems: England to Europe, America to itself.

I am not induced by motives of pride, party, or resentment to espouse the doctrine of separation and independence; I am clearly, positively, and conscientiously persuaded that it is the true interest of this continent to be so; that every thing short of *that* is mere patchwork, that it can afford no lasting felicity, – that it is leaving the sword to our children, and shrinking back at a time, when, a little more, a little farther, would have rendered this continent the glory of the earth.

As Britain hath not manifested the least inclination towards a compromise, we may be assured that no terms can be obtained worthy the acceptance of the continent, or any ways equal to the expense of blood and treasure we have been already put to.

The object contended for, ought always to bear some just proportion to the expense. The removal of N—, or the whole detestable junto, is a matter unworthy the millions we have expended. A temporary stoppage of trade, was an inconvenience, which would have sufficiently balanced the repeal of all the acts complained of, had such repeals been obtained; but if the whole continent must take up arms, if every man must be a soldier, it is scarcely worth our while to fight against a contemptible ministry only. Dearly, dearly, do we pay for the repeal of the acts, if that is all we fight for; for in a just estimation, it is as great a folly to pay a Bunker-hill price for law, as for land. As I have always considered the independency of this continent, as an event, which sooner or later must arrive, so from the late rapid progress of the continent to maturity, the event could not be far off. Wherefore, on the breaking out of hostilities, it was not worth the while to have disputed a matter, which time would have finally redressed, unless we meant to be in earnest; otherwise, it is like wasting an estate on a suit at law, to regulate the trespasses of a tenant, whose lease is just expiring. No man was a warmer wisher for reconciliation than myself, before the fatal nineteenth of April 1775,[1] but the moment the event of that day was made known, I rejected the hardened, sullen tempered Pharaoh of — for ever; and disdain the wretch, that with the pretended title of FATHER OF HIS PEOPLE can unfeelingly hear of their slaughter, and composedly sleep with their blood upon his soul.

But admitting that matters were now made up, what would be the event? I answer, the ruin of the continent. And that for several reasons.

First. The powers of governing still remaining in the hands of the k—, he will have a negative over the whole legislation of this continent. And as he hath shewn himself such an inveterate enemy to liberty, and discovered such a thirst for arbitrary power; is he, or is

1 Massacre at Lexington. – Paine.

he not, a proper man to say to these colonies, '*You shall make no laws but what I please*.' And is there any inhabitant in America so ignorant, as not to know, that according to what is called the *present constitution*, that this continent can make no laws but what the king gives leave to; and is there any man so unwise, as not to see, that (considering what has happened) he will suffer no Law to be made here, but such as suit his purpose. We may be as effectually enslaved by the want of laws in America, as by submitting to laws made for us in England. After matters are made up (as it is called) can there be any doubt but the whole power of the crown will be exerted, to keep this continent as low and humble as possible? Instead of going forward we shall go backward, or be perpetually quarrelling or ridiculously petitioning. – We are already greater than the king wishes us to be, and will he not hereafter endeavour to make us less? To bring the matter to one point. Is the power who is jealous of our prosperity, a proper power to govern us? Whoever says *No* to this question is an *independent*, for independency means no more, than, whether we shall make our own laws, or, whether the —, the greatest enemy this continent hath, or can have, shall tell us '*There shall be no laws but such as I like*.'

But the k— you will say has a negative in England; the people there can make no laws without his consent. In point of right and good order, there is something very ridiculous, that a youth of twenty-one (which hath often happened) shall say to several millions of people, older and wiser than himself, I forbid this or that act of yours to be law. But in this place I decline this sort of reply, tho' I will never cease to expose the absurdity of it, and only answer, that England being the king's residence, and America not so, makes quite another case. The k—'s negative *here* is ten times more dangerous and fatal than it can be in England, for *there* he will scarcely refuse his consent to a bill for putting England into as strong a state of defence as possible, and in America he would never suffer such a bill to be passed.

America is only a secondary object in the system of British politics. England consults the good of *this* country, no farther than it answers her *own* purpose. Wherefore, her own interest leads her to suppress the growth of *ours* in every case which doth not promote her advantage, or in the least interfere with it. A pretty stage we should soon be in under such a second-hand government, considering what has happened! Men do not change from enemies to friends by the alteration of a name: And in order to shew that reconciliation *now* is a dangerous doctrine, I affirm, *that it would be policy in the k— at this time, to repeal the acts for the sake of reinstating himself in the government of the provinces*; in order, that HE MAY ACCOMPLISH BY CRAFT AND SUBTLETY, IN THE LONG RUN, WHAT HE CANNOT DO BY FORCE AND VIOLENCE IN THE SHORT ONE. Reconciliation and ruin are nearly related.

Secondly, That as even the best terms, which we can expect to obtain, can amount to no more than a temporary expedient, or a kind of government by guardianship, which can last no longer than till the colonies come of age, so the general face and state of things, in the interim, will be unsettled and unpromising. Emigrants of property will not choose to come to a country whose form of government hangs but by a thread, and who is every day tottering on the brink of commotion and disturbance; and numbers of the present inhabitants would lay hold of the interval, to dispose of their effects, and quit the continent.

But the most powerful of all arguments, is, that nothing but independence, i.e. a continental form of government, can keep the peace of the continent and preserve it inviolate from civil wars. I dread the event of a reconciliation with Britain now, as it is more than probable, that it will be followed by a revolt somewhere or other, the consequences of which may be far more fatal than all the malice of Britain.

Thousands are already ruined by British barbarity; (thousands more will probably suffer the same fate). Those men have other feelings than us who have nothing suffered. All they *now* possess is liberty, what they before enjoyed is sacrificed to its service, and having nothing more to lose, they disdain submission. Besides, the general temper of the colonies, towards a British government, will be like that of a youth, who is nearly out of his time, they will care very little about her. And a government which cannot preserve the peace, is no government at all, and in that case we pay our money for nothing; and pray what is it that Britain can do, whose power will be wholly on paper, should a civil tumult break out the very day after reconciliation? I have heard some men say, many of whom I believe spoke without thinking, that they dreaded an independence, fearing that it would produce civil wars. It is but seldom that our first thoughts are truly correct, and that is the case here; for there are ten times more to dread from a patched up connection than from independence. I make the sufferers' case my own, and I protest, that were I driven from house and home, my property destroyed, and my circumstances ruined, that as a man, sensible of injuries, I could never relish the doctrine of reconciliation, or consider myself bound thereby.

The colonies have manifested such a spirit of good order and obedience to continental government, as is sufficient to make every reasonable person easy and happy on that head. No man can assign the least pretence for his fears, on any other grounds, that such as are truly childish and ridiculous, that one colony will be striving for superiority over another.

Where there are no distinctions there can be no superiority, perfect equality affords no temptation. The republics of Europe are all (and we may say always) in peace. Holland and Switzerland are without wars, foreign or domestic: Monarchical governments, it is true, are never long at rest; the crown itself is a temptation to enterprising ruffians at *home*; and that degree of pride and insolence ever attendant on regal authority, swells into a rupture with foreign powers, in instances, where a republican government, by being formed on more natural principles, would negotiate the mistake.

If there is any true cause of fear respecting independence, it is because no plan is yet laid down. Men do not see their way out — Wherefore, as an opening into that business, I offer the following hints; at the same time modestly affirming, that I have no other opinion of them myself, than that they may be the means of giving rise to something better. Could the straggling thoughts of individuals be collected, they would frequently form materials for wise and able men to improve to useful matter.

LET the assemblies be annual, with a President only. The representation more equal. Their business wholly domestic, and subject to the authority of a Continental Congress.

Let each colony be divided into six, eight, or ten, convenient districts, each district to send a proper number of delegates to Congress, so that each colony send at least thirty. The whole number in Congress will be at least 390. Each Congress to sit and to choose a president by the following method. When the delegates are met, let a colony be taken from the whole thirteen colonies by lot, after which let the whole Congress choose (by ballot) a president from out of the delegates of *that* province. In the next Congress, let a colony be taken by lot from twelve only, omitting that colony from which the president was taken in the former Congress, and so proceeding on till the whole thirteen shall have had their proper rotation. And in order that nothing may pass into a law but what is satisfactorily just, not less than three fifths of the Congress to be called a majority. – He that will promote discord, under a government so equally formed as this, would join Lucifer in his revolt.

But as there is a peculiar delicacy, from whom, or in what manner, this business must first arise, and as it seems most agreeable and consistent, that it should come from some intermediate body between the governed and the governors, that is between the Congress and the people, let a CONTINENTAL CONFERENCE be held, in the following manner, and for the following purpose.

A committee of twenty-six members of Congress, viz. two for each colony. Two members for each house of assembly, or Provincial convention; and five representatives of the people at large, to be chosen in the capital city or town of each province, for, and in behalf of the whole province, by as many qualified voters as shall think proper to attend from all parts of the province for that purpose; or, if more convenient, the representatives may be chosen in two or three of the most populous parts thereof. In this conference, thus assembled, will be united, the two grand principles of business, *knowledge* and *power*. The members of Congress, Assemblies, or Conventions, by having had experience in national concerns, will be able and useful counsellors, and the whole, being empowered by the people will have a truly legal authority.

The conferring members being met, let their business be to frame a CONTINENTAL CHARTER, or Charter of the United Colonies; (answering to what is called the Magna Charta of England) fixing the number and manner of choosing members of Congress, members of Assembly, with their date of sitting, and drawing the line of business and jurisdiction between them: (Always remembering, that our strength is continental, not provincial:) Securing freedom and property to all men, and above all things the free exercise of religion, according to the dictates of conscience; with such other matter as is necessary for a charter to contain. Immediately after which, the said conference to dissolve, and the bodies which shall be chosen conformable to the said charter, to be the legislators and governors of this continent and for the time being: Whose peace and happiness, may God preserve, Amen.

Should any body of men be hereafter delegated for this or some similar purpose, I offer them the following extracts from that wise observer on governments Dragonetti. 'The science', says he, 'of the politician consists in fixing the true point of happiness and freedom. Those men would deserve the gratitude of ages, who should discover a mode of government that contained the greatest sum of individual happiness, with the least national expense.' – Dragonetti on Virtue and Rewards.

But where says some is the King of America? I'll tell you Friend, he reigns above, and doth not make havoc of mankind like the Royal — of Britain. Yet that we may not appear to be defective even in earthly honours, let a day be solemnly set apart for proclaiming the charter; let it be brought forth placed on the divine law, the word of God; let a crown be placed thereon, by which the world may know, that so far as we approve of monarchy, that in America THE LAW IS KING. For as in absolute governments the King is law, so in free countries the law ought to be King; and there ought to be no other. But lest any ill use should afterwards arise, let the crown at the conclusion of the ceremony be demolished, and scattered among the people whose right it is.

A government of our own is our natural right: And when a man seriously reflects on the precariousness of human affairs, he will become convinced, that it is infinitely wiser and safer, to form a constitution of our own in a cool deliberate manner, while we have it in our power, than to trust such an interesting event to time and chance. If we omit it now, some Massenello [2] may hereafter arise, who laying hold of popular disquietudes, may collect together the desperate and the discontented, and by assuming to themselves the powers of government, may sweep away the liberties of the continent like a deluge. Should the government of America return again into the hands of Britain, the tottering situation of things, will be a temptation for some desperate adventurer to try his fortune; and in such a case, what relief can Britain give? Ere she could hear the news the fatal business might be done, and ourselves suffering like the wretched Britons under the oppression of the Conqueror. Ye that

---

2 Thomas Anello, otherwise Massenello, a fisherman of Naples, who after spiriting up his countrymen in the public market place, against the oppression of the Spaniards, to whom the place was then subject, prompted them to revolt, and in the space of a day became King. – Paine.

oppose independence now, ye know not what ye do; ye are opening a door to eternal tyranny, by keeping vacant the seat of government. There are thousands and tens of thousands, who would think it glorious to expel from the continent, that barbarous and hellish power, which hath stirred up the Indians and Negroes to destroy us; the cruelty hath a double guilt, it is dealing brutally by us, and treacherously by them.

To talk of friendship with those in whom our reason forbids us to have faith, and our affections wounded through a thousand pores instruct us to detest, is madness and folly. Every day wears out the little remains of kindred between us and them, and can there be any reason to hope, that as the relationship expires, the affection will increase, or that we shall agree better, when we have ten times more and greater concerns to quarrel over than ever?

Ye that tell us of harmony and reconciliation, can ye restore to us the time that is past? Can ye give to prostitution its former innocence? Neither can ye reconcile Britain and America. The last cord now is broken, the people of England are presenting addresses against us. There are injuries which nature cannot forgive; she would cease to be nature if she did. As well can the lover forgive the ravisher of his mistress, as the continent forgive the murders of Britain. The Almighty hath implanted in us these unextinguishable feelings for good and wise purposes. They are the guardians of his image in our hearts. They distinguish us from the herd of common animals. The social compact would dissolve, and justice be extirpated from the earth, or have only a casual existence were we callous to the touches of affection. The robber and the murderer, would often escape unpunished, did not the injuries which our tempers sustain, provoke us into justice.

O ye that love mankind! Ye that dare oppose, not only the tyranny, but the tyrant, stand forth! Every spot of the old world is over-run with oppression. Freedom hath been hunted round the globe. Asia, and Africa, have long expelled her. — Europe regards her like a stranger, and England hath given her warning to depart. O! receive the fugitive, and prepare in time an asylum for mankind.

ON THE PRESENT ABILITY OF AMERICA, WITH SOME
MISCELLANEOUS REFLECTIONS

I have never met with a man, either in England or America, who hath not confessed his opinion, that a separation between the countries, would take place one time or other. And there is no instance in which we have shewn less judgement, than in endeavouring to describe, what we call, the ripeness or fitness of the Continent for independence.

As all men allow the measure, and vary only in their opinion of the time, let us, in order to remove mistakes, take a general survey of things and endeavour if possible, to find out the *very* time. But we need not go far, the inquiry ceases at once, for the *time hath found us.* The general concurrence, the glorious union of all things prove the fact.

It is not in numbers but in unity, that our great strength lies; yet our present numbers are sufficient to repel the force of all the world. The Continent hath, at this time, the largest body of armed and disciplined men of any power under Heaven; and is just arrived at that pitch of strength, in which no single colony is able to support itself, and the whole, when united can accomplish the matter, and either more, or, less than this, might be fatal in its effects. Our land force is already sufficient, and as to naval affairs, we cannot be insensible, that Britain would never suffer an American man of war to be built while the continent remained in her hands. Wherefore we should be no forwarder an hundred years hence in that branch, than we are now; but the truth is, we should be less so, because the timber of the country is every day diminishing, and that which will remain at last, will be far off and difficult to procure.

Were the continent crowded with inhabitants, her sufferings under the present circumstances would be intolerable. The more sea port towns we had, the more should we have both to defend and to lose. Our present numbers are so happily proportioned to our wants, that no man need be idle. The diminution of trade affords an army, and the necessities of an army create a new trade.

Debts we have none; and whatever we may contract on this account will serve as a glorious memento of our virtue. Can we but leave posterity with a settled form of government, an independent constitution of its own, the purchase at any price will be cheap. But to expend millions for the sake of getting a few vile acts repealed, and routing the present ministry only, is unworthy the charge, and is using posterity with the utmost cruelty; because it is leaving them the great work to do, and a debt upon their backs, from which they derive no advantage. Such a thought is unworthy a man of honour, and is the true characteristic of a narrow heart and a pedling politician.

The debt we may contract doth not deserve our regard if the work be but accomplished. No nation ought to be without a debt. A national debt is a national bond; and when it bears no interest, is in no case a grievance. Britain is oppressed with a debt of upwards of one hundred and forty millions sterling, for which she pays upwards of four millions interest. And as a compensation for her debt, she has a large navy; America is without a debt, and without a navy; yet for the twentieth part of the English national debt, could have a navy as large again. The navy of England is not worth, at this time, more than three millions and a half sterling.

The first and second editions of this pamphlet were published without the following calculations, which are now given as a proof that the above estimation of the navy is a just one. *See Entic's naval history, intro.* page 56.

The charge of building a ship of each rate, and furnishing her with masts, yards, sails and rigging, together with a proportion of eight months boatswain's and carpenter's sea-stores, as calculated by Mr Burchett, Secretary to the navy.

	£
For a ship of 100 guns	35,553
90	29,886
80	23,638
70	17,785
60	14,197
50	10,606
40	7,558
30	5,846
20	3,710

And from hence it is easy to sum up the value, or cost rather, of the whole British navy, which in the year 1757, when it was at its greatest glory consisted of the following ships and guns:

Ships	Guns	Cost of one	Cost of all
6	100	35,553 *l.*	213,318 *l.*
12	90	29,886	358,632
12	80	23,638	283,656
43	70	17,785	746,755
35	60	14,197	496,895
40	50	10,606	424,240
45	40	7,558	340,110
58	20	3,710	215,180
85	Sloops, bombs, and fireships, one with another, at	2,000	170,000

Cost 3,266,786

Remains for guns   233,214

Total 3,500,000

No country on the globe is so happily situated, so internally capable of raising a fleet as America. Tar, timber, iron, and cordage are her natural produce. We need go abroad for nothing. Whereas the Dutch, who make large profits by hiring out their ships of war to the Spaniards and Portuguese, are obliged to import most of the materials they use. We ought to view the building of a fleet as an article of commerce, it being the natural manufactory of this country. It is the best money we can lay out. A navy when finished is worth more than it cost. And is that nice point in national policy, in which commerce and protection are united. Let us build; if we want them not, we can sell; and by that means replace our paper currency with ready gold and silver.

In point of manning a fleet, people in general run into great errors; it is not necessary that one-fourth part should be sailors. The Terrible privateer, Captain Death, stood the hottest engagement of any ship last war, yet had not twenty sailors on board, though her complement of men was upwards of two hundred. A few able and social sailors will soon instruct a sufficient number of active land-men in the common work of a ship. Wherefore, we never can be more capable to begin on maritime matters than now, while our timber is standing, our fisheries blocked up, and our sailors and shipwrights out of employ. Men of war of seventy and eighty guns were built forty years ago in New England, and why not the same now? Shipbuilding is America's greatest pride, and in which, she will in time excel the whole world. The great empires of the east are mostly inland, and consequently excluded from the possibility of rivalling her. Africa is in a state of barbarism; and no power in Europe, hath either such an extent or coast, or such an internal supply of materials. Where nature hath given the one, she has withheld the other; to America only hath she been liberal of both. The vast empire of Russia is almost shut out from the sea; wherefore, her boundless forests, her tar, iron, and cordage are only articles of commerce.

In point of safety, ought we to be without a fleet? We are not the little people now, which we were sixty years ago; at that time we might have trusted our property in the streets, or fields rather; and slept securely without locks or bolts to our doors or windows. The case now is altered, and our methods of defence ought to improve with our increase of property. A common pirate, twelve months ago, might have come up the Delaware, and laid the city of Philadelphia under instant contribution, for what sum he pleased; and the same might have happened to other places. Nay, any daring fellow, in a brig of fourteen or sixteen guns, might have robbed the whole Continent, and carried off half a million of money. These are circumstances which demand our attention, and point out the necessity of naval protection.

Some, perhaps, will say, that after we have made it up with Britain, she will protect us. Can we be so unwise as to mean, that she shall keep a navy in our harbours for that purpose? Common sense will tell us, that the power which hath endeavoured to subdue us, is of all others the most improper to defend us. Conquest may be effected under the pretence of friendship; and ourselves, after a long and brave resistance, be at last cheated into slavery. And if her ships are not to be admitted into our harbours, I would ask, how is she to protect us? A navy three or four thousand miles off can be of little use, and on sudden emergencies, none at all. Wherefore, if we must hereafter protect ourselves, why not do it for ourselves? Why do it for another?

The English list of ships of war is long and formidable, but not a tenth part of them are at any time fit for service, numbers of them not in being; yet their names are pompously continued in the list, if only a plank be left of the ship: and not a fifth part, of such as are fit for service, can be spared on any one station at one time. The East, and West Indies, Mediterranean, Africa, and other parts over which Britain extends her claim, make large demands upon her navy. From a mixture of prejudice and inattention, we have contracted a false notion respecting the navy of England, and have talked as if we should have the whole of it to encounter at once, and for that reason, supposed that we must have one as large; which not being instantly practicable, have been made use of by a set of disguised Tories to discourage our beginning thereon. Nothing can be farther from truth than this; for if America had only a twentieth part of the naval force of Britain, she would be by far an over match for her; because, as we neither have, nor claim any foreign dominion, our whole force would be employed on our own coast, where we should, in the long run, have two to one the advantage of those who had three or four thousand miles to sail over, before they could attack us, and the same distance to return in order to refit and recruit. And although Britain by her fleet, hath a check over our trade to Europe, we have as large a one over her trade to the West Indies, which, by laying in the neighbourhood of the Continent, is entirely at its mercy.

Some method might be fallen on to keep up a naval force in time of peace, if we should not judge it necessary to support a constant navy. If premiums were to be given to merchants, to build and employ in their service, ships mounted with twenty, thirty, forty, or fifty guns, (the premiums to be in proportion to the loss of bulk to the merchants) fifty or sixty of those ships, with a few guard ships on constant duty, would keep up a sufficient navy, and that without burdening ourselves with the evil so loudly complained of in England, of suffering their fleet, in time of peace to lie rotting in the docks. To unite the sinews of commerce and defence is sound policy; for when our strength and our riches, play into each other's hand, we need fear no external enemy.

In almost every article of defence we abound. Hemp flourishes even to rankness, so that we need not want cordage. Our iron is superior to that of other countries. Our small arms equal to any in the world. Cannon we can cast at pleasure. Saltpetre and gunpowder we are every day producing. Our knowledge is hourly improving. Resolution is our inherent character, and courage hath never yet forsaken us. Wherefore, what is it that we want? Why is it that we hesitate? From Britain we can expect nothing but ruin. If she is once admitted to the government of America again, this Continent will not be worth living in. Jealousies will be always arising; insurrections will be constantly happening; and who will go forth to quell them? Who will venture his life to reduce his own countrymen to a foreign obedience? The difference between Pennsylvania and Connecticut, respecting some unlocated lands, shews the insignificance of a B—sh government, and fully proves, that nothing but Continental authority can regulate Continental matters.

Another reason why the present time is preferable to all others, is, that the fewer our numbers are, the more land there is yet unoccupied, which instead of being lavished by the k— on his worthless dependants, may be hereafter applied, not only to the discharge of the present debt, but to the constant support of government. No nation under heaven hath such an advantage as this.

The infant state of the Colonies, as it is called, so far from being against, is an argument in favour of independence. We are sufficiently numerous, and were we more so, we might be less united. It is a matter worthy of observation, that the more a country is peopled, the smaller their armies are. In military numbers, the ancients far exceeded the moderns: and the reason is evident, for trade being the consequence of population, men become too much absorbed thereby to attend to any thing else. Commerce diminishes the spirit, both of patriotism and military defence. And history sufficiently informs us, that the bravest achievements were always accomplished in the nonage of a nation. With the increase of commerce, England hath lost its spirit. The city of London, notwithstanding its numbers, submits to continued insults with the patience of a coward. The more men have to lose, the less willing are they to venture. The rich are in general slaves to fear, and submit to courtly power with the trembling duplicity of a spaniel.

Youth is the seed time of good habits, as well in nations as in individuals. It might be difficult, if not impossible, to form the Continent into one government half a century hence. The vast variety of interests, occasioned by an increase of trade and population, would create confusion. Colony would be against colony. Each being able might scorn each other's assistance: and while the proud and foolish gloried in their little distinctions, the wise would lament that the union had not been formed before. Wherefore, the *present time* is the *true time* for establishing it. The intimacy which is contracted in infancy, and the friendship which is formed in misfortune, are, of all others, the most lasting and unalterable. Our present union is marked with both these characters: we are young, and we have been distressed; but our concord hath withstood our troubles, and fixes a memorable era for posterity to glory in.

The present time, likewise, is that peculiar time, which never happens to a nation but once, viz. the time of forming itself into a government. Most nations have let slip the opportunity, and by that means have been compelled to receive laws from their conquerors, instead of making laws for themselves. First, they had a king, and then a form of government; whereas, the articles or charter of government, should be formed first, and men delegated to execute them afterwards: but from the errors of other nations, let us learn wisdom, and lay hold of the present opportunity — *To begin government at the right end.*

When William the Conqueror subdued England he gave them law at the point of the sword; and until we consent that the seat of government in America, be legally and authoritatively occupied, we shall be in danger of having it filled by some fortunate ruffian, who may treat us in the same manner, and then, where will be our freedom? where our property?

As to religion, I hold it to be the indispensable duty of all government, to protect all conscientious professors thereof, and I know of no other business which government hath to do therewith. Let a man throw aside that narrowness of soul, that selfishness of principle, which the niggards of all professions are so unwilling to part with, and he will be at once delivered of his fears on that head. Suspicion is the companion of mean souls, and the bane of all good society. For myself I fully and conscientiously believe, that it is the will of the Almighty, that there should be diversity of religious opinions among us: It affords a larger field of our christian kindness. Were we all of one way of thinking, our religious dispositions would want matter for probation; and on this liberal principle, I look on the various denominations among us, to be like children of the same family, differing only, in what is called their Christian names.

In page fifty-four,[3] I threw out a few thoughts on the propriety of a Continental Charter, (for I only presume to offer hints not plans) and in this place, I take the liberty of rementioning the subject, by observing, that a charter is to be understood as a bond of solemn

3 Page 91 in this edition. — Editors.

obligation, which the whole enters into, to support the right of every separate part, whether of religion, personal freedom, or property. A firm bargain and a right reckoning make long friends.

In a former page I likewise mentioned the necessity of a large and equal representation; and there is no political matter which more deserves our attention. A small number of electors, or a small number of representatives, are equally dangerous. But if the number of the representatives be not only small, but unequal, the danger is increased. As an instance of this, I mention the following; when the Associators petition was before the House of Assembly of Pennsylvania; twenty-eight members only were present, all the Bucks county members, being eight, voted against it, and had seven of the Chester members done the same, this whole province had been governed by two counties only, and this danger it is always exposed to. The unwarrantable stretch likewise, which that House made in their last sitting, to gain an undue authority over the Delegates of that province, ought to warn the people at large, how they trust power out of their own hands. A set of instructions for the Delegates were put together, which in point of sense and business would have dishonoured a school-boy, and after being approved by a *few*, a *very few* without doors, were carried into the House, and there passed *in behalf of the whole colony*; whereas, did the whole colony know, with what ill-will that House hath entered on some necessary public measures, they would not hesitate a moment to think them unworthy of such a trust.

Immediate necessity makes many things convenient, which if continued would grow into oppressions. Expedience and right are different things. When the calamities of America required a consultation, there was no method so ready, or at that time so proper, as to appoint persons from the several Houses of Assembly for that purpose and the wisdom with which they have proceeded hath preserved this continent from ruin. But as it is more than probable that we shall never be without a CONGRESS, every well wisher to good order, must own, that the mode for choosing members of that body, deserves consideration. And I put it as a question to those, who make a study of mankind, whether *representation and election* is not too great a power for one and the same body of men to possess? When we are planning for posterity, we ought to remember that virtue is not hereditary.

It is from our enemies that we often gain excellent maxims, and are frequently surprised into reason by their mistakes. Mr Cornwall (one of the Lords of the Treasury) treated the petition of the New York Assembly with contempt, because *that* House, he said, consisted but of twenty-six members, which trifling number, he argued, could not with decency be put for the whole. We thank him for his involuntary honesty.[4]

TO CONCLUDE, however strange it may appear to some, or however unwilling they may be to think so, matters not, but many strong and striking reasons may be given, to shew, that nothing can settle our affairs so expeditiously as an open and determined declaration for independence. Some of which are,

First. — It is the custom of nations, when any two are at war, for some other powers, not engaged in the quarrel, to step in as mediators, and bring about the preliminaries of a peace: but while America calls herself the subject of Great Britain, no power, however well disposed she may be, can offer her mediation. Wherefore, in our present state we may quarrel on for ever.

Secondly. — It is unreasonable to suppose, that France or Spain will give us any kind of assistance, if we mean only to make use of that assistance for the purpose of repairing the breach, and strengthening the connection between Britain and America; because, those powers would be sufferers by the consequences.

Thirdly. — While we profess ourselves the subjects of Britain, we must, in the eye of foreign nations, be considered as rebels. The precedent is somewhat dangerous to *their peace*, for men to be in arms under the name of subjects; we on the spot, can solve the paradox: but to unite resistance and subjection, requires an idea much too refined for common understanding.

Fourthly. — Were a manifesto to be published, and dispatched to foreign courts, setting forth the miseries we have endured, and the peaceable methods we have ineffectually used for redress; declaring, at the same time, that not being able, any longer to live happily or safely under the cruel disposition of the B—sh court, we had been driven to the necessity of breaking off all connection with her; at the same time assuring all such courts of our peaceable disposition towards them, and of our desire of entering into trade with them: Such a memorial would produce more good effects to this Continent, than if a ship were freighted with petition to Britain.

4 Those who would fully understand of what great consequence a large and equal representation is to a state, should read Burgh's political Disquisitions. – Paine.

Under our present denomination of British subjects we can neither be received nor heard abroad: The custom of all courts is against us, and will be so, until, by an independence, we take rank with other nations.

These proceedings may at first appear strange and difficult; but, like all other steps which we have already passed over, will in a little time become familiar and agreeable; and, until an independence is declared, the Continent will feel itself like a man who continues putting off some unpleasant business from day to day, yet knows it must be done, hates to set about it, wishes it over, and is continually haunted with the thoughts of its necessity.

APPENDIX

Since the publication of the first edition of this pamphlet, or rather, on the same day on which it came out, the —'s Speech made its appearance in this city. Had the spirit of prophecy directed the birth of this production, it could not have brought it forth, at a more seasonable juncture, or a more necessary time. The bloody mindedness of the one, shew the necessity of pursuing the doctrine of the other. Men read by way of revenge. And the speech instead of terrifying, prepared a way for the manly principles of Independence.

Ceremony, and even, silence, from whatever motive they may arise, have a hurtful tendency, when they give the least degree of countenance to base and wicked performances; wherefore, if this maxim be admitted, it naturally follows, that the —'s Speech, as being a piece of finished villainy, deserved, and still deserves, a general execration both by the Congress and the people. Yet as the domestic tranquillity of a nation, depends greatly on the *chastity* of what may properly be called NATIONAL MATTERS, it is often better, to pass some things over in silent disdain, than to make use of such new methods of dislike, as might introduce the least innovation, on that guardian of our peace and safety. And perhaps, it is chiefly owing to this prudent delicacy, that the —'s Speech, hath not before now, suffered a public execution. The speech if it may be called one, is nothing better than a wilful audacious libel against the truth, the common good, and the existence of mankind; and is a formal and pompous method of offering up human sacrifices to the pride of tyrants. But this general massacre of mankind, is one of the privileges, and the certain consequences of K—s; for as nature knows them *not*, they know *not her*, and although they are beings of our *own* creating, they know not *us*, and are become the gods of their creators. The speech hath one good quality, which is, that it is not calculated to deceive, neither can we, even if we would, be deceived by it. Brutality and tyranny appear on the face of it. It leaves us at no loss: And every line convinces, even in the moment of reading, that He, who hunts the woods for prey, the naked and untutored Indian, is less a Savage than the — of B—.

Sir J—n D—e, the putative father of a whining Jesuitical piece, fallaciously called, '*The Address of the people of* ENGLAND *to the inhabitants of* AMERICA', hath, perhaps from a vain supposition, that the people *here* were to be frightened at the pomp and description of a king, given, (though very unwisely on his part) the real character of the present one: 'But,' says this writer, 'if you are inclined to pay compliments to an administration, which we do not complain of,' (meaning the Marquis of Rockingham's at the repeal of the Stamp Act) 'it is very unfair in you to withhold them from that prince, *by whose* NOD ALONE *they were permitted to do any thing*.' This is Toryism with a witness! Here is idolatry even without a mask: And he who can calmly hear, and digest such doctrine, hath forfeited his claim to rationality – an apostate from the order of manhood; and ought to be considered – as one, who hath, not only given up the proper dignity of a man, but sunk himself beneath the rank of animals, and contemptibly crawl through the world like a worm.

However, it matters very little now, what the — of E— either says or does; he hath wickedly broken through every moral and human obligation, trampled nature and conscience beneath his feet; and by a steady and constitutional spirit of insolence and cruelty, procured for himself an universal hatred. It is *now* the interest of America to provide for herself. She hath already a large and young family, whom it is more her duty to take care of, than to be granting away her property, to support a power who is become a reproach to the names of men and Christians – YE, whose office it is to watch over the morals of a nation, of whatsoever sect or denomination ye are of, as well as ye, who are more immediately the guardians of the public liberty, if ye wish to preserve your native country uncontaminated by European corruption, ye must in secret wish a separation – But leaving the moral part to private reflection, I shall chiefly confine my farther remarks to the following heads.

First. That it is the interest of America to be separated from Britain.

Secondly. Which is the easiest and most practicable plan, RE-CONCILIATION or INDEPENDENCE? with some occasional remarks.

In support of the first, I could, if I judged it proper, produce the opinion of some of the ablest and most experienced men on this continent; and whose sentiments, on that head, are not yet publicly known. It is in reality a self-evident position: For no nation in a state of foreign dependence, limited in its commerce, and cramped and fettered in its legislative powers, can ever arrive at any material eminence. America doth not yet know what opulence is; and although the progress which she hath made stands unparalleled in the history of other nations, it is but childhood, compared with what she would be capable of arriving at, had she, as she ought to have, the legislative powers in her own hands. England is, at this time, proudly coveting what would do her no good, were she to accomplish it; and the Continent hesitating on a matter, which will be her final ruin if neglected. It is the commerce and not the conquest of America, by which England is to be benefited, and that would in a great measure continue, were the countries as independent of each other as France and Spain; because in many articles, neither can go to a better market. But it is the independence of this country on Britain or any other, which is now the main and only object worthy of contention, and which, like all other truths discovered by necessity, will appear clearer and stronger every day.

First. Because it will come to that one time or other.

Secondly. Because the longer it is delayed the harder it will be to accomplish.

I have frequently amused myself both in public and private companies, with silently remarking the spacious errors of those who speak without reflecting. And among the many which I have heard, the following seems the most general, viz. that had this rupture happened forty or fifty years hence, instead of *now*, the Continent would have been more able to have shaken off the dependence. To which I reply, that our military ability *at this time*, arises from the experience gained in the last war, and which in forty or fifty years time, would have been totally extinct. The Continent, would not, by that time, have had a General, or even a military officer left; and we, or those who may succeed us, would have been as ignorant of martial matters as the ancient Indians: And this single position, closely attended to, will unanswerably prove, that the present time is preferable to all others: The argument turns thus – at the conclusion of the last war, we had experience, but wanted numbers; and forty or fifty years hence, we should have numbers, without experience; wherefore, the proper point of time, must be some particular point between the two extremes, in which a sufficiency of the former remains, and a proper increase of the latter is obtained: And that point of time is the present time.

The reader will pardon this digression, as it does not properly come under the head I first set out with, and to which I again return by the following position, viz.

Should affairs be patched up with Britain, and she to remain the governing and sovereign power of America, (which as matters are now circumstanced, is giving up the point entirely) we shall deprive ourselves of the very means of sinking the debt we have or may contract. The value of the back lands which some of the provinces are clandestinely deprived of, by the unjust extension of the limits of Canada, valued only at five pounds sterling per hundred acres, amount to upwards of twenty-five millions, Pennsylvania currency; and the quit-rents at one penny sterling per acre, to two millions yearly.

It is by the sale of those lands that the debt may be sunk, without burthen to any, and the quit-rent reserved thereon, will always lessen, and in time, will wholly support the yearly expense of government. It matters not how long the debt is in paying, so that the lands when sold be applied to the discharge of it, and for the execution of which, the Congress for the time being, will be the continental trustees.

I proceed now to the second head, viz. Which is the earliest and most practicable plan, RECONCILIATION or INDEPENDENCE? with some occasional remarks.

He who takes nature for his guide is not easily beaten out of his argument and on that ground, I answer *generally – That* INDEPENDENCE *being a* SINGLE SIMPLE LINE, *contained within ourselves; and reconciliation, a matter exceedingly perplexed and complicated, and in which, a treacherous capricious court is to interfere, gives the answer without a doubt.*

The present state of America is truly alarming to every man who is capable of reflection. Without law, without government, without any other mode of power than what is founded on, and granted by courtesy. Held together by an unexampled concurrence of sentiment, which is nevertheless subject to change, and which every secret enemy is endeavouring to dissolve. Our present condition, is, Legislation without law; wisdom without a plan; a constitution without a name; and, what is strangely astonishing, perfect Independence contending for Dependence. The instance is without a precedent; the case never existed before; and who can tell what may be the event? The property of no man is secure in the present unbraced system of things. The mind of the multitude is left at random, and feeling no fixed object before them, they pursue such as fancy or opinion starts. Nothing is criminal; there is no such thing as treason; wherefore, every one thinks himself at liberty to act as he pleases. The Tories dared not to have assembled offensively, had they known that their lives, by that act were forfeited to the laws of the state. A line of distinction should be drawn, between English soldiers taken in battle, and inhabitants of America taken in arms. The first are prisoners, but the latter traitors. The one forfeits his liberty, the other his head.

Notwithstanding our wisdom, there is a visible feebleness in some of our proceedings which gives encouragement to dissentions. The Continental belt is too loosely buckled. And if something is not done in time, it will be too late to do any thing, and we shall fall into a state, in which, neither *reconciliation* nor *independence* will be practicable. The — and his worthless adherents are got at their old game of dividing the Continent, and there are not wanting among us, Printers, who will be busy spreading specious falsehoods. The artful and hypocritical letter which appeared a few months ago in two of the New York papers, and likewise in two others, is an evidence that there are men who want either judgement or honesty.

It is easy getting into holes and corners and talking of reconciliation: But do such men seriously consider, how difficult the task is, and how dangerous it may prove, should the Continent divide thereon. Do they take within their view, all the various orders of men whose situation and circumstances, as well as their own, are to be considered therein. Do they put themselves in the place of the sufferer whose *all* is *already* gone, and of the soldier, who hath quitted *all* for the defence of his country. If their ill-judged moderation be suited to their own private situations *only*, regardless of others, the event will convince them, that 'they are reckoning without their Host'.

Put us, says some, on the footing we were on in sixty-three: To which I answer, the request is not *now* in the power of Britain to comply with, neither will she propose it; but if it were, and even should be granted, I ask, as a reasonable question, By what means is such a corrupt and faithless court to be kept to its engagements? Another parliament, nay, even the present, may hereafter repeal the obligation, on the pretence of its being violently obtained, or unwisely granted; and in that case, Where is our redress? – No going to law with nations; cannon are the barristers of crowns; and the sword, not of justice, but of war, decides the suit. To be on the footing of sixty-three, it is not sufficient, that the laws only be put on the same state, but, that our circumstances, likewise, be put on the same state; our burnt and destroyed towns repaired or built up, our private losses made good, our public debts (contracted for defence) discharged; otherwise, we shall be millions worse than we were at that enviable period. Such a request had it been complied with a year ago, would have won the heart and soul of the Continent – but now it is too late, 'The Rubicon is passed.'

Besides the taking up arms, merely to enforce the repeal of a pecuniary law, seems as unwarrantable by the divine law, and as repugnant to human feelings, as the taking up arms to enforce obedience thereto. The object, on either side, doth not justify the ways and means; for the lives of men are too valuable to be cast away on such trifles. It is the violence which is done and threatened to our persons; the destruction of our property by an armed force; the invasion of our country by fire and sword, which conscientiously qualifies the use of arms: And the instant, in which such a mode of defence became necessary, all subjection to Britain ought to have ceased; and the independency of America should have been considered, as dating its era from, and published by, *the first musket that was fired against her*. This line is a line of consistency; neither drawn by caprice, nor extended by ambition; but produced by a chain of events, of which the colonies were not the authors.

I shall conclude these remarks, with the following timely and well intended hints. We ought to reflect, that there are three different ways by which an independency may hereafter be effected; and that *one* of those *three,* will one day or other, be the fate of America, viz. By the legal voice of the people in Congress; by a military power; or by a mob: It may not always happen that our soldiers are citizens, and the multitude a body of reasonable men; virtue, as I have already remarked, is not hereditary, neither is it perpetual. Should an independency be brought about by the first of those means, we have every opportunity and every encouragement before us, to form the noblest, purest constitution on the face of the earth. We have it in our power to begin the world over again. A situation, similar to the present, hath not happened since the days of Noah until now. The birth-day of a new world is at hand, and a race of men perhaps as numerous as all Europe contains, are to receive their portion of freedom from the event of a few months. The Reflection is awful – and in this point of view, How trifling, how ridiculous, do the little, paltry cavellings, of a few weak or interested men appear, when weighed against the business of a world.

Should we neglect the present favourable and inviting period, and an independence be hereafter effected by any other means, we must charge the consequence to ourselves, or to those rather, whose narrow and prejudiced souls, are habitually opposing the measure, without either inquiring or reflecting. There are reasons to be given in support of Independence, which men should rather privately think of, than be publicly told of. We ought not now to be debating whether we shall be independent or not, but, anxious to accomplish it on a firm, secure, and honourable basis, and uneasy rather that it is not yet began upon. Every day convinces us of its necessity. Even the Tories (if such beings yet remain among us) should, of all men, be the most solicitous to promote it; for, as the appointment of committees at first, protected them from popular rage, so, a wise and well established form of government, will be the only certain means of continuing it securely to them. *Wherefore,* if they have not virtue enough to be Whigs, they ought to have prudence enough to wish for Independence.

In short, Independence is the only Bond that can tie and keep us together. We shall then see our object, and our ears will be legally shut against the schemes of an intriguing, as well as a cruel enemy. We shall then too, be on a proper footing, to treat with Britain; for there is reason to conclude, that the pride of that court, will be less hurt by treating with the American states for terms of peace, than with those, whom she denominates, 'rebellious subjects', for terms of accommodation. It is our delaying it that encourages her to hope for conquest, and our backwardness tends only to prolong the war. As we have, without any good effect therefrom, withheld our trade to obtain a redress of our grievances, let us *now* try the alternative, by *independently* redressing them ourselves, and then offering to open the trade. The mercantile and reasonable part of England will be still with us; because, peace *with* trade, is preferable to war *without* it. And if this offer be not accepted, other courts may be applied to.

On these grounds I rest the matter. And as no offer hath yet been made to refute the doctrine contained in the former editions of this pamphlet, it is a negative proof, that either the doctrine cannot be refuted, or, that the party in favour of it are too numerous to be opposed. WHEREFORE, instead of gazing at each other with suspicious or doubtful curiosity, let each of us, hold out to his neighbour the hearty hand of friendship, and unite in drawing a line, which, like an act of oblivion, shall bury in forgetfulness every former dissension. Let the names of Whig and Tory be extinct; and let none other be heard among us, than those of *a good citizen, an open and resolute friend, and a virtuous supporter of the* RIGHTS *of* MANKIND *and of the* FREE AND INDEPENDENT STATES OF AMERICA.

*

To the Representatives of the Religious Society of the People called Quakers, or to so many of them as were concerned in publishing a late piece, entitled 'The Ancient Testimony and Principles of the people called Quakers renewed, with respect to the King and Government, and Touching the Commotions now prevailing in these and other parts of America, addressed to the people in general'.

The Writer of this, is one of those few, who never dishonours religion either by ridiculing, or cavilling at any denomination whatsoever. To God, and not to man, are all men accountable on the score of religion. Wherefore, this epistle is not so properly addressed to you as a religious, but as a political body, dabbling in matters, which the professed Quietude of your Principles instructs you not to meddle with.

As you have, without a proper authority for so doing, put yourselves in the place of the whole body of the Quakers, so, the writer of this, in order to be on an equal rank with yourselves, is under the necessity, of putting himself in the place of all those who approve the very writings and principles, against which your testimony is directed: And he hath chosen their singular situation, in order that you might discover in him, that presumption of character which you cannot see in yourselves. For neither he nor you have any claim or title to *Political Representation*.

When men have departed from the right way, it is no wonder that they stumble and fall. And it is evident from the manner in which ye have managed your testimony, that politics, (as a religious body of men) is not your proper Walk; for however well adapted it might appear to you, it is, nevertheless, a jumble of good and bad put unwisely together, and the conclusion drawn therefore, both unnatural and unjust.

The two first pages, (and the whole doth not make four) we give you credit for, and expect the same civility from you, because the love and desire of peace is not confined to Quakerism, it is the *natural*, as well as the religious wish of all denominations of men. And on this ground, as men labouring to establish an Independent Constitution of our own, do we exceed all others in our hope, end, and aim. *Our plan is peace for ever*. We are tired of contention with Britain, and can see no real end to it but in a final separation. We act consistently, because for the sake of introducing an endless and uninterrupted peace, do we bear the evils and burthens of the present day. We are endeavouring, and will steadily continue to endeavour, to separate and dissolve a connection which hath already filled our land with blood; and which, while the name of it remains, will be the fatal cause of future mischiefs to both countries.

We fight neither for revenge nor conquest; neither from pride nor passion; we are not insulting the world with our fleets and armies, nor ravaging the globe for plunder. Beneath the shade of our own vines are we attacked; in our own houses, and on our own lands, is the violence committed against us. We view our enemies in the characters of Highwaymen and Housebreakers, and having no defence for ourselves in the civil law, are obliged to punish them by the military one, and apply the sword, in the very case, where you have before now, applied the halter. – Perhaps we feel for the ruined and insulted sufferers in all and every part of the continent, and with a degree of tenderness which hath not yet made its way into some of your bosoms. But be ye sure that ye mistake not the cause and ground of your Testimony. Call not coldness of soul, religion; nor put the *Bigot* in the place of the *Christian*.

O ye partial ministers of your own acknowledged principles. If the bearing arms be sinful, the first going to war must be more so, by all the difference between wilful attack and unavoidable defence. Wherefore, if ye really preach from conscience, and mean not to make a political hobby-horse of your religion, convince the world thereof, by proclaiming your doctrine to our enemies, *for they likewise bear* ARMS. Give us proof of your sincerity by publishing it at St James's, to the commanders in chief at Boston, to the Admirals and Captains who are piratically ravaging our coasts, and to all the murdering miscreants who are acting in authority under HIM whom ye profess to serve. Had ye the honest soul of *Barclay*[5] ye would preach repentance to *your* king; Ye would tell the Royal — his sins, and warn him of eternal ruin. Ye would not spend your partial invectives against the injured and the insulted only, but like faithful ministers, would cry aloud and *spare none*. Say not that ye are persecuted, neither endeavour to make us the authors of that reproach, which, ye are bringing upon yourselves; for we testify unto all men, that we do not complain against you because ye are *Quakers*, but because ye pretend to *be* and are NOT Quakers.

Alas! It seems by the particular tendency of some part of your testimony, and other parts of your conduct, as if all sin was reduced to, and comprehended in *the act of bearing arms*, and that by the *people only*. Ye appear to us, to have mistaken party for conscience, because the general tenor of your actions wants uniformity: And it is exceedingly difficult to us to give credit to many of your pretended scruples; because we see them made by the same men, who, in the very instant that they are exclaiming against the mammon of this

5 'Thou hast tasted of prosperity and adversity; thou knowest what it is to be banished thy native country, to be over-ruled as well as to rule, and set upon the throne; and being *oppressed* thou hast reason to know how *hateful* the *oppressor* is both to God and man: If after all these warnings and advertisements, thou dost not turn unto the Lord with all thy heart, but forget him who remembered thee in thy distress, and give up thyself to follow lust and vanity, surely great will be thy condemnation. — Against which snare, as well as the temptation of those who may or do feed thee, and prompt thee to evil, the most excellent and prevalent remedy will be, to apply thyself to that light of Christ which shineth in thy conscience and which neither can, nor will flatter thee, nor suffer thee to be at ease in thy sins.' — *Barclay's Address to Charles II.* — Paine.

world, are nevertheless, hunting after it with a step as steady as Time, and an appetite as keen as Death.

The quotation which ye have made from Proverbs, in the third page of your testimony, that, 'when a man's ways please the Lord, he maketh even his enemies to be at peace with him'; is very unwisely chosen on your part; because it amounts to a proof, that the king's ways (whom ye are so desirous of supporting) do *not* please the Lord, otherwise, his reign would be in peace.

I now proceed to the latter part of your testimony, and that, for which all the foregoing seems only an introduction, viz.

'It hath ever been our judgement and principle, since we were called to profess the light of Christ Jesus, manifested in our consciences unto this day, that the setting up and putting down kings and governments, is God's peculiar prerogative; for causes best known to himself: And that it is not our business to have any hand or contrivance therein; nor to be busy bodies above our station, much less to plot and contrive the ruin, or overturn any of them, but to pray for the king, and safety of our nation, and good of all men: That we may live a peaceable and quiet life, in all goodliness and honesty; *under the government which God is pleased to set over us.*' – If these are *really* your principles why do ye not abide by them? Why do ye not leave that, which ye call God's Work, to be managed by himself? These very principles instruct you to wait with patience and humility, for the event of all public measures, and to receive *that event* as the divine will towards you. *Wherefore*, what occasion is there for your *political testimony* if you fully believe what it contains? And the very publishing it proves, that either, ye do not believe what ye profess, or have not virtue enough to practise what ye believe.

The principles of Quakerism have a direct tendency to make a man the quiet and inoffensive subject of any, and every government *which is set over him.* And if the setting up and putting down of kings and governments is God's peculiar prerogative, he most certainly will not be robbed thereof by us; wherefore, the principle itself leads you to approve of every thing, which ever happened, or may happen to kings as being his work, OLIVER CROMWELL thanks you. – CHARLES, then, died not by the hands of man; and should the present Proud Imitator of him, come to the same untimely end, the writers and publishers of the testimony, are bound by the doctrine it contains, to applaud the fact. Kings are not taken away by miracles, neither are changes in governments brought about by any other means than such as are common and human; and such as we are now using. Even the dispersing of the Jews, though foretold by our Saviour, was effected by arms. Wherefore, as ye refuse to be the means on one side, ye ought not to be meddlers on the other; but to wait the issue in silence; and unless you can produce divine authority, to prove, that the Almighty who hath created and placed this *new* world, at the greatest distance it could possibly stand, east and west, from every part of the old, doth, nevertheless, disapprove of its being independent of the corrupt and abandoned court of B—n, unless I say, ye can show this, how can ye, on the ground of your principles, justify the exciting and stirring up of the people 'firmly to unite in the *abhorrence* of all such *writings*, and *measures*, as evidence a desire and design to break off the *happy* connection we have hitherto enjoyed, with the kingdom of Great Britain, and our just and necessary subordination to the king, and those who are lawfully placed in authority under him'. What a slap in the face is here! the men, who, in the very paragraph before, have quietly and passively resigned up the ordering, altering, and disposal of kings and governments, into the hands of God, are now recalling their principles, and putting in for a share of the business. Is it possible, that the conclusion, which is here justly quoted, can any ways follow from the doctrine laid down? The inconsistency is too glaring not to be seen; the absurdity too great not to be laughed at; and such as could only have been made by those, whose understandings were darkened by the narrow and crabby spirit of a despairing political party; for ye are not to be considered as the whole body of the Quakers but only as a factional and fractional part thereof.

Here ends the examination of your testimony; (which I call upon no man to abhor, as ye have done, but only to read and judge of fairly;) to which I subjoin the following remark; 'That the setting up and putting down of kings', most certainly mean, the making him a king, who is yet not so, and the making him no king who is already one. And pray what hath this to do in the present case? We neither mean to *set up* nor to *put down*, neither to *make* nor to *unmake*, but to have nothing to *do* with them. Wherefore, your testimony in whatever light it is viewed serves only to dishonour your judgement, and for many other reasons had better have been let alone than published.

First. Because it tends to the decrease and reproach of all religion whatever, and is of the utmost danger to society, to make it a party in political disputes.

Secondly. Because it exhibits a body of men, numbers of whom disavow the publishing political testimonies, as being concerned therein and approvers thereof.

Thirdly. Because it hath a tendency to undo that continental harmony and friendship which yourselves by your late liberal and charitable donations hath lent a hand to establish; and the preservation of which, is of the utmost consequence to us all.

And here without anger or resentment I bid you farewell. Sincerely wishing, that as men and Christians, ye may always fully and uninterruptedly enjoy every civil and religious right; and be, in your turn, the means of securing it to others; but that the example which ye have unwisely set, of mingling religion with politics, *may be disavowed and reprobated by every inhabitant of* AMERICA.

FINIS

[6] THE AMERICAN CRISIS

(1776–83)

From 1776 to 1783 America and Britain were locked in a bitter war marked by bloody battles in virtually every state. Throughout this period Paine sought to keep up the morale of newly independent Americans with periodic essays on war-related topics. There were sixteen papers in all, from 1776 to 1783, that Paine called The American Crisis. *The Crisis papers are full of the stirring phrases that so characterize Paine's writings and so contributed to his popularity. None surpasses the opening lines of the first paper. The text here is that first paper, written in December 1776 when the American cause seemed lost, with Washington's troops in full retreat across New Jersey.*

These are the times that try men's souls. The summer soldier and the sunshine patriot will, in this crisis, shrink from the service of their country; but he that stands it *now*, deserves the love and thanks of man and woman. Tyranny, like hell, is not easily conquered; yet we have this consolation with us, that the harder the conflict, the more glorious the triumph. What we obtain too cheap, we esteem too lightly: it is dearness only that gives every thing its value. Heaven knows how to put a proper price upon its goods; and it would be strange indeed if so celestial an article as FREEDOM should not be highly rated. Britain, with an army to enforce her tyranny, has declared that she has a right (*not only to* TAX) but 'TO BIND us in ALL CASES WHATSOEVER', and if being *bound in that manner*, is not slavery, then is there not such a thing as slavery upon earth. Even the expression is impious; for so unlimited a power can belong only to God.

Whether the independence of the continent was declared too soon, or delayed too long, I will not now enter into as an argument; my own simple opinion is, that had it been eight months earlier, it would have been much better. We did not make a proper use of last winter, neither could we, while we were in a dependent state. However, the fault, if it were one, was all our own; we have none to blame but ourselves. But no great deal is lost yet. All that Howe has been doing for this month past, is rather a ravage than a conquest, which the spirit of the Jerseys, a year ago, would have quickly repulsed, and which time and a little resolution will soon recover.

I have as little superstition in me as any man living, but my secret opinion has ever been, and still is, that God Almighty will not give up a people to military destruction, or leave them unsupportedly to perish, who have so earnestly and so repeatedly sought to avoid the calamities of war, by every decent method which wisdom could invent. Neither have I so much of the infidel in me, as to suppose that He has relinquished the government of the world, and given us up to the care of devils; and as I do not, I cannot see on what grounds the king of Britain can look up to heaven for help against us: a common murderer, a highwayman, or a house-breaker, has as good a pretence as he.

'Tis surprising to see how rapidly a panic will sometimes run through a country. All nations and ages have been subject to them. Britain has trembled like an ague at the report of a French fleet of flat-bottomed boats; and in the fourteenth [fifteenth] century the whole English army, after ravaging the kingdom of France, was driven back like men petrified with fear; and this brave exploit was performed by a few broken forces collected and headed by a woman, Joan of Arc. Would that heaven might inspire some Jersey maid to spirit up her countrymen, and save her fair fellow sufferers from ravage and ravishment! Yet panics, in some cases, have their uses; they produce as much good as hurt. Their duration is always short; the mind soon grows through them, and acquires a firmer habit than before. But their peculiar advantage is, that they are the touchstones of sincerity and hypocrisy, and bring things and men to light, which might otherwise have lain forever undiscovered. In fact, they have the same effect on secret traitors, which an imaginary apparition would have upon a private murderer. They sift out the hidden thoughts of man, and hold them up in public to the world. Many a disguised Tory has lately shown his head, that shall penitentially solemnize with curses the day on which Howe arrived upon the Delaware.

As I was with the troops at Fort Lee, and marched with them to the edge of Pennsylvania, I am well acquainted with many circumstances, which those who live at a distance know but little or nothing of. Our situation there was exceedingly cramped, the place being a narrow neck of land between the North River and the Hackensack. Our force was inconsiderable, being not one-fourth so great as Howe could bring against us. We had no army at hand to have relieved the garrison, had we shut ourselves up and stood on our defence. Our ammunition, light artillery, and the best part of our stores, had been removed, on the apprehension that Howe would endeavour to penetrate the Jerseys, in which case Fort Lee could be of no use to us; for it must occur to every thinking man, whether in the army or not, that these kind of field forts are only for temporary purposes, and last in use no longer than the enemy directs his force against the particular object which such forts are raised to defend. Such was our situation and condition at Fort Lee on the morning of the 20th of November, when an officer arrived with information that the enemy with 200 boats had landed about seven miles above; Major General [Nathanael] Greene, who commanded the garrison, immediately ordered them under arms, and sent express to General Washington at the town of Hackensack, distant by the way of the ferry = six miles. Our first object was to secure the bridge over the Hackensack, which laid up the river between the enemy and us, about six miles from us, and three from them. General Washington arrived in about three-quarters of an hour, and marched at the head of the troops towards the bridge, which place I expected we should have a brush for; however, they did not choose to dispute it with us, and the greatest part of our troops went over the bridge, the rest over the ferry, except some which passed at a mill on a small creek, between the bridge and the ferry, and made their way through some marshy grounds up to the town of Hackensack, and there passed the river. We brought off as much baggage as the wagons could contain, the rest was lost. The simple object was to bring off the garrison, and march them on till they could be strengthened by the Jersey or Pennsylvania militia, so as to be enabled to make a stand. We staid four days at Newark, collected our out-posts with some of the Jersey militia, and marched out twice to meet the enemy, on being informed that they were advancing, though our numbers were greatly inferior to theirs. Howe, in my little opinion, committed a great error in generalship in not throwing a body of forces off from Staten Island through Amboy, by which means he might have seized all our stores at Brunswick, and intercepted our march into Pennsylvania; but if we believe the power of hell to be limited, we must likewise believe that their agents are under some providential control.

I shall not now attempt to give all the particulars of our retreat to the Delaware; suffice it for the present to say, that both officers and men, though greatly harassed and fatigued, frequently without rest, covering, or provision, the inevitable consequences of a long retreat, bore it with a manly and martial spirit. All their wishes centred in one, which was, that the country would turn out and help them to drive the enemy back. Voltaire has remarked that King William never appeared to full advantage but in difficulties and in action; the same remark may be made on General Washington, for the character fits him. There is a natural firmness in some minds which cannot be unlocked by trifles, but which, when unlocked, discovers a cabinet of fortitude; and I reckon it among those kind of public blessings, which we do not immediately see, that God hath blessed him with uninterrupted health, and given him a mind that can even flourish upon care.

I shall conclude this paper with some miscellaneous remarks on the state of our affairs; and shall begin with asking the following question, Why is it that the enemy have left the New England provinces, and made these middle ones the seat of war? The answer is easy: New England is not infested with Tories, and we are. I have been tender in raising the cry against these men, and used numberless arguments to show them their danger, but it will not do to sacrifice a world either to their folly or their baseness. The period is now arrived, in which either they or we must change our sentiments, or one or both must fall. And what is a Tory? Good God! what is he? I should not be afraid to go with a hundred Whigs against a thousand Tories, were they to attempt to get into arms. Every Tory is a coward; for servile, slavish, self-interested fear is the foundation of Toryism; and a man under such influence, though he may be cruel, never can be brave.

But, before the line of irrecoverable separation be drawn between us, let us reason the matter together: Your conduct is an invitation to the enemy, yet not one in a thousand of you has heart enough to join him. Howe is as much deceived by you as the American cause is injured by you. He expects you will all take up arms, and flock to his standard, with muskets on your shoulders. Your opinions are of no use to him, unless you support him personally, for 'tis soldiers, and not Tories, that he wants.

I once felt all that kind of anger, which a man ought to feel, against the mean principles that are held by the Tories: a noted one, who kept a tavern at Amboy, was standing at his door, with as pretty a child in his hand, about eight or nine years old, as I ever saw, and after speaking his mind as freely as he thought was prudent, finished with this unfatherly expression, *'Well! give me peace in my day.'* Not a man lives on the continent but fully believes that a separation must some time or other finally take place, and a generous parent should have said, *'If there must be trouble, let it be in my day, that my child may have peace'*; and this single reflection, well applied, is sufficient to awaken every man to duty. Not a place upon earth might be so happy as America. Her situation is remote from all the wrangling world, and she has nothing to do but to trade with them. A man can distinguish himself between temper and principle, and I am as confident, as I am that God governs the world, that America will never be happy till she gets clear of foreign dominion. Wars, without ceasing, will break out till that period arrives, and the continent must in the end be conqueror; for though the flame of liberty may sometimes cease to shine, the coal can never expire.

America did not, nor does not want force; but she wanted a proper application of that force. Wisdom is not the purchase of a day, and it is no wonder that we should err at the first setting off. From an excess of tenderness, we were unwilling to raise an army, and trusted our cause to the temporary defence of a well-meaning militia. A summer's experience has now taught us better; yet with those troops, while they were collected, we were able to set bounds to the progress of the enemy, and, thank God! they are again assembling. I always considered militia as the best troops in the world for a sudden exertion, but they will not do for a long campaign. Howe, it is probable, will make an attempt on this city; should he fail on this side the Delaware, he is ruined. If he succeeds, our cause is not ruined. He stakes all on his side against a part on ours; admitting he succeeds, the consequence will be, that armies from both ends of the continent will march to assist their suffering friends in the middle states; for he cannot go everywhere, it is impossible. I consider Howe as the greatest enemy the Tories have; he is bringing a war in their country, which, had it not been for him and partly for themselves, they had been clear of. Should he now be expelled, I wish with all the devotion of a Christian, that the names of Whig and Tory may never more be mentioned; but should the Tories give him encouragement to come, or assistance if he come, I as sincerely wish that our next year's arms may expel them from the continent, and the Congress appropriate their possessions to the relief of those who have suffered in well-doing. A single successful battle next year will settle the whole. America could carry on a two years' war by the confiscation of the property of disaffected persons, and be made happy by their expulsion. Say not that this is revenge, call it rather the soft resentment of a suffering people, who, having no object in view but the *good* of *all,* have staked their *own all* upon a seemingly doubtful event. Yet it is folly to argue against determined hardness; eloquence may strike the ear, and the language of sorrow draw forth the tear of compassion, but nothing can reach the heart that is steeled with prejudice.

Quitting this class of men, I turn with the warm ardour of a friend to those who have nobly stood, and are yet determined to stand the matter out: I call not upon a few, but upon all: not on *this* state or *that* state, but on *every* state: up and help us; lay your shoulders to the wheel; better have too much force than too little, when so great an object is at stake. Let it be told to the future world, that in the depth of winter, when nothing but hope and virtue could survive, that the city and the country, alarmed at one common danger, came forth to meet and to repulse it. Say not that thousands are gone, turn out your tens of thousands; throw not the burden of the day upon Providence, but '*show your faith by your works*', that God may bless you. It matters not where you live, or what rank of life you hold, the evil or the blessing will reach you all. The far and the near, the home counties and the back, the rich and the poor, will suffer or rejoice alike. The heart that feels not now is dead; the blood of his children will curse his cowardice, who shrinks back at a time when a little might have saved the whole, and made *them* happy. I love the man that can smile in trouble, that can gather strength from distress, and grow brave by reflection. 'Tis the business of little minds to shrink; but he whose heart is firm, and whose conscience approves his conduct, will pursue his principles unto death. My own line of reasoning is to myself as straight and clear as a ray of light. Not all the treasures of the world, so far as I believe, could have induced me to support an offensive war, for I think it murder; but if a thief breaks into my house, burns and destroys my property, and kills or threatens to kill me, or those that are in it, and to *'bind me in all cases whatsoever'* to his absolute will, am I to suffer it? What signifies it to me, whether he who does it is a king or a common man; my countryman or not my countryman; whether it be done by an individual villain, or an army of them? If we reason to the root of things we shall find no difference; neither can any just cause be assigned why we should punish in the one case and pardon in the other. Let them call me rebel and welcome, I feel no concern from it; but I should suffer the misery of devils, were I to make a whore of my soul by swearing allegiance to one whose character is that of a sottish, stupid, stubborn, worthless, brutish man. I conceive likewise a horrid idea in receiving mercy from a being, who at the last day shall be shrieking to the rocks and mountains to cover him, and fleeing with terror from the orphan, the widow, and the slain of America.

There are cases which cannot be overdone by language, and this is one. There are persons, too, who see not the full extent of the evil which threatens them; they solace themselves with hopes that the enemy, if he succeed, will be merciful. It is the madness of folly, to expect mercy from those who have refused to do justice; and even mercy, where conquest is the object, is only a trick of war; the cunning of the fox is as murderous as the violence of the wolf, and we ought to guard equally against both. Howe's first object is, partly by threats and partly by promises, to terrify or seduce the people to deliver up their arms and receive mercy. The ministry recommended the same plan to Gage, and this is what the Tories call making their peace, *'a peace which passeth all understanding'* indeed! A peace which would be the immediate forerunner of a worse ruin than any we have yet thought of. Ye men of Pennsylvania, do reason upon these things! Were the back counties to give up their arms, they would fall an easy prey to the Indians, who are all armed: this perhaps is what some Tories would not be sorry for. Were the home counties to deliver up their arms, they would be exposed to the resentment of the back counties, who would then have it in their power to chastise their defection at pleasure. And were any one state to give up its arms, *that* state must be garrisoned by all Howe's army of Britons and Hessians to preserve it from the anger of the rest. Mutual fear is the principal link in the chain of mutual love, and woe be to that state that breaks the compact. Howe is mercifully inviting you to barbarous destruction, and men must be either rogues or fools that will not see it. I dwell not upon the vapours of imagination; I bring reason to your ears, and, in language as plain as A, B, C, hold up truth to your eyes.

I thank God, that I fear not. I see no real cause for fear. I know our situation well, and can see the way out of it. While our army was collected, Howe dared not risk a battle; and it is no credit to him that he decamped from the White Plains, and waited a mean opportunity to ravage the defenceless Jerseys; but it is great credit to us, that, with a handful of men, we sustained an orderly retreat for near an hundred miles, brought off our ammunition, all our field pieces, the greatest part of our stores, and had four rivers to pass. None can say that our retreat was precipitate, for we were near three weeks in performing it, that the country might have time to come in. Twice we marched back to meet the enemy, and remained out till dark. The sign of fear was not seen in our camp, and had not some of the cowardly and disaffected inhabitants spread false alarms through the country, the Jerseys had never been ravaged. Once more we are again collected and collecting; our new army at both ends of the continent is recruiting fast, and we shall be able to open the next campaign with sixty thousand men, well armed and clothed. This is our situation, and who will may know it. By perseverance and fortitude we have the prospect of a glorious issue; by cowardice and submission, the sad choice of a variety of evils – a ravaged country – a depopulated city – habitations without safety, and slavery without hope – our homes turned into barracks and bawdy-houses for Hessians, and a future race to provide for, whose fathers we shall doubt of. Look on this picture and weep over it! and if there yet remains one thoughtless wretch who believes it not, let him suffer it unlamented.

December 23, 1776.   COMMON SENSE.

[7] PUBLIC GOOD

(1780)

In December 1780 Paine wrote a pamphlet which he would later cite as proof that he had been an early advocate of a strengthened centralized government in America. Maryland had refused to ratify the Articles of Confederation, adopted by the Continental Congress in March 1777, because Virginia and other states claimed as theirs land in the western territories which Maryland felt should be ceded to the Federal Government. Paine agreed with the Maryland position and in this pamphlet attacked the trans-Allegheny claims of Virginia. The western lands, he wrote, belonged to all, and should some day be laid out as new states. Paine anticipates in Public Good *the developments of 1787; he calls for 'a continental convention, for the purpose of forming a continental constitution, defining and describing the powers and authority of Congress'. The text included here is an edited excerpt from the original.*

The following pages are on a subject hitherto little understood but highly interesting to the United States.

They contain an investigation of the claims of Virginia to the vacant western territory, and of the right of the United States to the same; with some outlines of a plan for laying out a new State, to be applied as a fund, for carrying on the war, or redeeming the national debt.

The reader, in the course of this publication, will find it studiously plain, and, as far as I can judge, perfectly candid. What materials I could get at I have endeavoured to place in a clear line, and deduce such arguments therefrom as the subject required. In the prosecution of it, I have considered myself as an advocate for the right of the States, and taken no other liberty with the subject than what a counsel would, and ought to do, in behalf of a client.

I freely confess that the respect I had conceived, and still preserve, for the character of Virginia, was a constant check upon those sallies of imagination, which are fairly and advantageously indulged against an enemy, but ungenerous when against a friend.

If there is anything I have omitted or mistaken, to the injury of the intentions of Virginia or her claims, I shall gladly rectify it, or if there is anything yet to add, should the subject require it, I shall as cheerfully undertake it; being fully convinced, that to have matters fairly discussed, and properly understood, is a principal means of preserving harmony and perpetuating friendship. . . .

When we take into view the mutual happiness and united interests of the States of America, and consider the vast consequences to arise from a strict attention of each, and of all, to everything which is just, reasonable, and honourable; or the evils that will follow from an inattention to those principles; there cannot, and ought not, to remain a doubt but the governing rule of right and of mutual good must in all public cases finally preside.

The hand of providence has cast us into one common lot, and accomplished the independence of America, by the unanimous consent of the several parts, concurring at once in time, manner and circumstances. No superiority of interest, at the expense of the rest, induced the one, more than the other, into the measure. Virginia and Maryland, it is true, might foresee that their staple commodity, tobacco, by being no longer monopolized by Britain, would bring them a better price abroad: for as the tax on it in England was treble its first purchase from the planter, and they being now no longer compelled to send it under that obligation, and in the restricted manner they formerly were, it is easy to see that the article, from the alteration of the circumstances of trade, will, and daily does, turn out to them with additional advantages.

But this being a natural consequence, produced by that common freedom and independence of which all are partakers, is therefore an advantage they are entitled to, and on which the rest of the States can congratulate them without feeling a wish to lessen, but rather to extend it. To contribute to the increased prosperity of another, by the same means which occasion our own, is an agreeable reflection; and the more valuable any article of export becomes, the more riches will be introduced into and spread over the continent.

Yet this is an advantage which those two States derive from the independence of America, superior to the local circumstances of the rest; and of the two it more particularly belongs to Virginia than Maryland, because the staple commodity of a considerable part of Maryland is flour, which, as it is an article that is the growth of Europe as well as of America, cannot obtain a foreign market but by underselling, or at least by limiting it to the current price abroad. But tobacco commands its own price. It is not a plant of almost universal growth, like wheat. There are but few soils and climes that produce it to advantage, and before the cultivation of it in Virginia and Maryland, the price was from four to sixteen shillings sterling a pound in England.

But the condition of the vacant western territory of America makes a very different case to that of the circumstances of trade in any of the States. Those very lands, formed, in contemplation, the fund by which the debt of America would in the course of years be redeemed. They were considered as the common right of all; and it is only till lately that any pretension of claim has been made to the contrary.

That difficulties and differences will arise in communities, ought always to be looked for. The opposition of interests, real or supposed, the variety of judgements, the contrariety of temper, and, in short, the whole composition of man, in his individual capacity, is tinctured with a disposition to contend; but in his social capacity there is either a right, which, being proved, terminates the disputes, or a reasonableness in the measure, where no direct right can be made out, which decides or comprises the matter.

As I shall have frequent occasion to mention the word *right*, I wish to be clearly understood in my definition of it. There are various senses in which this term is used, and custom has, in many of them, afforded it an introduction contrary to its true meaning. We are so naturally inclined to give the utmost degree of force to our own case, that we call every pretension, however founded, *a right*; and by this means the term frequently stands opposed to justice and reason.

After Theodore was elected King of Corsica, not many years ago, by the mere choice of the natives, for their own convenience in opposing the Genoese, he went over to England, ran himself in debt, got himself into jail, and on his release therefrom, by the benefit of an act of insolvency, he surrendered up what he called *his* kingdom of Corsica, as a part of his personal property, for the use of his creditors; some of whom may hereafter call this a charter, or by any other name more fashionable, and ground thereon what they may term a right to the sovereignty and property of Corsica. But does not justice abhor such an action both in him and them, under the prostituted name of a *right,* and must not laughter be excited wherever it is told?

A right, to be truly so, must be right within itself: yet many things have obtained the name of rights, which are originally founded in wrong. Of this kind are all rights by mere conquest, power or violence.

In the cool moments of reflection we are obliged to allow that the mode by which such a right is obtained is not the best suited to that spirit of universal justice which ought to preside equally over all mankind. There is something in the establishment of such a right that we wish to slip over as easily as possible, and say as little about as can be. But in the case of a *right founded in right,* the mind is carried cheerfully into the subject, feels no compunction, suffers no distress, subjects its sensations to no violence, nor sees anything in its way which requires an artificial smoothing.

From this introduction I proceed to examine into the claims of Virginia; first, as to the right, secondly as to the reasonableness, and lastly, as to the consequences.

The name, *Virginia,* originally bore a different meaning to what it does now. It stood in the place of the word North America, and seems to have been a name comprehensive of all the English settlements or colonies on the continent, and not descriptive of any one as distinguished from the rest. All to the southward of the Chesapeake, as low as the Gulf of Mexico, was called South Virginia, and all to the northward, North Virginia, in a similar line of distinction, as we now call the whole continent North and South America.

The first charter, or patent, was to Sir Walter Raleigh by Queen Elizabeth, of England, in the year 1583, and had neither name nor bounds. Upon Sir Walter's return, the name *Virginia* was given to the whole country, including the now United States. Consequently the present Virginia, either as a province or State, can set up no exclusive claim to the western territory under this patent, and that for two reasons: first, because the words of the patent run *to Sir Walter Raleigh, and such persons as he should nominate, themselves and their successors*; which is a line of succession Virginia does not pretend to stand in; and secondly, because a prior question would arise, namely, who are to be understood by Virginians under this patent? and the answer would be, all the inhabitants of America, from New England to Florida.

This patent, therefore, would destroy their exclusive claim, and invest the right collectively in the thirteen States.

But it unfortunately happened, that the settlers under this patent, partly from misconduct, the opposition of the Indians, and other calamities, discontinued the process, and the patent became extinct.

After this, James I, who, in the year 1602, succeeded Elizabeth, issued a new patent, which I come next to describe.

This patent differed from the former in this essential point, that it had limits, whereas the other had none: the former was intended to promote discoveries wherever they could be made, which accounts why no limits were affixed, and this to settle discoveries already made, which likewise assigns a reason why limits should be described.

In this patent were incorporated two companies, called the South Virginia Company, and the North Virginia Company, and sometimes the London Company, and the Plymouth Company. . . .

On these documents I shall make no remarks. They are their own evidence, and show what the limits of Virginia were while a British province; and as there was then no other authority by which they could be fixed, and as the grant to the London Company could not be a grant to any but themselves, and of consequence ceased to be when they ceased to exist, it remained a matter of choice in the Crown, on its reassumption of the lands, to limit or divide them into separate governments, as it judged best, and from which there was not, and could not, in the order of government, be any appeal. Neither was Virginia, as a province, affected by it, because the moneys, in any case, arising from the sale of lands, did not go into her treasury; and whether to the Crown or to the proprietors was to her indifferent. And it is likewise evident, from the secretary's letter, and the president's answer, that it was in contemplation to lay out a new colony on the *back* of Virginia, between the Allegheny Mountains and the Ohio.

Having thus gone through the several charters, or grants, and their relation to each other, and shown that Virginia cannot stand in succession to a private grant, which has been extinct for upwards of one hundred and fifty years – and that the western limits of Virginia, at the commencement of the Revolution, were at the heads of the rivers emptying themselves into the Atlantic, none of which are beyond the Allegheny Mountains; I now proceed to the second part, namely,

The reasonableness of her claims.

Virginia, as a British province, stood in a different situation with the Crown of England to any of the other provinces, because she had no ascertained limits, but such as arose from laying off new provinces and the proclamation of 1763. For the same name, Virginia, as I have before mentioned, was the general name of all the country, and the dominion out of which the several governments were laid off: and, in strict propriety, conformable to the origin of names, the province of Virginia was taken out of the dominion of Virginia. For the term, *dominion,* could not appertain to the province, which retained the name of Virginia, but the Crown, and from thence was applied to the whole country, and signified its being an appendage to the Crown of England, as they say now, *'our dominion of Wales'.*

It is not possible to suppose there could exist an idea that Virginia, as a British province, was to be extended to the South Sea, at the distance of three thousand miles. The dominion, as appertaining at that time to the Crown, might be claimed to extend so far, but as a province the thought was not conceivable, nor the practice possible.

And it is more than probable, that the deception made use of to obtain the patent of 1609, by representing the South Sea to be near where the Allegheny Mountains are, was one cause of its becoming extinct; and it is worthy of remarking, that no history (at least that I have met with) mentions any dispute or litigation, between the Crown and the Company, in consequence of the extinction of the patent, and the reassumption of the lands; and, therefore, the negative evidence corroborating with the positive, makes it as certain as such a case can possibly be, that either the Company received a compensation for the patent, or quitted it quietly, ashamed of the imposition they had practised, and their subsequent maladministration.

Men are not inclined to give up a claim where there is any ground to contend upon, and the silence in which the patent expired is a presumptive proof that its fate, from whatever cause, was just.

There is one general policy which seems to have prevailed with the English in laying off new governments, which was not to make them larger than their own country, that they might the easier hold them manageable: this was the case with everyone except Canada, the extension of whose limits was for the politic purpose of re-cognizing new acquisitions of territory not immediately convenient for colonization.

But, in order to give this matter a chance through all its cases, I will admit what no man can suppose, which is that there is an English charter that fixes Virginia to extend from the Atlantic to the South Sea, and contained within a due west line, set off two hundred miles below Cape Comfort, and a north-west line, set off two hundred miles above it. Her side, then, on the Atlantic (according to an explanation given in Mr Bradford's paper of Sept. 29, 1779, by an advocate for the Virginia claims) will be four hundred miles; her side to the south three thousand; her side to the west four thousand; and her north-west line about five thousand; and the quantity of land contained within these dimensions will be almost four thousand millions of acres, which is more than ten times the quantity contained within the present United States, and above an hundred times greater than the Kingdom of England.

To reason on a case like this is such a waste of time, and such an excess of folly, that it ought not to be reasoned upon. It is impossible to suppose that any patent to private persons could be so intentionally absurd, and the claim grounded thereon, is as wild as anything the imagination of man ever conceived.

But if, as I before mentioned, there was a charter which bore such an explanation, and Virginia stood in succession to it, what would that be to us, any more than the will of Alexander, had he taken it into his head to have bequeathed away the world? Such a charter, or grant, must have been obtained by imposition and a false representation of the country, or granted in error, or both; and in any of, or all these cases, the United States must reject the matter as something they cannot know, for the merits will not bear an argument, and the pretension of right stands upon no better ground.

Our case is an original one; and many matters attending it must be determined on their own merits and reasonableness. The territory of the rest of the States is, in general, within known bounds of moderate extent, and the quota which each state is to furnish towards the expense and service of the war, must be ascertained upon some rule of comparison. The number of inhabitants of each State formed the first rule; and it was naturally supposed that those numbers bore nearly the same proportion to each other, which the territory of each State did. Virginia on this scale, would be about one-fifth larger than Pennsylvania, which would be as much dominion as any state could manage with happiness and convenience.

When I first began this subject my intention was to be extensive on the merits, and concise on the matter of the right; instead of which, I have been extensive on the matter of right, and concise on the merits of reasonableness: and this alteration in my design arose, consequentially, from the nature of the subject; for as a reasonable thing the claim can be supported by no argument, and therefore, needs none to refute it; but as there is a strange propensity in mankind to shelter themselves under the sanction of right, however unreasonable that supposed right may be, I found it most conducive to the interest of the case to show that the right stands upon no better grounds than the reason. And shall therefore proceed to make some observations on the consequences of the claim.

The claim being unreasonable in itself, and standing on no ground of right, but such as, if true, must, from the quarter it is drawn, be offensive, has a tendency to create disgust, and sour the minds of the rest of the States. Those lands are capable, under the management of the United States, of repaying the charges of the war, and some of them, as I shall hereafter show, may, I presume, be made an immediate advantage of.

I distinguish three different descriptions of land in America at the commencement of the Revolution. Proprietary or chartered lands, as was the case in Pennsylvania; crown lands, within the described limits of any of the Crown governments; and crown residuary lands, that were without or beyond the limits of any province; and those last were held in reserve whereon to erect new governments, and lay out new provinces; as appears to have been the design by Lord Hillsborough's letter, and the president's answer, wherein he says, 'With respect to the establishment of a *new* colony on the *back* of Virginia, it is a subject of too great political importance for me to presume to give an opinion upon; however, permit me, My Lord, to observe, that when that part of the country shall become populated, it may be a wise and prudent measure.'

The expression is, a *'new colony* on the *back* of Virginia'; and referred to lands between the heads of the rivers and the Ohio. This is a proof that those lands were not considered within, but beyond the limits of Virginia, as a colony; and the other expression in the letter is equally descriptive, namely, *'We do not presume to say, to whom our Gracious Sovereign shall grant his vacant lands.'* Certainly then, the same right, which, at that time rested in the Crown, rests now in the more supreme authority of the United States; and therefore, addressing the president's letter to the circumstances of the Revolution, it will run thus:

'We do not presume to say to whom the *sovereign United States* shall grant their vacant lands, and with respect to the settlement of a *new colony* on the *back* of Virginia, it is a matter of too much political importance for me to give an opinion upon; however, permit me to observe, that when that part of the country shall become populated it may be a wise and prudent measure.'

It must occur to every person, on reflection, that those lands are too distant to be within the government of any of the present states; and, I may presume to suppose, that were a calculation justly made, Virginia has lost more by the decrease of taxables, than she has gained by what lands she has made sale of; therefore, she is not only doing the rest of the States wrong in point of equity, but herself and them an injury in point of strength, service, and revenue.

It is only the United States, and not any single State, that can lay off new States, and incorporate them in the Union by representation; therefore, the situation which the settlers on those lands will be in, under the assumed right of Virginia, will be hazardous and distressing, and they will feel themselves at last like the aliens to the Commonwealth of Israel, their habitations unsafe and their title precarious.

And when men reflect on that peace, harmony, quietude, and security, which are necessary to prosperity, especially in making new settlements, and think that when the war shall be ended, their happiness and safety will depend on a union with the States, and not a scattered people, unconnected with, and politically unknown to the rest, they will feel but little inclination to put themselves in a situation, which, however solitary and recluse it may appear at present, will then be uncertain and unsafe, and their troubles will have to begin where those of the United States shall end.

It is probable that some of the inhabitants of Virginia may be inclined to suppose that the writer of this, by taking up the subject in the manner he has done, is arguing unfriendly against their interest. To which he wishes to reply:

That the most extraordinary part of the whole is, that Virginia should countenance such a claim. For it is worthy of observing that, from the beginning of the contest with Britain, and long after, there was not a people in America who discovered, through all the variety and multiplicity of public business, a greater fund of true wisdom, fortitude, and disinterestedness than the then colony of Virginia. They were loved – they were reverenced. Their investigation of the assumed rights of Britain had a sagacity which was uncommon. Their reasonings were piercing, difficult to be equalled and impossible to be refuted, and their public spirit was exceeded by none. But since this unfortunate land scheme has taken place, their powers seem to be absorbed; a torpor has overshaded them, and everyone asks, What is become of Virginia?

It seldom happens that the romantic schemes of extensive dominion are of any service to a government, and never to a people. They assuredly end at last in loss, trouble, division and disappointment. And was even the title of Virginia good, and the claim admissible, she would derive more lasting and real benefit by participating in it than by attempting the management of an object so infinitely beyond her reach. Her share with the rest, under the supremacy of the United States, which is the only authority adequate to the purpose, would be worth more to her than what the whole would produce under the management of herself alone. And that for several reasons:

1st, Because her claim not being admissible nor yet manageable, she cannot make a good title to the purchasers, and consequently can get but little for the lands.

2d, Because the distance the settlers will be from her, will immediately put them out of all government and protection, so far, at least as relates to Virginia: and by this means she will render her frontiers a refuge to desperadoes, and a hiding place from justice; and the consequence will be perpetual unsafety to her own peace, and that of the neighbouring States.

3d, Because her quota of expense for carrying on the war, admitting her to engross such an immensity of territory, would be greater than she can either support or supply, and could not be less, upon a reasonable rule of proportion, than nine-tenths of the whole. And,

4th, Because she must sooner or later relinquish them; therefore to see her own interest wisely at first, is preferable to the alternative of finding it out by misfortune at last.

I have now gone through my examination of the claim of Virginia, in every case which I proposed; and for several reasons, wish the lot had fallen to another person. But as this is a most important matter, in which all are interested, and the substantial good of Virginia not injured but promoted, and as few men have leisure, and still fewer have inclination, to go into intricate investigation, I have at last ventured on the subject.

The succession of the United States to the vacant western territory is a right they originally set out upon; and in the pamphlet *Common Sense*, I frequently mentioned those lands as a national fund for the benefit of all; therefore, resuming the subject where I then left off, I shall conclude with concisely reducing to system what I then only hinted.

In my last piece, the *Crisis Extraordinary*, I estimated the annual amount of the charge of war and the support of the several governments at two million pounds sterling, and the peace establishment at three quarters of a million, and, by a comparison of the taxes of this country with those of England, proved that the whole yearly expense to us, to defend the country, is but a third of what Britain would have drawn from us by taxes, had she succeeded in her attempt to conquer; and our peace establishment only an eighth part; and likewise showed, that it was within the ability of the States to carry on the whole of the war by taxation, without having recourse to any other modes or funds. To have a clear idea of taxation is necessary to every country, and the more funds we can discover and organize, the less will be the hope of the enemy, and the readier their disposition to peace, which it is now *their* interest more than *ours* to promote.

I have already remarked that only the United States, and not any particular State, can lay off new States and incorporate them into the Union by representation; keeping, therefore, this idea in view, I ask, might not a substantial fund be quickly created by laying off a new State, so as to contain between twenty and thirty millions of acres, and opening a land office in all countries in Europe for hard money, and in this country for supplies in kind, at a certain price?

The tract of land that seems best adapted to answer this purpose is contained between the Allegheny Mountains and the river Ohio, as far north as the Pennsylvania line, thence extending down the said river to the falls thereof, thence due south into the latitude of the North Carolina line, and thence east to the Allegheny Mountains aforesaid. I the more readily mention this tract, because it is fighting the enemy with their own weapons, as it includes the same ground on which a new colony would have been erected, for the emolument of the Crown of England, as appears by the letters of Lords Hillsborough and Dartmouth, had not the Revolution prevented its being carried into effect.

It is probable that there may be some spots of private property within this tract, but to incorporate them into some government will render them more profitable to the owners, and the condition of the scattered settlers more eligible and happy than at present.

If twenty millions of acres of this new State be patented and sold at twenty pounds sterling per hundred acres, they will produce four million pounds sterling, which, if applied to Continental expenses only, will support the war for three years, should Britain be so unwise as to prosecute it against her own direct interest and against the interest and policy of all Europe. The several States will then have to raise taxes for their internal government only, and the Continental taxes, as soon as the fund begins to operate, will lessen, and if sufficiently productive, will cease.

Lands are the real riches of the habitable world, and the natural funds of America. The funds of other countries are, in general, artificially constructed; the creatures of necessity and contrivance dependent upon credit, and always exposed to hazard and uncertainty. But lands can neither be annihilated nor lose their value; on the contrary, they universally rise with population, and rapidly so, when under the security of effectual government. But this it is impossible for Virginia to give, and therefore, that which is capable of defraying the expenses of the empire, will, under the management of any single State, produce only a fugitive support to wandering individuals.

I shall now inquire into the effects which the laying out of a new State, under the authority of the United States, will have upon Virginia. It is the very circumstance she ought to, and must, wish for, when she examines the matter in all its bearings and consequences.

The present settlers beyond her reach, and her supposed authority over them remaining in herself, they will appear to her as revolters, and she to them as oppressors; and this will produce such a spirit of mutual dislike, that in a little time a total disagreement will take place, to the disadvantage of both. But under the authority of the United States the matter is manageable, and Virginia will be eased of a disagreeable consequence.

Besides this, a sale of the lands, continentally, for the purpose of supporting the expense of the war, will save her a greater share of taxes, than the small sale which she could make herself, and the small price she could get for them would produce.

She would likewise have two advantages which no other State in the Union enjoys; first, a frontier State for her defence against the incursions of the Indians; and the second is, that the laying out and peopling a new State on the back of an old one, situated as she is, is doubling the quantity of its trade.

The new State which is here proposed to be laid out, may send its exports down the Mississippi, but its imports must come through Chesapeake Bay, and consequently Virginia will become the market for the new State; because, though there is a navigation from it, there is none into it, on account of the rapidity of the Mississippi.

There are certain circumstances that will produce certain events whether men think of them or not. The events do not depend upon thinking, but are the natural consequence of acting; and according to the system which Virginia has gone upon, the issue will be, that she will get involved with the back settlers in a contention about *rights*, till they dispute with their own claims; and, soured by the contention, will go to any other State for their commerce; both of which may be prevented, a perfect harmony established, the strength of the States increased, and the expenses of the war defrayed, by settling the matter now on the plan of a general right; and every day it is delayed, the difficulty will be increased and the advantages lessened.

But if it should happen, as it possibly may, that the war should end before the money, which the new State may produce, be expended, the remainder of the lands therein may be set apart to reimburse those whose houses have been burned by the enemy, as this is a species of suffering which it was impossible to prevent, because houses are not movable property; and it ought not to be that because we cannot do everything, that we ought not to do what we can.

Having said this much on the subject, I think it necessary to remark that the prospect of a new fund, so far from abating our endeavours in making every immediate provision for the army, ought to quicken us therein; for should the States see it expedient to go upon the measure, it will be at least a year before it can be productive. I the more freely mention this, because there is a dangerous species of popularity, which, I fear, some men are seeking from their constituents by giving them grounds to believe that if they are elected they will lighten the taxes; a measure which, in the present state of things, cannot be done without exposing the country to the ravages of the enemy by disabling the army from defending it.

Where knowledge is a duty, ignorance is a crime; and if any man, whose duty it was to know better, has encouraged such an expectation, he has either deceived himself or them: besides, no country can be defended without expense, and let any man compare his portion of temporary inconveniences arising from taxation with the real distresses of the army for want of supplies, and the difference is not only sufficient to strike him dumb, but make him thankful that worse consequences have not followed.

In advancing this doctrine, I speak with an honest freedom to the country; for as it is their good to be defended, so it is their interest to provide that defence, at least till other funds can be organized.

As the laying out of new States will some time or other be the business of the country, and as it is yet a new business to us, and as the influence of the war has scarcely afforded leisure for reflecting on distant circumstances, I shall throw together a few hints for facilitating that measure whenever it may be proper for adopting it.

The United States now standing on the line of sovereignty, the vacant territory is their property collectively, but the persons by whom it may hereafter be peopled will also have an equal right with ourselves; and therefore, as new States shall be laid off and incorporated with the present, they will become partakers of the remaining territory with us who are already in possession. And this consideration ought to heighten the value of lands to new emigrants: because, in making the purchases, they not only gain an immediate property, but become initiated into the right and heirship of the States to a property in reserve, which is an additional advantage to what any purchasers under the late Government of England enjoyed.

The setting off the boundary of any new State will naturally be the first step, and as it must be supposed not to be peopled at the time it is laid off, a constitution must be formed by the United States, as the rule of government in any new state, for a certain term of years (perhaps ten) or until the state becomes peopled to a certain number of inhabitants; after which, the whole and sole right of modelling their government to rest with themselves.

A question may arise, whether a new State should immediately possess an equal right with the present ones in all cases which may come before Congress.

This, experience will best determine; but at a first view of the matter it appears thus: that it ought to be immediately incorporated into the Union on the ground of a family right, such a state standing in the line of a younger child of the same stock; but as new emigrants will have something to learn when they first come to America, and a new State requiring aid rather than capable of giving it, it might be most convenient to admit its immediate representation into Congress, there to sit, hear and debate on all questions and matters, but not to vote on any till after the expiration of seven years.

I shall in this place take the opportunity of renewing a hint which I formerly threw out in the pamphlet 'Common Sense', and which the several States will, sooner or later, see the convenience if not the necessity of adopting; which is, that of electing a Continental Convention, for the purpose of forming a Continental Constitution, defining and describing the powers and authority of Congress.

Those of entering into treaties, and making peace, they naturally possess, in behalf of the States, for their separate as well as their united good, but the internal control and dictatorial powers of Congress are not sufficiently defined, and appear to be too much in some cases and too little in others; and therefore, to have them marked out legally will give additional energy to the whole, and a new confidence to the several parts.

[8] SIX LETTERS TO RHODE ISLAND

(1782–3)

One of the provisions of the Articles of Confederation stipulated that any change in the original document be approved by all the states. It was this process which provided the context in December 1782 and January/February 1783 for Paine's Six Letters to Rhode Island. Congress had proposed a 5 per cent duty on imports, and Rhode Island stood alone in rejecting a revision in the Articles that would have allowed Congress to regulate commerce. The text here is from Paine's second and third Letters seeking to convince the people of Rhode Island that the national interest required the abandonment of claims to total state sovereignty.

The United States are, as Mr Burke very justly styles them, 'the greatest Commonwealth on the face of the earth'.[1] But all Commonwealths must have some laws in common, which regulate, preserve, and protect the whole.

What would the sovereignty of any one individual State be, if left to itself, to contend with a foreign power? It is on our united sovereignty, that our greatness and safety, and the security of our foreign commerce, rest. This united sovereignty then must be something more than a name, and requires to be as completely organized for the line it is to act in as that of any individual State, and, if any thing, more so, because more depends on it.

Every man in America stands in a two-fold order of citizenship. He is a citizen of the State he lives in, and of the United States; and without justly and truly supporting his citizenship in the latter, he will inevitably sacrifice the former. By his rank in the one, he is made secure with his neighbours; by the other, with the world. The one protects his domestic safety and property from internal robbers and injustice; the other his foreign and remote property from piracy and invasion, and puts him on a rank with other nations. Certainly then the one, like the other, must not and cannot be trusted to pleasure and caprice, lest, in the display of local authority, we forget the great line that made us great, and must keep us so.

1 See Mr Burke's speech on the case of Mr Laurens, Dec. 17, 1781, in the parliamentary debates, page 185. – Paine.

In introducing these remarks I have followed a thought naturally arising from the observations made by the Citizen of Rhode Island, and I find that experience begins to suggest the idea of an inadequacy in our confederated system to several cases which must necessarily happen; what I mean is, that the confederation is not adapted to fit all the cases which the empire of the United States, in the course of her sovereignty, may experience; and the case before us shows that it is not adequate to every purpose of internal benefit and commercial regulation.

Several new and important matters have arisen since the confederation was formed. The entering into foreign alliances and treaties of commerce; the borrowing foreign loans; the cessation of the emissions of the paper currency; the raising the supplies by taxes, and several others which might be enumerated. But as nothing can happen to which we are not equal, the thing necessary is to think wisely and deliberately of them, and provide accordingly. . . .

When the cause of America, like a new creation, rose into existence, it had something in it which confounded and yet enraptured the world. The boldness of the attempt, and the extent of its consequences, overawed the conjectures of mankind. A five per cent duty, levied for our support, either on land or commerce, would not then have swallowed up our attention, or produced a debate dishonourable to our patriotism. The defence of our country against an unprincipled and powerful enemy, the establishment of our natural rights, the exalting the human race to their original freedom, and guaranteeing the blessing of civil government, were the great objects of our heart, and we were a united, though a suffering people.

Why is it that so many little cares, unworthy our greatness, and injurious to our peace, have stolen upon our better thoughts? Are we tired of being successful? Is our domestic liberty of less value than formerly? Or are we disposed to surrender to contention that which the enemy could never take from us by force?

It would perhaps be quite as well were [we] to talk less about our independence, and more about our union. For if the union be justly supported, our independence is made secure. The former is the mother, the latter the infant at her breast. The nourishment of the one is drawn through the other, and to impoverish the mother is famishing her offspring.

Is there a country in the world that has so many openings to happiness as this? Masters of the land, and proprietors of the government, unchained from the evils of foreign subjection, and respected by sovereign powers, we have only to deserve prosperity, and its attainment is sure.

But it ever was and probably ever will be the unfortunate disposition of some men to encumber business with difficulties. The natural cast of their mind is to contention; and whatever is not to their particular wish, or their immediate interest, is sure to be magnified with invented calamities, and exhibited in terror. Such men can see the fate of empires in the snuff of a candle, and an eternity of public ruin wrapt up in every trifling disappointment to themselves. They build their hopes of popularity on error and accident; and subsist by flattering the mistakes and bewildering the judgement of others, till unable to discover the truth, or unwilling to confess it, they run into new inconsistencies, or retreat in angry discontent.

Never was a subject, simple and easy in itself (and which needed nothing but plain and temperate argument, if it needed any) more hideously tortured, and wilfully misrepresented, than by those who have wrote against the five per cent duty. Yet none of them have proposed a better or more eligible and practicable method of supporting public credit, and supplying the exigencies of the States. To them, I ask, can we rescue ourselves from a merciless enemy without charge? Can we defend our country or our property in it without expense? Can we borrow money without repaying it? Can we expect an army to subsist without supplies, or fight without reward? Or, in short, can we, who are to reap the benefit of independence, look for it as a mere boon from heaven, or hope to receive it at the expense of others?

We have to deal with a treacherous enemy, catching at every circumstance, and continuing the war on the hope of our mistakes. Their perfidiously withdrawing from the assurances they had given, in Carleton and Digby's letter, of acceding to our independence, serves to explain both their character and their politics. And another letter written by a Doctor Walters, a refugee Tory in New York, to Sir William Pepperil, a refugee Tory in England, and published in the London Morning Post on the 12th of last September (though false in its account of our finances) sufficiently shows that their expectations are founded solely on their hope of our neglecting to support the necessary defence. And shall we with our eyes open, and with the information of the enemy before us, encourage them in their deception, and add to the expenses of the war by prolonging it? They continue in our country not from a view of conquest, but to wait the issue of our internal difficulties. Every imprudent debate, every embarrassment that is started, is to them a matter of malignant joy, and a new ground for malicious hope. In this situation, watched by our enemies, and wounded by our mistakes, it becomes us to think and act with firm but deliberate patriotism, lest in the petulance of temper, or the hurry of imprudence, we sacrifice the prospects of a seven years contest.[2]

It was my original design to have confined the subject of this letter to the union of the States; but as that is a matter sufficiently forcible of itself, I shall wa[i]ve it for the present, and continue my remarks on the five per cent duty, not only as it respects the States generally, but as it more locally respects the State of Rhode Island.

That our condition, as a country engaged in a just and necessary war, requires money, needs not to be mentioned; and that the easiest way of raising it is the first subject for consideration, is equally clear. That the nature of a union requires and implies a disposition to act and draw together, and that the revenues are always within our control, are matters that require no proof. That Congress are as much the representatives of the people as the Assemblies are; that the members of it can in no instance exempt themselves from a share of the burdens necessary for the defence of the country, in common with their constituents, and that it is the duty of every legislature to support its faith, rank and reputation, in the union, are subjects which all are agreed in. That moneys cannot be borrowed without funds to pay with, and that those who are directed to borrow must be enabled to pay, needs no argument to support it; and that those who have it to lend will expect some better security than a promise, requires no explanation.

The question therefore is not *whether* we shall raise money, but *how* we shall raise it. The five per cent duty is part of the plan of finance adopted about a year ago, upon the failure of the paper currency. It was intendedly applied as a sinking fund for the discharge

2 The letter which I refer to, to Sir William Pepperil, has been seen by the Delegates of Rhode Island, now in Congress; for it fell into my hands, and I sent it there. And those gentlemen know full as well as I do, if they will confess it, that the hope of the enemy is fed up, by every imprudent dispute and inflammatory publication of ours, respecting revenue and supplies. – Paine.

of the debt we had contracted, at home or abroad, or might hereafter contract, in case the present taxes should not be sufficiently productive, which is now very well known to be the case. Therefore either the direct taxes on land and personal property must be increased, in the form they now are, or a duty of five per cent must be drawn through the medium of foreign articles, and the question is, which of the two will be the easiest, and most convenient to the community? The collected wisdom of the United States assembled in Congress has viewed a duty of five per cent as the easiest mode, and the several individual States have thought the same.

Those who have hitherto written against the five per cent duty have never either stated the case, or confined themselves to the subject, but have run out into extravagant language and wild imagination, and constantly endeavoured to keep the country and the community at large from properly understanding the measure, the propriety, or the necessity of it.

In this place I think it necessary to remark, that the United States are successors to a large landed property, and as Rhode Island has a share, in common with her sister States, so I hope she will never relinquish her right, or by any disagreement with them afford the least pretence for forfeiting it. But this property is not, in the present state of things, a practicable fund. To attempt to sell those lands at this time would be to give them away, neither are there purchasers for them at any price. Nay, it is our interest, at present, to prevent their being settled, because the settlement of them now, instead of enriching us, would draw off our inhabitants, and reduce both our force and our abilities.

But to return to my subject – We, I presume, are the only people in the world who have not taken in the aid of commerce, as a national fund. The landed interest, the stock and internal riches of the country, and almost every species of direct property, are subject, more or less, to some kind of taxation; while foreign imported articles, many of which are luxuries and trifles, have been suffered to pass without any tax at all, except that kind of tax which the importer lays on the community whenever he pleases, by raising the prices.

Whether this is good or ill policy, in a new country, whose first business is to settle and improve its lands, encourage agriculture, and restrain as much as possible the importation of foreign unnecessary articles, is a matter which I leave to the impartiality and honest judgement of every class of men. I am no enemy to genteel or fashionable dress, or to the moderate enjoyment of those articles of indulgence we are furnished with from abroad; but they ought to bear their proportion of the public expense as well as the soil we live on, and not be solely consigned as a revenue to the persons who import them, or the foreigners who bring them.

It is a matter which ought to strike Britain with forcible conviction, when she learns that we have the whole fund of commerce yet untouched. We have all that to begin upon which she has already exhausted; and so far as the debate may serve to explain to her our hitherto reserved funds and resources, I am the less concerned that it began.

How we came to leave so practicable and valuable a fund so long dormant, contrary to the custom and experience of all other nations, will, I believe, be best understood by the following observation:

Our non-importation agreement had exhausted us of almost every kind of supplies, and it was then necessary to hasten and encourage importations from all countries, except England, by every possible means. The then state of our commerce, therefore, permitted those indulgences, which, in any other case, would have been nationally improper. We suffered the produce and manufactures of other countries to be sold in America without duty, whereas none of our exports from America can enjoy the same privilege there; and thus having got into the habit of doing a thing from necessity, we have continued it to an impropriety.

This part of my argument naturally brings me to offer a remark on the five per cent duty, as a regulation of commerce.

Commerce is not the local property of any State, any more than it is the local property of any person, unless it can be proved, that such a State neither buys nor sells out of its own dominions. But as the commerce of every State is made up out of the produce and consumption of other States, as well as its own, therefore its regulation and protection can only be under the confederated patronage of all the States.

Besides, the European world, or any place we may trade to, knows us only through our national sovereignty, as UNITED STATES. Any infringement on our rights of commerce must be lodged before the United States, and every redress for any such injury must come to us through that line of sovereignty; consequently the regulation of it must reside in the same power.

The United States are likewise accountable to foreign powers for all misconduct committed under their flag; and as it is their flag which privileges our commerce abroad, and on the seas, it cannot therefore be expected, that the United States should be thus accountable on the one hand, and afford protection on the other, to all the rights of commerce, without receiving an aid and assistance from it.

I come now to consider a very striking injury that would accrue to Rhode Island, by not coming into the measure with the rest of the States.

The fidelity, patriotism, and well-affected disposition of Rhode Island, has never been made the least question of; neither does her present dissent proceed from any source of that kind, but from a misrepresentation of it on some part, and a misconception of it on another.

In the course of the debate she has taken up an idea, warranted by the articles of confederation, that each State has a prerogative to furnish its quota by such means as best suits its conveniency, and in this she is right. But the mistake is, that the five per cent duty is not of the nature of a quota, and that for the reason I have already mentioned, namely, that trade is not local property, but is diffused over and promiscuously drawn from all parts, beyond as well as within the State. Neither is she called upon, in the character of an individual State, for a particular thing limited like direct property, within her own jurisdiction only, but in her *united character*, to concur in a measure common to all the States, and yet the particular property of none.

But for the purpose of exemplifying this part of the argument, I will suppose her left out of the five per cent duty, and that she furnished a supply into the treasury, by laying on some new taxes in the room of it. The consequence to her in this case as a community would be, that, to avoid the five per cent duty, she would at least have to pay to the amount of ten per cent. For the prices of foreign articles would, by the imperceptible management of trade, get up to the same price in Rhode Island as they would be at in Boston, or other places where the duty was paid, and consequently would come as dear to the consumer as if they had undergone the duty; and yet the same consumer would have his part to pay in the additional tax laid on in the lieu [of] the five per cent. And thus an exemption from the duty would operate as a bounty, or an additional profit of the five per cent to the merchant only, and a double tax to the community.

Perhaps it is a circumstance worthy of remarking, that in all cases where a union of conduct and disposition is necessary, nothing can be gained and much may be lost by disagreement. The United States constitute one extended family, one imperial Commonwealth, the greatest and most equal in its rights and government of any ever known in the world: And while its principles permit the free exercise of debate, its manners ought to restrain every licentious abuse of it.

In offering the foregoing remarks, and those contained in my former letters, I have kept strictly to the point in question, without involving it with subjects foreign to the purpose, or treating it with wild and overheated language. All that is necessary, in a case like this, is calm discussion, and a disposition to agree and be understood. That measures and subjects do not strike every mind alike – that the necessity of them is not always equally known – and that, in a situation so remote as the several parts of the United States are from each other, some misconception may arise, is a circumstance we may naturally expect; but as our interest, like our object, is a united one, there can be no measure which is to operate equally over all, in matters common to all, that can, on a just consideration, be supposed to affect one more than another.

But if such a supposition could any way take place, it would apply to the merchants of Philadelphia, because it is the greatest seat of commerce, and extends it into parts of several other States. But they, convinced of its justice, necessity and true policy, have been among the promoters of the measure; and so likewise, on a just reflection, will be those of Rhode Island; and the country interest can adopt no other measure with equal ease.

A FRIEND TO RHODE ISLAND AND THE UNION. . . .

[9] LETTER TO THE ABBÉ RAYNAL

(1782)

In this pamphlet, written in 1782, Paine responded to the Abbé Raynal, a distin-
guished French historian, whose Révolution d'Amérique *had been translated into*
English in 1781. Paine sought to correct what he saw as numerous errors in the
Abbé's account of the American Revolution, none the least of which was his failure
to understand its true historical significance. For Paine it was more than just another
political rebellion. 'Our style and manner of thinking have undergone a revolution',
he wrote. 'We see with other eyes; we hear with other ears, and we think with other
thoughts, than those we formerly used.' The text included here is a shortened version
of the original.

A London translation of an original work in France, by the Abbé
Raynal, which treats of the Revolution of North America, having
been re-printed in Philadelphia and other parts of the continent, and
as the distance at which the Abbé is placed from the American
theatre of war and politics, has occasioned him to mistake several
facts, or misconceive the causes or principles by which they were
produced, the following tract, therefore, is published with a view to
rectify them, and prevent even accidental errors from intermixing
with history, under the sanction of time and silence.

The editor of the London edition has entitled it, 'The Revolution of
America, by the ABBÉ RAYNAL,' and the American printers have
followed the example. But I have understood, and I believe my
information just, that the piece, which is more properly reflections
on the Revolution, was unfairly purloined from the printer whom
the Abbé employed, or from the manuscript copy, and is only part
of a larger work then in the press, or preparing for it. The person
who procured it, appears to have been an Englishman, and though,
in an advertisement prefixed to the London edition, he has endeavoured to gloss over the embezzlement with professions of patriotism, and to soften it with high encomiums on the author, yet the
action in any view in which it can be placed, is illiberal and un-
pardonable.

In the course of his travels (says he), the translator happily succeeded in obtaining a copy of this exquisite little piece which has not made its appearance from any press. He publishes a French edition, in favour of those who feel its eloquent reasoning more forcibly in its native language, at the same time with the following translation of it: in which he has been desirous, perhaps in vain, that all the warmth, the grace, the strength, the dignity of the original, should not be lost. And he flatters himself, that the indulgence of the illustrious historian will not be wanting to a man, who, of his own motion, has taken the liberty to give this composition to the public, only from a strong persuasion, that its momentous argument will be useful in a critical conjuncture, to that country which he loves with an ardour that can be exceeded only by the nobler flame, which burns in the bosom of the philanthropic author, for the freedom and happiness of all the countries upon earth.

This plausibility of setting off a dishonourable action, may pass for patriotism and sound principles with those who do not enter into its demerits, and whose interest is not injured nor their happiness affected thereby. But it is more than probable, notwithstanding the declarations it contains, that the copy was obtained for the sake of profiting by the sale of a new and popular work, and that the professions are but a garb to the fraud.

It may with propriety be marked, that in all countries where literature is protected, and it never can flourish where it is not, the works of an author are his legal property; and to treat letters in any other light than this, is to banish them from the country, or strangle them in the birth.

The embezzlement from the Abbé Raynal, was, it is true, committed by one country upon another, and therefore shows no defect in the laws of either. But it is nevertheless a breach of civil manners and literary justice: neither can it be any apology, that because the countries are at war, literature shall be entitled to depradation.[1]

But the forestalling the Abbé's publication by London editions,

1 The state of literature in America must one day become a subject of legislative consideration. Hitherto it has been a disinterested volunteer in the service of the Revolution, and no man thought of profits: but when peace shall give time and opportunity for study, the country will deprive itself of the honour and service of letters and the improvement of science, unless sufficient laws are made to prevent depredations on literary property. It is well worth remarking, that Russia, who but a few years ago was scarcely known in Europe, owes a large share of her present greatness to the close attention she has paid, and the wise encouragement she has given, to every branch of science and learning: and we have almost the same instance in France, in the reign of Louis XIV. – Paine.

both in French and English, and thereby not only defrauding him and throwing an expensive publication on his hands by anticipating the sale, are only the smaller injuries which such conduct may occasion. A man's opinions, whether written or in thought, are his own, until he pleases to publish them himself; and it is adding cruelty to injustice, to make him the author of what future reflection, or better information, might occasion him to suppress or amend. There are declarations and sentiments in the Abbé's piece, which, for my own part, I did not expect to find, and such as himself, on a revisal, might have seen occasion to change; but the anticipated piracy effectually prevented his having the opportunity, and precipitated him into difficulties, which, had it not been for such ungenerous fraud, might not have happened.

This mode of making an author appear before his time, will appear still more ungenerous, when we consider how very few men there are in any country, who can at once, and without the aid of reflection and revisal, combine warm passions with a cool temper, and the full expansion of the imagination with the natural and necessary gravity of judgement, so as to be rightly balanced within themselves, and to make a reader feel, fancy, and understand justly at the same time. To call three powers of the mind into action at once, in a manner that neither shall interrupt, and that each shall aid and invigorate the other, is a talent very rarely possessed.

It often happens that the weight of an argument is lost by the wit of setting it off; or the judgement disordered by an intemperate irritation of the passions: yet a certain degree of animation must be felt by the writer, and raised in the reader, in order to interest the attention; and a sufficient scope given to the imagination, to enable it to create in the mind a sight of the persons, characters and circumstances of the subject: for without these, the judgement will feel little or no excitement to office, and its determinations will be cold, sluggish, and imperfect.

But if either or both of the two former are raised too high, or heated too much, the judgement will be jostled from its seat, and the whole matter, however important in itself, will diminish into a pantomime of the mind, in which we create images that promote no other purpose than amusement.

The Abbé's writings bear evident marks of that extension and rapidness of thinking and quickness of sensation, which of all others require revisal, and the more particularly so, when applied to the living characters of nations or individuals in a state of war. The least misinformation or misconception leads to some wrong conclusion, and an error believed, becomes the progenitor of others. And, as the Abbé has suffered such inconveniences in France, by mistaking certain circumstances of the war, and the characters of the parties therein, it becomes some apology for him that those errors were precipitated into the world by the avarice of an ungenerous enemy.

To an author of such distinguished reputation as the Abbé Raynal, it might very well become me to apologize for the present undertaking; but, as *to be right* is the first wish of philosophy, and the first principle of history, he will, I presume, accept from me a declaration of my motives, which are those of doing justice, in preference to any complimental apology I might otherwise make. The Abbé, in the course of his work, has, in some instances, extolled without a reason, and wounded without a cause. He has given fame where it was not deserved, and withheld it where it was justly due; and appears to be so frequently in and out of temper with his subjects and parties, that few or none of them are decisively and uniformly marked.

It is yet too soon to write the history of the Revolution, and whoever attempts it precipitately, will unavoidably mistake characters and circumstances, and involve himself in error and difficulty. Things, like men, are seldom understood rightly at first sight. But the Abbé is wrong even in the foundation of his work; that is, he has misconceived and mis-stated the causes which produced the rupture between England and her then colonies, and which led on, step by step, unstudied and uncontrived on the part of America, to a revolution, which has engaged the attention, and affected the interest of Europe.

To prove this, I shall bring forward a passage, which, though placed towards the latter part of the Abbé's work, is more intimately connected with the beginning; and in which, speaking of the original cause of the dispute, he declares himself in the following manner:

None (says he), of those energetic causes, which have produced so many revolutions upon the globe, existed in North America. Neither religion nor laws had there been outraged. The blood of martyrs or patriots had not there streamed from scaffolds. Morals had not there been insulted. Manners, customs, habits, no object dear to nations, had there been the sport of ridicule. Arbitrary power had not there torn any inhabitants from the arms of his family and friends, to drag him to a dreary dungeon. Public order had not been there inverted. The principles of administration had not been changed there; and the maxims of government had there always remained the same. The whole question was reduced to the knowing whether the mother country had, or had not, a right to lay, directly or indirectly, a slight tax upon the colonies.

On this extraordinary passage, it may not be improper, in general terms, to remark, that none can feel like those who suffer; and that for a man to be a competent judge of the provocatives, or as the Abbé styles them, the energetic causes of the Revolution, he must have resided at the time in America.

The Abbé, in saying that the several particulars he has enumerated, did not exist in America, and neglecting to point out the particular period, in which he means they did not exist, reduces thereby his declaration to a nullity, by taking away all meaning from the passage.

They did not exist in 1763, and they all existed before 1776; consequently as there was a time when they did *not*, and another, when they *did* exist, the *time when* constitutes the essence of the fact, and not to give it is to withhold the only evidence which proves the declaration right or wrong, and on which it must stand or fall. But the declaration as it now appears, unaccompanied by time, has an effect in holding out to the world, that there was no real cause for the Revolution, because it denies the existence of all those causes, which are supposed to be justifiable, and which the Abbé styles energetic.

I confess myself exceedingly at a loss to find out the time to which the Abbé alludes; because, in another part of the work, in speaking of the Stamp Act, which was passed in 1764, he styles it 'an *usurpation* of the Americans' *most precious and sacred rights*'. Consequently he here admits the most energetic of all causes, that is, *an usurpation of their most precious and sacred rights*, to have existed in America twelve years before the Declaration of Independence, and ten years before the breaking out of hostilities. The time, therefore, in which the paragraph is true, must be antecedent to the Stamp Act, but as at that time there was no revolution, nor any idea of one, it consequently applies without a meaning; and as it cannot, on the Abbé's own principle, be applied to any time *after* the Stamp Act, it is therefore a wandering, solitary paragraph, connected with nothing and at variance with everything.

The Stamp Act, it is true, was repealed in two years after it was passed, but it was immediately followed by one of infinitely more mischievous magnitude; I mean the Declaratory Act, which asserted the right, as it was styled, of the British Parliament, *'to bind America in all cases whatsoever'*.

If then the Stamp Act was an usurpation of the Americans' most precious and sacred rights, the Declaratory Act left them no rights at all; and contained the full grown seeds of the most despotic government ever exercised in the world. It placed America not only in the lowest, but in the basest state of vassalage; because it demanded an unconditional submission in everything, or as the act expressed it, *in all cases whatsoever*: and what renders this act the more offensive, is, that it appears to have been passed as an act of mercy; truly then may it be said, that *the tender mercies of the wicked are cruel*.

All the original charters from the Crown of England, under the faith of which the adventurers from the Old World settled in the New, were by this act displaced from their foundations; because, contrary to the nature of them, which was that of a compact, they were now made subject to repeal or alteration at the mere will of one party only. The whole condition of America was thus put into the hands of the Parliament or Ministry, without leaving to her the least right in any case whatsoever.

There is no despotism to which this iniquitous law did not extend; and though it might have been convenient in the execution of it, to have consulted manners and habits, the principle of the act made all tyranny legal. It stopped nowhere. It went to everything. It took in with it the whole life of a man, or if I may so express it, an eternity of circumstances. It is the nature of law to require obedience, but this demanded servitude; and the condition of an American, under the operation of it, was not that of a subject but a vassal. Tyranny has often been established *without* law and sometimes *against* it, but the history of mankind does not produce another instance, in which it has been established *by* law. It is an audacious outrage upon civil government, and cannot be too much exposed, in order to be sufficiently detested.

Neither could it be said after this, that the legislature of that country any longer made laws for this, but that it gave out commands; for wherein differed an act of Parliament constructed on this principle, and operating in this manner, over an unrepresented people, from the orders of a military establishment?

The Parliament of England, with respect to America, was not septennial but *perpetual*. It appeared to the latter a body always in being. Its election or expiration were to her the same as if its members succeeded by inheritance, or went out by death, or lived for ever, or were appointed to it as a matter of office. Therefore, for the people of England to have any just conception of the mind of America, respecting this extraordinary act, they must suppose all election and expiration in that country to cease for ever, and the present Parliament, its heirs, etc., to be perpetual; in this case, I ask, what would the most clamorous of them think, were an act to be passed, declaring the right of *such a Parliament* to bind *them* in all cases whatsoever? For this word *whatsoever* would go as effectually to their *Magna Charta, Bill of Rights, trial by juries, etc.,* as it went to the charters and forms of government in America.

I am persuaded, that the gentleman to whom I address these remarks, will not, after the passing of this act, say, 'that the *principles* of administration had not been *changed* in America, and that the maxims of government had been there *always the same*'. For here is, in principle, a total overthrow of the whole; and not a subversion only, but an annihilation of the foundation of liberty and absolute domination established in its stead.

The Abbé likewise states the case exceedingly wrong and injuriously, when he says, that '*the whole* question was reduced to the knowing whether the mother country had, or had not, a right to lay, directly or indirectly, a *slight* tax upon the colonies'. This was *not the whole* of the question; neither was the *quantity* of the tax the object either to the Ministry or to the Americans. It was the principle, of which the tax made but a part, and the quantity still less, that formed the ground on which America resisted.

The tax on tea, which is the tax here alluded to, was neither more nor less than an experiment to establish the practice of a declaratory law upon; modelled into the more fashionable phrase *of the universal supremacy of Parliament*. For until this time the declaratory law had lain dormant, and the framers of it had contented themselves with barely declaring an opinion.

Therefore the *whole* question with America, in the opening of the dispute, was, shall we be bound in all cases whatsoever by the British Parliament, or shall we not? For submission to the tea or tax act implied an acknowledgement of the Declaratory Act, or, in other words, of the universal supremacy of Parliament, which as they never intended to do, it was necessary they should oppose it, in its first stage of execution.

It is probable the Abbé had been led into this mistake by perusing detached pieces in some of the American newspapers; for, in a case where all were interested, everyone had a right to give his opinion; and there were many, who, with the best intentions, did not choose the best, nor indeed the true ground, to defend their cause upon. They felt themselves right by a general impulse, without being able to separate, analyse, and arrange the parts.

I am somewhat unwilling to examine too minutely into the whole of this extraordinary passage of the Abbé, lest I should appear to treat it with severity; otherwise I could show that not a single declaration is justly founded: for instance, the reviving an obsolete act of the reign of Henry VIII and fitting it to the Americans, by authority of which they were to be seized and brought from America to England, and there imprisoned and tried for any supposed offences, was, in the worst sense of the words, *to tear them, by the arbitrary power of Parliament, from the arms of their families and friends, and drag them not only to dreary but distant dungeons.* Yet this act was contrived some years before the breaking out of hostilities. And again, though the blood of martyrs and patriots had not streamed on the scaffolds, it streamed in the streets, in the massacre of the inhabitants of Boston, by the British soldiery in the year 1770.

Had the Abbé said that the causes which produced the Revolution in America were originally *different* from those which produced revolutions in other parts of the globe, he had been right. Here the value and quality of liberty, the nature of government, and the dignity of man, were known and understood, and the attachment of the Americans to these principles produced the Revolution, as a natural and almost unavoidable consequence. They had no particular family to set up or pull down. Nothing of personality was incorporated with their cause. They started even-handed with each other, and went no faster into the several stages of it, than they were driven by the unrelenting and imperious conduct of Britain. Nay, in the last act, the Declaration of Independence, they had nearly been too late; for had it not been declared at the exact time it was, I see no period in their affair since, in which it could have been declared with the same effect, and probably not at all.

But the object being formed before the reverse of fortunes took place, that is, before the operations of the gloomy campaign of 1776, their honour, their interest, their everything, called loudly on them to maintain it; and that glow of thought and energy of heart, which even a distant prospect of independence inspires, gave confidence to their hopes, and resolution to their conduct, which a state of dependence could never have reached. They looked forward to happier days and scenes of rest, and qualified the hardships of the campaign by contemplating the establishment of their new-born system.

If, on the other hand, we take a review of what part Britain has acted, we shall find everything which ought to make a nation blush – the most vulgar abuse, accompanied by that species of haughtiness which distinguishes the hero of a mob from the character of a gentleman. It was equally as much from her manners as from her injustice that she lost the colonies. By the latter she provoked their principles, by the former she wore out their temper; and it ought to be held out as an example to the world, to show how necessary it is to conduct the business of government with civility. In short, other revolutions may have originated in caprice, or generated in ambition; but here, the most unoffending humility was tortured into rage, and the infancy of existence made to weep.

A union so extensive, continued and determined, suffering with patience and never in despair, could not have been produced by common causes. It must be something capable of reaching the whole soul of man and arming it with perpetual energy. It is in vain to look for precedents among the revolutions of former ages, to find out, by comparison, the causes of this.

The spring, the progress, the object, the consequences, nay, the men, their habits of thinking, and all the circumstances of the country, are different. Those of other nations are, in general, little more than the history of their quarrels. They are marked by no important character in the annals of events; mixed in the mass of general matters, they occupy but a common page; and while the chief of the successful partisans stepped into power, the plundered multitude sat down and sorrowed. Few, very few of them are accompanied with reformation, either in government or manners; many of them with the most consummate profligacy. Triumph on the one side and misery on the other were the only events. Pains, punishments, torture, and death were made the business of mankind, until compassion, the fairest associate of the heart, was driven from its place, and the eye, accustomed to continual cruelty, could behold it without offence.

But as the principles of the present Revolution differed from those which preceded it, so likewise did the conduct of America both in government and war. Neither the foul finger of disgrace nor the bloody hand of vengeance has hitherto put a blot upon her fame. Her victories have received lustre from a greatness of lenity; and her laws have been permitted to slumber, where they might justly be awakened to punish. War, so much the trade of the world, has here been only the business of necessity; and when the necessity shall cease, her very enemies must confess, that as she drew the sword in her just defence, she used it without cruelty, and sheathed it without revenge.

As it is not my design to extend these remarks to a history, I shall now take my leave of this passage of the Abbé, with an observation, which, until something unfolds itself to convince me otherwise, I cannot avoid believing to be true; – which is, that it was the fixed determination of the British Cabinet to quarrel with America at all events.

They (the members who composed the Cabinet) had no doubt of success, if they could once bring it to the issue of a battle, and they expected from a conquest, what they could neither propose with decency, nor hope for by negotiation. The charters and constitutions of the colonies were become to them matters of offence, and their rapid progress in property and population were disgustingly beheld as the growing and natural means of independence. They saw no way to retain them long but by reducing them in time. A conquest would at once have made them both lords and landlords; and put them in the possession both of the revenue and the rental. The whole trouble of government would have ceased in a victory, and a final end put to remonstrance and debate.

The experience of the Stamp Act had taught them how to quarrel with the advantages of cover and convenience, and they had nothing to do but to renew the scene, and put contention into motion. They hoped for a rebellion, and they made one. They expected a declaration of independence, and they were not disappointed. But after this, they looked for victory, and they obtained a defeat.

If this be taken as the generating cause of the contest, then is every part of the conduct of the British Ministry consistent from the commencement of the dispute, until the signing the Treaty of Paris, after which, conquest becoming doubtful, they retreated to negotiation, and were again defeated.

Though the Abbé possesses and displays great powers of genius, and is a master of style and language, he seems not to pay equal attention to the office of an historian. His facts are coldly and carelessly stated. They neither inform the reader nor interest him. Many of them are erroneous, and most of them are defective and obscure. It is undoubtedly both an ornament and a useful addition to history, to accompany it with maxims and reflections. They afford likewise an agreeable change to the style, and a more diversified manner of expression; but it is absolutely necessary that the root from whence they spring, or the foundation on which they are raised, should be well attended to, which in this work is not. The Abbé hastens through his narrations as if he was glad to get from them, that he may enter the more copious field of eloquence and imagination. . . .

Though I am not surprised to see the Abbé mistaken in matters of history, acted at such a distance from his sphere of immediate observation, yet I am more than surprised to find him wrong (or at least what appears so to me) in the well enlightened field of philosophical reflection. Here the materials are his own; created by himself, and the error, therefore, is an act of the mind.

Hitherto my remarks have been confined to circumstance; the order in which they arose, and the events they produced. In these, my information being better than the Abbé's, my task was easy. How I may succeed in controverting matters of sentiment and opinion, with one whom years, experience, and long established reputation have placed in a superior line, I am less confident in; but as they fall within the scope of my observations it would be improper to pass them over.

From this part of the Abbe's work to the latter end, I find several expressions, which appear to me to start, with cynical complexion, from the path of liberal thinking, or at least they are so involved as to lose many of the beauties which distinguish other parts of the performance.

The Abbé having brought his work to the period when the Treaty of Alliance between France and the United States commenced, proceeds to make some remarks thereon.

In short (says he), philosophy, whose first sentiment is the desire to see all governments just and all people happy, in casting her eyes upon this alliance of a monarchy, with a people who are defending their liberty, *is curious to know its motive. She sees at once too clearly, that the happiness of mankind has no part in it.*

Whatever train of thinking or of temper the Abbé might be in, when he penned this expression, matters not. They will neither qualify the sentiment, nor add to its defect. If right, it needs no apology; if wrong, it merits no excuse. It is sent into the world as an opinion of philosophy, and may be examined without regard to the author.

It seems to be a defect, connected with ingenuity, that it often employs itself more in matters of curiosity, than usefulness. Man must be the privy councillor of fate, or something is not right. He must know the springs, the whys and wherefores of everything, or he sits down unsatisfied. Whether this be a crime, or only a caprice of humanity, I am not inquiring into. I shall take the passage as I find it, and place my objections against it.

It is not so properly the *motives* which produced the alliance, as the *consequences* which are to be *produced from it*, that mark out the field of philosophical reflection. In the one we only penetrate into the barren cave of secrecy, where little can be known, and everything may be misconceived; in the other, the mind is presented with a wide extended prospect of vegetative good, and sees a thousand blessings budding into existence.

But the expression, even within the compass of the Abbé's meaning, sets out with an error, because it is made to declare that which no man has authority to declare. Who can say that the happiness of mankind made *no part of the motives* which produced the alliance? To be able to declare this, a man must be possessed of the mind of all the parties concerned, and know that their motives were something else.

In proportion as the independence of America became contemplated and understood, the local advantages of it to the immediate actors, and the numerous benefits it promised mankind, appeared to be every day increasing; and we saw not a temporary good for the present race only, but a continued good to all posterity; these motives, therefore, added to those which preceded them, became the motives on the part of America, which led her to propose and agree to the Treaty of Alliance, as the best effectual method of extending and securing happiness; and therefore, with respect to us, the Abbé is wrong.

France, on the other hand, was situated very differently. She was not acted upon by necessity to seek a friend, and therefore her motive in becoming one, has the strongest evidence of being good, and that which is so, must have some happiness for its object. With regard to herself, she saw a train of conveniences worthy her attention. By lessening the power of an enemy, whom at the same time she sought neither to destroy nor distress, she gained an advantage without doing an evil, and created to herself a new friend by associating with a country in misfortune.

The springs of thought that lead to actions of this kind, however political they may be, are nevertheless naturally beneficent; for in all causes, good or bad, it is necessary there should be a fitness in the mind, to enable it to act in character with the object: therefore, as a bad cause cannot be prosecuted with a good motive, so neither can a good cause be long supported by a bad one: and as no man acts without a motive, therefore in the present instance, as they cannot be bad, they must be admitted to be good. But the Abbé sets out upon such an extended scale, that he overlooks the degrees by which it is measured, and rejects the beginning of good, because the end comes not out at once.

It is true that bad motives may in some degree be brought to support a good cause or prosecute a good object; but it never continues long, which is not the case with France; for either the object will reform the mind, or the mind corrupt the object, or else not being able, either way, to get into unison, they will separate in disgust: and this natural, though unperceived progress of association or contention between the mind and the object, is the secret cause of fidelity or defection. Every object a man pursues, is, for the time, a kind of mistress to his mind: if both are good or bad, the union is natural; but if they are in reverse, and neither can seduce nor yet reform the other, the opposition grows into dislike, and a separation follows.

When the cause of America first made its appearance on the stage of the universe, there were many, who, in the style of adventurers and fortune-hunters, were dangling in its train, and making their court to it with every profession of honour and attachment. They were loud in its praise and ostentatious in its service. Every place echoed with their ardour or their anger, and they seemed like men in love. But, alas! they were fortune-hunters. Their expectations were excited, but their minds were unimpressed; and finding it not to their purpose, not themselves reformed by its influence, they ceased their suit, and in some instances deserted and betrayed it.

There were others, who at first beheld America with indifference, and unacquainted with her character were cautious of her company. They treated her as one who, under the fair name of liberty, might conceal the hideous figure of anarchy, or the gloomy monster of tyranny. They knew not what she was. If fair, she was fair indeed. But still she was suspected and though born among us appeared to be a stranger.

Accident with some, and curiosity with others, brought on a distant acquaintance. They ventured to look at her. They felt an inclination to speak to her. One intimacy led to another, till the suspicion wore away, and a change of sentiment gradually stole upon the mind; and having no self-interest to serve, no passion of dishonour to gratify, they became enamoured of her innocence, and, unaltered by misfortune or uninfluenced by success, shared with fidelity in the varieties of her fate.

This declaration of the Abbé's respective motives, has led me unintentionally into a train of metaphysical reasoning; but there was no other avenue by which it could properly be approached. To place presumption against presumption, assertion against assertion, is a mode of opposition that has no effect; and therefore the more eligible method was to show that the declaration does not correspond with the natural progress of the mind, and the influence it has upon our conduct. I shall now quit this part and proceed to what I have before stated, namely, that it is not so properly the motives which produced the alliance, as the consequences to be procured from it, that mark out the field of philosophical reflection.

It is an observation I have already made in some former publications, that the circle of civilization is yet incomplete. Mutual wants have formed the individuals of each country into a kind of national society, and here the progress of civilization has stopped. For it is easy to see, that nations with regard to each other (notwithstanding the ideal civil law, which every one explains as it suits him) are like individuals in a state of nature. They are regulated by no fixed principle, governed by no compulsive law, and each does independently what it pleases or what it can.

Were it possible we could have known the world when in a state of barbarism, we might have concluded that it never could be brought into the order we now see it. The untamed was then as hard, if not harder, to work upon in its individual state, than the national mind is in its present one. Yet we have seen the accomplishment of one, why then should we doubt that of the other?

There is a greater fitness in mankind to extend and complete the civilization of nations with each other at this day, than there was to begin it with the unconnected individuals at first; in the same manner that it is somewhat easier to put together the materials of a machine after they are formed, than it was to form them from original matter. The present condition of the world, differing so exceedingly from what it formerly was, has given a new cast to the mind of man, more than what he appears to be sensible of. The wants of the individual, which first produced the idea of society, are now augmented into the wants of the nation, and he is obliged to seek from another country what before he sought from the next person.

Letters, the tongue of the world, have in some measure brought all mankind acquainted, and by an extension of their uses are every day promoting some new friendship. Through them distant nations became capable of conversation, and losing by degrees the awkwardness of strangers, and the moroseness of suspicion, they learn to know and understand each other. Science, the partisan of no country, but the beneficent patroness of all, has liberally opened a temple where all may meet. Her influence on the mind, like the sun on the chilled earth, has long been preparing it for higher cultivation and further improvement. The philosopher of one country sees not an enemy in the philosopher of another: he takes his seat in the temple of science, and asks not who sits beside him.

This was not the condition of the barbarian world. Then the wants of men were few and the objects within his reach. While he could acquire these, he lived in a state of individual independence; the consequence of which was, there were as many nations as persons, each contending with the other, to secure something which he had, or to obtain something which he had not. The world had then no business to follow, no studies to exercise the mind. Their time was divided between sloth and fatigue. Hunting and war were their chief occupations; sleep and food their principal enjoyments.

Now it is otherwise. A change in the mode of life has made it necessary to be busy; and man finds a thousand things to do now which before he did not. Instead of placing his ideas of greatness in the rude achievements of the savage, he studies arts, sciences, agriculture and commerce, the refinements of the gentleman, the principles of society, and the knowledge of the philosopher.

There are many things which in themselves are neither morally good nor bad, but they are productive of consequences, which are strongly marked with one or other of these characters. Thus commerce, though in itself a moral nullity, has had a considerable influence in tempering the human mind. It was the want of objects in the ancient world, which occasioned in them such a rude and perpetual turn for war. Their time hung on their hands without the means of employment. The indolence they lived in afforded leisure for mischief, and being all idle at once, and equal in their circumstances, they were easily provoked or induced to action.

But the introduction of commerce furnished the world with objects, which, in their extent, reach every man, and give him something to think about and something to do; by these his attention is mechanically drawn from the pursuits which a state of indolence and an unemployed mind occasioned, and he trades with the same countries, which in former ages, tempted by their productions, and too indolent to purchase them, he would have gone to war with.

Thus, as I have already observed, the condition of the world being materially changed by the influence of science and commerce, it is put into a fitness not only to admit of, but to desire, an extension of civilization. The principal and almost only remaining enemy, it now has to encounter, is *prejudice*; for it is evidently the interest of mankind to agree and make the best of life. The world has undergone its divisions of empire, the several boundaries of which are known and settled. The idea of conquering countries, like the Greeks and Romans, does not now exist; and experience has exploded the notion of going to war for the sake of profit. In short, the objects for war are exceedingly diminished, and there is now left scarcely anything to quarrel about, but what arises from that demon of society, prejudice, and the consequent sullenness and untractableness of the temper.

There is something exceedingly curious in the constitution and operation of prejudice. It has the singular ability of accommodating itself to all the possible varieties of the human mind. Some passions and vices are but thinly scattered among mankind, and find only here and there a fitness of reception. But prejudice, like the spider, makes every place its home. It has neither taste nor choice of situation, and all that it requires is room. Everywhere, except in fire or water, a spider will live.

So, let the mind be as naked as the walls of an empty and forsaken tenement, gloomy as a dungeon, or ornamented with the richest abilities of thinking, let it be hot, cold, dark or light, lonely or inhabited, still prejudice, if undisturbed, will fill it with cobwebs, and live, like the spider, where there seems nothing to live on. If the one prepares her food by poisoning it to her palate and her use, the other does the same; and as several of our passions are strongly characterized by the animal world, prejudice may be denominated the spider of the mind.

Perhaps no two events ever united so intimately and forcibly to combat and expel prejudice, as the Revolution of America and the alliance with France. Their effects are felt, and their influence already extends as well to the Old World as the New. Our style and manner of thinking have undergone a revolution more extraordinary than the political revolution of the country. We see with other eyes; we hear with other ears; and think with other thoughts, than those we formerly used. We can look back on our own prejudices, as if they had been the prejudices of other people.

We now see and know they were prejudices and nothing else; and, relieved from their shackles, enjoy a freedom of mind, we felt not before. It was not all the argument, however powerful, nor the reasoning, however eloquent, that could have produced this change, so necessary to the extension of the mind, and the cordiality of the world, without the two circumstances of the Revolution and the alliance.

Had America dropped quietly from Britain, no material change in sentiment had taken place. The same notions, prejudices, and conceits would have governed in both countries, as governed them before, and, still the slaves of error and education, they would have travelled on in the beaten track of vulgar and habitual thinking. But brought about by the means it has been, both with regard to ourselves, to France and England, every corner of the mind is swept of its cobwebs, poison and dust, and made fit for the reception of generous happiness.

Perhaps there never was an alliance on a broader basis, than that between America and France, and the progress of it is worth attending to. The countries had been enemies, not properly of themselves, but through the medium of England. They originally had no quarrel with each other, nor any cause for one, but what arose from the interest of England, and her arming America against France. At the same time, the Americans at a distance from, and unacquainted with, the world, and tutored in all the prejudices which governed those who governed them, conceived it their duty to act as they were taught. In doing this, they expended their substance to make conquests, not for themselves, but for their masters, who in return treated them as slaves.

A long succession of insolent severity, and the separation finally occasioned by the commencement of hostilities at Lexington, on the nineteenth of April, 1775, naturally produced a new disposition of thinking. As the mind closed itself towards England, it opened itself towards the world, and our prejudices like our oppressions, underwent, though less observed, a mental examination; until we found the former as inconsistent with reason and benevolence, as the latter were repugnant to our civil and political rights.

While we were thus advancing by degrees into the wide field of extended humanity, the alliance with France was concluded. An alliance not formed for the mere purpose of a day, but on just and generous grounds, and with equal and mutual advantages; and the easy, affectionate manner in which the parties have since communicated has made it an alliance not of courts only, but of countries. There is now an union of mind as well as of interest; and our hearts as well as our prosperity call on us to support it.

The people of England not having experienced this change, had likewise no ideas of it. They were hugging to their bosoms the same prejudices we were trampling beneath our feet; and they expected to keep a hold upon America, by that narrowness of thinking which America disdained. What they were proud of, we despised; and this is principal cause why all their negotiations, constructed on this ground, have failed. We are now really another people, and cannot again go back to ignorance and prejudice. The mind once enlightened cannot again become dark. There is no possibility, neither is there any term to express the supposition by, of the mind *un*knowing anything it already knows; and therefore all attempts on the part of England, fitted to the former habit of America, and on the expectation of their applying now, will be like persuading a seeing man to become blind, and a sensible one to turn an idiot. The first of which is unnatural and the other impossible. . . .

A total reformation is wanted in England. She wants an expanded mind — a heart which embraces the universe. Instead of shutting herself up in an island, and quarrelling with the world, she would derive more lasting happiness, and acquire more real riches, by generously mixing with it, and bravely saying, I am the enemy of none. It is not now a time for little contrivances or artful politics. The European world is too experienced to be imposed upon, and America too wise to be duped. It must be something new and masterly that can succeed. The idea of seducing America from her independence, or corrupting her from her alliance, is a thought too little for a great mind, and impossible for any honest one, to attempt. Whenever politics are applied to debauch mankind from their integrity, and dissolve the virtue of human nature, they become detestable; and to be a statesman on this plan, is to be a commissioned villain. He who aims at it, leaves a vacancy in his character, which may be filled up with the worst of epithets.

If the disposition of England should be such, as not to agree to a general and honourable peace, and the war must, at all events, continue longer, I cannot help wishing that the alliances which America has or may enter into, may become the only objects of the war. She wants an opportunity of showing to the world that she holds her honour as dear and sacred as her independence, and that she will in no situation forsake those whom no negotiations could induce to forsake her. Peace, to every reflecting mind, is a desirable object; but *that peace* which is accompanied with a ruined character, becomes a crime to the seducer, and a curse upon the seduced.

But where is the impossibility or even the great difficulty of England's forming a friendship with France and Spain, and making it a national virtue to renounce for ever those prejudiced inveteracies it has been her custom to cherish; and which, while they serve to sink her with an increasing enormity of debt, by involving her in fruitless wars, become likewise the bane of her repose, and the destruction of her manners? We had once the fetters that she has now, but experience has shown us the mistake, and thinking justly, has set us right.

The true idea of a great nation, is that which extends and promotes the principles of universal society; whose mind rises above the atmosphere of local thoughts, and considers mankind, of whatever nation or profession they may be, as the work of one Creator. The rage for conquest has had its fashion, and its day. Why may not the amiable virtues have the same? The Alexander and Caesars of antiquity have left behind them their monuments of destruction, and are remembered with hatred; while those more exalted characters, who first taught society and science, are blessed with the gratitude of every age and country. Of more use was *one* philosopher, though a heathen, to the world, than all the heathen conquerors that ever existed.

Should the present Revolution be distinguished by opening a new system of extended civilization, it will receive from heaven the highest evidence of approbation; and as this is a subject to which the Abbé's powers are so eminently suited, I recommend it to his attention with the affection of a friend, and the ardour of a universal citizen.

[10] DISSERTATIONS ON GOVERNMENT, THE AFFAIRS OF THE BANK, AND PAPER MONEY

(1786)

In 1786 a bitter controversy developed in Philadelphia over the Bank of North America, formerly the Bank of Pennsylvania. Farmers, deeply in debt, sought to increase the circulation of paper money. Fearful that the Bank of North America would not accept paper money, the farmers of Pennsylvania also demanded the repeal of the bank's charter. The wealthy merchants as well as the artisans of Philadelphia, on the other hand, were concerned about inflation and resisted both the agitation for paper money and the repeal of the bank's charter. Paine entered the dispute in February 1786 with this pamphlet endorsing the view of the merchants and artisans. Many farmers accused Paine of selling out to — indeed, of being bribed by — bank officials. Paine had been a friend of the bank since 1780, when he had played a role in its creation to help fund the war effort. The edited text included here indicates Paine's concern with the sanctity of contract as well as his optimistic assumptions about the benevolent effects of 'extending and facilitating' commerce.

I here present the public with a new performance. Some parts of it are more particularly adapted to the State of Pennsylvania, on the present state of its affairs; but there are others which are on a larger scale. The time bestowed on this work has not been long, the whole of it being written and printed during the short recess of the Assembly.

As to parties, merely considered as such, I am attached to no particular one. There are such things as right and wrong in the world, and so far as these are parties against each other, the signature of COMMON SENSE is properly employed. . . .

Every government, let its form be what it may, contains within itself a principle common to all, which is that of a sovereign power, or a power over which there is no control, and which controls all others; and as it is impossible to construct a form of government in which this power does not exist, so there must of necessity be a place, if it may be so called, for it to exist in.

In despotic monarchies this power is lodged in a single person, or sovereign. His will is law; which he declares, alters or revokes as he pleases, without being accountable to any power for so doing. Therefore, the only modes of redress, in countries so governed, are by petition or insurrection. And this is the reason we so frequently hear of insurrections in despotic governments; for as there are but two modes of redress, this is one of them.

Perhaps it may be said that as the united resistance of the people is able, by force to control the will of the sovereign, that therefore the controlling power lodges in them; but it must be understood that I am speaking of such powers only as are constituent parts of the government, not of those powers which are externally applied to resist and overturn it.

In republics, such as those established in America, the sovereign power, or the power over which there is no control, and which controls all others, remains where nature placed it – in the people; for the people in America are the fountain of power. It remains there as a matter of right, recognized in the constitutions of the country, and the exercise of it is constitutional and legal. This sovereignty is exercised in electing and deputing a certain number of persons to represent and act for the whole, and who, if they do not act right, may be displaced by the same power that placed them there, and others elected and deputed in their stead, and the wrong measures of former representatives corrected and brought right by this means. Therefore, the republican form and principle leaves no room for insurrection, because it provides and establishes a rightful means in its stead. . . .

Having already stated that the power of the representatives can never exceed the power of the people whom they represent, I now proceed to examine more particularly, what the power of the representatives is.

It is, in the first place, the power of acting as legislators in making laws – and in the second place, the power of acting in certain cases, as agents or negotiators for the commonwealth, for such purposes as the circumstances of the commonwealth require.

A very strange confusion of ideas, dangerous to the credit, stability, and the good and honour of the commonwealth, has arisen, by confounding those two distinct powers and things together and blending every act of the assembly, of whatever kind it may be, under one general name, of *Laws of the Commonwealth*, and thereby creating an opinion (which is truly of the despotic kind) that every succeeding assembly has an equal power over every transaction, as well as law, done by a former assembly.

All laws are acts, but all acts are not laws. Many of the acts of the assembly are acts of agency or negotiation, that is, they are acts of contract and agreement, on the part of the state, with certain persons therein mentioned, and for certain purposes therein recited. An act of this kind, after it has passed the house, is of the nature of a deed or contract, signed, sealed and delivered; and subject to the same general laws and principles of justice as all other deeds and contracts are: for in a transaction of this kind, the state stands as an individual, and can be known in no other character in a court of justice.

By '*laws*', as distinct from the agency transactions, or matters of negotiation, are to be comprehended all those public acts of the assembly or commonwealth, which have a universal operation, or apply themselves to every individual of the commonwealth. Of this kind are the laws for the distribution and administration of justice, for the preservation of the peace, for the security of property, for raising the necessary revenue by just proportions, etc.

Acts of this kind are properly *laws*, and they may be altered, amended and repealed, or others substituted in their places, as experience shall direct, for the better effecting the purpose for which they were intended: and the right and power of the assembly to do this is derived from the right and power which the people, were they all assembled together, instead of being represented, would have to do the same thing: because, in acts or laws of this kind, there is no other party than the public.

The law, or the alteration, or the repeal, is for themselves; – and whatever the effects may be, it falls on themselves; – if for the better, they have the benefit of it – if for the worse, they suffer the inconvenience. No violence to anyone is here offered – no breach of faith is here committed. It is therefore one of those rights and powers which is within the sense, meaning and limits of the original compact of justice which they formed with each other as the foundation-principle of the republic, and being one of those rights and powers, it devolves on their representatives by delegation.

As it is not my intention (neither is it within the limits assigned to this work) to define every species of what may be called *laws* (but rather to distinguish that part in which the representatives act as agents or negotiators for the state from the legislative part) I shall pass on to distinguish and describe those acts of the assembly which are acts of agency or negotiation, and to show that as they are different in their nature, construction and operation, from legislative acts, so likewise the power and authority of the assembly over them, after they are passed, is different.

It must occur to every person on the first reflection, that the affairs and circumstances of a commonwealth require other business to be done besides that of making laws, and, consequently, that the different kinds of business cannot all be classed under one name, or be subject to one and the same rule of treatment.

But to proceed –

By agency transactions, or matters of negotiation, done by the assembly, are to be comprehended all that kind of public business, which the assembly, as representatives of the republic, transact in its behalf, with a certain person or persons, or part or parts of the republic, for purposes mentioned in the act, and which the assembly confirm and ratify on the part of the commonwealth, by affixing to it the seal of the state.

An act of this kind, differs from a law of the before-mentioned kind; because here are two parties and there but one, and the parties are bound to perform different and distinct parts: whereas, in the before-mentioned law, every man's part was the same.

These acts, therefore, though numbered among the laws, are evidently distinct therefrom, and are not of the legislative kind. The former are laws for the government of the commonwealth; these are transactions of business, such as, selling and conveying an estate belonging to the public, or buying one; acts for borrowing money, and fixing with the lender the terms and modes of payment; acts of agreement and contract, with a certain person or persons, for certain purposes: and, in short, every act in which two parties, the state being one, are particularly mentioned or described, and in which the form and nature of a bargain or contract is comprehended.

These, if for custom and uniformity sake we call them by the name of *laws*, are not laws for the government of the common-wealth, but for the government of the contracting parties, as all deeds and contracts are; and are not, properly speaking, acts of the assembly, but joint acts, or acts of the assembly in behalf of the commonwealth on one part, and certain persons therein mentioned on the other part.

Acts of this kind are distinguishable into two classes:

First — Those wherein the matters inserted in the act have already been settled and adjusted between the state on one part, and the persons therein mentioned, on the other part. In this case the act is the completion and ratification of the contract or matters therein recited. It is in fact a deed signed, sealed and delivered.

Second — Those acts wherein the matters have not been already agreed upon, and wherein the act only holds forth certain propositions and terms to be accepted of and acceded to.

I shall give an instance of each of those acts. First, the state wants the loan of a sum of money; certain persons make an offer to government to lend that sum, and send in their proposals: the government accept these proposals, and all the matters of the loan and the payment are agreed on; and an act is passed according to the usual form of passing acts, ratifying and confirming this agreement. This act is final.

In the second case — the state, as in the preceding one, wants a loan of money — the assembly passes an act holding forth the terms on which it will borrow and pay: this act has no force until the propositions and terms are accepted of and acceded to by some person or persons, and when those terms are accepted of and complied with, the act is binding on the state.

But if at the meeting of the next assembly, or any other, the whole sum intended to be borrowed, should not be borrowed, that assembly may stop where they are, and discontinue proceeding with the loan, or make new propositions and terms for the remainder; but so far as the subscriptions have been filled up, and the terms complied with, it is, as in the first case, a signed deed; and in the same manner are all acts, let the manners in them be what they may, wherein, as I have before mentioned, the state on one part, and certain individuals on the other part, are parties in the act.

If the state should become a bankrupt, the creditors, as in all cases of bankruptcy, will be sufferers; they will have but a dividend for the whole: but this is not a dissolution of the contract, but an accommodation of it, arising from necessity. And so in all cases of this kind, if an inability takes place on either side, the contract cannot be performed, and some accommodation must be gone into, or the matter falls through of itself.

It may likewise, though it ought not to, happen that in performing the matters, agreeably to the terms of the act, inconveniences, unforeseen at the time of making the act, may arise to either or both parties: in this case, those inconveniences may be removed by the mutual consent and agreement of the parties, and each finds its benefit in so doing: for in a republic it is the harmony of its parts that constitutes their several and mutual good.

But the acts themselves are legally binding, as much as if they had been made between two private individuals. The greatness of one party cannot give it a superiority or advantage over the other. The state, or its representatives, the assembly, has no more power over an act of this kind, after it has passed, than if the state was a private person. It is the glory of a republic to have it so, because it secures the individual from becoming the prey of power, and prevents *might* from overcoming *right*.

If any difference or dispute arise afterwards between the state and the individuals with whom the agreement is made respecting the contract, or the meaning, or extent of any of the matters contained in the act, which may affect the property or interest of either, such difference or dispute must be judged of, and decided upon, by the laws of the land, in a court of justice and trial by jury; that is, by the laws of the land already in being at the time such act and contract was made.

No law made afterwards can apply to the case, either directly, or by construction or implication: for such a law would be a retrospective law, or a law made after the fact, and cannot even be produced in court as applying to the case before it for judgement.

That this is justice, that it is the true principle of republican government, no man will be so hardy as to deny. If, therefore, a lawful contract or agreement, sealed and ratified, cannot be affected or altered by any act made afterwards, how much more inconsistent and irrational, despotic and unjust would it be, to think of making an act with the professed intention of breaking up a contract already signed and sealed.

That it is possible an assembly, in the heat and indiscretion of party, and meditating on power rather than on the principle by which all power in a republican government is governed, that of equal justice, may fall into the error of passing such an act, is admitted; – but it would be an actless act, an act that goes for nothing, an act which the courts of justice and the established laws of the land, could know nothing of.

Because such an act would be an act of one party only, not only without, but against the consent of the other; and therefore, cannot be produced to affect a contract made between the two. That the violation of a contract should be set up as a justification to the violator, would be the same thing as to say, that a man by breaking his promise is freed from the obligation of it, or that by transgressing the laws, he exempts himself from the punishment of them.

Besides the constitutional and legal reasons why an assembly cannot, of its own act and authority, undo or make void a contract made between the state (by a former assembly) and certain individuals, may be added what may be called the natural reasons, or those reasons which the plain rules of common sense point out to every man. Among which are the following:

The principals, or real parties in the contract, are the state and the persons contracted with. The assembly is not a party, but an agent in behalf of the state, authorized and empowered to transact its affairs.

Therefore, it is the state that is bound on one part and certain individuals on the other part, and the performance of the contract, according to the conditions of it, devolves on succeeding assemblies, not as principals, but as agents.

Therefore, for the next or any other assembly to undertake to dissolve the state from its obligation is an assumption of power of a novel and extraordinary kind. It is the servant attempting to free his master.

The election of new assemblies following each other makes no difference in the nature of things. The state is still the same state. The public is still the same body. These do not annually expire, though the time of an assembly does. These are not new-created every year, nor can they be displaced from their original standing; but are a perpetual, permanent body, always in being and still the same.

But if we adopt the vague, inconsistent idea that every new assembly has a full and complete authority over every act done by the state in a former assembly, and confound together laws, contracts, and every species of public business, it will lead us into a wilderness of endless confusion and insurmountable difficulties. It would be declaring an assembly despotic, for the time being.

Instead of a government of established principles administered by established rules, the authority of government, by being strained so high, would, by the same rule, be reduced proportionately as low, and would be no other than that of a committee of the state, acting with discretionary powers for one year. Every new election would be a new revolution, or it would suppose the public of the former year dead and a new public in its place.

Having now endeavoured to fix a precise idea to, and distinguish between legislative acts and acts of negotiation and agency, I shall proceed to apply this distinction to the case now in dispute, respecting the charter of the bank.

The charter of the bank, or what is the same thing, the act for incorporating it, is to all intents and purposes an act of negotiation and contract, entered into, and confirmed between the state on one part, and certain persons mentioned therein on the other part. The purpose for which the act was done on the part of the state is therein recited, viz. the support which the finances of the country would derive therefrom. The incorporating clause is the condition or obligation on the part of the state; and the obligation on the part of the bank, is 'that nothing contained in that act shall be construed to authorize the said corporation to exercise any powers in this state repugnant to the laws or constitution thereof'.

Here are all the marks and evidences of a contract. The parties — the purport — and the reciprocal obligations.

That this is a contract, or a joint act, is evident from its being in the power of either of the parties to have forbidden or prevented its being done. The state could not force the stockholders of the bank to be a corporation, and therefore, as their consent was necessary to the making the act, their dissent would have prevented its being made; so, on the other hand, as the bank could not force the state to incorporate them, the consent or dissent of the state would have had the same effect to do, or to prevent its being done; and as neither of the parties could make the act alone, for the same reason can neither of them dissolve it alone: but this is not the case with a law or act of legislation, and therefore, the difference proves it to be an act of a different kind.

The bank may forfeit the charter by delinquency, but the delinquency must be proved and established by a legal process in a court of justice and trial by jury; for the state, or the assembly, is not to be a judge in its own case, but must come to the laws of the land for judgement; for that which is law for the individual, is likewise law for the state.

Before I enter further into this affair, I shall go back to the circumstances of the country, and the condition the government was in, for some time before, as well as at the time it entered into this engagement with the bank, and this act of incorporation was passed: for the government of this state, and I suppose the same of the rest, were then in want of two of the most essential matters which governments could be destitute of – money and credit.

In looking back to those times, and bringing forward some of the circumstances attending them, I feel myself entering on unpleasant and disagreeable ground; because some of the matters which the attacks on the bank now make it necessary to state, in order to bring the affair fully before the public, will not add honour to those who have promoted that measure and carried it through the late House of Assembly; and for whom, though my own judgement and opinion on the case oblige me to differ from, I retain my esteem, and the social remembrance of times past.

But, I trust, those gentlemen will do me the justice to recollect my exceeding earnestness with them, last spring, when the attack on the bank first broke out; for it clearly appeared to me one of those overheated measures, which, neither the country at large, not their own constituents, would justify them in, when it came to be fully understood; for however high a party measure may be carried in an assembly, the people out of doors are all the while following their several occupations and employments, minding their farms and their business, and take their own time and leisure to judge of public measures; the consequence of which is, that they often judge in a cooler spirit than their representatives act in.

It may be easily recollected that the present bank was preceded by, and rose out of a former one, called the Pennsylvania Bank which began a few months before; the occasion of which I shall briefly state.

In the spring of 1780, the Pennsylvania Assembly was composed of many of the same members, and nearly all of the same connection, which composed the late House that began the attack on the bank. I served as Clerk of the Assembly of 1780, which station I resigned at the end of the year, and accompanied a much lamented friend, the late Colonel John Laurens, on an embassy to France.

The spring of 1780 was marked with accumulation of misfortunes. The reliance placed on the defence of Charleston failed, and exceedingly lowered or depressed the spirits of the country. The measures of government, from the want of money, means and credit, dragged on like a heavy loaded carriage without wheels, and were nearly got to what a countryman would understand by a dead pull.

The Assembly of that year met, by adjournment, at an unusual time, the tenth of May, and what particularly added to the affliction, was that so many of the members, instead of spiriting up their constituents to the most nervous exertions, came to the Assembly furnished with petitions to be exempt from paying taxes. How the public measures were to be carried on, the country defended, and the army recruited, clothed, fed, and paid, when the only resource, and that not half sufficient, that of taxes, should be relaxed to almost nothing, was a matter too gloomy to look at.

A language very different from that of petitions ought at this time to have been the language of everyone. A declaration to have stood forth with their lives and fortunes, and a reprobation of every thought of partial indulgence would have sounded much better than petitions.

While the Assembly was sitting, a letter from the commander-in-chief was received by the executive council and transmitted to the House. The doors were shut, and it fell officially to me to read.

In this letter the naked truth of things was unfolded. Among other informations, the general said, that notwithstanding his confidence in the attachment of the army to the cause of the country, the distress of it, from the want of every necessary which men could be destitute of, had arisen to such a pitch, that the appearances of mutiny and discontent were so strongly marked on the countenance of the army, that he dreaded the event of every hour.

When the letter was read, I observed a despairing silence in the House. Nobody spoke for a considerable time. At length, a member, of whose fortitude to withstand misfortunes I had a high opinion, rose:

'If', said he, 'the account in that letter is a true state of things, and we are in the situation there represented, it appears to me in vain to contend the matter any longer. We may as well give up at first as at last.'

The gentleman who spoke next, was (to the best of my recollection) a member of Bucks County, who, in a cheerful note, endeavoured to dissipate the gloom of the House:

'Well, well,' said he, 'don't let the House despair. If things are not so well as we wish, we must endeavour to make them better.'

And on a motion for adjournment, the conversation went no further.

There was now no time to lose, and something absolutely necessary to be done, which was not within the immediate power of the House to do; for what with the depreciation of the currency, and slow operation of taxes, and the petitions to be exempted therefrom, the treasury was moneyless and the Government creditless.

If the Assembly could not give the assistance which the necessity of the case immediately required, it was very proper the matter should be known by those who either could or would endeavour to do it. To conceal the information within the House, and not provide the relief which that information required, was making no use of the knowledge, and endangering the public cause. The only thing that now remained, and was capable of reaching the case, was private credit, and the voluntary aid of individuals; and under this impression, on my return from the House, I drew out the salary due to me as clerk, enclosed $500 to a gentleman in this city, in part of the whole, and wrote fully to him on the subject of our affairs.

The gentleman to whom this letter was addressed is Mr Blair M'Clenaghan. I mentioned to him that, notwithstanding the current opinion that the enemy were beaten from before Charleston, there were too many reasons to believe the place was then taken and in the hands of the enemy: the consequence of which would be that a great part of the British force would return, and join at New York; that our own army required to be augmented, ten thousand men, to be able to stand against the combined force of the enemy.

I informed Mr M'Clenaghan of General Washington's letter, the extreme distresses he was surrounded with, and the absolute occasion there was for the citizens to exert themselves at this time, which there was no doubt they would do, if the necessity was made known to them; for that the ability of government was exhausted. I requested Mr M'Clenaghan to propose a voluntary subscription among his friends and added that I had enclosed five hundred dollars as my mite thereto, and that I would increase it as far as the last ability would enable me to go.

The next day Mr M'Clenaghan informed me that he had communicated the contents of the letter, at a meeting of gentlemen at the coffeehouse, and that a subscription was immediately begun; that Mr Robert Morris and himself had subscribed £200 each, in hard money, and that the subscription was going on very successfully. This subscription was intended as a donation, and to be given in bounties to promote the recruiting service. It is dated June 8, 1780. The original subscription list is now in my possession – it amounts to £400 hard money, and £101,360 Continental.

While this subscription was going forward, information of the loss of Charleston arrived, and on a communication from several members of Congress to certain gentlemen of this city, of the increasing distresses and dangers then taking place, a meeting was held of the subscribers, and such other gentlemen who chose to attend, at the city tavern. This meeting was on the seventeenth of June, nine days after the subscriptions had begun.

At this meeting it was resolved to open a security-subscription to the amount of £300,000, Pennsylvania currency, in real money; the subscribers to execute bonds to the amount of their subscriptions, and to form a bank thereon for supplying the army. This being resolved on and carried into execution, the plan of the first subscriptions was discontinued, and this extended one established in its stead.

By means of this bank the army was supplied through the campaign, and being at the same time recruited, was enabled to maintain its ground; and on the appointment of Mr Morris to be superintendent of the finances the spring following, he arranged the system of the present bank, styled the Bank of North America, and many subscribers of the former bank transferred their subscriptions into this.

Towards the establishment of this bank, Congress passed an ordinance of incorporation, December twenty-first, which the government of Pennsylvania recognized by sundry matters: and afterwards, on an application of the president and directors of the bank, through the mediation of the executive council, the Assembly agreed to, and passed the state act of incorporation 1 April, 1782.

Thus arose the bank – produced by the distresses of the times and the enterprising spirit of patriotic individuals. Those individuals furnished and risked the money, and the aid which the Government contributed was that of incorporating them.

It would have been well if the state had made all its bargains and contracts with as much true policy as it made this: for a greater service for so small a consideration, that only of an act of incorporation, has not been obtained since the Government existed.

Having now shown how the bank originated, I shall proceed with my remarks.

The sudden restoration of public and private credit, which took place on the establishment of the bank, is an event as extraordinary in itself as any domestic occurrence during the progress of the Revolution.

How far a spirit of envy might operate to produce the attack on the bank during the sitting of the late Assembly, is best known and felt by those who began or promoted the attack. The bank had rendered services which the Assembly of 1780 could not, and acquired an honour which many of its members might be unwilling to own, and wish to obscure.

But surely every government, acting on the principles of patriotism and public good, would cherish an institution capable of rendering such advantages to the community. The establishment of the bank in one of the most trying vicissitudes of the war, its zealous services in the public cause, its influence in restoring and supporting credit, and the punctuality with which all its business has been transacted, are matters, that so far from meriting the treatment it met with from the late Assembly, are an honour to the state, and what the body of her citizens may be proud to own.

But the attack on the bank, as a chartered institution, under the protection of its violators, however criminal it may be as an error of government, or impolitic as a measure of party, is not to be charged on the constituents of those who made the attack. It appears from every circumstance that has come to light, to be a measure which that Assembly contrived of itself. The members did not come charged with the affair from their constituents. There was no idea of such a thing when they were elected or when they met. The hasty and precipitate manner in which it was hurried through the House, and the refusal of the House to hear the directors of the bank in its defence, prior to the publication of the repealing bill for public consideration, operated to prevent their constituents comprehending the subject: therefore, whatever may be wrong in the proceedings lies not at the door of the public. The House took the affair on its own shoulders, and whatever blame there is lies on them.

The matter must have been prejudged and predetermined by a majority of the members out of the House before it was brought into it. The whole business appears to have been fixed at once, and all reasoning or debate on the case rendered useless. . . .

The subsequent conduct of the House, in resolving not to hear the directors of the bank, on their application for that purpose, prior to the publication of the bill for the consideration of the people, strongly corroborates this opinion; for why should not the House hear them, unless it was apprehensive that the bank, by such a public opportunity, would produce proofs of its services and usefulness, that would not suit the temper and views of its oppressors?

But if the House did not wish or choose to hear the defence of the bank, it was no reason that their constituents should not. The Constitution of this state, in lieu of having two branches of legislature, has substituted, that, 'to the end that laws before they are enacted may be more *maturely considered,* and the inconvenience of *hasty determinations* as much as possible prevented, all bills of a public nature shall be printed for the consideration of the people'. The people, therefore, according to the Constitution, stand in the place of another House; or, more properly speaking, are a house in their own right. But in this instance, the Assembly arrogates the whole power to itself, and places itself as a bar to stop the necessary information spreading among the people.

The application of the bank to be heard before the bill was published for public consideration had two objects. First, to the House – and secondly, through the House to the people, who are as another house. It was as a defence in the first instance, and as an appeal in the second. But the Assembly absorbs the right of the people to judge; because, by refusing to hear the defence, they barred the appeal. Were there no other cause which the constituents of that Assembly had for censuring its conduct, than the exceeding unfairness, partiality, and arbitrariness with which its business was transacted, it would be cause sufficient.

Let the constituents of assemblies differ, as they may, respecting certain peculiarities in the *form* of the constitution, they will all agree in supporting its *principles,* and in reprobating unfair proceedings and despotic measures. Every constituent is a member of the republic, which is a station of more consequence to him than being a member of a party, and though they may differ from each other in their choice of persons to transact the public business, it is of equal importance to all parties that the business be done on right principles; otherwise our laws and acts, instead of being founded in justice, will be founded in party, and be laws and acts of retaliation; and instead of being a republic of free citizens, we shall be alternately tyrants and slaves. But to return to the report.

The report begins by stating that, 'The committee to whom was referred the petitions concerning the bank established at Philadelphia, and who were instructed to *inquire* whether the said bank be compatible with the public safety, and that equality which ought ever to prevail between the individuals of a republic, beg leave to report' (not that they have made any *inquiry,* but) 'that it is the *opinion* of this committee, that the said bank, as at present established, is, in every view, incompatible with the public safety.' But why is it so? Here is an opinion unfounded and unwarranted. The committee have begun their report at the wrong end; for an opinion, when given as a matter of judgement, is an action of the mind which follows a fact, but here it is put in the room of one.

The report then says, 'that in the present state of our trade, the said bank has a direct tendency to banish a great part of the specie from the country, and to collect into the hands of the stockholders of the bank, almost the whole of the money which remains among us'.

Here is another mere assertion, just like the former, without a single fact or circumstance to show why it is made, or whereon it is founded. Now the very reverse of what the committee asserts is the natural consequence of a bank. Specie may be called the stock in trade of the bank, it is therefore its interest to prevent it from wandering out of the country, and to keep a constant standing supply to be ready for all domestic occasions and demands.

Were it true that the bank has a direct tendency to banish the specie from the country, there would soon be an end to the bank; and, therefore, the committee have so far mistaken the matter, as to put their fears in the place of their wishes: for if it is to happen as the committee states, let the bank alone and it will cease of itself, and the repealing act need not have been passed.

It is the interest of the bank that people should keep their cash there, and all commercial countries find the exceeding great convenience of having a general depository for their cash. But so far from banishing it, there are no two classes of people in America who are so much interested in preserving hard money in the country as the bank and the merchant. Neither of them can carry on their business without it. Their opposition to the paper money of the late Assembly was because it has a direct effect, as far as it is able, to banish the specie, and that without providing any means for bringing more in.

The committee must have been aware of this, and therefore chose to spread the first alarm, and, groundless as it was, to trust to the delusion.

As the keeping the specie in the country is the interest of the bank, so it has the best opportunities of preventing its being sent away, and the earliest knowledge of such a design. While the bank is the general depository of cash, no great sums can be obtained without getting it from thence, and as it is evidently prejudicial to its interest to advance money to be sent abroad, because in this case the money cannot by circulation return again, the bank, therefore, is interested in preventing what the committee would have it suspected of promoting.

It is to prevent the exportation of cash, and to retain it in the country, that the bank has, on several occasions, stopped the discounting notes till the danger had been passed.[1] The first part, therefore, of the assertion, that of banishing the specie, contains an apprehension as needless as it is groundless, and which, had the

1 The petitions say, 'That they have frequently seen the stopping of discounts at the bank operate on the trading part of the community, with a degree of violence scarcely inferior to that of a stagnation of the blood in the human body, hurrying the wretched merchant who hath debts to pay into the hands of griping usurers.'

As the persons who say or signed this live somewhere in Chester County, they are not, from situation, certain of what they say. Those petitions have every appearance of being contrived for the purpose of bringing the matter on. The petitions and the report have strong evidence in them of being both drawn by the same person: for the

committee understood, or been the least informed of the nature of a bank, they could not have made. It is very probable that some of the opposers of the bank are those persons who have been disappointed in their attempts to obtain specie for this purpose, and now disguise their opposition under other pretenses.

I now come to the second part of the assertion, which is, that when the bank has banished a great part of the specie from the country, 'it will collect into the hands of the stockholders almost the whole of the money which remains among us'. But how, or by what means, the bank is to accomplish this wonderful feat, the committee have not informed us. Whether people are to give their money to the bank for nothing, or whether the bank is to charm it from them as a rattlesnake charms a squirrel from a tree, the committee have left us as much in the dark about as they were themselves.

Is it possible the committee should know so very little of the matter, as not to know that no part of the money which at any time may be in the bank belongs to the stockholders? Not even the original capital which they put in is any part of it their own, until every person who has a demand upon the bank is paid, and if there is not a sufficiency for this purpose, on the balance of loss and gain, the original money of the stockholders must make up the deficiency.

The money, which at any time may be in the bank, is the property of every man who holds a bank note, or deposits cash there, or who

---

report is as clearly the echo of the petitions as ever the address of the British Parliament was the echo of the King's speech.

Besides the reason I have already given for occasionally stopping discounting notes at the bank, there are other necessary reasons. It is for the purpose of settling accounts; short reckonings make long friends. The bank lends its money for short periods, and by that means assists a great many different people: and if it did not sometimes stop discounting as a means of settling with the persons it has already lent its money to, those persons would find a way to keep what they had borrowed longer than they ought, and prevent others being assisted. It is a fact, and some of the committee know it to be so, that sundry of those persons who then opposed the bank acted this part.

The stopping the discounts do not, and cannot, operate to call in the loans sooner than the time for which they were lent, and therefore the charge is false that 'it hurries men into the hands of griping usurers': and the truth is that it operates to keep them from them.

If petitions are to be contrived to cover the design of a house of assembly, and give a pretence for its conduct, or if a house is to be led by the nose by the idle tale of any fifty or sixty signers to a petition, it is time for the public to look a little closer into the conduct of its representatives. – Paine.

has a just demand upon it from the city of Philadelphia up to Fort Pitt, or to any part of the United States; and he can draw the money from it when he pleases. Its being in the bank, does not in the least make it the property of the stockholders, any more than the money in the state treasury is the property of the state treasurer. They are only stewards over it for those who please to put it, or let it remain there: and, therefore, this second part of the assertion is somewhat ridiculous.

The next paragraph in the report is, 'that the accumulation of *enormous wealth* in the hands of a *society* who claim perpetual duration, will necessarily produce a degree of influence and power which cannot be entrusted in the hands of any set of men whatsoever' (the committee I presume excepted) 'without endangering public safety'. There is an air of solemn fear in this paragraph which is something like introducing a ghost in a play to keep people from laughing at the players.

I have already shown that whatever wealth there may be, at any time, in the bank, is the property of those who have demands upon the bank, and not the property of the stockholders. As a society they hold no property, and most probably never will, unless it should be a house to transact their business in, instead of hiring one. Every half year the bank settles its accounts, and each individual stockholder takes his dividend of gain or loss to himself, and the bank begins the next half year in the same manner it began the first, and so on. This being the nature of a bank, there can be no accumulation of wealth among them as a society.

For what purpose the word *'society'* is introduced into the report I do not know, unless it be to make a false impression upon people's minds. It has no connection with the subject, for the bank is not a society, but a company, and denominated so in the charter. There are several religious societies incorporated in this state, which hold property as the right of those societies, and to which no person can belong that is not of the same religious profession. But this is not the case with the bank. The bank is a company for the promotion and convenience of commerce, which is a matter in which all the state is interested, and holds no property in the manner which those societies do.

But there is a direct contradiction in this paragraph to that which goes before it. The committee, there, accuses the bank of banishing the specie, and here, of accumulating enormous sums of it. So here are two enormous sums of specie; one enormous sum going out, and another enormous sum remaining. To reconcile this contradiction, the committee should have added to their report, *that they suspected the bank had found out the philosopher's stone, and kept it a secret.*

The next paragraph is, 'that the said bank, in its corporate capacity, is empowered to hold estates to the amount of ten millions of dollars, and by the tenor of the present charter is to exist for ever, without being obliged to yield any emolument to the government, or be in the least dependent on it'.

The committee have gone so vehemently into this business, and so completely shown their want of knowledge in every point of it, as to make, in the first part of this paragraph, a fear of what, the greater fear is, will never happen. Had the committee known anything of banking, they must have known, that the objection against banks has been (not that they held great estates but) that they held none; that they had no real, fixed, and visible property, and that it is the maxim and practice of banks not to hold any.

The Honourable Chancellor Livingston, late Secretary for Foreign Affairs, did me the honour of showing, and discoursing with me on a plan of a bank he had drawn up for the State of New York. In this plan it was made a condition or obligation, that whatever the capital of the bank amounted to in specie, there should be added twice as much in real estates. But the mercantile interest rejected the proposition.

It was a very good piece of policy in the Assembly which passed the charter act, to add the clause to empower the bank to purchase and hold real estates. It was as an inducement to the bank to do it, because such estates being held as the property of the bank would be so many mortgages to the public in addition to the money capital of the bank.

But the doubt is that the bank will not be induced to accept the opportunity. The bank has existed five years, and has not purchased a shilling of real property: and as such property or estates cannot be purchased by the bank but with the interest money which the stock produces, and as that is divided every half year among the stockholders, and each stockholder chooses to have the management of his own dividend, and if he lays it out in purchasing an estate to have that estate his own private property, and under his own immediate management, there is no expectation, so far from being any fear, that the clause will be accepted.

Where knowledge is a duty, ignorance is a crime; and the committee are criminal in not understanding this subject better. Had this clause not been in the charter, the committee might have reported the want of it as a defect, in not empowering the bank to hold estates as a real security to its creditors: but as the complaint now stands, the accusation of it is, that the charter empowers the bank to *give real security* to its creditors. A complaint never made, heard of, or thought of before.

The second article in this paragraph is, 'that the bank, according to the tenor of the present charter, is to exist for ever'. Here I agree with the committee, and am glad to find that among such a list of errors and contradictions there is one idea which is not wrong, although the committee have made a wrong use of it.

As we are not to live for ever ourselves, and other generations are to follow us, we have neither the power nor the right to govern them, or to say how they shall govern themselves. It is the summit of human vanity, and shows a covetousness of power beyond the grave, to be dictating to the world to come. It is sufficient that we do that which is right in our own day, and leave them with the advantage of good examples.

As the generations of the world are every day both commencing and expiring, therefore, when any public act, of this sort, is done, it naturally supposes the age of that generation to be then beginning, and the time contained between coming of age, and the natural end of life, is the extent of time it has a right to go to, which may be about thirty years; for though many may die before, others will live beyond; and the mean time is equally fair for all generations.

If it was made an article in the Constitution, that all laws and acts should cease of themselves in thirty years, and have no legal force beyond that time, it would prevent their becoming too numerous and voluminous, and serve to keep them within view in a compact compass. Such as were proper to be continued, would be enacted again, and those which were not, would go into oblivion. There is the same propriety that a nation should fix a time for a full settlement of its affairs, and begin again from a new date, as that an individual should; and to keep within the distance of thirty years would be a convenient period.

The British, from the want of some general regulation of this kind, have a great number of obsolete laws; which, though out of use and forgotten, are not out of force, and are occasionally brought up for particular purposes, and innocent, unwary persons trepanned thereby.

To extend this idea still further – it would probably be a considerable improvement in the political system of nations, to make all treaties of peace for a limited time. It is the nature of the mind to feel uneasy under the idea of a condition perpetually existing over it, and to excite in itself apprehensions that would not take place were it not from that cause.

Were treaties of peace made for, and renewable every seven or ten years, the natural effect would be, to make peace continue longer than it does under the custom of making peace for ever. If the parties felt, or apprehended, any inconveniences under the terms already made, they would look forward to the time when they should be eventually relieved therefrom, and might renew the treaty on improved conditions.

This opportunity periodically occurring, and the recollection of it always existing, would serve as a chimney to the political fabric, to carry off the smoke and fume of national fire. It would naturally abate and honourably take off the edge and occasion for fighting: and however the parties might determine to do it, when the time of the treaty should expire, it would then seem like fighting in cool blood: the fighting temper would be dissipated before the fighting time arrived, and negotiation supply its place. To know how probable this may be, a man need do no more than observe the progress of his own mind on any private circumstance similar in its nature to a public one. But to return to my subject.

To give limitation is to give duration: and though it is not a justifying reason, that because an act or contract is not to last for ever, that it shall be broken or violated to-day, yet, where no time is mentioned, the omission affords an opportunity for the abuse. When we violate a contract on this pretence, we assume a right that belongs to the next generation; for though they, as a following generation, have the right of altering or setting it aside, as not being concerned in the making it, or not being done in their day, we, who made it, have not that right; and, therefore, the committee, in this part of their report, have made a wrong use of a right principle; and as this clause in the charter might have been altered by the consent of the parties, it cannot be produced to justify the violation. And were it not altered there would be no inconvenience from it.

The term 'for ever' is an absurdity that would have no effect. The next age will think for itself, by the same rule of right that we have done, and not admit any assumed authority of ours to encroach upon the system of their day. Our *for ever* ends, where their *for ever* begins.

The third article in this paragraph is, that the bank holds its charter 'without being obliged to yield any emolument to the Government'.

Ingratitude has a short memory. It was on the failure of the Government to support the public cause, that the bank originated. It stepped in as a support, when some of the persons then in the Government, and who now oppose the bank, were apparently on the point of abandoning the cause, not from disaffection, but from despair. While the expenses of the war were carried on by emissions of Continental money, any set of men, in government, might carry it on. The means being provided to their hands, required no great exertions of fortitude or wisdom; but when this means failed, they would have failed with it, had not a public spirit awakened itself with energy out-of-doors. It was easy times to the Government while Continental money lasted. The dream of wealth supplied the reality of it; but when the dream vanished, the Government did not awake.

But what right has the Government to expect any emolument from the bank? Does the committee mean to set up acts and charters for sale, or what do they mean? Because it is the practice of the British Ministry to grind a toll out of every public institution they can get a power over, is the same practice to be followed here?

The war being now ended, and the bank having rendered the service expected, or rather hoped for, from it, the principal public use of it, at this time, is for the promotion and extension of commerce. The whole community derives benefit from the operation of the bank. It facilitates the commerce of the country. It quickens the means of purchasing and paying for country produce, and hastens on the exportation of it. The emolument, therefore, being to the community, it is the office and duty of government to give protection to the bank.

Among many of the principal conveniences arising from the bank, one of them is, that it gives a kind of life to, what would otherwise be, dead money. Every merchant and person in trade, has always in his hands some quantity of cash, which constantly remains with him; that is, he is never entirely without: this remnant money, as it may be called, is of no use to him till more is collected to it. He can neither buy produce nor merchandise with it, and this being the case with every person in trade, there will be (though not all at the same time) as many of those sums lying uselessly by, and scattered throughout the city, as there are persons in trade, besides many that are not in trade.

I should not suppose the estimate overrated, in conjecturing, that half the money in the city, at any one time, lies in this manner. By collecting those scattered sums together, which is done by means of the bank, they become capable of being used, and the quantity of circulating cash is doubled, and by the depositors alternately lending them to each other, the commercial system is invigorated: and as it is the interest of the bank to preserve this money in the country for domestic uses only, and as it has the best opportunity of doing so, the bank serves as a sentinel over the specie.

If a farmer, or a miller, comes to the city with produce, there are but few merchants that can individually purchase it with ready money of their own; and those few would command nearly the whole market for country produce; but, by means of the bank, this monopoly is prevented, and the chance of the market enlarged.

It is very extraordinary that the late Assembly should promote monopolizing; yet such would be the effect of suppressing the bank; and it is much to the honour of those merchants, who are capable by their fortunes of becoming monopolizers, that they support the bank. In this case, honour operates over interest. They were the persons who first set up the bank, and their honour is now engaged to support what it is their interest to put down.

If merchants, by this means, or farmers, by similar means, among themselves, can mutually aid and support each other, what has the Government to do with it? What right has it to expect emolument from associated industry, more than from individual industry? It would be a strange sort of government, that should make it illegal for people to assist each other, or pay a tribute for doing so.

But the truth is, that the Government has already derived emoluments, and very extraordinary ones. It has already received its full share, by the services of the bank during the war; and it is every day receiving benefits, because whatever promotes and facilitates commerce, serves likewise to promote and facilitate the revenue.

The last article in this paragraph is, 'that the bank is not the least dependent on the Government'.

Have the committee so soon forgotten the principles of republican government and Constitution, or are they so little acquainted with them, as not to know, that this article in their report partakes of the nature of treason? Do they not know, that freedom is destroyed by dependence, and the safety of the state endangered thereby? Do they not see, that to hold any part of the citizens of the state, as yearly pensioners on the favour of an assembly, is striking at the root of free elections?

If other parts of their report discover a want of knowledge on the subjects of banks, this shows a want of principle in the science of government.

Only let us suppose this dangerous idea carried into practice, and then see what it leads to. If corporate bodies are, after their incorporation to be annually dependent on an assembly for the continuance of their charter, the citizens which compose those corporations, are not free. The Government holds an authority and influence over them, in a manner different from what it does over other citizens, and by this means destroys that equality of freedom, which is the bulwark of the republic and the Constitution.

By this scheme of government any party, which happens to be uppermost in a state, will command all the corporations in it, and may create more for the purpose of extending that influence. The dependent borough towns in England are the rotten parts of their government and this idea of the committee has a very near relation to it.

'If you do not do so and so,' expressing what was meant, 'take care of your charter', was a threat thrown out against the bank. But as I do not wish to enlarge on a disagreeable circumstance and hope that what is already said is sufficient to show the anti-constitutional conduct and principles of the committee, I shall pass on to the next paragraph in the report. Which is –

'That the great profits of the bank, which will daily increase as money grows scarcer, and which already far exceed the profits of

European banks, have tempted foreigners to vest their money in this bank, and thus to draw from us large sums for interest.'

Had the committee understood the subject, some dependence might be put on their opinion which now cannot. Whether money will grow scarcer, and whether the profits of the bank will increase, are more than the committee know, or are judges sufficient to guess at. The committee are not so capable of taking care of commerce, as commerce is capable of taking care of itself.

The farmer understands farming, and the merchant understands commerce; and as riches are equally the object of both, there is no occasion that either should fear that the other will seek to be poor. The more money the merchant has, so much the better for the farmer who has produce to sell; and the richer the farmer is, so much the better for the merchant, when he comes to his store.

As to the profits of the bank, the stockholders must take their chance for it. It may some years be more and others less, and upon the whole may not be so productive as many other ways that money may be employed. It is the convenience which the stockholders, as commercial men, derive from the establishment of the bank, and not the mere interest they receive, that is the inducement to them. It is the ready opportunity of borrowing alternately of each other that forms the principal object: and as they pay as well as receive a great part of the interest among themselves, it is nearly the same thing, both cases considered at once, whether it is more or less.

The stockholders are occasionally depositors and sometimes borrowers of the bank. They pay interest for what they borrow, and receive none for what they deposit; and were a stockholder to keep a nice account of the interest he pays for the one and loses on the other, he would find, at the year's end, that ten per cent on his stock would probably not be more than common interest on the whole, if so much.

As to the committee complaining 'that foreigners by vesting their money in the bank will draw large sums from us for interest', it is like a miller complaining, in a dry season, that so much water runs into his dam and some of it runs over.

Could those foreigners draw this interest without putting in any capital, the complaint would be well founded; but as they must first put money in before they can draw any out, as they must draw many years before they can draw even the numerical sum they put in at first, the effect for at least twenty years to come, will be directly contrary to what the committee states; because we draw *capital* from them and they only *interest* from us, and as we shall have the use of the money all the while it remains with us, the advantage will always be in our favour. In framing this part of the report, the committee must have forgotten which side of the Atlantic they were on, for the case would be as they state it if we put money into their bank instead of their putting it into ours. . . .

I proceed to the third and last subject – that of paper money.

I remember a German farmer expressing as much in a few words as the whole subject requires; *'Money is money, and paper is paper.'*

All the invention of man cannot make them otherwise. The alchemist may cease his labours, and the hunter after the philosopher's stone go to rest, if paper can be metamorphosed into gold and silver, or made to answer the same purpose in all cases.

Gold and silver are the emissions of nature: paper is the emission of art. The value of gold and silver is ascertained by the quantity which nature has made in the earth. We cannot make that quantity more or less than it is, and therefore the value being dependent upon the quantity, depends not on man. Man has no share in making gold or silver; all that his labours and ingenuity can accomplish is, to collect it from the mine, refine it for use and give it an impression, or stamp it into coin.

Its being stamped into coin adds considerably to its convenience but nothing to its value. It has then no more value than it had before. Its value is not in the impression but in itself. Take away the impression and still the same value remains. Alter it as you will, or expose it to any misfortune that can happen, still the value is not diminished. It has a capacity to resist the accidents that destroy other things. It has, therefore, all the requisite qualities that money can have, and is a fit material to make money of; and nothing which has not all those properties, can be fit for the purpose of money.

Paper, considered as a material whereof to make money, has none of the requisite qualities in it. It is too plentiful, and too easily come at. It can be had anywhere, and for a trifle.

There are two ways in which I shall consider paper.

The only proper use for paper, in the room of money, is to write promissory notes and obligations of payment in specie upon. A piece of paper, thus written and signed, is worth the sum it is given for, if the person who gives it is able to pay it; because in this case, the law will oblige him. But if he is worth nothing, the paper note is worth nothing. The value, therefore, of such a note, is not in the note itself, for that is but paper and promise, but in the man who is obliged to redeem it with gold or silver.

Paper, circulating in this manner, and for this purpose, continually points to the place and person where, and of whom, the money is to be had, and at last finds its home; and, as it were, unlocks its master's chest and pays the bearer.

But when an assembly undertake to issue paper *as* money, the whole system of safety and certainty is overturned, and property set afloat. Paper notes given and taken between individuals as a promise of payment is one thing, but paper issued by an assembly *as* money is another thing. It is like putting an apparition in the place of a man; it vanishes with looking at it, and nothing remains but the air.

Money, when considered as the fruit of many years' industry, as the reward of labour, sweat and toil, as the widow's dowry and children's portion, and as the means of procuring the necessaries and alleviating the afflictions of life, and making old age a scene of rest, has something in it sacred that is not to be sported with, or trusted to the airy bubble of paper currency.

By what power or authority an assembly undertakes to make paper money, is difficult to say. It derives none from the Constitution, for that is silent on the subject. It is one of those things which the people have not delegated, and which, were they at any time assembled together, they would not delegate. It is, therefore, an assumption of power which an assembly is not warranted in, and which may, one day or other, be the means of bringing some of them to punishment.

I shall enumerate some of the evils of paper money and conclude with offering means for preventing them.

One of the evils of paper money is, that it turns the whole country into stock jobbers. The precariousness of its value and the uncertainty of its fate continually operate, night and day, to produce this destructive effect. Having no real value in itself it depends for support upon accident, caprice and party, and as it is the interest of some to depreciate and of others to raise its value, there is a continual invention going on that destroys the morals of the country.

It was horrid to see, and hurtful to recollect, how loose the principles of justice were left, by means of the paper emissions during the war. The experience then had, should be a warning to any assembly how they venture to open such a dangerous door again.

As to the romantic, if not hypocritical, tale that a virtuous people need no gold and silver, and that paper will do as well, it requires no other contradiction than the experience we have seen. Though some well-meaning people may be inclined to view it in this light, it is certain that the sharper always talks this language.

There are a set of men who go about making purchases upon credit, and buying estates they have not wherewithal to pay for; and having done this, their next step is to fill the newspapers with paragraphs of the scarcity of money and the necessity of a paper emission, then to have a legal tender under the pretence of supporting its credit, and when out, to depreciate it as fast as they can, get a deal of it for a little price, and cheat their creditors; and this is the concise history of paper money schemes.

But why, since the universal custom of the world has established money as the most convenient medium of traffic and commerce, should paper be set up in preference to gold and silver? The productions of nature are surely as innocent as those of art; and in the case of money, are abundantly, if not infinitely, more so. The love of gold and silver may produce covetousness, but covetousness, when not connected with dishonesty, is not properly a vice. It is frugality run to an extreme.

But the evils of paper money have no end. Its uncertain and fluctuating value is continually awakening or creating new schemes of deceit. Every principle of justice is put to the rack, and the bond of society dissolved: the suppression, therefore, of paper money might very properly have been put into the act for preventing vice and immorality.

The pretence for paper money has been, that there was not a sufficiency of gold and silver. This, so far from being a reason for paper emissions, is a reason against them.

As gold and silver are not the productions of North America, they are, therefore, articles of importation; and if we set up a paper manufactory of money it amounts, as far as it is able, to prevent the importation of hard money, or to send it out again as fast it comes in; and by following this practice we shall continually banish the specie, till we have none left, and be continually complaining of the grievance instead of remedying the cause.

Considering gold and silver as articles of importation, there will in time, unless we prevent it by paper emissions, be as much in the country as the occasions of it require, for the same reasons there are as much of other imported articles. But as every yard of cloth manufactured in the country occasions a yard the less to be imported, so it is by money, with this difference, that in the one case we manufacture the thing itself and in the other we do not. We have cloth for cloth, but we have only paper dollars for silver ones.

As to the assumed authority of any assembly in making paper money, or paper of any kind, a legal tender, or in other language, a compulsive payment, it is a most presumptuous attempt at arbitrary power. There can be no such power in a republican government: the people have no freedom, and property no security where this practice can be acted: and the committee who shall bring in a report for this purpose, or the member who moves for it, and he who seconds it merits impeachment, and sooner or later may expect it.

Of all the various sorts of base coin, paper money is the basest. It has the least intrinsic value of anything that can be put in the place of gold and silver. A hobnail or a piece of wampum far exceeds it. And there would be more propriety in making those articles a legal tender than to make paper so. . . .

Most of the advocates for tender laws are those who have debts to discharge, and who take refuge in such a law, to violate their contracts and cheat their creditors. But as no law can warrant the doing an unlawful act, therefore the proper mode of proceeding, should any such laws be enacted in future, will be to impeach and execute the members who moved for and seconded such a bill, and put the debtor and the creditor in the same situation they were in, with respect to each other, before such a law was passed. Men ought to be made to tremble at the idea of such a bare-faced act of injustice. It is in vain to talk of restoring credit, or complain that money cannot be borrowed at legal interest, until every idea of tender laws is totally and publicly reprobated and extirpated from among us.

As to paper money, in any light it can be viewed, it is at best a bubble. Considered as property, it is inconsistent to suppose that the breath of an assembly, whose authority expires with the year, can give to paper the value and duration of gold. They cannot even engage that the next assembly shall receive it in taxes. And by the precedent (for authority there is none), that one assembly makes paper money, another may do the same, until confidence and credit are totally expelled, and all the evils of depreciation acted over again. The amount, therefore, of paper money is this, that it is the illegitimate offspring of assemblies, and when their year expires, they leave a vagrant on the hands of the public.

Having now gone through the three subjects proposed in the title to this work, I shall conclude with offering some thoughts on the present affairs of the state.

My idea of a single legislature was always founded on a hope, that whatever personal parties there might be in the state, they would all unite and agree in the general principles of good government – that these party differences would be dropped at the threshold of the state house, and that the public good, or the good of the whole, would be the governing principle of the legislature within it.

Party dispute, taken on this ground, would only be, who should have the honour of making the laws; not what the laws should be. But when party operates to produce party laws, a single house is a single person, and subject to the haste, rashness and passion of individual sovereignty. At least, it is an aristocracy.

The form of the present Constitution is now made to trample on its principles, and the constitutional members are anti-constitutional legislators. They are fond of supporting the form for the sake of the power, and they dethrone the principle to display the sceptre.

The attack of the late Assembly on the bank, discovers such a want of moderation and prudence, of impartiality and equity, of fair and candid inquiry and investigation, of deliberate and unbiased judgement, and such a rashness of thinking and vengeance of power, as is inconsistent with the safety of the republic. It was judging without hearing, and executing without trial.

By such rash, injudicious and violent proceedings, the interest of the state is weakened, its prosperity diminished, and its commerce and its specie banished to other places. Suppose the bank had not been in an immediate condition to have stood such a sudden attack, what a scene of instant distress would the rashness of that Assembly have brought upon this city and state. The holders of bank notes, whoever they might be, would have been thrown into the utmost confusion and difficulties. It is no apology to say the House never thought of this, for it was their duty to have thought of everything.

But by the prudent and provident management of the bank

(though unsuspicious of the attack), it was enabled to stand the run upon it, without stopping payment a moment, and to prevent the evils and mischiefs taking place which the rashness of the Assembly had a direct tendency to bring on; a trial that scarcely a bank in Europe, under a similar circumstance, could have withstood.

I cannot see reason sufficient to believe that the hope of the House to put down the bank was placed on the withdrawing the charter, so much as on the expectation of producing a bankruptcy of the bank, by starting a run upon it. If this was any part of their project it was a very wicked one, because hundreds might have been ruined to gratify a party spleen.

But this not being the case, what has the attack amounted to, but to expose the weakness and rashness, the want of judgement as well as justice, of those who made it, and to confirm the credit of the bank more substantially than it was before?

The attack, it is true, has had one effect, which is not in the power of the Assembly to remedy; it has banished many thousand hard dollars from the state. By means of the bank, Pennsylvania had the use of a great deal of hard money belonging to citizens of other states, and that without any interest, for it laid here in the nature of deposit, the depositors taking bank notes in its stead. But the alarm called those notes in and the owners drew out their cash.

The banishing the specie served to make room for the paper money of the Assembly and we have now paper dollars where we might have had silver ones. So that the effect of the paper money has been to make less money in the state than there was before. Paper money is like dram-drinking, it relieves for a moment by deceitful sensation, but gradually diminishes the natural heat, and leaves the body worse than it found it. Were not this the case, and could money be made of paper at pleasure, every sovereign in Europe would be as rich as he pleased. But the truth is, that it is a bubble and the attempt vanity. Nature has provided the proper materials for money, gold and silver, and any attempt of ours to rival her is ridiculous.

But to conclude. If the public will permit the opinion of a friend who is attached to no party, and under obligation to none, nor at variance with any, and who through a long habit of acquaintance with them has never deceived them, that opinion shall be freely given.

The bank is an institution capable of being made exceedingly beneficial to the state, not only as the means of extending and facilitating its commerce, but as a means of increasing the quantity of hard money in the state. The Assembly's paper money serves directly to banish or crowd out the hard, because it is issued *as* money and put in the place of hard money. But bank notes are of a very different kind, and produce a contrary effect. They are promissory notes payable on demand, and may be taken to the bank and exchanged for gold or silver without the least ceremony or difficulty.

The bank, therefore, is obliged to keep a constant stock of hard money sufficient for this purpose; which is what the Assembly neither does, nor can do by their paper; because the quantity of hard money collected by taxes into the treasury is trifling compared with the quantity that circulates in trade and through the bank.

The method, therefore, to increase the quantity of hard money would be to combine the security of the government and the bank into one. And instead of issuing paper money that serves to banish the specie, to borrow the sum wanted of the bank in bank notes, on the condition of the bank exchanging those notes at stated periods and quantities, with hard money.

Paper issued in this manner, and directed to this end, would, instead of banishing, work itself into gold and silver; because it will then be both the advantage and duty of the bank and of all the mercantile interests connected with it, to procure and import gold and silver from any part of the world, to give in exchange for the notes. The English Bank is restricted to the dealing in no other articles of importation than gold and silver, and we may make the same use of our bank if we proceed properly with it.

Those notes will then have a double security, that of the Government and that of the bank: and they will not be issued *as* money, but as hostages to be exchanged for hard money, and will, therefore, work the contrary way to what the paper of the assembly, uncombined with the security of the bank, produces: and the interest allowed the bank will be saved to the Government, by a saving of the expenses and charged attending paper emissions.

It is, as I have already observed in the course of this work, the harmony of all the parts of a republic, that constitutes their several and mutual good. A government that is constructed only to govern, is not a republican government. It is combining authority with usefulness, that in a great measure distinguishes the republican system from others.

Paper money appears, at first sight, to be a great saving, or rather that it costs nothing; but it is the dearest money there is. The ease with which it is emitted by an assembly at first, serves as a trap to catch people in at last. It operates as an anticipation of the next year's taxes. If the money depreciates, after it is out, it then, as I have already remarked, has the effect of fluctuating stock, and the people become stock-jobbers to throw the loss on each other.

If it does not depreciate, it is then to be sunk by taxes at the price of *hard money*; because the same quantity of produce, or goods, that would procure a paper dollar to pay taxes with, would procure a silver one for the same purpose. Therefore, in any case of paper money, it is dearer to the country than hard money, by all the expense which the paper, printing, signing, and other attendant charges come to, and at last goes into the fire.

Suppose one hundred thousand dollars in paper money to be emitted every year by the assembly, and the same sum to be sunk every year by taxes, there will then be no more than one hundred thousand dollars out at any one time. If the expense of paper and printing, and of persons to attend the press while the sheets are striking off, signers, etc., be five per cent, it is evident that in the course of twenty years' emissions, the one hundred thousand dollars will cost the country two hundred thousand dollars. Because the papermaker's and printer's bills, and the expense of supervisors and signers, and other attendant charges, will in that time amount to as much as the money amounts to; for the successive emissions are but a re-coinage of the same sum.

But gold and silver require to be coined but once, and will last an hundred years, better than paper will one year, and at the end of that time be still gold and silver. Therefore, the saving to government, in combining its aid and security with that of the bank in procuring hard money, will be an advantage to both, and to the whole community.

The case to be provided against, after this, will be, that the Government do not borrow too much of the bank, nor the bank lend more notes than it can redeem; and, therefore, should anything of this kind be undertaken, the best way will be to begin with a moderate sum, and observe the effect of it. The interest given the bank operates as a bounty on the importation of hard money, and which may not be more than the money expended in making paper emissions.

But nothing of this kind, nor any other public undertaking, that requires security and duration beyond the year, can be gone upon under the present mode of conducting government. The late Assembly, by assuming a sovereign power over every act and matter done by the state in former assemblies, and thereby setting up a precedent of overhauling, and overturning, as the accident of elections shall happen or party prevail, have rendered government incompetent to all the great objects of the state. They have eventually reduced the public to an annual body like themselves; whereas the public are a standing, permanent body, holding annual elections.

There are several great improvements and undertakings, such as inland navigation, building bridges, opening roads of communication through the state, and other matters of a public benefit, that might be gone upon, but which now cannot, until this governmental error or defect is remedied. The faith of government, under the present mode of conducting it, cannot be relied on. Individuals will not venture their money in undertakings of this kind, on an act that may be made by one assembly and broken by another.

When a man can say that he cannot trust the Government, the importance and dignity of the public is diminished, sapped and undermined; and, therefore, it becomes the public to restore their own honour by setting these matters to rights.

Perhaps this cannot be effectually done until the time of the next convention, when the principles, on which they are to be regulated and fixed, may be made a part of the constitution.

In the meantime the public may keep their affairs in sufficient good order, by substituting prudence in the place of authority, and electing men into the Government, who will at once throw aside the narrow prejudices of party, and make the good of the whole the ruling object of their conduct. And with this hope, and a sincere wish for their prosperity, I close my book.

[11] THE RIGHTS OF MAN

(1791–2)

In this his largest and most important work Paine spells out the principles of his radical liberal faith. Part One, dedicated to George Washington, is a point-by-point rebuttal of Edmund Burke's Reflections on the Revolution in France *(1790). Shortly after its publication in London in February 1791, Part One was translated into French and also published in America with an accompanying letter from Jefferson hailing once again 'the standard of Common Sense'. President Andrew Jackson would later claim that* The Rights of Man *would 'be more enduring than all the piles of marble and granite man can erect'. Along with excerpts from Part One, the text here includes chapters from Part Two, published in February 1792. Dedicated to Lafayette, Part Two of* The Rights of Man *is said to have sold nearly a million and a half copies during Paine's lifetime. Part Two contains Paine's most progressive social programmes. Shortly after its publication Paine fled Britain for France. Three months later he was found guilty of seditious libel for having written* The Rights of Man. *Paine never returned to Britain.*

PART ONE

Among the incivilities by which nations or individuals provoke and irritate each other, Mr Burke's pamphlet on the French Revolution is an extraordinary instance. Neither the People of France, nor the National Assembly, were troubling themselves about the affairs of England, or the English Parliament; and why Mr Burke should commence an unprovoked attack upon them, both in parliament and in public, is a conduct that cannot be pardoned on the score of manners, nor justified on that of policy.

There is scarcely an epithet of abuse to be found in the English language, with which Mr Burke has not loaded the French Nation and the National Assembly. Everything which rancour, prejudice, ignorance, or knowledge could suggest, are poured forth in the copious fury of near four hundred pages. In the strain and on the plan Mr Burke was writing, he might have written on to as many thousands. When the tongue or the pen is let loose in a frenzy of passion, it is the man, and not the subject, that becomes exhausted.

Hitherto Mr Burke has been mistaken and disappointed in the opinions he had formed of the affairs of France; but such is the ingenuity of his hope, or the malignancy of his despair, that it furnishes him with new pretences to go on. There was a time when it was impossible to make Mr Burke believe there would be any revolution in France. His opinion then was, that the French had neither spirit to undertake it, nor fortitude to support it; and now that there is one, he seeks an escape, by condemning it.

Not sufficiently content with abusing the National Assembly, a great part of his work is taken up with abusing Dr Price (one of the best-hearted men that lives), and the two societies in England known by the name of the Revolution Society, and the Society for Constitutional Information.

Dr Price had preached a sermon on the 4th of November 1789, being the anniversary of what is called in England, the Revolution which took place 1688. Mr Burke, speaking of this sermon, says, 'The Political Divine proceeds dogmatically to assert, that, by the principles of the Revolution, the people of England have acquired three fundamental rights:

'1. To choose our own governors.

2. To cashier them for misconduct.

3. To frame a government for ourselves.'

Dr Price does not say that the right to do these things exists in this or in that person, or in this or in that description of persons, but that it exists in the *whole*; that it is a right resident in the nation. – Mr Burke, on the contrary, denies that such a right exists in the nation, either in whole or in part, or that it exists anywhere; and, what is still more strange and marvellous, he says, 'that the people of England utterly disclaim such a right, and that they will resist the practical assertion of it with their lives and fortunes'. That men should take up arms, and spend their lives and fortunes, *not* to maintain their rights, but to maintain they have *not* rights, is an entirely new species of discovery, and suited to the paradoxical genius of Mr Burke.

The method which Mr Burke takes to prove that the people of England have no such rights, and that such rights do not now exist in the nation, either in whole or in part, or anywhere at all, is of the same marvellous and monstrous kind with what he has already said; for his arguments are, that the persons, or the generation of persons, in whom they did exist, are dead, and with them the right is dead also. To prove this, he quotes a declaration made by parliament about a hundred years ago, to William and Mary, in these words: 'The Lords Spiritual and Temporal, and Commons, do, in the name of the people aforesaid' – (meaning the people of England then living) – 'most humbly and faithfully *submit* themselves, their *heirs* and *posterities*, for EVER.' He also quotes a clause of another act of parliament made in the same reign, the terms of which, he says, 'bind us' – (meaning the people of that day) – 'our *heirs*, and our *posterity*, to *them*, their *heirs* and *posterity*, to the end of time'.

Mr Burke conceives his point sufficiently established by producing those clauses, which he enforces by saying that they exclude the right of the nation for *ever*: And not yet content with making such declarations, repeated over and over again, he farther says, 'that if the people of England possessed such a right before the Revolution', (which he acknowledges to have been the case, not only in England, but throughout Europe, at an early period), 'yet that the *English nation* did, at the time of the Revolution, most solemnly renounce and abdicate it, for themselves, and for *all their posterity, for ever*'.

As Mr Burke occasionally applies the poison drawn from his horrid principles, not only to the English nation, but to the French Revolution and the National Assembly, and charges that august, illuminated and illuminating body of men with the epithet of *usurpers*, I shall, *sans ceremonie*, place another system of principles in opposition to his.

The English Parliament of 1688 did a certain thing, which, for themselves and their constituents, they had a right to do, and which it appeared right should be done: But, in addition to this right, which they possessed by delegation, *they set up another right by assumption*, that of binding and controlling posterity to the end of time. The case, therefore, divides itself into two parts; the right which they possessed by delegation, and the right which they set up by assumption. The first is admitted; but, with respect to the second, I reply –

There never did, there never will, and there never can exist a parliament, or any description of men, or any generation of men, in any country, possessed of the right or the power of binding and controlling posterity to the '*end of time*', or of commanding for ever how the world shall be governed, or who shall govern it; and therefore, all such clauses, acts or declarations, by which the makers of them attempt to do what they have neither the right nor the power to do, nor the power to execute, are in themselves null and void. — Every age and generation must be as free to act for itself, *in all cases*, as the ages and generations which preceded it. The vanity and presumption of governing beyond the grave, is the most ridiculous and insolent of all tyrannies. Man has no property in man; neither has any generation a property in the generations which are to follow. The parliament or the people of 1688, or of any other period, has no more right to dispose of the people of the present day, or to bind or to control them *in any shape whatever*, than the parliament or the people of the present day have to dispose of, bind or control those who are to live a hundred or a thousand years hence. Every generation is, and must be, competent to all the purposes which its occasions require. It is the living, and not the dead, that are to be accommodated. When man ceases to be, his power and his wants cease with him; and having no longer any participation in the concerns of this world, he has no longer any authority in directing who shall be its governors, or how its government shall be organized, or how administered.

I am not contending for nor against any form of government, nor for nor against any party here or elsewhere. That which a whole nation chooses to do, it has a right to do. Mr Burke says, No. Where then *does* the right exist? I am contending for the rights of the *living*, and against their being willed away, and controlled and contracted for, by the manuscript assumed authority of the dead; and Mr Burke is contending for the authority of the dead over the rights and freedom of the living. There was a time when kings disposed of their crowns by will upon their deathbeds, and consigned the people, like beasts of the field, to whatever successor they appointed. This is now so exploded as scarcely to be remembered, and so monstrous as hardly to be believed: But the parliamentary clauses upon which Mr Burke builds his political church, are of the same nature.

The laws of every country must be analogous to some common principle. In England, no parent or master, nor all the authority of parliament, omnipotent as it has called itself, can bind or control the personal freedom even of an individual beyond the age of twenty-one years: On what ground of right, then, could the parliament of 1688, or any other parliament, bind all posterity for ever?

Those who have quitted the world, and those who are not yet arrived at it, are as remote from each other, as the utmost stretch of mortal imagination can conceive: What possible obligation, then, can exist between them; what rule or principle can be laid down, that of two non-entities, the one out of existence, and the other not in, and who never can meet in this world, the one should control the other to the end of time?

In England, it is said that money cannot be taken out of the pockets of the people without their consent: But who authorized, or who could authorize the parliament of 1688 to control and take away the freedom of posterity, (who were not in existence to give or to withhold their consent), and limit and confine their right of acting in certain cases for ever?

A greater absurdity cannot present itself to the understanding of man, than what Mr Burke offers to his readers. He tells them, and he tells the world to come, that a certain body of men, who existed a hundred years ago, made a law; and that there does not now exist in the nation, nor ever will, nor ever can, a power to alter it. Under how many subtleties, or absurdities, has the divine right to govern been imposed on the credulity of mankind! Mr Burke has discovered a new one, and he has shortened his journey to Rome, by appealing to the power of this infallible parliament of former days; and he produces what it has done, as of divine authority: for that power must certainly be more than human, which no human power to the end of time can alter.

But Mr Burke has done some service, not to his cause, but to his country, by bringing those clauses into public view. They serve to demonstrate how necessary it is at all times to watch against the attempted encroachment of power, and to prevent its running to excess. It is somewhat extraordinary, that the offence for which James II was expelled, that of setting up power by *assumption*, should be re-acted, under another shape and form, by the parliament that expelled him. It shows, that the rights of man were but imperfectly understood at the Revolution; for, certain it is, that the right which that parliament set up by *assumption* (for by delegation it had it not, and could not have it, because none could give it) over the persons and freedom of posterity for ever, was of the same tyrannical unfounded kind which James attempted to set up over the parliament and the nation, and for which he was expelled. The only difference is, (for in principle they differ not), that the one was an usurper over the living, and the other over the unborn; and as the one has no better authority to stand upon than the other, both of them must be equally null and void, and of no effect.

From what, or from whence, does Mr Burke prove the right of any human power to bind posterity for ever? He has produced his clauses; but he must produce also his proofs, that such a right existed, and show how it existed. If it ever existed, it must now exist; for whatever appertains to the nature of man, cannot be annihilated by man. It is the nature of man to die, and he will continue to die as long as he continues to be born. But Mr Burke has set up a sort of political Adam, in whom all posterity are bound for ever, he must therefore prove that his Adam possessed such a power, or such a right.

The weaker any cord is, the less will it bear to be stretched, and the worse is the policy to stretch it, unless it is intended to break it. Had any one purposed the overthrow of Mr Burke's positions, he would have proceeded as Mr Burke has done. He would have magnified the authorities, on purpose to have called the *right* of them into question; and the instant the question of right was started, the authorities must have been given up.

It requires but a very small glance of thought to perceive, that although laws made in one generation often continue in force through succeeding generations, yet that they continue to derive their force from the consent of the living. A law not repealed continues in force, not because it *cannot* be repealed, but because it *is not* repealed; and the non-repealing passes for consent.

But Mr Burke's clauses have not even this qualification in their favour. They become null, by attempting to become immortal. The nature of them precludes consent. They destroy the right which they *might* have, by grounding it on a right which they *cannot* have. Immortal power is not a human right, and therefore cannot be a right of parliament. The parliament of 1688 might as well have passed an act to have authorized themselves to live for ever, as to make their authority live for ever. All therefore that can be said of those clauses is, that they are a formality of words, of as much import, as if those who used them had addressed a congratulation to themselves, and, in the oriental style of antiquity, had said, O Parliament, live for ever!

The circumstances of the world are continually changing, and the opinions of men change also; and as government is for the living, and not for the dead, it is the living only that has any right in it. That which may be thought right and found convenient in one age, may be thought wrong and found inconvenient in another. In such cases, Who is to decide, the living, or the dead?

As almost one hundred pages of Mr Burke's book are employed upon these clauses, it will consequently follow, that if the clauses themselves, so far as they set up an *assumed, usurped* dominion over posterity for ever, are unauthoritative, and in their nature null and void; that all his voluminous inferences and declamation drawn therefrom, or founded thereon, are null and void also: and on this ground I rest the matter.

We now come more particularly to the affairs of France. Mr Burke's book has the appearance of being written as instruction to the French nation; but if I may permit myself the use of an extravagant metaphor, suited to the extravagance of the case, It is darkness attempting to illuminate light.

While I am writing this, there are accidentally before me some proposals for a declaration of rights by the Marquis de Lafayette (I ask his pardon for using his former address, and do it only for distinction's sake) to the National Assembly, on the 11th of July 1789, three days before the taking of the Bastille; and I cannot but remark with astonishment how opposite the sources are from which that Gentleman and Mr Burke draw their principles. Instead of referring to musty records and mouldy parchments to prove that the rights of the living are lost, 'renounced and abdicated for ever', by those who are now no more, as Mr Burke has done, M. de Lafayette applies to the living world, and emphatically says, 'Call to mind the sentiments which Nature has engraved in the heart of every citizen, and which take a new force when they are solemnly recognized by all: – For a nation to love liberty, it is sufficient that she knows it; and to be free, it is sufficient that she wills it.' How dry, barren and obscure, is the source from which Mr Burke labours! and how ineffectual, though gay with flowers, are all his declamation and his arguments, compared with these clear, concise, and soul-animating sentiments! Few and short as they are, they lead on to a vast field of generous and manly thinking, and do not finish, like Mr Burke's periods, with music in the ear, and nothing in the heart.

As I have introduced M. de Lafayette, I will take the liberty of adding an anecdote respecting his farewell address to the Congress of

America in 1783, and which occurred fresh to my mind when I saw
Mr Burke's thundering attack on the French Revolution. – M. de
Lafayette went to America at an early period of the war, and continued a volunteer in her service to the end. His conduct through the
whole of that enterprise is one of the most extraordinary that is to be
found in the history of a young man, scarcely then twenty years of
age. Situated in a country that was like the lap of sensual pleasure,
and with the means of enjoying it, how few are there to be found
who would exchange such a scene for the woods and wildernesses of
America, and pass the flowery years of youth in unprofitable danger
and hardship! but such is the fact. When the war ended, and he was
on the point of taking his final departure, he presented himself to
Congress, and contemplating, in his affectionate farewell, the revolution he had seen, expressed himself in these words: *'May this
great monument, raised to Liberty, serve as a lesson to the oppressor, and an
example to the oppressed!'* – When this address came to the hands of
Dr Franklin, who was then in France, he applied to Count Vergennes
to have it inserted in the French Gazette, but never could obtain his
consent. The fact was, that Count Vergennes was an aristocratical
despot at home, and dreaded the example of the American Revolution in France, as certain other persons now dread the example of the
French Revolution in England; and Mr Burke's tribute of fear (for in
this light his book must be considered) runs parallel with Count
Vergennes' refusal. But, to return more particularly to his work –
'We have seen' (says Mr Burke) 'the French rebel against a mild and
lawful Monarch, with more fury, outrage, and insult, than any people
has been known to rise against the most illegal usurper, or the most
sanguinary tyrant.' – This is one among a thousand other instances,
in which Mr Burke shows that he is ignorant of the springs and
principles of the French Revolution.

It was not against Louis the XVIth, but against the despotic principles of the government, that the nation revolted. These principles
had not their origin in him, but in the original establishment, many
centuries back; and they were become too deeply rooted to be
removed, and the augean stable of parasites and plunderers too
abominably filthy to be cleansed, by anything short of a complete
and universal revolution. When it becomes necessary to do a thing,
the whole heart and soul should go into the measure, or not attempt
it. That crisis was then arrived, and there remained no choice but to

act with determined vigour, or not to act at all. The king was known to be the friend of the nation, and this circumstance was favourable to the enterprise. Perhaps no man bred up in the style of an absolute King, ever possessed a heart so little disposed to the exercise of that species of power as the present King of France. But the principles of the government itself still remained the same. The Monarch and the Monarchy were distinct and separate things; and it was against the established despotism of the latter, and not against the person or principles of the former, that the revolt commenced, and the revolution has been carried.

Mr Burke does not attend to the distinction between *men* and *principles*; and therefore, he does not see that a revolt may take place against the despotism of the latter, while there lies no charge of despotism against the former.

The natural moderation of Louis XVI contributed nothing to alter the hereditary despotism of the monarchy. All the tyrannies of former reigns, acted under that hereditary despotism, were still liable to be revived in the hands of a successor. It was not the respite of a reign that would satisfy France, enlightened as she was then become. A casual discontinuance of the *practice* of despotism, is not a discontinuance of its *principles*; the former depends on the virtue of the individual who is in immediate possession of the power; the latter, on the virtue and fortitude of the nation. In the case of Charles I and James II of England, the revolt was against the personal despotism of the men; whereas in France, it was against the hereditary despotism of the established government. But men who can consign over the rights of posterity for ever on the authority of a mouldy parchment, like Mr Burke, are not qualified to judge of this revolution. It takes in a field too vast for their views to explore, and proceeds with a mightiness of reason they cannot keep pace with.

But there are many points of view in which this revolution may be considered. When despotism has established itself for ages in a country, as in France, it is not in the person of the King only that it resides. It has the appearance of being so in show, and in nominal authority; but it is not so in practice, and in fact. It has its standard everywhere. Every office and department has its despotism, founded upon custom and usage. Every place has its Bastille, and every Bastille its despot. The original hereditary despotism resident in the person of the King, divides and subdivides itself into a thousand shapes and forms, till at last the whole of it is acted by deputation. This was the case in France; and against this species of despotism, proceeding on through an endless labyrinth of office till the source of it is scarcely perceptible, there is no mode of redress. It strengthens itself by assuming the appearance of duty, and tyrannizes under the pretence of obeying.

When a man reflects on the condition which France was in from the nature of her government, he will see other causes for revolt than those which immediately connect themselves with the person or character of Louis XVI. There were, if I may so express it, a thousand despotisms to be reformed in France, which had grown up under the hereditary despotism of the monarchy, and became so rooted as to be in a great measure independent of it. Between the monarchy, the parliament, and the church, there was a *rivalship* of despotism, besides the feudal despotism operating locally, and the ministerial despotism operating everywhere. But Mr Burke, by considering the King as the only possible object of a revolt, speaks as if France was a village, in which everything that passed must be known to its commanding officer, and no oppression could be acted but what he could immediately control. Mr Burke might have been in the Bastille his whole life, as well under Louis XVI as Louis XIV and neither the one nor the other have known that such a man as Mr Burke existed. The despotic principles of the government were the same in both reigns, though the dispositions of the men were as remote as tyranny and benevolence.

What Mr Burke considers as a reproach to the French Revolution, (that of bringing it forward under a reign more mild than the preceding ones), is one of its highest honours. The revolutions that have taken place in other European countries, have been excited by personal hatred. The rage was against the man, and he became the victim. But, in the instance of France, we see a revolution generated in the rational contemplation of the rights of man, and distinguishing from the beginning between persons and principles.

But Mr Burke appears to have no idea of principles, when he is contemplating governments. 'Ten years ago' (says he) 'I could have felicitated France on her having a government, without inquiring what the nature of that government was, or how it was administered.' Is this the language of a rational man? Is it the language of a heart feeling as it ought to feel for the rights and happiness of the human race? On this ground, Mr Burke must compliment all the governments in the world, while the victims who suffer under them, whether sold into slavery, or tortured out of existence, are wholly forgotten. It is power, and not principles, that Mr Burke venerates; and under this abominable depravity, he is disqualified to judge between them. – Thus much for his opinion as to the occasions of the French Revolution. I now proceed to other considerations.

I know a place in America called Point-no-Point; because as you proceed along the shore, gay and flowery as Mr Burke's language, it continually recedes and presents itself at a distance before you; but when you have got as far as you can go, there is no point at all. Just thus it is with Mr Burke's three hundred and fifty-six pages. It is therefore difficult to reply to him. But as the points he wishes to establish, may be inferred from what he abuses, it is in his paradoxes that we must look for his arguments.

As the tragic paintings by which Mr Burke has outraged his own imagination, and seeks to work upon that of his readers, they are very well calculated for theatrical representation, where facts are manufactured for the sake of show, and accommodated to produce, through the weakness of sympathy, a weeping effect. But Mr Burke should recollect that he is writing History, and not *Plays*; and that his readers will expect truth, and not the spouting rant of high-toned exclamation.

When we see a man dramatically lamenting in a publication intended to be believed, that, '*The age of chivalry is gone!*' that '*The glory of Europe is extinguished for ever!*' that '*The unbought grace of life*' (if any one knows what it is), '*the cheap defences of nations, the nurse of manly sentiment and heroic enterprise, is gone!*' and all this because the Quixote age of chivalry nonsense is gone, what opinion can we form of his judgement, or what regard can we pay to his facts? In the rhapsody of his imagination, he had discovered a world of windmills, and his sorrows are, that there are no Quixotes to attack them. But if the age of aristocracy, like that of chivalry, should fall, (and they had originally some connection), Mr Burke, the trumpeter of the Order, may continue his parody to the end, and finish with exclaiming, '*Othello's occupation's gone!*'

Notwithstanding Mr Burke's horrid paintings, when the French Revolution is compared with the revolutions of other countries, the astonishment will be, that it is marked with so few sacrifices; but this astonishment will cease when we reflect that *principles*, and not *persons*, were the meditated objects of destruction. The mind of the nation was acted upon by a higher stimulus than what the consideration of persons could inspire, and sought a higher conquest than could be produced by the downfall of an enemy. Among the few who fell, there do not appear to be any that were intentionally singled out. They all of them had their fate in the circumstances of the moment, and were not pursued with that long, cold-blooded, unabated revenge which pursued the unfortunate Scotch in the affair of 1745.

Through the whole of Mr Burke's book I do not observe that the Bastille is mentioned more than once, and that with a kind of implication as if he were sorry it was pulled down, and wished it were built up again. 'We have rebuilt Newgate' (says he), 'and tenanted the mansion; and we have prisons almost as strong as the Bastille for those who dare to libel the Queens of France.'[1] As to what a madman, like the person called Lord G— G—, might say, and to whom Newgate is rather a bedlam than a prison, it is unworthy a rational consideration. It was a madman that libelled — and that is sufficient apology; and it afforded an opportunity for confining him, which was the thing that was wished for: But certain it is that Mr Burke, who does not call himself a madman, (whatever other people may do), has libelled, in the most unprovoked manner, and in the grossest style of the most vulgar abuse, the whole representative authority of France; and yet Mr Burke takes his seat in the British House of Commons! From his violence and his grief, his silence on some points, and his excess on others, it is difficult not to believe that Mr Burke is sorry, extremely sorry, that arbitrary power, the power of the Pope, and the Bastille, are pulled down.

Not one glance of compassion, not one commiserating reflection, that I can find throughout his book, has he bestowed on those who

1 Since writing the above, two other places occur in Mr Burke's pamphlet, in which the name of the Bastille is mentioned, but in the same manner. In the one, he introduces it in a sort of obscure question, and asks — 'Will any ministers who now serve such a king, with but a decent appearance of respect, cordially obey the orders of those whom but the other day, *in his name*, they had committed to the Bastille?' In the other, the taking it is mentioned as implying criminality in the French guards who assisted in demolishing it. — 'They have not' (says he) 'forgot the taking the king's castles at Paris.' — This is Mr Burke, who pretends to write on constitutional freedom. — Paine.

lingered out the most wretched of lives, a life without hope, in the most miserable of prisons. It is painful to behold a man employing his talents to corrupt himself. Nature has been kinder to Mr Burke than he is to her. He is not affected by the reality of distress touching his heart, but by the showy resemblance of it striking his imagination. He pities the plumage, but forgets the dying bird. Accustomed to kiss the aristocratical hand that hath purloined him from himself, he degenerates into a composition of art, and the genuine soul of nature forsakes him. His hero or his heroine must be a tragedy-victim expiring in show, and not the real prisoner of misery, sliding into death in the silence of a dungeon. . . .

Lay then the axe to the root, and teach governments humanity. It is their sanguinary punishments which corrupt mankind. In England, the punishment in certain cases, is by *hanging, drawing*, and *quartering*; the heart of the sufferer is cut out, and held up to the view of the populace. In France, under the former government, the punishments were not less barbarous. Who does not remember the execution of Damien, torn to pieces by horses? The effect of those cruel spectacles exhibited to the populace, is to destroy tenderness, or excite revenge; and by the base and false idea of governing men by terror, instead of reason, they become precedents. It is over the lowest class of mankind that government by terror is intended to operate, and it is on them that it operates to the worst effect. They have sense enough to feel they are the objects aimed at; and they inflict in their turn the examples of terror they have been instructed to practise.

There is in all European countries, a large class of people of that description which in England is called the '*mob*'. Of this class were those who committed the burnings and devastations in London in 1780, and of this class were those who carried the heads upon spikes in Paris. Foulon and Berthier were taken up in the country, and sent to Paris, to undergo their examination at the Hôtel de Ville; for the National Assembly, immediately on the new ministry coming into office, passed a decree, which they communicated to the King and Cabinet, that they (the National Assembly) would hold the ministry, of which Foulon was one, responsible for the measures they were advising and pursuing; but the mob, incensed at the appearance of Foulon and Berthier, tore them from their conductors before they were carried to the Hôtel de Ville, and executed them on the spot. Why then does Mr Burke charge outrages of this kind on a whole people? As well may he charge the riots and outrages of 1780 on all the people of London, or those in Ireland on all his countrymen.

But everything we see or hear offensive to our feelings, and derogatory to the human character, should lead to other reflections than those of reproach. Even the beings who commit them have some claim to our consideration. How then is it that such vast classes of mankind as are distinguished by the appellation of the vulgar, or the ignorant mob, are so numerous in all old countries? The instant we ask ourselves this question, reflection feels an answer. They arise, as an unavoidable consequence, out of the ill construction of all old governments in Europe, England included with the rest. It is by distortedly exalting some men, that others are distortedly debased, till the whole is out of nature. A vast mass of mankind are degradedly thrown into the background of the human picture, to bring forward with greater glare, the puppet-show of State and aristocracy. In the commencement of a revolution, those men are rather the followers of the *camp* than of the *standard* of liberty, and have yet to be instructed how to reverence it.

I give to Mr Burke all his theatrical exaggerations for facts, and I then ask him, if they do not establish the certainty of what I here lay down? Admitting them to be true, they show the necessity of the French Revolution, as much as any one thing he could have asserted. These outrages were not the effect of the principles of the revolution, but of the degraded mind that existed before the revolution, and which the revolution is calculated to reform. Place them then to their proper cause, and take the reproach of them to your own side.

It is to the honour of the National Assembly, and the city of Paris, that during such a tremendous scene of arms and confusion, beyond the control of all authority, they have been able, by the influence of example and exhortation, to restrain so much. Never were more pains taken to instruct and enlighten mankind, and to make them see that their interest consisted in their virtue, and not in their revenge, than have been displayed in the Revolution of France. . . .

Mr Burke, with his usual outrage, abuses the *Declaration of the Rights of Man*, published by the National Assembly of France as the basis on which the constitution of France is built. This he calls 'paltry and blurred sheets of paper about the rights of man'. – Does Mr Burke mean to deny that *man* has any rights? If he does, then he must mean that there are no such things as rights anywhere, and that he has none himself; for who is there in the world but man? But if Mr Burke means to admit that man has rights, the question then will be, What are those rights, and how came man by them originally?

The error of those who reason by precedents drawn from antiquity, respecting the rights of man, is, that they do not go far enough into antiquity. They do not go the whole way. They stop in some of the intermediate stages of an hundred or a thousand years, and produce what was then done, as a rule for the present day. This is no authority at all. If we travel still farther into antiquity, we shall find a direct contrary opinion and practice prevailing; and if antiquity is to be authority, a thousand such authorities may be produced, successively contradicting each other: But if we proceed on, we shall at last come out right; we shall come to the time when man came from the hand of his Maker. What was he then? Man. Man was his high and only title, and a higher cannot be given him. – But of titles I shall speak hereafter.

We are now got at the origin of man, and at the origin of his rights. As to the manner in which the world has been governed from that day to this, it is no further any concern of ours than to make a proper use of the errors or the improvements which the history of it presents. Those who lived a hundred or a thousand years ago, were then moderns, as we are now. They had *their* ancients, and those ancients had others, and we also shall be ancients in our turn. If the mere name of antiquity is to govern in the affairs of life, the people who are to live an hundred or a thousand years hence, may as well take us for a precedent, as we make a precedent of those who lived an hundred or a thousand years ago. The fact is, that portions of antiquity, by proving everything, establish nothing. It is authority against authority all the way, till we come to the divine origin of the rights of man at the creation. Here our inquiries find a resting-place, and our reason finds a home. If a dispute about the rights of man had arisen at the distance of an hundred years from the creation, it is to this source of authority they must have referred, and it is to the same source of authority that we must now refer.

Though I mean not to touch upon any sectarian principle of religion, yet it may be worth observing, that the genealogy of Christ is traced to Adam. Why then not trace the rights of man to the creation of man? I will answer the question. Because there have been upstart governments, thrusting themselves between, and pre-sumptuously working to *un-make* man.

If any generation of men ever possessed the right of dictating the mode by which the world should be governed for ever, it was the first generation that existed; and if that generation did it not, no succeeding generation can show any authority for doing it, nor can set any up. The illuminating and divine principle of the equal rights of man, (for it has its origin from the Maker of man) relates, not only to the living individuals, but to generations of men succeeding each other. Every generation is equal in rights to the generations which preceded it, by the same rule that every individual is born equal in rights with his contemporary.

Every history of the creation, and every traditionary account, whether from the lettered or unlettered world, however they may vary in their opinion or belief of certain particulars, all agree in establishing one point, *the unity of man*; by which I mean, that men are all of *one degree*, and consequently that all men are born equal, and with equal natural right, in the same manner as if posterity had been continued by *creation* instead of *generation*, the latter being only the mode by which the former is carried forward; and consequently, every child born into the world must be considered as deriving its existence from God. The world is as new to him as it was to the first man that existed, and his natural right in it is of the same kind.

The Mosaic account of the creation, whether taken as divine authori-ty, or merely historical, is full to this point, *the unity or equality of man*. The expressions admit of no controversy. 'And God said. Let us make man in our own image. In the image of God created he him; male and female created he them.' The distinction of sexes is pointed out, but no other distinction is even implied. If this be not divine authority, it is at least historical authority, and shows that the equality of man, so far from being a modern doctrine, is the oldest open record.

It is also to be observed, that all the religions known in the world are founded, so far as they relate to man, on the *unity of man*, as being all of one degree. Whether in heaven or in hell, or in whatever state man may be supposed to exist hereafter, the good and the bad are the only distinctions. Nay, even the laws of governments are obliged to slide into this principle, by making degrees to consist in crimes, and not in persons.

It is one of the greatest of all truths, and of the highest advantage to cultivate. By considering man in this light, and by instructing him to consider himself in this light, it places him in a close connection with all his duties, whether to his Creator, or to the creation of which he is a part; and it is only when he forgets his origin, or, to use a more fashionable phrase, his *birth and family*, that he becomes dissolute. It is not among the least of the evils of the present existing governments in all parts of Europe, that man, considered as man, is thrown back to a vast distance from his Maker, and the artificial chasm filled up by a succession of barriers, or sort of turnpike gates, through which he has to pass. I will quote Mr Burke's catalogue of barriers that he has set up between man and his Maker. Putting himself in the character of a herald, he says – 'We fear God – we look with *awe* to kings – with affection to parliaments – with duty to magistrates – with reverence to priests, and with respect to nobility.' Mr Burke has forgotten to put in '*chivalry*'. He has also forgotten to put in Peter.

The duty of man is not a wilderness of turnpike gates, through which he is to pass by tickets from one to the other. It is plain and simple, and consists but of two points. His duty to God, which every man must feel; and with respect to his neighbour, to do as he would be done by. If those to whom power is delegated do well, they will be respected; if not, they will be despised: and with regard to those to whom no power is delegated, but who assume it, the rational world can know nothing of them.

Hitherto we have spoken only (and that but in part) of the natural rights of man. We have now to consider the civil rights of man, and to show how the one originates from the other. Man did not enter into society to become *worse* than he was before, nor to have fewer rights than he had before, but to have those rights better secured. His natural rights are the foundation of all his civil rights. But in order to pursue this distinction with more precision, it will be necessary to mark the different qualities of natural and civil rights.

A few words will explain this. Natural rights are those which appertain to man in right of his existence. Of this kind are all the intellectual rights, or rights of the mind, and also all those rights of acting as an individual for his own comfort and happiness, which are not injurious to the natural rights of others. – Civil rights are those which appertain to man in right of his being a member of society.

Every civil right has for its foundation, some natural right pre-existing in the individual, but to the enjoyment of which his individual power is not, in all cases, sufficiently competent. Of this kind are all those which relate to security and protection.

From this short review, it will be easy to distinguish between that class of natural rights which man retains after entering into society, and those which he throws into the common stock as a member of society.

The natural rights which he retains, are all those in which the *power* to execute is as perfect in the individual as the right itself. Among this class, as is before mentioned, are all the intellectual rights, or rights of the mind: consequently, religion is one of those rights. The natural rights which are not retained, are all those in which, though the right is perfect in the individual, the power to execute them is defective. They answer not his purpose. A man, by natural right, has a right to judge in his own cause; and so far as the right of mind is concerned, he never surrenders it: But what availeth it him to judge, if he has not power to redress? He therefore deposits this right in the common stock of society, and takes the arm of society, of which he is a part, in preference and in addition to his own. Society *grants* him nothing. Every man is a proprietor in society, and draws on the capital as a matter of right.

From these premises, two or three certain conclusions will follow.

First, That every civil right grows out of a natural right; or, in other words, is a natural right exchanged.

Secondly, That civil power, properly considered as such, is made up of the aggregate of that class of the natural rights of man, which becomes defective in the individual in point of power, and answers not his purpose; but when collected to a focus, becomes competent to the purpose of every one.

Thirdly, That the power produced from the aggregate of natural rights, imperfect in power in the individual, cannot be applied to invade the natural rights which are retained in the individual, and in which the power to execute is as perfect as the right itself.

We have now, in a few words, traced man from a natural individual to a member of society, and shown, or endeavoured to show, the quality of the natural rights retained, and of those which are exchanged for civil rights. Let us now apply these principles to governments.

In casting our eyes over the world, it is extremely easy to distinguish the governments which have arisen out of society, or out of the social compact, from those which have not: but to place this in a clearer light than what a single glance may afford, it will be proper to take a review of the several sources from which governments have arisen, and on which they have been founded.

They may be all comprehended under three heads. First, Superstition. Secondly, Power. Thirdly, The common interest of society, and the common rights of man.

The first was a government of priestcraft, the second of conquerors, and the third of reason.

When a set of artful men pretended, through the medium of oracles, to hold intercourse with the Deity, as familiarly as they now march up the back-stairs in European courts, the world was completely under the government of superstition. The oracles were consulted, and whatever they were made to say, became the law; and this sort of government lasted as long as this sort of superstition lasted.

After these a race of conquerors arose, whose government, like that of William the Conqueror, was founded in power, and the sword assumed the name of a sceptre. Governments thus established, last as long as the power to support them lasts; but that they might avail themselves of every engine in their favour, they united fraud to force, and set up an idol which they called *Divine Right*, and which, in imitation of the Pope, who affects to be spiritual and temporal, and in contradiction to the Founder of the Christian religion, twisted itself afterwards into an idol of another shape, called *Church and State*. The key of St Peter, and the key of the Treasury, became quartered on one another, and the wondering cheated multitude worshipped the invention.

When I contemplate the natural dignity of man; when I feel (for Nature has not been kind enough to me to blunt my feelings) for the honour and happiness of its character, I become irritated at the attempt to govern mankind by force and fraud, as if they were all knaves and fools, and can scarcely avoid disgust at those who are thus imposed upon.

We have now to review the governments which arise out of society, in contradistinction to those which arose out of superstition and conquest.

It has been thought a considerable advance towards establishing the principles of Freedom, to say, that government is a compact between those who govern and those who are governed: but this cannot be true, because it is putting the effect before the cause; for as man must have existed before governments existed, there necessarily was a time when governments did not exist, and consequently there could originally exist no governors to form such a compact with. The fact therefore must be, that the *individuals themselves*, each in his own personal and sovereign right, *entered into a compact with each other* to produce a government: and this is the only mode in which governments have a right to arise, and the only principle on which they have a right to exist.

To possess ourselves of a clear idea of what government is, or ought to be, we must trace it to its origin. In doing this, we shall easily discover that governments must have arisen, either *out* of the people, or *over* the people. Mr Burke has made no distinction. He investigates nothing to its source, and therefore he confounds everything: but he has signified his intention of undertaking at some future opportunity, a comparison between the constitutions of England and France. As he thus renders it a subject of controversy by throwing the gauntlet, I take him up on his own ground. It is in high challenges that high truths have the right of appearing; and I accept it with the more readiness, because it affords me, at the same time, an opportunity of pursuing the subject with respect to governments arising out of society.

But it will be first necessary to define what is meant by a *constitution*. It is not sufficient that we adopt the word; we must fix also a standard signification to it.

A constitution is not a thing in name only, but in fact. It has not an ideal, but a real existence; and wherever it cannot be produced in a visible form, there is none. A constitution is a thing *antecedent* to a government, and a government is only the creature of a constitution. The constitution of a country is not the act of its government, but of the people constituting a government. It is the body of elements, to which you can refer, and quote article by article; and which contains the principles on which the government shall be established, the manner in which it shall be organized, the powers it shall have, the mode of elections, the duration of parliaments, or by what other name such bodies may be called; the powers which the executive part of the government shall have; and, in fine, everything that relates to the complete organization of a civil government, and the principles on which it shall act, and by which it shall be bound. A constitution, therefore, is to a government, what the laws made afterwards by that government are to a court of judicature. The court of judicature does not make the laws, neither can it alter them; it only acts in conformity to the laws made: and the government is in like manner governed by the constitution.

Can then Mr Burke produce the English Constitution? If he cannot, we may fairly conclude, that though it has been so much talked about, no such thing as a constitution exists, or ever did exist, and consequently that the people have yet a constitution to form.

Mr Burke will not, I presume, deny the position I have already advanced; namely, that governments arise, either *out* of the people, or *over* the people. The English government is one of those which arose out of a conquest, and not out of society, and, consequently it arose over the people; and though it has been much modified from the opportunity of circumstances since the time of William the Conqueror, the country has never yet regenerated itself, and is therefore without a constitution.

I readily perceive the reason why Mr Burke declined going into the comparison between the English and French constitutions, because he could not but perceive, when he sat down to the task, that no such thing as a constitution existed on his side the question. His book is certainly bulky enough to have contained all he could say on this subject, and it would have been the best manner in which people could have judged of their separate merits. Why then has he declined the only thing that was worth while to write upon? It was the strongest ground he could take, if the advantages were on his side; but the weakest, if they were not: and his declining to take, is either a sign that he could not possess it, or could not maintain it.

Mr Burke said in a speech last winter in parliament, That when the National Assembly first met in three Orders, (the Tiers Etats, the Clergy, and the Noblesse), France had then a good constitution. This shows, among numerous other instances, that Mr Burke does not understand what a constitution is. The persons so met, were not a *constitution*, but a *convention*, to make a constitution.

The present National Assembly of France is, strictly speaking, the personal social compact. – The members of it are the delegates of the nation in its *original* character; future assemblies will be the delegates of the nation in its *organized* character. The authority of the present Assembly is different to what the authority of future Assemblies will be. The authority of the present one is to form a constitution: the authority of future Assemblies will be to legislate according to the principles and forms prescribed in that constitution; and if experience should hereafter show that alterations, amendments, or additions, are necessary, the constitution will point out the mode by which such things shall be done, and not leave it to the discretionary power of the future government.

A government on the principles on which constitutional governments arising out of society are established, cannot have the right of altering itself. If it had, it would be arbitrary. It might make itself what it pleased; and wherever such a right is set up, it shows there is no constitution. The act by which the English Parliament empowered itself to sit seven years, shows there is no constitution in England. It might, by the same self-authority, have sat any greater number of years, or for life. The Bill which the present Mr Pitt brought into parliament some years ago, to reform parliament, was on the same erroneous principle. The right to reform is in the nation in its original character, and the constitutional method would be by a general convention elected for the purpose. There is, moreover, a paradox in the idea of vitiated bodies reforming themselves.

From these preliminaries I proceed to draw some comparisons. I have already spoken of the declaration of rights; and as I mean to be as concise as possible, I shall proceed to other parts of the French constitution.

The constitution of France says, That every man who pays a tax of sixty sous *per annum*, (2s. and 6d. English), is an elector. – What article will Mr Burke place against this? Can anything be more limited, and at the same time more capricious, than the qualifications of electors are in England? Limited – because not one man in an hundred (I speak much within compass) is admitted to vote: Capricious – because the lowest character that can be supposed to exist, and who has not so much as the visible means of an honest livelihood, is an elector in some places; while, in other places, the man who pays very large taxes, and has a known fair character, and the farmer who rents to the amount of three or four hundred pounds a year, with a property on that farm to three or four times that amount, is not admitted to be an elector. Everything is out of nature, as Mr Burke says on another occasion, in this strange chaos, and all sorts of follies are blended with all sorts of crimes. William the Conqueror and his descendants parcelled out the country in this manner, and bribed some parts of it by what they called Charters, to hold the other parts of it the better subjected to their will. This is the reason why so many of those charters abound in Cornwall; the people were averse to the government established at the Conquest, and the towns were garrisoned and bribed to enslave the country. All the old charters are the badges of this conquest, and it is from this source that the capriciousness of elections arises.

The French constitution says, That the number of representatives for any place shall be in a ratio to the number of taxable inhabitants or electors. What article will Mr Burke place against this? The county of Yorkshire, which contains near a million of souls, sends two county members; and so does the county of Rutland, which contains not an hundredth part of that number. The town of old Sarum, which contains not three houses, sends two members; and the town of Manchester, which contains upwards of sixty thousand souls, is not admitted to send any. Is there any principle in these things? Is there anything by which you can trace the marks of freedom, or discover those of wisdom? No wonder, then, Mr Burke has declined the comparison, and endeavoured to lead his readers from the point by a wild unsystematical display of paradoxical rhapsodies.

The French constitution says, That the National Assembly shall be elected every two years. – What article will Mr Burke place against this? Why, that the nation has no right at all in the case: that the government is perfectly arbitrary with respect to this point; and he can quote for his authority, the precedent of a former parliament.

The French constitution says, There shall be no game laws; that the farmer on whose lands wild game shall be found (for it is by the produce of his lands they are fed) shall have a right to what he can take: That there shall be no monopolies of any kind – that all trade shall be free, and every man free to follow any occupation by which he can procure an honest livelihood, and in any place, town or city throughout the nation. – What will Mr Burke say to this? In England, game is made the property of those at whose expense it is not fed; and with respect to monopolies, the country is cut up into monopolies. Every chartered town is an aristocratical monopoly in itself, and the qualification of electors proceeds out of those chartered monopolies. Is this freedom? Is this what Mr Burke means by a constitution?

In these chartered monopolies, a man coming from another part of the country, is hunted from them as if he were a foreign enemy. An Englishman is not free of his own country: every one of those places presents a barrier in his way, and tells him he is not a freeman – that he has no rights. Within these monopolies, are other monopolies. In a city, such for instance as Bath, which contains between twenty and thirty thousand inhabitants, the right of electing representatives to parliament is monopolized by about thirty-one persons. And within these monopolies are still others. A man even of the same town, whose parents were not in circumstances to give him an occupation, is debarred, in many cases, from the natural right of acquiring one, be his genius or industry what it may.

Are these things examples to hold out to a country regenerating itself from slavery, like France? – Certainly they are not; and certain am I, that when the people of England come to reflect upon them, they will, like France, annihilate those badges of ancient oppression, those traces of a conquered nation. – Had Mr Burke possessed talents similar to the author of 'On the Wealth of Nations', he would have comprehended all the parts which enter into, and, by assemblage, form a constitution. He would have reasoned from minutiae to magnitude. It is not from his prejudices only, but from the disorderly cast of his genius, that he is unfitted for the subject he writes upon. Even his genius is without a constitution. It is a genius at random, and not a genius constituted. But he must say something – He has therefore mounted in the air like a balloon, to draw the eyes of the multitude from the ground they stand upon.

Much is to be learned from the French constitution. Conquest and tyranny transplanted themselves with William the Conqueror from Normandy into England, and the country is yet disfigured with the marks. May then the example of all France contribute to regenerate the freedom which a province of it destroyed!

The French constitution says, That to preserve the national representation from being corrupt, no member of the National Assembly shall be an officer of the government, a place-man, or a pensioner. – What will Mr Burke place against this? I will whisper his answer: *Loaves* and *fishes*. Ah! this government of loaves and fishes has more mischief in it than people have yet reflected on. The National Assembly has made the discovery, and it holds out the example to the world. Had governments agreed to quarrel on purpose to fleece their countries by taxes, they would not have succeeded better than they have done.

Many things in the English government appear to me the reverse of what they ought to be, and of what they are said to be. The Parliament, imperfectly and capriciously elected as it is, is nevertheless *supposed* to hold the national purse in *trust* for the nation: but in the manner in which an English parliament is constructed, it is like a man being both mortgager and mortgagee; and in the case of misapplication of trust, it is the criminal sitting in judgement upon himself. If those who vote the supplies are the same persons who receive the supplies when voted, and are to account for the expenditure of those supplies to those who voted them, it is *themselves accountable to themselves*, and the Comedy of Errors concludes with the Pantomime of HUSH. Neither the ministerial party, nor the opposition, will touch upon this case. The national purse is the common hack which each mounts upon. It is like what the country people call, 'Ride and tie – You ride a little way, and then I' [2] – They order these things better in France.

The French constitution says, That the right of war and peace is in the nation. Where else should it reside, but in those who are to pay the expense?

In England, this right is said to reside in a *metaphor*, shown at the Tower for sixpence or a shilling apiece: So are the lions; and it would be a step nearer to reason to say it resided in them, for any inanimate metaphor is no more than a hat or a cap. We can all see the absurdity of worshipping Aaron's molten calf, or Nebuchadnezzar's golden image; but why do men continue to practise themselves the absurdities they despise in others?

It may with reason be said, that in the manner the English nation is represented, it signifies not where this right resides, whether in the Crown, or in the Parliament. War is the common harvest of all those who participate in the division and expenditure of public money, in

2 It is a practice in some parts of the country, when two travellers have but one horse, which like the national purse will not carry double, that the one mounts and rides two or three miles ahead, and then ties the horse to a gate, and walks on. When the second traveller arrives, he takes the horse, rides on, and passes his companion a mile or two, and ties again; and so on – *Ride and tie.* – Paine.

all countries. It is the art of *conquering at home*: the object of it is an increase of revenue; and as revenue cannot be increased without taxes, a pretence must be made for expenditures. In reviewing the history of the English Government, its wars and its taxes, a bystander, not blinded by prejudice, nor warped by interest, would declare, that taxes were not raised to carry on wars, but that wars were raised to carry on taxes.

Mr Burke, as a Member of the House of Commons, is a part of the English Government; and though he professes himself an enemy to war, he abuses the French Constitution, which seeks to explode it. He holds up the English Government as a model in all its parts, to France; but he should first know the remarks which the French make upon it. They contend, in favour of their own, that the portion of liberty enjoyed in England, is just enough to enslave a country by, more productively than by despotism; and that as the real object of all despotism is revenue, a government so formed obtains more than it could do either by direct despotism, or in a full state of freedom, and is therefore, on the ground of interest, opposed to both. They account also for the readiness which always appears in such governments for engaging in wars, by remarking on the different motives which produce them. In despotic governments, wars are the effect of pride; but in those governments in which they become the means of taxation, they acquire thereby a more permanent promptitude.

The French Constitution, therefore, to provide against both these evils, has taken away the power of declaring war from kings and ministers, and placed the right where the expense must fall. . . .

The French Constitution says, *There shall be no titles*; and of consequence, all that class of equivocal generation, which in some countries is called '*aristocracy*', and in others '*nobility*', is done away, and the *peer* is exalted into MAN.

Titles are but nick-names, and every nick-name is a title. The thing is perfectly harmless in itself; but it marks a sort of foppery in the human character, which degrades it. It reduces man into the diminutive of man in things which are great, and the counterfeit of woman in things which are little. It talks about its fine *blue ribbon* like a girl, and shows its new *garter* like a child. A certain writer of some antiquity, says, 'When I was a child, I thought as a child; but when I became a man, I put away childish things.'

It is, properly, from the elevated mind of France, that the folly of titles has fallen. It has outgrown the baby-clothes of *Count* and *Duke*, and breeched itself in manhood. France has not levelled; it has exalted. It has put down the dwarf, to set up the man. The punyism of a senseless word like *Duke*, or *Count*, or *Earl*, has ceased to please. Even those who possessed them have disowned the gibberish, and as they outgrew the rickets, have despised the rattle. The genuine mind of man, thirsting for its native home, society, condemns the gewgaws that separate him from it. Titles are like circles drawn by the magician's wand, to contract the sphere of man's felicity. He lives immured within the Bastille of a word, and surveys at a distance the envied life of man.

Is it then any wonder that titles should fall in France? Is it not a greater wonder they should be kept up anywhere? What are they? What is their worth, and 'what is their amount'? When we think or speak of a *Judge* or a *General*, we associate with it the ideas of office and character; we think of gravity in the one, and bravery in the other: but when we use a word *merely as a title*, no ideas associate with it. Through all the vocabulary of Adam, there is not such an animal as a Duke or a Count; neither can we connect any certain idea with the words. Whether they mean strength or weakness, wisdom or folly, a child or a man, or the rider or the horse, is all equivocal. What respect then can be paid to that which describes nothing, and which means nothing? Imagination has given figure and character to centaurs, satyrs, and down to all the fairy tribe; but titles baffle even the powers of fancy, and are a chimerical nondescript.

But this is not all. – If a whole country is disposed to hold them in contempt, all their value is gone, and none will own them. It is common opinion only that makes them anything, or nothing, or worse than nothing. There is no occasion to take titles away, for they take themselves away when society concurs to ridicule them. This species of imaginary consequence has visibly declined in every part of Europe, and it hastens to its exit as the world of reason continues to rise. There was a time when the lowest class of what are called nobility was more thought of than the highest is now, and when a man in armour riding throughout Christendom in quest of adventures was more stared at than a modern Duke. The world has seen his folly fall, and it has fallen by being laughed at, and the farce of titles will follow its fate. – The patriots of France have discovered in good time, that rank and dignity in society must take a new ground. The old one has fallen through. – It must now take the substantial ground of character, instead of the chimerical ground of titles; and they have brought their titles to the altar, and made of them a burnt-offering to Reason.

If no mischief had annexed itself to the folly of titles, they would not have been worth a serious and formal destruction, such as the National Assembly have decreed them: and this makes it necessary to inquire farther into the nature and character of aristocracy.

That, then, which is called aristocracy in some countries, and nobility in others, arose out of the governments founded upon conquest. It was originally a military order, for the purpose of supporting military government, (for such were all governments founded in conquest); and to keep up a succession of this order for the purpose for which it was established, all the younger branches of those families were disinherited, and the law of *primogenitureship* set up.

The nature and the character of aristocracy shows itself to us in this law. It is a law against every law of nature, and Nature herself calls for its destruction. Establish family justice, and aristocracy falls. By the aristocratical law of primogenitureship, in a family of six children, five are exposed. Aristocracy has never more than *one* child. The rest are begotten to be devoured. They are thrown to the cannibal for prey, and the natural parent prepares the unnatural repast.

As everything which is out of nature in man, affects, more or less, the interest of society, so does this. All the children which the aristocracy disowns (which are all, except the eldest) are, in general, cast like orphans on a parish, to be provided for by the public, but at a greater charge. – Unnecessary offices and places in governments and courts are created at the expense of the public, to maintain them.

With what kind of parental reflections can the father or mother contemplate their younger offspring. By nature they are children, and by marriage they are heirs; but by aristocracy they are bastards and orphans. They are the flesh and blood of their parents in one line, and nothing akin to them in the other. To restore, therefore, parents to their children, and children to their parents – relations to each other, and man to society – and to exterminate the monster Aristocracy, root and branch – the French constitution has destroyed the law of PRIMOGENITURESHIP. Here then lies the monster; and Mr Burke, if he pleases, may write its epitaph.

Hitherto we have considered aristocracy chiefly in one point of view. We have now to consider it in another. But whether we view it before or behind, or sideways, or any way else, domestically or publicly, it is still a monster.

In France, aristocracy had one feature less in its countenance, than what it has in some other countries. It did not compose a body of hereditary legislators. It was not '*a corporation of aristocracy*', for such I have heard M. de Lafayette describe an English House of Peers. Let us then examine the grounds upon which the French constitution has resolved against having such a House in France.

Because, in the first place, as is already mentioned, aristocracy is kept up by family tyranny and injustice.

Secondly, Because there is an unnatural unfitness in an aristocracy to be legislators for a nation. Their ideas of *distributive justice* are corrupted at the very source. They begin life by trampling on all their younger brothers and sisters, and relations of every kind, and are taught and educated so to do. With what ideas of justice or honour can that man enter a house of legislation, who absorbs in his own person the inheritance of a whole family of children, or doles out to them some pitiful portion with the insolence of a gift?

Thirdly, Because the idea of hereditary legislation is as inconsistent as that of hereditary judges, or hereditary juries; and as absurd as an hereditary mathematician, or an hereditary wise man; and as ridiculous as an hereditary poet-laureate.

Fourthly, Because a body of men holding themselves accountable to nobody, ought not to be trusted by anybody.

Fifthly, Because it is continuing the uncivilized principle of governments founded in conquest, and the base idea of man having property in man, and governing him by personal right.

Sixthly, Because aristocracy has a tendency to degenerate the human species. – By the universal economy of nature it is known, and by the instance of the Jews it is proved, that the human species has a tendency to degenerate, in any small number of persons, when separated from the general stock of society, and intermarrying constantly with each other. It defeats even its pretended end, and becomes in time the opposite of what is noble in man. Mr Burke talks of nobility; let him show what it is. The greatest characters the world have known, have risen on the democratic floor. Aristocracy has not been able to keep a proportionate pace with democracy. The artificial NOBLE shrinks into a dwarf before the NOBLE of Nature; and in the few instances of those (for there are some in all countries) in whom nature, as by a miracle, has survived in aristocracy, THOSE MEN DESPISE IT. – But it is time to proceed to a new subject.

The French constitution has reformed the condition of the clergy. It has raised the income of the lower and middle classes, and taken from the higher. None is now less than twelve hundred livres (fifty pounds sterling), nor any higher than about two or three thousand pounds. What will Mr Burke place against this? Hear what he says.

He says, 'That the people of England can see without pain or grudging, an archbishop precede a duke; they can see a bishop of Durham, or a bishop of Winchester, in possession of £10,000 a year; and cannot see why it is in worse hands than estates to the like amount in the hands of this earl or that 'squire.' And Mr Burke offers this as an example to France.

As to the first part, whether the archbishop precedes the duke, or the duke the bishop, it is, I believe, to the people in general, somewhat like *Sternhold* and *Hopkins*, or *Hopkins* and *Sternhold*; you may put which you please first: and as I confess that I do not understand the merits of this case, I will not contend it with Mr Burke.

But with respect to the latter, I have something to say. – Mr Burke has not put the case right. – The comparison is out of order, by being put between the bishop and the earl or the 'squire. It ought to be put between the bishop and the curate, and then it will stand thus: – *The people of England can see without pain or grudging, a bishop of Durham, or a bishop of Winchester, in possession of ten thousand pounds a year, and a curate on thirty or forty pounds a year, or less.* – No, Sir, they certainly do not see those things without great pain or grudging. It is a case that applies itself to every man's sense of justice, and is one among many that calls aloud for a constitution.

In France, the cry of '*The church! the church!*' was repeated as often as in Mr Burke's book, and as loudly as when the dissenters' bill was before the English parliament; but the generality of the French clergy were not to be deceived by this cry any longer. They knew, that whatever the pretence might be, it was themselves who were one of the principal objects of it. It was the cry of the high beneficed clergy, to prevent any regulation of income taking place between those of ten thousand pounds a year and the parish priest. They, therefore, joined their case to those of every other oppressed class of men, and by this union obtained redress.

The French constitution has abolished tithes, that source of perpetual discontent between the tithe-holder and the parishioner. When land is held on tithe, it is in the condition of an estate held between two parties; the one receiving one-tenth, and the other nine-tenths of the produce; and, consequently, on principles of equity, if the estate can be improved, and made to produce by that improvement double or treble what it did before, or in any other ratio, the expense of such improvement ought to be borne in like proportion between the parties who are to share the produce. But this is not the case in tithes; the farmer bears the whole expense, and the tithe-holder takes a tenth of the improvement, in addition to the original tenth, and by this means gets the value of two-tenths instead of one. This is another case that calls for a constitution.

The French constitution hath abolished or renounced *Toleration*, and *Intolerance* also, and hath established UNIVERSAL RIGHT OF CONSCIENCE.

Toleration is not the *opposite* of Intolerance, but is the *counterfeit* of it. Both are despotisms. The one assumes to itself the right of withholding Liberty of Conscience, and the other of granting it. The one is the pope armed with fire and faggot, and the other is the pope selling or granting indulgences. The former is church and State, and the latter is church and traffic.

But Toleration may be viewed in a much stronger light. Man worships not himself, but his Maker; and the liberty of conscience which he claims, is not for the service of himself, but of his God. In this case, therefore, we must necessarily have the associated idea of two beings; the *mortal* who renders the worship, and the IMMORTAL BEING who is worshipped. Toleration, therefore, places itself, not between man and man, nor between church and church, nor between one denomination of religion and another, but between God and man; between the being who worships, and the BEING who is worshipped; and by the same act of assumed authority by which it tolerates man to pay his worship, it presumptuously and blasphemously sets itself up to tolerate the Almighty to receive it.

Were a bill brought into any parliament, entitled 'AN ACT to tolerate or grant liberty to the Almighty to receive the worship of a

Jew or a Turk', or 'to prohibit the Almighty from receiving it', all men would startle, and call it blasphemy. There would be an uproar. The presumption of toleration in religious matters would then present itself unmasked: but the presumption is not the less because the name of 'man' only appears to those laws, for the associated idea of the *worshipper* and the *worshipped* cannot be separated. – Who, then, art thou, vain dust and ashes! by whatever name thou art called, whether a King, a Bishop, a Church or a State, a Parliament, or anything else, that obtrudest thine insignificance between the soul of man and its Maker? Mind thine own concerns. If he believes not as thou believest, it is a proof that thou believest not as he believeth, and there is no earthly power can determine between you.

With respect to what are called denominations of religion, if every-one is left to judge of his own religion, there is no such thing as a religion that is wrong; but if they are to judge of each other's religion, there is no such thing as a religion that is right; and therefore, all the world is right, or all the world is wrong. But with respect to religion itself, without regard to names, and as directing itself from the uni-versal family of mankind to the Divine object of all adoration, *it is man bringing to his Maker the fruits of his heart*; and though those fruits may differ from each other like the fruits of the earth, the grateful tribute of everyone is accepted.

A Bishop of Durham, or a Bishop of Winchester, or the Arch-bishop who heads the Dukes, will not refuse a tithe-sheaf of wheat, because it is not a cock of hay; nor a cock of hay, because it is not a sheaf of wheat; nor a pig, because it is neither one nor the other: but these same persons, under the figure of an established church, will not permit their Maker to receive the varied tithes of man's devo-tion.

One of the continual choruses of Mr Burke's book is, 'Church and State'. He does not mean some one particular church, or some one particular State, but any church and State; and he uses the term as a general figure to hold forth the political doctrine of always uniting the church with the State in every country, and he censures the National Assembly for not having done this in France. – Let us bestow a few thoughts on this subject.

All religions are in their nature kind and benign, and united with principles of morality. They could not have made proselytes at first, by professing anything that was vicious, cruel, persecuting, or immoral. Like everything else, they had their beginning; and they proceeded by persuasion, exhortation, and example. How then is it that they lose their native mildness, and become morose and intolerant?

It proceeds from the connection which Mr Burke recommends. By engendering the church with the State, a sort of mule-animal, capable only of destroying, and not of breeding up, is produced, called *The Church established by Law*. It is a stranger, even from its birth, to any parent mother on which it is begotten, and whom in time it kicks out and destroys.

The inquisition in Spain does not proceed from the religion originally professed, but from this mule-animal, engendered between the church and the State. The burnings in Smithfield proceeded from the same heterogeneous production; and it was the regeneration of this strange animal in England afterwards, that renewed rancour and irreligion among the inhabitants, and that drove the people called Quakers and Dissenters to America. Persecution is not an original feature in any religion; but it is always the strongly marked feature of all law-religion; or religions established by law. Take away the law-establishment, and every religion reassumes its original benignity. In America, a Catholic Priest is a good citizen, a good character, and a good neighbour; an Episcopalian Minister is of the same description: and this proceeds, independently of the men, from there being no law-establishment in America.

If also we view this matter in a temporal sense, we shall see the ill effects it has had on the prosperity of nations. The union of church and State has impoverished Spain. The revoking the edict of Nantes drove the silk manufacture from France into England; and church and State are now driving the cotton manufacture from England to America and France. Let then Mr Burke continue to preach his antipolitical doctrine of Church and State. It will do some good. The National Assembly will not follow his advice, but will benefit by his folly. It was by observing the ill effects of it in England, that America has been warned against it; and it is by experiencing them in France, that the National Assembly have abolished it, and, like America, have established UNIVERSAL RIGHT OF CONSCIENCE, AND UNIVERSAL RIGHT OF CITIZENSHIP.[3]

3 When in any country we see extraordinary circumstances taking place, they naturally lead any man who has a talent for observation and investigation, to inquire

I will here cease the comparison with respect to the principles of the French constitution, and conclude this part of the subject with a few observations on the organization of the formal parts of the French and English governments.

The executive power in each country is in the hands of a person styled the King; but the French constitution distinguishes between the King and the Sovereign: It considers the station of King as official, and places Sovereignty in the nation.

The representatives of the nation, who compose the National Assembly, and who are the legislative power, originate in and from the people by election, as an inherent right in the people. – In England it is otherwise; and this arises from the original establishment of what is called its monarchy; for, as by the conquest all the rights of the people or the nation were absorbed into the hands of the Conqueror, and who added the title of King to that of Conqueror, those same matters which in France are now held as rights in the people, or in the nation, are held in England as grants from what is called the Crown. The Parliament in England, in both its branches, was erected

---

into the causes. The manufactures of Manchester, Birmingham, and Sheffield, are the principal manufactures in England. From whence did this arise? A little observation will explain the case. The principal, and the generality of the inhabitants of those places, are not of what is called in England, *the church established by law*; and they, or their fathers, (for it is within but a few years), withdrew from the persecution of the chartered towns, where test-laws more particularly operate, and established a sort of asylum for themselves in those places. It was the only asylum that then offered, for the rest of Europe was worse. – But the case is now changing. France and America bid all comers welcome, and initiate them into all the rights of citizenship. Policy and interest, therefore, will, but perhaps too late, dictate in England, what reason and justice could not. Those manufactures are withdrawing, and are arising in other places. There is now erecting at Passy, three miles from Paris, a large cotton-mill, and several are already erected in America. Soon after the rejecting the Bill for repealing the test-law, one of the richest manufacturers in England said in my hearing, 'England, Sir, is not a country for a dissenter to live in – we must go to France.' These are truths, and it is doing justice to both parties to tell them. It is chiefly the dissenters who have carried English manufactures to the height they are now at, and the same men have it in their power to carry them away; and though those manufactures will afterwards continue to be made in those places, the foreign market will be lost. There are frequently appearing in the London Gazette, extracts from certain acts to prevent machines and persons, as far as they can extend to persons, from going out of the country. It appears from these, that the ill effects of the test-laws and church-establishment begin to be much suspected; but the remedy of force can never supply the remedy of reason. In the progress of less than a century, all the unrepresented part of England, of all denominations, which is at least a hundred times the most numerous, may begin to feel the necessity of a constitution, and then all those matters will come regularly before them.—Paine.

by patents from the descendants of the Conqueror. The House of Commons did not originate as a matter of right in the people to delegate or elect, but as a grant or boon.

By the French constitution, the Nation is always named before the King. The third article of the Declaration of rights says, '*The nation is essentially the source*' (or fountain) '*of all sovereignty.*' Mr Burke argues, that, in England, a King is the fountain – that he is the fountain of all honour. But as this idea is evidently descended from the Conquest, I shall make no other remark upon it, than that it is the nature of conquest to turn everything upside down; and as Mr Burke will not be refused the privilege of speaking twice, and as there are but two parts in the figure, the *fountain* and the *spout*, he will be right the second time.

The French constitution puts the legislative before the executive; the Law before the King; *La Loi, Le Roi*. This also is in the natural order of things; because laws must have existence, before they can have execution.

A King in France does not, in addressing himself to the National Assembly, say, 'My assembly', similar to the phrase used in England of *my* 'Parliament'; neither can he use it consistently with the constitution, nor could it be admitted. There may be propriety in the use of it in England, because, as is before mentioned, both Houses of Parliament originated from what is called the Crown by patent or boon – and not from the inherent rights of the people, as the National Assembly does in France, and whose name designates its origin.

The President of the National Assembly does not ask the King *to grant to the Assembly liberty of speech*, as is the case with the English House of Commons. The constitutional dignity of the National Assembly cannot debase itself. Speech is, in the first place, one of the natural rights of man always retained; and with respect to the National Assembly, the use of it is their *duty*, and the nation is their *authority*. They were elected by the greatest body of men exercising the right of election the European world ever saw. They sprung not from the filth of rotten boroughs, nor are they the vassal representatives of aristocratical ones. Feeling the proper dignity of their character, they support it. Their parliamentary language, whether for or against a question, is free, bold, and manly, and extends to all the parts and circumstances of the case. If any matter or subject respecting the executive department, or the person who presides in it, (the King), comes before them, it is debated on with the spirit of men, and the language of gentlemen; and their answer, or their address, is returned in the same style. They stand not aloof with the gaping vacuity of vulgar ignorance, nor bend with the cringe of sycophantic insignificance. The graceful pride of truth knows no extremes, and preserves, in every latitude of life, the right-angled character of man.

Let us now look to the other side of the question. — In the addresses of the English Parliaments to their Kings, we see neither the intrepid spirit of the old Parliaments of France, nor the serene dignity of the present National Assembly; neither do we see in them anything of the style of English manners, which border somewhat on bluntness. Since then they are neither of foreign extraction, nor naturally of English production, their origin must be sought for elsewhere, and that origin is the Norman Conquest. They are evidently of the vassalage class of manners, and emphatically mark the prostrate distance that exists in no other condition of men than between the conqueror and the conquered. That this vassalage idea and style of speaking was not got rid of even at the Revolution of 1688, is evident from the declaration of Parliament to William and Mary, in these words: 'We do most humbly and faithfully *submit* ourselves, our heirs and posterities, for ever.' Submission is wholly a vassalage term, repugnant to the dignity of Freedom, and an echo of the language used at the Conquest.

As the estimation of all things is by comparison, the Revolution of 1688, however from circumstances it may have been exalted beyond its value, will find its level. It is already on the wane, eclipsed by the enlarging orb of reason, and the luminous revolutions of America and France. In less than another century, it will go, as well as Mr Burke's labours, 'to the family vault of all the Capulets'. Mankind will then scarcely believe that a country calling itself free, would send to Holland for a man, and clothe him with power, on purpose to put themselves in fear of him, and give him almost a million sterling a year for leave to *submit* themselves and their posterity, like bond-men and bond-women, for ever.

But there is a truth that ought to be made known: I have had the opportunity of seeing it; which is, *that, notwithstanding appearances, there is not any description of men that despise monarchy so much as courtiers.* But they well know, that if it were seen by others, as it is seen by them, the juggle could not be kept up. They are in the condition of men who get their living by a show, and to whom the folly of that show is so familiar that they ridicule it; but were the audience to be made as wise in this respect as themselves, there would be an end to the show and the profits with it. The difference between a republican and a courtier with respect to monarchy, is, that the one opposes monarchy, believing it to be something; and the other laughs at it, knowing it to be nothing.

As I used sometimes to correspond with Mr Burke, believing him then to be a man of sounder principles than his book shows him to be, I wrote to him last winter from Paris, and gave him an account how prosperously matters were going on. Among other subjects in that letter, I referred to the happy situation the National Assembly were placed in; that they had taken a ground on which their moral duty and their political interest were united. They have not to hold out a language which they do not themselves believe, for the fraudulent purpose of making others believe it. Their station requires no artifice to support it, and can only be maintained by enlightening mankind. It is not their interest to cherish ignorance, but to dispel it. They are not in the case of a ministerial or an opposition party in England, who, though they are opposed, are still united to keep up the common mystery. The National Assembly must throw open a magazine of light. It must show man the proper character of man; and the nearer it can bring him to that standard, the stronger the National Assembly becomes.

In contemplating the French constitution, we see in it a rational order of things. The principles harmonize with the forms, and both with their origin. It may perhaps be said as an excuse for bad forms, that they are nothing more than forms; but this is a mistake. Forms grow out of principles, and operate to continue the principles they grow from. It is impossible to practise a bad form on anything but a bad principle. It cannot be ingrafted on a good one; and wherever the forms in any government are bad, it is a certain indication that the principles are bad also.

I will here finally close this subject. I began it by remarking that Mr Burke had *voluntarily* declined going into a comparison of the English and French constitutions. He apologizes (in page 241) for not doing it, by saying that he had not time. Mr Burke's book was upwards of eight months in hand, and is extended to a volume of three hundred and sixty-six pages. As his omission does injury to his cause, his apology makes it worse; and men on the English side of the water will begin to consider, whether there is not some radical defect in what is called the English constitution, that made it necessary for Mr Burke to suppress the comparison, to avoid bringing it into view.

As Mr Burke has not written on constitutions, so neither has he written on the French Revolution. He gives no account of its commencement or its progress. He only expresses his wonder. 'It looks', says he, 'to me, as if I were in a great crisis, not of the affairs of France alone, but of all Europe, perhaps of more than Europe. All circumstances taken together, the French Revolution is the most astonishing that has hitherto happened in the world.'

As wise men are astonished at foolish things, and other people at wise ones, I know not on which ground to account for Mr Burke's astonishment; but certain it is, that he does not understand the French Revolution. It has apparently burst forth like a creation from a chaos, but it is no more than the consequence of a mental revolution priorily existing in France. The mind of the nation had changed beforehand, and the new order of things has naturally followed the new order of thoughts. – I will here, as concisely as I can, trace out the growth of the French Revolution, and mark the circumstances that have contributed to produce it.

The despotism of Louis XIV united with the gaiety of his Court, and the gaudy ostentation of his character, had so humbled, and at the same time so fascinated the mind of France, that the people appeared to have lost all sense of their own dignity, in contemplating that of their Grand Monarch: and the whole reign of Louis XV, remarkable only for weakness and effeminacy, made no other alteration than that of spreading a sort of lethargy over the nation, from which it showed no disposition to rise.

The only signs which appeared of the spirit of Liberty during those periods, are to be found in the writings of the French philosophers. Montesquieu, president of the Parliament of Bordeaux, went as far as a writer under a despotic government could well proceed; and being obliged to divide himself between principle and prudence, his mind often appears under a veil, and we ought to give him credit for more than he has expressed.

Voltaire, who was both the flatterer and the satirist of despotism, took another line. His forte lay in exposing and ridiculing the superstitions which priestcraft united with statecraft had interwoven with governments. It was not from the purity of his principles, or his love of mankind, (for satire and philanthropy are not naturally concordant), but from his strong capacity of seeing folly in its true shape, and his irresistible propensity to expose it, that he made those attacks. They were however as formidable as if the motives had been virtuous; and he merits the thanks, rather than the esteem of mankind.

On the contrary, we find in the writings of Rousseau, and the Abbé Raynal, a loveliness of sentiment in favour of Liberty, that excites respect, and elevates the human faculties; but having raised this animation, they do not direct its operations, and leave the mind in love with an object, without describing the means of possessing it.

The writings of Quesnay, Turgot, and the friends of those authors, are of the serious kind; but they laboured under the same disadvantage with Montesquieu: their writings abound with moral maxims of government, but are rather directed to economize and reform the administration of the government, than the government itself.

But all those writings and many others had their weight; and by the different manner in which they treated the subject of government, Montesquieu by his judgement and knowledge of laws, Voltaire by his wit, Rousseau and Raynal by their animation, and Quesnay and Turgot by their moral maxims and systems of economy, readers of every class met with something to their taste, and a spirit of political inquiry began to diffuse itself through the nation at the time the dispute between England and the then colonies of America broke out.

In the war which France afterwards engaged in, it is very well known that the nation appeared to be beforehand with the French ministry. Each of them had its view: but those views were directed to different objects; the one fought liberty, and the other retaliation on England. The French officers and soldiers who after this went to America, were eventually placed in the school of Freedom, and learned the practice as well as the principles of it by heart.

As it was impossible to separate the military events which took place in America from the principles of the American Revolution, the publication of those events in France necessarily connected themselves with the principles which produced them. Many of the facts were in themselves principles; such as the declaration of American independence, and the treaty of alliance between France and America, which recognized the natural right of man, and justified resistance to oppression.

The then Minister of France, Count Vergennes, was not the friend of America; and it is both justice and gratitude to say, that it was the Queen of France who gave the cause of America a fashion at the French Court. Count Vergennes was the personal and social friend of Dr Franklin; and the Doctor had obtained, by his sensible gracefulness, a sort of influence over him; but with respect to principles, Count Vergennes was a despot.

The situation of Dr Franklin as Minister from America to France, should be taken into the chain of circumstances. The diplomatic character is of itself the narrowest sphere of society that man can act in. It forbids intercourse by a reciprocity of suspicion; and a diplomatic is a sort of unconnected atom, continually repelling and repelled. But this was not the case with Dr Franklin. He was not the diplomatic of a Court, but of MAN. His character as a philosopher had been long established, and his circle of society in France was universal.

Count Vergennes resisted for a considerable time the publication in France of the American constitutions, translated into the French language; but even in this he was obliged to give way to public opinion, and a sort of propriety in admitting to appear what he had undertaken to defend. The American constitutions were to liberty, what a grammar is to language: they define its parts of speech, and practically construct them into syntax.

The peculiar situation of the then Marquis de Lafayette is another link in the great chain. He served in America as an American officer under a commission of Congress, and by the universality of his acquaintance, was in close friendship with the civil government of America, as well as with the military line. He spoke the language of the country, entered into the discussions on the principles of government, and was always a welcome friend at any election.

When the war closed, a vast reinforcement to the cause of Liberty spread itself over France, by the return of the French officers and soldiers. A knowledge of the practice was then joined to the theory; and all that was wanting to give it real existence, was opportunity. Man cannot, properly speaking, make circumstances for his purpose, but he always has it in his power to improve them when they occur; and this was the case in France. . . .

The States-General were to meet at Versailles in April 1789, but did not assemble till May. They situated themselves in three separate chambers, or rather the Clergy and the Aristocracy withdrew each into a separate chamber. The majority of the aristocracy claimed what they called the privilege of voting as a separate body, and of giving their consent or their negative in that manner; and many of the bishops and the high-beneficed clergy claimed the same privilege on the part of their Order.

The *Tiers Etat* (as they were then called) disowned any knowledge of artificial Orders and artificial privileges; and they were not only resolute on this point, but somewhat disdainful. They began to consider aristocracy as a kind of fungus growing out of the corruption of society, that could not be admitted even as a branch of it; and from the disposition the aristocracy had shown by upholding Lettres de Cachet, and in sundry other instances, it was manifest that no constitution could be formed by admitting men in any other character than as National Men.

After various altercations on this head, the Tiers Etat or Commons (as they were then called) declared themselves (on a motion made for that purpose by the Abbé Sieyès) 'THE REPRESENTATIVES OF THE NATION; *and that the two Orders could be considered but as deputies of corporations, and could only have a deliberative voice when they assembled in a national character with the national representatives*'. This proceeding extinguished the style of *Etats Généraux*, or States-General, and erected it into the style it now bears, that of L'Assemblée Nationale, or National Assembly.

This motion was not made in a precipitate manner: It was the result of cool deliberation, and concerted between the national representatives and the patriotic members of the two chambers, who saw into the folly, mischief, and injustice of artificial privileged distinctions. It was become evident, that no constitution, worthy of being called by that name, could be established on any thing less than a national ground. The aristocracy had hitherto opposed the despotism of the Court, and affected the language of patriotism; but it opposed it as its rival (as the English Barons opposed King John), and it now opposed the nation from the same motives.

On carrying this motion, the national representatives, as had been concerted, sent an invitation to the two chambers, to unite with them in a national character, and proceed to business. A majority of the clergy, chiefly of the parish priests, withdrew from the clerical chamber, and joined the nation; and forty-five from the other chamber joined in like manner. There is a sort of secret history belonging to this last circumstance, which is necessary to its explanation: It was not judged prudent that all the patriotic members of the chamber styling itself the Nobles, should quit it at once; and in consequence of this arrangement, they drew off by degrees, always leaving some, as well to reason the case, as to watch the suspected. In a little time, the numbers increased from forty-five to eighty, and soon after to a greater number; which, with a majority of the clergy, and the whole of the national representatives, put the malcontents in a very diminutive condition.

The King, who, very different from the general class called by that name, is a man of a good heart, showed himself disposed to recommend an union of the three chambers, on the ground the National Assembly had taken; but the malcontents exerted themselves to prevent it, and began now to have another project in view. Their numbers consisted of a majority of the aristocratical chamber, and a minority of the clerical chamber, chiefly of bishops and high-beneficed clergy; and these men were determined to put everything to issue, as well by strength as by stratagem. They had no objection to a constitution; but it must be such a one as themselves should dictate, and suited to their own views and particular situations. On the other hand, the Nation disowned knowing anything of them but as citizens, and was determined to shut out all such upstart pretensions. The more aristocracy appeared, the more it was despised; there was a visible imbecility and want of intellects in the majority, a sort of *je ne sais quoi*, that while it affected to be more than citizen, was less than man. It lost ground from contempt more than from hatred; and was rather jeered at as an ass, than dreaded as a lion. This is the general character of aristocracy, or what are called Nobles or Nobility, or rather No-ability, in all countries.

The plan of the malcontents consisted now of two things; either to deliberate and vote by chambers, (or orders), more especially on all questions respecting a constitution, (by which the aristocratical chamber would have had a negative on any article of the constitution); or, in case they could not accomplish this object, to overthrow the National Assembly entirely.

To effect one or other of these objects, they began now to cultivate a friendship with the despotism they had hitherto attempted to rival, and the Count D'Artois became their chief. The King (who has since declared himself deceived into their measures) held, according to the old form, *a Bed of Justice*, in which he accorded to the deliberation and vote *par tête* (by head) upon several subjects; but reserved the deliberation and vote upon all questions respecting a constitution, to the three chambers separately. This declaration of the King was made against the advice of M. Necker, who now began to perceive that he was growing out of fashion at Court, and that another minister was in contemplation.

As the form of sitting in separate chambers was yet apparently kept up, though essentially destroyed, the national representatives, immediately after this declaration of the King, resorted to their own chambers to consult on a protest against it; and the minority of the chamber (calling itself the Nobles), who had joined the national cause, retired to a private house to consult in like manner. The malcontents had by this time concerted their measures with the Court, which Count D'Artois undertook to conduct; and as they saw from the discontent which the declaration excited, and the opposition making against it, that they could not obtain a control over the intended constitution by a separate vote, they prepared themselves for their final object – that of conspiring against the National Assembly, and overthrowing it.

The next morning, the door of the chamber of the National Assembly was shut against them, and guarded by troops; and the Members were refused admittance. On this, they withdrew to a tennis ground in the neighbourhood of Versailles, as the most convenient place they could find, and, after renewing their session, took an oath never to separate from each other, under any circumstance whatever, death excepted, until they had established a constitution. As the experiment of shutting up the house had no other effect than that of producing a closer connection in the Members, it was opened again the next day, and the public business recommenced in the usual place. . . .

It is worth remarking, that the National Assembly neither pursued those fugitive conspirators, nor took any notice of them, nor sought to retaliate in any shape whatever. Occupied with establishing a constitution founded on the Rights of Man and the Authority of the People, the only authority on which government has a right to exist in any country, the National Assembly felt none of those mean passions which mark the character of impertinent governments, founding themselves on their own authority, or on the absurdity of hereditary succession. It is the faculty of the human mind to become what it contemplates, and to act in unison with its object.

The conspiracy being thus dispersed, one of the first works of the National Assembly, instead of vindictive proclamations, as has been the case with other governments, published a Declaration of the Rights of Man, as the basis on which the new constitution was to be built. . . .

MISCELLANEOUS CHAPTER

The opinions of men with respect to government, are changing fast in all countries. The revolutions of America and France have thrown a beam of light over the world, which reaches into man. The enormous expense of governments have provoked people to think, by making them feel: and when once the veil begins to rend, it admits not of repair. Ignorance is of a peculiar nature: and once dispelled, and it is impossible to re-establish it. It is not originally a thing of itself, but is only the absence of knowledge; and though man may be *kept* ignorant, he cannot be *made* ignorant. The mind, in discovering truth, acts in the same manner as it acts through the eye in discovering objects; when once any object has been seen, it is impossible to put the mind back to the same condition it was in before it saw it. Those who talk of a counter-revolution in France, show how little they understand of man. There does not exist in the compass of language, an arrangement of words to express so much as the means of effecting a counter-revolution. The means must be an obliteration of knowledge; and it has never yet been discovered, how to make man *unknow* his knowledge, or *unthink* his thoughts.

Mr Burke is labouring in vain to stop the progress of knowledge; and it comes with the worse grace from him, as there is a certain transaction known in the city, which renders him suspected of being a pensioner in a fictitious name. This may account for some strange doctrine he has advanced in his book, which, though he points it at the Revolution Society, is effectually directed against the whole Nation.

'The King of England', says he, 'holds *his* Crown' (for it does not belong to the Nation, according to Mr Burke) 'in *contempt* of the choice of the Revolution Society, who have not a single vote for a King among them either *individually* or *collectively*; and his Majesty's heirs, each in their time and order, will come to the Crown *with the same contempt* of their choice, with which his Majesty has succeeded to that which he now wears.'

As to who is King in England or elsewhere, or whether there is any King at all, or whether the people choose a Cherokee Chief, or a Hessian Hussar for a King, it is not a matter that I trouble myself about – be that to themselves; but with respect to the doctrine, so far as it relates to the Rights of Men and Nations, it is as abominable as anything ever uttered in the most enslaved country under heaven. Whether it sounds worse to my ear, by not being accustomed to hear such despotism, than what it does to the ear of another person, I am not so well a judge of; but of its abominable principle I am at no loss to judge.

It is not the Revolution Society that Mr Burke means; it is the Nation, as well in its *original*, as in its *representative* character; and he has taken care to make himself understood, by saying that they have not a vote either *collectively* or *individually*. The Revolution Society is composed of citizens of all denominations, and of members of both the Houses of Parliament; and consequently, if there is not a right to vote in any of the characters, there can be no right to any, either in the nation, or in its parliament. This ought to be a caution to every country, how it imports foreign families to be kings. It is somewhat curious to observe, that although the people of England have been in the habit of talking about kings, it is always a Foreign House of kings; hating Foreigners, yet governed by them. – It is now the House of Brunswick, one of the petty tribes of Germany.

It has hitherto been the practice of the English Parliaments, to regulate what was called the succession, (taking it for granted, that the Nation then continued to accord to the form of annexing a monarchical branch to its government; for without this, the Parliament could not have had authority to have sent either to Holland or to Hanover, or to impose a King upon the Nation against its will). And this must be the utmost limit to which Parliament can go upon the case; but the right of the Nation goes to the *whole* case, because it has the right of changing its *whole* form of government. The right of a Parliament is only a right in trust, a right by delegation, and that but from a very small part of the Nation; and one of its Houses has not even this. But the right of the Nation is an original right, as universal as taxation. The Nation is the paymaster of everything, and everything must conform to its general will.

I remember taking notice of a speech in what is called the English House of Peers, by the then Earl of Shelburne, and I think it was at the time he was Minister, which is applicable to this case. I do not directly charge my memory with every particular; but the words and the purport, as nearly as I remember, were these: *That the form of a Government was a matter wholly at the will of a Nation, at all times; that if it chose a monarchical form, it had a right to have it so; and if it afterwards chose to be a Republic, it had a right to be a Republic, and to say to a King, 'We have no longer any occasion for you.'*

When Mr Burke says that 'His Majesty's heirs and successors, each in their time and order, will come to the crown with the *same contempt* of their choice with which His Majesty has succeeded to that he wears', it is saying too much even to the humblest individual in the country; part of whose daily labour goes towards making up the million sterling a year, which the country gives the person it styles a King. Government with insolence, is despotism; but when contempt is added, it becomes worse; and to pay for contempt, is the excess of slavery. This species of government comes from Germany; and reminds me of what one of the Brunswick soldiers told me, who was taken prisoner by the Americans in the late war: 'Ah!' said he, 'America is a fine free country, it is worth the people's fighting for; I know the difference by knowing my own: in my country, if the prince says, Eat straw, we eat straw.' God help that country, thought I, be it England or elsewhere, whose liberties are to be protected by German principles of government, and Princes of Brunswick!

As Mr Burke sometimes speaks of England, sometimes of France, and sometimes of the world, and of government in general, it is difficult to answer his book without apparently meeting him on the same ground. Although principles of government are general subjects, it is next to impossible in many cases to separate them from the idea of place and circumstance; and the more so when circumstances are put for arguments, which is frequently the case with Mr Burke.

In the former part of his book, addressing himself to the people of France, he says, 'No experience has taught us', (meaning the English), 'that in any other course or method than that of an *hereditary crown*, can our liberties be regularly perpetuated and preserved sacred as our *hereditary right*.' I ask Mr Burke, who is to take them away? – M. de Lafayette, in speaking to France, says, '*For a Nation to be free, it is sufficient that she wills it*.' But Mr Burke represents England as wanting capacity to take care of itself, and that its liberties must be taken care of by a King holding it in 'contempt'. If England is sunk to this, it is preparing itself to eat straw, as in Hanover or in Brunswick. But besides the folly of the declaration, it happens that the facts are all against Mr Burke. It was by the government *being hereditary*, that the liberties of the people were endangered. Charles I and James II are instances of this truth; yet neither of them went so far as to hold the Nation in contempt.

As it is sometimes of advantage to the people of one country, to hear what those of other countries have to say respecting it, it is possible that the people of France may learn something from Mr Burke's book, and that the people of England may also learn something from the answers it will occasion. When Nations fall out about freedom, a wide field of debate is opened. The argument commences with the rights of war, without its evils; and as knowledge is the object contended for, the party that sustains the defeat obtains the prize.

Mr Burke talks about what he calls an hereditary crown, as if it were some production of Nature; or as if, like Time, it had a power to operate, not only independently, but in spite of man; or as if it were a thing or a subject universally consented to. Alas! it has none of those properties, but is the reverse of them all. It is a thing in imagination, the propriety of which is more than doubted, and the legality of which in a few years will be denied.

But, to arrange this matter in a clearer view than what general expressions can convey, it will be necessary to state the distinct heads under which (what is called) an hereditary crown, or, more properly speaking, an hereditary succession to the government of a Nation, can be considered; which are,

First, The right of a particular Family to establish itself.

Secondly, The right of a Nation to establish a particular Family.

With respect to the *first* of these heads, that of a Family establishing itself with hereditary powers on its own authority, and independent of the consent of a Nation, all men will concur in calling it despotism;

and it would be trespassing on their understanding to attempt to prove it.

But the *second* head, that of a Nation establishing a particular Family with *hereditary powers*, does not present itself as despotism on the first reflection; but if men will permit a second reflection to take place, and carry that reflection forward but one remove out of their own persons to that of their offspring, they will then see that hereditary succession becomes in its consequences the same despotism to others, which they reprobated for themselves. It operates to preclude the consent of the succeeding generation; and the preclusion of consent is despotism. When the person who at any time shall be in possession of a government, or those who stand in succession to him, shall say to a Nation, I hold this power in 'contempt' of you, it signifies not on what authority he pretends to say it. It is no relief, but an aggravation to a person in slavery, to reflect that he was sold by his parent; and as that which heightens the criminality of an act cannot be produced to prove the legality of it, hereditary succession cannot be established as a legal thing.

In order to arrive at a more perfect decision on this head, it will be proper to consider the generation which undertakes to establish a Family with *hereditary powers*, apart and separate from the generations which are to follow; and also to consider the character in which the *first* generation acts with respect to succeeding generations.

The generation which first selects a person, and puts him at the head of its government, either with the title of King, or any other distinction, acts its *own choice*, be it wise or foolish, as a free agent for itself. The person so set up is not hereditary, but selected and appointed; and the generation who sets him up, does not live under an hereditary government, but under a government of its own choice and establishment. Were the generation who sets him up, and the person so set up, to live for ever, it never could become hereditary succession; and of consequence, hereditary succession can only follow on the death of the first parties.

As therefore hereditary succession is out of the question with respect to the *first* generation, we have now to consider the character in which *that* generation acts with respect to the commencing generation, and to all succeeding ones.

It assumes a character, to which it has neither right nor title. It changes itself from a *Legislator* to a *Testator*, and affects to make its

Will, which is to have operation after the demise of the makers, to bequeath the government; and it not only attempts to bequeath, but to establish on the succeeding generation, a new and different form of government under which itself lived. Itself, as is already observed, lived not under an hereditary government, but under a government of its own choice and establishment; and it now attempts, by virtue of a will and testament, (and which it has not authority to make), to take from the commencing generation, and all future ones, the rights and free agency by which itself acted.

But, exclusive of the right which any generation has to act collectively as a testator, the objects to which it applies itself in this case, are not within the compass of any law, or of any will or testament.

The rights of men in society, are neither devisable, nor transferable, nor annihilable, but are descendable only; and it is not in the power of any generation to intercept finally, and cut off the descent. If the present generation, or any other, are disposed to be slaves, it does not lessen the right of the succeeding generation to be free: wrongs cannot have a legal descent. When Mr Burke attempts to maintain, that the *English Nation did at the Revolution of* 1688, *most solemnly renounce and abdicate their rights for themselves, and for all their posterity for ever*, he speaks a language that merits not reply, and which can only excite contempt for his prostitute principles, or pity for his ignorance.

In whatever light hereditary succession, as growing out of the will and testament of some former generation, presents itself, it is an absurdity. A cannot make a will to take from B the property of B, and give it to C; yet this is the manner in which (what is called) hereditary succession by law operates. A certain former generation made a will, to take away the rights of the commencing generation, and all future ones, and convey those rights to a third person, who afterwards comes forward, and tells them, in Mr Burke's language, that they have *no rights*, that their rights are already bequeathed to him, and that he will govern in *contempt* of them. From such principles, and such ignorance, Good Lord deliver the world!

But, after all, what is this metaphor called a crown, or rather what is monarchy? Is it a thing, or is it a name, or is it a fraud? Is it 'a contrivance of human wisdom', or of human craft to obtain money from a nation under specious pretences? Is it a thing necessary to a nation? If it is, in what does that necessity consist, what services does it perform, what is its business, and what are its merits? Doth the virtue consist in the metaphor, or in the man? Doth the goldsmith that makes the crown, make the virtue also? Doth it operate like Fortunatus's wishing-cap, or Harlequin's wooden sword? Doth it make a man a conjuror? In fine, what is it? It appears to be a something going much out of fashion, falling into ridicule, and rejected in some countries both as unnecessary and expensive. In America it is considered as an absurdity; and in France it has so far declined, that the goodness of the man, and the respect for his personal character, are the only things that preserve the appearance of its existence.

If government be what Mr Burke describes it, 'a contrivance of human wisdom', I might ask him, if wisdom was at such a low ebb in England, that it was become necessary to import it from Holland and from Hanover? But I will do the country the justice to say, that was not the case; and even if it was, it mistook the cargo. The wisdom of every country, when properly exerted, is sufficient for all its purposes; and there could exist no more real occasion in England to have sent for a Dutch Stadtholder, or a German Elector, than there was in America to have done a similar thing. If a country does not understand its own affairs, how is a foreigner to understand them, who knows neither its laws, its manners, nor its language? If there existed a man so transcendently wise above all others, that his wisdom was necessary to instruct a nation, some reason might be offered for monarchy; but when we cast our eyes about a country, and observe how every part understands its own affairs; and when we look around the world, and see that of all men in it, the race of kings are the most insignificant in capacity, our reason cannot fail to ask us – What are those men kept for?

If there is anything in monarchy which we people of America do not understand, I wish Mr Burke would be so kind as to inform us. I see in America, a government extending over a country ten times as large as England, and conducted with regularity, for a fortieth part of the expense which government costs in England. If I ask a man in America, if he wants a King? he retorts, and asks me if I take him for an idiot? How is it that this difference happens? are we more or less wise than others? I see in America, the generality of people living in a style of plenty unknown in monarchical countries; and I see that the principle of its government, which is that of the *equal Rights of Man*, is making a rapid progress in the world.

If monarchy is a useless thing, why is it kept up anywhere? and if a necessary thing, how can it be dispensed with? That *civil government* is necessary, all civilized nations will agree; but civil government is republican government. All that part of the government of England which begins with the office of constable, and proceeds through the department of magistrate, quarter-session, and general assize, including trial by jury, is republican government. Nothing of monarchy appears in any part of it, except the name which William the Conqueror imposed upon the English, that of obliging them to call him 'Their Sovereign Lord the King'.

It is easy to conceive, that a band of interested men, such as Placemen, Pensioners, Lords of the bed-chamber, Lords of the kitchen, Lords of the necessary-house, and the Lord knows what besides, can find as many reasons for monarchy as their salaries, paid at the expense of the country, amount to; but if I ask the farmer, the manufacturer, the merchant, the tradesman, and down through all the occupations of life to the common labourer, what service monarchy is to him? he can give me no answer. If I ask him what monarchy is, he believes it is something like a sinecure.

Notwithstanding the taxes of England amount to almost seventeen millions a year, said to be for the expenses of government, it is still evident that the sense of the Nation is left to govern itself, and does govern itself by magistrates and juries, almost at its own charge, on republican principles, exclusive of the expense of taxes. The salaries of the Judges are almost the only charge that is paid out of the revenue. Considering that all the internal government is executed by the people, the taxes of England ought to be the lightest of any nation in Europe; instead of which, they are the contrary. As this cannot be accounted for on the score of civil government, the subject necessarily extends itself to the monarchical part.

When the people of England sent for George the First, (and it would puzzle a wiser man than Mr Burke to discover for what he could be wanted, or what service he could render), they ought at least to have conditioned for the abandonment of Hanover. Besides the endless German intrigues that must follow from a German Elector being King of England, there is a natural impossibility of uniting in the same person the principles of Freedom and the principles of Despotism, or, as it is usually called in England, Arbitrary Power. A German Elector is in his electorate a despot: How then could it be expected that he should be attached to principles of liberty in one country, while his interest in another was to be supported by despotism? The union cannot exist; and it might easily have been foreseen, that German Electors would make German Kings, or, in Mr Burke's words, would assume government with 'contempt'. The English have been in the habit of considering a King of England only in the character in which he appears to them: whereas the same person, while the connection lasts, has a home-seat in another country, the interest of which is different to their own, and the principles of the governments in opposition to each other – To such a person England will appear as a town-residence, and the Electorate as the estate. The English may wish, as I believe they do, success to the principles of Liberty in France, or in Germany; but a German Elector trembles for the fate of despotism in his electorate: and the Duchy of Mecklenburgh, where the present Queen's family governs, is under the same wretched state of arbitrary power, and the people in slavish vassalage.

There never was a time when it became the English to watch continental intrigues more circumspectly than at the present moment, and to distinguish the politics of the Electorate from the politics of the Nation. The revolution of France has entirely changed the ground with respect to England and France, as nations: but the German despots, with Prussia at their head, are combining against Liberty; and the fondness of Mr Pitt for office, and the interest which all his family-connections have obtained, do not give sufficient security against this intrigue.

As everything which passes in the world becomes matter for history, I will now quit this subject, and take a concise review of the state of parties and politics in England, as Mr Burke has done in France.

Whether the present reign commenced with contempt, I leave to Mr Burke: certain however it is, that it had strongly that appearance. The animosity of the English Nation, it is very well remembered, ran high; and, had the true principles of Liberty been as well under-stood then as they now promise to be, it is probable the Nation would not have patiently submitted to so much. George the First and Second were sensible of a rival in the remains of the Stuarts; and as they could not but consider themselves as standing on their good behaviour, they had prudence to keep their German principles of government to themselves; but as the Stuart family wore away, the prudence became less necessary.

The contest between rights, and what were called prerogatives, continued to heat the Nation till some time after the conclusion of the American War, when all at once it fell a calm – Execration exchanged itself for applause, and Court popularity sprang up like a mushroom in a night.

To account for this sudden transition, it is proper to observe, that there are two distinct species of popularity; the one excited by merit, the other by resentment. As the Nation had formed itself into two parties, and each was extolling the merits of its parliamentary champions for and against prerogative, nothing could operate to give a more general shock than an immediate coalition of the champions themselves. The partisans of each being thus suddenly left in the lurch, and mutually heated with disgust at the measure, felt no other relief than uniting in a common execration against both. A higher stimulus of resentment being thus excited, than what the contest on prerogatives had occasioned, the Nation quitted all former objects of rights and wrongs, and sought only that of gratification. The indignation at the Coalition, so effectually superseded the indignation against the Court, as to extinguish it; and without any change of principles on the part of the Court, the same people who had reprobated its despotism, united with it, to revenge themselves on the Coalition Parliament. The case was not, which they liked best, – but, which they hated most; and the least hated passed for love. The dissolution of the Coalition Parliament, as it afforded the means of gratifying the resentment of the Nation, could not fail to be popular; and from hence arose the popularity of the Court.

Transitions of this kind exhibit a Nation under the government of temper, instead of a fixed and steady principle; and having once committed itself, however rashly, it feels itself urged along to justify by continuance its first proceeding. – Measures which at other times it would censure, it now approves, and acts persuasion upon itself to suffocate its judgement.

On the return of a new Parliament, the new Minister, Mr Pitt, found himself in a secure majority: and the nation gave him credit, not out of regard to himself, but because it had resolved to do it out of resentment to another. He introduced himself to public notice by a proposed Reform of Parliament, which in its operation would have amounted to a public justification of corruption. The Nation was to be at the expense of buying up the rotten boroughs, whereas it ought to punish the persons who deal in the traffic.

Passing over the two bubbles, of the Dutch business, and the million a year to sink the national debt, the matter which most presents itself, is the affair of the Regency. Never, in the course of my observation, was delusion more successfully acted, nor a nation more completely deceived. – But, to make this appear, it will be necessary to go over the circumstances.

Mr Fox had stated in the House of Commons, that the Prince of Wales, as heir in succession, had a right in himself to assume the government. This was opposed by Mr Pitt; and, so far as the opposition was confined to the doctrine, it was just. But the principles which Mr Pitt maintained on the contrary side, were as bad, or worse in their extent, than those of Mr Fox; because they went to establish an aristocracy over the Nation, and over the small representation it has in the House of Commons.

Whether the English form of government be good or bad, is not in this case the question; but, taking it as it stands, without regard to its merits or demerits, Mr Pitt was farther from the point than Mr Fox.

It is supposed to consist of three parts: – while therefore the Nation is disposed to continue this form, the parts have a *national standing*, independent of each other, and are not the creatures of each other. Had Mr Fox passed through Parliament, and said, that the person alluded to claimed on the ground of the Nation, Mr Pitt must then have contended (what he called) the right of the Parliament, against the right of the Nation.

By the appearance which the contest made, Mr Fox took the hereditary ground, and Mr Pitt the parliamentary ground; but the fact is, they both took hereditary ground, and Mr Pitt took the worst of the two.

What is called the Parliament, is made up of two Houses; one of which is more hereditary, and more beyond the control of the Nation, than what the Crown (as it is called) is supposed to be. It is an hereditary aristocracy, assuming and asserting indefeasible, irrevocable rights and authority, wholly independent of the Nation. Where then was the merited popularity of exalting this hereditary power over another hereditary power less independent of the Nation than what itself assumed to be, and of absorbing the rights of the Nation into a House over which it has neither election nor control?

The general impulse of the Nation was right; but it acted without reflection. It approved the opposition made to the right set up by Mr Fox, without perceiving that Mr Pitt was supporting another indefeasible right, more remote from the Nation, in opposition to it.

With respect to the House of Commons, it is elected but by a small part of the Nation; but were the election as universal as taxation, which it ought to be, it would still be only the organ of the Nation, and cannot possess inherent rights. – When the National Assembly of France resolves a matter, the resolve is made in right of the Nation; but Mr Pitt, on all national questions, so far as they refer to the House of Commons, absorbs the rights of the nation into the organ, and makes the organ into a Nation, and the Nation itself into a cipher.

In a few words, the question on the Regency was a question of a million a year, which is appropriated to the executive department: and Mr Pitt could not possess himself of any management of this sum, without setting up the supremacy of Parliament; and when this was accomplished it was indifferent who should be Regent, as he must be Regent at his own cost. Among the curiosities which this contentious debate afforded, was that of making the Great Seal into a King; the affixing of which to an act, was to be royal authority. If, therefore, Royal Authority is a Great Seal, it consequently is in itself nothing; and a good constitution would be of infinitely more value to the Nation, than what the three Nominal Powers, as they now stand, are worth.

The continual use of the word *constitution* in the English Parliament, shows there is none; and that the whole is merely a form of government without a constitution, and constituting itself with what powers it pleases. If there were a constitution, it certainly could be referred to; and the debate on any constitutional point, would terminate by producing the constitution. One member says, This is constitution; and another says, That is constitution – Today it is one thing; and tomorrow, it is something else – while the maintaining the debate proves there is none. Constitution is now the cant word of Parliament, turning itself to the ear of the Nation. Formerly it was the *universal supremacy of Parliament – the omnipotence of Parliament*: But since the progress of Liberty in France, those phrases have a despotic harshness in their note; and the English Parliament have caught the fashion from the National Assembly, but without the substance, of speaking of *constitution*.

As the present generation of people in England did not make the Government, they are not accountable for any of its defects; but that sooner or later it must come into their hands to undergo a constitutional reformation, is as certain as that the same thing has happened in France. If France, with a revenue of nearly twenty-four million sterling, with an extent of rich and fertile country above four times larger than England, with a population of twenty-four millions of inhabitants to support taxation, with upwards of ninety millions sterling of gold and silver circulating in the nation, and with a debt less than the present debt of England – still found it necessary, from whatever cause, to come to a settlement of its affairs, it solves the problem of funding for both countries.

It is out of the question to say how long what is called the English constitution has lasted, and to argue from thence how long it is to last; the question is, how long can the funding system last? It is a thing but of modern invention, and has not yet continued beyond the life of a man; yet in that short space it has so far accumulated, that, together with the current expenses, it requires an amount of taxes at least equal to the whole landed rental of the nation in acres to defray the annual expenditure. That a government could not always have gone on by the same system which has been followed for the last seventy years, must be evident to every man; and for the same reason it cannot always go on. . . .

CONCLUSION

Reason and Ignorance, the opposites of each other, influence the great bulk of mankind. If either of these can be rendered sufficiently extensive in a country, the machinery of government goes easily on. Reason obeys itself; and Ignorance submits to whatever is dictated to it.

The two modes of government which prevail in the world, are, *first*, government by election and representation: *Secondly*, government by hereditary succession. The former is generally known by the name of republic; the latter by that of monarchy and aristocracy.

Those two distinct and opposite forms, erect themselves on the two distinct and opposite bases of Reason and Ignorance. — As the exercise of government requires talents and abilities, and as talents and abilities cannot have hereditary descent, it is evident that hereditary succession requires a belief from man, to which his reason cannot subscribe, and which can only be established upon his ignorance; and the more ignorant any country is, the better it is fitted for this species of government.

On the contrary, government in a well-constituted republic, requires no belief from man beyond what his reason can give. He sees the *rationale* of the whole system, its origin and its operation; and as it is best supported when best understood, the human faculties act with boldness, and acquire, under this form of government, a gigantic manliness.

As, therefore, each of those forms acts on a different base, the one moving freely by the aid of reason, the other by ignorance; we have next to consider, what it is that gives motion to that species of government which is called mixed government, or, as it is sometimes ludicrously styled, a government of *this*, *that*, and *t'other*.

The moving power in this species of government, is of necessity, Corruption. However imperfect election and representation may be in mixed governments, they still give exercise to a greater portion of reason than is convenient to the hereditary part; and therefore it becomes necessary to buy the reason up. A mixed government is an imperfect everything, cementing and soldering the discordant parts together by corruption, to act as a whole. Mr Burke appears highly disgusted, that France, since she had resolved on a revolution, did not adopt what he calls '*A British Constitution*'; and the regretful manner in which he expresses himself on this occasion, implies a suspicion, that the British Constitution needed something to keep its defects in countenance.

In mixed governments there is no responsibility: the parts cover each other till responsibility is lost; and the corruption which moves the machine, contrives at the same time its own escape. When it is laid down as a maxim, that a *King can do no wrong*, it places him in a state of similar security with that of idiots and persons insane, and responsibility is out of the question with respect to himself. It then descends upon the Minister, who shelters himself under a majority in Parliament, which, by places, pensions, and corruption, he can always command; and that majority justifies itself by the same authority with which it protects the Minister. In this rotatory motion, responsibility is thrown off from the parts, and from the whole.

When there is a part in a government which can do no wrong, it implies that it does nothing; and is only the machine of another power, by whose advice and direction it acts. What is supposed to be the King in mixed governments, is the Cabinet; and as the Cabinet is always a part of the Parliament, and the members justifying in one character what they advise and act in another, a mixed government becomes a continual enigma; entailing upon a country, by the quantity of corruption necessary to solder the parts, the expense of supporting all the forms of government at once, and finally resolving itself into a government by committee; in which the advisers, the actors, the approvers, the justifiers, the persons responsible, and the persons not responsible, are the same persons.

By this pantomimical contrivance, and change of scene and character, the parts help each other out in matters which neither of them singly would assume to act. When money is to be obtained, the mass of variety apparently dissolves, and a profusion of parliamentary praises passes between the parts. Each admires with astonishment, the wisdom, the liberality, the disinterestedness of the other; and all of them breathe a pitying sigh at the burdens of the Nation.

But in a well-constituted republic, nothing of this soldering, praising, and pitying, can take place; the representation being equal throughout the country, and complete in itself, however it may be arranged into legislative and executive, they have all one and the same natural source. The parts are not foreigners to each other, like democracy, aristocracy, and monarchy. As there are no discordant distinctions, there is nothing to corrupt by compromise, nor confound by contrivance. Public measures appeal of themselves to the understanding of the Nation, and, resting on their own merits, disown any flattering application to vanity. The continual whine of lamenting the burden of taxes, however successfully it may be practised in mixed governments, is inconsistent with the sense and spirit of a republic. If taxes are necessary, they are of course advantageous; but if they require an apology, the apology itself implies an impeachment. Why then is man thus imposed upon, or why does he impose upon himself?

When men are spoken of as kings and subjects, or when

government is mentioned under the distinct or combined heads of monarchy, aristocracy, and democracy, what is it that *reasoning* man is to understand by the terms? If there really existed in the world two or more distinct and separate *elements* of human power, we should then see the several origins to which those terms would descriptively apply: but as there is but one species of man, there can be but one element of human power; and that element is man himself. Monarchy, aristocracy, and democracy, are but creatures of imagination; and a thousand such may be contrived, as well as three.

*

From the revolutions of America and France, and the symptoms that have appeared in other countries, it is evident that the opinion of the world is changed with respect to systems of government, and that revolutions are not within the compass of political calculations. The progress of time and circumstances, which men assign to the accomplishment of great changes, is too mechanical to measure the force of the mind, and the rapidity of reflection, by which revolutions are generated: All the old governments have received a shock from those that already appear, and which were once more improbable, and are a greater subject of wonder, than a general revolution in Europe would be now.

When we survey the wretched condition of man under the monarchical and hereditary systems of government, dragged from his home by one power, or driven by another, and impoverished by taxes more than by enemies, it becomes evident that those systems are bad, and that a general revolution in the principle and construction of governments is necessary.

What is government more than the management of the affairs of a Nation? It is not, and from its nature cannot be, the property of any particular man or family, but of the whole community, at whose expense it is supported; and though by force or contrivance it has been usurped into an inheritance, the usurpation cannot alter the right of things. Sovereignty, as a matter of right, appertains to the Nation only, and not to any individual; and a Nation has at all times an inherent indefeasible right to abolish any form of government it finds inconvenient, and establish such as accords with its interest, disposition, and happiness. The romantic and barbarous distinction of men into Kings and subjects, though it may suit the condition of courtiers, cannot that of citizens; and is exploded by the principle upon which governments are now founded. Every citizen is a member of the Sovereignty, and, as such, can acknowledge no personal subjection; and his obedience can be only to the laws.

When men think of what government is, they must necessarily suppose it to possess a knowledge of all the objects and matters upon which its authority is to be exercised. In this view of government, the republican system, as established by America and France, operates to embrace the whole of a Nation; and the knowledge necessary to the interest of all the parts, is to be found in the centre, which the parts by representation form: But the old governments are on a construction that excludes knowledge as well as happiness; government by monks, who know nothing of the world beyond the walls of a convent, is as consistent as government by Kings.

What were formerly called revolutions, were little more than a change of persons, or an alteration of local circumstances. They rose and fell like things of course, and had nothing in their existence or their fate that could influence beyond the spot that produced them. But what we now see in the world, from the revolutions of America and France, are a renovation of the natural order of things, a system of principles as universal as truth and the existence of man, and combining moral with political happiness and national prosperity.

'I. *Men are born and always continue free, and equal in respect of their rights. Civil distinctions, therefore, can be founded only on public utility.*

'II. *The end of all political associations is the preservation of the natural and imprescriptible rights of man; and these rights are liberty, property, security, and resistance of oppression.*

'III. *The Nation is essentially the source of all Sovereignty; nor can any* INDIVIDUAL, *or* ANY BODY OF MEN, *be entitled to any authority which is not expressly derived from it.*'

In these principles, there is nothing to throw a Nation into confusion by inflaming ambition. They are calculated to call forth wisdom and abilities, and to exercise them for the public good, and not for the emolument or aggrandizement of particular descriptions of men or families. Monarchical sovereignty, the enemy of mankind, and the source of misery, is abolished; and sovereignty itself is restored to its natural and original place, the Nation. Were this the case through Europe, the cause of wars would be taken away.

It is attributable to Henry the Fourth of France, a man of an enlarged and benevolent heart, that he proposed, about the year 1610, a plan for abolishing war in Europe. The plan consisted in constituting an European Congress, or as the French Authors style it, a Pacific Republic; by appointing delegates from the several Nations, who were to act as a Court of arbitration in any disputes that might arise between nation and nation.

Had such a plan been adopted at the time it was proposed, the taxes of England and France, as two of the parties, would have been at least ten millions sterling annually to each Nation less than they were at the commencement of the French Revolution.

To conceive a cause why such a plan has not been adopted, (and that instead of a Congress for the purpose of *preventing* war, it has been called only to *terminate* a war, after a fruitless expense of several years), it will be necessary to consider the interest of governments as a distinct interest to that of Nations.

Whatever is the cause of taxes to a Nation, becomes also the means of revenue to a government. Every war terminates with an addition of taxes, and consequently with an addition of revenue; and in any event of war, in the manner they are now commenced and concluded, the power and interest of governments are increased. War, therefore, from its productiveness, as it easily furnishes the pretence of necessity for taxes and appointments to places and offices, becomes a principal part of the system of old governments; and to establish any mode to abolish war, however advantageous it might be to Nations, would be to take from such government the most lucrative of its branches. The frivolous matters upon which war is made, show the disposition and avidity of governments to uphold the system of war, and betray the motives upon which they act.

Why are not republics plunged into war, but because the nature of their government does not admit of an interest distinct from that of the Nation? Even Holland, though an ill-constructed republic, and with a commerce extending over the world, existed nearly a century without war: and the instant the form of government was changed in France, the republican principles of peace and domestic prosperity and economy arose with the new government; and the same conse-quences would follow the same causes in other Nations.

As war is the system of government on the old construction, the animosity which Nations reciprocally entertain, is nothing more than what the policy of their governments excites, to keep up the spirit of the system. Each government accuses the other of perfidy, intrigue, and ambition, as a means of heating the imagination of their respective Nations, and incensing them to hostilities. Man is not the enemy of man, but through the medium of a false system of government. Instead, therefore, of exclaiming against the ambition of Kings, the exclamation should be directed against the principle of such governments; and instead of seeking to reform the individual, the wisdom of a Nation should apply itself to reform the system.

Whether the forms and maxims of governments which are still in practice, were adapted to the condition of the world at the period they were established, is not in this case the question. The older they are, the less correspondence can they have with the present state of things. Time, and change of circumstances and opinions, have the same progressive effect in rendering modes of government obsolete, as they have upon customs and manners. – Agriculture, commerce, manufactures, and the tranquil arts, by which the prosperity of Nations is best promoted, require a different system of government, and a different species of knowledge to direct its operations, than what might have been required in the former condition of the world.

As it is not difficult to perceive, from the enlightened state of mankind, that hereditary governments are verging to their decline, and that Revolutions on the broad basis of national sovereignty, and government by representation, are making their way in Europe, it would be an act of wisdom to anticipate their approach, and produce Revolutions by reason and accommodation, rather than commit them to the issue of convulsions.

From what we now see, nothing of reform in the political world ought to be held improbable. It is an age of Revolutions, in which everything may be looked for. The intrigue of Courts, by which the system of war is kept up, may provoke a confederation of Nations to abolish it: and an European Congress, to patronize the progress of free government, and promote the civilization of Nations with each other, is an event nearer in probability, than once were the Revolutions and Alliance of France and America.

FINIS

PART TWO

INTRODUCTION

What Archimedes said of the mechanical powers, may be applied to Reason and Liberty: '*Had we*', said he, '*a place to stand upon, we might raise the world.*'

The revolution of America presented in politics what was only theory in mechanics. So deeply rooted were all the governments of the old world, and so effectually had the tyranny and the antiquity of habit established itself over the mind, that no beginning could be made in Asia, Africa, or Europe, to reform the political condition of man. Freedom had been hunted round the globe; reason was considered as rebellion; and the slavery of fear had made men afraid to think.

But such is the irresistible nature of truth, that all it asks, and all it wants, is the liberty of appearing. The sun needs no inscription to distinguish him from darkness; and no sooner did the American governments display themselves to the world, than despotism felt a shock, and man began to contemplate redress.

The independence of America, considered merely as a separation from England, would have been a matter but of little importance, had it not been accompanied by a revolution in the principles and practice of governments. She made a stand, not for herself only, but for the world, and looked beyond the advantages herself could receive. Even the Hessian, though hired to fight against her, may live to bless his defeat; and England, condemning the viciousness of its government, rejoice in its miscarriage.

As America was the only spot in the political world, where the principles of universal reformation could begin, so also was it the best in the natural world. An assemblage of circumstances conspired, not only to give birth, but to add gigantic maturity to its principles. The scene which that country presents to the eye of a spectator, has something in it which generates and encourages great ideas. Nature appears to him in magnitude. The mighty objects he beholds, act upon his mind by enlarging it, and he partakes of the greatness he contemplates. – Its first settlers were emigrants from different European nations, and of diversified professions of religion, retiring from the governmental persecutions of the old world, and meeting in the new, not as enemies, but as brothers. The wants which necessarily accompany the cultivation of a wilderness produced among them a state of society, which countries, long harassed by the quarrels and intrigues of governments, had neglected to cherish. In such a situation man becomes what he ought. He sees his species, not with the inhuman idea of a natural enemy, but as kindred; and the example shows to the artificial world, that man must go back to Nature for information.

From the rapid progress which America makes in every species of improvement, it is rational to conclude, that if the governments of Asia, Africa, and Europe, had begun on a principle similar to that of America, or had not been very early corrupted therefrom, that those countries must, by this time, have been in a far superior condition to what they are. Age after age has passed away, for no other purpose than to behold their wretchedness. – Could we suppose a spectator who knew nothing of the world, and who was put into it merely to make his observations, he would take a great part of the old world to be new, just struggling with the difficulties and hardship of an infant settlement. He could not suppose that the hordes of miserable poor, with which old countries abound, could be any other than those who had not yet had time to provide for themselves. Little would he think they are the consequences of what in such countries is called government.

If, from the more wretched parts of the old world, we look at those which are in an advanced stage of improvement, we still find the greedy hand of government thrusting itself into every corner and crevice of industry, and grasping the spoil of the multitude. Invention is continually exercised, to furnish new pretences for revenue and taxation. It watches prosperity as its prey, and permits none to escape without a tribute.

As revolutions have begun, (and as the probability is always greater against a thing beginning, than of proceeding after it has begun), it is natural to expect that other revolutions will follow. The amazing and still increasing expenses with which old governments are conducted, the numerous wars they engage in or provoke, the embarrassments they throw in the way of universal civilization and commerce, and the oppression and usurpation they practise at home, have wearied out the patience, and exhausted the property of the world. In such a situation, and with the examples already existing, revolutions are to be looked for. They are become subjects of universal conversation, and may be considered as the *order of the day*.

If systems of government can be introduced, less expensive, and more productive of general happiness, than those which have existed, all attempts to oppose their progress will in the end be fruitless. Reason, like time, will make its own way, and prejudice will fall in a combat with interest. If universal peace, civilization, and commerce, are ever to be the happy lot of man, it cannot be accomplished but by a revolution in the system of governments. All the monarchical governments are military. War is their trade, plunder and revenue their objects. While such governments continue, peace has not the absolute security of a day. What is the history of all monarchical governments, but a disgustful picture of human wretchedness, and the accidental respite of a few years' repose? Wearied with war, and tired with human butchery, they sat down to rest, and called it peace. This certainly is not the condition that Heaven intended for man; and if *this be monarchy*, well might monarchy be reckoned among the sins of the Jews.

The revolutions which formerly took place in the world, had nothing in them that interested the bulk of mankind. They extended only to a change of persons and measures, but not of principles, and rose or fell among the common transactions of the moment. What we now behold, may not improperly be called a '*counter-revolution*'. Conquest and tyranny, at some early period, dispossessed man of his rights, and he is now recovering them. And as the tide of all human affairs has its ebb and flow in directions contrary to each other, so also is it in this. Government founded on a *moral theory, on a system of universal peace, on the indefeasible hereditary Rights of Man*, is now revolving from west to east, by a stronger impulse than the government of the sword revolved from east to west. It interests not particular individuals, but nations, in its progress, and promises a new era to the human race.

The danger to which the success of revolutions is most exposed, is that of attempting them before the principles on which they proceed, and the advantages to result from them, are sufficiently seen and understood. Almost everything appertaining to the circumstances of a nation, has been absorbed and confounded under the general and mysterious word *government*. Though it avoids taking to its account the errors it commits, and the mischiefs it occasions, it fails not to arrogate to itself whatever has the appearance of prosperity. It robs industry of its honours, by pedantically making itself the cause of its effects; and purloins from the general character of man, the merits that appertain to him as a social being.

It may therefore be of use, in this day of revolutions, to discriminate between those things which are the effect of government, and those which are not. This will best be done by taking a review of society and civilization, and the consequences resulting therefrom, as things distinct from what are called governments. By beginning with this investigation, we shall be able to assign effects to their proper cause, and analyse the mass of common errors.

CHAPTER I
OF SOCIETY AND CIVILIZATION

Great part of that order which reigns among mankind is not the effect of government. It has its origin in the principles of society and the natural constitution of man. It existed prior to government, and would exist if the formality of government was abolished. The mutual dependence and reciprocal interest which man has upon man, and all the parts of a civilized community upon each other, create that great chain of connection which holds it together. The land-holder, the farmer, the manufacturer, the merchant, the tradesman, and every occupation, prospers by the aid which each receives from the other, and from the whole. Common interest regulates their concerns, and forms their law; and the laws which common usage ordains, have a greater influence than the laws of government. In fine, society performs for itself almost everything which is ascribed to government.

To understand the nature and quantity of government proper for man, it is necessary to attend to his character. As Nature created him for social life, she fitted him for the station she intended. In all cases she made his natural wants greater than his individual powers. No one man is capable, without the aid of society, of supplying his own wants; and those wants, acting upon every individual, impel the whole of them into society, as naturally as gravitation acts to a centre.

But she has gone further. She has not only forced man into society, by a diversity of wants, which the reciprocal aid of each other can supply, but she has implanted in him a system of social affections, which, though not necessary to his existence, are essential to his happiness. There is no period in life when this love for society ceases to act. It begins and ends with our being.

If we examine, with attention, into the composition and constitution of man, the diversity of his wants, and the diversity of talents in different men for reciprocally accommodating the wants of each other, his propensity to society, and consequently to preserve the advantages resulting from it, we shall easily discover, that a great deal of what is called government is mere imposition.

Government is no farther necessary than to supply the few cases to which society and civilization are not conveniently competent; and instances are not wanting to show, that everything which government can usefully add thereto, has been performed by the common consent of society, without government.

For upwards of two years from the commencement of the American war, and to a longer period in several of the American States, there were no established forms of government. The old governments had been abolished, and the country was too much occupied in defence, to employ its attention in establishing new governments; yet during this interval, order and harmony were preserved as inviolate as in any country in Europe. There is a natural aptness in man, and more so in society, because it embraces a greater variety of abilities and resources, to accommodate itself to whatever situation it is in. The instant formal government is abolished, society begins to act. A general association takes place, and common interest produces common security.

So far is it from being true, as has been pretended, that the abolition of any formal government is the dissolution of society, that it acts by a contrary impulse, and brings the latter the closer together. All that part of its organization which it had committed to its government, devolves again upon itself, and acts through its medium. When men, as well from natural instinct, as from reciprocal benefits, have habituated themselves to social and civilized life, there is always enough of its principles in practice to carry them through any changes they may find necessary or convenient to make in their government. In short, man is so naturally a creature of society, that it is almost impossible to put him out of it.

Formal government makes but a small part of civilized life; and when even the best that human wisdom can devise is established, it is a thing more in name and idea, than in fact. It is to the great and fundamental principles of society and civilization – to the common usage universally consented to, and mutually and reciprocally maintained – to the unceasing circulation of interest, which, passing through its million channels, invigorates the whole mass of civilized man – it is to these things, infinitely more than to anything else which even the best instituted government can perform, that the safety and prosperity of the individual and of the whole depends.

The more perfect civilization is, the less occasion has it for government, because the more does it regulate its own affairs, and govern itself; but so contrary is the practice of old governments to the reason of the case, that the expenses of them increase in the proportion they ought to diminish. It is but few general laws that civilized life requires, and those of such common usefulness, that whether they are enforced by the forms of government or not, the effect will be nearly the same. If we consider what the principles are that first condense men into society, and what the motives that regulate their mutual intercourse afterwards, we shall find, by the time we arrive at what is called government, that nearly the whole of the business is performed by the natural operation of the parts upon each other.

Man, with respect to all those matters, is more a creature of consistency than he is aware, or than governments would wish him to believe. All the great laws of society are laws of nature. Those of trade and commerce, whether with respect to the intercourse of individuals, or of nations, are laws of mutual and reciprocal interest. They are followed and obeyed, because it is the interest of the parties so to do, and not on account of any formal laws their governments may impose or interpose.

But how often is the natural propensity to society disturbed or destroyed by the operations of government! When the latter, instead of being ingrafted on the principles of the former, assumes to exist for itself, and acts by partialities of favour and oppression, it becomes the cause of the mischiefs it ought to prevent.

If we look back to the riots and tumults, which at various times have happened in England, we shall find, that they did not proceed from the want of a government, but that government was itself the generating cause; instead of consolidating society it divided it; it deprived it of its natural cohesion, and engendered discontents and

disorders, which otherwise would not have existed. In those associations which men promiscuously form for the purpose of trade, or
of any concern, in which government is totally out of the question,
and in which they act merely on the principles of society, we see
how naturally the various parties unite; and this shows, by comparison, that governments, so far from being always the cause or
means of order, are often the destruction of it. The riots of 1780 had
no other source than the remains of those prejudices, which the
government itself had encouraged. But with respect to England there
are also other causes.

Excess and inequality of taxation, however disguised in the means,
never fail to appear in their effects. As a great mass of the community
are thrown thereby into poverty and discontent, they are constantly
on the brink of commotion; and deprived, as they unfortunately are,
of the means of information, are easily heated to outrage. Whatever
the apparent cause of any riots may be, the real one is always want of
happiness. It shows that something is wrong in the system of
government, that injures the felicity by which society is to be preserved.

But as fact is superior to reasoning, the instance of America presents
itself to confirm these observations. – If there is a country in the
world, where concord, according to common calculation, would be
least expected, it is America. Made up, as it is, of people from
different nations,[4] accustomed to different forms and habits of
government, speaking different languages, and more different in
their modes of worship, it would appear that the union of such a
people was impracticable; but by the simple operation of constructing
government on the principles of society and the rights of man, every
difficulty retires, and all the parts are brought into cordial unison.
There, the poor are not oppressed, the rich are not privileged. Indus-

4 That part of America which is generally called New England, including New
Hampshire, Massachusetts, Rhode Island, and Connecticut, is peopled chiefly by English
descendants. In the state of New York, about half are Dutch, the rest English, Scottish,
and Irish. In New Jersey, a mixture of English and Dutch, with some Scottish and
Irish. In Pennsylvania, about one-third are English, another Germans, and the remainder Scottish and Irish, with some Swedes. The States to the southward have a
greater proportion of English than the middle States, but in all of them there is a
mixture; and besides those enumerated, there are a considerable number of French,
and some few of all the European nations lying on the coast. The most numerous
religious denomination are the Presbyterians; but no one sect is established above
another, and all men are equally citizens. – Paine.

try is not mortified by the splendid extravagance of a court rioting at its expense. Their taxes are few, because their government is just; and as there is nothing to render them wretched, there is nothing to engender riots and tumults.

A metaphysical man, like Mr Burke, would have tortured his invention to discover how such a people could be governed. He would have supposed that some must be managed by fraud, others by force, and all by some contrivance; that genius must be hired to impose upon ignorance, and show and parade to fascinate the vulgar. Lost in the abundance of his researches, he would have resolved and re-resolved, and finally overlooked the plain and easy road that lay directly before him.

One of the great advantages of the American Revolution has been, that it led to a discovery of the principles, and laid open the imposition, of governments. All the revolutions till then had been worked within the atmosphere of a court, and never on the great floor of a nation. The parties were always of the class of courtiers; and whatever was their rage for reformation, they carefully preserved the fraud of the profession.

In all cases they took care to represent government as a thing made up of mysteries, which only themselves understood; and they hid from the understanding of the nation, the only thing that was beneficial to know, namely, *That government is nothing more than a national association acting on the principles of society*.

Having thus endeavoured to show, that the social and civilized state of man is capable of performing within itself, almost everything necessary to its protection and government, it will be proper, on the other hand, to take a review of the present old governments, and examine whether their principles and practice are correspondent thereto.

CHAPTER 2

OF THE ORIGIN OF THE PRESENT
OLD GOVERNMENTS

It is impossible that such governments as have hitherto existed in the world, could have commenced by any other means than a total violation of every principle sacred and moral. The obscurity in which the origin of all the present old governments is buried, implies the iniquity and disgrace with which they began. The origin of the present government of America and France will ever be remembered, because it is honourable to record it; but with respect to the rest, even Flattery has consigned them to the tomb of time, without an inscription.

It could have been no difficult thing in the early and solitary ages of the world, while the chief employment of men was that of attending flocks and herds, for a banditti of ruffians to overrun a country, and lay it under contributions. Their power being thus established, the chief of the band contrived to lose the name of Robber in that of Monarch; and hence the origin of Monarchy and Kings.

The origin of the government of England, so far as relates to what is called its line of monarchy, being one of the latest, is perhaps the best recorded. The hatred which the Norman invasion and tyranny begat, must have been deeply rooted in the nation, to have outlived the contrivance to obliterate it. Though not a courtier will talk of the curfew-bell, not a village in England has forgotten it.

Those bands of robbers having parcelled out the world, and divided it into dominions, began, as is naturally the case, to quarrel with each other. What at first was obtained by violence, was considered by others as lawful to be taken, and a second plunderer succeeded the first. They alternately invaded the dominions which each had assigned to himself, and the brutality with which they treated each other explains the original character of monarchy. It was ruffian torturing ruffian. The conqueror considered the conquered, not as his prisoner, but his property. He led him in triumph rattling in chains, and doomed him, at pleasure, to slavery or death. As time obliterated the history of their beginning, their successors assumed new appearances, to cut off the entail of their disgrace, but their principles and objects remained the same. What at first was plunder, assumed the foster name of revenue; and the power originally usurped, they affected to inherit.

From such beginning of governments, what could be expected, but a continual system of war and extortion? It has established itself into a trade. The vice is not peculiar to one more than to another, but is the common principle of all. There does not exist within such governments sufficient stamina whereon to ingraft reformation; and the shortest, easiest, and most effectual remedy, is to begin anew on the ground of the oration.

What scenes of horror, what perfection of iniquity, present themselves in contemplating the character, and reviewing the history of such governments! If we would delineate human nature with a baseness of heart, and hypocrisy of countenance, that reflection would shudder at and humanity disown, it is kings, courts, and cabinets, that must sit for the portrait. Man, naturally as he is, with all his faults about him, is not up to the character.

Can we possibly suppose that if governments had originated in a right principle, and had not an interest in pursuing a wrong one, that the world could have been in the wretched and quarrelsome condition we have seen it? What inducement has the farmer, while following the plough, to lay aside his peaceful pursuit, and go to war with the farmer of another country? or what inducement has the manufacturer? What is dominion to them, or to any class of men in a nation? Does it add an acre to any man's estate, or raise its value? Are not conquest and defeat each of the same price, and taxes the never-failing consequence? – Though this reasoning may be good to a nation, it is not so to a government. War is the Faro table of governments, and nations the dupes of the games.

If there is anything to wonder at in this miserable scene of governments, more than might be expected, it is the progress which the peaceful arts of agriculture, manufacture and commerce have made, beneath such a long accumulating load of discouragement and oppression. It serves to show, that instinct in animals does not act with stronger impulse, than the principles of society and civilization operate in man. Under all discouragements, he pursues his object, and yields to nothing but impossibilities.

CHAPTER 3

OF THE OLD AND NEW SYSTEMS
OF GOVERNMENT

Nothing can appear more contradictory than the principles on which the old governments began, and the condition to which society, civilization, and commerce, are capable of carrying mankind. Government on the old system, is an assumption of power, for the aggrandizement of itself; on the new, a delegation of power, for the common benefit of society. The former supports itself by keeping up a system of war; the latter promotes a system of peace, as the true means of enriching a nation. The one encourages national prejudices; the other promotes universal society, as the means of universal commerce. The one measures its prosperity, by the quantity of revenue it extorts; the other proves its excellence, by the small quantity of taxes it requires.

Mr Burke has talked of old and new whigs. If he can amuse himself with childish names and distinctions, I shall not interrupt his pleasure. It is not to him, but to the Abbé Sieyès, that I address this chapter. I am already engaged to the latter gentleman, to discuss the subject of monarchical government; and as it naturally occurs in comparing the old and new systems, I make this the opportunity of presenting to him my observations. I shall occasionally take Mr Burke in my way.

Though it might be proved that the system of government now called the NEW, is the most ancient in principle of all that have existed, being founded on the original inherent Rights of Man: yet, as tyranny and the sword have suspended the exercise of those rights for many centuries past, it serves better the purpose of distinction to call it the *new*, than to claim the right of calling it the old.

The first general distinction between those two systems, is, that the one now called the old is *hereditary*, either in whole or in part; and the new is entirely *representative*. It rejects all hereditary government:

First, As being an imposition on mankind.

Secondly, As inadequate to the purposes for which government is necessary.

With respect to the first of these heads – It cannot be proved by what right hereditary government could begin: neither does there exist within the compass of mortal power, a right to establish it. Man has no authority over posterity in matters of personal right; and therefore, no man, or body of men, had, or can have, a right to set up hereditary government. Were even ourselves to come again into existence, instead of being succeeded by posterity, we have not now the right of taking from ourselves the rights which would then be ours. On what ground, then, do we pretend to take them from others?

All hereditary government is in its nature tyranny. An heritable crown, or an heritable throne, or by what other fanciful name such things may be called, have no other significant explanation than that mankind are heritable property. To inherit a government, is to inherit the people, as if they were flocks and herds.

With respect to the second head, that of being inadequate to the purposes for which government is necessary, we have only to consider what government essentially is, and compare it with the circumstances to which hereditary succession is subject.

Government ought to be a thing always in full maturity. It ought to be so constructed as to be superior to all the accidents to which individual man is subject; and therefore, hereditary succession, by being *subject to them all*, is the most irregular and imperfect of all the systems of government.

We have heard the *Rights of Man* called a *levelling* system; but the only system to which the word *levelling* is truly applicable is the hereditary monarchical system. It is a system of *mental levelling*. It indiscriminately admits every species of character to the same authority. Vice and virtue, ignorance and wisdom, in short, every quality, good or bad, is put on the same level. Kings succeed each other, not as rationals, but as animals. It signifies not what their mental or moral characters are. Can we then be surprised at the abject state of the human mind in monarchical countries, when the government itself is formed on such an abject levelling system? – It has no fixed character. Today it is one thing; tomorrow it is something else. It changes with the temper of every succeeding individual, and is subject to all the varieties of each. It is government through the medium of passions and accidents. It appears under all the various characters of childhood, decrepitude, dotage, a thing at nurse, in leading-strings, or in crutches. It reverses the wholesome order of nature. It occasionally puts children over men, and the conceits of nonage over wisdom and experience. In short, we cannot conceive a more ridiculous figure of government, than hereditary succession, in all its cases, presents.

Could it be made a decree in nature, or an edict registered in heaven, and man could know it, that virtue and wisdom should invariably appertain to hereditary succession, the objections to it would be removed; but when we see that nature acts as if she disowned and sported with the hereditary system; that the mental characters of successors, in all countries, are below the average of human understanding; that one is a tyrant, another an idiot, a third insane, and some all three together, it is impossible to attach confidence to it, when reason in man has power to act.

It is not to the Abbé Sieyès that I need apply this reasoning; he has already saved me that trouble, by giving his own opinion upon the case. 'If it be asked', says he, 'what is my opinion with respect to hereditary right, I answer, without hesitation, That, in good theory, an hereditary transmission of any power or office, can never accord with the laws of a true representation. Hereditaryship is, in this sense, as much an attaint upon principle, as an outrage upon society. But let us', continues he, 'refer to the history of all elective monarchies and principalities: Is there one in which the elective mode is not worse than the hereditary succession?'

As to debating on which is the worst of the two, it is admitting both to be bad; and herein we are agreed. The preference which the Abbé has given, is a condemnation of the thing that he prefers. Such a mode of reasoning on such a subject is inadmissible, because it finally amounts to an accusation upon Providence, as if she had left to man no other choice with respect to government than between two evils, the best of which he admits to be '*an attaint upon principle, and an outrage upon society*'.

Passing over, for the present, all the evils and mischiefs which monarchy has occasioned in the world, nothing can more effectually prove its uselessness in a state of *civil government*, than making it hereditary. Would we make any office hereditary that required wisdom and abilities to fill it? and where wisdom and abilities are not necessary, such an office, whatever it may be, is superfluous or insignificant.

Hereditary succession is a burlesque upon monarchy. It puts it in the most ridiculous light, by presenting it as an office which any child or idiot may fill. It requires some talents to be a common mechanic; but, to be a king, requires only the animal figures of man – a sort of breathing automaton. This sort of superstition may last a few years more, but it cannot long resist the awakened reason and interest of man.

As to Mr Burke, he is a stickler for monarchy, not altogether as a pensioner, if he is one, which I believe, but as a political man. He has taken up a contemptible opinion of mankind, who, in their turn, are taking up the same of him. He considers them as a herd of beings that must be governed by fraud, effigy and show; and an idol would be as good a figure of monarchy with him, as a man. I will, however, do him the justice to say, that, with respect to America, he has been very complimentary. He always contended, at least in my hearing, that the people of America were more enlightened than those of England, or of any country in Europe; and that therefore the imposition of show was not necessary in their governments.

Though the comparison between hereditary and elective monarchy, which the Abbé has made, is unnecessary to the case, because the representative system rejects both; yet, were I to make the comparison, I should decide contrary to what he has done.

The civil wars which have originated from contested hereditary claims, are more numerous, and have been more dreadful, and of longer continuance, than those which have been occasioned by election. All the civil wars in France arose from the hereditary system; they were either produced by hereditary claims, or by the imperfection of the hereditary form, which admits of regencies, or monarchy at nurse. With respect to England, its history is full of the same misfortunes. The contests for succession between the houses of York and Lancaster, lasted a whole century; and others of a similar nature, have renewed themselves since that period. Those of 1715 and 1745, were of the same kind. The succession war for the crown of Spain, embroiled almost half Europe. The disturbances in Holland are generated from the hereditaryship of the Stadtholder. A government calling itself free, with an hereditary office, is like a thorn in the flesh, that produces a fermentation which endeavours to discharge it.

But I might go further, and place also foreign wars, of whatever kind, to the same cause. It is by adding the evil of hereditary succession to that of monarchy, that a permanent family interest is created, whose constant objects are dominion and revenue. Poland, though an elective monarchy, has had fewer wars than those which are hereditary; and it is the only government that has made a voluntary essay, though but a small one, to reform the condition of the country.

Having thus glanced at a few of the defects of the old, or hereditary systems of government, let us compare it with the new, or representative system.

The representative system takes society and civilization for its basis; nature, reason, and experience, for its guide.

Experience, in all ages, and in all countries, has demonstrated, that it is impossible to control Nature in her distribution of mental powers. She gives them as she pleases. Whatever is the rule by which she, apparently to us, scatters them among mankind, that rule remains a secret to man. It would be as ridiculous to attempt to fix the hereditaryship of human beauty, as of wisdom. Whatever wisdom constituently is, it is like a seedless plant; it may be reared when it appears, but it cannot be voluntarily produced. There is always a sufficiency somewhere in the general mass of society for all purposes; but with respect to the parts of society, it is continually changing its place. It rises in one today, in another tomorrow, and has most probably visited in rotation every family of the earth, and again withdrawn.

As this is the order of nature, the order of government must necessarily follow it, or government will, as we see it does, degenerate into ignorance. The hereditary system, therefore, is as repugnant to human wisdom, as to human right; and is as absurd, as it is unjust.

As the republic of letters brings forward the best literary productions, by giving to genius a fair and universal chance; so the representative system of government is calculated to produce the wisest laws, by collecting wisdom from where it can be found. I smile to myself when I contemplate the ridiculous insignificance into which literature and all the sciences would sink, were they made hereditary; and I carry the same idea into governments. An hereditary governor is as inconsistent as an hereditary author. I know not whether Homer or Euclid had sons: but I will venture an opinion, that if they had, and had left their works unfinished, those sons could not have completed them.

Do we need a stronger evidence of the absurdity of hereditary government, than is seen in the descendants of those men, in any line of life, who once were famous? Is there scarcely an instance in which there is not a total reverse of the character? It appears as if the tide of mental faculties flowed as far as it could in certain channels, and then forsook its course, and arose in others. How irrational then is the hereditary system which establishes channels of power, in company with which wisdom refuses to flow! By continuing this absurdity, man is perpetually in contradiction with himself; he accepts, for a king, or a chief magistrate, or a legislator, a person whom he would not elect for a constable.

It appears to general observation, that revolutions create genius and talents; but those events do no more than bring them forward. There is existing in man, a mass of sense lying in a dormant state, and which, unless something excites it to action, will descend with him, in that condition, to the grave. As it is to the advantage of society that the whole of its faculties should be employed, the construction of government ought to be such as to bring forward, by a quiet and regular operation, all that extent of capacity which never fails to appear in revolutions.

This cannot take place in the insipid state of hereditary government, not only because it prevents, but because it operates to benumb. When the mind of a nation is bowed down by any political superstition in its government, such as hereditary succession is, it loses a considerable portion of its powers on all other subjects and objects. Hereditary succession requires the same obedience to ignorance, as to wisdom; and when once the mind can bring itself to pay this indiscriminate reverence, it descends below the stature of mental manhood. It is fit to be great only in little things. It acts a treachery upon itself, and suffocates the sensations that urge the detection.

Though the ancient governments present to us a miserable picture of the condition of man, there is one which above all others exempts itself from the general description. I mean the democracy of the Athenians. We see more to admire, and less to condemn, in that great, extraordinary people, than in any thing which history affords.

Mr Burke is so little acquainted with constituent principles of government, that he confounds democracy and representation together. Representation was a thing unknown in the ancient democracies. In those the mass of the people met and enacted laws (grammatically speaking) in the first person. Simple democracy was no other than the common-hall of the ancients. It signifies the *form*, as well as the public principle of the government. As these democracies increased in population, and the territory extended, the simple democratical form became unwieldy and impracticable; and as the system of representation was not known, the consequence was, they either degenerated convulsively into monarchies, or became absorbed into such as then existed. Had the system of representation been then understood, as it now is, there is no reason to believe that those forms of government, now called monarchical or aristocratical, would ever have taken place. It was the want of some method to consolidate the parts of society, after it became too populous, and too extensive for the simple democratical form, and also the lax and solitary condition of shepherds and herdsmen in other parts of the world, that afforded opportunities to those unnatural modes of government to begin.

As it is necessary to clear away the rubbish of errors, into which the subject of government has been thrown, I shall proceed to remark on some others.

It has always been the political craft of courtiers and court-governments, to abuse something which they called republicanism; but what republicanism was, or is, they never attempt to explain. Let us examine a little into this case.

The only forms of government are, the democratical, the aristocratical, the monarchical, and what is now called the representative.

What is called a *republic*, is not any *particular form* of government. It is wholly characteristical of the purport, matter, or object for which government ought to be instituted, and on which it is to be employed, RES-PUBLICA, the public affairs, or the public good; or, literally translated, the *public thing*. It is a word of a good original, referring to what ought to be the character and business of government; and in this sense it is naturally opposed to the word *monarchy*, which has a base original signification. It means arbitrary power in an individual person; in the exercise of which, *himself*, and not the *res-publica*, is the object.

Every government that does not act on the principle of a *republic*, or in other words that does not make the *res-publica* its whole and sole object, is not a good government. Republican government is no other than government established and conducted for the interest of the public, as well individually as collectively. It is not necessarily connected with any particular form, but it most naturally associates with the representative form, as being best calculated to secure the end for which a nation is at the expense of supporting it.

Various forms of government have affected to style themselves a republic. Poland calls itself a republic, which is an hereditary aristocracy, with what is called an elective monarchy. Holland calls itself a republic, which is chiefly aristocratical, with an hereditary stadtholdership. But the government of America, which is wholly on the system of representation, is the only real republic in character and in practice, that now exists. Its government has no other object than the public business of the nation, and therefore it is properly a republic;

and the Americans have taken care that THIS, and no other, shall always be the object of their government, by their rejecting everything hereditary, and establishing government on the system of representation only.

Those who have said that a republic is not a *form* of government calculated for countries of great extent, mistook, in the first place, the *business* of a government, for a *form* of government; for the *respublica* equally appertains to every extent of territory and population. And, in the second place, if they meant anything with respect to *form*, it was the simple democratical form, such as was the mode of government in the ancient democracies, in which there was no representation. The case, therefore is, not, that a republic cannot be extensive, but that it cannot be extensive on the simple democratical form; and the question naturally presents itself, *What is the best form of government for conducting the* RES-PUBLICA, *or the* PUBLIC BUSINESS *of a nation, after it becomes too extensive and populous for the simple democratical form?*

It cannot be monarchy, because monarchy is subject to an objection of the same amount to which the simple democratical form was subject.

It is possible that an individual may lay down a system of principles, on which government shall be constitutionally established to any extent of territory. This is no more than an operation of the mind, acting by its own powers. But the practice upon those principles, as applying to the various and numerous circumstances of a nation, its agriculture, manufacture, trade, commerce, etc., requires a knowledge of a different kind, and which can be had only from the various parts of society. It is an assemblage of practical knowledge, which no one individual can possess; and therefore the monarchical form is as much limited, in useful practice, from the incompetency of knowledge, as was the democratical form, from the multiplicity of population. The one degenerates, by extension, into confusion; the other, into ignorance and incapacity, of which all the great monarchies are an evidence. The monarchical form, therefore, could not be a substitute for the democratical, because it has equal inconveniences.

Much less could it when made hereditary. This is the most effectual of all forms to preclude knowledge. Neither could the high democratical mind have voluntarily yielded itself to be governed by children and idiots, and all the motley insignificance of character, which attends such a mere animal system, the disgrace and the reproach of reason and of man.

As to the aristocratical form, it has the same vices and defects with the monarchical, except that the chance of abilities is better from the proportion of numbers, but there is still no security for the right use and application of them.

Referring, then, to the original simple democracy, it affords the true data from which government on a large scale can begin. It is incapable of extension, not from its principle, but from the inconvenience of its form; and monarchy and aristocracy, from their incapacity. Retaining, then, democracy as the ground, and rejecting the corrupt systems of monarchy and aristocracy, the representative system naturally presents itself; remedying at once the defects of the simple democracy as to form, and the incapacity of the other two with respect to knowledge.

Simple democracy was society governing itself without the aid of secondary means. By ingrafting representation upon democracy, we arrive at a system of government capable of embracing and confederating all the various interests and every extent of territory and population; and that also with advantages as much superior to hereditary government, as the republic of letters is to hereditary literature.

It is on this system that the American government is founded. It is representation ingrafted upon democracy. It has fixed the form by a scale parallel in all cases to the extent of the principle. What Athens was in miniature, America will be in magnitude. The one was the wonder of the ancient world; the other is becoming the admiration and model of the present. It is the easiest of all the forms of government to be understood, and the most eligible in practice; and excludes at once the ignorance and insecurity of the hereditary mode, and the inconvenience of the simple democracy.

It is impossible to conceive a system of government capable of acting over such an extent of territory, and such a circle of interests, as is immediately produced by the operation of representation. France, great and populous as it is, is but a spot in the capaciousness of the system. It adapts itself to all possible cases. It is preferable to simple democracy even in small territories. Athens, by representation, would have outrivalled her own democracy.

That which is called government, or rather that which we ought to conceive government to be, is no more than some common centre, in which all the parts of society unite. This cannot be accomplished by any method so conducive to the various interests of the community, as by the representative system. It concentrates the knowledge necessary to the interest of the parts, and of the whole. It places government in a state of constant maturity. It is, as has been already observed, never young, never old. It is subject neither to nonage, nor dotage. It is never in the cradle, nor on crutches. It admits not of a separation between knowledge and power, and is superior, as government always ought to be, to all the accidents of individual man, and is therefore superior to what is called monarchy.

A nation is not a body, the figure of which is to be represented by the human body; but is like a body contained within a circle, having a common centre, in which every radius meets; and that centre is formed by representation. To connect representation with what is called monarchy, is eccentric government. Representation is of itself the delegated monarchy of a nation, and cannot debase itself by dividing it with another.

Mr Burke has two or three times, in his parliamentary speeches, and in his publications, made use of a jingle of words that convey no ideas. Speaking of government, he says, 'It is better to have monarchy for its basis, and republicanism for its corrective, than republicanism for its basis, and monarchy for its corrective.' – If he means that it is better to correct folly with wisdom, than wisdom with folly, I will no otherwise contend with him, than that it would be much better to reject the folly entirely.

But what is this thing which Mr Burke calls monarchy? Will he explain it? All men can understand what representation is; and that it must necessarily include a variety of knowledge and talents. But, what security is there for the same qualities on the part of monarchy? or, when this monarchy is a child, where then is the wisdom? What does it know about government? Who then is the monarch, or where is the monarchy? If it is to be performed by regency, it proves it to be a farce. A regency is a mock species of republic, and the whole of monarchy deserves no better description. It is a thing as various as imagination can paint. It has none of the stable character that government ought to possess. Every succession is a revolution, and every regency a counter-revolution. The whole of it is a scene of perpetual court cabal and intrigue, of which Mr Burke is himself an instance. To render monarchy consistent with government, the next in succession should not be born a child, but a man at once, and that man a Solomon. It is ridiculous that nations are to wait, and government be interrupted, till boys grow to be men.

Whether I have too little sense to see, or too much to be imposed upon; whether I have too much or too little pride, or of anything else, I leave out of the question; but certain it is, that what is called monarchy, always appears to me a silly, contemptible thing. I compare it to something kept behind a curtain, about which there is a great deal of bustle and fuss, and a wonderful air of seeming solemnity; but when, by any accident, the curtain happens to be open, and the company see what it is, they burst into laughter.

In the representative system of government, nothing of this can happen. Like the nation itself, it possesses a perpetual stamina, as well of body as of mind, and presents itself on the open theatre of the world in a fair and manly manner. Whatever are its excellences or its defects, they are visible to all. It exists not by fraud and mystery; it deals not in cant and sophistry; but inspires a language, that, passing from heart to heart, is felt and understood.

We must shut our eyes against reason, we must basely degrade our understanding, not to see the folly of what is called monarchy. Nature is orderly in all her works; but this is a mode of government that counteracts nature. It turns the progress of the human faculties upside down. It subjects age to be governed by children, and wisdom by folly.

On the contrary, the representative system is always parallel with the order and immutable laws of nature, and meets the reason of man in every part. For example:

In the American federal government, more power is delegated to the President of the United States, than to any other individual member of congress.[5] He cannot, therefore, be elected to this office under the age of thirty-five years. By this time the judgement of man becomes matured, and he has lived long enough to be acquainted with men and things, and the country with him. – But on the monarchical plan, (exclusive of the numerous chances there are against every man born into the world, of drawing a prize in the lottery of human faculties), the next in succession, whatever he may

5 Paine is mistaken here. The President was not then, nor is now, a member of Congress. – Editors.

be, is put at the head of a nation, and of a government, at the age of eighteen years. Does this appear like an act of wisdom? Is it consistent with the proper dignity and the manly character of a nation? Where is the propriety of calling such a lad the father of the people? — In all other cases, a person is a minor until the age of twenty-one years. Before this period, he is not trusted with the management of an acre of land, or with the heritable property of a flock of sheep, or an herd of swine; but, wonderful to tell! he may, at the age of eighteen years, be trusted with a nation.

That monarchy is all a bubble, a mere court artifice to procure money, is evident, (at least to me), in every character in which it can be viewed. It would be impossible, on the rational system of representative government, to make out a bill of expenses to such an enormous amount as this deception admits. Government is not of itself a very chargeable institution. The whole expense of the federal government of America, founded, as I have already said, on the system of representation, and extending over a country nearly ten times as large as England, is but six hundred thousand dollars, or one hundred and thirty-five thousand pounds sterling.

I presume, that no man in his sober senses, will compare the character of any of the kings of Europe with that of General Washington. Yet, in France, and also in England, the expense of the civil list only, for the support of one man, is eight times greater than the whole expense of the federal government in America. To assign a reason for this, appears almost impossible. The generality of people in America, especially the poor, are more able to pay taxes, than the generality of people either in France or England.

But the case is, that the representative system diffuses such a body of knowledge throughout a nation, on the subject of government, as to explode ignorance and preclude imposition. The craft of courts cannot be acted on that ground. There is no place for mystery; nowhere for it to begin. Those who are not in the representation, know as much of the nature of business as those who are. An affectation of mysterious importance would there be scouted. Nations can have no secrets; and the secrets of courts, like those of individuals, are always their defects.

In the representative system, the reason for everything must publicly appear. Every man is a proprietor in government, and considers it a necessary part of his business to understand. It concerns his interest, because it affects his property. He examines the cost, and compares it with the advantages; and above all, he does not adopt the slavish custom of following what in other governments are called LEADERS.

It can only be by blinding the understanding of man, and making him believe that government is some wonderful mysterious thing, that excessive revenues are obtained. Monarchy is well calculated to ensure this end. It is the popery of government; a thing kept up to amuse the ignorant, and quiet them into taxes.

The government of a free country, properly speaking, is not in the persons, but in the laws. The enacting of those requires no great expense; and when they are administered, the whole of civil government is performed – the rest is all court contrivance.

CHAPTER 4

OF CONSTITUTIONS

That men mean distinct and separate things when they speak of constitutions and of governments, is evident; or, why are those terms distinctly and separately used? A constitution is not the act of a government, but of a people constituting a government; and government without a constitution, is power without a right.

All power exercised over a nation, must have some beginning. It must be either delegated, or assumed. There are no other sources. All delegated power is trust, and all assumed power is usurpation. Time does not alter the nature and quality of either.

In viewing this subject, the case and circumstances of America present themselves as in the beginning of a world; and our inquiry into the origin of government is shortened, by referring to the facts that have arisen in our own day. We have no occasion to roam for information into the obscure field of antiquity, nor hazard ourselves upon conjecture. We are brought at once to the point of seeing government begin, as if we had lived in the beginning of time. The real volume, not of history, but of facts, is directly before us, un-mutilated by contrivance, or the errors of tradition.

I will here concisely state the commencement of the American constitutions; by which the difference between constitutions and governments will sufficiently appear.

It may not be improper to remind the reader, that the United States of America consist of thirteen separate states, each of which established a government for itself, after the declaration of independence, done the fourth of July 1776. Each state acted independently of the rest, in forming its government; but the same general principle pervades the whole. When the several state governments were formed, they proceeded to form the federal government, that acts over the whole in all matters which concern the interest of the whole, or which relate to the intercourse of the several states with each other, or with foreign nations. I will begin with giving an instance from one of the state governments. (that of Pennsylvania), and then proceed to the federal government.

The state of Pennsylvania, though nearly of the same extent of territory as England, was then divided into only twelve counties. Each of those counties had elected a committee at the commencement of the dispute with the English government; and as the city of Philadelphia, which also had its committee, was the most central for intelligence, it became the centre of communication to the several county committees. When it became necessary to proceed to the formation of a government, the committee of Philadelphia proposed a conference of all the county committees, to be held in that city, and which met the latter end of July 1776.

Though these committees had been elected by the people, they were not elected expressly for the purpose, nor invested with the authority of forming a constitution; and as they could not, consistently with the American idea of rights, assume such a power, they could only confer upon the matter, and put it into a train of operation. The conferees, therefore, did no more than state the case, and recommend to the several counties to elect six representatives for each county, to meet in convention at Philadelphia, with powers to form a constitution, and propose it for public consideration.

This convention, of which Benjamin Franklin was president, having met and deliberated, and agreed upon a constitution, they next ordered it to be published, not as a thing established, but for the consideration of the whole people, their approbation or rejection, and then adjourned to a stated time. When the time of adjournment was expired, the convention re-assembled; and as the general opinion of the people in approbation of it was then known, the constitution was signed, sealed, and proclaimed on the *authority of the people* and the original instrument deposited as a public record. The convention then appointed a day for the general election of the representatives who were to compose the government, and the time it should commence; and having done this, they dissolved, and returned to their several homes and occupations.

In this constitution were laid down, first, a declaration of rights. Then followed the form which the government should have, and the powers it should possess – the authority of the courts of judicature, and of juries – the manner in which elections should be conducted, and the proportion of representatives to the number of electors – the time which each succeeding assembly should continue, which was one year – the mode of levying, and of accounting for the expenditure, of public money – of appointing public officers, etc.

No article of this constitution could be altered or infringed at the discretion of the government that was to ensue. It was to that government a law. But as it would have been unwise to preclude the benefit of experience, and in order also to prevent the accumulation of errors, if any should be found, and to preserve a unison of government with the circumstances of the state at all times, the constitution provided, that, at the expiration of every seven years, a convention should be elected, for the express purpose of revising the constitution, and making alterations, additions, or abolitions therein, if any such should be found necessary.

Here we see a regular process – a government issuing out of a constitution, formed by the people in their original character; and that constitution serving, not only as an authority, but as a law of control to the government. It was the political bible of the state. Scarcely a family was without it. Every member of the government had a copy; and nothing was more common, when any debate arose on the principle of a bill, or on the extent of any species of authority, than for the members to take the printed constitution out of their pocket, and read the chapter with which such matter in debate was connected.

Having thus given an instance from one of the states, I will show the proceedings by which the federal constitution of the United States arose and was formed.

Congress, at its two first meetings, in September 1774, and May 1775, was nothing more than a deputation from the legislatures of the several provinces, afterwards states; and had no other authority than what arose from common consent, and the necessity of its acting as a public body. In everything which related to the internal affairs of America, congress went no further than to issue recommendations to the several provincial assemblies, who at discretion adopted them or not. Nothing on the part of congress was compulsive; yet, in this situation, it was more faithfully and affectionately obeyed, than was any government in Europe. This instance, like that of the national assembly in France, sufficiently shows, that the strength of government does not consist in anything *within* itself, but in the attachment of a nation, and the interest which the people feel in supporting it. When this is lost, government is but a child in power; and though, like the old government of France, it may harass individuals for a while, it but facilitates its own fall.

After the declaration of independence, it became consistent with the principle on which representative government is founded, that the authority of congress should be defined and established. Whether that authority should be more or less than congress then discretionarily exercised, was not the question. It was merely the rectitude of the measure.

For this purpose, the act, called the act of confederation, (which was a sort of imperfect federal constitution), was proposed, and, after long deliberation, was concluded in the year 1781. It was not the act of congress, because it is repugnant to the principles of representative government that a body should give power to itself. Congress first informed the several states of the powers which it conceived were necessary to be invested in the union, to enable it to perform the duties and services required from it; and the states severally agreed with each other, and concentrated in congress those powers.

It may not be improper to observe, that in both those instances, (the one of Pennsylvania, and the other of the United States), there is no such thing as the idea of a compact between the people on one side, and the government on the other. The compact was that of the people with each other, to produce and constitute a government. To suppose that any government can be a party in a compact with the whole people, is to suppose it to have existence before it can have a right to exist. The only instance in which a compact can take place between the people and those who exercise the government, is, that the people shall pay them, while they choose to employ them.

Government is not a trade which any man or body of men has a right to set up and exercise for his own emolument, but is altogether a trust, in right of those by whom that trust is delegated, and by whom it is always resumable. It has of itself no rights; they are altogether duties.

Having thus given two instances of the original formation of a constitution, I will show the manner in which both have been changed since their first establishment.

The powers vested in the governments of the several states, by the state constitutions, were found, upon experience, to be too great; and those vested in the federal government, by the act of confederation, too little. The defect was not in the principle, but in the distribution of power.

Numerous publications, in pamphlets and in the newspapers, appeared, on the propriety and necessity of new modelling the federal government. After some time of public discussion, carried on through the channel of the press, and in conversations, the state of Virginia, experiencing some inconvenience with respect to commerce, proposed holding a continental conference; in consequence of which, a deputation from five or six of the state assemblies met at Annapolis in Maryland, in 1786. This meeting, not conceiving itself sufficiently authorized to go into the business of a reform, did no more than state their general opinions of the propriety of the measure, and re-commend that a convention of all the states should be held the year following.

This convention met at Philadelphia in May 1787, of which Gen-eral Washington was elected president. He was not at that time connected with any of the state governments, or with congress. He delivered up his commission when the war ended, and since then had lived a private citizen.

The convention went deeply into all the subjects; and having, after a variety of debate and investigation, agreed among themselves upon the several parts of a federal constitution, the next question was, the manner of giving it authority and practice.

For this purpose, they did not, like a cabal of courtiers, send for a Dutch Stadtholder, or a German Elector; but they referred the whole matter to the sense and interest of the country.

They first directed, that the proposed constitution should be pub-lished. Secondly, that each state should elect a convention, expressly for the purpose of taking it into consideration, and of ratifying or rejecting it; and that as soon as the approbation and ratification of any nine states should be given, that those states should proceed to the election of their proportion of members to the new federal government; and that the operation of it should then begin, and the former federal government cease.

The several states proceeded accordingly to elect their conventions. Some of those conventions ratified the constitution by very large majorities, and two or three unanimously. In others there were much debate and division of opinion. In the Massachusetts convention, which met at Boston, the majority was not above nineteen or twenty, in about three hundred members; but such is the nature of representative government, that it quietly decides all matters by majority. After the debate in the Massachusetts convention was closed, and the vote taken, the objecting members rose, and declared, *'That though they had argued and voted against it, because certain parts appeared to them in a different light to what they appeared to other members; yet, as the vote had decided in favour of the constitution as proposed, they should give it the same practical support as if they had voted for it.'*

As soon as nine states had concurred, (and the rest followed in the order their conventions were elected), the old fabric of the federal government was taken down, and the new one erected, of which General Washington is President. – In this place I cannot help remarking, that the character and services of this gentleman are sufficient to put all those men called kings to shame. While they are receiving from the sweat and labours of mankind, a prodigality of pay, to which neither their abilities nor their services can entitle them, he is rendering every service in his power, and refusing every pecuniary reward. He accepted no pay as commander in chief; he accepts none as President of the United States.

After the new federal constitution was established, the state of Pennsylvania, conceiving that some parts of its own constitution required to be altered, elected a convention for that purpose. The proposed alterations were published, and the people concurring therein, they were established.

In forming those constitutions, or in altering them, little or no inconvenience took place. The ordinary course of things was not interrupted, and the advantages have been much. It is always the interest of a far greater number of people in a nation to have things right, than to let them remain wrong; and when public matters are open to debate, and the public judgement free, it will not decide wrong, unless it decides too hastily.

In the two instances of changing the constitutions, the governments then in being were not actors either way. Government has no right to make itself a party in any debate respecting the principles or modes of forming, or of changing, constitutions. It is not for the benefit of those who exercise the powers of government, that constitutions, and the governments issuing from them, are established. In all those matters, the right of judging and acting are in those who pay, and not in those who receive.

A constitution is the property of a nation, and not of those who exercise the government. All the constitutions of America are declared to be established on the authority of the people. In France, the word nation is used instead of the people; but in both cases, a constitution is a thing antecedent to the government, and always distinct therefrom.

In England, it is not difficult to perceive that everything has a constitution, except the nation. Every society and association that is established, first agreed upon a number of original articles, digested into form, which are its constitution. It then appointed its officers, whose powers and authorities are described in that constitution, and the government of that society then commenced. Those officers, by whatever name they are called, have no authority to add to, alter, or abridge the original articles. It is only to the constituting power that this right belongs.

From the want of understanding the difference between a constitution and a government, Dr Johnson, and all writers of his description, have always bewildered themselves. They could not but perceive, that there must necessarily be a *controlling* power existing somewhere, and they placed this power in the discretion of the persons exercising the government, instead of placing it in a constitution formed by the nation. When it is in a constitution, it has the nation for its support, and the natural and the political controlling powers are together. The laws which are enacted by governments, control men only as individuals, but the nation, through its constitution, controls the whole government, and has a natural ability so to do. The final controlling power, therefore, and the original constituting power, are one and the same power.

Dr Johnson could not have advanced such a position in any country where there was a constitution; and he is himself an evidence, that no such thing as a constitution exists in England. – But it may be put as a question, not improper to be investigated, That if a constitution does not exist, how came the idea of its existence so generally established?

In order to decide this question, it is necessary to consider a constitution in both its cases: – First, as creating a government and giving it powers. Secondly, as regulating and restraining the powers so given.

If we begin with William of Normandy, we find that the government of England was originally a tyranny, founded on an invasion and conquest of the country. This being admitted, it will then appear, that the exertion of the nation, at different periods, to abate that tyranny, and render it less intolerable, has been credited for a constitution.

Magna Carta, as it was called, (it is now like an almanac of the same date), was no more than compelling the government to renounce a part of its assumptions. It did not create and give powers to government in the manner a constitution does; but was, as far as it went, of the nature of reconquest, and not of a constitution; for could the nation have totally expelled the usurpation, as France has done its despotism, it would then have had a constitution to form.

The history of the Edwards and the Henries, and up to the commencement of the Stuarts, exhibits as many instances of tyranny as could be acted within the limits to which the nation had restricted it. The Stuarts endeavoured to pass those limits, and their fate is well known. In all those instances we see nothing of a constitution, but only of restrictions on assumed power.

After this, another William, descended from the same stock, and claiming from the same origin, gained possession; and of the two evils, *James* and *William*, the nation preferred what it thought the least; since, from circumstances, it must take one. The act, called the Bill of Rights, comes here into view. What is it, but a bargain, which the parts of the government made with each other to divide powers, profits, and privileges? You shall have so much, and I will have the rest; and with respect to the nation, it said, for *your share*, YOU *shall have the right of petitioning*. This being the case, the bill of rights is more properly a bill of wrongs, and of insult. As to what is called the convention parliament, it was a thing that made itself, and then made the authority by which it acted. A few persons got together, and called themselves by that name. Several of them had never been elected, and none of them for the purpose.

From the time of William, a species of government arose, issuing out of this coalition bill of rights; and more so, since the corruption introduced at the Hanover succession, by the agency of Walpole; that can be described by no other name than a despotic legislation. Though the parts may embarrass each other, the whole has no bounds; and the only right it acknowledges out of itself, is the right of petitioning. Where then is the constitution either that gives or that restrains power?

It is not because a part of the government is elective, that makes it less a despotism, if the persons so elected possess afterwards, as a parliament, unlimited powers. Election, in this case, becomes separated from representation, and the candidates are candidates for despotism.

I cannot believe that any nation, reasoning on its own rights, would have thought of calling those things *a constitution*, if the cry of constitution had not been set up by the government. It has got into circulation like the words *bore* and *quoz*, by being chalked up in the speeches of parliament, as those words were on window shutters and door posts; but whatever the constitution may be in other respects, it has undoubtedly been *the most productive machine of taxation that was ever invented*. The taxes in France, under the new constitution, are not quite thirteen shillings per head,[6] and the taxes in England, under what is called its present constitution, are forty-eight shillings and sixpence per head, men, women, and children, amounting to nearly seventeen millions sterling, besides the expense of collection, which is upwards of a million more.

In a country like England, where the whole of the civil government is executed by the people of every town and county, by means of parish officers, magistrates, quarterly sessions, juries, and assize; without any trouble to what is called the government, or any other

6 The whole amount of the assessed taxes of France, for the present year, is three hundred millions of livres, which is twelve millions and a half sterling; and the incidental taxes are estimated at three millions, making in the whole fifteen millions and a half; which, among twenty-four millions of people, is not quite thirteen shillings per head. France has lessened her taxes since the revolution, nearly nine millions sterling annually. Before the revolution, the city of Paris paid a duty of upwards of thirty per cent on all articles brought into the city. This tax was collected at the city gates. It was taken off on the first of last May, and the gates taken down. – Paine.

expense to the revenue than the salary of the judges, it is astonishing how such a mass of taxes can be employed. Not even the internal defence of the country is paid out of the revenue. On all occasions, whether real or contrived, recourse is continually had to new loans and new taxes. No wonder, then, that a machine of government so advantageous to the advocates of a court, should be so triumphantly extolled! No wonder, that St James's or St Stephen's should echo with the continual cry of constitution; No wonder, that the French Revolution should be reprobated, and the *res-publica* treated with reproach! The *red book* of England, like the red book of France will explain the reason.[7]

I will now, by way of relaxation, turn a thought or two to Mr Burke. I ask his pardon for neglecting him so long.

'America', says he, (in his speech on the Canada constitution bill) 'never dreamed of such absurd doctrine as the *Rights of Man*.'

Mr Burke is such a bold presumer, and advances his assertions and his premises with such a deficiency of judgement, that, without troubling ourselves about principles of philosophy or politics, the mere logical conclusions they produce, are ridiculous. For instance,

If governments, as Mr Burke asserts, are not founded on the Rights of MAN, and are founded on *any rights* at all, they consequently must be founded on the rights of *something* that is *not man*. What then is that something?

Generally speaking, we know of no other creatures that inhabit the earth than man and beast; and in all cases, where only two things offer themselves, and one must be admitted, a negation proved on anyone, amounts to an affirmative on the other; and therefore, Mr Burke, by proving against the Rights of *Man*, proves in behalf of the *beast*; and consequently, proves that government is a beast: and as difficult things sometimes explain each other, we now see the origin of keeping wild beasts in the Tower; for they certainly can be of no other use than to show the origin of the government. They are in the place of a constitution. O John Bull, what honours thou hast lost by not being a wild beast. Thou mightest, on Mr Burke's system, have been in the Tower for life.

7 What was called the *livre rouge*, or the red book, in France, was not exactly similar to the court calendar in England; but it sufficiently showed how a great part of the taxes was lavished. – Paine.

If Mr Burke's arguments have not weight enough to keep one serious, the fault is less mine than his; and as I am willing to make an apology to the reader for the liberty I have taken, I hope Mr Burke will also make his for giving the cause.

Having thus paid Mr Burke the compliment of remembering him, I return to the subject.

From the want of a constitution in England to restrain and regulate the wild impulse of power, many of the laws are irrational and tyrannical, and the administration of them vague and problematical.

The attention of the government of England, (for I rather choose to call it by this name, than the English government) appears, since its political connection with Germany, to have been so completely engrossed and absorbed by foreign affairs, and the means of raising taxes, that it seems to exist for no other purposes. Domestic concerns are neglected; and with respect to regular law, there is scarcely such a thing.

Almost every case now must be determined by some precedent, be that precedent good or bad, or whether it properly applies or not; and the practice is become so general, as to suggest a suspicion, that it proceeds from a deeper policy than at first sight appears.

Since the revolution of America, and more so since that of France, this preaching up the doctrine of precedents, drawn from times and circumstances antecedent to those events, has been the studied practice of the English government. The generality of those precedents are founded on principles and opinions, the reverse of what they ought; and the greater distance of time they are drawn from, the more they are to be suspected. But by associating those precedents with a superstitious reverence for ancient things, as monks show relics and call them holy, the generality of mankind are deceived into the design. Governments now act as if they were afraid to awaken a single reflection in man. They are softly leading him to the sepulchre of precedents, to deaden his faculties and call his attention from the scene of revolutions. They feel that he is arriving at knowledge faster than they wish, and their policy of precedents is the barometer of their fears. This political popery, like the ecclesiastical popery of old, has had its day, and is hastening to its exit. The ragged relic and the antiquated precedent, the monk and the monarch, will moulder together.

Government by precedent, without any regard to the principle of the precedent, is one of the vilest systems that can be set up. In numerous instances, the precedent ought to operate as a warning, and not as an example, and requires to be shunned instead of imitated; but instead of this, precedents are taken in the lump, and put at once for constitution and for law.

Either the doctrine of precedents is policy to keep a man in a state of ignorance, or it is a practical confession that wisdom degenerates in governments as governments increase in age, and can only hobble along by the stilts and crutches of precedents. How is it that the same persons who would proudly be thought wiser than their predecessors, appear at the same time only as the ghosts of departed wisdom? How strangely is antiquity treated! To answer some purposes it is spoken of as the times of darkness and ignorance, and to answer others, it is put for the light of the world.

If the doctrine of precedents is to be followed, the expenses of government need not continue the same. Why pay men extravagantly, who have but little to do? If everything that can happen is already in precedent, legislation is at an end, and precedent, like a dictionary, determines every case. Either, therefore, government has arrived at its dotage, and requires to be renovated, or all the occasions for exercising its wisdom have occurred.

We now see all over Europe, and particularly in England, the curious phenomenon of a nation looking one way, and a government the other – the one forward and the other backward. If governments are to go on by precedent, while nations go on by improvement, they must at last come to a final separation; and the sooner, and the more civilly they determine this point, the better.[8]

Having thus spoken of constitutions generally, as things distinct from actual governments, let us proceed to consider the parts of which a constitution is composed.

8 In England the improvements in agriculture, useful arts, manufactures, and commerce, have been made in opposition to the genius of its government, which is that of following precedents. It is from the enterprise and industry of the individuals, and their numerous associations, in which, tritely speaking, government is neither pillow nor bolster, that these improvements have proceeded. No man thought about the government, or who was *in*, or who was *out*, when he was planning or executing those things; and all he had to hope, with respect to government, was, *that it would let him alone*. Three or four very silly ministerial newspapers are continually offending against the spirit of national improvement, by ascribing it to a minister. They may with as much truth ascribe this book to a minister. – Paine.

Opinions differ more on this subject, than with respect to the whole. That a nation ought to have a constitution, as a rule for the conduct of its government, is a simple question in which all men, not directly courtiers, will agree. It is only on the component parts that questions and opinions multiply.

But this difficulty, like every other, will diminish when put into a train of being rightly understood.

The first thing is, that a nation has a right to establish a constitution.

Whether it exercises this right in the most judicious manner at first, is quite another case. It exercises it agreeably to the judgement it possesses; and by continuing to do so, all errors will at last be exploded.

When this right is established in a nation, there is no fear that it will be employed to its own injury. A nation can have no interest in being wrong.

Though all the constitutions of America are on one general principle, yet no two of them are exactly alike in their component parts, or in the distribution of the powers which they give to the actual governments. Some are more, and others less complex.

In forming a constitution, it is first necessary to consider what are the ends for which government is necessary? Secondly, what are the best means, and the least expensive, for accomplishing those ends?

Government is nothing more than a national association; and the object of this association is the good of all, as well individually as collectively. Every man wishes to pursue his occupation, and to enjoy the fruits of his labours, and the produce of his property in peace and safety, and with the least possible expense. When these things are accomplished, all the objects for which government ought to be established are answered.

It has been customary to consider government under three distinct general heads. The legislative, the executive, and the judicial.

But if we permit our judgement to act unencumbered by the habit of multiplied terms, we can perceive no more than two divisions of power, of which civil government is composed, namely, that of legislating or enacting laws, and that of executing or administering them. Everything, therefore, appertaining to civil government, classes itself under one or other of these two divisions.

So far as regards the execution of the laws, that which is called the judicial power, is strictly and properly the executive power of every country. It is that power to which every individual has appeal, and which causes the laws to be executed; neither have we any other clear idea with respect to the official execution of the laws. In England, and also in America and France, this power begins with the magistrate, and proceeds up through all the courts of judicature.

I leave to courtiers to explain what is meant by calling monarchy the executive power. It is merely a name in which acts of government are done; and any other, or none at all, would answer the same purpose. Laws have neither more nor less authority on this account. It must be from the justness of their principles, and the interest which a nation feels therein, that they derive support; if they require any other than this, it is a sign that something in the system of government is imperfect. Laws difficult to be executed cannot be generally good.

With respect to the organization of the *legislative power*, different modes have been adopted in different countries. In America it is generally composed of two houses. In France it consists but of one, but in both countries it is wholly by representation.

The case is, that mankind (from the long tyranny of assumed power) have had so few opportunities of making the necessary trials on modes and principles of government, in order to discover the best, *that government is but now beginning to be known*, and experience is yet wanting to determine many particulars.

The objections against two houses, are, first, that there is an inconsistency in any part of a whole legislature, coming to a final determination by vote on any matter, whilst *that matter*, with respect to *that whole*, is yet only in a train of deliberation, and consequently open to new illustrations.

Secondly, That by taking the vote on each, as a separate body, it always admits of the possibility, and is often the case in practice, that the minority governs the majority, and that, in some instances, to a degree of great inconsistency.

Thirdly, That two houses arbitrarily checking or controlling each other is inconsistent; because it cannot be proved, on the principles of just representation, that either should be wiser or better than the other. They may check in the wrong as well as in the right, – and therefore, to give the power where we cannot give the wisdom to use it, nor be assured of its being rightly used, renders the hazard at least equal to the precaution.[9]

The objection against a single house is, that it is always in a condition of committing itself too soon. – But it should at the same time be remembered, that when there is a constitution which defines the power, and establishes the principles within which a legislature shall act, there is already a more effectual check provided, and more powerfully operating, than any other check can be. For example.

Were a bill to be brought into any of the American legislatures, similar to that which was passed into an act by the English Parliament, at the commencement of George the First, to extend the duration of the assemblies to a longer period than they now sit, the check is in the constitution, which in effect says, *Thus far shalt thou go and no further*.

But in order to remove the objection against a single house, (that of acting with too quick an impulse), and at the same time to avoid the inconsistencies, in some cases absurdities, arising from two houses, the following method has been proposed as an improvement upon both.

First, To have but one representation.

Secondly, To divide that representation, by lot, into two or three parts.

9 With respect to the two houses, of which the English Parliament is composed, they appear to be effectually influenced into one, and, as a legislature, to have no temper of its own. The minister, whoever he at any time may be, touches it as with an opium wand, and it sleeps obedience.

But if we look at the distinct abilities of the two houses, the difference will appear so great, as to show the inconsistency of placing power where there can be no certainty of the judgement to use it. Wretched as the state of representation is in England, it is manhood compared with what is called the House of Lords; and so little is this nick-named house regarded, that the people scarcely inquire at any time what it is doing. It appears also to be most under influence, and the furthest removed from the general interest of the nation. In the debate on engaging in the Russian and Turkish war, the majority in the house of peers in favour of it was upwards of ninety, when in the other house, which is more than double its numbers, the majority was sixty-three.

The proceedings on Mr Fox's bill, respecting the rights of juries, merits also to be noticed. The persons called the peers were not the objects of that bill. They are already in possession of more privileges than that bill gave to others. They are their own jury, and if any of that house were prosecuted for a libel, he would not suffer, even upon conviction, for the first offence. Such inequality in laws ought not to exist, in any country. The French constitution says, That *the law is the same to every individual, whether to protect or to punish. All are equal in its sight.* – Paine.

Thirdly, That every proposed bill, shall be first debated in those parts by succession, that they may become the hearers of each other, but without taking any vote. After which the whole representation to assemble for a general debate and determination by vote.

To this proposed improvement has been added another, for the purpose of keeping the representation in a state of constant renovation; which is, that one-third of the representation of each county, shall go out at the expiration of one year, and the number be replaced by new elections. – Another third at the expiration of the second year replaced in like manner, and every third year to be a general election.[10]

But in whatever manner the separate parts of a constitution may be arranged, there is *one* general principle that distinguishes freedom from slavery, which is, that all *hereditary government over a people is to them a species of slavery, and representative government is freedom.*

Considering government in the only light in which it should be considered, that of a NATIONAL ASSOCIATION; it ought to be so constructed as not to be disordered by any accident happening among the parts; and, therefore, no extraordinary power, capable of producing such an effect, should be lodged in the hands of any individual. The death, sickness, absence, or defection, of any one individual in a government, ought to be a matter of no more consequence, with respect to the nation, than if the same circumstance had taken place in a member of the English Parliament, or the French National Assembly.

Scarcely anything presents a more degrading character of national greatness, than its being thrown into confusion by anything happening to, or acted by, an individual; and the ridiculousness of the scene is often increased by the natural insignificance of the person by whom it is occasioned. Were a government so constructed, that it could not go on unless a goose or a gander were present in the senate, the difficulties would be just as great and as real on the flight or sickness of the goose, or the gander, as if it were called a King. We laugh at individuals for the silly difficulties they make to themselves,

10 As to the state of representation in England, it is too absurd to be reasoned upon. Almost all the represented parts are decreasing in population, and the unrepresented parts are increasing. A general convention of the nation is necessary to take the whole state of its government into consideration. – Paine.

without perceiving, that the greatest of all ridiculous things are acted in governments.[11]

All the constitutions of America are on a plan that excludes the childish embarrassments which occur in monarchical countries. No suspension of government can there take place for a moment, from any circumstance whatever. The system of representation provides for everything, and is the only system in which nations and governments can always appear in their proper character.

As extraordinary power ought not to be lodged in the hands of any individual, so ought there to be no appropriations of public money to any person, beyond what his services in a state may be worth. It signifies not whether a man be called a president, a king, an emperor, a senator, or by any other name, which propriety or folly may devise, or arrogance assume; it is only a certain service he can perform in the state; and the service of any such individual in the routine of office, whether such office be called monarchical, presidential, senatorial, or by any other name or title, can never exceed the value of ten thousand pounds a year. All the great services that are done in the world are performed by volunteer characters, who accept nothing for them; but the routine of office is always regulated to such a general standard of abilities as to be within the compass of numbers in every country to perform, and therefore cannot merit very extraordinary recompense. *Government*, says Swift, *is a plain thing, and fitted to the capacity of many heads.*

It is inhuman to talk of a million sterling a year, paid out of the public taxes of any country, for the support of any individual, whilst thousands who are forced to contribute thereto, are pining with want, and struggling with misery. Government does not consist in a

11 It is related that in the canton of Berne, in Switzerland, it had been customary, from time immemorial, to keep a bear at the public expense, and the people had been taught to believe, that if they had not a bear they should all be undone. It happened some years ago, that the bear, then in being, was taken sick, and died too suddenly to have his place immediately supplied with another. During this interregnum the people discovered, that the corn grew, and the vintage flourished, and the sun and moon continued to rise and set, and everything went on the same as before, and, taking courage from these circumstances, they resolved not to keep any more bears; for, said they, 'a bear is a very voracious, expensive animal, and we were obliged to pull out his claws, lest he should hurt the citizens'.

The story of the bear of Berne was related in some of the French newspapers, at the time of the flight of Louis XVI, and the application of it to monarchy could not be mistaken in France; but it seems, that the aristocracy of Berne applied it to themselves, and have since prohibited the reading of French newspapers. – Paine.

contrast between prisons and palaces, between poverty and pomp; it is not instituted to rob the needy of his mite, and increase the wretchedness of the wretched. – But of this part of the subject I shall speak hereafter, and confine myself at present to political observations.

When extraordinary power and extraordinary pay are allotted to any individual in a government, he becomes the centre, round which every kind of corruption generates and forms. Give to any man a million a year, and add thereto the power of creating and disposing of places, at the expense of a country, and the liberties of that country are no longer secure. What is called the splendour of a throne is no other than the corruption of the state. It is made up of a band of parasites, living in luxurious indolence, out of the public taxes.

When once such a vicious system is established it becomes the guard and protection of all inferior abuses. The man who is in the receipt of a million a year is the last person to promote a spirit of reform, lest, in the event, it should reach to himself. It is always his interest to defend inferior abuses, as so many outworks to protect the citadel; and in this species of political fortification, all the parts have such a common dependence that it is never to be expected they will attack each other.[12]

Monarchy would not have continued so many ages in the world, had it not been for the abuses it protects. It is the master-fraud, which shelters all others. By admitting a participation of the spoil, it makes itself friends; and when it ceases to do this, it will cease to be the idol of courtiers.

12 It is scarcely possible to touch on any subject, that will not suggest an allusion to some corruption in governments. The simile of '*fortifications*', unfortunately involves with it a circumstance, which is directly in point with the matter above alluded to.

Among the numerous instances of abuse which have been acted or protected by governments, ancient or modern, there is not a greater than that of quartering a man and his heirs upon the public, to be maintained at its expense.

Humanity dictates a provision for the poor; but by what right, moral or political, does any government assume to say, that the person called the Duke of Richmond, shall be maintained by the public? Yet, if common report is true, not a beggar in London can purchase his wretched pittance of coal, without paying towards the civil list of the Duke of Richmond. Were the whole produce of this imposition but a shilling a year, the iniquitous principle would be still the same; but when it amounts, as it is said to do, to not less than twenty thousand pounds *per ann.* the enormity is too serious to be permitted to remain – This is one of the effects of monarchy and aristocracy.

In stating this case, I am led by no personal dislike. Though I think it mean in any man to live upon the public, the vice originates in the government; and so general is it become, that whether the parties are in the ministry or in the opposition, it makes no difference: they are sure of the guarantee of each other. – Paine.

As the principle on which constitutions are now formed rejects all hereditary pretensions to government, it also rejects all that catalogue of assumptions known by the name of prerogatives.

If there is any government where prerogatives might with apparent safety be entrusted to any individual, it is in the federal government of America. The President of the United States of America is elected only for four years. He is not only responsible in the general sense of the word, but a particular mode is laid down in the constitution for trying him. He cannot be elected under thirty-five years of age; and he must be a native of the country.

In a comparison of these cases with the government of England, the difference when applied to the latter amounts to an absurdity. In England the person who exercises prerogative is often a foreigner; always half a foreigner, and always married to a foreigner. He is never in full natural or political connection with the country, is not responsible for anything, and becomes of age at eighteen years; yet such a person is permitted to form foreign alliances, without even the knowledge of the nation, and to make war and peace without its consent.

But this is not all. Though such a person cannot dispose of the government, in the manner of a testator, he dictates the marriage connections, which, in effect, accomplishes a great part of the same end. He cannot directly bequeath half the government to Prussia, but he can form a marriage partnership that will produce almost the same thing. Under such circumstances, it is happy for England that she is not situated on the continent, or she might, like Holland, fall under the dictatorship of Prussia. Holland, by marriage, is as effectually governed by Prussia, as if the old tyranny of bequeathing the government had been the means.

The presidency in America, (or, as it is sometimes called, the executive) is the only office from which a foreigner is excluded, and in England it is the only one to which he is admitted. A foreigner cannot be a member of parliament, but he may be what is called a king. If there is any reason for excluding foreigners, it ought to be from those offices where mischief can most be acted, and where, by uniting every bias of interest and attachment, the trust is best secured.

But as nations proceed in the great business of forming constitutions, they will examine with more precision into the nature and business of that department which is called the executive. What the legislative and judicial departments are, everyone can see; but with respect to what, in Europe, is called the executive, as distinct from those two, it is either a political superfluity or a chaos of unknown things.

Some kind of official department to which reports shall be made from the different parts of a nation, or from abroad, to be laid before the national representatives, is all that is necessary; but there is no consistency in calling this the executive; neither can it be considered in any other light than as inferior to the legislative. The sovereign authority in any country is the power of making laws, and everything else is an official department.

Next to the arrangement of the principles and the organization of the several parts of a constitution, is the provision to be made for the support of the persons to whom the nation shall confide the administration of the constitutional powers.

A nation can have no right to the time and services of any person at his own expense, whom it may choose to employ or entrust in any department whatever; neither can any reason be given for making provision for the support of any one part of a government and not for the other.

But, admitting that the honour of being entrusted with any part of a government, is to be considered a sufficient reward, it ought to be so to every person alike. If the members of the legislature of any country are to serve at their own expense, that which is called the executive, whether monarchical, or by any other name, ought to serve in like manner. It is inconsistent to pay the one, and accept the service of the other gratis.

In America, every department in the government is decently provided for; but no one is extravagantly paid. Every member of Congress, and of the assemblies, is allowed a sufficiency for his expenses. Whereas in England, a most prodigal provision is made for the support of one part of the government, and none for the other, the consequence of which is, that the one is furnished with the means of corruption, and the other is put into the condition of being corrupted. Less than a fourth part of such expense, applied as it is in America, would remedy a great part of the corruption.

Another reform in the American constitution, is the exploding all oaths of personality. The oath of allegiance in America is to the nation only. The putting any individual as a figure for a nation is improper. The happiness of a nation is the superior object, and therefore the intention of an oath of allegiance ought not to be obscured by being figuratively taken, to, or in the name of, any person. The oath, called the civic oath, in France, viz. '*the nation, the law, and the king*', is improper. If taken at all, it ought to be as in America, to the nation only. The law may or may not be good; but, in this place, it can have no other meaning, than as being conducive to the happiness of the nation and therefore is included in it. The remainder of the oath is improper, on the ground, that all personal oaths ought to be abolished. They are the remains of tyranny on one part, and slavery on the other; and the name of the CREATOR ought not to be introduced to witness the degradation of his creation; or if taken, as is already mentioned, as figurative of the nation, it is in this place redundant. But whatever apology may be made for oaths at the first establishment of a government, they ought not to be permitted afterwards. If a government requires the support of oaths, it is a sign that it is not worth supporting, and ought not to be supported. Make government what it ought to be, and it will support itself.

To conclude this part of the subject: – One of the greatest improvements that has been made for the perpetual security and progress of constitutional liberty, is the provision which the new constitutions make for occasionally revising, altering, and amending them.

The principle upon which Mr Burke formed his political creed, that '*of binding and controlling posterity to the end of time, and of renouncing and abdicating the rights of all posterity, for ever*', is now become too detestable to be made a subject of debate; and therefore, I pass it over with no other notice than exposing it.

Government is but now beginning to be known. Hitherto it has been the mere exercise of power, which forbade all effectual inquiry into rights, and grounded itself wholly on possession. While the enemy of liberty was its judge, the progress of its principles must have been small indeed.

The constitutions of America, and also that of France, have either affixed a period for their revision, or laid down the mode by which improvements shall be made. It is perhaps impossible to establish anything that combines principles with opinions and practice, which the progress of circumstances, through a length of years, will not in some measure derange, or render inconsistent; and, therefore, to prevent inconveniencies accumulating, till they discourage reformations or provoke revolutions, it is best to provide the means of regulating them as they occur. The Rights of Man are the rights of all generations of men, and cannot be monopolized by any. That which is worth following, will be followed for the sake of its worth; and it is in this that its security lies, and not in any conditions with which it may be encumbered. When a man leaves property to his heirs, he does not connect it with an obligation that they shall accept it. Why then should we do otherwise with respect to constitutions?

The best constitution that could now be devised, consistent with the condition of the present moment, may be far short of that excellence which a few years may afford. There is a morning of reason rising upon man on the subject of government, that has not appeared before. As the barbarism of the present old governments expires, the moral condition of nations with respect to each other will be changed. Man will not be brought up with the savage idea of considering his species as his enemy, because the accident of birth gave the individuals existence in countries distinguished by different names; and as constitutions have always some relation to external as well as to domestic circumstances, the means of benefiting by every change, foreign or domestic, should be a part of every constitution.

We already see an alteration in the national disposition of England and France towards each other, which, when we look back to only a few years, is itself a revolution. Who could have foreseen, or who would have believed, that a French National Assembly would ever have been a popular toast in England, or that a friendly alliance of the two nations should become the wish of either. It shows, that man, were he not corrupted by governments, is naturally the friend of man, and that human nature is not of itself vicious. That spirit of jealousy and ferocity, which the governments of the two countries inspired, and which they rendered subservient to the purpose of taxation, is now yielding to the dictates of reason, interest, and humanity. The trade of courts is beginning to be understood, and the affectation of mystery, with all the artificial sorcery by which they imposed upon mankind, is on the decline. It has received its death-wound; and though it may linger, it will expire.

Government ought to be as much open to improvement as anything which appertains to man, instead of which it has been monopolized from age to age, by the most ignorant and vicious of the human race. Need we any other proof of their wretched management, than the excess of debts and taxes with which every nation groans, and the quarrels into which they have precipitated the world?

Just emerging from such a barbarous condition, it is too soon to determine to what extent of improvement government may yet be carried. For what we can foresee, all Europe may form but one great republic, and man be free of the whole.

CHAPTER 5

WAYS AND MEANS

OF IMPROVING THE CONDITION OF EUROPE, INTERSPERSED
WITH MISCELLANEOUS OBSERVATIONS

In contemplating a subject that embraces with equatorial magnitude the whole region of humanity, it is impossible to confine the pursuit in one single direction. It takes ground on every character and condition that appertains to man, and blends the individual, the nation, and the world.

From a small spark, kindled in America, a flame has arisen, not to be extinguished. Without consuming, like the *Ultima Ratio Regum*, it winds its progress from nation to nation, and conquers by a silent operation. Man finds himself changed, he scarcely perceives how. He acquires a knowledge of his rights by attending justly to his interest, and discovers in the event that the strength and powers of despotism consist wholly in the fear of resisting it, and that, in order '*to be free, it is sufficient that he wills it*'.

Having in all the preceding parts of this work endeavoured to establish a system of principles as a basis, on which governments ought to be erected, I shall proceed in this, to the ways and means of rendering them into practice. But in order to introduce this part of the subject with more propriety, and stronger effect, some preliminary observation, deducible from, or connected with, those principles, are necessary.

Whatever the form or constitution of government may be, it ought to have no other object than the *general* happiness. When, instead of this, it operates to create and increase wretchedness in any of the parts of society, it is on a wrong system, and reformation is necessary.

Customary language has classed the condition of man under the two descriptions of civilized and uncivilized life. To the one it has ascribed felicity and affluence; to the other hardship and want. But however our imagination may be impressed by painting and comparison, it is nevertheless true, that a great portion of mankind, in what are called civilized countries, are in a state of poverty and wretchedness, far below the condition of an Indian. I speak not of one country, but of all. It is so in England, it is so all over Europe. Let us inquire into the cause.

It lies not in any natural defect in the principles of civilization, but in preventing those principles having a universal operation; the consequence of which is, a perpetual system of war and expense, that drains the country, and defeats the general felicity of which civilization is capable.

All the European governments (France now excepted) are constructed not on the principle of universal civilization, but on the reverse of it. So far as those governments relate to each other, they are in the same condition as we conceive of savage uncivilized life; they put themselves beyond the law as well of GOD as of man, and are, with respect to principle and reciprocal conduct, like so many individuals in a state of nature.

The inhabitants of every country, under the civilization of laws, easily civilize together, but governments being yet in an uncivilized state, and almost continually at war, they pervert the abundance which civilized life produces to carry on the uncivilized part to a greater extent. By thus engrafting the barbarism of government upon the internal civilization of a country, it draws from the latter, and more especially from the poor, a great portion of those earnings, which should be applied to their own subsistence and comfort. — Apart from all reflections of morality and philosophy, it is a melancholy fact, that more than one-fourth of the labour of mankind is annually consumed by this barbarous system.

What has served to continue this evil, is the pecuniary advantage which all the governments of Europe have found in keeping up this state of uncivilization. It affords to them pretences for power, and revenue, for which there would be neither occasion nor apology, if the circle of civilization were rendered complete. Civil government alone, or the government of laws, is not productive of pretences for many taxes; it operates at home, directly under the eye of the country, and precludes the possibility of much imposition. But when the scene is laid in the uncivilized contention of governments, the field of pretences is enlarged, and the country, being no longer a judge, is open to every imposition, which governments please to act.

Not a thirtieth, scarcely a fortieth, part of the taxes which are raised in England are either occasioned by, or applied to, the purposes of civil government. It is not difficult to see, that the whole which the actual government does in this respect, is to enact laws, and that the country administers and executes them, at its own expense, by means of magistrates, juries, sessions, and assize, over and above the taxes which it pays.

In this view of the case, we have two distinct characters of government; the one the civil government, or the government of laws, which operates at home, the other the court or cabinet government, which operates abroad, on the rude plan of uncivilized life; the one attended with little charge, the other with boundless extravagance; and so distinct are the two, that if the latter were to sink, as it were by a sudden opening of the earth, and totally disappear, the former would not be deranged. It would still proceed, because it is the common interest of the nation that it should, and all the means are in practice.

Revolutions, then, have for their object, a change in the moral condition of governments, and with this change the burden of public taxes will lessen, and civilization will be left to the enjoyment of that abundance, of which it is now deprived.

In contemplating the whole of this subject, I extend my views into the department of commerce. In all my publications, where the matter would admit, I have been an advocate for commerce, because I am a friend to its effects. It is a pacific system, operating to cordialize mankind, by rendering nations, as well as individuals, useful to each other. As to mere theoretical reformation, I have never preached it up. The most effectual process is that of improving the condition of man by means of his interest; and it is on this ground that I take my stand.

If commerce were permitted to act to the universal extent it is capable, it would extirpate the system of war, and produce a revolution in the uncivilized state of governments. The invention of commerce has arisen since those governments began, and is the greatest approach towards universal civilization, that has yet been made by any means not immediately flowing from moral principles.

Whatever has a tendency to promote the civil intercourse of nations, by an exchange of benefits, is a subject as worthy of philosophy as of politics. Commerce is no other than the traffic of two individuals, multiplied on a scale of numbers; and by the same rule that nature intended the intercourse of two, she intended that of all. For this purpose she has distributed the materials of manufactures and commerce, in various and distant parts of a nation and of the world; and as they cannot be procured by war so cheaply or so commodiously as by commerce, she has rendered the latter the means of extirpating the former.

As the two are nearly the opposites of each other, consequently, the uncivilized state of European governments is injurious to commerce. Every kind of destruction or embarrassment serves to lessen the quantity, and it matters but little in what part of the commercial world the reduction begins. Like blood, it cannot be taken from any of the parts, without being taken from the whole mass in circulation, and all partake of the loss. When the ability in any nation to buy is destroyed, it equally involves the seller. Could the government of England destroy the commerce of all other nations, she would most effectually ruin her own.

It is possible that a nation may be the carrier for the world, but she cannot be the merchant. She cannot be the seller and the buyer of her own merchandize. The ability to buy must reside out of herself; and, therefore, the prosperity of any commercial nation is regulated by the prosperity of the rest. If they are poor she cannot be rich, and her condition, be it what it may, is an index of the height of the commercial tide in other nations.

That the principles of commerce, and its universal operation may be understood, without understanding the practice, is a position that reason will not deny; and it is on this ground only that I argue the subject. It is one thing in the counting-house, in the world it is another. With respect to its operation it must necessarily be contemplated as a reciprocal thing; that only one half its powers resides within the nation, and that the whole is as effectually destroyed by destroying the half that resides without, as if the destruction had been committed on that which is within; for neither can act without the other.

When in the last, as well as in former wars, the commerce of England sunk, it was because the general quantity was lessened everywhere; and it now rises, because commerce is in a rising state in every nation. If England, at this day, imports and exports more than at any former period, the nations with which she trades must necessarily do the same; her imports are their exports, and vice versa.

There can be no such thing as a nation flourishing alone in commerce; she can only participate; and the destruction of it in any part must necessarily affect all. When, therefore, governments are at war, the attack is made upon the common stock of commerce, and the consequence is the same as if each had attacked his own.

The present increase of commerce is not to be attributed to ministers, or to any political contrivances, but to its own natural operations in consequence of peace. The regular markets had been destroyed, the channels of trade broken up, the high road of the seas infested with robbers of every nation, and the attention of the world called to other objects. Those interruptions have ceased, and peace has restored the deranged condition of things to their proper order.[13]

It is worth remarking, that every nation reckons the balance of trade in its own favour; and therefore something must be irregular in the common ideas upon this subject.

The fact, however, is true, according to what is called a balance; and it is from this cause that commerce is universally supported. Every nation feels the advantage, or it would abandon the practice: but the deception lies in the mode of making up the accounts, and in attributing what are called profits to a wrong cause.

Mr Pitt has sometimes amused himself, by showing what he called a balance of trade from the custom-house books. This mode of calculation, not only affords no rule that is true, but one that is false.

In the first place, Every cargo that departs from the custom house, appears on the books as an export; and, according to the custom-house balance, the losses at sea, and by foreign failures, are all reckoned on the side of profit, because they appear as exports.

Secondly, Because the importation by the smuggling trade does

13 In America, the increase of commerce is greater in proportion than in England. It is, at this time, at least one-half more than at any period prior to the revolution. The greatest number of vessels cleared out of the port of Philadelphia, before the commencement of the war, was between eight and nine hundred. In the year 1788, the number was upwards of twelve hundred. As the state of Pennsylvania is estimated as an eighth part of the United States in population, the whole number of vessels must now be nearly ten thousand. – Paine.

not appear on the custom-house books, to arrange against the exports.

No balance, therefore, as applying to superior advantages, can be drawn from those documents; and if we examine the natural operation of commerce, the idea is fallacious; and if true, would soon be injurious. The great support of commerce consists in the balance being a level of benefits among all nations.

Two merchants of different nations trading together, will both become rich, and each makes the balance in his own favour; consequently, they do not get rich out of each other; and it is the same with respect to the nations in which they reside. The case must be, that each nation must get rich out of its own means, and increases that riches by something which it procures from another in exchange.

If a merchant in England sends an article of English manufacture abroad, which costs him a shilling at home, and imports something which sells for two, he makes a balance of one shilling in his own favour: but this is not gained out of the foreign nation or the foreign merchant, for he also does the same by the article he receives, and neither has a balance of advantage upon the other. The original value of the two articles in their proper countries were but two shillings; but by changing their places, they acquire a new idea of value, equal to double what they had at first, and that increased value is equally divided.

There is not otherwise a balance on foreign than on domestic commerce. The merchants of London and Newcastle trade on the same principles, as if they resided in different nations, and make their balances in the same manner: yet London does not get rich out of Newcastle, any more than Newcastle out of London: but coals, the merchandize of Newcastle, have an additional value at London, and London merchandize has the same at Newcastle.

Though the principle of all commerce is the same, the domestic, in a national view, is the part the most beneficial; because the whole of the advantages, on both sides, rests within the nation; whereas, in foreign commerce, it is only a participation of one half.

The most unprofitable of all commerce is that connected with foreign dominion. To a few individuals it may be beneficial, merely because it is commerce; but to the nation it is a loss. The expense of maintaining dominion more than absorbs the profits of any trade. It does not increase the general quantity in the world, but operates to lessen it; and as a greater mass would be afloat by relinquishing dominion, the participation without the expense would be more valuable than a greater quantity with it.

But it is impossible to engross commerce by dominion; and therefore it is still more fallacious. It cannot exist in confined channels, and necessarily breaks out by regular or irregular means, that defeat the attempt: and to succeed would be still worse. France, since the revolution, has been more than indifferent as to foreign possessions; and other nations will become the same, when they investigate the subject with respect to commerce.

To the expense of dominion is to be added that of navies, and when the amount of the two are subtracted from the profits of commerce, it will appear, that what is called the balance of trade, even admitting it to exist, is not enjoyed by the nation but absorbed by the government.

The idea of having navies for the protection of commerce is delusive. It is putting the means of destruction for the means of protection. Commerce needs no other protection than the reciprocal interest which every nation feels in supporting it – it is common stock – it exists by a balance of advantages to all, and the only interruption it meets, is from the present uncivilized state of governments, and which it is its common interest to reform.[14]

Quitting this subject, I now proceed to other matters. – As it is necessary to include England in the prospect of a general reformation, it is proper to inquire into the defects of its government. It is only by each nation reforming its own, that the whole can be improved, and the full benefit of reformation enjoyed. Only partial advantages can flow from partial reforms.

France and England are the only two countries in Europe where a reformation in government could have successfully begun. The one secure by the ocean, and the other by the immensity of its internal strength, could defy the malignancy of foreign despotism. But it is with revolutions as with commerce, the advantages increase by their

14 When I saw Mr Pitt's mode of estimating the balance of trade, in one of his parliamentary speeches, he appeared to me to know nothing of the nature and interest of commerce; and no man has more wantonly tortured it than himself. During a period of peace, it has been havocked with the calamities of war. Three times has it been thrown into stagnation, and the vessels unmanned by impressing, within less than four years of peace. – Paine.

becoming general, and double to either what each would receive alone.

As a new system is now opening to the view of the world, the European courts are plotting to counteract it. Alliances, contrary to all former systems, are agitating, and a common interest of courts is forming against the common interest of man. This combination draws a line that runs throughout Europe, and presents a cause so entirely new, as to exclude all calculations from former circumstances. While despotism warred with despotism, man had no interest in the contest; but in a cause that unites the soldier with the citizen, and nation with nation, the despotism of courts, though it feels the danger, and meditates revenge, is afraid to strike.

No question has arisen within the records of history that pressed with the importance of the present. It is not whether this or that party shall be in or not, or Whig or Tory, or high or low shall prevail; but whether man shall inherit his rights, and universal civilization take place? Whether the fruits of his labours shall be enjoyed by himself, or consumed by the profligacy of governments? Whether robbery shall be banished from courts, and wretchedness from countries?

When, in countries that are called civilized, we see age going to the workhouse and youth to the gallows, something must be wrong in the system of government. It would seem, by the exterior appearance of such countries, that all was happiness; but there lies hidden from the eye of common observation, a mass of wretchedness that has scarcely any other chance, than to expire in poverty or infamy. Its entrance into life is marked with the presage of its fate; and until this is remedied, it is in vain to punish.

Civil government does not consist in executions; but in making that provision for the instruction of youth, and the support of age, as to exclude, as much as possible, profligacy from the one, and despair from the other. Instead of this, the resources of a country are lavished upon kings, upon courts, upon hirelings, impostors, and prostitutes; and even the poor themselves, with all their wants upon them, are compelled to support the fraud that oppresses them.

Why is it, that scarcely any are executed but the poor? The fact is a proof, among other things, of a wretchedness in their condition. Bred up without morals, and cast upon the world without a prospect, they are the exposed sacrifice of vice and legal barbarity. The millions that are superfluously wasted upon governments, are more than sufficient to reform those evils, and to benefit the condition of every man in a nation, not included within the purlieus of a court. This I hope to make appear in the progress of this work.

It is the nature of compassion to associate with misfortune. In taking up this subject I seek no recompense – I fear no consequence. Fortified with that proud integrity, that disdains to triumph or to yield, I will advocate the Rights of Man.

It is to my advantage that I have served an apprenticeship to life. I know the value of moral instruction, and I have seen the danger of the contrary.

At an early period, little more than sixteen years of age, raw and adventurous, and heated with the false heroism of a master who had served in a man of war, I began the carver of my own fortune, and entered on board the Terrible privateer, Capt. Death. From this adventure I was happily prevented by the affectionate and moral remonstrance of a good father, who, from his own habits of life, being of the Quaker profession, must begin to look upon me as lost. But the impression, much as it effected at the time, began to wear away, and I entered afterwards in the King of Prussia privateer, Capt. Mendez, and went with her to sea. Yet, from such a beginning, and with all the inconvenience of early life against me, I am proud to say, that with a perseverence undismayed by difficulties, a disinterestedness that compelled respect, I have not only contributed to raise a new empire in the world, founded on a new system of government, but I have arrived at an eminence in political literature, the most difficult of all lines to succeed and excel in, which aristocracy, with all its aids, has not been able to reach or to rival.

Knowing my own heart, and feeling myself, as I now do, superior to all the skirmish of party, the inveteracy of interested or mistaken opponents, I answer not to falsehood or abuse, but proceed to the defects of the English government.[15]

15 Politics and self-interest have been so uniformly connected, that the world, from being so often deceived, has a right to be suspicious of public characters: but with regard to myself, I am perfectly easy on this head. I did not, at my first setting out in public life, nearly seventeen years ago, turn my thoughts to subjects of government from motives of interest; and my conduct from that moment to this, proves the fact. I saw an opportunity, in which I thought I could do some good, and I followed exactly what my heart dictated. I neither read books, nor studied other people's opinions. I thought for myself. The case was this:

During the suspension of the old governments in America, both prior to, and at the breaking out of hosilities, I was struck with the order and decorum with which everything was conducted: and impressed with the idea, that a little more than what society naturally performed, was all the government that was necessary; and that monarchy and aristocracy were frauds and impositions upon mankind. On these principles I published the pamphlet *Common Sense*. The success it met with was beyond anything since the invention of printing. I gave the copyright up to every state in the union, and the demand ran to not less than one hundred thousand copies. I continued the subject in the same manner, under the title of *Crisis*, till the complete establishment of the revolution.

After the declaration of independence, Congress unanimously, and unknown to me, appointed me as secretary in the foreign department. This was agreeable to me, because it gave me the opportunity of seeing into the abilities of foreign courts, and their manner of doing business. But a misunderstanding arising between Congress and me, respecting one of their commissioners then in Europe, Mr Silas Deane, I resigned the office, and declined, at the same time, the pecuniary offers made me by the ministers of France and Spain, M. Gérard and Don Juan Mirralles.

I had by this time so completely gained the ear and confidence of America, and my own independence was become so visible as to give me a range in political writing, beyond, perhaps, what any man ever possessed in any country; and what is more extraordinary, I held it undiminished to the end of the war, and enjoy it in the same manner to the present moment. As my object was not myself, I set out with the determination, and happily with the disposition, of not being moved by praise or censure, friendship or calumny, nor of being drawn from my purpose by any personal altercation; and the man who cannot do this, is not fit for a public character.

When the war ended, I went from Philadelphia to Borden-Town, on the east bank of the Delaware, where I have a small place. Congress was at this time at Prince-Town, fifteen miles distant; and General Washington had taken his headquarters at Rocky-Hill, within the neighbourhood of Congress, for the purpose of resigning up his commission, (the object for which he accepted it being accomplished), and of retiring to private life. While he was on this business, he wrote me the letter which I here subjoin.

Rocky-Hill, Sept. 10, 1783

I have learned since I have been at this place, that you are at Borden-Town. Whether for the sake of retirement or economy, I know not. Be it for either, for both, or whatever it may, if you will come to this place, and partake with me, I shall be exceedingly happy to see you at it.

Your presence may remind Congress of your past services to this country; and if it is in my power to impress them, command my best exertions with freedom, as they will be rendered cheerfully by one, who entertains a lively sense of the importance of your works, and who, with much pleasure, subscribes himself,

Your sincere friend,
G. WASHINGTON

During the war, in the latter end of the year 1780, I formed to myself a design of coming over to England; and communicated it to General Greene, who was then in Philadelphia, on his route to the southward, General Washington being then at too great a distance to communicate with immediately. I was strongly impressed with the idea, that if I could get over to England, without being known, and only remain in safety till I could get out a publication, that I could open the eyes of the country with respect to the madness and stupidity of its government. I saw that the parties in parliament had pitted themselves as far as they could go, and could make no new

I begin with charters and corporations.

It is a perversion of terms to say, that a charter gives rights. It operates by a contrary effect, that of taking rights away. Rights are inherently in all the inhabitants; but charters, by annulling those rights in the majority, leave the right by exclusion in the hands of a few. If charters were constructed so as to express in direct terms, '*that every inhabitant, who is not a member of a corporation, shall not exercise the right of voting*', such charters would, in the face, be charters, not of the rights, but of exclusion. The effect is the same under the form they now stand; and the only persons on whom they operate, are the persons whom they exclude. Those whose rights are guaranteed, by not being taken away, exercise no other rights, than as members of the community they are entitled to without a charter; and, therefore, all charters have no other than an indirect negative operation. They do not give rights to A, but they make a difference in favour of A by taking away the right of B, and consequently are instruments of injustice.

But charters and corporations have a more extensive evil effect than what relates merely to elections. They are sources of endless contentions in the places where they exist; and they lessen the

---

impressions on each other. General Greene entered fully into my views; but the affair of Arnold and André happening just after, he changed his mind, and, under strong apprehensions for my safety, wrote very pressingly to me from Annapolis, in Maryland, to give up the design, which, with some reluctance, I did. Soon after this I accompanied Col Lawrens, son of Mr Lawrens, who was then in the Tower, to France, on business from Congress. We landed at L'Orient; and while I remained there, he being gone forward, a circumstance occurred, that renewed my former design. An English packet from Falmouth to New York, with the government dispatches on board, was brought into L'Orient. That a packet should be taken, is no extraordinary thing; but that the dispatches should be taken with it, will scarcely be credited, as they are always slung at the cabin window, in a bag loaded with cannon ball, and ready to be sunk at a moment. The fact, however, is as I have stated it, for the dispatches came into my hands, and I read them. The capture, as I was informed, succeeded by the following stratagem: – The captain of the Madame privateer, who spoke English, on coming up with the packet, passed himself for the captain of an English frigate, and invited the captain of the packet on board, which, when done, he sent some of his own hands back, and secured the mail. But be the circumstance of the capture what it may, I speak with certainty as to the government dispatches. They were sent up to Paris, to Count Vergennes, and when Col Lawrens and myself returned to America, we took the originals to Congress.

By these dispatches I saw into the stupidity of the English cabinet, far more than I otherwise could have done, and I renewed my former design. But Col Lawrens was so unwilling to return alone; more especially, as, among other matters, we had a charge of upwards of two hundred thousand pounds sterling in money, that I gave in to his wishes, and finally gave up my plan. But I am now certain, that if I could have executed it, that it would not have been altogether unsuccessful. – Paine.

common rights of national society. A native of England, under the operation of these charters and corporations, cannot be said to be an Englishman in the full sense of the word, He is not free of the nation, in the same manner that a Frenchman is free of France, and an American of America. His rights are circumscribed to the town, and, in some cases, to the parish of his birth; and all other parts, though in his native land, are to him as a foreign country. To acquire a residence in these, he must undergo a local naturalization by purchase, or he is forbidden or expelled the place. This species of feudality is kept up to aggrandize the corporations at the ruin of towns; and the effect is visible.

The generality of corporation towns are in a state of solitary decay, and prevented from further ruin, only by some circumstance in their situation, such as a navigable river, or a plentiful surrounding country. As population is one of the chief sources of wealth, (for without it land itself has no value), everything which operates to prevent it must lessen the value of property; and as corporations have not only this tendency, but directly this effect, they cannot but be injurious. If any policy were to be followed, instead of that of general freedom to every person to settle where he chose, (as in France or America), it would be more consistent to give encouragement to newcomers, than to preclude their admission by exacting premiums from them.[16]

The persons most immediately interested in the abolition of corporations, are the inhabitants of the towns where corporations are established. The instances of Manchester, Birmingham, and Sheffield, show, by contrast, the injury which those Gothic institutions are to property and commerce. A few examples may be found, such as that of London, whose natural and commercial advantage, owing to its situation on the Thames, is capable of bearing up against the political

16 It is difficult to account for the origin of charter and corporation towns, unless we suppose them to have arisen out of, or been connected with, some species of garrison service. The times in which they began justify this idea. The generality of those towns have been garrisons; and the corporations were charged with the care of the gates of the towns, when no military garrison was present. Their refusing or granting admission to strangers, which has produced the custom of giving, selling, and buying freedom, has more of the nature of garrison authority than civil government. Soldiers are free of all corporations throughout the nation, by the same propriety that every soldier is free of every garrison, and no other persons are. He can follow any employment, with the permission of his officers, in any corporation town throughout the nation. — Paine.

evils of a corporation; but in almost all other cases the fatality is too visible to be doubted or denied.

Though the whole nation is not so directly affected by the depression of property in corporation towns as the inhabitants themselves, it partakes of the consequence. By lessening the value of property, the quantity of national commerce is curtailed. Every man is a customer in proportion to his ability; and as all parts of a nation trade with each other, whatever affects any of the parts, must necessarily communicate to the whole.

As one of the houses of the English Parliament is, in a great measure, made up of elections from these corporations; and as it is unnatural that a pure stream should flow from a foul fountain, its vices are but a continuation of the vices of its origin. A man of moral honour and good political principles, cannot submit to the mean drudgery and disgraceful arts, by which such elections are carried. To be a successful candidate, he must be destitute of the qualities that constitute a just legislator: and being thus disciplined to corruption by the mode of entering into parliament, it is not to be expected that the representative should be better than the man.

Mr Burke, in speaking of the English representation, has advanced as bold a challenge as ever was given in the days of chivalry. 'Our representation', says he, 'has been found *perfectly adequate to all the purposes* for which a representation of the people can be desired or devised. I defy', continues he, 'the enemies of our constitution to show the contrary.' – This declaration from a man who has been in constant opposition to all the measures of parliament the whole of his political life, a year or two excepted, is most extraordinary; and, comparing him with himself, admits of no other alternative, than that he acted against his judgement as a member, or has declared contrary to it as an author.

But it is not in the representation only that the defects lie, and therefore I proceed in the next place to the aristocracy.

What is called the House of Peers, is constituted on a ground very similar to that, against which there is a law in other cases. It amounts to a combination of persons in one common interest. No reason can be given, why an house of legislation should be composed entirely of men whose occupation consists in letting landed property, than why it should be composed of those who hire, or of brewers, or bakers, or any other separate class of men.

Mr Burke calls this house, '*the great ground and pillar of security to the landed interest*'. Let us examine this idea.

What pillar of security does the landed interest require more than any other interest in the state, or what right has it to a distinct and separate representation from the general interest of a nation? The only use to be made of this power, (and which it has always made), is to ward off taxes from itself, and throw the burden upon such articles of consumption by which itself would be least affected.

That this has been the consequence, (and will always be the consequence of constructing governments on combinations), is evident with respect to England, from the history of its taxes.

Notwithstanding taxes have increased and multiplied upon every article of common consumption, the land-tax, which more particularly affects this 'pillar', has diminished. In 1788, the amount of the land-tax was £1,950,000, which is half a million less than it produced almost a hundred years ago,[17] notwithstanding the rentals are in many instances doubled since that period.

Before the coming of the Hanoverians, the taxes were divided in nearly equal proportions between the land and articles of consumption, the land bearing rather the largest share: but since that era, nearly thirteen millions annually of new taxes have been thrown upon consumption. The consequence of which has been a constant increase in the number and wretchedness of the poor, and in the amount of the poor-rates. Yet here again the burden does not fall in equal proportions on the aristocracy with the rest of the community. Their residences, whether in town or country, are not mixed with the habitations of the poor. They live apart from distress, and the expense of relieving it. It is in manufacturing towns and labouring villages that those burdens press the heaviest; in many of which it is one class of poor supporting another.

Several of the most heavy and productive taxes are so contrived, as to give an exemption to this pillar, thus standing in its own defence. The tax upon beer brewed for sale does not affect the aristocracy, who brew their own beer free of this duty. It falls only on those who have not conveniency or ability to brew, and who must purchase it in small quantities. But what will mankind think of the justice of taxation, when they know that this tax alone, from which the aris-

17 See Sir John Sinclair's History of the Revenue. The land-tax in 1646 was £2,473,499. – Paine.

tocracy are from circumstances exempt, is nearly equal to the whole of the land-tax, being in the year 1788, and it is not less now, £1,666,152, and with its proportion of the taxes on malt and hops, it exceeds it. – That a single article, thus partially consumed, and that chiefly by the working part, should be subject to a tax, equal to that on the whole rental of a nation, is, perhaps, a fact not to be paralleled in the histories of revenues.

This is one of the consequences resulting from an house of legislation, composed on the ground of a combination of common interest; for whatever their separate politics as to parties may be, in this they are united. Whether a combination acts to raise the price of any article for sale, or the rate of wages; or whether it acts to throw taxes from itself upon another class of the community, the principle and the effect are the same; and if the one be illegal, it will be difficult to show that the other ought to exist.

It is no use to say that taxes are first proposed in the House of Commons; for as the other house has always a negative, it can always defend itself; and it would be ridiculous to suppose that its acquiescence in the measures to be proposed were not understood beforehand. Besides which, it has obtained so much influence by borough-traffic, and so many of its relations and connections are distributed on both sides of the Commons, as to give it, besides an absolute negative in one house, a preponderancy in the other, in all matters of common concern.

It is difficult to discover what is meant by the *landed interest*, if it does not mean a combination of aristocratical land-holders, opposing their own pecuniary interest to that of the farmer, and every branch of trade, commerce, and manufacture. In all other respects it is the only interest that needs no partial protection. It enjoys the general protection of the world. Every individual, high or low, is interested in the fruits of the earth; men, women, and children, of all ages and degrees, will turn out to assist the farmer, rather than a harvest should not be got in; and they will not act thus by any other property. It is the only one for which the common prayer of mankind is put up, and the only one that can never fail from the want of means. It is the interest, not of the policy, but of the existence of man, and when it ceases, he must cease to be.

No other interest in a nation stands on the same united support. Commerce, manufactures, arts, sciences, and everything else, compared with this, are supported but in parts. Their prosperity or their decay has not the same universal influence. When the valleys laugh and sing, it is not the farmer only, but all creation that rejoice. It is a prosperity that excludes all envy; and this cannot be said of anything else.

Why then does Mr Burke talk of his house of peers, as the pillar of the landed interest? Were that pillar to sink into the earth, the same landed property would continue, and the same ploughing, sowing, and reaping would go on. The aristocracy are not the farmers who work the land, and raise the produce, but are the mere consumers of the rent; and when compared with the active world are the drones, a seraglio of males, who neither collect the honey nor form the hive, but exist only for lazy enjoyment.

Mr Burke, in his first essay, called aristocracy, '*the Corinthian capital of polished society*'. Towards completing the figure, he has now added the *pillar*; but still the base is wanting; and whenever a nation choose to act a Samson, not blind, but bold, down go the temple of Dagon, the Lords and the Philistines.

If a house of legislation is to be composed of men of one class, for the purpose of protecting a distinct interest, all the other interests should have the same. The inequality, as well as the burden of taxation, arises from admitting it in one case, and not in all. Had there been a house of farmers, there had been no game laws; or a house of merchants and manufacturers, the taxes had neither been so unequal nor so excessive. It is from the power of taxation being in the hands of those who can throw so great a part of it from their own shoulders, that it has raged without a check.

Men of small or moderate estates are more injured by the taxes being thrown on articles of consumption than they are eased by warding it from landed property, for the following reasons:

First, They consume more of the productive taxable articles, in proportion to their property, than those of large estates.

Secondly, Their residence is chiefly in towns, and their property in houses; and the increase of the poor-rates, occasioned by taxes on consumption, is in much greater proportion than the land-tax has been favoured. In Birmingham, the poor-rates are not less than seven shillings in the pound. From this, as already observed, the aristocracy are in a great measure exempt.

These are but a part of the mischiefs flowing from the wretched scheme of an house of peers.

As a combination, it can always throw a considerable portion of taxes from itself; and as an hereditary house, accountable to nobody, it resembles a rotten borough, whose consent is to be courted by interest. There are but few of its members who are not in some mode or other participators, or disposers of the public money. One turns a candle-holder, or a lord in waiting; another a lord of the bed-chamber, a groom of the stole, or any insignificant nominal office, to which a salary is annexed, paid out of the public taxes, and which avoids the direct appearance of corruption. Such situations are derogatory to the character of man; and where they can be submitted to, honour cannot reside.

To all these are to be added the numerous dependants, the long list of younger branches and distant relations, who are to be provided for at the public expense: in short, were an estimation to be made of the charge of aristocracy to a nation, it will be found nearly equal to that of supporting the poor. The Duke of Richmond alone (and there are cases similar to his) takes away as much for himself as would maintain two thousand poor and aged persons. Is it, then, any wonder, that under such a system of government, taxes and rates have multiplied to their present extent?

In stating these matters, I speak an open and disinterested language, dictated by no passion but that of humanity. To me, who have not only refused offers, because I thought them improper, but have declined rewards I might with reputation have accepted, it is no wonder that meanness and imposition appear disgustful. Independence is my happiness, and I view things as they are, without regard to place or person; my country is the world, and my religion is to do good.

Mr Burke, in speaking of the aristocratical law of primogeniture, says, 'it is the standing law of our landed inheritance; and which, without question, has a tendency, and I think', continues he, 'a happy tendency, to preserve a character of weight and consequence'.

Mr Burke may call this law what he pleases, but humanity and impartial reflection will denounce it a law of brutal injustice. Were we not accustomed to the daily practice, and did we only hear of it as the law of some distant part of the world, we should conclude that the legislators of such countries had not yet arrived at a state of civilization.

As to its preserving a character of *weight and consequence*, the case appears to me directly the reverse. It is an attaint upon character; a sort of privateering of family property. It may have weight among dependent tenants, but it gives none on a scale of national, and much less of universal character. Speaking for myself, my parents were not able to give me a shilling, beyond what they gave me in education; and to do this they distressed themselves: yet, I possess more of what is called consequence in the world, than anyone in Mr Burke's catalogue of aristocrats.

Having thus glanced at some of the defects of the two houses of parliament, I proceed to what is called the crown, upon which I shall be very concise.

It signifies a nominal office of a million sterling a year, the business of which consists in receiving the money. Whether the person be wise or foolish, sane or insane, a native or a foreigner, matters not. Every ministry acts upon the same idea that Mr Burke writes, namely, that the people must be hoodwinked, and held in superstitious ignorance by some bugbear or other; and what is called the crown answers this purpose, and therefore it answers all the purposes to be expected from it. This is more than can be said of the other two branches.

The hazard to which this office is exposed in all countries, is not from anything that can happen to the man, but from what may happen to the nation – the danger of its coming to its senses.

It has been customary to call the crown the executive power, and the custom is continued, though the reason has ceased.

It was called the *executive*, because the person whom it signified used, formerly, to sit in the character of a judge, in administering or executing the laws. The tribunals were then a part of the court. The power, therefore, which is now called the judicial, is what was called the executive; and, consequently, one or other of the terms is redundant, and one of the offices useless. When we speak of the crown now, it means nothing; it signifies neither a judge nor a general: besides which it is the laws that govern, and not the man. The old terms are kept up, to give an appearance of consequence to empty forms; and the only effect they have is that of increasing expenses.

Before I proceed to the means of rendering governments more conducive to the general happiness of mankind than they are at present, it will not be improper to take a review of the progress of taxation in England.

It is a general idea, that when taxes are once laid on, they are never taken off. However true this may have been of late, it was not always so. Either, therefore, the people of former times were more watchful over government than those of the present, or government was administered with less extravagance.

It is now seven hundred years since the Norman conquest, and the establishment of what is called the crown. Taking this portion of time in seven separate periods of one hundred years each, the amount of the annual taxes, at each period, will be as follows: —

Annual amount of taxes levied by William the Conqueror, beginning in the year 1066	£400,000
Annual amount of taxes at one hundred years from the conquest, (1166)	200,000
Annual amount of taxes at two hundred years from the conquest, (1266)	150,000
Annual amount of taxes at three hundred years from the conquest, (1366)	130,000
Annual amount of taxes at four hundred years from the conquest, (1466)	100,000

These statements, and those which follow, are taken from Sir John Sinclair's History of the Revenue; by which it appears, that taxes continued decreasing for four hundred years, at the expiration of which time they were reduced three-fourths, viz. from four hundred thousand pounds to one hundred thousand. The people of England of the present day, have a traditionary and historical idea of the bravery of their ancestors; but whatever their virtues or their vices might have been, they certainly were a people who would not be imposed upon, and who kept government in awe as to taxation, if not as to principle. Though they were not able to expel the monarchical usurpation, they restricted it to a republican economy of taxes.

Let us now review the remaining three hundred years.

Annual amount of taxes at five hundred years from the conquest, (1566)	£500,000
Annual amount of taxes at six hundred years from the conquest, (1666)	1,800,000
Annual amount of taxes at the present time, (1791)	17,000,000

The difference between the first four hundred years and the last three, is so astonishing, as to warrant an opinion, that the national character of the English has changed. It would have been impossible to have dragooned the former English, into the excess of taxation that now exists; and when it is considered that the pay of the army, the navy, and of all the revenue officers, is the same now as it was above a hundred years ago, when the taxes were not above a tenth part of what they are at present, it appears impossible to account for the enormous increase in expenditure, on any other ground, than extravagance, corruption, and intrigue.[18]

With the Revolution of 1688, and more so since the Hanover succession, came the destructive system of continental intrigues, and

18 Several of the court newspapers have of late made frequent mention of Wat Tyler. That his memory should be traduced by court sycophants, and all those who live on the spoil of a public, is not to be wondered at. He was, however, the means of checking the rage and injustice of taxation in his time, and the nation owed much to his valour. The history is concisely this: – In the time of Richard the Second, a poll-tax was levied, of one shilling per head, upon every person in the nation, of whatever estate or condition, on poor as well as rich, above the age of fifteen years. If any favour was shown in the law, it was to the rich rather than to the poor; as no person could be charged more than twenty shillings for himself, family, and servants, though ever so numerous; while all other families, under the number of twenty, were charged per head. Poll-taxes had always been odious; but this being also oppressive and unjust, it excited, as it naturally must, universal detestation among the poor and middle classes. The person known by the name of Wat Tyler, whose proper name was Walter, and a tiler by trade, lived at Deptford. The gatherer of the poll-tax, on coming to his house, demanded tax for one of his daughters, whom Tyler declared was under the age of fifteen. The tax-gatherer insisted on satisfying himself, and began an indecent examination of the girl, which enraging the father, he struck him with a hammer, that brought him to the ground, and was the cause of his death.

This circumstance served to bring the discontents to an issue. The inhabitants of the neighbourhood espoused the cause of Tyler, who in a few days was joined, according to some histories, by upwards of fifty thousand men, and chosen their chief. With this force he marched to London, to demand an abolition of the tax, and a redress of other grievances. The court, finding itself in a forlorn condition, and unable to make resistance, agreed, with Richard at its head, to hold a conference with Tyler in Smithfield, making many fair professions, courtier like, of its dispositions to redress the oppressions. While Richard and Tyler were in conversation on these matters, each being on horseback, Walworth then mayor of London, and one of the creatures of the court, watched an opportunity, and like a cowardly assassin, stabbed Tyler with a dagger; and two or three other falling upon him, he was instantly sacrificed.

Tyler appears to have been an intrepid disinterested man, with respect to himself. All his proposals made to Richard, were on a more just and public ground, than those which had been made to John by the Barons; and notwithstanding the sycophancy of historians, and men like Mr Burke, who seek to gloss over a base action of the court by traducing Tyler, his fame will outlive their falsehood. If the Barons merited a monument to be erected in Runnymede, Tyler merits one in Smithfield. – Paine.

the rage for foreign wars and foreign dominion; systems of such secure mystery that the expenses admit of no accounts; a single line stands for millions. To what excess taxation might have extended, had not the French Revolution contributed to break up the system, and put an end to pretences, is impossible to say. Viewed, as that revolution ought to be, as the fortunate means of lessening the load of taxes of both countries, it is of as much importance to England as to France; and, if properly improved to all the advantage of which it is capable, and to which it leads, deserve as much celebration in one country as the other.

In pursuing this subject, I shall begin with the matter that first presents itself, that of lessening the burden of taxes; and shall then add such matters and propositions, respecting the three countries of England, France, and America, as the present prospect of things appears to justify: I mean, an alliance of the three, for the purposes that will be mentioned in their proper place.

What has happened may happen again. By the statement before shown of the progress of taxation, it is seen, that taxes have been lessened to a fourth part of what they had formerly been. Though the present circumstances do not admit of the same reduction, yet it admits of such a beginning, as may accomplish that end in less time, than in the former case.

The amount of taxes for the year, ending at Michaelmas 1788, was as follows:

Land-tax,	1,950,000
Customs,	3,789,274
Excise, (including old and new malt),	6,751,727
Stamps,	1,278,214
Miscellaneous taxes and incidents,	1,803,755
	£15,572,970

Since the year 1788, upwards of one million of new taxes have been laid on, besides the produce from the lotteries; and as the taxes have in general been more productive since than before, the amount may be taken, in round numbers, at £17,000,000.

N B. The expense of collection and the drawbacks, which together amount to nearly two millions, are paid out of the gross amount; and the above is the net sum paid into the exchequer.

This sum of seventeen millions is applied to two different purposes; the one to pay the interest of the national debt, the other to the current expenses of each year. About nine millions are appropriated to the former; and the remainder, being nearly eight millions, to the latter. As to the million, said to be applied to the reduction of the debt, it is so much like paying with one hand and taking out with the other, as not to merit much notice.

It happened, fortunately for France, that she possessed national domains for paying off her debt, and thereby lessening her taxes: but as this is not the case in England, her reduction of taxes can only take place by reducing the current expenses, which may now be done to the amount of four or five millions annually, as will hereafter appear. When this is accomplished, it will more than counterbalance the enormous charge of the American war; and the saving will be from the same source from whence the evil arose.

As to the national debt, however heavy the interest may be in taxes; yet, as it serves to keep alive a capital, useful to commerce, it balances by its effects a considerable part of its own weight; and as the quantity of gold and silver in England is, by some means or other, short of its proper proportion,[19] (being not more than twenty millions, whereas it should be sixty), it would, besides the injustice, be bad policy to extinguish a capital that serves to supply that defect. But with respect to the current expense, whatever is saved therefrom is gain. The excess may serve to keep corruption alive, but it has no reaction on credit and commerce, like the interest of the debt.

It is now very probable, that the English government (I do not mean the nation) is unfriendly to the French Revolution. Whatever serves to expose the intrigue and lessen the influence of courts, by lessening taxation, will be unwelcome to those who feed upon the spoil. Whilst the clamour of French intrigue, arbitrary power, popery, and wooden shoes could be kept up, the nation was easily allured and alarmed into taxes. Those days are now past; deception, it is to be hoped, has reaped its last harvest, and better times are in prospect for both countries, and for the world.

Taking it for granted that an alliance may be formed between England, France, and America, for the purposes hereafter to be mentioned, the national expenses of France and England may conse-

19 Foreign intrigue, foreign wars, and foreign dominions, will in a great measure account for the deficiency. – Paine.

quently be lessened. The same fleets and armies will no longer be necessary to either, and the reduction can be made ship for ship on each side. But to accomplish these objects, the governments must necessarily be fitted to a common and correspondent principle. Confidence can never take place while an hostile disposition remains in either, or where mystery and secrecy on one side, is opposed to candour and openness on the other.

These matters admitted, the national expenses might be put back, *for the sake of a precedent*, to what they were at some period when France and England were not enemies. This, consequently, must be prior to the Hanover succession, and also to the Revolution of 1688.[20] The first instance that presents itself, antecedent to those dates, is in the very wasteful and profligate times of Charles the Second, at which time England and France acted as allies. If I have chosen a period of great extravagance, it will serve to show modern extravagance in a still worse light; especially as the pay of the navy, the army, and the revenue officers has not increased since that time.

The peace establishment was then as follows: — (See Sir John Sinclair's History of the Revenue.)

Navy,	300,000
Army,	212,000
Ordnance,	40,000
Civil List,	462,115

£1,014,115

The parliament, however, settled the whole annual peace establish-

20 I happened to be in England at the celebration of the centenary of the Revolution of 1688. The characters of William and Mary have always appeared to me detestable; the one seeking to destroy his uncle, and the other her father, to get possession of power themselves; yet, as the nation was disposed to think something of that event, I felt hurt at seeing it ascribe the whole reputation of it to a man who had undertaken it as a job, and who, besides what he otherwise got, charged six hundred thousand pounds for the expense of the little fleet that brought him from Holland. George the First acted the same close-fisted part as William had done, and bought the Duchy of Bremen with the money he got from England, two hundred and fifty thousand pounds over and above his pay as king; and having thus purchased it at the expense of England, added it to his Hanoverian dominions for his own private profit. In fact, every nation that does not govern itself, is governed as a job. England has been the prey of jobs ever since the Revolution.   Paine.

ment at 1,200,000.[21] If we go back to the time of Elizabeth, the amount of all the taxes was but half a million, yet the nation sees nothing during that period, that reproaches it with want of consequence.

All circumstances then taken together, arising from the French Revolution, from the approaching harmony and reciprocal interest of the two nations, the abolition of court intrigue on both sides, and the progress of knowledge in the science of government, the annual expenditure might be put back to one million and a half, viz.

Navy,	500,000
Army,	500,000
Expenses of government,	500,000
	£1,500,000

Even this sum is six times greater than the expenses of government are in America, yet the civil internal government in England, (I mean that administered by means of quarter sessions, juries, and assize, and which, in fact, is nearly the whole, and performed by the nation), is less expense upon the revenue, than the same species and portion of government is in America.

It is time that nations should be rational, and not be governed like animals, for the pleasure of their riders. To read the history of kings, a man would be almost inclined to suppose that government consisted in stag-hunting, and that every nation paid a million a year to a huntsman. Man ought to have pride, or shame enough to blush at being thus imposed upon, and when he feel his proper character, he will. Upon all subjects of this nature, there is often passing in the mind, a train of ideas he has not yet accustomed himself to encourage and communicate. Restrained by something that puts on the character of prudence, he acts the hypocrite upon himself as well as to others. It is, however, curious to observe how soon this spell can be dissolved. A single expression, boldly conceived and uttered, will sometimes put a whole company into their proper feelings; and whole nations are acted upon in the same manner.

As to the offices of which any civil government may be composed, it matters but little by what names they are described. In

21 Charles, like his predecessors and successors, finding that war was the harvest of governments, engaged in a war with the Dutch, the expense of which increased the annual expenditure to £1,800,000, as stated under the date of 1666; but the peace establishment was but £1,200,000. – Paine.

the routine of business, as before observed, whether a man be styled a president, a king, an emperor, a senator, or anything else, it is impossible that any service he can perform, can merit from a nation more than ten thousand pounds a year; and as no man should be paid beyond his services, so every man of a proper heart will not accept more. Public money ought to be touched with the most scrupulous consciousness of honour. It is not the produce of riches only, but of the hard earnings of labour and poverty. It is drawn even from the bitterness of want and misery. Not a beggar passes, or perishes in the streets, whose mite is not in that mass.

Were it possible that the Congress of America, could be so lost to their duty, and to the interest of their constituents, as to offer George Washington, as president of America, a million a year, he would not, and he could not, accept it. His sense of honour is of another kind. It has cost England almost seventy millions sterling, to maintain a family imported from abroad, of very inferior capacity to thousands in the nation; and scarcely a year has passed that has not produced some new mercenary application. Even the physicians' bills have been sent to the public to be paid. No wonder that jails are crowded, and taxes and poor-rates increased. Under such systems, nothing is to be looked for but what has already happened; and as to reformation, whenever it comes, it must be from the nation, and not from the government.

To show that the sum of five hundred thousand pounds is more than sufficient to defray all the expenses of government, exclusive of navies and armies, the following estimate is added for any country, of the same extent as England.

In the first place, three hundred representatives, fairly elected, are sufficient for all the purposes to which legislation can apply, and preferable to a larger number. They may be divided into two or three houses, or meet in one, as in France, or in any manner a constitution shall direct.

As representation is always considered, in free countries, as the most honourable of all stations, the allowance made to it is merely to defray the expense which the representatives incur by that service, and not to it as an office.

If an allowance, at the rate of five hundred pounds *per ann.* be made to every representative, deducting for non-attendance, the expense, if the whole number attended for six months, each year, would be $\left.\begin{array}{r}\\\\\\\\\end{array}\right\}$ £75,000

The official departments cannot reasonably exceed the following number, with the salaries annexed:

Three offices, at ten thousand pounds each,		30,000
Ten ditto,	at £5,000 each	50,000
Twenty ditto,	at £2,000 each	40,000
Forty ditto,	at £1,000 each	40,000
Two hundred ditto,	at £ 500 each	100,000
Three hundred ditto,	at £ 200 each	60,000
Five hundred ditto,	at £ 100 each	50,000
Seven hundred ditto,	at £ 75 each	52,500
		£497,500

If a nation choose, it can deduct four per cent, from all offices, and make one of twenty thousand *per ann*.

All revenue officers are paid out of the moneys they collect, and therefore, are not in this estimation.

The foregoing is not offered as an exact detail of offices, but to show the number and rate of salaries which five hundred thousand pounds will support; and it will, on experience, be found impracticable to find business sufficient to justify even this expense. As to the manner in which office business is now performed, the Chiefs, in several offices, such as the post office, and certain offices in the exchequer, etc., do little more than sign their names three of four times a year; and the whole duty is performed by under clerks.

Taking, therefore, one million and an half as a sufficient peace establishment for all the honest purposes of government, which is three hundred thousand pounds more than the peace establishment in the profligate and prodigal times of Charles the Second, (notwithstanding, as has been already observed, the pay and salaries of the army, navy, and revenue officers, continue the same as at that period), there will remain a surplus of upwards of six millions out of the present current expenses. The question then will be, how to dispose of this surplus.

Whoever has observed the manner in which trade and taxes twist themselves together, must be sensible of the impossibility of separating them suddenly.

First. Because the articles now on hand are already charged with the duty, and the reduction cannot take place on the present stock.

Secondly. Because, on all those articles on which the duty is charged in the gross, such as per barrel, hogshead, hundredweight, or ton, the abolition of the duty does not admit of being divided down so as fully to relieve the consumer, who purchases by the pint, or the pound. The last duty laid on strong beer and ale, was three shillings per barrel, which, if taken off, would lessen the purchase only half a farthing per pint, and consequently, would not reach to practical relief.

This being the condition of a great part of the taxes, it will be necessary to look for such others as are free from this embarrassment, and where the relief will be direct and visible, and capable of immediate operation.

In the first place, then, the poor-rates are a direct tax which every housekeeper feels, and who knows also, to a farthing, the sum which he pays. The national amount of the whole of the poor-rates is not positively known, but can be procured. Sir John Sinclair, in his History of the Revenue, had stated it at £2,100,587. A considerable part of which is expended in litigations, in which the poor, instead of being relieved, are tormented. The expense, however, is the same to the parish from whatever cause it arises.

In Birmingham, the amount of the poor-rates is fourteen thousand pounds a year. This, though a large sum, is moderate, compared with the population. Birmingham is said to contain seventy thousand souls, and on a proportion of seventy thousand to fourteen thousand pounds poor-rates, the national amount of poor-rates, taking the population of England at seven millions, would be but one million four hundred thousand pounds. It is, therefore, most probable, that the population of Birmingham is over-rated. Fourteen thousand pounds is the proportion upon fifty thousand souls, taking two millions of poor-rates as the national amount.

Be it, however, what it may, it is no other than the consequence of the excessive burden of taxes, for, at the time when the taxes were very low, the poor were able to maintain themselves; and there were no poor-rates.[22] In the present state of things, a labouring man, with a wife and two or three children, does not pay less than between seven and eight pounds a year in taxes. He is not sensible of this, because it is disguised to him in the articles which he buys, and he

22 Poor-rates began about the time of Henry the Eighth, when the taxes began to increase, and they have increased as the taxes increased ever since. – Paine.

thinks only of their dearness; but as the taxes take from him, at least, a fourth part of his yearly earnings, he is consequently disabled from providing for a family, especially, if himself, or any of them, are afflicted with sickness.

The first step, therefore, of practical relief, would be to abolish the poor-rates entirely, and in lieu thereof, to make a remission of taxes to the poor of double the amount of the present poor-rates, viz. four millions annually out of the surplus taxes. By this measure, the poor will be benefited two millions, and the housekeepers two millions. This alone would be equal to a reduction of one hundred and twenty millions of the national debt, and consequently equal to the whole expense of the American war.

It will then remain to be considered, which is the most effectual mode of distributing this remission of four millions.

It is easily seen, that the poor are generally composed of large families of children, and old people past their labour. If these two classes are provided for, the remedy will so far reach to the full extent of the case, that what remains will be incidental and in a great measure, fall within the compass of benefit clubs, which, though of humble invention, merit to be ranked among the best of modern institutions.

Admitting England to contain seven million of souls; if one-fifth thereof are of that class of poor which need support, the number will be one million four hundred thousand. Of this number, one hundred and forty thousand will be aged poor, as will be hereafter shown, and for which a distinct provision will be proposed.

There will then remain one million two hundred and sixty thousand, which, at five souls to each family, amount to two hundred and fifty-two thousand families, rendered poor from the expense of children and the weight of taxes.

The number of children under fourteen years of age, in each of those families, will be found to be about five to every two families; some having two, and others three; some one, and others four; some none, and others five; but it rarely happens that more than five are under fourteen years of age, and after this age they are capable of service or of being apprenticed.

Allowing five children (under fourteen years) to every two families,

| The number of children will be | 630,000 |
| The number of parents were they all living, would be | 504,000 |

It is certain, that if the children are provided for, the parents are relieved of consequence, because it is from the expense of bringing up children that their poverty arises.

Having thus ascertained the greatest number that can be supposed to need support on account of young families, I proceed to the mode of relief or distribution, which is,

To pay as a remission of taxes to every poor family, out of the surplus taxes, and in room of poor-rates, four pounds a year for every child under fourteen years of age; enjoining the parents of such children to send them to school, to learn reading, writing, and common arithmetic; the ministers of every parish, of every denomination, to certify jointly to an office, for that purpose, that this duty is performed.

The amount of this expense will be,

| For six hundred and thirty thousand children, at four pounds *per ann.* each, | £2,520,000 |

By adopting this method, not only the poverty of the parents will be relieved, but ignorance will be banished from the rising generation, and the number of poor will hereafter become less, because their abilities, by the aid of education, will be greater. Many a youth, with good natural genius, who is apprenticed to a mechanical trade, such as a carpenter, joiner, millwright, shipwright, blacksmith, etc., is prevented getting forward the whole of his life, from the want of a little common education when a boy.

I now proceed to the case of the aged.

I divide age into two classes. First, the approach of age beginning at fifty. Secondly, old age commencing at sixty.

At fifty, though the mental faculties of man are in full vigour, and his judgement better than at any preceding date, the bodily powers for laborious life are on the decline. He cannot bear the same quantity of fatigue as at an earlier period. He begins to earn less, and is less capable of enduring wind and weather; and in those more retired employments where much sight is required, he fails apace, and sees himself, like an old horse, beginning to be turned adrift.

At sixty his labour ought to be over, at least from direct necessity.

It is painful to see old age working itself to death, in what are called civilized countries, for daily bread.

To form some judgement of the number of those above fifty years of age, I have several times counted the persons I met in the streets of London, men, women, and children, and have generally found that the average is about one in sixteen or seventeen. If it be said that aged persons do not come much in the streets, so neither do infants; and a great proportion of grown children are in school, and in work-shops as apprentices. Taking then sixteen for a divisor, the whole number of persons in England, of fifty years and upwards of both sexes, rich and poor, will be four hundred and twenty thousand.

The persons to be provided for out of this gross number will be, husbandmen, common labourers, journeymen of every trade and their wives, sailors, and disbanded soldiers, worn-out servants of both sexes, and poor widows.

There will be also a considerable number of middling tradesmen, who having lived decently in the former part of life, begin, as age approaches, to lose their business, and at last fall to decay.

Besides these, there will be constantly thrown off from the re-volutions of that wheel, which no man can stop, nor regulate, a number from every class of life connected with commerce and adven-ture.

To provide for all those accidents, and whatever else may befall, I take the number of persons, who at one time or other of their lives, after fifty years of age, may feel it necessary or comfortable to be better supported, than they can support themselves, and that not as a matter of grace and favour, but of right, at one-third of the whole number, which is one hundred and forty thousand . . . and for whom a distinct provision was proposed to be made. If there be more, society, notwithstanding the show and pomposity of government, is in a deplorable condition in England.

Of this one hundred and forty thousand, I take one-half, seventy thousand, to be of the age of fifty and under sixty, and the other half to be sixty years and upwards. – Having thus ascertained the probable proportion of the number of aged persons, I proceed to the mode of rendering their condition comfortable, which is,

To pay to every such person of the age of fifty years, and until he shall arrive at the age of sixty, the sum of six pounds *per ann.* out of the surplus taxes; and ten pounds *per ann.* during life after the age of sixty. The expense of which will be,

Seventy thousand persons at £6 *per ann.*	420,000
Seventy thousand ditto at £10 *per ann.*	700,000
	£1,120,000

This support, as already remarked, is not of the nature of a charity, but of a right. Every person in England, male and female, pays on an average in taxes, two pounds eight shillings and sixpence *per ann.* from the day of his (or her) birth; and, if the expense of collection be added, he pays two pounds eleven shillings and sixpence; consequently, at the end of fifty years he has paid one hundred and twenty-eight pounds fifteen shillings; and at sixty, one hundred and fifty-four pounds ten shillings. Converting, therefore, his (or her) individual tax into a tontine, the money he shall receive after fifty years, is but little more than the legal interest of the net money he has paid; the rest is made up from those whose circumstances do not require them to draw such support, and the capital in both cases defrays the expenses of government. It is on this ground that I have extended the probable claims to one third of the number of aged persons in the nation. – Is it then better that the lives of one hundred and forty thousand aged persons be rendered comfortable, or that a million a year of public money be expended on any one individual, and him often of the most worthless or insignificant character? Let reason and justice, let honour and humanity, let even hypocrisy, sycophancy and Mr Burke, let George, let Louis, Leopold, Frederic, Catherine, Cornwallis, or Tippoo Saib, answer the question.[23]

23 Reckoning the taxes by families, five to a family, each family pays on an average, 12*l.* 16*s.* 6*d. per ann.* To this sum are to be added the poor-rates. Though all pay taxes in the articles they consume, all do not pay poor-rates. About two millions are exempted, some as not being housekeepers, others as not being able, and the poor themselves who receive the relief. The average, therefore, of poor-rates on the remaining number, is forty shillings for every family of five persons, which makes the whole average amount of taxes and rates, 14*l.* 17*s.* 6*d.* For six persons, 17*l.* 17*s.* For seven persons, 20*l.* 16*s.* 6*d.*

The average of taxes in America, under the new or representative system of government, including the interest of the debt contracted in the war, and taking the population at four million of souls, which it now amounts to, and it is daily increasing, is five shillings per head, men, women, and children. The difference, therefore, between the two governments, is as under,

	England			America		
	l.	*s.*	*d.*	*l.*	*s.*	*d.*
For a family of five persons	14	17	6	1	5	0
For a family of six persons	17	17	0	1	10	0
For a family of seven persons	20	16	6	1	15	0

Paine.

The sum thus remitted to the poor will be,

To two hundred and fifty-two thousand poor families, containing six hundred and thirty thousand children,	2,520,000
To one hundred and forty thousand aged persons	1,120,000
	£3,640,000

There will then remain three hundred and sixty thousand pounds out of the four millions, part of which may be applied as follows:

After all the above cases are provided for, there will still be a number of families who, though not properly of the class of poor, yet find it difficult to give education to their children; and such children, under such a case, would be in a worse condition than if their parents were actually poor. A nation under a well-regulated government, should permit none to remain uninstructed. It is monarchical and aristocratical government only that requires ignorance for its support.

Suppose then four hundred thousand children to be in this condition, which is a greater number than ought to be supposed, after the provisions already made, the method will be,

To allow for each of those children ten shillings a year for the expense of schooling, for six years each, which will give them six months schooling each year and half a crown a year for paper and spelling books.

The expense of this will be annually [24] £250,000.

There will then remain one hundred and ten thousand pounds.

Notwithstanding the great modes of relief which the best instituted and best principled government may devise, there will be a

---

24 Public schools do not answer the general purpose of the poor. They are chiefly in corporation towns, from which the country towns and villages are excluded; or, if admitted, the distance occasions a great loss of time. Education, to be useful to the poor, should be on the spot; and the best method, I believe, to accomplish this, is to enable the parents to pay the expense themselves. There are always persons of both sexes to be found in every village, especially when growing into years, capable of such an undertaking. Twenty children, at ten shillings each, (and that not more than six months each year) would be as much as some livings amount to in the remote parts of England; and there are often distressed clergymen's widows to whom such an income would be acceptable. Whatever is given on this account to children answers two purposes, to them it is education, to those who educate them it is a livelihood. – Paine.

number of smaller cases, which it is good policy as well as beneficence in a nation to consider.

Were twenty shillings to be given immediately on the birth of a child, to every woman who should make the demand, and none will make it whose circumstances do not require it, it might relieve a great deal of instant distress.

There are about two hundred thousand births yearly in England, and if claimed, by one-fourth, the amount would be £50,000.

And twenty shillings to every new-married couple who should claim in like manner. This would not exceed the sum of £20,000.

Also twenty thousand pounds to be appropriated to defray the funeral expenses of persons, who, travelling for work, may die at a distance from their friends. By relieving parishes from this charge, the sick stranger will be better treated.

I shall finish this part of the subject with a plan adapted to the particular condition of a metropolis, such as London.

Cases are continually occurring in a metropolis, different to those which occur in the country, and for which a different, or rather an additional mode of relief is necessary. In the country, even in large towns, people have a knowledge of each other, and distress never rises to that extreme height it sometimes does in a metropolis. There is no such thing in the country as persons, in the literal sense of the word, starved to death, or dying with cold from the want of a lodging. Yet such cases, and others equally as miserable, happen in London.

Many a youth comes up to London full of expectations, and with little or no money, and unless he gets immediate employment he is already half undone; and boys bred up in London, without any means of a livelihood, and as it often happens of dissolute parents, are in a still worse condition; and servants long out of place are not much better off. In short, a world of little cases are continually arising, which busy or affluent life knows not of, to open the first door to distress. Hunger is not among the postponable wants, and a day, even a few hours, in such a condition, is often the crisis of a life of ruin.

These circumstances, which are the general cause of the little thefts and pilferings that lead to greater, may be prevented. There yet remain twenty thousand pounds out of the four millions of surplus taxes, which, with another fund hereafter to be mentioned, amounting to about twenty thousand pounds more, cannot be better applied than to this purpose. The plan then will be,

First, To erect two or more buildings, or take some already erected, capable of containing at least six thousand persons, and to have in each of these places as many kinds of employment as can be contrived, so that every person who shall come may find something which he or she can do.

Secondly, To receive all who shall come, without inquiring who or what they are. The only condition to be, that for so much, or so many hours work, each person shall receive so many meals of wholesome food, and a warm lodging, at least as good as a barrack. That a certain portion of what each person's work shall be worth shall be reserved, and given to him, or her, on their going away; and that each person shall stay as long, or as short time, or come as often as he choose, on these conditions.

If each person stayed three months, it would assist by rotation twenty-four thousand persons annually, though the real number, at all times, would be but six thousand. By establishing an asylum of this kind, persons to whom temporary distresses occur, would have an opportunity to recruit themselves, and be enabled to look out for better employment.

Allowing that their labour paid but one-half the expense of supporting them, after reserving a portion of their earnings for themselves, the sum of forty thousand pounds additional would defray all other charges for even a greater number than six thousand.

The fund very properly convertible to this purpose, in addition to the twenty thousand pounds, remaining of the former fund, will be the produce of the tax upon coals, so iniquitously and wantonly applied to the support of the Duke of Richmond. It is horrid that any man, more especially at the price coals now are, should live on the distresses of a community; and any government permitting such an abuse, deserves to be dismissed. This fund is said to be about twenty thousand pounds *per annum*.

I shall now conclude this plan with enumerating the several particulars, and then proceed to other matters.

The enumeration is as follows:

First, Abolition of two million poor-rates.

Secondly, Provision for two hundred and fifty-two thousand poor families.

Thirdly, Education for one million and thirty thousand children.

Fourthly, Comfortable provision for one hundred and forty thousand aged persons.

Fifthly, Donation of twenty shillings each for fifty thousand births.

Sixthly, Donation of twenty shillings each for twenty thousand marriages.

Seventhly, Allowance of twenty thousand pounds for the funeral expenses of persons travelling for work, and dying at a distance from their friends.

Eighthly, Employment, at all times, for the casual poor in the cities of London and Westminster.

By the operation of this plan, the poor laws, those instruments of civil torture, will be superseded, and the wasteful expense of litigation prevented. The hearts of the humane will not be shocked by ragged and hungry children, and persons of seventy and eighty years of age begging for bread. The dying poor will not be dragged from place to place to breathe their last, as a reprisal of parish upon parish. Widows will have a maintenance for their children, and not be carried away, on the death of their husbands, like culprits and criminals; and children will no longer be considered as increasing the distresses of their parents. The haunts of the wretched will be known, because it will be to their advantage; and the number of petty crimes, the offspring of distress and poverty, will be lessened. The poor, as well as the rich, will then be interested in the support of government, and the cause and apprehension of riots and tumults will cease. – Ye who sit in ease, and solace yourselves in plenty, and such there are in Turkey and Russia, as well as in England, and who say to yourselves, 'Are we not well off', have ye thought of these things? When ye do, ye will cease to speak and feel for yourselves alone.

The plan is easy in practice. It does not embarrass trade by a sudden interruption in the order of taxes, but effects the relief by changing the application of them; and the money necessary for the purpose can be drawn from the excise collections, which are made eight times a year in every market town in England.

Having now arranged and concluded this subject, I proceed to the next.

Taking the present current expenses at seven millions and a half, which is the least amount they are now at, there will remain (after the sum of one million and an half be taken for the new current expenses, and four millions for the before-mentioned service) the sum of two millions; part of which to be applied as follows:

Though fleets and armies, by an alliance with France, will, in great measure, become useless, yet the persons who have devoted themselves to those services, and have thereby unfitted themselves for other lines of life, are not to be sufferers by the means that make others happy. They are a different description of men to those who form or hang about a court.

A part of the army will remain at least for some years, and also of the navy, for which a provision is already made in the former part of this plan of one million, which is almost half a million more than the peace establishment of the army and navy in the prodigal times of Charles the Second.

Suppose then fifteen thousand soldiers to be disbanded, and that an allowance be made to each of three shillings a week during life, clear of all deductions, to be paid in the same manner as the Chelsea College pensioners are paid, and for them to return to their trades and their friends; and also that an addition of fifteen thousand sixpences per week be made to the pay of the soldiers who shall remain; the annual expense will be,

To the pay of fifteen thousand disbanded soldiers, at three shillings per week,	117,000
Additional pay to the remaining soldiers,	19,500
	136,500
Suppose that the pay to the officers of the disbanded corps be of the same amount as the sum allowed to the men,	117,000
	253,500
To prevent bulky estimations, admit the same sum to the disbanded navy as to the army, and the same increase of pay,	253,500
Total	£507,000

Every year some part of this sum of half a million (I omit the odd seven thousand pounds for the purpose of keeping the account unembarrassed) will fall in, and the whole of it in time, as it is on the ground of life annuities, except the increased pay of twenty-nine thousand pounds. As it falls in, a part of the taxes may be taken off; for instance, when thirty thousand pounds fall in, the duty on hops may be wholly taken off; and as other parts fall in, the duties on candles and soap may be lessened, till at last they will totally cease.

There now remains at least one million and an half of surplus taxes.

The tax on houses and windows is one of those direct taxes, which, like the poor-rates, is not confounded with trade; and, when taken off, the relief will be instantly felt. This tax falls heavy on the middling class of people.

The amount of this tax by the returns of 1788, was,

		l.	*s.*	*d.*
Houses and windows by the act of 1766,		385,459	11	7
Ditto	ditto by the act of 1779,	130,739	14	$5\frac{1}{2}$
	Total	516,199	6	$0\frac{1}{2}$

If this tax be struck off, there will then remain about one million of surplus taxes, and as it is always proper to keep a sum in reserve, for incidental matters, it may be best not to extend reductions further, in the first instance, but to consider what may be accomplished by other modes of reform.

Among the taxes most heavily felt is the commutation-tax. I shall, therefore, offer a plan for its abolition, by substituting another in its place, which will affect three objects at once:

First, That of removing the burden to where it can best be borne.

Secondly, Restoring justice among families by a distribution of property.

Thirdly, Extirpating the overgrown influence arising from the unnatural law of primogeniture, and which is one of the principal sources of corruption at elections.

The amount of the commutation tax by the returns
of 1788, was,   £771,657 0 0

When taxes are proposed, the country is amused by the plausible language of taxing luxuries. One thing is called a luxury at one time, and something else at another; but the real luxury does not consist in the article, but in the means of procuring it, and this is always kept out of sight.

I know not why any plant or herb of the field should be a greater luxury in one country than another, but an overgrown estate in either is a luxury at all times, and as such is the proper object of taxation. It is, therefore, right to take those kind tax-making gentlemen up on their own word, and argue on the principle themselves have laid down, that of *taxing luxuries*. If they, or their champion Mr Burke, who, I fear, is growing out of date like the man in armour, can prove that an estate of twenty, thirty, or forty thousand pounds a year is not a luxury, I will give up the argument.

Admitting that any annual sum, say for instance, one thousand pounds, is necessary or sufficient for the support of a family, consequently the second thousand is of the nature of a luxury, the third still more so, and by proceeding on, we shall at last arrive at a sum that may not improperly be called a prohibitable luxury. It would be impolitic to set bounds to property acquired by industry, and therefore it is right to place the prohibition beyond the probable acquisition to which industry can extend; but there ought to be a limit to property, or the accumulation of it, by bequest. It should pass in some other line. The richest in every nation have poor relations, and those often very near in consanguinity.

The following table of progressive taxation is constructed on the above principles, and as a substitute for the commutation-tax. It will reach the point of prohibition by a regular operation, and thereby supersede the aristocratical law of primogeniture.

TABLE I

A tax on all estates of the clear yearly value of fifty pounds, after deducting the land-tax, and up

	s.	d.
To £500	0	3 per pound
From 500 to 1000	0	6 per pound
On the second thousand	0	9 per pound
On the third ditto	1	0 per pound
On the fourth ditto	1	6 per pound
On the fifth ditto	2	0 per pound
On the sixth ditto	3	0 per pound
On the seventh ditto	4	0 per pound
On the eighth ditto	5	0 per pound
On the ninth ditto	6	0 per pound
On the tenth ditto	7	0 per pound
On the eleventh ditto	8	0 per pound

	s.	d.	
On the twelfth ditto	9	0	per pound
On the thirteenth ditto	10	0	per pound
On the fourteenth ditto	11	0	per pound
On the fifteenth ditto	12	0	per pound
On the sixteenth ditto	13	0	per pound
On the seventeenth ditto	14	0	per pound
On the eighteenth ditto	15	0	per pound
On the nineteenth ditto	16	0	per pound
On the twentieth ditto	17	0	per pound
On the twenty-first ditto	18	0	per pound
On the twenty-second ditto	19	0	per pound
On the twenty-third ditto	20	0	per pound

The foregoing table shows the progression per pound on every progressive thousand. The following table shows the amount of the tax on every thousand separately, and in the last column, the total amount of all the separate sums collected.

TABLE II

	d.	l.	s.	d.
An estate of £50 *per ann.* at 3 per pd. pays		0	12	6
100	3	1	5	0
200	3	2	10	0
300	3	3	15	0
400	3	5	0	0
500	3	7	5	0

After 500*l.* – the tax of sixpence per pound takes place on the second 500*l.* consequently an estate of 1,000*l. per ann.* pays 21*l.* 15*s.* and so on.

		l.	s.	d.		l.	s.	Total amount l.	s.
For the	1st	500 at	0	3 per pound		7	5 ⎫		
	2d	500 at	0	6		14	10 ⎭	21	15
	2d	1000 at	0	9		37	10	59	5
	3rd	1000 at	1	0		50	0	109	5
	4th	1000 at	1	6		75	0	184	5
	5th	1000 at	2	0		100	0	284	5
	6th	1000 at	3	0		150	0	434	5
	7th	1000 at	4	0		200	0	634	5

					Total amount	
	l.	*s.*	*d.*	*l.*	*s.*	*l.*	*s.*
For the 8th 1000 at	5	0	per pound	250	0	880	5
9th 1000 at	6	0		300	0	1180	5
10th 1000 at	7	0		350	0	1530	5
11th 1000 at	8	0		400	0	1930	5
12th 1000 at	9	0		450	0	2380	5
13th 1000 at	10	0		500	0	2880	5
14th 1000 at	11	0		550	0	3430	5
15th 1000 at	12	0		600	0	4030	5
16th 1000 at	13	0		650	0	4680	5
17th 1000 at	14	0		700	0	5380	5
18th 1000 at	15	0		750	0	6130	5
19th 1000 at	16	0		800	0	6930	5
20th 1000 at	17	0		850	0	7780	5
21st 1000 at	18	0		900	0	8680	5
22d 1000 at	19	0		950	0	9630	5
23rd 1000 at	20	0		1000	0	10630	5

At the twenty-third thousand the tax becomes twenty shillings in the pound, and consequently every thousand beyond that sum can produce no profit but by dividing the estate. Yet formidable as this tax appears, it will not, I believe, produce so much as the commutation-tax; should it produce more, it ought to be lowered to that amount upon estates under two or three thousand a year.

On small and middling estates it is lighter (as it is intended to be) than the commutation-tax. It is not till after seven or eight thousand a year that it begins to be heavy. The object is not so much the produce of the tax, as the justice of the measure. The aristocracy has screened itself too much, and this serves to restore a part of the lost equilibrium.

As an instance of its screening itself, it is only necessary to look back to the first establishment of the excise laws, at what is called the Restoration, or the coming of Charles the Second. The aristocratical interest then in power, commuted the feudal services itself was under by laying a tax on beer brewed for *sale*; that is, they compounded with Charles for an exemption from those services for themselves and their heirs, by a tax to be paid by other people. The aristocracy do not purchase beer brewed for sale, but brew their own beer free of the duty, and if any commutation at that time were necessary, it ought to have been at the expense of those for whom the exemptions from those services were intended;[25] instead of which it was thrown on an entire different class of men.

But the chief object of this progressive tax (besides the justice of rendering taxes more equal than they are) is, as already stated, to extirpate the overgrown influence arising from the unnatural law of primogeniture, and which is one of the principal sources of corruption at elections.

It would be attended with no good consequences to inquire how such vast estates as thirty, forty, or fifty thousand a year could commence, and that at a time when commerce and manufactures were not in a state to admit of such acquisitions. Let it be sufficient to remedy the evil by putting them in a condition of descending again to the community, by the quiet means of apportioning them among all the heirs and heiresses of those families. This will be the more necessary, because hitherto the aristocracy have quartered their younger children and connections upon the public in useless posts, places, and offices, which when abolished will leave them destitute, unless the law of primogeniture be also abolished or superseded.

A progressive tax will, in a great measure, effect this object, and that as a matter of interest to the parties most immediately concerned, as will be seen by the following table; which shows the net produce upon every estate, after substracting the tax. By this it will appear, that after an estate exceeds thirteen or fourteen thousand a year, the remainder produces but little profit to the holder, and consequently will pass either to the younger children, or to other kindred.

TABLE III

Showing the net produce of every estate from one thousand to twenty-three thousand pounds a year.

No. of thousands per ann.	Total tax subtracted £	Net produce £
1000	21	979
2000	59	1941

---

25 The tax on beer brewed for sale, from which the aristocracy are exempt, is almost one million more than the present commutation-tax, being by the returns of 1788, 1,666,152*l*. and consequently they ought to take on themselves the amount of the commutation-tax, as they are already exempted from one which is almost one million greater. – Paine.

No. of thousands per ann.	Total tax subtracted £	Net produce £
3000	109	2891
4000	184	3816
5000	284	4716
6000	434	5566
7000	634	6366
8000	880	7120
9000	1100	7820
10,000	1530	8470
11,000	1930	9070
12,000	2380	9620
13,000	2880	10,120
14,000	3430	10,570
15,000	4030	10,970
16,000	4680	11,320
17,000	5380	11,620
18,000	6130	11,870
19,000	6930	12,170
20,000	7780	12,220
21,000	8680	12,320
22,000	9630	12,370
23,000	10,360	12,370

NB. The odd shillings are dropped in this table.

According to this table, an estate cannot produce more than 12,370*l*. clear of the land tax and the progressive tax, and therefore the dividing such estates will follow as a matter of family interest. An estate of 23,000*l*. a year, divided into five estates of four thousand each and one of three, will be charged only 1129*l*. *which is but five per cent*, but if held by one possessor will be charged 10,630*l*.

Although an inquiry into the origin of those estates be unnecessary, the continuation of them in their present state is another subject. It is a matter of national concern. As hereditary estates, the law has created the evil, and it ought also to provide the remedy. Primogeniture ought to be abolished, not only because it is unnatural and unjust, but because the country suffers by its operation. By cutting off (as before observed) the younger children from their proper portion of inheritance, the public is loaded with the expense of maintaining them; and the freedom of elections violated by the overbearing influence which this unjust monopoly of family property produces. Nor is this all. It occasions a waste of national property. A considerable part of the land of the country is rendered unproductive by the great extent of parks and chases which this law serves to keep up, and this at a time when the annual production of grain is not equal to the national consumption. – In short, the evils of the aristocratical system are so great and numerous, so inconsistent with everything that is just, wise, natural, and beneficent, that when they are considered, there ought not to be a doubt that many, who are now classed under that description, will wish to see such a system abolished.

What pleasure can they derive from contemplating the exposed condition, and almost certain beggary of their younger offspring? Every aristocratical family has an appendage of family beggars hanging round it, which in a few ages, or a few generations, are shook off, and console themselves with telling their tale in almshouses, work-houses, and prisons. This is the natural consequence of aristocracy. The peer and the beggar are often of the same family. One extreme produces the other: to make one rich many must be made poor; neither can the system be supported by other means.

There are two classes of people to whom the laws of England are particularly hostile, and those the most helpless; younger children and the poor. Of the former I have just spoken; of the latter I shall mention one instance out of the many that might be produced, and with which I shall close this subject.

Several laws are in existence for regulating and limiting workmen's wages. Why not leave them as free to make their own bargains, as the law-makers are to let their farms and houses? Personal labour is all the property they have. Why is that little, and the little freedom they enjoy to be infringed? But the injustice will appear stronger, if we consider the operation and effect of such laws. When wages are fixed by what is called a law, the legal wages remain stationary, while everything else is in progression; and as those who make that law, still continue to lay on new taxes by other laws, they increase the expense of living by one law, and take away the means by another.

But if those gentlemen law-makers and tax-makers thought it right to limit the poor pittance which personal labour can produce, and on which a whole family is to be supported, they certainly must feel themselves happily indulged in a limitation on their own part, of not less than twelve thousand a year, and that of property they never acquired, (nor probably any of their ancestors) and of which they have made so ill a use.

Having now finished this subject, I shall bring the several particulars into one view, and then proceed to other matters.

The first EIGHT ARTICLES are brought forward ...

1. Abolition of two million poor-rates.

2. Provision for two hundred and fifty-two thousand poor families, at the rate of four pounds per head for each child under fourteen years of age; which, with the addition of two hundred and fifty thousand pounds, provides also education for one million and thirty thousand children.

3. Annuity of six pounds (*per ann.*) each for all poor persons, decayed tradesmen, or others (supposed seventy thousand) of the age of fifty years, and until sixty.

4. Annuity of ten pounds each for life for all poor persons, decayed tradesmen, and others (supposed seventy thousand) of the age of sixty years.

5. Donation of twenty shillings each for fifty thousand births.

6. Donation of twenty shillings each for twenty thousand marriages.

7. Allowance of twenty thousand pounds for the funeral expenses of persons travelling for work, and dying at a distance from their friends.

8. Employment at all times for the casual poor in the cities of London and Westminster.

SECOND ENUMERATION:

9. Abolition of the tax on houses and windows.

10. Allowance of three shillings per week for life to fifteen thousand disbanded soldiers, and a proportionable allowance to the officers of the disbanded corps.

11. Increase of pay to the remaining soldiers of 19,500*l*. annually.

12. The same allowance to the disbanded navy, and the same increase of pay, as to the army.

13. Abolition of the commutation-tax.

14. Plan of a progressive tax, operating to extirpate the unjust and

unnatural law of primogeniture, and the vicious influence of the aristocratical system.[26]

There yet remains, as already stated, one million of surplus taxes. Some parts of this will be required for circumstances that do not immediately present themselves, and such part as shall not be wanted, will admit a further reduction of taxes equal to that amount.

Among the claims that justice requires to be made, the condition of the inferior revenue officers will merit attention. It is a reproach to any government to waste such an immensity of revenue in sinecures and nominal and unnecessary places and offices, and not allow even a decent livelihood to those on whom the labour falls. The salary of the inferior officers of the revenue has stood at the petty pittance of less than fifty pounds a year for upwards of one hundred years. It ought to be seventy. About one hundred and twenty thousand pounds applied to this purpose, will put all those salaries in a decent condition.

This was proposed to be done almost twenty years ago, but the treasury-board then in being startled at it, as it might lead to similar expectations from the army and navy; and the event was, that the King, or somebody for him, applied to parliament to have his own salary raised a hundred thousand a year, which being done, everything else was laid aside.

26 When inquiries are made into the condition of the poor, various degrees of distress will most probably be found, to render a different arrangement preferable to that which is already proposed. Widows with families will be in greater want than where there are husbands living. There is also a difference in the expense of living in different countries; and more so in fuel.

	£
Suppose then fifty thousand extraordinary cases, at the rate of 10l. per family per ann.	500,000
100,000 Families, at 8l. per family per ann.	800,000
100,000 Families, at 7l. per family per ann.	700,000
104,000 Families, at 5l. per family per ann.	520,000
And instead of ten shilling per head for the education of other children, to allow fifty shillings per family for that purpose to fifty thousand families	250,000
	2,770,000
140,000 Aged persons as before,	1,120,000
	3,890,000

This arrangement amounts to the same sum as stated [earlier], including the 250,000l. for education; but it provides (including the aged people) for four hundred and four thousand families, which is almost one-third of all the families in England. – Paine.

With respect to another class of men, the inferior clergy, I forbear to enlarge on their condition; but all partialities and prejudices for, or against, different modes and forms of religion aside, common justice will determine, whether there ought to be an income of twenty or thirty pounds a year to one man, and of ten thousand to another. I speak on this subject with the more freedom, because I am known not to be a Presbyterian; and therefore the cant cry of court sycophants, about church and meeting, kept up to amuse and bewilder the nation, cannot be raised against me.

Ye simple men, on both sides the question, do ye not see through this courtly craft? If ye can be kept disputing and wrangling about church and meeting, ye just answer the purpose of every courtier, who lives the while on the spoil of the taxes, and laughs at your credulity. Every religion is good that teaches man to be good; and I know of none that instructs him to be bad.

All the before-mentioned calculations, suppose only sixteen millions and a half of taxes paid into the exchequer, after the expense of collection and drawbacks at the custom-house and excise-office are deducted; whereas the sum paid into the exchequer is very nearly, if not quite, seventeen millions. The taxes raised in Scotland and Ireland are expended in those countries, and therefore their savings will come out of their own taxes; but if any part be paid into the English exchequer, it might be remitted. This will not make one hundred thousand pounds a year difference.

There now remains only the national debt to be considered. In the year 1789, the interest, exclusive of the tontine, was 9,150,138*l*. How much the capital has been reduced since that time the minister best knows. But after paying the interest, abolishing the tax on houses and windows, the commutation-tax, and the poor-rates; and making all the provisions for the poor, for the education of children, the support of the aged, the disbanded part of the army and navy, and increasing the pay of the remainder, there will be a surplus of one million.

The present scheme of paying off the national debt appears to me, speaking as an indifferent person, to be an ill-concerted, if not a fallacious job. The burden of the national debt consists not in its being so many millions, or so many hundred millions, but in the quantity of taxes collected every year to pay the interest. If this quantity continue the same, the burden of the national debt is the same to all intents and purposes, be the capital more or less. The only knowledge which the public can have of the reduction of the debt, must be through the reduction of taxes for paying the interest. The debt, therefore, is not reduced one farthing to the public by all the millions that have been paid; and it would require more money now to purchase up the capital, than when the scheme began.

Digressing for a moment at this point, to which I shall return again, I look back to the appointment of Mr Pitt, as minister.

I was then in America. The war was over; and though resentment had ceased, memory was still alive.

When the news of the coalition arrived, though it was a matter of no concern to me as a citizen of America, I felt it as a man. It had something in it which shocked, by public sporting with decency, if not with principle. It was impudence in Lord North; it was want of firmness in Mr Fox.

Mr Pitt was, at that time, what may be called a maiden character in politics. So far from being hackneyed, he appeared not to be initiated into the first mysteries of court intrigue. Everything was in his favour. Resentment against the coalition served as friendship to him, and his ignorance of vice was credited for virtue. With the return of peace, commerce and prosperity would rise of itself; yet even this increase was thrown to his account.

When he came to the helm the storm was over, and he had nothing to interrupt his course. It required even ingenuity to be wrong, and he succeeded. A little time showed him the same sort of man as his predecessors had been. Instead of profiting by those errors which had accumulated a burden of taxes unparalleled in the world, he sought, I might almost say, he advertised for enemies, and provoked means to increase taxation. Aiming at something, he knew not what, he ransacked Europe and India for adventures, and abandoning the fair pretensions he began with, became the knight-errant of modern times.

It is unpleasant to see character throw itself away. It is more so to see oneself deceived. Mr Pitt had merited nothing, but he promised much. He gave symptoms of a mind superior to the meanness and corruption of courts. His apparent candour encouraged expectations; and the public confidence, stunned, wearied, and confounded by a chaos of parties, revived and attached itself to him. But mistaking, as he has done, the disgust of the nation against the coalition, for merit in himself, he has rushed into measures, which a man less supported would not have presumed to act.

All this seems to show that change of ministers amounts to nothing. One goes out, another comes in, and still the same measures, vices, and extravagance are pursued. It signifies not who is minister. The defect lies in the system. The foundation and the superstructure of the government is bad. Prop it as you please, it continually sinks into court government, and ever will.

I return, as I promised, to the subject of the national debt, that off-spring of the Dutch-Anglo Revolution, and its handmaid the Hanover succession.

But it is now too late to inquire how it began. Those to whom it is due have advanced the money; and whether it was well or ill spent, or pocketed, is not their crime. It is, however, easy to see, that as the nation proceeds in contemplating the nature and principles of government, and to understand taxes, and make comparisons between those of America, France, and England, it will be next to impossible to keep it in the same torpid state it has hitherto been. Some reform must, from the necessity of the case, soon begin. It is not whether these principles press with little or much force in the present moment. They are out. They are abroad in the world, and no force can stop them. Like a secret told, they are beyond recall; and he must be blind indeed that does not see that a change is already beginning.

Nine millions of dead taxes is a serious thing; and this not only for bad, but in a great measure for foreign government. By putting the power of making war into the hands of foreigners who came for what they could get, little else was to be expected than what has happened.

Reasons are already advanced in this work showing that, whatever the reforms in the taxes may be, they ought to be made in the current expenses of government, and not in the part applied to the interest of the national debt. By remitting the taxes of the poor, *they* will be totally relieved, and all discontent on their part will be taken away; and by striking off such of the taxes as are already mentioned, the nation will more than recover the whole expense of the mad American War.

There will then remain only the national debt as a subject of discontent; and in order to remove, or rather to prevent this, it would be good policy in the stock-holders themselves to consider it as property, subject like all other property, to bear some portion of the taxes. It would give to it both popularity and security, and as a great part of its present inconvenience is balanced by the capital which it keeps alive, a measure of this kind would so far add to that balance as to silence objections.

This may be done by such gradual means as to accomplish all that is necessary with the greatest ease and convenience.

Instead of taxing the capital, the best method would be to tax the interest by some progressive ratio, and to lessen the public taxes in the same proportion as the interest diminished.

Suppose the interest was taxed one halfpenny in the pound the first year, a penny more the second, and to proceed by a certain ratio to be determined upon, always less than any other tax upon property. Such a tax would be subtracted from the interest at the time of payment, without any expense of collection.

One halfpenny in the pound would lessen the interest and consequently the taxes, twenty thousand pounds. The tax on waggons amounts to this sum, and this tax might be taken off the first year. The second year the tax on female servants, or some other of the like amount might also be taken off, and by proceeding in this manner, always applying the tax raised from the property of the debt towards its extinction, and not carry it to the current services, it would liberate itself.

The stock-holders, notwithstanding this tax, would pay less taxes than they do now. What they would save by the extinction of the poor-rates, and the tax on houses and windows, and the commutation-tax, would be confidently greater than what this tax, slow, but certain in its operation, amounts to.

It appears to me to be prudence to look out for measures that may apply under any circumstance that may approach. There is, at this moment, a crisis in the affairs of Europe that requires it. Preparation now is wisdom. If taxation be once let loose, it will be difficult to reinstate it; neither would the relief be so effectual, as to proceed by some certain and gradual reduction.

The fraud, hypocrisy, and imposition of governments, are now beginning to be too well understood to promise them any long career. The farce of monarchy and aristocracy, in all countries, is following that of chivalry, and Mr Burke is dressing for the funeral. Let it then pass quietly to the tomb of all other follies, and the mourners be comforted.

The time is not very distant when England will laugh at itself for sending to Holland, Hanover, Zell, or Brunswick for men, at the expense of a million a year, who understood neither her laws, her language, nor her interest, and whose capacities would scarcely have fitted them for the office of a parish constable. If government could be trusted to such hands, it must be some easy and simple thing indeed, and materials fit for all the purposes may be found in every town and village in England.

When it shall be said in any country in the world, my poor are happy; neither ignorance nor distress is to be found among them; my jails are empty of prisoners, my streets of beggars; the aged are not in want, the taxes are not oppressive; the rational world is my friend, because I am the friend of its happiness: when these things can be said, then may that country boast its constitution and its government.

Within the space of a few years we have seen two revolutions, those of America and France. In the former, the contest was long, and the conflict severe; in the latter, the nation acted with such a consolidated impulse, that having no foreign enemy to contend with, the revolution was complete in power the moment it appeared. From both those instances it is evident, that the greatest forces that can be brought into the field of revolutions, are reason and common interest. Where these can have the opportunity of acting, opposition dies with fear, or crumbles away by conviction. It is a great standing which they have now universally obtained; and we may hereafter hope to see revolutions, or changes in governments, produced with the same quiet operation by which any measure, determinable by reason and discussion, is accomplished.

When a nation changes its opinion and habits of thinking, it is no longer to be governed as before; but it would not only be wrong, but bad policy, to attempt by force what ought to be accomplished by reason. Rebellion consists in forcibly opposing the general will of a nation, whether by a party or by a government. There ought, therefore, to be in every nation a method of occasionally ascertaining the state of public opinion with respect to government. On this point the old government of France was superior to the present government of England, because, on extraordinary occasions, recourse could be had to what was then called the States General. But in England there are no such occasional bodies; and as to those who are now called Representatives, a great part of them are mere machines of the court, placemen, and dependants.

I presume, that though all the people of England pay taxes, not an hundredth part of them are electors, and the members of one of the houses of parliament represent nobody but themselves. There is, therefore, no power but the voluntary will of the people that has a right to act in any matter respecting a general reform; and by the same right that two persons can confer on such a subject, a thousand may. The object, in all such preliminary proceedings, is to find out what the general sense of a nation is, and to be governed by it. If it prefer a bad or defective government to a reform, or choose to pay ten times more taxes than there is occasion for, it has a right so to do; and so long as the majority do not impose conditions on the minority, different to what they impose on themselves, though there may be much error, there is no injustice. Neither will the error continue long. Reason and discussion will soon bring things right, however wrong they may begin. By such a process no tumult is to be apprehended. The poor, in all countries, are naturally both peaceable and grateful in all reforms in which their interest and happiness is included. It is only by neglecting and rejecting them that they become tumultuous.

The objects that now press on the public attention are, the French Revolution, and the prospect of a general revolution in governments. Of all nations in Europe, there is none so much interested in the French Revolution as England. Enemies for ages, and that at a vast expense, and without any national object, the opportunity now presents itself of amicably closing the scene, and joining their efforts to reform the rest of Europe. By doing this, they will not only prevent the further effusion of blood, and increase of taxes, but be in a condition of getting rid of a considerable part of their present burdens, as has been already stated. Long experience however has shown, that reforms of this kind are not those which old governments wish to promote; and therefore it is to nations, and not to such governments, that these matters present themselves.

In the preceding part of this work, I have spoken of an alliance between England, France, and America, for purposes that were to be afterwards mentioned. Though I have no direct authority on the part of America, I have good reason to conclude, that she is disposed to enter into a consideration of such a measure, provided, that the governments with which she might ally, acted as national governments, and not as courts enveloped in intrigue and mystery. That France as a nation, and a national government, would prefer an alliance with England, is a matter of certainty. Nations, like individuals, who have long been enemies, without knowing each other, or knowing why, become the better friends when they discover the errors and impositions under which they had acted.

Admitting, therefore, the probability of such a connection, I will state some matters by which such an alliance, together with that of Holland, might render service, not only to the parties immediately concerned, but to all Europe.

It is, I think, certain, that if the fleets of England, France, and Holland were confederated, they could propose, with effect, a limitation to, and a general dismantling of all the navies in Europe, to a certain proportion to be agreed upon.

First, That no new ship of war shall be built by any power in Europe, themselves included.

Secondly, That all the navies now in existence shall be put back, suppose to one-tenth of their present force. This will save to France and England at least two millions sterling annually to each, and their relative force be in the same proportion as it is now. If men will permit themselves to think, as rational beings ought to think, nothing can appear more ridiculous and absurd, exclusive of all moral reflections, than to be at the expense of building navies, filling them with men, and then hauling them into the ocean, to try which can sink each other fastest. Peace, which costs nothing, is attended with infinitely more advantage, than any victory with all its expense. But this, though it best answers the purpose of nations, does not that of court governments, whose habited policy is pretence for taxation, places, and offices.

It is, I think, also certain, that the above confederated powers, together with that of the United States of America, can propose with effect, to Spain, the independence of South America, and the opening those countries of immense extent and wealth to the general commerce of the world, as North America now is.

With how much more glory, and advantage to itself, does a nation act, when it exerts its powers to rescue the world from bondage, and to create itself friends, than when it employs those powers to increase ruin, desolation, and misery. The horrid scene that is now acting by the English government in the East Indies, is fit only to be told of Goths and Vandals, who, destitute of principles, robbed and tortured the world they were incapable of enjoying.

The opening of South America would produce an immense field of commerce, and a ready money market for manufactures, which the eastern world does not. The East is already a country full of manufactures, the importation of which is not only an injury to the manufactures of England, but a drain upon its specie. The balance against England by this trade is regularly upwards of half a million annually sent out in the East India ships in silver; and this is the reason, together with German intrigue, and German subsidies, there is so little silver in England.

But any war is harvest to such governments, however ruinous it may be to a nation. It serves to keep up deceitful expectations which prevent a people looking into the defects and abuses of government. It is the *lo here!* and the *lo there!* that amuses and cheats the multitude.

Never did so great an opportunity offer itself to England, and to all Europe, as is produced by the two revolutions of America and France. By the former, freedom has a national champion in the Western world; and by the latter, in Europe. When another nation shall join France, despotism and bad government will scarcely dare to appear. To use a trite expression, the iron is becoming hot all over Europe. The insulted German and the enslaved Spaniard, the Russ and the Pole, are beginning to think. The present age will hereafter merit to be called the Age of Reason, and the present generation will appear to the future as the Adam of a new world.

When all the governments of Europe shall be established on the representative system, nations will become acquainted, and the animosities and prejudices fomented by the intrigue and artifice of courts, will cease. The oppressed soldier will become a freeman; and the tortured sailor, no longer dragged along the streets like a felon, will pursue his mercantile voyage in safety. It would be better that nations should continue the pay of their soldiers during their lives, and give them their discharge and restore them to freedom and their friends, and cease recruiting, than retain such multitudes at the same expense, in a condition useless to society and themselves. As soldiers have hitherto been treated in most countries, they might be said to be without a friend. Shunned by the citizen on an apprehension of being enemies to liberty, and too often insulted by those who commanded them, their condition was a double oppression. But where genuine principle of liberty pervade a people, everything is restored to order; and the soldier civilly treated, returns the civility.

In contemplating revolutions, it is easy to perceive that they may arise from two distinct causes; the one, to avoid or get rid of some great calamity; the other, to obtain some great and positive good; and the two may be distinguished by the names of active and passive revolutions. In those which proceed from the former cause, the temper becomes incensed and soured; and the redress, obtained by danger, is too often sullied by revenge. But in those which proceed from the latter, the heart, rather animated than agitated, enters serenely upon the subject. Reason and discussion, persuasion and conviction, become the weapons in the contest, and it is only when those are attempted to be suppressed that recourse is had to violence. When men unite in agreeing that a *thing is good*, could it be obtained, such as relief from a burden of taxes and the extinction of corruption, the object is more than half accomplished. What they approve as the end, they will promote in the means.

Will any man say, in the present excess of taxation, falling so heavily on the poor, that a remission of five pounds annually of taxes to one hundred and four thousand poor families is not a *good thing*? Will he say, that a remission of seven pounds annually to one hundred thousand other poor families – of eight pounds annually to another hundred thousand poor families, and of ten pounds annually to fifty thousand poor and widowed families, are not *good things*? And to proceed a step farther in this climax, will he say, that to provide against the misfortunes to which all human life is subject, by securing six pounds annually for all poor, distressed, and reduced persons of the age of fifty and until sixty, and of ten pounds annually after sixty is not a *good thing*?

Will he say, that an abolition of two million of poor-rates to the housekeepers, and of the whole of the house and window-light tax and of the commutation-tax is not a *good thing*? Or will he say, that to abolish corruption is a *bad thing*?

If, therefore, the good to be obtained be worthy of a passive, rational, and costless revolution, it would be bad policy to prefer waiting for a calamity that should force a violent one. I have no idea, considering the reforms which are now passing and spreading through-out Europe, that England will permit herself to be the last; and where the occasion and the opportunity quietly offer, it is better than to wait for a turbulent necessity. It may be considered as an honour to the animal faculties of man to obtain redress by courage and danger, but it is far greater honour to the rational faculties to accomplish the same object by reason, accommodation, and general consent.[27]

As reforms, or revolutions, call them which you please, extend themselves among nations, those nations will form connections and conventions, and when a few are thus confederated, the progress will be rapid, till despotism and corrupt government be totally expelled, at least out of two quarters of the world, Europe and America. The Algerine piracy may then be commanded to cease, for it is only by the malicious policy of old governments, against each other, that it exists.

Throughout this work, various and numerous as the subjects are, which I have taken up and investigated, there is only a single para-graph upon religion, viz. '*that every religion is good, that teaches man to be good*'.

I have carefully avoided to enlarge upon the subject, because I am inclined to believe, that what is called the present ministry wish to see contentions about religion kept up, to prevent the nation turning its attention to subjects of government. It is, as if they were to say, '*Look that way, or any way, but this.*'

But as religion is very improperly made a political machine, and

27 I know it is the opinion of many of the most enlightened characters in France (there always will be those who see farther into events than others) not only among the general mass of citizens, but of many of the principal members of the former National Assembly, that the monarchical plan will not continue many years in that country. They have found out that as wisdom cannot be made hereditary, power ought not; and that, for a man to merit a million sterling a year from a nation, he ought to have a mind capable of comprehending from an atom to a universe; which, if he had, he would be above receiving the pay. But they wished not to appear to lead the nation faster than its own reason and interest dictated. In all the conversations where I have been present upon this subject, the idea always was, that when such a time, from the general opinion of the nation, shall arrive, that the honourable and liberal method would be, to make a handsome present in fee simple to the person whoever he may be, that shall then be in the monarchical office, and for him to retire to the enjoyment of private life, possessing his share of general rights and privileges, and to be no more accountable to the public for his time and his conduct than any other citizen. – Paine.

the reality of it is thereby destroyed, I will conclude this work with stating in what light religion appears to me.

If we suppose a large family of children, who, on any particular day, or particular circumstance, made it a custom to present to their parent some token of their affection and gratitude, each of them would make a different offering, and most probably in a different manner. Some would pay their congratulations in themes of verse or prose, by some little devices, as their genius dictated, or according to what they thought would please; and perhaps, the least of all, not able to do any of those things, would ramble into the garden, or the field, and gather what it thought the prettiest flower it could find, though, perhaps, it might be but a simple weed. The parent would be more gratified by such variety, than if the whole of them had acted on a concerted plan, and each had made exactly the same offering. This would have the cold appearance of contrivance, or the harsh one of control. But of all unwelcome things, nothing could more afflict the parent than to know, that the whole of them had afterwards gotten together by the ears, boys and girls, fighting, scratching, reviling, and abusing each other about which was the best or the worst present.

Why may we not suppose, that the great Father of all is pleased with variety of devotion; and that the greatest offence we can act, is that by which we seek to torment and render each other miserable. For my own part, I am fully satisfied that what I am now doing, with an endeavour to conciliate mankind, to render their condition happy, to unite nations that have hitherto been enemies, and to extirpate the horrid practice of war, and break the chains of slavery and oppression, is acceptable in his sight, and being the best service I can perform, I act it cheerfully.

I do not believe that any two men, on what are called doctrinal points, think alike who think at all. It is only those who have not thought that appear to agree. It is in this case as with what is called the British constitution. It has been taken for granted to be good, and encomiums have supplied the place of proof. But when the nation comes to examine into its principles and the abuses it admits, it will be found to have more defects than I have pointed out in this work and the former.

As to what are called national religions, we may, with as much propriety, talk of national Gods. It is either political craft or the remains of the Pagan system, when every nation had its separate and particular deity. Among all the writers of the English church clergy, who have treated on the general subject of religion, the present Bishop of Llandaff has not been excelled, and it is with much pleasure that I take the opportunity of expressing this token of respect.

I have now gone through the whole of the subject, at least, as far as it appears to me at present. It has been my intention for the five years I have been in Europe, to offer an address to the people of England on the subject of government, if the opportunity presented itself before I returned to America. Mr Burke has thrown it in my way, and I thank him. On a certain occasion three years ago, I pressed him to propose a national convention to be fairly elected for the purpose of taking the state of the nation into consideration; but I found, that however strongly the parliamentary current was then setting against the party he acted with, their policy was to keep everything within that field of corruption, and trust to accidents. Long experience had shown that parliaments would follow any change of ministers, and on this they rested their hopes and their expectations.

Formerly, when divisions arose respecting governments, recourse was had to the sword, and a civil war ensued. That savage custom is exploded by the new system, and reference is had to national conventions. Discussion and the general will arbitrates the question, and to this, private opinion yields with a good grace, and order is preserved uninterrupted.

Some gentlemen have affected to call the principles upon which this work and the former part of *Rights of Man* are founded, 'a new fangled doctrine'. The question is not whether those principles are new or old, but whether they are right or wrong. Suppose the former, I will show their effect by a figure easily understood.

It is now towards the middle of February. Were I to take a turn into the country, the trees would present a leafless winterly appearance. As people are apt to pluck twigs as they walk along, I perhaps might do the same, and by chance might observe, that a *single bud* on that twig had begun to swell. I should reason very unnaturally, or rather not reason at all, to suppose *this* was the *only* bud in England which had this appearance. Instead of deciding thus, I should instantly conclude, that the same appearance was beginning, or about to begin, everywhere; and though the vegetable sleep will continue longer on some trees and plants than on others, and though some of them may not *blossom* for two or three years, all will be in leaf in the summer, except those which are *rotten*. What pace the political summer may keep with the natural, no human foresight can determine. It is, however, not difficult to perceive that the spring is begun. – Thus wishing, as I sincerely do, freedom and happiness to all nations, I close the

SECOND PART.

[12] LETTER
ADDRESSED TO THE ADDRESSERS
ON THE LATE PROCLAMATION

━━━◆◆◆◆◆━━━

(1792)

This pamphlet was written in the summer of 1792, just before Paine fled to France, and was published immediately after he arrived there. In the edited text included here Paine answered the charge of seditious libel with one of his most stirring passages:

If, to expose the fraud and imposition of monarchy, and every species of hereditary government — to lessen the oppression of taxes — to propose plans for the education of helpless infancy, and the comfortable support of the aged and distressed — to endeavour to conciliate nations to each other — to extirpate the horrid practice of war — to promote universal peace, civilization, and commerce — and to break the chains of political superstition, and raise degraded man to his proper rank; — if these things be libellous, let me live the life of a libeller, and let the name of LIBELLER *be engraved on my tomb.*

Could I have commanded circumstances with a wish, I know not of any that would have more generally promoted the progress of knowledge, than the late Proclamation, and the numerous rotten borough and corporation addresses thereon. They have not only served as advertisements, but they have excited a spirit of inquiry into the principles of government, and a desire to read the *Rights of Man*, in places where that spirit and that work were before unknown.

The people of England, wearied and stunned with parties, and alternately deceived by each, had almost resigned the prerogative of thinking. Even curiosity had expired, and a universal languor had spread itself over the land. The opposition was visibly no other than a contest for power, whilst the mass of the nation stood torpidly by as the prize.

In this hopeless state of things, the first part of the *Rights of Man* made its appearance. It had to combat with a strange mixture of prejudice and indifference; it stood exposed to every species of newspaper abuse; and besides this, it had to remove the obstructions which Mr Burke's rude and outrageous attack on the French Revolution had artfully raised.

But how easy does even the most illiterate reader distinguish the spontaneous sensations of the heart, from the laboured productions of the brain. Truth, whenever it can fully appear, is a thing so naturally familiar to the mind, that an acquaintance commences at first sight. No artificial light, yet discovered, can display all the properties of daylight; so neither can the best invented fiction fill the mind with every conviction which truth begets.

To overthrow Mr Burke's fallacious book was scarcely the operation of a day. Even the phalanx of placemen and pensioners, who had given the tone to the multitude by clamouring forth his political fame, became suddenly silent; and the final event to himself has been, that as he rose like a rocket, he fell like the stick.

It seldom happens that the mind rests satisfied with the simple detection of error or imposition. Once put in motion, *that* motion soon becomes accelerated; where it had intended to stop, it discovers new reasons to proceed, and renews and continues the pursuit far beyond the limits it first prescribed to itself. Thus it has happened to the people of England. From a detection of Mr Burke's incoherent rhapsodies, and distorted facts, they began an inquiry into the first principles of government, whilst himself like an object left far behind, became invisible and forgotten.

Much as the first part of *Rights of Man* impressed at its first appearance, the progressive mind soon discovered that it did not go far enough. It detected errors; it exposed absurdities; it shook the fabric of political superstition; it generated new ideas; but it did not produce a regular system of principles in the room of those which it displaced. And, if I may guess at the mind of the Government-party, they beheld it as an unexpected gale that would soon blow over, and they forbore, like sailors in threatening weather, to whistle, lest they should increase the wind. Everything, on their part, was profound silence.

When the second part of *Rights of Man*, *combining Principle and Practice*, was preparing to appear, they affected, for a while, to act with the same policy as before; but finding their silence had no more influence in stifling the progress of the work, than it would have in stopping the progress of time, they changed their plan, and affected to treat it with clamorous contempt. The speech-making placemen and pensioners, and place-expectants, in both Houses of Parliament, the *Outs* as well as the *Ins,* represented it as a silly, insignificant performance; as a work incapable of producing any effect; as something which they were sure the good sense of the people would either despise or indignantly spurn; but such was the overstrained awkwardness with which they harangued and encouraged each other, that in the very act of declaring their confidence they betrayed their fears. . . .

Ye silly swains, thought I to myself, why do you torment yourselves thus? The *Rights of Man* is a book calmly and rationally written; why then are you so disturbed? Did you see how little or how suspicious such conduct makes you appear, even cunning alone, had you no other faculty, would hush you into prudence. The plans, principles, and arguments, contained in that work, are placed before the eyes of the nation, and of the world, in a fair, open, and manly manner, and nothing more is necessary than to refute them. Do this, and the whole is done; but if ye cannot, so neither can ye suppress the reading, nor convict the author; for the law, in the opinion of all good men, would convict itself, that should condemn what cannot be refuted.

Having now shown the Addressers the several stages of the business, prior to their being called upon, like Caesar in the Tiber, crying to Cassius, '*Help, Cassius, or I sink!*' I next come to remark on the policy of the Government, in promotion addresses; on the consequences naturally resulting therefrom; and on the conduct of the persons concerned.

With respect to the policy, it evidently carries with it every mark and feature of disguised fear. And it will hereafter be placed in the history of extraordinary things, that a pamphlet should be produced by an individual, unconnected with any sect or party, and not seeking to make any, and almost a stranger in the land, that should completely frighten a whole government, and that in the midst of its most triumphant security. Such a circumstance cannot fail to prove that either the pamphlet has irresistible powers, or the Government very extraordinary defects, or both. The nation exhibits no signs of fear at the *Rights of Man*; why then should the Government, unless the interests of the two are really opposite to each other, and the secret is beginning to be known? That there are two distinct classes of men in the nation, those who pay taxes, and those who receive and live upon the taxes, is evident at first sight; and when taxation is carried to excess, it cannot fail to disunite those two, and something of this kind is now beginning to appear. . . .

That the success of the Proclamation has been less than the success of the work it was intended to discourage, is a matter within my own knowledge; for a greater number of the cheap edition of the first and second parts of the *Rights of Man* has been sold in the space only of one month, than the whole number of addressers (admitting them to be thirty-two thousand) have amounted to in three months.

It is a dangerous attempt in any government to say to a nation, '*thou shalt not read.*' This is now done in Spain, and was formerly done under the old government of France; but it served to procure the downfall of the latter, and is subverting that of the former; and it will have the same tendency in all countries; because *thought* by some means or other, is got abroad in the world, and cannot be restrained, though reading may.

If *Rights of Man* were a book that deserved the vile description which promoters of the addresses have given of it, why did not these men prove their charge, and satisfy the people, by producing it, and reading it publicly? This most certainly ought to have been done, and would also have been done, had they believed it would have answered their purpose. But the fact is, that the book contains truths which those time-servers dreaded to hear, and dreaded that the people should know; and it is now following up the addresses in every part of the nation, and convicting them of falsehoods.

Among the unwarrantable proceedings to which the Proclamation has given rise, the meetings of the justices in several of the towns and counties ought to be noticed. Those men have assumed to re-act the farce of general warrants, and to suppress, by their own authority, whatever publications they please. This is an attempt at power equalled only by the conduct of the minor despots of the most despotic governments in Europe, and yet those justices affect to call England a free country. But even this, perhaps, like the scheme for garrisoning the country by building military barracks, is necessary to awaken the country to a sense of its rights, and, as such, it will have a good effect.

Another part of the conduct of such justices has been, that of threatening to take away the licences from taverns and public-houses, where the inhabitants of the neighbourhood associated to read and discuss the principles of government, and to inform each other thereon. This, again, is similar to what is doing in Spain and Russia; and the reflection which it cannot fail to suggest is, that the principles and conduct of any government must be bad, when that government dreads and startles at discussion, and seeks security by a prevention of knowledge.

If the Government, or the Constitution, or by whatever name it be called, be that miracle of perfection which the Proclamation and the addresses have trumpeted it forth to be, it ought to have defied discussion and investigation, instead of dreading it. Whereas, every attempt it makes, either by proclamation, prosecution, or address, to suppress investigation, is a confession that it feels itself unable to bear it. It is error only, and not truth, that shrinks from inquiry. All the numerous pamphlets, and all the newspaper falsehood and abuse, that have been published against the *Rights of Man*, have fallen before it like pointless arrows; and, in like manner would any work have fallen before the Constitution, had the Constitution, as it is called, been founded on as good political principles as those on which the *Rights of Man* is written.

It is a good constitution for courtiers, placemen, pensioners, borough-holders, and the leaders of parties, and these are the men that have been the active leaders of addresses; but it is a bad constitution for at least ninety-nine parts of the nation out of an hundred, and this truth is every day making its way.

It is bad, first, because it entails upon the nation the unnecessary expense of supporting three forms and systems of government at once, namely, the monarchical, the aristocratical, and the democratical.

Secondly, because it is impossible to unite such a discordant composition by any other means than perpetual corruption; and therefore the corruption so loudly and so universally complained of, is no other than the natural consequence of such an unnatural compound of governments; and in this consists that excellence which the numerous herd of placemen and pensioners so loudly extol, and which at the same time occasions that enormous load of taxes under which the rest of the nation groans.

Among the mass of national delusions calculated to amuse and impose upon the multitude, the standing one has been that of flattering them into taxes, by calling the Government (or as they please to express it, the English Constitution) *'the envy and the admiration of the world'*. Scarcely an address has been voted in which some of the speakers have not uttered this hackneyed, nonsensical falsehood.

Two revolutions have taken place, those of America and France; and both of them have rejected the unnatural compounded system of the English Government. America has declared against all hereditary government, and established the representative system of government only. France has entirely rejected the aristocratical part, and is now discovering the absurdity of the monarchical, and is approaching fast to the representative system. On what ground then, do these men continue a declaration, respecting what they call the *envy and admiration of other nations,* which the voluntary practice of such nations, as have had the opportunity of establishing government, contradicts and falsifies? Will such men never confine themselves to truth? Will they be for ever the deceivers of the people?

But I will go further, and show, that were government now to begin in England, the people could not be brought to establish the same system they now submit to.

In speaking on this subject (or on any other) *on the pure ground of principle*, antiquity and precedent cease to be authority, and hoary-headed error loses its effect. The reasonableness and propriety of things must be examined abstractedly from custom and usage; and, in this point of view, the right which grows into practice today is as much a right, and as old in principle and theory, as if it had the customary sanction of a thousand ages. Principles have no connection with time, nor characters with names.

To say that the Government of this country is composed of Kings, Lords, and Commons, is the mere phraseology of custom. It is composed of men; and whoever the men be to whom the government of any country be entrusted, they ought to be the best and wisest that can be found, and if they are not so, they are not fit for the station. A man derives no more excellence from the change of a name, or calling him king, or calling him lord, than I should do by changing my name from Thomas to George, or from Paine to Guelph. I should not be a whit more able to write a book because my name was altered; neither would any man, now called a king or a lord, have a whit more sense than he now has, were he to call himself Thomas Paine.

As to the word 'Commons', applied as it is in England, it is a term of degradation and reproach, and ought to be abolished. It is a term unknown in free countries.

But to the point. Let us suppose that government was now to begin in England, and that the plan of government, offered to the nation for its approbation or rejection, consisted of the following parts:

First – That some one individual should be taken from all the rest of the nation, and to whom all the rest should swear obedience, and never be permitted to sit down in his presence, and that they should give to him one million sterling a year. That the nation should never after have power or authority to make laws but with his express consent; and that his sons and his sons' sons, whether wise or foolish, good men or bad, fit or unfit, should have the same power, and also the same money annually paid to them for ever.

Secondly – That there should be two houses of legislators to assist in making laws, one of which should, in the first instance, be entirely appointed by the aforesaid person, and that their sons and their sons' sons, whether wise or foolish, good men or bad, fit or unfit, should for ever after be hereditary legislators.

Thirdly – That the other house should be chosen in the same manner as the house now called the House of Commons is chosen, and should be subject to the control of the two aforesaid hereditary powers in all things.

It would be impossible to cram such a farrago of imposition and absurdity down the throat of this or any other nation that was capable of reasoning upon its rights and its interest.

They would ask, in the first place, on what ground of right, or on what principle, such irrational and preposterous distinctions could, or ought to be made; and what pretensions any man could have, or what services he could render, to entitle him to a million a year? They would go further, and revolt at the idea of consigning their children, and their children's children, to the domination of persons hereafter to be born, who might, for anything they could foresee, turn out to be knaves or fools; and they would finally discover, that the project of hereditary governors and legislators *was a treasonable usurpation over the rights of posterity*. Not only the calm dictates of reason, and the force of natural affection, but the integrity of manly pride, would impel men to spurn such proposals.

From the grosser absurdities of such a scheme, they would extend their examination to the practical defects – They would soon see that it would end in tyranny accomplished by fraud. That in the operation of it, it would be two to one against them, because the two parts that were to be made hereditary would form a common interest, and stick to each other; and that themselves and representatives would become no better than hewers of wood and drawers of water for the other parts of the government. Yet call one of those powers King, the other Lords, and the third the Commons, and it gives the model of what is called the English Government.

I have asserted, and have shown, both in the first and second parts of *Rights of Man*, that there is not such a thing as an English Constitution, and that the people have yet a constitution to form. *A constitution is a thing antecedent to a government; it is the act of a people creating a government and giving it powers, and defining the limits and exercise of the powers so given.* But whenever did the people of England, acting in their original, constituent character, by a delegation elected for that express purpose, declare and say, '*We, the people of this land, do constitute and appoint this to be our system and form of government*'? The government has assumed to constitute itself, but it never was constituted by the people, in whom alone the right of constituting resides.

I will here recite the preamble to the Federal Constitution of the United States of America. I have shown in the second part of *Rights of Man*, the manner by which the Constitution was formed and afterwards ratified; and to which I refer the reader. The preamble is in the following words:

WE, THE PEOPLE, of the United States, in order to form a more perfect union, establish justice, insure domestic tranquillity, provide for common defence, promote the general welfare, and secure the blessings of liberty to ourselves and our posterity, DO ORDAIN AND ESTABLISH THIS CON-STITUTION for the United States of America.

Then follow the several articles which appoint the manner in which the several component parts of the government, legislative and executive, shall be elected, and the period of their duration, and the powers they shall have: also, the manner by which future additions, alterations, or amendments, shall be made to the Constitution. Consequently, every improvement that can be made in the science of government, follows in that country as a matter of order. It is only in governments founded on assumption and false principles, that reasoning upon, and investigating systems and principles of government, and showing their several excellencies and defects, are termed libellous and seditious. These terms were made part of the charge brought against Locke, Hampden, and Sydney, and will continue to be brought against all good men, so long as bad government shall continue.

The Government of this country has been ostentatiously giving challenges for more than a hundred years past, upon what is called its own excellence and perfection. Scarcely a king's speech, or a parliamentary speech, has been uttered, in which this glove has not been thrown, till the world has been insulted with their challenges. But it now appears that all this was vapour and vain boasting, or that it was intended to conceal abuses and defects, and hush the people into taxes.

I have taken the challenge up, and in behalf of the public, have shown, in a fair, open, and candid manner, both the radical and practical defects of the system; when lo! those champions of civil list have fled away, and sent the Attorney-general to deny the challenge, by turning the acceptance of it into an attack, and defending their places and pensions by a prosecution.

I will here drop this part of the subject, and state a few particulars respecting the prosecution now pending, by which the Addressers will see that they have been used as tools to the prosecuting party and their dependents. The case is as follows:

The original edition of the first and second bill in the first part of the *Rights of Man*; expensively printed (in the modern style of printing pamphlets, that they might be bound up with Mr Burke's *Reflections on the French Revolution*), the high price precluded the generality of people from purchasing; and many applications were made to me from various parts of the country to print the work in a cheaper manner. The people of Sheffield requested leave to print two thousand copies for themselves, with which request I immediately complied.

The same request came to me from Rotherham, from Leicester, from Chester, for several towns in Scotland; and Mr James Mackintosh, author of *Vindiciae Gallicae*, brought me a request from Warwickshire, for leave to print ten thousand copies in that county. I had already sent a cheap edition to Scotland; and finding the applications increase, I concluded that the best method of complying therewith, would be to print a very numerous edition in London, under my own direction, by which means the work would be more perfect, and the price be reduced lower than it could be by *printing* small editions in the country, of only a few thousands each. . . .

And conscious as I now am, that the work entitled *Rights of Man* so far from being, as has been maliciously or erroneously represented, a false, wicked, and seditious libel, is a work abounding with unanswerable truths, with principles of the purest morality and benevolence, and with arguments not to be controverted – Conscious, I say, of these things, and having no object in view but the happiness of mankind, I have now put the matter to the best proof in my power, by giving to the public a cheap edition of the first and second parts of that work.

Let every man read and judge for himself, not only of the merits and demerits of the work, but of the matters therein contained, which relate to his own interest and happiness.

If, to expose the fraud and imposition of monarchy, and every species of hereditary government – to lessen the oppression of taxes – to propose plans for the education of helpless infancy, and the comfortable support of the aged and distressed – to endeavour to conciliate nations to each other – to extirpate the horrid practice of war – to promote universal peace, civilization, and commerce – and to break the chains of political superstition, and raise degraded man to his proper rank; – if these things be libellous, let me live the life of a libeller, and let the name of LIBELLER be engraved on my tomb.

Of all the weak and ill-judged measures which fear, ignorance, or arrogance could suggest, the Proclamation, and the project for addresses, are two of the worst. They served to advertise the work which the promoters of those measures wished to keep unknown; and in doing this they offered violence to the judgement of the people, by calling on them to condemn what they forbade them to know, and put the strength of their party to that hazardous issue that prudence would have avoided. – The county meeting for Middlesex was attended by only one hundred and eighteen Addressers. They, no doubt, expected that thousands would flock to their standard, and clamour against the *Rights of Man*. But the case most probably is, that men in all countries, are not so blind to their rights and their interest as governments believe.

Having thus shown the extraordinary manner in which the Government party commenced their attack, I proceed to offer a few observations on the prosecution, and on the mode of trial by special jury.

In the first place, I have written a book; and if it cannot be refuted, it cannot be condemned. But I do not consider the prosecution as particularly levelled against me, but against the general right, or the right of every man, of investigating systems and principles of government, and showing their several excellencies or defects. If the press be free only to flatter Government, as Mr Burke has done, and to cry up and extol what certain Court sycophants are pleased to call a 'glorious Constitution', and not free to examine into its errors or abuses, or whether a Constitution really exists or not, such freedom is no other than that of Spain, Turkey, or Russia; and a jury in this case, would not be a jury to try, but an inquisition to condemn.

I have asserted, and by fair and open argument maintained, the right of every nation at all times to establish such a system and form of government for itself as best accords with its disposition, interest, and happiness; and to change and alter it as it sees occasion. Will any jury deny to the nation this right? If they do, they are traitors, and their verdict would be null and void. And if they admit the right, the means must be admitted also; for it would be the highest absurdity to say, that the right existed, but the means did not. The question then is, What are the means by which the possession and exercise of this national right are to be secured? The answer will be, that of maintaining, inviolably, the right of free investigation; for investigation always serves to detect error, and to bring forth truth.

I have, as an individual, given my opinion upon what I believe to be not only the best, but the true system of government, which is the representative system, and I have given reasons for that opinion.

First, Because in the representative system, no office of very extraordinary power, or extravagant pay, is attached to any individual; and consequently there is nothing to excite those national contentions and civil wars with which countries under monarchical governments are frequently convulsed, and of which the history of England exhibits such numerous instances.

Secondly, Because the representative is a system of government always in maturity; whereas monarchical government fluctuates through all the stages, from nonage to dotage.

Thirdly, Because the representative system admits of none but men properly qualified into the government, or removes them if they prove to be otherwise. Whereas, in the hereditary system, a nation may be encumbered with a knave or an idiot for a whole lifetime, and not be benefited by a successor.

Fourthly, Because there does not exist a right to establish hereditary government, or, in other words, hereditary successors, because hereditary government always means a government yet to come, and the case always is, that those who are to live afterwards have the same right to establish government for themselves, as the people had who lived before them; and, therefore, all laws attempting to establish hereditary government, are founded on assumption and political fiction.

If these positions be truths, and I challenge any man to prove the contrary; if they tend to instruct and enlighten mankind, and to free them from error, oppression, and political superstition, which are the objects I have in view in publishing them, that jury would commit an act of injustice to their country, and to me, if not an act of perjury, that should call them *false, wicked,* and *malicious.*

Dragonetti, in his treatise *On Virtues and Rewards*, has a paragraph worthy of being recorded in every country in the world – 'The science (says he), of the politician, consists, in fixing the true point of happiness and freedom. Those men deserve the gratitude of ages who should discover a mode of government that contained the greatest sum of *individual happiness* with the least *national expense.*' But if juries are to be made use of to prohibit inquiry, to suppress truth, and to stop the progress of knowledge, this boasted palladium of liberty becomes the most successful instrument of tyranny.

Among the arts practised at the bar, and from the bench, to impose upon the understanding of a jury, and to obtain a verdict where the consciences of men could not otherwise consent, one of the most successful has been that of calling *truth a libel*, and of insinuating that the words '*falsely, wickedly, and maliciously*', though they are made the formidable and high sounding part of the charge, are not matters of consideration with a jury. For what purpose, then, are they retained, unless it be for that of imposition and wilful defamation?

I cannot conceive a greater violation of order, nor a more abominable insult upon morality, and upon human understanding, than to see a man sitting in the judgement seat, affecting by an antiquated foppery of dress to impress the audience with awe; then causing witnesses and jury to be sworn to truth and justice, himself having officially sworn the same; then causing to be read a prosecution against a man charging him with having *wickedly and maliciously written and published a certain false, wicked, and seditious book*; and having gone through all this with a show of solemnity, as if he saw the eye of the Almighty darting through the roof of the building like a ray of light, turn, in an instant, the whole into a farce, and, in order to obtain a verdict that could not be otherwise obtained, tell the jury that the charge of *falsely, wickedly, and seditiously*, meant nothing; that *truth* was out of the question; and that whether the person accused spoke truth or falsehood, or intended *virtuously or wickedly*, was the same thing; and finally conclude the wretched inquisitorial scene, by stating some antiquated precedent, equally as abominable as that which is then acting, or giving some opinion of his own, and *falsely calling the one and the other − Law*. It was, most probably, to such a judge as this, that the most solemn of all reproofs was given − 'The Lord will smite thee, thous whitened wall.' (Paul to Ananias. Acts xxiii. 2.) . . .

I consider the reform of Parliament, by an application to Parliament, as proposed by the Society, to be a worn-out, hackneyed subject, about which the nation is tired, and the parties are deceiving each other. It is not a subject that is cognizable before Parliament, because no government has a right to alter itself, either in whole or in part. The right, and the exercise of that right, appertains to the nation only, and the proper means is by a national convention, elected for the purpose, by all the people. By this, the will of the nation, whether to reform or not, or what the reform shall be, or how far it shall extend, will be known, and it cannot be known by any other means. Partial addresses, or separate associations, are not testimonies of the general will.

It is, however, certain that the opinions of men, with respect to systems and principles of government, are changing fast in all countries. The alteration in England, within the space of a little more than a year, is far greater than could have been believed, and it is daily and hourly increasing. It moves along the country with the silence of thought. The enormous expense of government has provoked men to think, by making them feel; and the Proclamation has served to increase jealousy and disgust. To prevent, therefore, those commotions which too often and too suddenly arise from suffocated discontents, it is best that the general W I L L should have the full and free opportunity of being publicly ascertained and known.

Wretched as the state of representation is in England, it is every day becoming worse, because the unrepresented parts of the nation are increasing in population and property, and the represented parts are decreasing. It is, therefore, no ill-grounded estimation to say that as not one person in seven is represented, at least fourteen millions of taxes out of the seventeen millions, are paid by the unrepresented part; for although copyholds and leaseholds are assessed to the land-tax the holders are unrepresented. Should then a general demur take place as to the obligation of paying taxes, on the ground of not being represented, it is not the representatives of rotten boroughs, nor special juries, that can decide the question. This is one of the possible cases that ought to be foreseen, in order to prevent the inconveniences that might arise to numerous individuals, by provoking it.

I confess I have no idea of petitioning for rights. Whatever the rights of people are, they have a right to them, and none have a right either to withhold them, or to grant them. Government ought to be established on such principles of justice as to exclude the occasion of all such applications, for wherever they appear they are virtually accusations. . . .

There ought to be, in the constitution of every country, a mode of referring back, on any extraordinary occasion, to the sovereign and original constituent power, which is the nation itself. The right of altering any part of government, cannot, as already observed, reside in the government, or that government might make itself what it pleased.

It ought also to be taken for granted, that though a nation may feel inconveniences, either in the excess of taxation, or in the mode of expenditure, or in anything else, it may not at first be sufficiently assured in what part of its government the defect lies, or where the evil originates. It may be supposed to be in one part, and an inquiry be found to be in another; or partly in all. This obscurity is naturally interwoven with what are called mixed governments.

Be, however, the reform to be accomplished whatever it may, it can only follow in consequence of obtaining a full knowledge of all the causes that have rendered such reform necessary, and everything short of this is guess-work or frivolous cunning. In this case, it cannot be supposed that any application to Parliament can bring forward this knowledge. That body is itself the supposed cause, or one of the supposed causes, of the abuses in question; and cannot be expected, and ought not to be asked, to give evidence against itself. The inquiry, therefore, which is of necessity the first step in the business, cannot be trusted to Parliament, but must be undertaken by a distinct body of men, separated from every suspicion of corruption or influence.

Instead, then, of referring to rotten boroughs and absurd corporations for addresses, or hawking them about the country to be signed by a few dependent tenants, the real and effectual mode would be to come at once to the point, and ascertain the sense of the nation by electing a national convention. By this method, as already observed, the general WILL, whether to reform or not, or what the reform shall be, or how far it shall extend, will be known, and it cannot be known by any other means.

Such a body, empowered and supported by the nation, will have authority to demand information upon all matters necessary to be inquired into; and no minister, nor any person, will dare to refuse it. It will then be seen whether seventeen millions of taxes are necessary, and for what purposes they are expended. The concealed pensioners will then be obliged to unmask; and the source of influence and corruption, if any such there be, will be laid open to the nation, not for the purpose of revenge, but of redress.

By taking this public and national ground, all objections against partial addresses on the one side, or private associations on the other, will be done away; THE NATION WILL DECLARE ITS OWN RE-FORMS; and the clamour about party and faction, or ins or outs, will become ridiculous.

The plan and organization of a convention is easy in practice.

In the first place, the number of inhabitants in every county can be sufficiently ascertained from the number of houses assessed to the house and window-light tax in each county. This will give the rule for apportioning the number of members to be elected to the national convention in each of the counties.

If the total number of inhabitants in England be seven millions and the total number of members to be elected to the convention be one thousand, the number of members to be elected in a county containing one hundred and fifty thousand inhabitants will be *twenty-one,* and in like proportion for any other county.

As the election of a convention must, in order to ascertain the general sense of the nation, go on grounds different from that of parliamentary elections, the mode that best promises this end will have no difficulties to combat with from absurd customs and pretended rights. The right of every man will be the same, whether he lives in a city, a town, or a village. The custom of attaching rights to *place,* or in other words, to inanimate matter, instead of to the *person,* independently of place, is too absurd to make any part of a rational argument.

As every man in the nation, of the age of twenty-one years, pays taxes, either out of the property he possesses, or out of the product of his labour, which is property to him; and is amenable in his own person to every law of the land; so has everyone the same equal right to vote, and no one part of the nation, nor any individual, has a right to dispute the rights of another. The man who should do this ought to forfeit the exercise of his *own* right, for a term of years. This would render the punishment consistent with the crime.

When a qualification to vote is regulated by years, it is placed on the firmest possible ground; because the qualification is such, as nothing but dying before the time can take away; and the equality of rights, as a principle, is recognized in the act of regulating the exercise. But when rights are placed upon, or made dependent upon property, they are on the most precarious of all tenures. 'Riches make themselves wings, and fly away', and the rights fly with them; and thus they become lost to the man when they would be of most value.

It is from a strange mixture of tyranny and cowardice, that exclusions have been set up and continued. The boldness to do wrong at first, changes afterwards into cowardly craft, and at last into fear. The representatives in England appear now to act as if they were afraid to do right, even in part, lest it should awaken the nation to a sense of all the wrongs it has endured. This case serves to show that the same conduct that best constitutes the safety of an individual, namely, a strict adherence to principle, constitutes also the safety of a government, and that without it safety is but an empty name. When the rich plunder the poor of his rights, it becomes an example to the poor to plunder the rich of his property; for the rights of the one are as much property to him, as wealth is property to the other, and the *little all* is as dear as the *much*. It is only by setting out on just principles that men are trained to be just to each other; and it will always be found, that when the rich protect the rights of the poor, the poor will protect the property of the rich. But the guarantee, to be effectual, must be parliamentarily reciprocal.

Exclusions are not only unjust, but they frequently operate as injuriously to the party who monopolizes, as to those who are excluded. When men seek to exclude others from participating in the exercise of any right, they should at least, be assured, that they can effectually perform the whole of the business they undertake; for, unless they do this, themselves will be losers by the monopoly. This has been the case with respect to the monopolized right of election. The monopolizing party has not been able to keep the parliamentary representation, to whom the power of taxation was intrusted, in the state it ought to have been, and have thereby multiplied taxes upon themselves equally with those who were excluded.

A great deal has been, and will continue to be said, about disqualifications, arising from the commission of offences; but were this subject urged to its full extent, it would disqualify a great number of the present electors, together with their representatives; for, of all offences, none are more destructive to the morals of society than bribery and corruption. It is, therefore, civility to such persons to pass this subject over, and give them a fair opportunity of recovering, or rather of creating character.

Everything, in the present mode of electioneering in England, is the reverse of what it ought to be, and the vulgarity that attends elections is no other than the natural consequence of inverting the order of the system.

In the first place, the candidate seeks the elector, instead of the elector seeking for a representative; and the electors are advertised as being in the interest of the candidate, instead of the candidate being in the interest of the electors. The candidate pays the elector for his vote, instead of the nation paying the representative for his time and attendance on public business. The complaint for an undue election is brought by the candidate, as if he, and not the electors, were the party aggrieved; and he takes on himself, at any period of the election, to break it up, by declining, as if the election was in his right and not in theirs.

The compact that was entered into at the last Westminster election between two of the candidates (Mr Fox and Lord Hood), was an indecent violation of the principles of election. The candidates assumed, in their own persons, the rights of the electors; for, it was only in the body of the electors, and not at all in the candidates, that the right of making such compact, or compromise, could exist. But the principle of election and representation is so completely done away in every stage thereof, that inconsistency has no longer the power of surprising.

Neither from elections thus conducted, nor from rotten borough addressers, nor from county-meetings, promoted by placemen and pensioners, can the sense of the nation be known. It is still corruption appealing to itself. But a convention of a thousand persons, fairly elected, would bring every matter to a decided issue.

As to county-meetings, it is only persons of leisure, or those who live near to a place of meeting, that can attend, and the number on such occasions is but like a drop in the bucket compared with the whole. The only consistent service which such meetings could render, would be that of apportioning the county into convenient districts, and when this is done, each district might, according to its number of inhabitants, elect its quota of county members to the national convention; and the vote of each elector might be taken in the parish where he resided, either by ballot or by voice, as he should choose to give it.

A national convention thus formed, would bring together the sense and opinions of every part of the nation, fairly taken. The science of government, and the interest of the public, and of the several parts thereof, would then undergo an ample and rational discussion, freed from the language of parliamentary disguise.

But in all deliberations of this kind, though men have a right to reason with, and endeavour to convince each other, upon any matter that respects their common good, yet, in point of practice, the majority of opinions, when known, forms a rule for the whole, and to this rule every good citizen practically conforms.

Mr Burke, as if he knew (for every concealed pensioner has the opportunity of knowing), that the abuses acted under the present system, are too flagrant to be palliated, and that the majority of opinions, when ever such abuses should be made public, would be for a general and effectual reform, has endeavoured to preclude the event, by sturdily denying the right of a majority of a nation to act as a whole. Let us bestow a thought upon this case.

When any matter is proposed as a subject for consultation, it necessarily implies some mode of decision. Common consent, arising from absolute necessity, has placed this in a majority of opinions; because, without it, there can be no decision, and consequently no order. It is, perhaps, the only case in which mankind, however various in their ideas upon other matters, can consistently be unanimous; because it is a mode of decision derived from the primary original rights of every individual concerned; *that* right being first individually exercised in giving an opinion, and whether that opinion shall arrange with the minority or the majority, is a subsequent accidental thing that neither increases nor diminishes the individual, original right itself. Prior to any debate, inquiry, or investigation, it is not supposed to be known on which side the majority of opinions will fall, and therefore, while this mode of decision secures to everyone the right of giving an opinion, it admits to everyone an equal chance in the ultimate event.

Among the matters that will present themselves to the consideration of a national convention, there is one, wholly of a domestic nature, but so marvellously loaded with confusion, as to appear at first sight, almost impossible to be reformed. I mean the condition of what is called law.

But, if we examine into the cause from whence this confusion, now so much the subject of universal complaint, is produced, not only the remedy will immediately present itself, but, with it, the means of preventing the like case hereafter.

In the first place, the confusion has generated itself from the absurdity of every Parliament assuming to be eternal in power, and the laws partake in a similar manner, of this assumption. They have no period of legal or natural expiration; and, however absurd in principle, or inconsistent in practice many of them have become, they still are, if not especially repealed, considered as making a part of the general mass. By this means the body of what is called law, is spread over a space of *several hundred years*, comprehending laws obsolete, laws repugnant, laws ridiculous, and every other kind of laws forgotten or remembered; and what renders the case still worse, is, that the confusion multiplies with the progress of time.[1]

To bring this misshapen monster into form, and to prevent its lapsing again into a wilderness state, only two things, and those very simple, are necessary.

The first is, to review the whole mass of laws, and to bring forward such only as are worth retaining, and let all the rest drop; and to give to the laws so brought forward a new era, commencing from the time of such reform.

Secondly; that at the expiration of every twenty-one years (or any other stated period) a like review shall again be taken, and the laws, found proper to be retained, be again carried forward, commencing with that date, and the useless laws dropped and discontinued.

By this means there can be no obsolete laws, and scarcely such a thing as laws standing in direct or equivocal contradiction to each other, and every person will know the period of time to which he is to look back for all the laws in being.

It is worth remarking, that while every other branch of science is brought within some commodious system, and the study of it simplified by easy methods, the laws take the contrary course, and become every year more complicated, entangled, confused, and obscure.

Among the paragraphs which the Attorney-general has taken from the *Rights of Man*, and put into his information, one is, that where I have said, 'that with respect to regular law, there is a *scarcely such a thing*'.

As I do not know whether the Attorney-general means to show this expression to be libellous, because it is TRUE, or because it is FALSE, I shall make no other reply to him in this place, than by remarking, that if almanac-makers had not been more judicious than law-makers, the study of almanacs would by this time have become as abstruse as the study of law, and we should hear of a library of almanacs as we now do of statutes; but by the simple operation of letting the obsolete matter drop, and carrying forward that only which is proper to be retained, all that is necessary to be known is

1 In the time of Henry IV a law was passed making it felony 'to multiply gold or silver, or to make use of the craft of multiplication', and this law remained two hundred and eighty-six years upon the statute books. It was then repealed as being ridiculous and injurious. – Paine.

found within the space of a year, and laws also admit of being kept within some given period.

I shall here close this letter, so far as it respects the addresses, the Proclamation, and the prosecution; and shall offer a few observations to the Society, styling itself 'THE FRIENDS OF THE PEOPLE'.

That the science of government is beginning to be better understood than in former times, and that the age of fiction and political superstition, and of craft and mystery, is passing away, are matters which the experience of every day proves to be true, as well in England as in other countries.

As therefore it is impossible to calculate the silent progress of opinion, and also impossible to govern a nation after it has changed its habits of thinking, by the craft or policy that it was governed by before, the only true method to prevent popular discontents and commotions is, to throw, by every fair and rational argument, all the light upon the subject that can possibly be thrown; and at the same time, to open the means of collecting the general sense of the nation; and this cannot, as already observed, be done by any plan so effectually as a national convention. Here individual opinion will quiet itself by having a centre to rest upon.

The Society already mentioned (which is made of men of various descriptions, but chiefly of those called Foxites), appears to me, either to have taken wrong grounds from want of judgement, or to have acted with cunning reserve. It is now amusing the people with a new phrase, namely, that of 'a temperate and moderate reform', the interpretation of which is, *a continuance of the abuses as long as possible. If we cannot hold all let us hold some.*

Who are those that are frightened at reforms? Are the public afraid that their taxes should be lessened too much? Are they afraid that sinecure places and pensions should be abolished too fast? Are the poor afraid that their condition should be rendered too comfortable? Is the worn-out mechanic, or the aged and decayed tradesman, frightened at the prospect of receiving ten pounds a year out of the surplus taxes? Is the soldier frightened at the thoughts of his discharge, and three shillings per week during life? Is the sailor afraid that press-warrants will be abolished? The Society mistakes the fears of borough mongers, placemen, and pensioners, for the fears of the people; and the *temperate and moderate reform* it talks of is calculated to suit the condition of the former.

Those words, 'temperate and moderate', are words either of political cowardice, or of cunning, or seduction. A thing, moderately good, is not so good as it ought to be. Moderation in temper is always a virtue; but moderation in principle, is a species of vice. But who is to be the judge of what is a temperate and moderate reform? The Society is the representative of nobody; neither can the unrepresented part of the nation commit this power to those in Parliament, in whose election they had no choice; and, therefore, even, upon the ground the Society has taken, recourse must be had to a national convention. . . .

[13] AN ESSAY FOR THE USE
OF NEW REPUBLICANS
IN THEIR OPPOSITION TO MONARCHY

(1792)

In August 1792 the French National Assembly awarded Paine the title of 'citizen of France', and in September he was elected to represent the district that included Calais in the new National Convention. That same month the Convention voted to abolish the monarchy; 22 September was decreed as the first day of the new French Republic. Paine wrote this essay in October 1792 to reinforce the anti-monarchical convictions that lay behind these dramatic developments.

The attainment of any important possession that we have long been ardently coveting is at once a source of subsequent self-congratulation. Indeed, the feeling that we have triumphed so absorbs us that we immediately lose the sense of the cause of our success. But, after dwelling awhile on our new happiness, we verify all the incidents that have produced it, and the examination of each of them separately still further enhances our satisfaction. It is our present purpose to develop fully the reasons why our readers should participate in our enjoyment.

All French citizens have joined in celebrating the downfall of Royalty and the creation of a Republic, yet, among those who applaud, there are some persons who have not an entirely clear comprehension of their former situation or of that upon which they are now entering.

All Frenchmen have shuddered at the perjuries of the King, the plots of his Court and the profligacy of his brothers; so that the race of Louis was deposed from the throne of their hearts long before it was deposed by legislative decree. We do not effect much, however, if we merely dethrone an idol; we must also break to pieces the pedestal upon which it rested. It is the office of royalty rather than the holder of the office that is fatal in its consequences. But everyone has not a vivid conception of this fact.

Yet all Frenchmen should be able in the present conjuncture to prove the absurdity of Royalty and the reasonableness of a Republic, whenever these forms of government are discussed; because if you now enjoy freedom and happiness, you should be conscious of the reasons for your contentment.

As a distinction is drawn frequently between Royalty and Monarchy, we had better examine into the question of the pertinency of this distinction.

The system of Royalty has begun in the same fashion in all countries and among all peoples. A band of robbers, gathered together under a leader, throw themselves on a country and make slaves of its people; then they elect their leader king. Next comes another robber chief, who conquers and kills the first, and makes himself king in his stead. After a time, the recollection of all this violence is obliterated, and the successors of the robber are held to reign quite legitimately. They are shrewd enough to confer a few benefits now and then on their subjects; they corrupt those about them, and, to give an air of sanctity to their origin, they devise pedigrees that are purely fictitious; afterwards, they are aided by the dishonesty of the priests, and religion befriends their usurped power, which will henceforth be regarded as their hereditary possession.

The consequences that flow from Royalty are such as might be expected from its source. The annals of monarchy abound in such hideous wickedness, such horrible cruelties that only by reading them can we form any idea of the baseness of which human nature is capable. The pictures that we there behold of kings and their ministers and courtiers are so horrifying that humanity is forced to turn away from them with a shudder.

And yet what else could be expected? Kings are monsters in the natural order, and what can we expect from monsters but miseries and crimes? Now, what is Monarchy? Whatever effort may have been made to conceal its true nature and to familiarize the people with that hateful term, its real meaning cannot be disguised: it signifies *absolute power vested in a single person,* although that person be a fool, a traitor or a tyrant. Do we not outrage national honour when we suggest the possibility of any people being ruled by such a person as I have denoted?

But, apart from the defects of the individual, government by a single person is vicious in itself. A prince is too small a person himself to be capable of governing even the smallest state. What an absurdity it is, then, to believe in his capacity for the government of a great nation!

However, you will say, there have been kings who were men of genius. Granted: but such intelligent rulers have been a greater curse to nations than those who were intellectually deficient. Kings of that class have always been ambitious, and have compelled their subjects to pay dearly for the conquests and *Te-deums* that were celebrated over the land while its inhabitants were dying of hunger. We have only to turn to the career of Louis XIV and of other sovereigns in proof of the truth of this statement.

What, however, of those rulers who have no claim to ability, and who substitute for it the vices that seem inherent in Royalty? We have the following description of them in the *Contrat Social* of J. J. Rousseau: 'The men who take the foremost place in monarchies are often simply base marplots, ordinary rogues, mean intriguers. The trivial intellectual qualities that have raised these people to high positions in courts but serve to make more apparent to the public their real insignificance.' In a word, the story of all monarchies supplies proof that, while monarchs do nothing, their ministers do nothing but evil.

While Royalty is harmful from its very nature, hereditary Royalty is, in addition, absurd and disgusting. Just think of it! Yonder is a man who claims that he has a hereditary right to rule me! Where did he get it? From his ancestors, he says, and from mine. But how could they give him a right they did not possess? No man has power over posterity. I can no more be the slave of those who went before me than I can of those who now exist. If we returned to life, we could not rob ourselves of the rights acquired in a second existence; still less could we rob posterity of their rights.

A hereditary crown! A throne to be handed over to a successor! Why, it is to treat our posterity as a herd of cattle who are entirely destitute of either rights or will. No more infamous and indecent illusion ever disgraced humanity than that the people is a herd which may be transmitted from one king to another.

From one point of view, we should not, perhaps, censure kings for their savage cruelty, their brutality and their oppressions; it is not they who are in fault; it is hereditary succession: a swamp breeds serpents; hereditary succession breeds oppressors.

The following is the system of logic upon which are founded the claims of Royalty: 'I', says the hereditary prince, 'owe my authority to my birth; I owe my birth to God; therefore, I owe nothing to men.' When he has a subservient minister, he then proceeds to commit all the crimes of which tyranny is capable, and he never has any idea that he is acting wrongfully. We have plenty of evidence of this fact in the history of all countries.

You must also see clearly that there must be an entire absence of sympathy between ruler and people. What renders us kind and humane? Is it not sympathy, the power which I have of putting myself in my neighbour's place? How can a monarch have sympathy? He can never put himself in anybody's place, for the simple reason that he can never be in any place but his own.

A monarch is naturally and preëminently an egotist. We have innumerable proofs which show that such a person is altogether separated from humanity. When Charles II was asked to punish Lauderdale for his cruelty to the Scots, his reply was: 'Lauderdale may have oppressed the Scots, but he has always supported my interests.' A frequent expression of Louis XIV was: 'If I were to comply with the will of my people, I should not be King.' He lost his temper when anyone spoke of the 'safety of the State', or 'the calamities of the State'.

We might not object to the hereditary succession of kings, if we could always be certain that the throne should be occupied by a wise and virtuous prince. If, however, we but consider the character of those who sit on the thrones of Europe at the present hour, what do we discover? We find that the men who fill them are either fools or tyrants or traitors or libertines, and that in some of them are combined all imaginable vices. It would thus seem that nature and destiny have agreed in the present age to supply us with tangible evidence of the atrocious wickedness and folly of Royalty.

Yet, after all, there is nothing distinctive about the present age in this relation. Hereditary succession is so essentially vicious that it is impossible for the people to hope for the advent of a virtuous prince. A person educated in the belief that he has a right to command others is inevitably bound by his surroundings to lose all sense of reason and justice.

In fact, were not this notion of hereditary kings a serious matter, we might feel inclined to laugh at the absurdity of such an institution. We have to imagine that, as in the case of racehorses, a prince has certain peculiar characteristics that destine him for the throne, just as the courser has certain physical qualities which destine him for the race-track. But in the case of the noble race of Andalusian steeds, certain precautions are taken to insure its genuineness. Surely, in the case of princes, except similar precautions are adopted, no matter how much they violate the laws of decency, it is impossible to discover whether the offspring of a queen is a legitimate prince or a bastard.

Everything connected with hereditary Royalty bears the mark of infamy or folly. Just consider: a person cannot be a mere workman without some sort of ability; to be a king all that a man requires is to be born. The story told by Montaigne of the dog Barkouf who was appointed governor of a province by an Asiatic monarch, excites our amusement. We laugh at the folly of the Egyptians, who set up a pebble on a throne and acknowledged it as their King. But a pebble or a dog would be less harmful to the people who bowed before them than are kings to the nations that pay them servile homage.

An irrational animal or a piece of lifeless rock is less dangerous to a nation than a human idol. Hardly a single example can be adduced where a man of genius has left behind him children worthy of their parentage. And yet the authority vested in a sovereign, must descend to his son! It is like saying that a wise father always has a wise son! A good governor by inheritance is as likely as a good author by inheritance.

Common sense, therefore, is as much outraged by the idea of Royalty as common right is. Still, it is more than an absurdity; it is a plague, because a nation that prostrates itself in presences of an absurdity is degraded. Can that people which reveres equally vice and virtue, ignorance and wisdom, ever have the capacity for managing important affairs? For this reason, it will be noticed that the inhabitants of a monarchical country are often intellectually degenerate and are distinguished for their servile disposition.

Another consequence of this baleful institution is that it destroys equality and introduces what is called 'Nobility'. Evil a thing as Nobility is, it is less so than government by inheritance. All that the noble asks of me is that I recognize his superiority because of his birth, while the King requires my submission: I am amused by the noble; I feel like setting my foot upon the King.

It was thought that when the Convention voted the abolition of Royalty, someone would speak in its favour. In this relation, a certain philosopher, who believed that no decree should be issued without a preliminary discussion of the question, moved for the appointment of an orator who should bring forward all the arguments that could be adduced in favour of Royalty, so that everything that could be said in its justification should be made clear to the world. It was on the principle that counsel is assigned to the defence, no matter how strong is the evidence of the prisoner's guilt. In the Republic of Venice there was an official whose function it was to assail all testimony, however indisputable. Royalty, however, has plenty of defenders. It is only fitting that we should examine the cogency of their arguments.

1. *The people need a King to protect them from the tyranny of the powerful.*

Let the Rights of Man be established, Equality enthroned, a sound Constitution drafted, with its powers clearly defined; let all privileges, distinctions of birth and monopolies be annulled; establish liberty of trade and industry, the freedom of the press, equal division of family inheritances, publicity of all government measures, and you will be certain to have excellent laws, and may dispel from your mind the dread of the powerful; for, whether they like it or not, all citizens will then be subject to the law.

2. *A King will prevent the Legislature from usurping authority.*

If representatives, who cannot act as administrators or judges, are often renewed, if their functions are determined by law, if the people can summon at any moment their national conventions and primary assemblies, the tyranny of a legislature would have only a very short existence, especially among a people capable of self-defence, who can read, and have newspapers, guns and pikes. Why assume an evil solely for the purposes of providing a remedy?

3. *To strengthen the executive power, we should have a King.*

Such a proposition might have a certain force when we had nobles, priests, parliaments, and other privileged classes. Now, however, the law is all powerful, and as it is the expression of the general will, it is the interest of everyone to see that it is executed. On the contrary, the presence of a hereditary king tends to weaken the executive power, as was clearly demonstrated recently when we attempted to unite Royalty and Liberty in marriage bonds.

For that matter, those who hold this opinion are persons who identify the king with the Executive Power. My readers, I fancy, entertain more enlightened sentiments.

The following is another not uncommon fallacy: 'We must have either an hereditary chief or an elective chief. If we have an elective chief, the citizens will quarrel about the candidates, and every election will be followed by a civil war.' In the first place, such civil wars as have arisen in England and France were the result, not of election, but of hereditary succession; and, in addition, the scourge of foreign war has, for a score of times, devastated these kingdoms, because of the claims asserted by certain royal families. In fine, all the disturbances that occurred during the Regency had their source in hereditary succession.

The great point, however, to be considered is this: an elective chief will not be followed by a train of courtiers, will not be surrounded with royal pageantry, will not be puffed up with servile adulation, and will not have an income of thirty millions; and besides, his fellow-citizens will not elect him to an office of several years' duration without limiting his authority and keeping his income within due bounds.

Moreover, the presence of a king entails the presence of an aristocracy and of taxation reaching thirty millions. This is doubtless why Franklin styled Royalism *a crime as bad as poisoning.*

The sole reason why Royalty, with all its visionary spendour, its assumed necessity, the superstitious idolatry that follows in its train, was created was for the purpose of exacting from its victims excessive taxation and willing submission.

Royalty and Popery have had the same goal to attain and have been supported by the same deceptions; they are now falling into the same decay under the rays of the same Light.

[14] REASONS FOR PRESERVING THE LIFE OF LOUIS CAPET

(1793)

After abolishing the monarchy, the National Convention debated the fate of Louis XVI. The Girondins, Paine's party, opposed bringing the King to trial. Paine disagreed and, like the more radical Jacobins, preferred trying the King. Louis was tried in late 1792 and found guilty of treason. The Jacobins then demanded his death, while the Girondins sought the lesser punishment of banishment or jail. Paine sided at this point with his Girondin colleagues and pleaded that Louis's life be spared. This text is the speech he gave to the National Convention on 15 January 1793. He urges that Capet deserves his life, if for no other reason, because he gave assistance to America during its war with Britain.

Citizen President: My hatred and abhorrence of monarchy are sufficiently known: they originate in principles of reason and conviction, nor, except with life, can they ever be extirpated; but my compassion for the unfortunate, whether friend or enemy, is equally lively and sincere.

I voted that Louis should be tried, because it was necessary to afford proofs to the world of the perfidy, corruption and abomination of the monarchical system. The infinity of evidence that has been produced exposes them in the most glaring and hideous colours; thence it results that monarchy, whatever form it may assume, arbitrary or otherwise, becomes necessarily a centre round which are united every species of corruption, and the kingly trade is no less destructive of all morality in the human breast, than the trade of an executioner is destructive of its sensibility. I remember, during my residence in another country, that I was exceedingly struck with a sentence of M. Autheine at the Jacobins [Club], which corresponds exactly with my own idea – 'Make me a king to-day,' said he, 'and I shall be a robber to-morrow.'

Nevertheless, I am inclined to believe that if Louis Capet had been born in obscure condition, had he lived within the circle of an amiable and respectable neighbourhood, at liberty to practise the duties of domestic life, had he been thus situated, I cannot believe that he would have shown himself destitute of social virtues; we are, in a moment of fermentation like this, naturally little indulgent to his vices, or rather to those of his government; we regard them with additional horror and indignation; not that they are more heinous than those of his predecessors, but because our eyes are now open, and the veil of delusion at length withdrawn; yet the lamentable, degraded state to which he is actually reduced, is surely far less imputable to him than to the Constituent Assembly, which, of its own authority, without consent or advice of the people, restored him to the throne.

I was in Paris at the time of the flight, or abdication of Louis XVI, and when he was taken and brought back. The proposal of restoring him to supreme power struck me with amazement; and although at that time I was not a French citizen, yet as a citizen of the world I employed all the efforts that depended on me to prevent it.

A small society, composed only of five persons, two of whom are now members of the Convention, took at that time the name of the Republican Club (Société Républicaine). This society opposed the restoration of Louis, not so much on account of his personal offences, as in order to overthrow the monarchy, and to erect on its ruins the republican system and an equal representation.

With this design, I traced out in the English language certain propositions, which were translated with some trifling alterations, and signed by Achille Duchâtelet, now Lieutenant-General in the army of the French Republic, and at that time one of the five members which composed our little party: the law requiring the signature of a citizen at the bottom of each printed paper.

The paper was indignantly torn by Malouet; and brought forth in this very room as an article of accusation against the person who had signed it, the author and the adherents; but such is the revolution of events, that this paper is now received and brought forth for a very opposite purpose – to remind the nation of the errors of that unfortunate day, that fatal error of not having then banished Louis XVI from its bosom, and to plead this day in favour of his exile, preferable to his death. . . .

Having thus explained the principles and the exertions of the republicans at that fatal period, when Louis was reinstated in full possession of the executive power which by his flight had been suspended, I return to the subject, and to the deplorable situation in which the man is now actually involved.

What was neglected at the time of which I have been speaking, has been since brought about by the force of necessity. The wilful, treacherous defects in the former Constitution have been brought to light; the continual alarm of treason and conspiracy aroused the nation, and produced eventually a second revolution. The people have beat down royalty, never, never to rise again; they have brought Louis Capet to the bar, and demonstrated in the face of the whole world, the intrigues, the cabals, the falsehood, corruption, and rooted depravity, the inevitable effects of monarchical government. There remains then only one question to be considered, what is to be done with this man?

For myself I seriously confess, that when I reflect on the unaccountable folly that restored the executive power to his hands, all covered as he was with perjuries and treason, I am far more ready to condemn the Constituent Assembly than the unfortunate prisoner Louis Capet.

But abstracted from every other consideration, there is one circumstance in his life which ought to cover or at least to palliate a great number of his transgressions, and this very circumstance affords to the French nation a blessed occasion of extricating itself from the yoke of kings, without defiling itself in the impurities of their blood.

It is to France alone, I know, that the United States of America owe that support which enabled them to shake off the unjust and tyrannical yoke of Britain. The ardour and zeal which she displayed to provide both men and money, were the natural consequence of a thirst for liberty. But as the nation at that time, restrained by the shackles of her own government, could only act by the means of a monarchical organ, this organ – whatever in other respects the object might be – certainly performed a good, a great action.

Let then those United States be the safeguard and asylum of Louis Capet. There, hereafter, far removed from the miseries and crimes of royalty, he may learn, from the constant aspect of public prosperity, that the true system of government consists not in kings, but in fair, equal and honourable representation.

In relating this circumstance, and in submitting this proposition, I consider myself as a citizen of both countries. I submit it as a citizen of America, who feels the debt of gratitude which he owes to every

Frenchman. I submit it also as a man, who, although the enemy of kings, cannot forget that they are subject to human frailties. I support my proposition as a citizen of the French Republic, because it appears to me the best, the most politic measure that can be adopted.

As far as my experience in public life extends, I have ever observed, that the great mass of the people are invariably just, both in their intentions and in their objects; but the true method of accomplishing an effect does not always show itself in the first instance. For example; the English nation had groaned under the despotism of the Stuarts. Hence Charles I lost his life; yet Charles II was restored to all the plenitude of power, which his father had lost. Forty years had not expired when the same family strove to re-establish their ancient oppression; so the nation then banished from its territories the whole race. The remedy was effectual. The Stuart family sank into obscurity, confounded itself with the multitude, and is at length extinct.

The French nation has carried her measures of government to a greater length. France is not satisfied with exposing the guilt of the monarch. She has penetrated into the vices and horrors of the monarchy. She has shown them clear as daylight, and forever crushed that system; and he, whoever he may be, that should ever dare to reclaim those rights would be regarded not as a pretender, but punished as a traitor.

Two brothers of Louis Capet have banished themselves from the country; but they are obliged to comply with the spirit and etiquette of the courts where they reside. They can advance no pretensions on their own account, so long as Louis Capet shall live.

Monarchy, in France, was a system pregnant with crime and murders, cancelling all natural ties, even those by which brothers are united. We know how often they have assassinated each other to pave a way to power. As those hopes which the emigrants had reposed in Louis XVI, are fled, the last that remains rests upon his death, and their situation inclines them to desire this catastrophe, that they may once again rally around a more active chief, and try one further effort under the fortune of the ci-devant Monsieur and D'Artois. That such an enterprise would precipitate them into a new abyss of calamity and disgrace, it is not difficult to foresee; yet it might be attended with mutual loss, and it is our duty as legislators not to spill a drop of blood when our purpose may be effectually accomplished without it.

It has already been proposed to abolish the punishment of death, and it is with infinite satisfaction that I recollect the humane and excellent oration pronounced by Robespierre on that subject in the Constituent Assembly. This cause must find its advocates in every corner where enlightened politicians and lovers of humanity exist, and it ought above all to find them in this assembly.

Monarchical governments have trained the human race, and inured it to the sanguinary arts and refinements of punishment; and it is exactly the same punishment which has so long shocked the sight and tormented the patience of the people, that now, in their turn, they practise in revenge upon their oppressors. But it becomes us to be strictly on our guard against the abomination and perversity of monarchical examples: as France has been the first of European nations to abolish royalty, let her also be the first to abolish the punishment of death, and to find out a milder and more effectual substitute.

In the particular case now under consideration, I submit the following propositions: 1st, That the National Convention shall pronounce sentence of banishment on Louis and his family, 2d, That Louis Capet shall be detained in prison till the end of the war, and at that epoch the sentence of banishment to be executed.

[15] THE AGE OF REASON, PART ONE

(1794)

Nothing Paine wrote brought such notoriety as his Age of Reason. *No matter that one of Paine's motives for writing it in 1794 was to rescue natural Christianity from unbelievers, he would still for ever after be regarded, as Teddy Roosevelt put it, as 'that filthy little atheist'. Paine's offence was to take deism out of the hands of the aristocracy and intellectuals and bring it to the people. From the early years of the eighteenth century philosophers in England and France had been attacking the miraculous, supernatural and political aspects of Christianity and calling instead for a religion committed to the moral teachings of Christ and compatible with a scientific reading of the world organized around rational Newtonian principles. By the end of the century religious deists and political progressives, like Jefferson, agreed that priests and tyrants were co-conspirators against liberty and progress. Paine's* Age of Reason, *published in Paris in 1794, became the manifesto for such views. It has endured since then, depending on one's viewpoint, as the bible of rational Christianity or as blasphemy and the devil's doing. The text here is Part One of what were the two parts of the original essay.*

TO MY FELLOW-CITIZENS OF THE UNITED STATES OF AMERICA

I put the following work under your protection. It contains my opinion upon religion. You will do me the justice to remember, that I have always strenuously supported the right of every man to his own opinion, however different that opinion might be to mine. He who denies to another this right, makes a slave of himself to his present opinion, because he precludes himself the right of changing it.

The most formidable weapon against errors of every kind is reason. I have never used any other, and I trust I never shall.

Your affectionate friend and fellow-citizen,

THOMAS PAINE.

Paris, 8th Pluvôise.
Second year of the French Republic, one and indivisible.
January 27th, O.S. 1794.

THE AUTHOR'S PROFESSION OF FAITH

It has been my intention, for several years past, to publish my thoughts upon religion. I am well aware of the difficulties that attend the subject, and from that consideration, had reserved it to a more advanced period of life. I intended it to be the last offering I should make to my fellow-citizens of all nations, and that at a time when the purity of the motive that induced me to it could not admit of a question, even by those who might disapprove the work. The circumstance that has now taken place in France of the total abolition of the whole national order of priesthood, and of everything appertaining to compulsive systems of religion, and compulsive articles of faith, has not only precipitated my intention, but rendered a work of this kind exceedingly necessary, lest in the general wreck of superstition, of false systems of government and false theology, we lose sight of morality, of humanity and of the theology that is true.

As several of my colleagues, and others of my fellow-citizens of France, have given me the example of making their voluntary and individual profession of faith, I also will make mine; and I do this with all that sincerity and frankness with which the mind of man communicates with itself.

I believe in one God, and no more; and I hope for happiness beyond this life.

I believe in the equality of man; and I believe that religious duties consist in doing justice, loving mercy, and endeavouring to make our fellow-creatures happy.

But, lest it should be supposed that I believe many other things in addition to these, I shall, in the progress of this work, declare the things I do not believe, and my reasons for not believing them.

I do not believe in the creed professed by the Jewish Church, by the Roman Church, by the Greek Church, by the Turkish Church, by the Protestant Church, nor by any church that I know of. My own mind is my own church.

All national institutions of churches, whether Jewish, Christian or Turkish, appear to me no other than human inventions, set up to terrify and enslave mankind, and monopolize power and profit.

I do not mean by this declaration to condemn those who believe otherwise; they have the same right to their belief as I have to mine. But it is necessary to the happiness of man that he be mentally faithful to himself. Infidelity does not consist in believing, or in disbelieving; it consists in professing to believe what he does not believe.

It is impossible to calculate the moral mischief, if I may so express it, that mental lying has produced in society. When a man has so far corrupted and prostituted the chastity of his mind as to subscribe his professional belief to things he does not believe he has prepared himself for the commission of every other crime.

He takes up the trade of a priest for the sake of gain, and in order to qualify himself for that trade he begins with a perjury. Can we conceive any thing more destructive to morality than this?

Soon after I had published the pamphlet *Common Sense*, in America, I saw the exceeding probability that a revolution in the system of government would be followed by a revolution in the system of religion. The adulterous connection of church and state, wherever it has taken place, whether Jewish, Christian or Turkish, has so effectually prohibited by pains and penalties every discussion upon established creeds, and upon first principles of religion, that until the system of government should be changed, those subjects could not be brought fairly and openly before the world; but that whenever this should be done, a revolution in the system of religion would follow. Human inventions and priestcraft would be detected; and man would return to the pure, unmixed and unadulterated belief of one God, and no more.

CONCERNING MISSIONS AND REVELATIONS

Every national church or religion has established itself by pretending some special mission from God, communicated to certain individuals. The Jews have their Moses; the Christians their Jesus Christ, their apostles and saints; and the Turks their Mahomet, as if the way to God was not open to every man alike.

Each of those churches show certain books, which they call *revelation*, or the Word of God. The Jews say that their Word of God was given by God to Moses, face to face; the Christians say that their Word of God came by divine inspiration; and the Turks say that their Word of God (the Koran) was brought by an angel from heaven. Each of those churches accuses the other of unbelief; and for my own part, I disbelieve them all.

As it is necessary to affix right ideas to words, I will, before I proceed further into the subject, offer some observations on the word *revelation*. Revelation, when applied to religion, means something communicated *immediately* from God to man.

No one will deny or dispute the power of the Almighty to make such a communication, if He pleases. But admitting, for the sake of a case, that something has been revealed to a certain person, and not revealed to any other person, it is revelation to that person only. When he tells it to a second person, a second to a third, a third to a fourth, and so on, it ceases to be a revelation to all those persons. It is revelation to the first person only, and *hearsay* to every other, and consequently they are not obliged to believe it.

It is a contradiction in terms and ideas, to call anything a revelation that comes to us at second-hand, either verbally or in writing. Revelation is necessarily limited to the first communication – after this it is only an account of something which that person says was a revelation made to him; and though he may find himself obliged to believe it, it cannot be incumbent on me to believe it in the same manner; for it was not a revelation made to *me*, and I have only his word for it that it was made to him. When Moses told the children of Israel that he received the two tables of the commandments from the hands of God, they were not obliged to believe him, because they had no other authority for it than his telling them so; and I have no other authority for it than some historian telling me so. The commandments carry no internal evidence of divinity with them; they contain some good moral precepts, such as any man qualified to be a lawgiver, or a legislator, could produce himself, without having recourse to supernatural intervention.[1]

When I am told that the Koran was written in heaven and brought to Mahomet by an angel, the account comes too near the same kind of hearsay evidence and second-hand authority as the former. I did not see the angel myself and, therefore, I have a right not to believe it.

When also I am told that a woman called the Virgin Mary, said, or gave out, that she was with child without any cohabitation with a man, and that her betrothed husband, Joseph, said that an angel told

---

1 It is, however, necessary to except the declaration which says that God *visits the sins of the fathers upon the children*; it is contrary to every principle of moral justice. – Paine.

him so, I have a right to believe them or not; such a circumstance
required a much stronger evidence than their bare word for it; but
we have not even this – for neither Joseph nor Mary wrote any such
matter themselves; it is only reported by others that *they said so* – it is
hearsay upon hearsay, and I do not choose to rest my belief upon
such evidence.

It is, however, not difficult to account for the credit that was given
to the story of Jesus Christ being the Son of God. He was born at a
time when the heathen mythology had still some fashion and repute
in the world, and that mythology had prepared the people for the
belief of such a story. Almost all the extraordinary men that lived
under the heathen mythology were reputed to be the sons of some of
their gods. It was not a new thing, at that time, to believe a man to
have been celestially begotten; the intercourse of gods with women
was then a matter of familiar opinion.

Their Jupiter, according to their accounts, had cohabited with
hundreds: the story, therefore, had nothing in it either new, wonderful or obscene; it was conformable to the opinions that then
prevailed among the people called Gentiles, or Mythologists, and it
was those people only that believed it.

The Jews, who had kept strictly to the belief of one God, and no
more, and who had always rejected the heathen mythology, never
credited the story.

It is curious to observe how the theory of what is called the
Christian Church sprung out of the tail of the heathen mythology. A
direct incorporation took place in the first instance, by making the
reputed founder to be celestially begotten. The trinity of gods that
then followed was no other than a reduction of the former plurality,
which was about twenty or thirty thousand; the statue of Mary
succeeded the statue of Diana of Ephesus; the deification of heroes
changed into the canonization of saints; the Mythologists had gods
for everything; the Christian Mythologists had saints for everything;
the Church became as crowded with the one as the Pantheon had
been with the other, and Rome was the place of both. The Christian
theory is little else than the idolatry of the ancient Mythologists,
accommodated to the purposes of power and revenue; and it yet
remains to reason and philosophy to abolish the amphibious fraud.

AN APPRECIATION OF THE CHARACTER OF JESUS CHRIST, AND HIS HISTORY

Nothing that is here said can apply, even with the most distant disrespect, to the real character of Jesus Christ. He was a virtuous and an amiable man. The morality that he preached and practised was of the most benevolent kind; and though similar systems of morality had been preached by Confucius, and by some of the Greek philosophers, many years before; by the Quakers since; and by many good men in all ages, it has not been exceeded by any.

Jesus Christ wrote no account of himself, of his birth, parentage, or anything else; not a line of what is called the New Testament is of his own writing. The history of him is altogether the work of other people; and as to the account given of his resurrection and ascension, it was the necessary counterpart to the story of his birth. His historians, having brought him into the world in a supernatural manner, were obliged to take him out again in the same manner, or the first part of the story must have fallen to the ground.

The wretched contrivance with which this latter part is told exceeds every thing that went before it. The first part, that of the miraculous conception, was not a thing that admitted of publicity; and therefore the tellers of this part of the story had this advantage, that though they might not be credited, they could not be detected. They could not be expected to prove it, because it was not one of those things that admitted of proof, and it was impossible that the person of whom it was told could prove it himself.

But the resurrection of a dead person from the grave, and his ascension through the air, is a thing very different as to the evidence it admits of, to the invisible conception of a child in the womb. The resurrection and ascension, supposing them to have taken place, admitted of public and ocular demonstration, like that of the ascension of a balloon, or the sun at noon-day, to all Jerusalem at least.

A thing which everybody is required to believe requires that the proof and evidence of it should be equal to all, and universal; and as the public visibility of this last related act was the only evidence that could give sanction to the former part, the whole of it falls to the ground, because that evidence never was given. Instead of this, a small number of persons, not more than eight or nine, are introduced as proxies for the whole world to say they saw it, and all the rest of the world are called upon to believe it. But it appears that Thomas did not believe the resurrection, and, as they say, would not believe without having ocular and manual demonstration himself. *So neither will I,* and the reason is equally as good for me, and for every other person, as for Thomas.

It is in vain to attempt to palliate or disguise this matter. The story, so far as relates to the supernatural part, has every mark of fraud and imposition stamped upon the face of it. Who were the authors of it is as impossible for us now to know, as it is for us to be assured that the books in which the account is related were written by the persons whose names they bear; the best surviving evidence we now have respecting this affair is the Jews. They are regularly descended from the people who lived in the times this resurrection and ascension is said to have happened, and they say, *it is not true.* It has long appeared to me a strange inconsistency to cite the Jews as a proof of the truth of the story. It is just the same as if a man were to say, I will prove the truth of what I have told you by producing the people who say it is false.

That such a person as Jesus existed, and that he was crucified, which was the mode of execution at that day, are historical relations strictly within the limits of probability. He preached most excellent morality and the equality of man; but he preached also against the corruptions and avarice of the Jewish priests, and this brought upon him the hatred and vengeance of the whole order of priesthood.

The accusation which those priests brought against him was that of sedition and conspiracy against the Roman government, to which the Jews were then subject and tributary; and it is not improbable that the Roman government might have some secret apprehensions of the effects of his doctrine, as well as the Jewish priests; neither is it improbable that Jesus Christ had in contemplation the delivery of the Jewish nation from the bondage of the Romans. Between the two, however, this virtuous reformer and revolutionist lost his life.

FABULOUS BASES OF CHRISTIANITY

It is upon this plain narrative of facts, together with another case I am going to mention, that the Christian Mythologists, calling themselves the Christian Church, have erected their fable, which, for absurdity and extravagance, is not exceeded by anything that is to be found in the mythology of the ancients.

The ancient Mythologists tell that the race of Giants made war against Jupiter, and that one of them threw a hundred rocks against him at one throw; that Jupiter defeated him with thunder, and confined him afterwards under Mount Etna, and that every time the giant turns himself Mount Etna belches fire. It is here easy to see that the circumstance of the mountain, that of its being a volcano, suggested the idea of the fable; and that the fable is made to fit and wind itself up with that circumstance.

The Christian Mythologists tell that their Satan made war against the Almighty, who defeated him, and confined him afterwards, not under a mountain, but in a pit. It is here easy to see that the first fable suggested the idea of the second; for the fable of Jupiter and the Giants was told many hundred years before that of Satan.

Thus far the ancient and the Christian Mythologists differ very little from each other. But the latter have contrived to carry the matter much farther.

They have contrived to connect the fabulous part of the story of Jesus Christ with the fable originating from Mount Etna; and in order to make all the parts of the story tie together they have taken to their aid the traditions of the Jews; for the Christian mythology is made up partly from the ancient mythology and partly from the Jewish traditions.

The Christian Mythologists, after having confined Satan in a pit, were obliged to let him out again to bring on the sequel of the fable. He is then introduced into the Garden of Eden, in the shape of a snake or a serpent, and in that shape he enters into familiar conversation with Eve, who is no way surprised to hear a snake talk; and the issue of this *tête-à-tête* is that he persuades her to eat an apple, and the eating of that apple damns all mankind.

After giving Satan this triumph over the whole creation, one would have supposed that the Church Mythologists would have been kind enough to send him back again to the pit: or, if they had not done this, that they would have put a mountain upon him (for they say that their faith can remove a mountain), or have put him *under* a mountain, as the former mythologists had done, to prevent his getting again among the women and doing more mischief. But instead of this they leave him at large, without even obliging him to give his parole – the secret of which is that they could not do without him; and after being at the trouble of making him, they bribed him to stay. They promised him ALL the Jews, ALL the Turks by anticipation, nine-tenths of the world beside, and Mahomet into the bargain. After this, who can doubt the bountifulness of the Christian Mythology?

Having thus made an insurrection and a battle in heaven, in which none of the combatants could be either killed or wounded – put Satan into the pit – let him out again – gave him a triumph over the whole creation – damned all mankind by the eating of an apple, these Christian Mythologists bring the two ends of their fable together. They represent this virtuous and amiable man, Jesus Christ, to be at once both God and Man, and also the Son of God, celestially begotten, on purpose to be sacrificed, because they say that Eve in her longing had eaten an apple.

EXAMINATION OF THE PRECEDING BASES

Putting aside everything that might excite laughter by its absurdity, or detestation by its profaneness, and confining ourselves merely to an examination of the parts, it is impossible to conceive a story more derogatory to the Almighty, more inconsistent with His wisdom, more contradictory to His power, than this story is.

In order to make for it a foundation to rise upon, the inventors were under the necessity of giving to the being whom they call Satan, a power equally as great, if not greater than they attribute to the Almighty. They have not only given him the power of liberating himself from the pit, after what they call his fall, but they have made that power increase afterwards to infinity. Before this fall they represent him only as an angel of limited existence, as they represent the rest. After his fall, he becomes, by their account, omnipresent. He exists everywhere, and at the same time. He occupies the whole immensity of space.

Not content with this deification of Satan, they represent him as defeating, by stratagem, in the shape of an animal of the creation, all the power and wisdom of the Almighty. They represent him as having compelled the Almighty to the *direct necessity* either of surrendering the whole of the creation to the government and sovereignty of this Satan, or of capitulating for its redemption by coming down upon earth, and exhibiting Himself upon a cross in the shape of a man.

Had the inventors of this story told it the contrary way, that is, had they represented the Almighty as compelling Satan to exhibit *himself* on a cross, in the shape of a snake, as a punishment for his new transgression, the story would have been less absurd – less contradictory. But instead of this, they make the transgressor triumph, and the Almighty fall.

That many good men have believed this strange fable, and lived very good lives under that belief (for credulity is not a crime), is what I have no doubt of. In the first place, they were educated to believe it, and they would have believed anything else in the same manner.

There are also many who have been so enthusiastically enraptured by what they conceived to be the infinite love of God to man, in making a sacrifice of Himself, that the vehemence of the idea has forbidden and deterred them from examining into the absurdity and profaneness of the story. The more unnatural anything is, the more it is capable of becoming the object of dismal admiration.

OF THE TRUE THEOLOGY

But if objects for gratitude and admiration are our desire, do they not present themselves every hour to our eyes? Do we not see a fair creation prepared to receive us the instant we are born – a world furnished to our hands, that cost us nothing? Is it we that light up the sun, that pour down the rain, and fill the earth with abundance? Whether we sleep or wake, the vast machinery of the universe still goes on.

Are these things, and the blessings they indicate in future, nothing to us? Can our gross feelings be excited by no other subjects than tragedy and suicide? Or is the gloomy pride of man become so intolerable, that nothing can flatter it but a sacrifice of the Creator?

I know that this bold investigation will alarm many, but it would be paying too great a compliment to their credulity to forbear it upon that account; the times and the subject demand it to be done. The suspicion that the theory of what is called the Christian Church is fabulous is becoming very extensive in all countries; and it will be a consolation to men staggering under that suspicion, and doubting what to believe and what to disbelieve, to see the object freely investigated. I therefore pass on to an examination of the books called the Old and New Testaments.

EXAMINATION OF THE OLD TESTAMENT

These books, beginning with Genesis and ending with Revelation (which, by the bye, is a book of riddles that requires a revelation to explain it), are, we are told, the Word of God. It is, therefore, proper for us to know who told us so, that we may know what credit to give to the report. The answer to this question is that nobody can tell, except that we tell one another so. The case, however, historically appears to be as follows:

When the Church Mythologists established their system, they collected all the writings they could find and managed them as they pleased. It is a matter altogether of uncertainty to us whether such of the writings as now appear under the name of the Old and New Testaments are in the same state in which those collectors say they found them, or whether they added, altered, abridged or dressed them up.

Be this as it may, they decided by *vote* which of the books out of the collection they had made should be the WORD OF GOD, and which should not. They rejected several; they voted others to be doubtful, such as the books called the Apocrypha; and those books which had a majority of votes were voted to be the Word of God. Had they voted otherwise, all the people, since calling themselves Christians, had believed otherwise – for the belief of the one comes from the vote of the other. Who the people were that did all this, we know nothing of; they called themselves by the general name of the Church, and this is all we know of the matter.

As we have no other external evidence or authority for believing these books to be the Word of God than what I have mentioned, which is no evidence or authority at all, I come in the next place to examine the internal evidence contained in the books themselves.

In the former part of this essay, I have spoken of revelation; I now proceed further with that subject for the purpose of applying it to the books in question.

Revelation is a communication of something which the person to whom that thing is revealed did not know before. For if I have done a thing, or seen it done, it needs no revelation to tell me I have done it, or seen it, nor to enable me to tell it, or to write it.

Revelation, therefore, cannot be applied to anything done upon earth, of which man himself is the actor or the witness; and consequently all the historical and anecdotal parts of the Bible, which is almost the whole of it, is not within the meaning and compass of the word revelation, and, therefore, is not the Word of God.

When Samson ran off with the gate-posts of Gaza, if he ever did so (and whether he did or not is nothing to us), or when he visited his Delilah, or caught his foxes, or did anything else, what has revelation to do with these things? If they were facts, he could tell them himself, or his secretary, if he kept one, could write them, if they were worth either telling or writing; and if they were fictions, revelation could not make them true; and whether true or not, we are neither the better nor the wiser for knowing them. When we contemplate the immensity of that Being who directs and governs the incomprehensible WHOLE, of which the utmost ken of human sight can discover but a part, we ought to feel shame at calling such paltry stories the Word of God.

As to the account of the Creation, with which the book of Genesis opens, it has all the appearance of being a tradition which the Israelites had among them before they came into Egypt; and after their departure from that country they put it at the head of their history, without telling (as it is most probable) that they did not know how they came by it. The manner in which the account opens shows it to be traditionary. It begins abruptly; it is nobody that speaks; it is nobody that hears; it is addressed to nobody; it has neither first, second, nor third person; it has every criterion of being a tradition; it has no voucher. Moses does not take it upon himself by introducing it with the formality that he used on other occasions, such as that of saying, '*The Lord spake unto Moses, saying*'.

Why it has been called the Mosaic account of the Creation, I am at a loss to conceive. Moses, I believe, was too good a judge of such subjects to put his name to that account. He had been educated among the Egyptians, who were a people as well skilled in science, and particularly in astronomy, as any people of their day; and the silence and caution that Moses observes in not authenticating the account is a good negative evidence that he neither told it nor believed it.

The case is that every nation of people has been world-makers, and the Israelites had as much right to set up the trade of world-making as any of the rest; and as Moses was not an Israelite, he might not choose to contradict the tradition. The account, however, is harmless; and this is more than can be said for many other parts of the Bible.

Whenever we read the obscene stories, the voluptuous debaucheries, the cruel and torturous executions, the unrelenting vindictiveness, with which more than half the Bible is filled, it would be more consistent that we called it the word of a demon than the Word of God. It is a history of wickedness that has served to corrupt and brutalize mankind; and, for my part, I sincerely detest it as I detest everything that is cruel.[2]

We scarcely meet with anything, a few phrases excepted, but what deserves either our abhorrence or our contempt, till we come to the miscellaneous parts of the Bible. In the anonymous publications, the Psalms, and the book of Job, more particularly in the latter, we find a great deal of elevated sentiment reverentially expressed of the power and benignity of the Almighty; but they stand on no higher rank than many other compositions on similar subjects, as well before that time as since.

The Proverbs which are said to be Solomon's, though most probably a collection (because they discover a knowledge of life which his situation excluded him from knowing), are an instructive table of ethics. They are inferior in keenness to the proverbs of the Spaniards, and not more wise and economical than those of the American Franklin.

All the remaining parts of the Bible, generally known by the name of the Prophets, are the works of the Jewish poets and itinerant preachers, who mixed poetry,[3] anecdote, and devotion together — and those works still retain the air and style of poetry, though in translation.

2 Paine's references to the Bible usually denote the Old Testament. — Editors.
3 As there are many readers who do not see that a composition is poetry unless it be in rhyme, it is for their information that I add this note.
Poetry consists principally in two things — imagery and composition. The composition of poetry differs from that of prose in the manner of mixing long and short syllables together. Take a long syllable out of a line of poetry, and put a short one in the room of it, or put a long syllable where a short one should be, and that line will lose its poetical harmony. It will have an effect upon the line like that of misplacing a

There is not, throughout the whole book called the Bible, any word that describes to us what we call a poet, nor any word which describes what we call poetry. The case is that the word *prophet,* to which latter times have affixed a new idea, was the Bible word for poet, and the word *prophesying* meant the art of making poetry. It also meant the art of playing poetry to a tune upon any instrument of music.

We read of prophesying with pipes, tabrets and horns – of prophesying with harps, with psalteries, with cymbals and with every other instrument of music then in fashion. Were we now to speak of prophesying with a fiddle, or with a pipe and tabor, the expression would have no meaning or would appear ridiculous, and to some people contemptuous, because we have changed the meaning of the word.

We are told of Saul being among the *prophets,* and also that he prophesied; but we are not told what *they prophesied* nor what *he prophesied.* The case is, there was nothing to tell; for these prophets were a company of musicians and poets, and Saul joined in the concert, and this was called *prophesying.*

The account given of this affair in the book called Samuel is that Saul met a *company* of prophets; a whole company of them! coming down with a psaltery, a tabret, a pipe and a harp, and that they prophesied, and that he prophesied with them. But it appears afterward that Saul prophesied badly; and that is, he performed his part

---

note in a song. The imagery in those books, called the Prophets, appertains altogether to poetry. It is fictitious, and often extravagant, and not admissible in any other kind of writing than poetry. To show that these writings are composed in poetical numbers, I will take ten syllables, as they stand in the book, and make a line of the same number of syllables, (heroic measure) that shall rhyme with the last word. It will then be seen that the composition of these books is poetical measure. The instance I shall produce is from Isaiah:

> '*Hear, O ye heavens, and give ear, O earth!*'
> 'Tis God himself that calls attention forth.

Another instance I shall quote is from the mournful Jeremiah, to which I shall add two other lines, for the purpose of carrying out the figure, and showing the intention of the poet:

> '*O! that mine head were waters and mine eyes*'
> Were fountains flowing like the liquid skies;
> Then would I give the mighty flood release,
> And weep a deluge for the human race. – Paine.

badly; for it is said, that an *'evil spirit from God'* [4] came upon Saul, and he prophesied.

Now, were there no other passage in the book called the Bible than this to demonstrate to us that we have lost the original meaning of the word *prophesy,* and substituted another meaning in its place, this alone would be sufficient; for it is impossible to use and apply the word *prophesy,* in the place it is here used and applied, if we give to it the sense which latter times have affixed to it. The manner in which it is here used strips it of all religious meaning, and shows that a man might then be a prophet, or he might *prophesy,* as he may now be a poet or a musician, without any regard to the morality or immorality of his character. The word was originally a term of science, promiscuously applied to poetry and music, and not restricted to any subject upon which poetry and music might be exercised.

Deborah and Barak are called prophets, not because they predicted anything, but because they composed the poem or song that bears their name in celebration of an act already done. David is ranked among the prophets, for he was a musician, and was also reputed to be (though perhaps very erroneously) the author of the Psalms. But Abraham, Isaac and Jacob are not called prophets; it does not appear from any accounts we have that they could either sing, play music or make poety.

We are told of the greater and the lesser prophets. They might as well tell us of the greater and the lesser God; for there cannot be degrees in prophesying consistently with its modern sense. But there are degrees in poetry, and therefore the phrase is reconcilable to the case, when we understand by it the greater and the lesser poets.

It is altogether unnecessary, after this, to offer any observations upon what those men, styled prophets, have written. The axe goes at once to the root, by showing that the original meaning of the word has been mistaken and consequently all the inferences that have been drawn from those books, the devotional respect that has been paid to them, and the laboured commentaries that have been written upon them, under that mistaken meaning, are not worth disputing about. In many things, however, the writings of the Jewish poets deserve a

---

4 As those men who call themselves divines and commentators are very fond of puzzling one another, I leave them to contest the meaning of the first part of the phrase, that of *an evil spirit from God.* I keep to my text – I keep to the meaning of the word prophesy. – Paine.

better fate than that of being bound up, as they now are with the trash that accompanies them, under the abused name of the Word of God.

If we permit ourselves to conceive right ideas of things, we must necessarily affix the idea, not only of unchangeableness, but of the utter impossibility of any change taking place, by any means or accident whatever, in that which we would honour with the name of the Word of God; and therefore the Word of God cannot exist in any written or human language.

The continually progressive change to which the meaning of words is subject, the want of a universal language which renders translation necessary, the errors to which translations are again subject, the mistakes of copyists and printers, together with the possibility of wilful alteration, are of themselves evidences that the human language, whether in speech or in print, cannot be the vehicle of the Word of God. The Word of God exists in something else.

Did the book called the Bible excel in purity of ideas and expression all the books that are now extant in the world, I would not take it for my rule of faith, as being the Word of God, because the possibility would nevertheless exist of my being imposed upon. But when I see throughout the greater part of this book scarcely anything but a history of the grossest vices and a collection of the most paltry and contemptible tales, I cannot dishonour my Creator by calling it by His name.

OF THE NEW TESTAMENT

Thus much for the Bible; I now go on to the book called the New Testament. The *New* Testament! that is, the *new* will, as if there could be two wills of the Creator.

Had it been the object or the intention of Jesus Christ to establish a new religion, he would undoubtedly have written the system himself, or *procured it to be written* in his life-time. But there is no publication extant authenticated with his name. All the books called the New Testament were written after his death. He was a Jew by birth and by profession; and he was the Son of God in like manner that every other person is – for the Creator is the Father of All.

The first four books, called Matthew, Mark, Luke and John, do not give a history of the life of Jesus Christ, but only detached anecdotes of him. It appears from these books that the whole time of his being a preacher was not more than eighteen months; and it was only during this short time that those men became acquainted with him. They make mention of him at the age of twelve years, sitting, they say, among the Jewish doctors, asking and answering them questions. As this was several years before their acquaintance with him began, it is most probable they had this anecdote from his parents.

From this time there is no account of him for about sixteen years. Where he lived, or how he employed himself during this interval, is not known. Most probably he was working at his father's trade, which was that of a carpenter. It does not appear that he had any school education and the probability is that he could not write, for his parents were extremely poor, as appears from their not being able to pay for a bed when he was born.

It is somewhat curious that the three persons whose names are the most universally recorded, were of very obscure parentage. Moses was a foundling; Jesus Christ was born in a stable; and Mahomet was a mule driver. The first and last of these men were founders of different systems of religion; but Jesus Christ founded no new system. He called men to the practice of moral virtues and the belief of one God. The great trait in his character is philanthropy.

The manner in which he was apprehended shows that he was not much known at that time; and it shows also, that the meetings he then held with his followers were in secret; and that he had given over or suspended preaching publicly. Judas could not otherwise betray him than by giving information where he was, and pointing him out to the officers that went to arrest him; and the reason for employing and paying Judas to do this could arise only from the cause already mentioned, that of his not being much known and living concealed.

The idea of his concealment not only agrees very ill with his reputed divinity, but associates with it something of pusillanimity; and his being betrayed or, in other words, his being apprehended on the information of one of his followers shows that he did not intend to be apprehended, and consequently that he did not intend to be crucified.

The Christian Mythologists tell us that Christ died for the sins of the world, and that he came on *purpose to die*. Would it not then have been the same if he had died of a fever or of the small-pox, of old age, or of anything else?

The declaratory sentence which, they say, was passed upon Adam, in case he ate of the apple, was not, that *thou shalt surely be crucified,* but, *thou shalt surely die* – the sentence of death, and not the manner of dying. Crucifixion, therefore, or any other particular manner of dying, made no part of the sentence that Adam was to suffer, and consequently, even upon their own tactics, it could make no part of the sentence that Christ was to suffer in the room of Adam. A fever would have done as well as a cross, if there was any occasion for either.

The sentence of death, which they tell us was thus passed upon Adam, must either have meant dying naturally, that is, ceasing to live, or have meant what these Mythologists call damnation; and, consequently, the act of dying on the part of Jesus Christ, must, according to their system, apply as a prevention to one or other of these two *things* happening to Adam and to us.

That it does not prevent our dying is evident, because we all die; and if their accounts of longevity be true, men die faster since the crucifixion than before; and with respect to the second explanation (including with it the *natural death* of Jesus Christ as a substitute for the *eternal death or damnation* of all mankind), it is impertinently representing the Creator as coming off, or revoking the sentence, by a pun or a quibble upon the word *death.*

That manufacturer of quibbles, St Paul, if he wrote the books that bear his name, has helped this quibble on by making another quibble upon the word *Adam.* He makes there to be two Adams; the one who sins in fact and suffers by proxy; the other who sins by proxy and suffers in fact. A religion thus interlarded with quibble, subterfuge and pun has a tendency to instruct its professors in the practice of these arts. They acquire the habit without being aware of the cause.

If Jesus Christ was the being which those Mythologists tell us he was, and that he came into this world to *suffer,* which is a word they sometimes use instead of to *die,* the only real suffering he could have endured would have been *to live.* His existence here was a state of exilement or transportation from heaven, and the way back to his original country was to die. In fine, everything in this strange system is the reverse of what it pretends to be. It is the reverse of truth, and I become so tired of examining into its inconsistencies and absurdities that I hasten to the conclusion of it in order to proceed to something better.

How much or what parts of the books called the New Testament were written by the persons whose names they bear is what we can know nothing of; neither are we certain in what language they were originally written. The matters they now contain may be classed under two heads – anecdote and epistolary correspondence.

The four books already mentioned, Matthew, Mark, Luke and John, are altogether anecdotal. They relate events after they have taken place. They tell what Jesus Christ did and said, and what others did and said to him; and in several instances they relate the same event differently. Revelation is necessarily out of the question with respect to those books; not only because of the disagreement of the writers, but because revelation cannot be applied to the relating of facts by the person who saw them done, nor to the relating or recording of any discourse or conversation by those who heard it. The book called the Acts of the Apostles (an anonymous work) belongs also to the anecdotal part.

All the other parts of the New Testament, except the book of enigmas called the Revelations, are a collection of letters under the name of epistles; and the forgery of letters has been such a common practice in the world that the probability is at least equal, whether they are genuine or forged.

One thing, however, is much less equivocal, which is, that out of the matters contained in those books, together with the assistance of some old stories, the Church has set up a system of religion very contradictory to the character of the person whose name it bears. It has set up a religion of pomp and of revenue, in pretended imitation of a person whose life was humility and poverty.

The invention of a purgatory, and of the releasing of souls therefrom by prayers bought of the church with money; the selling of pardons, dispensations and indulgences, are revenue laws, without bearing that name or carrying that appearance.

But the case nevertheless is that those things derive their origin from the paroxysm of the crucifixion and the theory deduced therefrom, which was that one person could stand in the place of another, and could perform meritorious services for him.

The probability, therefore, is that the whole theory or doctrine of what is called the redemption (which is said to have been accomplished by the act of one person in the room of another) was originally fabricated on purpose to bring forward and build all those secondary and pecuniary redemptions upon; and that the passages in the books upon which the idea or theory of redemption is built have been manufactured and fabricated for that purpose.

Why are we to give this Church credit when she tells us that those books are genuine in every part, any more than we give her credit for everything else she has told us, or for the miracles she says she has performed? That she *could* fabricate writings is certain, because she could write; and the composition of the writings in question is of that kind that anybody might do it; and that she *did* fabricate them is not more inconsistent with probability than that she should tell us, as she has done, that she could and did work miracles.

Since, then, no external evidence can, at this long distance of time, be produced to prove whether the Church fabricated the doctrine called redemption or not (for such evidence whether for or against, would be subject to the same suspicion of being fabricated), the case can only be referred to the internal evidence which the thing carries of itself; and this affords a very strong presumption of its being a fabrication. For the internal evidence is that the theory or doctrine of redemption has for its basis an idea of pecuniary justice and not that of moral justice.

If I owe a person money and cannot pay him, and he threatens to put me in prison, another person can take the debt upon himself and pay it for me; but if I have committed a crime, every circumstance of the case is changed; moral justice cannot take the innocent for the guilty, even if the innocent would offer itself. To suppose justice to do this is to destroy the principle of its existence, which is the thing itself; it is then no longer justice, it is indiscriminate revenge. This single reflection will show that the doctrine of redemption is founded on a mere pecuniary idea corresponding to that of a debt which another person might pay; and as this pecuniary idea corresponds again with the system of second redemption, obtained through the means of money given to the church for pardons, the probability is that the same persons fabricated both the one and the other of those theories; and that in truth there is no such thing as redemption – that it is fabulous, and that man stands in the same relative condition with his

Maker as he ever did stand since man existed, and that it is his greatest consolation to think so.

Let him believe this, and he will live more consistently and morally than by any other system; it is by his being taught to contemplate himself as an outlaw, as an outcast, as a beggar, as a mumper, as one thrown, as it were, on a dunghill at an immense distance from his Creator, and who must make his approaches by creeping and cringing to intermediate beings, that he conceives either a contemptuous disregard for everything under the name of religion, or becomes indifferent, or turns what he calls devout.

In the latter case, he consumes his life in grief, or the affectation of it; his prayers are reproaches; his humility is ingratitude; he calls himself a worm, and the fertile earth a dunghill; and all the blessings of life by the thankless name of vanities; he despises the choicest gift of God to man, the GIFT OF REASON; and having endeavoured to force upon himself the belief of a system against which reason revolts, he ungratefully calls it *human reason,* as if man could give reason to himself.

Yet, with all this strange appearance of humility and this contempt for human reason, he ventures into the boldest presumptions; he finds fault with everything; his selfishness is never satisfied; his ingratitude is never at an end.

He takes on himself to direct the Almighty what to do, even in the government of the universe; he prays dictatorially; when it is sunshine, he prays for rain, and when it is rain, he prays for sunshine; he follows the same idea in everything that he prays for; for what is the amount of all his prayers but an attempt to make the Almighty change His mind, and act otherwise than He does? It is as if he were to say: Thou knowest not so well as I.

DEFINING THE TRUE REVELATION

But some, perhaps, will say: Are we to have no Word of God – no revelation? I answer, Yes; there is a Word of God; there is a revelation.

THE WORD OF GOD IS THE CREATION WE BEHOLD and it is in *this word,* which no human invention can counterfeit or alter, that God speaketh universally to man.

Human language is local and changeable, and is therefore incapable of being used as the means of unchangeable and universal information. The idea that God sent Jesus Christ to publish, as they say, the glad tidings to all nations, from one end of the earth unto the other, is consistent only with the ignorance of those who knew nothing of the extent of the world, and who believed, as those world-saviours believed, and continued to believe for several centuries (and that in contradiction to the discoveries of philosophers and the experience of navigators), that the earth was flat like a trencher, and that man might walk to the end of it.

But how was Jesus Christ to make anything known to all nations? He could speak but one language, which was Hebrew, and there are in the world several hundred languages. Scarcely any two nations speak the same language, or understand each other; and as to translations, every man who knows anything of languages knows that it is impossible to translate from one language into another, not only without losing a great part of the original, but frequently mistaking the sense; and besides all this, the art of printing was wholly unknown at the time Christ lived.

It is always necessary that the means that are to accomplish any end be equal to the accomplishment of that end, or the end cannot be accomplished. It is in this that the difference between finite and infinite power and wisdom discovers itself. Man frequently fails in accomplishing his ends, from a natural inability of the power to the purpose, and frequently from the want of wisdom to apply power properly. But it is impossible for infinite power and wisdom to fail as man faileth. The means it uses are always equal to the end; but human language, more especially as there is not an universal language, is incapable of being used as an universal means of unchangeable and uniform information, and therefore it is not the means that God uses in manifesting himself universally to man.

It is only in the CREATION that all our ideas and conceptions of a *Word of God* can unite. The Creation speaks a universal language, independently of human speech or human language, multiplied and various as they be. It is an ever-existing original, which every man can read. It cannot be forged; it cannot be counterfeited; it cannot be lost; it cannot be altered; it cannot be suppressed. It does not depend upon the will of man whether it shall be published or not; it publishes itself from one end of the earth to the other. It preaches to all nations and to all worlds; and this *Word of God* reveals to man all that is necessary for man to know of God.

Do we want to contemplate His power? We see it in the immensity of the creation. Do we want to contemplate His wisdom? We see it in the unchangeable order by which the incomprehensible whole is governed. Do we want to contemplate His munificence? We see it in the abundance with which He fills the earth. Do we want to contemplate His mercy? We see it in His not withholding that abundance even from the unthankful. In fine, do we want to know that God is? Search not the book called the Scripture, which any human hand might make, but the Scripture called the creation.

CONCERNING GOD, AND THE LIGHTS CAST ON HIS EXISTENCE AND ATTRIBUTES BY THE BIBLE

The only idea man can affix to the name of God is that of a *first cause*, the cause of all things. And incomprehensible and difficult as it is for a man to conceive what a first cause is, he arrives at the belief of it from the tenfold greater difficulty of disbelieving it.

It is difficult beyond description to conceive that space can have no end; but it is more difficult to conceive an end. It is difficult beyond the power of man to conceive an eternal duration of what we call time; but it is more impossible to conceive a time when there shall be no time.

In like manner of reasoning, everything we behold carries in itself the internal evidence that it did not make itself. Every man is an evidence to himself that he did not make himself; neither could his father make himself, nor his grandfather, nor any of his race; neither could any tree, plant or animal make itself; and it is the conviction arising from this evidence that carries us on, as it were, by necessity to the belief of a first cause eternally existing, of a nature totally different to any material existence we know of, and by the power of which all things exist; and this first cause man calls God.

It is only by the exercise of reason that man can discover God. Take away that reason, and he would be incapable of understanding anything; and, in this case, it would be just as consistent to read even the book called the Bible to a horse as to a man. How, then, is it that people pretend to reject reason?

Almost the only parts of the book called the Bible that convey to us any idea of God are some chapters in Job and the 19th Psalm; I recollect no other. Those parts are true *deistical* compositions, for they treat of the *Deity* through His works. They take the book of creation as the Word of God, they refer to no other book, and all the inferences they make are drawn from that volume.

I insert in this place the 19th Psalm, as paraphrased into English verse by Addison. I recollect not the prose, and where I write this I have not the opportunity of seeing it.

> The spacious firmament on high,
> With all the blue ethereal sky,
> And spangled heavens, a shining frame
> Their great original proclaim.
> The unwearied sun, from day to day,
> Does his Creator's power display;
> And publishes to every land
> The work of an Almighty hand.
>
> Soon as the evening shades prevail,
> The moon takes up the wondrous tale,
> And nightly to the list'ning earth
> Repeats the story of her birth;
> While all the stars that round her burn,
> And all the planets in their turn,
> Confirm the tidings as they roll,
> And spread the truth from pole to pole.
>
> What, though in solemn silence all
> Move round this dark, terrestrial ball?
> What though no real voice, nor sound,
> Amidst their radiant orbs be found?
> In reason's ear they all rejoice
> And utter forth a glorious voice,
> Forever singing, as they shine,
> THE HAND THAT MADE US IS DIVINE.

What more does man want to know than that the hand or power that made these things is divine, in omnipotent? Let him believe this with the force it is impossible to repel, if he permits his reason to act, and his rule of moral life will follow of course.

The allusions in Job have, all of them, the same tendency with this

Psalm; that of deducing or proving a truth that would be otherwise unknown, from truths already known.

I recollect not enough of the passages in Job to insert them correctly; but there is one occurs to me that is applicable to the subject I am speaking upon. 'Canst thou by searching find out God? Canst thou find out the Almighty to perfection?'

I know not how the printers have pointed this passage, for I keep no Bible; but it contains two distinct questions that admit of distinct answers.

First, – Canst thou by searching find out God? Yes; because, in the first place, I know I did not make myself, and yet I have existence; and by *searching* into the nature of other things, I find that no other thing could make itself; and yet millions of other things exist; therefore it is, that I know, by positive conclusion resulting from this search, that there is a power superior to all those things, and that power is God.

Secondly, – Canst thou find out the Almighty to *perfection*? No; not only because the power and wisdom He has manifested in the structure of the creation that I behold is to me incomprehensible, but because even this manifestation, great as it is, is probably but a small display of that immensity of power and wisdom by which millions of other worlds, to me invisible by their distance, were created and continue to exist.

It is evident that both these questions were put to the reason of the person to whom they are supposed to have been addressed; and it is only by admitting the first question to be answered affirmatively that the second could follow. It would have been unnecessary, and even absurd, to have put a second question, more difficult than the first, if the first question had been answered negatively.

The two questions have different objects; the first refers to the existence of God; the second to His attributes; reason can discover the one, but it falls infinitely short in discovering the whole of the other.

I recollect not a single passage in all the writings ascribed to the men called apostles that conveys any idea of what God is. Those writings are chiefly controversial; and the subjects they dwell upon, that of a man dying in agony on a cross, is better suited to the gloomy genius of a monk in a cell, by whom it is not impossible they were written, than to any man breathing the open air of the creation.

The only passage that occurs to me that has any reference to the works of God, by which only His power and wisdom can be known, is related to have been spoken by Jesus Christ as a remedy against distrustful care. 'Behold the lilies of the field, they toil not, neither do they spin.' This, however, is far inferior to the allusions in Job and in the 19th Psalm; but it is similar in idea, and the modesty of the imagery is correspondent to the modesty of the man.

TRUE THEOLOGY AND THAT OF SUPERSTITION

As to the Christian system of faith, it appears to me a species of Atheism – a sort of religious denial of God. It professes to believe in a man rather than in God. It is a compound made up chiefly of Manism with but little Deism, and is as near to Atheism as twilight is to darkness. It introduces between man and his Maker an opaque body, which it calls a Redeemer, as the moon introduces her opaque self between the earth and the sun, and it produces by this means a religious, or an irreligious, eclipse of light. It has put the whole orbit of reason into shade.

The effect of this obscurity has been that of turning everything upside down, and representing it in reverse, and among the revolutions it has thus magically produced it has made a revolution in theology.

That which is now called natural philosophy, embracing the whole circle of science, of which astronomy occupies the chief place, is the study of the works of God, and of the power and wisdom of God in His works and is the true theology.

As to the theology that is now studied in its place, it is the study of human opinions and of human fancies *concerning* God. It is not the study of God Himself in the works that He has made, but in the works or writings that man has made; and it is not among the least of the mischiefs that the Christian system has done to the world, that it has abandoned the original and beautiful system of theology, like a beautiful innocent, to distress and reproach, to make room for the hag of superstition.

The Book of Job and the 19th Psalm, which even the Church admits to be more ancient than the chronological order in which they stand in the book called the Bible, are theological orations conformable to the original system of theology.

The internal evidence of those orations proves to a demonstration that the study and contemplation of the works of creation, and of the power and wisdom of God, revealed and manifested in those works, made a great part in the religious devotion of the times in which they were written; and it was this devotional study and contemplation that led to the discovery of the principles upon which what are now called sciences are established; and it is to the discovery of these principles that almost all the arts that contribute to the convenience of human life owe their existence.

Every principal art has some science for its parent, though the person who mechanically performs the work does not always, and but very seldom, perceive the connection.

It is a fraud of the Christian system to call the sciences *human invention*; it is only the application of them that is human. Every science has for its basis a system of principles as fixed and unalterable as those by which the universe is regulated and governed. Man cannot make principles, he can only discover them.

For example: Every person who looks at an almanac sees an account when an eclipse will take place, and he sees also that it never fails to take place according to the account there given. This shows that man is acquainted with the laws by which the heavenly bodies move. But it would be something worse than ignorance, were any church on earth to say that those laws are a human invention.

It would also be ignorance, or something worse, to say that the scientific principles by the aid of which man is enabled to calculate and foreknow when an eclipse will take place are a human invention. Man cannot invent anything that is eternal and immutable; and the scientific principles he employs for this purpose must be, and are of necessity, as eternal and immutable as the laws by which the heavenly bodies move, or they could not be used as they are to ascertain the time when, and the manner how, an eclipse will take place.

The scientific principles that man employs to obtain the foreknowledge of an eclipse, or of anything else relating to the motion of the heavenly bodies, are contained chiefly in that part of science which is called trigonometry, or the properties of a triangle, which, when applied to the study of the heavenly bodies, is called astronomy; when applied to direct the course of a ship on the ocean it is called navigation; when applied to the construction of figures drawn by rule and compass it is called geometry; when applied to the construction of plans or edifices it is called architecture; when applied to the measurement of any portion of the surface of the earth it is called land surveying. In fine, it is the soul of science; it is an eternal truth; it contains the *mathematical demonstration* of which man speaks, and the extent of its uses is unknown.

It may be said that man can make or draw a triangle, and therefore a triangle is a human invention.

But the triangle, when drawn, is no other than the image of the principle; it is a delineation to the eye, and from thence to the mind, of a principle that would otherwise be imperceptible. The triangle does not make the principle, any more than a candle taken into a room that was dark makes the chairs and tables that before were invisible. All the properties of a triangle exist independently of the figure, and existed before any triangle was drawn or thought of by man. Man had no more to do in the formation of these properties or principles than he had to do in making the laws by which the heavenly bodies move; and therefore the one must have the same divine origin as the other.

In the same manner, as it may be said, that man can make a triangle, so also, may it be said, he can make the mechanical instrument called a lever; but the principle by which the lever acts is a thing distinct from the instrument, and would exist if the instrument did not; it attaches itself to the instrument after it is made; the instrument, therefore, cannot act otherwise than it does act; neither can all the efforts of human invention make it act otherwise – that which, in all such cases, man calls the *effect* is no other than the principle itself rendered perceptible to the senses.

Since, then, man cannot make principles, from whence did he gain a knowledge of them, so as to be able to apply them, not only to things on earth, but to ascertain the motion of bodies so immensely distant from him as all the heavenly bodies are? From whence, I ask, *could* he gain that knowledge, but from the study of the true theology?

It is the structure of the universe that has taught this knowledge to man. That structure is an ever-existing exhibition of every principle upon which every part of mathematical science is founded. The offspring of this science is mechanics; for mechanics is no other than the principles of science applied practically.

The man who proportions the several parts of a mill uses the same scientific principles as if he had the power of constructing a universe; but as he cannot give to matter that invisible agency by which all the component parts of the immense machine of the universe have influence upon each other and act in motional unison together, without any apparent contact, and to which man has given the name of attraction, gravitation and repulsion, he supplies the place of that agency by the humble imitation of teeth and cogs.

All the parts of a man's microcosm must visibly touch; but could he gain a knowledge of that agency so as to be able to apply it in practice we might then say that another *canonical book* of the Word of God had been discovered.

If man could alter the properties of the lever, so also could he alter the properties of the triangle, for a lever (taking that sort of lever which is called a steelyard, for the sake of explanation) forms, when in motion, a triangle. The line it descends from (one point of that line being in the fulcrum), the line it descends to, and the chord of the arc which the end of the lever describes in the air, are the three sides of a triangle.

The other arm of the lever describes also a triangle; and the corresponding sides of those two triangles, calculated scientifically, or measured geometrically, and also the sines, tangents and secants generated from the angles, and geometrically measured, have the same proportions to each other as the different weights have that will balance each other on the lever, leaving the weight of the lever out of the case.

It may also be said that man can make a wheel and axis; that he can put wheels of different magnitudes together, and produce a mill. Still the case comes back to the same point, which is that he did not make the principle that gives the wheels those powers. That principle is as unalterable as in the former cases, or rather it is the same principle under a different appearance to the eye.

The power that two wheels of different magnitudes have upon each other is in the same proportion as if the semi-diameter of the two wheels were joined together and made into that kind of lever I have described, suspended at the part where the semi-diameters join; for the two wheels, scientifically considered, are no other than the two circles generated by the motion of the compound lever.

It is from the study of the true theology that all our knowledge of science is derived, and it is from that knowledge that all the arts have originated.

The Almighty Lecturer, by displaying the principles of science in the structure of the universe, has invited man to study and to imitation. It is as if He had said to the inhabitants of this globe that we call ours, 'I have made an earth for man to dwell upon, and I have rendered the starry heavens visible, to teach him science and the arts. He can now provide for his own comfort, AND LEARN FROM MY MUNIFICENCE TO ALL, TO BE KIND TO EACH OTHER.'

Of what use is it, unless it be to teach man something, that his eye is endowed with the power of beholding to an incomprehensible distance an immensity of worlds revolving in the ocean of space? Of what use is it that this immensity of worlds is visible to man? What has man to do with the Pleiades, with Orion, with Sirius, with the star he calls the North Star, with the moving orbs he has named Saturn, Jupiter, Mars, Venus, and Mercury, if no uses are to follow from their being visible? A less power of vision would have been sufficient for man, if the immensity he now possesses were given only to waste itself, as it were, on an immense desert of space glittering with shows.

It is only by contemplating what he calls the starry heavens, as the book and school of science, that he discovers any use in their being visible to him, or any advantage resulting from his immensity of vision. But when he contemplates the subject of this light, he sees an additional motive for saying, that *nothing was made in vain*; for in vain would be this power of vision if it taught man nothing.

CHRISTIANITY AND EDUCATION, IN THE LIGHT OF HISTORY

As the Christian system of faith has made a revolution in theology, so also has it made a revolution in the state of learning. That which is now called learning was not learning originally. Learning does not consist, as the schools now make it consist, in the knowledge of languages, but in the knowledge of things to which language gives names.

The Greeks were a learned people, but learning with them did not consist in speaking Greek any more than in a Roman's speaking Latin, or a Frenchman's speaking French, or an Englishman's speaking English. From what we know of the Greeks, it does not appear that they knew or studied any language but their own, and this was one cause of their becoming so learned; it afforded them more time to apply themselves to better studies. The schools of the Greeks were schools of science and philosophy, and not of languages; and it is in the knowledge of the things that science and philosophy teach, that learning consists.

Almost all the scientific learning that now exists came to us from the Greeks, or the people who spoke the Greek language. It, therefore, became necessary to the people of other nations who spoke a different language that some among them should learn the Greek language in order that the learning of the Greeks might be made known in those nations, by translating the Greek books of science and philosophy into the mother tongue of each nation.

The study, therefore, of the Greek language (and in the same manner for the Latin) was no other than the drudgery business of a linguist; and the language thus obtained was no other than the means, as it were the tools, employed to obtain the learning the Greeks had. It made no part of the learning itself, and was so distinct from it as to make it exceedingly probable that the persons who had studied Greek sufficiently to translate those works, such, for instance, as Euclid's 'Elements', did not understand any of the learning the works contained.

As there is now nothing new to be learned from the dead languages, all the useful books being already translated, the languages are become useless, and the time expended in teaching and learning them is wasted. So far as the study of languages may contribute to the progress and communication of knowledge (for it has nothing to do with the *creation* of knowledge), it is only in the living languages that new knowledge is to be found; and certain it is that, in general, a youth will learn more of a living language in one year than of a dead language in seven, and it is but seldom that the teacher knows much of it himself.

The difficulty of learning the dead languages does not arise from any superior abstruseness in the languages themselves, but in their *being dead,* and the pronunciation entirely lost. It would be the same with any other language when it becomes dead. The best Greek linguist that now exists does not understand Greek so well as a Grecian ploughman did or a Grecian milkmaid; and the same for the Latin, compared with a ploughman or milkmaid of the Romans; and with respect to pronunciation and idiom, not so well as the cows that she milked. It would therefore be advantageous to the state of learning to abolish the study of dead languages and to make learning consist, as it originally did, in scientific knowledge.

The apology that is sometimes made for continuing to teach the dead languages is that they are taught at a time when a child is not capable of exerting any other mental faculty than that of memory; but that is altogether erroneous. The human mind has a natural disposition to scientific knowledge and to the things connected with it.

The first and favourite amusement of a child, even before it begins to play, is that of imitating the works of man. It builds houses with cards or sticks: it navigates the little ocean of a bowl of water with a paper boat, or dams the stream of a gutter and contrives something which it calls a mill; and it interests itself in the fate of its works with a care that resembles affection. It afterwards goes to school, where its genius is killed by the barren study of a dead language, and the philosopher is lost in the linguist.

But the apology that is now made for continuing to teach the dead languages could not be the cause, at first, of cutting down learning to the narrow and humble sphere of linguistry; the cause, therefore, must be sought for elsewhere. In all researches of this kind the best evidence that can be produced is the internal evidence the thing carries with itself, and the evidence of circumstances that unite with it; both of which, in this case, are not difficult to be discovered.

Putting then aside, as a matter of distinct consideration, the outrage offered to the moral justice of God by supposing Him to make the innocent suffer for the guilty, and also the loose morality and low contrivance of supposing Him to change Himself into the shape of a man, in order to make an excuse to Himself for not executing His supposed sentence upon Adam – putting, I say, those things aside as matter of distinct consideration, it is certain that what is called the Christian system of faith, including in it the whimsical account of the Creation – the strange story of Eve – the snake and the apple – the ambiguous idea of a man-god – the corporeal idea of the death of a god – the mythological idea of a family of gods, and the Christian system of arithmetic, that three are one, and one is three, are all irreconcilable, not only to the divine gift of reason that God has given to man, but to the knowledge that man gains of the power and wisdom of God, by the aid of the sciences and by studying the structure of the universe that God has made.

The setters-up, therefore, and the advocates of the Christian system of faith could not but foresee that the continually progressive knowledge that man would gain, by the aid of science, of the power and wisdom of God, manifested in the structure of the universe and in all the works of creation, would militate against, and call into question, the truth of their system of faith; and therefore it became necessary to their purpose to cut learning down to a size less dangerous to their project, and this they effected by restricting the idea of learning to the dead study of dead languages.

They not only rejected the study of science out of the Christian schools, but they persecuted it, and it is only within about the last two centuries that the study has been revived. So late as 1610, Galileo, a Florentine, discovered and introduced the use of telescopes, and by applying them to observe the motions and appearances of the heavenly bodies afforded additional means for ascertaining the true structure of the universe.

Instead of being esteemed for those discoveries, he was sentenced to renounce them, or the opinions resulting from them, as a damnable heresy. And, prior to that time, Virgilius was condemned to be burned for asserting the antipodes, or in other words that the earth was a globe, and habitable in every part where there was land; yet the truth of this is now too well known even to be told.

If the belief of errors not morally bad did no mischief, it would make no part of the moral duty of man to oppose and remove them. There was no moral ill in believing the earth was flat like a trencher, any more than there was moral virtue in believing it was round like a globe; neither was there any moral ill in believing that the Creator made no other world than this, any more than there was moral virtue in believing that He made millions and that the infinity of space is filled with worlds.

But when a system of religion is made to grow out of a supposed system of creation that is not true, and to unite itself therewith in a manner almost inseparable therefrom, the case assumes an entirely different ground. It is then that errors not morally bad become fraught with the same mischiefs as if they were. It is then that the truth, though otherwise indifferent itself, becomes an essential by becoming the criterion that either confirms by corresponding evidence, or denies by contradictory evidence the reality of the religion itself.

In this view of the case, it is the moral duty of man to obtain every possible evidence that the structure of the heavens or any other part of creation affords, with respect to systems of religion. But this, the supporters or partisans of the Christian system, as if dreading the result, incessantly opposed, and not only rejected the sciences, but persecuted the professors.

Had Newton or Descartes lived three or four hundred years ago and pursued their studies as they did, it is most probable they would not have lived to finish them; and had Franklin drawn lightning from the clouds at the same time, it would have been at the hazard of expiring for it in the flames.

Later times have laid all the blame upon the Goths and the Vandals; but, however unwilling the partisans of the Christian system may be to believe or to acknowledge it, it is nevertheless true that the age of ignorance commenced with the Christian system. There was more knowledge in the world before that period than for many centuries afterwards; and as to religious knowledge, the Christian system, as already said, was only another species of mythology, and the mythology to which it succeeded was a corruption of an ancient system of theism.[5]

5 It is impossible for us now to know at what time the heathen mythology began; but it is certain, from the internal evidence that it carries, that it did not begin in the same state or condition in which it ended. All the gods of that mythology, except Saturn, were of modern invention. The supposed reign of Saturn was prior to that which is called the heathen mythology, and was so far a species of theism, that it admitted the belief of only one God. Saturn is supposed to have abdicated the government in favour of his three sons and one daughter, Jupiter, Pluto, Neptune and Juno; after this, thousands of other gods and demi-gods were imaginarily created, and the calendar of gods increased as fast as the calendar of saints and the calendars of courts have increased since.

All the corruptions that have taken place in theology and in religion have been produced by admitting of what man calls *revealed religion*. The Mythologists pretended to more revealed religion than the Christians do. They had their oracles and their priests, who were supposed to receive and deliver the word of God verbally, on almost all occasions.

Since then, all corruptions, down from Moloch to modern predestinarianism, and the human sacrifices of the heathens to the Christian sacrifice of the Creator, have been produced by admitting of what is called *revealed religion*. The most effectual means to prevent all such evils and impositions is not to admit of any other revelation than that which is manifested in the book of creation, and to contemplate the creation as the only true and real Word of God that ever did or ever will exist; and that everything else, called the Word of God, is fable and imposition. – Paine.

It is owing to this long interregnum of science, *and to no other cause*, that we have now to look back through a vast chasm of many hundred years to the respectable characters we call the ancients. Had the progression of knowledge gone on proportionably with that stock that before existed, that chasm would have been filled up with characters rising superior in knowledge to each other; and those ancients we now so much admire would have appeared respectably in the background of the scene. But the Christian system laid all waste; and if we take our stand about the beginning of the sixteenth century, we look back through that long chasm to the times of the ancients, as over a vast sandy desert, in which not a shrub appears to intercept the vision to the fertile hills beyond.

It is an inconsistency scarcely possible to be credited that anything should exist, under the name of a religion, that held it to be *irreligious* to study and contemplate the structure of the universe that God has made. But the fact is too well established to be denied. The event that served more than any other to break the first link in this long chain of despotic ignorance is that known by the name of the Reformation by Luther.

From that time, though it does not appear to have made any part of the intention of Luther, or of those who are called reformers, the sciences began to revive, and liberality, their natural associate, began to appear. This was the only public good the Reformation did; for with respect to religious good it might as well not have taken place. The mythology still continued the same, and a multiplicity of National Popes grew out of the downfall of the Pope of Christendom.

COMPARING CHRISTIANISM WITH PANTHEISM

Having thus shown from the internal evidence of things the cause that produced a change in the state of learning, and the motive for substituting the study of the dead languages in the place of the sciences, I proceed, in addition to the several observations already made in the former part of this work, to compare, or rather to confront, the evidence that the structure of the universe affords with the Christian system of religion; but, as I cannot begin this part better than by referring to the ideas that occurred to me at an early part of life, and which I doubt not have occurred in some degree to almost every person at one time or other, I shall state what those ideas were and add thereto such other matter as shall arise out of the subject, giving to the whole, by way of preface, a short introduction.

My father being of the Quaker profession, it was my good fortune to have an exceedingly good moral education, and a tolerable stock of useful learning. Though I went to the grammar school, I did not learn Latin, not only because I had no inclination to learn languages, but because of the objection the Quakers have against the books in which the language is taught. But this did not prevent me from being acquainted with the subjects of all the Latin books used in the school.

The natural bent of my mind was to science. I had some turn, and I believe some talent, for poetry; but this I rather repressed than encouraged, as leading too much into the field of imagination. As soon as I was able I purchased a pair of globes, and attended the philosophical lectures of Martin and Ferguson, and became afterwards acquainted with Dr Bevis, of the society called the Royal Society, then living in the Temple, and an excellent astronomer.

I had no disposition for what is called politics. It presented to my mind no other idea than as contained in the word Jockeyship. When, therefore, I turned my thoughts towards matter of government I had to form a system for myself that accorded with the moral and philosophic principles in which I have been educated. I saw, or at least I thought I saw, a vast scene opening itself to the world in the affairs of America, and it appeared to me that unless the Americans changed the plan they were pursuing with respect to the government of England, and declared themselves independent, they would not only involve themselves in a multiplicity of new difficulties, but shut out the prospect that was then offering itself to mankind through their means. It was from these motives that I published the work known by the name of *Common Sense*, which was the first work I ever did publish; and so far as I can judge of myself, I believe I should never have been known in the world as an author on any subject whatever had it not been for the affairs of America. I wrote *Common Sense* the latter end of the year 1775, and published it the first of January, 1776. Independence was declared the fourth of July following.

Any person who has made observations on the state and progress of the human mind by observing his own cannot but have observed that there are two distinct classes of what are called thoughts – those that we produce in ourselves by reflection and the act of thinking, and those that bolt into the mind of their own accord. I have always made it a rule to treat these voluntary visitors with civility, taking care to examine, as well as I was able, if they were worth entertaining, and it is from them I have acquired almost all the knowledge that I have. As to the learning that any person gains from school education, it serves only, like a small capital, to put him in a way of beginning learning for himself afterwards.

Every person of learning is finally his own teacher, the reason of which is that principles, being a distinct quality to circumstances, cannot be impressed upon the memory; their place of mental residence is the understanding and they are never so lasting as when they begin by conception. Thus much for the introductory part.

From the time I was capable of conceiving an idea and acting upon it by reflection, I either doubted the truth of the Christian system or thought it to be a strange affair; I scarcely knew which it was, but I well remember, when about seven or eight years of age, hearing a sermon read by a relation of mine, who was a great devotee of the Church, upon the subject of what is called *redemption by the death of the Son of God*.

After the sermon was ended, I went into the garden, and as I was going down the garden steps (for I perfectly recollect the spot) I revolted at the recollection of what I had heard, and thought to myself that it was making God Almighty act like a passionate man who killed His son when He could not revenge Himself in any other way, and, as I was sure a man would be hanged who did such a thing, I could not see for what purpose they preached such sermons.

This was not one of that kind of thoughts that had anything in it of childish levity; it was to me a serious reflection, arising from the idea I had that God was too good to do such an action, and also too almighty to be under any necessity of doing it. I believe in the same manner at this moment; and I moreover believe that any system of religion that has anything in it that shocks the mind of a child cannot be a true system.

It seems as if parents of the Christian profession were ashamed to tell their children anything about the principles of their religion. They sometimes instruct them in morals and talk to them of the goodness of what they call Providence, for the Christian mythology has five deities – there is God the Father, God the Son, God the Holy

Ghost, the God Providence and the Goddess Nature. But the Christian story of God the Father putting His son to death, or employing people to do it (for that is the plain language of the story) cannot be told by a parent to a child; and to tell him that it was done to make mankind happier and better is making the story still worse − as if mankind could be improved by the example of murder; and to tell him that all this is a mystery is only making an excuse for the incredibility of it.

How different is this to the pure and simple profession of Deism! The true Deist has but one Deity, and his religion consists in contemplating the power, wisdom and benignity of the Deity in His works, and in endeavouring to imitate Him in everything moral, scientifical and mechanical.

The religion that approaches the nearest of all others to true Deism, in the moral and benign part thereof, is that professed by the Quakers; but they have contracted themselves too much by leaving the works of God out of their system. Though I reverence their philanthropy, I cannot help smiling at the conceit that if the taste of a Quaker could have been consulted at the Creation what a silent and drab-coloured Creation it would have been! Not a flower would have blossomed its gayeties, nor a bird been permitted to sing.

Quitting these reflections, I proceed to other matters. After I had made myself master of the use of the globes and of the orrery,[6] and conceived an idea of the infinity of space, and the eternal divisibility of matter, and obtained at least a general knowledge of what is called natural philosophy, I began to compare, or, as I have before said, to confront the eternal evidence those things afford with the Christian system of faith.

Though it is not a direct article of the Christian system, that this world that we inhabit is the whole of the habitable creation, yet it is so worked up therewith, from what is called the Mosaic account of the Creation, the story of Eve and the apple, and the counterpart of

6 As this book may fall into the hands of persons who do not know what an orrery is, it is for their information I add this note, as the name gives no idea of the uses of the thing. The orrery has its name from the person who invented it. It is a machinery of clock-work, representing the universe in miniature, and in which the revolution of the earth round itself and round the sun, the revolution of the moon round the earth, the revolution of the planets round the sun, their relative distances from the sun, as the centre of the whole system, their relative distances from each other and their different magnitudes, are represented as they really exist in what we call the heavens. − Paine.

that story, the death of the Son of God, that to believe otherwise, that is, to believe that God created a plurality of worlds, at least as numerous as what we call stars, renders the Christian system of faith at once little and ridiculous, and scatters it in the mind like feathers in the air. The two beliefs cannot be held together in the same mind, and he who thinks that he believes both has thought but little of either.

Though the belief of a plurality of worlds was familiar to the ancients, it is only within the last three centuries that the extent and dimensions of this globe that we inhabit have been ascertained. Several vessels following the tract of the ocean have sailed entirely around the world, as a man may march in a circle and come round by the contrary side of the circle to the spot he set out from.

The circular dimensions of our world, in the widest part, as a man would measure the widest round of an apple or ball, is only twenty-five thousand and twenty English miles, reckoning sixty-nine miles and a half to an equatorial degree, and may be sailed round in the space of about three years.[7]

A world of this extent may, at first thought, appear to us to be great; but if we compare it with the immensity of space in which it is suspended, like a bubble or balloon in the air, it is infinitely less in proportion than the smallest grain of sand is to the size of the world, or the finest particle of dew to the whole ocean, and is therefore but small; and, as will be hereafter shown, is only one of a system of worlds of which the universal creation is composed.

It is not difficult to gain some faint idea of the immensity of space in which this and all other worlds are suspended if we follow a progression of ideas. When we think of the size or dimensions of a room our ideas limit themselves to the walls, and there they stop; but when our eye or our imagination darts into space, that is, when it looks upward into what we call the open air, we cannot conceive any walls or boundaries it can have, and if for the sake of resting our ideas we suppose a boundary, the question immediately renews itself, and asks what is beyond that boundary? — and in the same manner, what is beyond the next boundary? And so on till the fatigued imagination returns and says, *There is no end.* Certainly, then, the

7 Allowing a ship to sail, on an average, three miles in an hour, she would sail entirely round the world in less than one year, if she could sail in a direct circle; but she is obliged to follow the course of the ocean.   Paine.

Creator was not pent for room when He made this world no larger than it is, and we have to seek the reason in something else.

If we take a survey of our own world, or rather of this of which the Creator has given us the use as our portion of the immense system of creation, we find every part of it – the earth, the waters, and the air that surrounds it – filled, and, as it were, crowded with life, down from the largest animals that we know of to the smallest insects the naked eye can behold, and from thence to others still smaller, and totally invisible without the assistance of the microscope. Every tree, every plant, every leaf serves not only as a habitation but as a world to some numerous race, till animal existence becomes so exceedingly refined that the effluvia of a blade of grass would be food for thousands.

Since, then, no part of our earth is left unoccupied, why is it to be supposed that the immensity of space is a naked void, lying in eternal waste? There is room for millions of worlds as large or larger than ours, and each of them millions of miles apart from each other. Having now arrived at this point, if we carry our ideas only one thought further, we shall see, perhaps, the true reason, at least a very good reason for our happiness, why the Creator, instead of making one immense world extending over an immense quantity of space, has preferred dividing that quantity of matter into several distinct and separate worlds, which we call planets, of which our earth is one. But before I explain my ideas upon this subject, it is necessary (not for the sake of those who already know, but for those who do not) to show what the system of the universe is.

THE PLAN AND ORDER OF THE UNIVERSE

That part of the universe that is called the solar system (meaning the system of worlds to which our earth belongs, and of which Sol, or in English language, the Sun, is the centre) consists, besides the Sun, of six distinct orbs, or planets, or worlds, besides the secondary bodies, called the satellites or moons, of which our earth has one that attends her in her annual revolution around the Sun, in like manner as the other satellites or moons attend the planets or worlds to which they severally belong, as may be seen by the assistance of the telescope.

The Sun is the centre, round which those six worlds or planets revolve at different distances therefrom, and in circles concentric to each other. Each world keeps constantly in nearly the same track round the Sun, and continues, at the same time, turning round itself in nearly an upright position, as a top turns round itself when it is spinning on the ground, and leans a little sideways.

It is this leaning of the earth (23½ degrees) that occasions summer and winter, and the different length of days and nights. If the earth turned round itself in a position perpendicular to the plane or level of the circle it moves in around the Sun, as a top turns round when it stands erect on the ground, the days and nights would be always of the same length, twelve hours day and twelve hours night, and the seasons would be uniformly the same throughout the year.

Every time that a planet (our earth for example) turns round itself, it makes what we call day and night; and every time it goes entirely round the Sun it makes what we call a year; consequently our world turns three hundred and sixty-five times round itself in going once round the Sun.[8]

The names that the ancients gave to those six worlds, and which are still called by the same names, are Mercury, Venus, this world that we call ours, Mars, Jupiter and Saturn. They appear larger to the eye than the stars, being many million miles nearer to our earth than any of the stars are. The planet Venus is that which is called the evening star, and sometimes the morning star, as she happens to set after or rise before the Sun, which in either case is never more than three hours.

The Sun, as before said, being the centre, the planet or world nearest the Sun is Mercury; his distance from the Sun is thirty-four million miles, and he moves round in a circle always at that distance from the Sun, as a top may be supposed to spin round in the track in which a horse goes in a mill.

The second world is Venus; she is fifty-seven million miles distant from the Sun, and consequently moves round in a circle much greater than that of Mercury. The third world is this that we inhabit, and which is eighty-eight million miles distant from the Sun, and consequently moves round in a circle greater than that of Venus.

The fourth world is Mars; he is distant from the Sun one hundred and thirty-four million miles, and consequently moves round in a

8 Those who supposed that the Sun went round the earth every 24 hours made the same mistake in idea that a cook would do in fact, that should make the fire go round the meat, instead of the meat turning round itself towards the fire. – Paine.

circle greater than that of our earth. The fifth is Jupiter; he is distant from the Sun five hundred and fifty-seven million miles, and consequently moves round in a circle greater than that of Mars.

The sixth world is Saturn; he is distant from the Sun seven hundred and sixty-three million miles, and consequently moves round in a circle that surrounds the circles, or orbits, of all the other worlds or planets.

The space, therefore, in the air, or in the immensity of space, that our solar system takes up for the several worlds to perform their revolutions in round the Sun, is of the extent in a straight line of the whole diameter of the orbit, or circle, in which Saturn moves round the Sun, which being double his distance from the Sun, is fifteen hundred and twenty-six million miles and its circular extent is nearly five thousand million, and its globular contents are almost three thousand five hundred million times three thousand five hundred million square miles.[9]

But this, immense as it is, is only one system of worlds. Beyond this, at a vast distance into space, far beyond all power of calculation, are the stars called the fixed stars. They are called fixed because they have no revolutionary motion, as the six worlds or planets have that I have been describing. Those fixed stars continue always at the same distance from each other, and always in the same place, as the Sun does in the centre of our system. The probability, therefore, is that each of those fixed stars is also a Sun, round which another system of worlds or planets, though too remote for us to discover, performs its revolutions, as our system of worlds does round our central Sun.

By this easy progression of ideas, the immensity of space will appear to us to be filled with systems of worlds, and that no part of

9 If it should be asked, how can man know these things? I have one plain answer to give, which is, that man knows how to calculate an eclipse, and also how to calculate to a minute of time when the planet Venus in making her revolutions around the Sun will come in a straight line between our earth and the Sun, and will appear to us about the size of a large pea passing across the face of the Sun. This happens but twice in about a hundred years, at the distance of about eight years from each other, and has happened twice in our time, both of which were foreknown by calculation. It can also be known when they will happen again for a thousand years to come, or to any other portion of time. As, therefore, man could not be able to do these things if he did not understand the solar system, and the manner in which the revolutions of the several planets or worlds are performed, the fact of calculating an eclipse, or a transit of Venus, is a proof in point that the knowledge exists; and as to a few thousand, or even a few million miles, more or less, it makes scarcely any sensible difference in such immense distances. – Paine.

space lies at waste, any more than any part of the globe of earth and water is left unoccupied.

Having thus endeavoured to convey, in a familiar and easy manner, some idea of the structure of the universe, I return to explain what I before alluded to, namely, the great benefits arising to man in consequence of the Creator having made a *plurality* of worlds, such as our system is, consisting of a central sun and six worlds, besides satellites, in preference to that of creating one world only of a vast extent.

ADVANTAGES OF LIFE IN A PLURALITY OF WORLDS

It is an idea I have never lost sight of that all our knowledge of science is derived from the revolutions (exhibited to our eye and from thence to our understanding) which those several planets or worlds of which our system is composed make in their circuit round the Sun.

Had, then, the quantity of matter which these six worlds contain been blended into one solitary globe, the consequence to us would have been that either no revolutionary motion would have existed, or not a sufficiency of it to give us the idea and the knowledge of science we now have; and it is from the sciences that all the mechanical arts that contribute so much to our earthly felicity and comfort are derived.

As, therefore, the Creator made nothing in vain, so also must it be believed that He organized the structure of the universe in the most advantageous manner for the benefit of man; and as we see, and from experience feel, the benefits we derive from the structure of the universe formed as it is, which benefits we should not have had the opportunity of enjoying, if the structure, so far as relates to our system, had been a solitary globe – we can discover at least one reason why a *plurality* of words has been made, and that reason calls forth the devotional gratitude of man as well as his admiration.

But it is not to us, the inhabitants of this globe, only, that the benefits arising from a plurality of worlds are limited. The inhabitants of each of the worlds of which our system is composed enjoy the same opportunities of knowledge as we do. They behold the revolutionary motions of our earth, as we behold theirs. All the planets revolve in sight of each other and, therefore, the same universal school of science presents itself to all. Neither does the knowledge stop here. The system of worlds next to us exhibits, in its revolutions, the same principles and school of science to the inhabitants of their system as our system does to us, and in like manner throughout the immensity of space.

Our ideas, not only of the almightiness of the Creator, but of His wisdom and His beneficence, become enlarged in proportion as we contemplate the extent and the structure of the universe. The solitary idea of a solitary world rolling or at rest in the immense ocean of space gives place to the cheerful idea of a society of worlds so happily contrived as to administer, even by their motion, instruction to man. We see our own earth filled with abundance, but we forget to consider how much of that abundance is owing to the scientific knowledge the vast machinery of the universe has unfolded.

But, in the midst of those reflections, what are we to think of the Christian system of faith that forms itself upon the idea of only one world, and that of no greater extent, as is before shown, than twenty-five thousand miles? An extent which a man walking at the rate of three miles an hour, for twelve hours in the day, could he keep on in a circular direction, would walk entirely round in less than two years. Alas! what is this to the mighty ocean of space, and the almighty power of the Creator?

From whence, then, could arise the solitary and strange conceit that the Almighty, who had millions of worlds equally dependent on His protection, should quit the care of all the rest, and come to die in our world, because, they say, one man and one woman had eaten an apple?

And, on the other hand, are we to suppose that every world in the boundless creation had an Eve, an apple, a serpent and a redeemer? In this case, the person who is irreverently called the Son of God, and sometimes God Himself, would have nothing else to do than to travel from world to world, in an endless succession of deaths, with scarcely a momentary interval of life.

CONCERNING THE MULTIPLICITY OF RELIGIONS

It has been by rejecting the evidence that the world or works of God in the creation afford to our senses, and the action of our reason upon that evidence, that so many wild and whimsical systems of faith and of religion have been fabricated and set up.

There may be many systems of religion that, so far from being morally bad, are in many respects morally good; but there can be but ONE that is true; and that one necessarily must, as it ever will, be in all things consistent with the ever-existing word of God that we behold in His works. But such is the strange construction of the Christian system of faith that every evidence the heavens afford to man either directly contradicts it or renders it absurd.

It is possible to believe, and I always feel pleasure in encouraging myself to believe it, that there have been men in the world who persuade themselves that what is called a *pious fraud* might, at least under particular circumstances, be productive of some good. But the fraud being once established, could not afterwards be explained, for it is with a pious fraud as with a bad action, it begets a calamitous necessity of going on.

The persons who first preached the Christian system of faith, and in some measure combined with it the morality preached by Jesus Christ, might persuade themselves that it was better than the heathen mythology that then prevailed. From the first preachers the fraud went on to the second and to the third, till the idea of its being a pious fraud became lost in the belief of its being true; and that belief became again encouraged by the interests of those who made a livelihood by preaching it.

But though such a belief might by such means be rendered almost general among the laity, it is next to impossible to account for the continued persecution carried on by the Church for several hundred years against the sciences and against the professors of science, if the Church had not some record or some tradition that it was originally no other than a pious fraud, or did not foresee that it could not be maintained against the evidence that the structure of the universe afforded.

Having thus shown the irreconcilable inconsistencies between the real word of God existing in the universe and that which is called *the Word of God,* as shown to us in a printed book that any man might make, I proceed to speak of the three principal means that have been employed in all ages, and perhaps in all countries, to impose upon mankind.

Those three means are mystery, miracle and prophecy. The two first are incompatible with true religion, and the third ought always to be suspected.

With respect to mystery, everything we behold is, in one sense, a mystery to us. Our own existence is a mystery; the whole vegetable world is a mystery. We cannot account how it is that an acorn, when put into the ground, is made to develop itself and become an oak. We know not how it is that the seed we sow unfolds and multiplies itself, and returns to us such an abundant interest for so small a capital.

The fact, however, as distinct from the operating cause, is not a mystery, because we see it, and we know also the means we are to use, which is no other than putting the seed into the ground. We know, therefore, as much as is necessary for us to know; and that part of the operation that we do not know, and which, if we did, we could not perform, the Creator takes upon Himself and performs it for us. We are, therefore, better off than if we had been let into the secret, and left to do it for ourselves.

But though every created thing is, in this sense a mystery, the word mystery cannot be applied to *moral truth,* any more than obscurity can be applied to light. The God in whom we believe is a God of moral truth, and not a God of mystery or obscurity. Mystery is the antagonist of truth. It is a fog of human invention, that obscures truth, and represents it in distortion. Truth never envelops *itself* in mystery, and the mystery in which it is at any time enveloped is the work of its antagonist, and never of itself.

THE BEST WAY TO SERVE GOD

Religion, therefore, being the belief of a God and the practice of moral truth, cannot have connection with mystery. The belief of a God, so far from having anything of mystery in it, is of all beliefs the most easy, because it arises to us, as is before observed, out of necessity. And the practice of moral truth, or, in other words, a practical imitation of the moral goodness of God, is no other than our acting towards each other as He acts benignly toward all.

We cannot *serve* God in the manner we serve those who cannot do without such service; and, therefore, the only idea we can have of serving God is that of contributing to the happiness of the living creation that God has made. This cannot be done by retiring ourselves from the society of the world and spending a recluse life in selfish devotion.

The very nature and design of religion, if I may so express it, prove even to demonstration that it must be free from everything of mystery, and unencumbered with everything that is mysterious. Religion, considered as a duty, is incumbent upon every living soul alike, and, therefore, must be on a level with the understanding and comprehension of all.

Man does not learn religion as he learns the secrets and mysteries of a trade. He learns the theory of religion by reflection. It arises out of the action of his own mind upon the things which he sees, or upon what he may happen to hear or to read, and the practice joins itself thereto.

When men, whether from policy or pious fraud, set up systems of religion incompatible with the word or works of God in the creation, and not only above, but repugnant to human comprehension, they were under the necessity of inventing or adopting a word that should serve as a bar to all questions, inquiries and speculations. The word *mystery* answered this purpose, and thus it has happened that religion, which is in itself without mystery, has been corrupted into a fog of mysteries.

As *mystery* answered all general purposes, *miracle* followed as an occasional auxiliary. The former served to bewilder the mind, the latter to puzzle the senses. The one was the lingo, the other the legerdemain.

But before going further into this subject, it will be proper to inquire what is to be understood by a miracle.

In the same sense that everything may be said to be a mystery, so also may it be said that everything is a miracle, and that no one thing is a greater miracle than another. The elephant, though larger, is not a greater miracle than a mite, nor a mountain a greater miracle than an atom. To an almighty power, it is no more difficult to make the one than the other, and no more difficult to make millions of worlds than to make one.

Everything, therefore, is a miracle in one sense, while in the other sense there is no such thing as a miracle. It is a miracle when compared to our power and to our comprehension, it is not a miracle compared to the power that performs it; but as nothing in this description conveys the idea that is affixed to the word miracle, it is necessary to carry the inquiry further.

Mankind have conceived to themselves certain laws by which

what they call nature is supposed to act; and that a miracle is something contrary to the operation and effect of those laws; but unless we know the whole extent of those laws, and of what are commonly called the powers of nature, we are not able to judge whether anything that may appear to us wonderful or miraculous be within, or be beyond, or be contrary to, her natural power of acting.

The ascension of man several miles high in the air would have everything in it that constitutes the idea of a miracle if it were not known that a species of air can be generated several times lighter than the common atmospheric air and yet possess elasticity enough to prevent the balloon in which that light air is inclosed from being compressed into as many times less bulk by the common air that surrounds it.

In like manner, extracting flashes or sparks of fire from the human body, as visibly as from a steel struck with a flint, and causing iron or steel to move without any visible agent, would also give the idea of a miracle if we were not acquainted with electricity and magnetism. So also would many other experiments in natural philosophy, to those who are not acquainted with the subject.

The restoring of persons to life who are to appearance dead, as is practised upon drowned persons, would also be a miracle if it were not known that animation is capable of being suspended without being extinct.

Besides these, there are performances by sleight-of-hand, and by persons acting in concert that have a miraculous appearance, which when known are thought nothing of. And besides these, there are mechanical and optical deceptions. There is now an exhibition in Paris of ghosts or spectres, which, though it is not imposed upon the spectators as a fact, has an astonishing appearance. As, therefore, we know not the extent to which either nature or art can go, there is no positive criterion to determine what a miracle is, and mankind, in giving credit to appearances, under the idea of there being miracles, are subject to be continually imposed upon.

Since, then, appearances are so capable of deceiving, and things not real have a strong resemblance to things that are, nothing can be more inconsistent than to suppose that the Almighty would make use of means such as are called miracles that would subject the person who performed them to the suspicion of being an impostor, and the person who related them to be suspected of lying, and the doctrine intended to be supported thereby to be suspected as a fabulous invention.

Of all the modes of evidence that ever were invented to obtain belief to any system or opinion to which the name of religion has been given, that of miracle, however successful the imposition may have been, is the most inconsistent. For, in the first place, whenever recourse is had to show, for the purpose of procuring that belief (for a miracle, under any idea of the word, is a show), it implies a lameness or weakness in the doctrine that is preached.

And, in the second place, it is degrading the Almighty into the character of a showman, playing tricks to amuse and make the people stare and wonder. It is also the most equivocal sort of evidence that can be set up; for the belief is not to depend upon the thing called a miracle, but upon the credit of the reporter who says that he saw it; and, therefore, the thing, were it true, would have no better chance of being believed than if it were a lie.

Suppose I were to say that when I sat down to write this book a hand presented itself in the air, took up the pen and wrote every word that is herein written; would anybody believe me? Certainly they would not. Would they believe me a whit more if the thing had been a fact? Certainly they would not.

Since, then, a real miracle, were it to happen, would be subject to the same fate as the falsehood, the inconsistency becomes the greater of supposing the Almighty would make use of means that would not answer the purpose for which they were intended, even if they were real.

If we are to suppose a miracle to be something so entirely out of the course of what is called nature that she must go out of that course to accomplish it, and we see an account given of such miracle by the person who said he saw it, it raises a question in the mind very easily decided, which is, is it more probable that nature should go out of her course or that a man should tell a lie? We have never seen, in our time, nature go out of her course; but we have good reason to believe that millions of lies have been told in the same time; it is, therefore, at least millions to one that the reporter of a miracle tells a lie.

The story of the whale swallowing Jonah, though a whale is large enough to do it, borders greatly on the marvellous; but it would have approached nearer to the idea of a miracle if Jonah had swallowed the whale. In this, which may serve for all cases of miracles, the matter would decide itself, as before stated, namely, is it more probable that a man should have swallowed a whale or told a lie?

But suppose that Jonah had really swallowed the whale, and gone with it in his belly to Nineveh and, to convince the people that it was true, had cast it up in their sight, of the full length and size of a whale, would they not have believed him to have been the devil instead of a prophet? Or, if the whale had carried Jonah to Nineveh, and cast him up in the same public manner, would they not have believed the whale to have been the devil, and Jonah one of his imps?

The most extraordinary of all the things called miracles, related in the New Testament, is that of the devil flying away with Jesus Christ, and carrying him to the top of a high mountain, and to the top of the highest pinnacle of the temple, and showing him and promising to him *all the kingdoms of the World*. How happened it that he did not discover America, or is it only with *kingdoms* that his sooty highness has any interest?

I have too much respect for the moral character of Christ to believe that he told this whale of a miracle himself; neither is it easy to account for what purpose it could have been fabricated, unless it were to impose upon the connoisseurs of miracles as is sometimes practised upon the connoisseurs of Queen Anne's farthings and collectors of relics and antiquities; or to render the belief of miracles ridiculous by outdoing miracles, as Don Quixote outdid chivalry; or to embarrass the belief of miracles by making it doubtful by what power, whether of God or of the devil, anything called a miracle was performed. It requires, however, a great deal of faith in the devil to believe this miracle.

In every point of view in which those things called miracles can be placed and considered, the reality of them is improbable and their existence unnecessary. They would not, as before observed, answer any useful purpose even if they were true; for it is more difficult to obtain belief to a miracle than to a principle evidently moral without any miracle.

Moral principle speaks universally for itself. Miracle could be but a thing of the moment, and seen but by a few; after this it requires a transfer of faith from God to man to believe a miracle upon man's report. Instead, therefore, of admitting the recitals of miracles as evidence of any system of religion being true, they ought to be considered as symptoms of its being fabulous. It is necessary to the full and upright character of truth that it rejects the crutch, and it is consistent with the character of fable to seek the aid that truth rejects. Thus much for mystery and miracle.

As mystery and miracle took charge of the past and the present, prophecy took charge of the future and rounded the tenses of faith. It was not sufficient to know what had been done, but what would be done. The supposed prophet was the supposed historian of times to come; and if he happened, in shooting with a long bow of a thousand years, to strike within a thousand miles of a mark, the ingenuity of posterity could make it point-blank; and if he happened to be directly wrong, it was only to suppose, as in the case of Jonah and Nineveh, that God had repented Himself and changed His mind. What a fool do fabulous systems make of man!

PROPHETS AND THEIR PROPHECIES

It has been shown, in a former part of this work, that the original meaning of the words *prophet* and *prophesying* has been changed, and that a prophet, in the sense of the word as now used, is a creature of modern invention; and it is owing to this change in the meaning of the words, that the flights and metaphors of the Jewish poets, and phrases and expressions now rendered obscure by our not being acquainted with the local circumstances to which they applied at the time they were used, have been erected into prophecies and made to bend to explanations at the will and whimsical conceits of sectaries, expounders and commentators.

Everything unintelligible was prophetical, and everything insignificant was typical. A blunder would have served for a prophecy, and a dish-clout for a type.

If by a prophet we are to suppose a man to whom the Almighty communicated some event that would take place in future, either there were such men or there were not. If there were, it is consistent to believe that the event so communicated would be told in terms that could be understood, and not related in such a loose and obscure manner as to be out of the comprehension of those that heard it, and so equivocal as to fit almost any circumstance that might happen afterwards. It is conceiving very irreverently of the Almighty to suppose that He would deal in this jesting manner with mankind, yet all the things called prophecies in the book called the Bible come under this description.

But it is with prophecy as it is with miracle; it could not answer the purpose even if it were real. Those to whom a prophecy should be told, could not tell whether the man prophesied or lied, or whether it had been revealed to him, or whether he conceited it; and if the thing that he prophesied, or intended to prophesy, should happen, or something like it, among the multitude of things that are daily happening, nobody could again know whether he foreknew it, or guessed at it, or whether it was accidental.

A prophet, therefore, is a character useless and unnecessary; and the safe side of the case is to guard against being imposed upon by not giving credit to such relations.

Upon the whole, mystery, miracle and prophecy are appendages that belong to fabulous and not to true religion. They are the means by which so many *Lo, heres!* and *Lo, theres!* have been spread about the world, and religion been made into a trade. The success of one impostor gave encouragement to another, and the quieting salvo of doing *some good* by keeping up a *pious fraud* protected them from remorse.

RECAPITULATION

Having now extended the subject to a greater length than I first intended, I shall bring it to a close by abstracting a summary from the whole.

First – That the idea or belief of a Word of God existing in print, or in writing, or in speech, is inconsistent in itself for reasons already assigned. These reasons, among many others, are the want of a universal language; the mutability of language; the errors to which translations are subject; the possibility of totally suppressing such a word; the probability of altering it, or of fabricating the whole, and imposing it upon the world.

Secondly – That the creation we behold is the real and ever-existing Word of God, in which we cannot be deceived. It proclaims His power, it demonstrates His wisdom, it manifests His goodness and beneficence.

Thirdly – That the moral duty of man consists in imitating the moral goodness and beneficence of God, manifested in the creation towards all His creatures. That seeing, as we daily do, the goodness of God to all men, it is an example calling upon all men to practise the same towards each other; and, consequently, that everything of persecution and revenge between man and man, and everything of cruelty to animals, is a violation of moral duty.

I trouble not myself about the manner of future existence. I content myself with believing, even to positive conviction, that the Power that gave me existence is able to continue it, in any form and manner He pleases, either with or without this body; and it appears more probable to me that I shall continue to exist hereafter, than that I should have had existence, as I now have, before that existence began.

It is certain that, in one point, all the nations of the earth and all religions agree – all believe in a God; the things in which they disagree are the redundancies annexed to that belief; and, therefore, if ever a universal religion should prevail, it will not be by believing anything new, but in getting rid of redundancies and believing as man believed at first. Adam, if ever there were such a man, was created a Deist; but in the meantime, let every man follow, as he has a right to do, the religion and the worship he prefers.

[16] DISSERTATION ON
FIRST PRINCIPLES OF GOVERNMENT
———————•◆◆◆•———————

(1795)

*Written in the summer of 1795 after his release from jail and after his readmission to
the National Convention, The Dissertation on First Principles of Government
offers the most succinct rendition of Paine's philosophy of rights. While it was
written primarily to familiarize Dutch readers with his general political views,
Paine could not resist offering his opinions on a controversial issue of that moment,
the proposed restriction on manhood suffrage contained in the new French Constitution.*

There is no subject more interesting to every man than the subject of
government. His security, be he rich or poor, and in a great measure
his prosperity, are connected therewith; it is therefore his interest as
well as his duty to make himself acquainted with its principles, and
what the practice ought to be.

Every art and science, however imperfectly known at first, has
been studied, improved and brought to what we call perfection by
the progressive labours of succeeding generations; but the science of
government has stood still. No improvement has been made in the
principle and scarcely any in the practice till the American Revolution began. In all the countries of Europe (except in France) the
same forms and systems that were erected in the remote ages of
ignorance still continue, and their antiquity is put in the place of
principle; it is forbidden to investigate their origin, or by what right
they exist. If it be asked how has this happened, the answer is easy:
they are established on a principle that is false, and they employ their
power to prevent detection.

Notwithstanding the mystery with which the science of
government has been enveloped, for the purpose of enslaving,
plundering and imposing upon mankind, it is of all things the least
mysterious and the most easy to be understood. The meanest capacity
cannot be at a loss, if it begins its inquiries at the right point. Every
art and science has some point, or alphabet, at which the study of
that art or science begins, and by the assistance of which the progress

is facilitated. The same method ought to be observed with respect to the science of government.

Instead then of embarrassing the subject in the outset with the numerous subdivisions under which different forms of government have been classed, such as aristocracy, democracy, oligarchy, monarchy, etc., the better method will be to begin with what may be called primary divisions, or those under which all the several subdivisions will be comprehended.

The primary divisions are but two:

First, government by election and representation.

Secondly, government by hereditary succession.

All the several forms and systems of government, however numerous or diversified, class themselves under one or other of those primary divisions; for either they are on the system of representation, or on that of hereditary succession. As to that equivocal thing called mixed government, such as the late Government of Holland, and the present Government of England, it does not make an exception to the general rule, because the parts separately considered are either representative or hereditary.

Beginning then our inquiries at this point, we have first to examine into the nature of those two primary divisions. If they are equally right in principle, it is mere matter of opinion which we prefer. If the one be demonstratively better than the other that difference directs our choice; but if one of them should be so absolutely false as not to have a right of existence the matter settles itself at once; because a negative proved on one thing, where two only are offered, and one must be accepted, amounts to an affirmative on the other.

The revolutions that are now spreading themselves in the world have their origin in this state of the case, and the present war is a conflict between the representative system founded on the rights of the people, and the hereditary system founded in usurpation. As to what are called monarchy, royalty and aristocracy, they do not, either as things or as terms, sufficiently describe the hereditary system; they are but secondary things or signs of the hereditary system, and which fall of themselves if that system has not a right to exist.

Were there no such terms as monarchy, royalty and aristocracy, or were other terms substituted in their place, the hereditary system, if it continued, would not be altered thereby. It would be the same system under any other titulary name as it is now.

The character therefore of the revolutions of the present day distinguishes itself most definitely by grounding itself on the system of representative government, in opposition to the hereditary. No other distinction reaches the whole of the principle.

Having thus opened the case generally, I proceed, in the first place, to examine the hereditary system because it has the priority in point of time. The representative system is the invention of the modern world; and, that no doubt may arise as to my own opinion, I declare it beforehand, which is, *that there is not a problem in Euclid more mathematically true than that hereditary government has not a right to exist. When therefore we take from any man the exercise of hereditary power we take away that which he never had the right to possess, and which no law or custom could, or ever can, give him a title to.*

The arguments that have hitherto been employed against the hereditary system have been chiefly founded upon the absurdity of it, and its incompetency to the purpose of good government. Nothing can present to our judgement, or to our imagination, a figure of greater absurdity, than that of seeing the government of a nation fall, as it frequently does, into the hands of a lad necessarily destitute of experience, and often little better than a fool. It is an insult to every man of years, of character, and of talents, in a country.

The moment we begin to reason upon the hereditary system, it falls into derision; let but a single idea begin and a thousand will soon follow. Insignificance, imbecility, childhood, dotage, want of moral character; in fine, every defect, serious or laughable, unite to hold up the hereditary system as a figure of ridicule. Leaving, however, the ridiculousness of the thing to the reflections of the reader, I proceed to the more important part of the question, namely, whether such a system has a right to exist.

To be satisfied of the right of a thing to exist, we must be satisfied that it had a right to begin. If it had not a right to begin, it has not the right to continue. By what right then did the hereditary system begin? Let a man but ask himself this question, and he will find that he cannot satisfy himself with an answer.

The right which any man or any family had to set itself up at first to govern a nation, and to establish itself hereditarily, was no other than the right which Robespierre had to do the same thing in France. If he had none, they had none. If they had any, he had as much; for it is impossible to discover superiority of right in any family, by virtue of which hereditary government could begin. The Capets, the Guelphs, the Robespierres, the Marats, are all on the same standing as to the question of right. It belongs exclusively to none.

It is one step towards liberty to perceive that hereditary government could not begin as an exclusive right in any family. The next point will be whether, having once begun, it could grow into a right by the influence of time.

This would be supposing an absurdity; for either it is putting time in the place of principle, or making it superior to principle; whereas time has no more connection with, or influence upon principle, than principle has upon time. The wrong which began a thousand years ago is as much a wrong as if it began to-day; and the right which originates to-day is as much a right as if it had the sanction of a thousand years.

Time with respect to principles is an eternal N O W: it has no operation upon them: it changes nothing of their nature and qualities. But what have we to do with a thousand years? Our lifetime is but a short portion of that period, and if we find the wrong in existence as soon as we begin to live, that is the point of time at which it begins to us; and our right to resist it is the same as if it never existed before.

As hereditary government could not begin as a natural right in any family, nor derive after its commencement any right from time, we have only to examine whether there exist in a nation a right to set it up, and establish it by what is called law, as has been done in England. I answer N O; and that any law or any constitution made for that purpose is an act of treason against the right of every minor in the nation, at the time it is made, and against the rights of all succeeding generations.

I shall speak upon each of those cases. First, of the minor at the time such law is made. Secondly, of the generations that are to follow.

A nation, in a collective sense, comprehends all the individuals of whatever age, from just born to just dying. Of these, one part will be minors and the other aged. The average of life is not exactly the same in every climate and country, but in general the minority in years are the majority in numbers; that is, the number of persons under twenty-one years, is greater than the number of persons above that age.

This difference in number is not necessary to the establishment of the principle I mean to lay down, but it serves to show the justice of it more strongly. The principle would be equally as good if the majority in years were also the majority in numbers.

The rights of minors are as sacred as the rights of the aged. The difference is altogether in the different age of the two parties, and nothing in the nature of the rights; the rights are the same rights; and are to be preserved inviolate for the inheritance of the minors when they shall come of age. During the minority of minors their rights are under the sacred guardianship of the aged.

The minor cannot surrender them; the guardian cannot dispossess him; consequently, the aged part of a nation, who are the law-makers for the *time being,* and who, in the march of life are but a few years ahead of those who are yet minors, and to whom they must shortly give place, have not and cannot have the right to make a law to set up and establish hereditary government, or, to speak more distinctly, *an hereditary succession of governors*; because it is an attempt to deprive every minor in the nation, at the time such a law is made, of his inheritance of rights when he shall come of age, and to sub-jugate him to a system of government to which, during his minority, he could neither consent nor object.

If a person who is a minor at the time such a law is proposed, had happened to have been born a few years sooner, so as to be of the age of twenty-one years at the time of proposing it, his right to have objected against it, to have exposed the injustice and tyrannical principles of it and to have voted against it, will be admitted on all sides.

If, therefore, the law operates to prevent his exercising the same rights after he comes of age as he would have had a right to exercise had he been of age at the time, it is undeniably a law to take away and annul the rights of every person in the nation who shall be a minor at the time of making such a law, and consequently the right to make it cannot exist.

I come now to speak of government by hereditary succession, as it applies to succeeding generations; and to show that in this case, as in the case of minors, there does not exist in a nation a right to set it up.

A nation, though continually existing, is continually in a state of renewal and succession. It is never stationary. Every day produces new births, carries minors forward to maturity, and old persons from the stage. In this ever running flood of generations there is no part superior in authority to another. Could we conceive an idea of superiority in any, at what point of time, or in what century of the world, are we to fix it? To what cause are we to ascribe it? By what evidence are we to prove it? By what criterion are we to know it?

A single reflection will teach us that our ancestors, like ourselves, were but tenants for life in the great freehold of rights. The fee-absolute was not in them, it is not in us, it belongs to the whole family of man through all ages. If we think otherwise than this we think either as slaves or as tyrants. As slaves, if we think that any former generation had a right to bind us; as tyrants, if we think that we have authority to bind the generations that are to follow.

It may not be inapplicable to the subject, to endeavour to define what is to be understood by a generation in the sense the word is here used.

As a natural term its meaning is sufficiently clear. The father, the son, the grandson, are so many distinct generations. But when we speak of a generation as describing the persons in whom legal authority resides, as distinct from another generation of the same description who are to succeed them, it comprehends all those who are above the age of twenty-one years, at the time that we count from; and a generation of this kind will continue in authority between fourteen and twenty-one years, that is, until the number of minors, who shall have arrived at age, shall be greater than the number of persons remaining of the former stock.

For example: If France, at this or any other moment, contains twenty-four millions of souls, twelve millions will be males, and twelve females. Of the twelve millions of males, six millions will be of the age of twenty-one years, and six will be under, and the authority to govern will reside in the first six.

But every day will make some alteration, and in twenty-one years every one of those minors who survives will have arrived at age, and the greater part of the former stock will be gone: the majority of persons then living, in whom the legal authority resides, will be composed of those who, twenty-one years before, had no legal existence. Those will be fathers and grandfathers in their turn, and, in the next twenty-one years (or less) another race of minors, arrived at age, will succeed them, and so on.

As this is ever the case, and as every generation is equal in rights to another, it consequently follows, that there cannot be a right in any to establish government by hereditary succession, because it would be supposing itself possessed of a right superior to the rest, namely, that of commanding by its own authority how the world shall be hereafter governed, and who shall govern it.

Every age and generation is, and must be (as a matter of right), as free to act for itself in all cases, as the age and generation that preceded it. The vanity and presumption of governing beyond the grave is the most ridiculous and insolent of all tyrannies. Man has no property in man, neither has one generation a property in the generations that are to follow.

In the first part of the *Rights of Man* I have spoken of government by hereditary succession . . .

The history of the English Parliament furnishes an example of this kind; and which merits to be recorded as being the greatest instance of legislative ignorance and want of principle that is to be found in any country. The case is as follows:

The English Parliament of 1688, imported a man and his wife from Holland, *William* and *Mary,* and made them King and Queen of England. Having done this, the said Parliament made a law to convey the government of the country to the heirs of William and Mary, in the following words: 'We, the Lords Spiritual and Temporal, and Commons, do, in the name of the people of England, most humbly and faithfully submit *ourselves, our heirs and posterities,* to William and Mary, *their heirs and posterities,* for ever.' And in a subsequent law, as quoted by Edmund Burke, the said Parliament, in the name of the people of England then living, *binds the said people, their heirs and posterities, to William and Mary, their heirs and posterities, to the end of time.*

It is not sufficient that we laugh at the ignorance of such law-makers; it is necessary that we reprobate their want of principle. The Constituent Assembly of France, 1789, fell into the same vice as the Parliament of England had done, and assumed to establish an hereditary succession in the family of the Capets as an act of the Constitution of that year.

That every nation, *for the time being,* has a right to govern itself as it pleases, must always be admitted; but government by hereditary succession is government for another race of people, and not for itself; and as those on whom it is to operate are not in existence, or are minors, so neither is the right in existence to set it up for them, and to assume such a right is treason against the right of posterity.

I here close the arguments on the first head, that of government by hereditary succession; and proceed to the second, that of government by election and representation; or, as it may be concisely expressed, *representative government*, in contradistinction to *hereditary government*.

Reasoning by exclusion, if *hereditary government* has not a right to exist, and that it has not is provable, *representative government* is admitted of course.

In contemplating government by election and representation, we amuse not ourselves in inquiring when or how, or by what right, it began. Its origin is ever in view. Man is himself the origin and the evidence of the right. It appertains to him in right of his existence, and his person is the title deed.

The true and only true basis of representative government is equality of rights. Every man has a right to one vote, and no more in the choice of representatives. The rich have no more right to exclude the poor from the right of voting, or of electing and being elected, than the poor have to exclude the rich; and wherever it is attempted, or proposed, on either side, it is a question of force and not of right. Who is he that would exclude another? That other has a right to exclude him.

That which is now called aristocracy implies an inequality of rights; but who are the persons that have a right to establish this inequality? Will the rich exclude themselves? No. Will the poor exclude themselves? No. By what right then can any be excluded? It would be a question, if any man or class of men have a right to exclude themselves; but, be this as it may, they cannot have the right to exclude another. The poor will not delegate such a right to the rich, nor the rich to the poor, and to assume it is not only to assume arbitrary power, but to assume a right to commit robbery.

Personal rights, of which the right of voting for representatives is one, are a species of property of the most sacred kind: and he that would employ his pecuniary property, or presume upon the influence it gives him, to dispossess or rob another of his property or rights, uses that pecuniary property as he would use fire-arms, and merits to have it taken from him.

Inequality of rights is created by a combination in one part of the community to exclude another part from its rights. Whenever it be made an article of a constitution, or a law, that the right of voting, or of electing and being elected, shall appertain exclusively to persons possessing a certain quantity of property, be it little or much, it is a combination of the persons possessing that quantity to exclude those who do not possess the same quantity. It is investing themselves with powers as a self-created part of society, to the exclusion of the rest.

It is always to be taken for granted, that those who oppose an equality of rights never mean the exclusion should take place on themselves; and in this view of the case, pardoning the vanity of the thing, aristocracy is a subject of laughter. This self-soothing vanity is encouraged by another idea not less selfish, which is that the opposers conceive they are playing a safe game, in which there is a chance to gain and none to lose; that at any rate the doctrine of equality includes *them,* and that if they cannot get more rights than those whom they oppose and would exclude they shall not have less.

This opinion has already been fatal to thousands, who, not contented with *equal rights,* have sought more till they lost all, and experienced in themselves the degrading *inequality* they endeavoured to fix upon others.

In any view of the case it is dangerous and impolitic, sometimes ridiculous, and always unjust to make property the criterion of the right of voting. If the sum or value of the property upon which the right is to take place be considerable it will exclude a majority of the people and unite them in a common interest against the government and against those who support it; and as the power is always with the majority, they can overturn such a government and its supporters whenever they please.

If, in order to avoid this danger, a small quantity of property be fixed, as the criterion of the right, it exhibits liberty in disgrace, by putting it in competition with accident and insignificance. When a broodmare shall fortunately produce a foal or a mule that, by being worth the sum in question, shall convey to its owner the right of voting, or by its death take it from him, in whom does the origin of such a right exist? Is it in the man, or in the mule? When we consider how many ways property may be acquired without merit, and lost without crime, we ought to spurn the idea of making it a criterion of rights.

But the offensive part of the case is that this exclusion from the right of voting implies a stigma on the moral character of the persons excluded; and this is what no part of the community has a right to pronounce upon another part. No external circumstance can justify it: wealth is no proof of moral character; nor poverty of the want of it.

On the contrary, wealth is often the presumptive evidence of dishonesty; and poverty the negative evidence of innocence. If therefore property, whether little or much, be made a criterion, the means by which that property has been acquired ought to be made a criterion also.

The only ground upon which exclusion from the right of voting is consistent with justice would be to inflict it as a punishment for a certain time upon those who should propose to take away that right from others. The right of voting for representatives is the primary right by which other rights are protected.

To take away this right is to reduce a man to slavery, for slavery consists in being subject to the will of another, and he that has not a vote in the election of representatives is in this case. The proposal therefore to disfranchise any class of men is as criminal as the proposal to take away property.

When we speak of right we ought always to unite with it the idea of duties: rights become duties by reciprocity. The right which I enjoy becomes my duty to guarantee it to another, and he to me; and those who violate the duty justly incur a forfeiture of the right.

In a political view of the case, the strength and permanent security of government is in proportion to the number of people interested in supporting it. The true policy therefore is to interest the whole by an equality of rights, for the danger arises from exclusions. It is possible to exclude men from the right of voting, but it is impossible to exclude them from the right of rebelling against that exclusion; and when all other rights are taken away the right of rebellion is made perfect.

While men could be persuaded they had no rights, or that rights appertained only to a certain class of men, or that government was a thing existing in right of itself, it was not difficult to govern them authoritatively. The ignorance in which they were held, and the superstition in which they were instructed, furnished the means of doing it.

But when the ignorance is gone, and the superstition with it; when they perceive the imposition that has been acted upon them; when they reflect that the cultivator and the manufacturer are the primary means of all the wealth that exists in the world, beyond what nature spontaneously produces; when they begin to feel their consequences by their usefulness, and their right as members of society, it is then no longer possible to govern them as before. The fraud once detected cannot be re-acted. To attempt it is to provoke derision, or invite destruction.

That property will ever be unequal is certain. Industry, superiority of talents, dexterity of management, extreme frugality, fortunate opportunities, or the opposite, or the means of those things, will ever produce that effect, without having recourse to the harsh, ill-sounding names of avarice and oppression; and besides this there are some men who, though they do not despise wealth, will not stoop to the drudgery or the means of acquiring it, nor will be troubled with it beyond their wants or their independence; while in others there is an avidity to obtain it by every means not punishable; it makes the sole business of their lives, and they follow it as a religion. All that is required with respect to property is to obtain it honestly, and not employ it criminally; but it is always criminally employed when it is made a criterion for exclusive rights.

In institutions that are purely pecuniary, such as that of a bank or a commercial company, the rights of the members composing that company are wholly created by the property they invest therein; and no other rights are represented in the government of that company than what arise out of that property; neither has that government cognizance of *anything but property*.

But the case is totally different with respect to the institution of civil government, organized on the system of representation. Such a government has cognizance of *everything*, and of *every man* as a member of the national society, whether he has property or not; and, therefore, the principle requires that *every man*, and *every kind of right*, be represented, of which the right to acquire and to hold property is but one, and that not of the most essential kind.

The protection of a man's person is more sacred than the protection of property; and besides this, the faculty of performing any kind of work or services by which he acquires a livelihood, or maintaining his family, is of the nature of property. It is property to him; he has acquired it; and it is as much the object of his protection as exterior property, possessed without that faculty, can be the object of protection in another person.

I have always believed that the best security for property, be it much or little, is to remove from every part of the community, as far as can possibly be done, every cause of complaint, and every motive to violence; and this can only be done by an equality of rights. When rights are secure, property is secure in consequence. But when property is made a pretence for unequal or exclusive rights, it weakens the right to hold the property, and provokes indignation and tumult; for it is unnatural to believe that property can be secure under the guarantee of a society injured in its rights by the influence of that property.

Next to the injustice and ill-policy of making property a pretence for exclusive rights, is the unaccountable absurdity of giving to mere *sound* the idea of property, and annexing to it certain rights; for what else is a *title* but sound? Nature is often giving to the world some extraordinary men who arrive at fame by merit and universal consent, such as Aristotle, Socrates, Plato, etc. They were truly great or noble. But when government sets up a manufactory of nobles, it is as absurd as if she undertook to manufacture wise men. Her nobles are all counterfeits.

This wax-work order has assumed the name of aristocracy; and the disgrace of it would be lessened if it could be considered only as childish imbecility. We pardon foppery because of its insignificance, and on the same ground we might pardon the foppery of titles. But the origin of aristocracy was worse than foppery. It was robbery. The first aristocrats in all countries were brigands. Those of later times, sycophants.

It is very well known that in England (and the same will be found in other countries), the great landed estates now held in descent were plundered from the quiet inhabitants at the Conquest. The possibility did not exist of acquiring such estates honestly. If it be asked how they could have been acquired, no answer but that of robbery can be given. That they were not acquired by trade, by commerce, by manufactures, by agriculture, or by any reputable employment, is certain.

How then were they acquired! Blush, aristocracy, to hear your origin, for your progenitors were thieves. They were the Robespierres and the Jacobins of that day. When they had committed the robbery, they endeavoured to lose the disgrace of it by sinking their real names under fictitious ones, which they called titles. It is ever the practice of felons to act in this manner. They never pass by their real names.

As property, honestly obtained, is best secured by an equality of rights, so ill-gotten property depends for protection on a monopoly of rights. He who has robbed another of his property, will next endeavour to disarm him of his rights, to secure that property; for when the robber becomes the legislator he believes himself secure. That part of the Government of England that is called the House of Lords, was originally composed of persons who had committed the robberies of which I have been speaking. It was an association for the protection of the property they had stolen.

But besides the criminality of the origin of aristocracy, it has an injurious effect on the moral and physical character of man. Like slavery it debilitates the human faculties; for as the mind bowed down by slavery loses in silence its elastic powers, so, in the contrary extreme, when it is buoyed up by folly, it becomes incapable of exerting them, and swindles into imbecility. It is impossible that a mind employed upon ribands and titles can ever be great. The childishness of the objects consumes the man.

It is at all times necessary, and more particularly so during the progress of a revolution, and until right ideas confirm themselves by habit, that we frequently refresh our patriotism by reference to first principles. It is by tracing things to their origin that we learn to understand them: and it is by keeping that line and that origin always in view that we never forget them.

An inquiry into the origin of rights will demonstrate to us that *rights* are not *gifts* from one man to another, nor from one class of men to another; for who is he who could be the first giver, or by what principle, or on what authority, could he possess the right of giving?

A declaration of rights is not a creation of them, nor a donation of them. It is a manifest of the principle by which they exist, followed by a detail of what the rights are; for every civil right has a natural right for its foundation, and it includes the principle of a reciprocal guarantee of those rights from man to man. As, therefore, it is impossible to discover any origin of rights otherwise than in the origin of man, it consequently follows, that rights appertain to man in right of his existence only, and must therefore be equal to every man.

The principle of an *equality of rights* is clear and simple. Every man can understand it, and it is by understanding his rights that he learns his duties; for where the rights of men are equal, every man must finally see the necessity of protecting the rights of others as the most effectual security for his own.

But if, in the formation of a constitution, we depart from the principle of equal rights, or attempt any modification of it, we plunge into a labyrinth of difficulties from which there is no way out but by retreating. Where are we to stop? Or by what principle are we to find out the point to stop at, that shall discriminate between men of the same country, part of whom shall be free, and the rest not?

If property is to be made the criterion, it is a total departure from every moral principle of liberty, because it is attaching rights to mere matter, and making man the agent of that matter. It is, moreover, holding up property as an apple of discord, and not only exciting but justifying war against it; for I maintain the principle, that when property is used as an instrument to take away the rights of those who may happen not to possess property, it is used to an unlawful purpose, as fire-arms would be in a similar case.

In a state of nature all men are equal in rights, but they are not equal in power; the weak cannot protect themselves against the strong. This being the case, the institution of civil society is for the purpose of making an equalization of powers that shall be parallel to, and a guarantee of, the equality of rights. The laws of a country, when properly constructed, apply to this purpose.

Every man takes the arm of the law for his protection as more effectual than his own; and therefore every man has an equal right in the formation of the government, and of the laws by which he is to be governed and judged. In extensive countries and societies, such as America and France, this right in the individual can only be exercised by delegation, that is, by election and representation; and hence it is that the institution of representative government arises.

Hitherto, I have confined myself to matters of principle only. First, that hereditary government has not a right to exist; that it cannot be established on any principle of right; and that it is a violation of all principle. Secondly, that government by election and representation has its origin in the natural and eternal rights of man; for whether a man be his own lawgiver, as he would be in a state of nature; or whether he exercises his portion of legislative sovereignty in his own person, as might be the case in small democracies where all could assemble for the formation of the laws by which they were to be governed; or whether he exercises it in the choice of persons to represent him in a national assembly of representatives, the origin of the right is the same in all cases. The first, as is before observed, is defective in power; the second, is practicable only in democracies of small extent; the third, is the greatest scale upon which human government can be instituted.

Next to matters of *principle* are matters of *opinion*, and it is necessary to distinguish between the two. Whether the rights of men shall be equal is not a matter of opinion but of right, and consequently of principle; for men do not hold their rights as grants from each other, but each one in right of himself. Society is the guardian but not the giver. And as in extensive societies, such as America and France, the right of the individual in matters of government cannot be exercised but by election and representation, it consequently follows that the only system of government consistent with principle, where simple democracy is impracticable, is the representative system.

But as to the organical part, or the manner in which the several parts of government shall be arranged and composed, it is altogether *matter of opinion*. It is necessary that all the parts be conformable with the *principle of equal rights*; and so long as this principle be religiously adhered to, no very material error can take place, neither can any error continue long in that part which falls within the province of opinion.

In all matters of opinion, the social compact, or the principle by which society is held together, requires that the majority of opinions becomes the rule for the whole, and that the minority yields practical obedience thereto. This is perfectly conformable to the principle of equal rights; for, in the first place, every man has *a right to give an opinion* but no man has a right that his opinion should *govern the rest*. In the second place, it is not supposed to be known beforehand on which side of any question, whether for or against, any man's opinion will fall. He may happen to be in a majority upon some questions, and in a minority upon others; and by the same rule that he expects obedience in the one case, he must yield it in the other.

All the disorders that have arisen in France during the progress of the Revolution have had their origin, not in the *principle of equal rights*, but in the violation of that principle. The principle of equal rights has been repeatedly violated, and that not by the majority but by the minority, and *that minority has been composed of men possessing property, as well as of men without property; property, therefore, even upon the experience already had, is no more a criterion of character than it is of rights.*

It will sometimes happen that the minority are right, and the majority are wrong, but as soon as experience proves this to be the case, the minority will increase to a majority, and the error will reform itself by the tranquil operation of freedom of opinion and equality of rights. Nothing, therefore, can justify an insurrection, neither can it ever be necessary where rights are equal and opinions free.

Taking then the principle of equal rights as the foundation of the Revolution, and consequently of the Constitution, the organical part, or the manner in which the several parts of the Government shall be arranged in the Constitution, will, as is already said, fall within the province of opinion.

Various methods will present themselves upon a question of this kind, and though experience is yet wanting to determine which is the best, it has, I think, sufficiently decided which is the worst. That is the worst, which in its deliberations and decisions is subject to the precipitancy and passion of an individual; and when the whole legislature is crowded into one body it is an individual in mass. In all cases of deliberation it is necessary to have a corps of reserve, and it would be better to divide the representation by lot into two parts, and let them revise and correct each other, than that the whole should sit together, and debate at once.

Representative government is not necessarily confined to any one particular form. The principle is the same in all the forms under which it can be arranged. The equal rights of the people is the root from which the whole springs, and the branches may be arranged as present opinion or future experience shall best direct. As to that *hospital of incurables* (as Chesterfield calls it), the British House of Peers, it is an excrescence growing out of corruption; and there is no more affinity or resemblance between any of the branches of a legislative body originating from the right of the people, and the aforesaid House of Peers, than between a regular member of the human body and an ulcerated wen.

As to that part of government that is called the *executive*, it is necessary in the first place to fix a precise meaning to the word.

There are but two divisions into which power can be arranged. First, that of willing or decreeing the laws; secondly, that of executing or puting them in practice. The former corresponds to the intellectual faculties of the human mind which reasons and determines what shall be done; the second, to the mechanical powers of the human body that puts that determination into practice.

If the former decides, and the latter does not perform, it is a state of imbecility; and if the latter acts without the predetermination of the former, it is a state of lunacy. The executive department therefore is official, and is subordinate to the legislative, as the body is to the mind in a state of health; for it is impossible to conceive the idea of two sovereignties, a sovereignty to *will* and a sovereignty to *act*.

The executive is not invested with the power of deliberating whether it shall act or not; it has no discretionary authority in the case; for it can *act no other thing* than what the laws decree, and it is *obliged* to act conformably thereto; and in this view of the case the executive is made up of all the official departments that execute the laws, of which that which is called the judiciary is the chief.

But mankind have conceived an idea that *some kind of authority* is necessary to *superintend* the execution of the laws and to see that they are faithfully performed; and it is by confounding this superintending authority with the official execution that we get embarrassed about the term *executive power*. All the parts in the governments of the United States of America that are called THE EXECUTIVE, are no other than authorities to superintend the execution of the laws; and they are so far independent of the legislative that they know the legislative only through the laws, and cannot be controlled or directed by it through any other medium.

In what manner this superintending authority shall be appointed, or composed, is a matter that falls within the province of opinion. Some may prefer one method and some another; and in all cases, where opinion only and not principle is concerned, the majority of opinions forms the rule for all.

There are however some things deducible from reason, and evidenced by experience, that serve to guide our decision upon the case. The one is never to invest any individual with extraordinary power; for besides his being tempted to misuse it, it will excite contention and commotion in the nation for the office. Secondly, never to invest power long in the hands of any number of individuals. The inconveniences that may be supposed to accompany frequent changes are less to be feared than the danger that arises from long continuance.

I shall conclude this discourse with offering some observations on the means of *preserving liberty*; for it is not only necessary that we establish it, but that we preserve it.

It is, in the first place, necessary that we distinguish between the means made use of to overthrow despotism, in order to prepare the way for the establishment of liberty, and the means to be used after the despotism is overthrown.

The means made use of in the first case are justified by necessity. Those means are, in general, insurrections; for while the established government of despotism continues in any country it is scarcely possible that any other means can be used. It is also certain that in the commencement of a revolution, the revolutionary party permit to themselves a *discretionary exercise of power* regulated more by circumstances than by principle, which, were the practice to continue, liberty would never be established, or if established would soon be overthrown. It is never to be expected in a revolution that every man is to change his opinion at the same moment.

There never yet was any truth or any principle so irresistibly obvious that all men believed it at once. Time and reason must cooperate with each other to the final establishment of any principle; and therefore those who may happen to be first convinced have not a right to persecute others, on whom conviction operates more slowly. The moral principle of revolutions is to instruct, not to destroy.

Had a constitution been established two years ago (as ought to have been done), the violence's that have since desolated France and injured the character of the Revolution, would, in my opinion, have been prevented. The nation would then have had a bond of union, and every individual would have known the line of conduct he was to follow. But, instead of this, a revolutionary government, a thing without either principle or authority, was substituted in its place; virtue and crime depended upon accident; and that which was patriotism one day became treason the next.

All these things have followed from the want of a constitution; for it is the nature and intention of a constitution to *prevent governing by party,* by establishing a common principle that shall limit and control the power and impulse of party, and that says to all parties, *thus far shalt thou go and no further.* But in the absence of a constitution, men look entirely to party; and instead of principle governing party, party governs principle.

An avidity to punish is always dangerous to liberty. It leads men to stretch, to misinterpret, and to misapply even the best of laws. He that would make his own liberty secure must guard even his enemy from oppression; for if he violates this duty he establishes a precedent that will reach to himself.

[17] AGRARIAN JUSTICE

———◆◆◆◆◆———

(1795)

Agrarian Justice was the last of Paine's major works. Published in the winter of 1795, it saw Paine returning to the themes of poverty and inequality which preoccupied him in Part Two of The Rights of Man. *The essay contains his most extensive discussion of property and social justice and includes a proposal for the creation of a public fund to repay all English men and women for what Paine labels 'the loss of his or her natural inheritance, by the introduction of the system of landed property'.*

TO THE LEGISLATURE AND THE EXECUTIVE DIRECTORY OF THE FRENCH REPUBLIC

The plan contained in this work is not adapted for any particular country alone: the principle on which it is based is general. But as the rights of man are a new study in this world, and one needing protection from priestly imposture, and the insolence of oppressions too long established, I have thought it right to place this little work under your safeguard.

When we reflect on the long and dense night in which France and all Europe have remained plunged by their governments and their priests, we must feel less surprise than grief at the bewilderment caused by the first burst of light that dispels the darkness. The eye accustomed to darkness can hardly bear at first the broad daylight. It is by usage the eye learns to see, and it is the same in passing from any situation to its opposite.

As we have not at one instant renounced all our errors, we cannot at one stroke acquire knowledge of all our rights. France has had the honour of adding to the word *Liberty* that of *Equality*; and this word signifies essentially a principle that admits of no gradation in the things to which it applies. But equality is often misunderstood, often misapplied, and often violated.

Liberty and *Property* are words expressing all those of our possessions which are not of an intellectual nature. There are two kinds of property. Firstly, natural property, or that which comes to us from the Creator of the universe – such as the earth, air, water. Secondly, artificial or acquired property – the invention of men.

In the latter, equality is impossible; for to distribute it equally it would be necessary that all should have contributed in the same proportion, which can never be the case; and this being the case, every individual would hold on to his own property, as his right share. Equality of natural property is the subject of this little essay. Every individual in the world is born therein with legitimate claims on a certain kind of property, or its equivalent.

The right of voting for persons charged with the execution of the laws that govern society is inherent in the word liberty, and constitutes the equality of personal rights. But even if that right (of voting) were inherent in property, which I deny, the right of suffrage would still belong to all equally, because, as I have said, all individuals have legitimate birthrights in a certain species of property.

I have always considered the present Constitution of the French Republic the *best organized system* the human mind has yet produced. But I hope my former colleagues will not be offended if I warn them of an error which has slipped into its principle. Equality of the right of suffrage is not maintained. This right is in it connected with a condition on which it ought not to depend; that is, with a proportion of a certain tax called 'direct'.

The dignity of suffrage is thus lowered; and, in placing it in the scale with an inferior thing, the enthusiasm that right is capable of inspiring is diminished. It is impossible to find any equivalent counterpoise for the right of suffrage, because it is alone worthy to be its own basis, and cannot thrive as a graft, or an appendage.

Since the Constitution was established we have seen two conspiracies stranded – that of Babeuf, and that of some obscure personages who decorate themselves with the despicable name of 'royalists'. The defect in principle of the Constitution was the origin of Babeuf's conspiracy.

He availed himself of the resentment caused by this flaw, and instead of seeking a remedy by legitimate and constitutional means, or proposing some measure useful to society, the conspirators did their best to renew disorder and confusion, and constituted themselves personally into a Directory, which is formally destructive of election and representation. They were, in fine, extravagant enough to suppose that society, occupied with its domestic affairs, would blindly yield to them a directorship usurped by violence.

The conspiracy of Babeuf was followed in a few months by that of the royalists, who foolishly flattered themselves with the notion of doing great things by feeble or foul means. They counted on all the discontented, from whatever cause, and tried to rouse, in their turn, the class of people who had been following the others. But these new chiefs acted as if they thought society had nothing more at heart than to maintain courtiers, pensioners, and all their train, under the contemptible title of royalty. My little essay will disabuse them, by showing that society is aiming at a very different end – maintaining itself.

We all know or should know, that the time during which a revolution is proceeding is not the time when its resulting advantages can be enjoyed. But had Babeuf and his accomplices taken into consideration the condition of France under this Constitution, and compared it with what it was under the tragical revolutionary government, and during the execrable Reign of Terror, the rapidity of the alteration must have appeared to them very striking and astonishing. Famine has been replaced by abundance, and by the well-founded hope of a near and increasing prosperity.

As for the defect in the Constitution, I am fully convinced that it will be rectified constitutionally, and that this step is indispensable; for so long as it continues it will inspire the hopes and furnish the means of conspirators; and for the rest, it is regrettable that a Constitution so wisely organized should err so much in its principle. This fault exposes it to other dangers which will make themselves felt.

Intriguing candidates will go about among those who have not the means to pay the direct tax and pay it for them, on condition of receiving their votes. Let us maintain inviolably equality in the sacred right of suffrage: public security can never have a basis more solid. *Salut et Fraternité*.

Your former colleague,
THOMAS PAINE.

AUTHOR'S ENGLISH PREFACE

The following little piece was written in the winter of 1795 and '96; and, as I had not determined whether to publish it during the present war, or to wait till the commencement of a peace, it has lain by me, without alteration or addition, from the time it was written.

What has determined me to publish it now is a sermon preached by Watson, Bishop of Llandaff. Some of my readers will recollect, that this Bishop wrote a book entitled *An Apology for the Bible*, in answer to my second part of *The Age of Reason*. I procured a copy of his book, and he may depend upon hearing from me on that subject.

At the end of the Bishop's book is a list of the works he has written. Among which is the sermon alluded to; it is entitled: 'The Wisdom and Goodness of God, in having made both Rich and Poor; with an Appendix, containing Reflections on the Present State of England and France'.

The error contained in this sermon determined me to publish my *Agrarian Justice*. It is wrong to say God made *rich* and *poor*; He made only *male* and *female*; and He gave them the earth for their inheritance. . . .

Instead of preaching to encourage one part of mankind in insolence . . . it would be better that priests employed their time to render the general condition of man less miserable than it is. Practical religion consists in doing good: and the only way of serving God is that of endeavouring to make His creation happy. All preaching that has not this for its object is nonsense and hypocrisy.

                                                        THOMAS PAINE.

AGRARIAN JUSTICE

To preserve the benefits of what is called civilized life, and to remedy at the same time the evil which it has produced, ought to be considered as one of the first objects of reformed legislation.

Whether that state that is proudly, perhaps erroneously, called civilization, has most promoted or most injured the general happiness of man, is a question that may be strongly contested. On one side, the spectator is dazzled by splendid appearances; on the other, he is shocked by extremes of wretchedness; both of which it has erected.

The most affluent and the most miserable of the human race are to be found in the countries that are called civilized.

To understand what the state of society ought to be, it is necessary to have some idea of the natural and primitive state of man; such as it is at this day among the Indians of North America. There is not, in that state, any of those spectacles of human misery which poverty and want present to our eyes in all the towns and streets in Europe.

Poverty, therefore, is a thing created by that which is called civilized life. It exists not in the natural state. On the other hand, the natural state is without those advantages which flow from agriculture, arts, science and manufactures.

The life of an Indian is a continual holiday, compared with the poor of Europe; and, on the other hand it appears to be abject when compared to the rich. Civilization, therefore, or that which is so called, has operated two ways: to make one part of society more affluent, and the other more wretched, than would have been the lot of either in a natural state.

It is always possible to go from the natural to the civilized state, but it is never possible to go from the civilized to the natural state. The reason is that man in a natural state, subsisting by hunting, requires ten times the quantity of land to range over to procure himself sustenance, than would support him in a civilized state, where the earth is cultivated.

When, therefore, a country becomes populous by the additional aids of cultivation, art and science, there is a necessity of preserving things in that state; because without it there cannot be sustenance for more, perhaps, than a tenth part of its inhabitants. The thing, therefore, now to be done is to remedy the evils and preserve the benefits that have arisen to society by passing from the natural to that which is called the civilized state.

In taking the matter upon this ground, the first principle of civilization ought to have been, and ought still to be, that the condition of every person born into the world, after a state of civilization commences, ought not to be worse than if he had been born before that period.

But the fact is that the condition of millions, in every country in Europe, is far worse than if they had been born before civilization began, or had been born among the Indians of North America at the present day. I will show how this fact has happened.

It is a position not to be controverted that the earth, in its natural, uncultivated state was, and ever would have continued to be, *the common property of the human race*. In that state every man would have been born to property. He would have been a joint life proprietor with the rest in the property of the soil, and in all its natural productions, vegetable and animal.

But the earth in its natural state, as before said, is capable of supporting but a small number of inhabitants compared with what it is capable of doing in a cultivated state. And as it is impossible to separate the improvement made by cultivation from the earth itself, upon which that improvement is made, the idea of landed property arose from that inseparable connection; but it is nevertheless true, that it is the value of the improvement, only, and not the earth itself, that is individual property.

Every proprietor, therefore, of cultivated lands, owes to the community a *ground-rent* (for I know of no better term to express the idea) for the land which he holds; and it is from this ground-rent that the fund proposed in this plan is to issue.

It is deducible, as well from the nature of the things as from all the histories transmitted to us, that the idea of landed property commenced with cultivation, and that there was no such thing as landed property before that time. It could not exist in the first state of man, that of hunters. It did not exist in the second state, that of shepherds: neither Abraham, Isaac, Jacob, nor Job, so far as the history of the Bible may be credited in probable things, were owners of land.

Their property consisted, as is always enumerated in flocks and herds, and they travelled with them from place to place. The frequent contentions at that time about the use of a well in the dry country of Arabia, where those people lived, also show that there was no landed property. It was not admitted that land could be claimed as property.

There could be no such thing as landed property originally. Man did not make the earth, and, though he had a natural right to *occupy* it, he had no right to *locate as his property* in perpetuity any part of it; neither did the Creator of the earth open a land-office, from whence the first title-deeds should issue. Whence then, arose the idea of landed property? I answer as before, that when cultivation began the idea of landed property began with it, from the impossibility of separating the improvement made by cultivation from the earth itself, upon which that improvement was made.

The value of the improvement so far exceeded the value of the natural earth, at that time, as to absorb it; till, in the end, the common right of all became confounded into the cultivated right of the individual. But there are, nevertheless, distinct species of rights, and will continue to be, so long as the earth endures.

It is only by tracing things to their origin that we can gain rightful ideas of them, and it is by gaining such ideas that we discover the boundary that divides right from wrong, and teaches every man to know his own. I have entitled this tract 'Agrarian Justice' to distinguish it from 'Agrarian Law'.

Nothing could be more unjust than agrarian law in a country improved by cultivation; for though every man, as an inhabitant of the earth, is a joint proprietor of it in its natural state, it does not follow that he is a joint proprietor of cultivated earth. The additional value made by cultivation, after the system was admitted, became the property of those who did it, or who inherited it from them, or who purchased it. It had originally no owner. While, therefore, I advocate the right, and interest myself in the hard case of all those who have been thrown out of their natural inheritance by the introduction of the system of landed property, I equally defend the right of the possessor to the part which is his.

Cultivation is at least one of the greatest natural improvements ever made by human invention. It has given to created earth a tenfold value. But the landed monopoly that began with it has produced the greatest evil. It has dispossessed more than half the inhabitants of every nation of their natural inheritance, without providing for them, as ought to have been done, an indemnification for that loss, and has thereby created a species of poverty and wretchedness that did not exist before.

In advocating the case of the persons thus dispossessed, it is a right, and not a charity, that I am pleading for. But it is that kind of right which, being neglected at first, could not be brought forward afterwards till heaven had opened the way by a revolution in the system of government. Let us then do honour to revolutions by justice, and give currency to their principles by blessings.

Having thus in a few words, opened the merits of the case, I shall now proceed to the plan I have to propose, which is,

To create a national fund, out of which there shall be paid to every person, when arrived at the age of twenty-one years, the sum of fifteen pounds sterling, as a compensation in part, for the loss of his or her natural inheritance, by the introduction of the system of landed property:

And also, the sum of ten pounds per annum, during life, to every person now living, of the age of fifty years, and to all others as they shall arrive at that age.

MEANS BY WHICH THE FUND IS TO BE CREATED

I have already established the principle, namely, that the earth, in its natural uncultivated state was, and ever would have continued to be, the *common property of the human race*; that in that state, every person would have been born to property; and that the system of landed property, by its inseparable connection with cultivation, and with what is called civilized life, has absorbed the property of all those whom it dispossessed, without providing, as ought to have been done, an indemnification for that loss.

The fault, however, is not in the present possessors. No complaint is intended, or ought to be alleged against them, unless they adopt the crime by opposing justice. The fault is in the system, and it has stolen imperceptibly upon the world, aided afterwards by the agrarian law of the sword. But the fault can be made to reform itself by successive generations; and without diminishing or deranging the property of any of the present possessors, the operation of the fund can yet commence, and be in full activity, the first year of its establishment, or soon after, as I shall show.

It is proposed that the payments, as already stated, be made to every person, rich or poor. It is best to make it so, to prevent invidious distinctions. It is also right it should be so, because it is in lieu of the natural inheritance, which, as a right, belongs to every man, over and above the property he may have created, or inherited from those who did. Such persons as do not choose to receive it can throw it into the common fund.

Taking it then for granted that no person ought to be in a worse condition when born under what is called a state of civilization, than he would have been had he been born in a state of nature, and that civilization ought to have made, and ought still to make, provision for that purpose, it can only be done by subtracting from property a portion equal in value to the natural inheritance it has absorbed.

Various methods may be proposed for this purpose, but that which appears to be the best (not only because it will operate without deranging any present possessors, or without interfering with the collection of taxes or *emprunts* necessary for the purposes of government and the Revolution, but because it will be the least troublesome and the most effectual, and also because the subtraction will be made at a time that best admits it) is at the moment that property is passing by the death of one person to the possession of another. In this case, the bequeather gives nothing: the receiver pays nothing. The only matter to him is that the monopoly of natural inheritance, to which there never was a right, begins to cease in his person. A generous man would not wish it to continue, and a just man will rejoice to see it abolished.

My state of health prevents my making sufficient inquiries with respect to the doctrine of probabilities, whereon to found calculations with such degrees of certainty as they are capable of. What, therefore, I offer on this head is more the result of observation and reflection than of received information; but I believe it will be found to agree sufficiently with fact. In the first place, taking twenty-one years as the epoch of maturity, all the property of a nation, real and personal, is always in the possession of persons above that age. It is then necessary to know, as a datum of calculation, the average of years which persons above that age will live. I take this average to be about thirty years, for though many persons will live forty, fifty, or sixty years, after the age of twenty-one years, others will die much sooner, and some in every year of that time.

Taking, then, thirty years as the average of time, it will give, without any material variation one way or other, the average of time in which the whole property or capital of a nation, or a sum equal thereto, will have passed through one entire revolution in descent, that is, will have gone by deaths to new possessors; for though, in many instances, some parts of this capital will remain forty, fifty, or sixty years in the possession of one person, other parts will have revolved two or three times before those thirty years expire, which will bring it to that average; for were one-half the capital of a nation to revolve twice in thirty years, it would produce the same fund as if the whole revolved once.

Taking, then, thirty years as the average of time in which the whole capital of a nation, or a sum equal thereto, will revolve once, the thirtieth part thereof will be the sum that will revolve every year, that is, will go by deaths to new possessors; and this last sum being thus known, and the ratio per cent to be subtracted from it determined, it will give the annual amount or income of the proposed fund, to be applied as already mentioned.

In looking over the discourse of the English Minister, Pitt, in his opening of what is called in England the budget (the scheme of finance for the year 1796), I find an estimate of the national capital of that country. As this estimate of a national capital is prepared ready to my hand, I take it as a datum to act upon. When a calculation is made upon the known capital of any nation, combined with its population, it will serve as a scale for any other nation, in proportion as its capital and population be more or less.

I am the more disposed to take this estimate of Mr Pitt, for the purpose of showing to that minister, upon his own calculation, how much better money may be employed than in wasting it, as he has done, on the wild project of setting up Bourbon kings. What, in the name of heaven, are Bourbon kings to the people of England? It is better that the people have bread.

Mr Pitt states the national capital of England, real and personal, to be one thousand three hundred millions sterling, which is about one-fourth part of the national capital of France, including Belgia. The event of the last harvest in each country proves that the soil of France is more productive than that of England, and that it can better support twenty-four or twenty-five millions of inhabitants than that of England can seven or seven and a half millions.

The thirtieth part of this capital of £1,3000,000,000 is £43,333,333 which is the part that will revolve every year by deaths in that country to new possessors; and the sum that will annually revolve in France in the proportion of four to one, will be about one hundred and seventy-three millions sterling. From this sum of £43,333,333 annually revolving, is to be subtracted the value of the natural inheritance absorbed in it, which, perhaps, in fair justice, cannot be taken at less, and ought not to be taken for more, than a tenth part.

It will always happen that of the property thus revolving by deaths every year a part will descend in a direct line to sons and daughters, and the other part collaterally, and the proportion will be found to be about three to one; that is, about thirty millions of the above sum will descend to direct heirs, and the remaining sum of £13,333,333 to more distant relations, and in part to strangers.

Considering, then, that man is always related to society, that relationship will become comparatively greater in proportion as the next of kin is more distant; it is therefore consistent with civilization to say that where there are no direct heirs society shall be heir to a part over and above the tenth part *due* to society.

If this additional part be from five to ten or twelve per cent, in proportion as the next of kin be nearer or more remote, so as to average with the escheats that may fall, which ought always to go to society and not to the government (an addition of ten per cent more), the produce from the annual sum of £43,333,333 will be:

From £30,000,000 at ten per cent	£3,000,000
From £13,333,333 at ten per cent with the addition of ten per cent more }	2,666,666
£43,333,333	£5,666,666

Having thus arrived at the annual amount of the proposed fund, I come, in the next place, to speak of the population proportioned to this fund and to compare it with the uses to which the fund is to be applied.

The population (I mean that of England) does not exceed seven millions and a half, and the number of persons above the age of fifty will in that case be about four hundred thousand. There would not, however, be more than that number that would accept the proposed ten pounds sterling per annum, though they would be entitled to it. I have no idea it would be accepted by many persons who had a yearly income of two or three hundred pounds sterling. But as we often see instances of rich people falling into sudden poverty, even at the age of sixty, they would always have the right of drawing all the arrears due to them. Four millions, therefore, of the above annual sum of £5,666,666 will be required for four hundred thousand aged persons, at ten pounds sterling each.

I come now to speak of the persons annually arriving at twenty-one years of age. If all the persons who died were above the age of twenty-one years, the number of persons annually arriving at that age must be equal to the annual number of deaths, to keep the population stationary. But the greater part die under the age of twenty-one, and therefore the number of persons annually arriving at twenty-one will be less than half the number of deaths.

The whole number of deaths upon a population of seven millions and an half will be about 220,000 annually. The number arriving at twenty-one years of age will be about 100,000. The whole number of these will not receive the proposed fifteen pounds, for the reasons already mentioned, though, as in the former case, they would be entitled to it. Admitting then that a tenth part declined receiving it, the amount would stand thus:

Fund annually		£5,666,666
To 400,000 aged persons at £10 each	£4,000,000	
To 90,000 persons of 21 yrs, £15 ster. each	1,350,000	
		5,350,000
	Remains	£ 316,666

There are, in every country, a number of blind and lame persons totally incapable of earning a livelihood. But as it will always happen that the greater number of blind persons will be among those who are above the age of fifty years, they will be provided for in that class. The remaining sum of £316,666 will provide for the lame and blind under that age, at the same rate of £10 annually for each person.

Having now gone through all the necessary calculations, and stated the particulars of the plan, I shall conclude with some observations.

It is not charity but a right, not bounty but justice, that I am pleading for. The present state of civilization is as odious as it is unjust. It is absolutely the opposite of what it should be, and it is necessary that a revolution should be made in it. The contrast of affluence and wretchedness continually meeting and offending the eye, is like dead and living bodies chained together. Though I care as little about riches as any man, I am a friend to riches because they are capable of good.

I care not how affluent some may be, provided that none be miserable in consequence of it. But it is impossible to enjoy affluence with the felicity it is capable of being enjoyed, while so much misery is mingled in the scene. The sight of the misery, and the unpleasant sensations it suggests, which, though they may be suffocated cannot be extinguished, are a greater drawback upon the felicity of affluence than the proposed ten per cent upon property is worth. He that would not give the one to get rid of the other has no charity, even for himself.

There are, in every country, some magnificent charities established by individuals. It is, however, but little that any individual can do, when the whole extent of the misery to be relieved is considered. He may satisfy his conscience, but not his heart. He may give all that he has, and that all will relieve but little. It is only by organizing civilization upon such principles as to act like a system of pulleys, that the whole weight of misery can be removed.

The plan here proposed will reach the whole. It will immediately relieve and take out of view three classes of wretchedness – the blind, the lame, and the aged poor; and it will furnish the rising generation with means to prevent their becoming poor; and it will do this without deranging or interfering with any national measures.

To show that this will be the case, it is sufficient to observe that the operation and effect of the plan will, in all cases, be the same as if every individual were *voluntarily* to make his will and dispose of his property in the manner here proposed.

But it is justice, and not charity, that is the principle of the plan. In all great cases it is necessary to have a principle more universally active than charity; and, with respect to justice, it ought not to be left to the choice of detached individuals whether they will do justice or not. Considering, then, the plan on the ground of justice, it ought to be the act of the whole growing spontaneously out of the principles of the revolution, and the reputation of it ought to be national and not individual.

A plan upon this principle would benefit the revolution by the energy that springs from the consciousness of justice. It would multiply also the national resources; for property, like vegetation, increases by offsets. When a young couple begin the world, the difference is exceedingly great whether they begin with nothing or with fifteen pounds apiece. With this aid they could buy a cow, and implements to cultivate a few acres of land; and instead of becoming burdens upon society, which is always the case where children are produced faster than they can be fed, would be put in the way of becoming useful and profitable citizens. The national domains also would sell the better if pecuniary aids were provided to cultivate them in small lots.

It is the practice of what has unjustly obtained the name of civilization (and the practice merits not to be called either charity or policy) to make some provision for persons becoming poor and wretched only at the time they become so. Would it not, even as a matter of economy, be far better to adopt means to prevent their becoming poor? This can best be done by making every person when arrived at the age of twenty-one years an inheritor of something to begin with.

The rugged face of society, chequered with the extremes of affluence and want, proves that some extraordinary violence has been committed upon it, and calls on justice for redress. The great mass of the poor in all countries are become an hereditary race, and it is next to impossible for them to get out of that state of themselves. It ought also to be observed that this mass increases in all countries that are called civilized. More persons fall annually into it than get out of it.

Though in a plan of which justice and humanity are the foundation-principles, interest ought not to be admitted into the calculation, yet it is always of advantage to the establishment of any plan to show that it is beneficial as a matter of interest. The success of any proposed plan submitted to public consideration must finally depend on the numbers interested in supporting it, united with the justice of its principles.

The plan here proposed will benefit all, without injuring any. It will consolidate the interest of the republic with that of the individual. To the numerous class dispossessed of their natural inheritance by the system of landed property it will be an act of national justice. To persons dying possessed of moderate fortunes it will operate as a tontine to their children, more beneficial than the sum of money paid into the fund: and it will give to the accumulation of riches a degree of security that none of the old governments of Europe, now tottering on their foundations, can give.

I do not suppose that more than one family in ten, in any of the countries of Europe, has, when the head of the family dies, a clear property left of five hundred pounds sterling. To all such the plan is advantageous. That property would pay fifty pounds into the fund, and if there were only two children under age they would receive fifteen pounds each (thirty pounds), on coming of age, and be entitled to ten pounds a year after fifty.

It is from the overgrown acquisition of property that the fund will support itself; and I know that the possessors of such property in England, though they would eventually be benefited by the protection of nine-tenths of it, will exclaim against the plan. But without entering into any inquiry how they came by that property, let them recollect that they have been the advocates of this war, and that Mr Pitt has already laid on more new taxes to be raised annually upon the people of England, and that for supporting the despotism of Austria and the Bourbons against the liberties of France, than would pay annually all the sums proposed in this plan.

I have made the calculations stated in this plan, upon what is called personal, as well as upon landed property. The reason for making it upon land is already explained; and the reason for taking personal property into the calculation is equally well founded though on a different principle. Land, as before said, is the free gift of the Creator in common to the human race. Personal property is the *effect of society*; and it is as impossible for an individual to acquire personal property without the aid of society, as it is for him to make land originally.

Separate an individual from society, and give him an island or a continent to possess, and he cannot acquire personal property. He cannot be rich. So inseparably are the means connected with the end, in all cases, that where the former do not exist the latter cannot be obtained. All accumulation, therefore, of personal property, beyond what a man's own hands produce, is derived to him by living in society; and he owes on every principle of justice, of gratitude, and of civilization, a part of that accumulation back again to society from whence the whole came.

This is putting the matter on a general principle, and perhaps it is best to do so; for if we examine the case minutely it will be found that the accumulation of personal property is, in many instances, the effect of paying too little for the labour that produced it; the consequence of which is that the working hand perishes in old age, and the employer abounds in affluence.

It is, perhaps, impossible to proportion exactly the price of labour to the profits it produces; and it will also be said, as an apology for the injustice, that were a workman to receive an increase of wages daily he would not save it against old age, nor be much better for it in the interim. Make, then, society the treasurer to guard it for him in a common fund; for it is no reason that, because he might not make a good use of it for himself, another should take it.

The state of civilization that has prevailed throughout Europe, is as unjust in its principle, as it is horrid in its effects; and it is the consciousness of this, and the apprehension that such a state cannot continue when once investigation begins in any country, that makes the possessors of property dread every idea of a revolution. It is the hazard and not the principle of revolutions that retards their progress. This being the case, it is necessary as well for the protection of property as for the sake of justice and humanity, to form a system that, while it preserves one part of society from wretchedness, shall secure the other from depredation.

The superstitious awe, the enslaving reverence, that formerly surrounded affluence, is passing away in all countries, and leaving the possessor of property to the convulsion of accidents. When wealth and splendour, instead of fascinating the multitude, excite emotions of disgust; when, instead of drawing forth admiration, it is beheld as an insult upon wretchedness; when the ostentatious appearance it makes serves to call the right of it in question, the case of property becomes critical, and it is only in a system of justice that the possessor can contemplate security.

To remove the danger, it is necessary to remove the antipathies, and this can only be done by making property productive of a national blessing, extending to every individual. When the riches of one man above another shall increase the national fund in the same proportion; when it shall be seen that the prosperity of that fund depends on the prosperity of individuals; when the more riches a man acquires, the better it shall be for the general mass; it is then that antipathies will cease, and property be placed on the permanent basis of national interest and protection.

I have no property in France to become subject to the plan I propose. What I have, which is not much, is in the United States of America. But I will pay one hundred pounds sterling towards this fund in France, the instant it shall be established; and I will pay the same sum in England, whenever a similar establishment shall take place in that country.

A revolution in the state of civilization is the necessary companion of revolutions in the system of government. If a revolution in any country be from bad to good, or from good to bad, the state of what is called civilization in that country, must be made conformable thereto, to give that revolution effect.

Despotic government supports itself by abject civilization, in which debasement of the human mind, and wretchedness in the mass of the people, are the chief criterions. Such governments consider man merely as an animal; that the exercise of intellectual faculty is not his privilege; *that he has nothing to do with the laws but to obey them;*[1] and they politically depend more upon breaking the spirit of the people by poverty, than they fear enraging it by desperation.

It is a revolution in the state of civilization that will give perfection to the Revolution of France. Already the conviction that government by representation is the true system of government is spreading itself fast in the world. The reasonableness of it can be seen by all. The justness of it makes itself felt even by its opposers. But when a system of civilization, growing out of that system of government, shall be so organized that not a man or woman born in the Republic but shall inherit some means of beginning the world, and see before them the certainty of escaping the miseries that under other governments accompany old age, the Revolution of France will have an advocate and an ally in the heart of all nations.

An army of principles will penetrate where an army of soldiers cannot; it will succeed where diplomatic management would fail: it is neither the Rhine, the Channel, nor the ocean that can arrest its progress: it will march on the horizon of the world, and it will conquer.

MEANS FOR CARRYING THE PROPOSED PLAN INTO EXECUTION, AND TO RENDER IT AT THE SAME TIME CONDUCIVE TO THE PUBLIC INTEREST

I. Each canton shall elect in its primary assemblies, three persons, as commissioners for that canton, who shall take cognizance, and keep a register of all matters happening in that canton, conformable to the charter that shall be established by law for carrying this plan into execution.

1 An expression used by Bishop Horsley in the Parliament of England. – Paine.

II. The law shall fix the manner in which the property of deceased persons shall be ascertained.

III. When the amount of the property of any deceased persons shall be ascertained, the principal heir to that property, or the eldest of the co-heirs, if of lawful age, or if under age, the person authorized by the will of the deceased to represent him or them, shall give bond to the commissioners of the canton to pay the said tenth part thereof in four equal quarterly payments, within the space of one year or sooner, at the choice of the payers. One-half of the whole property shall remain as a security until the bond be paid off.

IV. The bond shall be registered in the office of the commissioners of the canton, and the original bonds shall be deposited in the national bank at Paris. The bank shall publish every quarter of a year the amount of the bonds in its possession, and also the bonds that shall have been paid off, or what parts thereof, since the last quarterly publication.

V. The national bank shall issue bank notes upon the security of the bonds in its possession. The notes so issued, shall be applied to pay the pensions of aged persons, and the compensations to persons arriving at twenty-one years of age. It is both reasonable and generous to suppose, that persons not under immediate necessity, will suspend their right of drawing on the fund, until it acquire, as it will do, a greater degree of ability. In this case, it is proposed, that an honorary register be kept, in each canton, of the names of the persons thus suspending that right, at least during the present war.

VI. As the inheritors of property must always take up their bonds in four quarterly payments, or sooner if they choose, there will always be *numéraire* [cash] arriving at the bank after the expiration of the first quarter, to exchange for the bank notes that shall be brought in.

VII. The bank notes being thus put in circulation, upon the best of all possible security, that of actual property, to more than four times the amount of the bonds upon which the notes are issued, and with *numéraire* continually arriving at the bank to exchange or pay them off whenever they shall be presented for that purpose, they will acquire a permanent value in all parts of the Republic. They can therefore be received in payments of taxes, or *emprunts* equal to *numéraire*, because the Government can always receive *numéraire* for them at the bank.

VIII. It will be necessary that the payments of the ten per cent be made in *numéraire* for the first year from the establishment of the plan. But after the expiration of the first year, the inheritors of property may pay ten per cent either in bank notes issued upon the fund, or in *numéraire*.

If the payments be in *numéraire*, it will lie as a deposit at the bank, to be exchanged for a quantity of notes equal to that amount; and if in notes issued upon the fund, it will cause a demand upon the fund equal thereto; and thus the operation of the plan will create means to carry itself into execution.

[18] LETTER TO GEORGE WASHINGTON

◆◆◆◆

(1795)

Surely the strangest of Paine's writings, this bitter attack on America's first President was written in Paris during 1795. Paine had been in jail from late December 1793 to November 1794. Throughout imprisonment he had assumed that it was only George Washington's failure to intervene that prevented his release. He poured this anger, against the man to whom he had dedicated Part One of The Rights of Man, *into the* Letter, *which he sent to be published in America, against the advice of James Monroe. Monroe, the Jeffersonian American envoy, had just replaced the real culprit, Gouverneur Morris. The publication of the intemperate* Letter to Washington *in America, excerpts from which are included here, did little to enhance the reputation of Paine, already severely damaged by* The Age of Reason.

As censure is but awkwardly softened by apology, I shall offer to you no apology for this letter. The eventful crisis to which your double politics have conducted the affairs of your country, requires an investigation uncramped by ceremony.

There was a time when the fame of America, moral and political, stood fair and high in the world. The lustre of her Revolution extended itself to every individual; and to be a citizen of America gave a title to respect in Europe. Neither meanness nor ingratitude had been mingled in the composition of her character. Her resistance to the attempted tyranny of England left her unsuspected of the one, and her open acknowledgement of the aid she received from France precluded all suspicion of the other. The Washington of politics had not then appeared.

At the time I left America (April, 1787) the Continental Convention, that formed the Federal Constitution, was on the point of meeting. Since that time new schemes of politics, and new distinctions of parties, have arisen. The term *Anti-federalist* has been applied to all those who combated the defects of that Constitution, or opposed the measures of your administration.

It was only to the absolute necessity of establishing some Federal authority, extending equally over all the States, that an instrument so inconsistent as the present Federal Constitution is, obtained a suffrage.

I would have voted for it myself, had I been in America, or even for a worse, rather than have had none, provided it contained the means of remedying its defects by the same appeal to the people by which it was to be established. It is always better policy to leave removable errors to expose themselves than to hazard too much in contending against them theoretically.

I have introduced these observations, not only to mark the general difference between Anti-federalist and Anti-constitutionalist, but to preclude the effect, and even the application, of the former of these terms to myself.

I declare myself opposed to several matters in the Constitution, particularly to the manner in which what is called the Executive is formed, and to the long duration of the Senate; and if I live to return to America, I will use all my endeavours to have them altered.[1] I also declare myself opposed to almost the whole of your administration; for I know it to have been deceitful, if not perfidious, as I shall show in the course of this letter.

But as to the point of consolidating the States into a Federal Government, it so happens, that the proposition for that purpose came originally from myself. I proposed it in a letter to Chancellor Livingston in the spring of 1782, while that gentleman was Minister for Foreign Affairs. The five per cent duty recommended by Congress had then fallen through, having been adopted by some of the States, altered by others, rejected by Rhode Island, and repealed by Virginia after it had been consented to.

The proposal in the letter I allude to, was to get over the whole difficulty at once, by annexing a Continental legislative body to Congress; for in order to have any law of the Union uniform, the case could only be that either Congress, as it then stood, must frame the law, and the States severally adopt it without alteration, or the States must erect a Continental legislature for the purpose.

Chancellor Livingston, Robert Morris, Gouverneur Morris and myself had a meeting at the house of Robert Morris on the subject of that letter. There was no diversity of opinion on the proposition for a Continental legislature: the only difficulty was on the manner of

1 I have always been opposed to the mode of refining government up to an individual or what is called a single executive. Such a man will always be the chief of a party. A plurality is far better: It combines the mass of a nation better together: And besides this, it is necessary to the manly mind of a republic that it loses the debasing idea of obeying an individual. – Paine.

bringing the proposition forward. For my own part, as I considered it as a remedy in reserve, that could be applied at any time *when the states saw themselves wrong enough to be put right* (which did not appear to be the case at that time), I did not see the propriety of urging it precipitately, and declined being the publisher of it myself.

After this account of a fact, the leaders of your party will scarcely have the hardiness to apply to me the term of Anti-federalist. But I can go to a date and to a fact beyond this; for the proposition for electing a Continental convention to form the Continental Government is one of the subjects treated of in the pamphlet *Common Sense*.

Having thus cleared away a little of the rubbish that might otherwise have lain in my way, I return to the point of time at which the present Federal Constitution and your administration began.

It was very well said by an anonymous writer in Philadelphia, about a year before that period, that *'thirteen staves and ne'er a hoop will not make a barrel'*, and as any kind of hooping the barrel, however defectively executed, would be better than none, it was scarcely possible but that considerable advantages must arise from the Federal hooping of the States. It was with pleasure that every sincere friend of America beheld, as the natural effect of union, her rising prosperity; and was with grief they saw that prosperity mixed, even in the blossom, with the germ of corruption.

Monopolies of every kind marked your administration almost in the moment of its commencement. The lands obtained by the Revolution were lavished upon partisans; the interest of the disbanded soldier was sold to the speculator; injustice was acted under the pretence of faith; and the chief of the army became the patron of the fraud. From such a beginning what else could be expected than what has happened? A mean and servile submission to the insults of one nation; treachery and ingratitude to another.

Some vices make their approach with such a splendid appearance that we scarcely know to what class of moral distinctions they belong. They are rather virtues corrupted than vices, originally. But meanness and ingratitude have nothing equivocal in their character. There is not a trait in them that renders them doubtful. They are so originally vice that they are generated in the dung of other vices, and crawl into existence with the filth upon their back. The fugitives have found protection in you, and the levee-room is their place of rendez-vous.

As the Federal Constitution is a copy, though not quite so base as the original, of the form of the British Government, an imitation of its vices was naturally to be expected. So intimate is the connection between *form* and *practice*, that to adopt the one is to invite the other. Imitation is naturally progressive and is rapidly so in matters that are vicious.

Soon after the Federal Constitution arrived in England, I received a letter from a female literary correspondent (a native of New York), very well mixed with friendship, sentiment and politics. In my answer to that letter, I permitted myself to ramble into the wilderness of imagination, and to anticipate what might hereafter be the con-dition of America. I had no idea that the picture I then drew was realizing so fast, and still less that Mr Washington was hurrying it on. As the extract I allude to is congenial with the subject I am upon, I here transcribe it:

You touch me on a very tender point when you say that my friends on your side the water cannot be reconciled to the idea of my abandoning America. They are right. I had rather see my horse Button eating the grass of Bord-entown or Morrisania than see all the pomp and show of Europe.

A thousand years hence (for I must indulge a few thoughts), perhaps in less, America may be what Europe now is. The innocence of her character, that won the hearts of all nations in her favour, may sound like a romance and her inimitable virtue as if it had never been. The ruin of that liberty which thousands bled for or struggled to obtain may just furnish materials for a village tale or extort a sigh from rustic sensibility, whilst the fashionable of that day, enveloped in dissipation, shall deride the principle and deny the fact.

When we contemplate the fall of empires and the extinction of the nations of the Ancient World, we see but little to excite our regret than the moul-dering ruins of pompous palaces, magnificent museums, lofty pyramids and walls and towers of the most costly workmanship; but when the empire of America shall fall, the subject for contemplative sorrow will be infinitely greater than crumbling brass and marble can inspire. It will not then be said, here stood a temple of vast antiquity; here rose a babel of invisible height; or there a place of sumptuous extravagance; but here, Ah, painful thought! the noblest work of human wisdom, the grandest scene of human glory, the fair cause of Freedom rose and fell. Read this, and then ask if I forget America.

Impressed, as I was, with apprehensions of this kind, I had America constantly in my mind in all the publications I afterwards made. The first and still more the second part of the *Rights of Man* bear evident marks of this watchfulness; and the *Dissertation on First Principles of Government* goes more directly to the point than either of the former. I now pass on to other subjects.

It will be supposed by those into whose hands this letter may fall that I have some personal resentment against you; I will therefore settle this point before I proceed further.

If I have any resentment you must acknowledge that I have not been hasty in declaring it; neither would it now be declared (for what are private resentments to the public) if the cause of it did not unite itself as well with your public as with your private character, and with the motives of your political conduct.

The part I acted in the American Revolution is well known; I shall not here repeat it. I know also that had it not been for the aid received from France, in men, money and ships, that your cold and unmilitary conduct (as I shall show in the course of this letter) would in all probability have lost America; at least she would not have been the independent nation she now is. You slept away your time in the field, till the finances of the country were completely exhausted, and you have but little share in the glory of the final event. It is time, Sir, to speak the undisguised language of historical truth.

Elevated to the chair of the Presidency, you assumed the merit of everything to yourself, and the natural ingratitude of your constitution began to appear. You commenced your Presidential career by encouraging and swallowing the grossest adulation, and you travelled America from one end to the other to put yourself in the way of receiving it. You have as many addresses in your chest as James II. As to what were your views, for, if you are not great enough to have ambition, you are little enough to have vanity, they cannot be directly inferred from expressions of your own; but the partisans of your politics have divulged the secret.

John Adams has said (and John it is known was always a speller after places and offices, and never thought his little services were highly enough paid), John has said, that as Mr Washington had no child, the Presidency should be made hereditary in the family of Lund Washington. John might then have counted upon some sinecure himself, and a provision for his descendants. He did not go so far as to say, also, that the Vice-Presidency should be hereditary in the family of John Adams. He prudently left that to stand on the ground that one good turn deserves another.[2]

John Adams is one of those men who never contemplated the origin of government, or comprehended anything of first principles. If he had, he might have seen that the right to set up and establish hereditary government never did, and never can, exist in any generation at any time whatever; that it is of the nature of treason; because it is an attempt to take away the rights of all the minors living at that time, and of all succeeding generations. It is of a degree beyond common treason. It is a sin against nature. The equal right of every generation is a right fixed in the nature of things. It belongs to the son when of age, as it belonged to the father before him.

John Adams would himself deny the right that any former deceased generation could have to decree authoritatively a succession of governors over him, or over his children; and yet he assumes the pretended right, treasonable as it is, of acting it himself. His ignorance is his best excuse.

John Jay has said (and this John was always the sycophant of everything in power, from Mr Gerard in America, to Grenville in England), – John Jay has said that the Senate should have been appointed for life. He would then have been sure of never wanting a lucrative appointment for himself, and have had no fears about impeachment. These are the disguised traitors that call themselves Federalists.[3]

Could I have known to what degree of corruption and perfidy the administrative part of the Government of America had descended, I could have been at no loss to have understood the reservedness of Mr Washington towards me, during my imprisonment in the Luxembourg. There are cases in which silence is a loud language. I will here explain the cause of that imprisonment, and return to Mr Washington afterwards.

In the course of that rage, terror and suspicion which the brutal letter of the Duke of Brunswick first started into existence in France,

2 Two persons to whom John Adams said this, told me of it. The secretary of Mr Jay was present when it was told to me. – Paine.
3 If Mr John Jay desires to know on what authority I say this, I will give that authority publicly when he chooses to call for it. – Paine.

it happened that almost every man who was opposed to violence, or who was not violent himself, became suspected. I had constantly been opposed to everything which was of the nature or of the appearance of violence; but as I had always done it in a manner that showed it to be a principle founded in my heart, and not a political manoeuvre, it precluded the pretence of accusing me. I was reached, however, under another pretence.

A decree was passed to imprison all persons born in England; but as I was a member of the convention, and had been complimented with the honorary style of Citizen of France, as Mr Washington and some other Americans had been, this decree fell short of reaching me. A motion was afterwards made and carried, supported chiefly by Bourdon de l'Oise, for expelling foreigners from the Convention. My expulsion being thus effected, the two committees of Public Safety and of General Surety, of which Robespierre was the dictator, put me in arrestation under the former decree for imprisoning persons born in England. Having thus shown under what pretence the imprisonment was effected, I come to speak of such parts of the case as apply between me and Mr Washington, either as a President or as an individual.

I have always considered that a foreigner, such as I was in fact, with respect to France, might be a member of a convention for framing a constitution, without affecting his right of citizenship in the country to which he belongs, but not a member of a government after a constitution is formed; and I have uniformly acted upon this distinction. To be a member of a government requires that a person be in allegiance to that government and to the country locally. But a constitution, being a thing of principle, and not of action, and which, after it is formed, is to be referred to the people for their approbation or rejection, does not require allegiance in the persons forming and proposing it; and besides this, it is only to the thing after it be formed and established, and to the country after its governmental character is fixed by the adoption of a constitution, that the allegiance can be given.

No oath of allegiance or of citizenship was required of the members who composed the Convention: there was nothing existing in form to swear allegiance to. If any such condition had been required, I could not, as citizen of America in fact, though citizen of France by compliment, have accepted a seat in the Convention.

As my citizenship in America was not altered or diminished by anything I had done in Europe (on the contrary, it ought to be considered as strengthened, for it was the American principle of government that I was endeavouring to spread in Europe), and as it is the duty of every government to charge itself with the care of any of its citizens who may happen to fall under an arbitrary persecution abroad, and is also one of the reasons for which ambassadors or ministers are appointed – it was the duty of the Executive Department in America, to have made (at least) some inquiries about me, as soon as it heard of my imprisonment.

But if this had not been the case, the government owed it to me on every ground and principle of honour and gratitude. Mr Washington owed it to me on every score of private acquaintance, I will not now say, friendship; for it has some time been known by those who know him, that he has no friendships; that he is incapable of forming any; he can serve or desert a man, or a cause, with constitutional indifference; and it is this cold, hermaphrodite faculty that imposed itself upon the world and was credited for a while, by enemies as by friends, for prudence, moderation and impartiality . . . .

A stranger might be led to suppose, from the egotism with which Mr Washington speaks, that himself, and himself only, had generated, conducted, completed, and established the Revolution: in fine, that it was all his own doing.

In the first place, as to the political part, he had no share in it; and, therefore, the whole of *that* is out of the question with respect to him. There remains, then, only the military part; and it would have been prudent in Mr Washington not to have awakened inquiry upon that subject. Fame then was cheap; he enjoyed it cheaply; and nobody was disposed to take away the laurels that, whether they were *acquired* or not, had been *given*.

Mr Washington's merit consisted in constancy. But constancy was the common virtue of the Revolution. Who was there that was inconstant? I know but of one military defection, that of Arnold; and I know of no political defection among those who made themselves eminent when the Revolution was formed by the Declaration of Independence. Even Silas Deane, though he attempted to defraud, did not betray.

But when we speak of military character, something more is to be understood than constancy; and something more *ought* to be understood than the Fabian system of *doing nothing*. The *nothing* part can be done by anybody. Old Mrs Thompson, the housekeeper of head-quarters (who threatened to make the sun and the *wind* shine through Rivington of New York), could not have done it as well as Mr Washington. Deborah would have been as good as Barak.

Mr Washington had the nominal rank of Commander-in-Chief, but he was not so in fact. He had, in reality, only a separate command. He had no control over, or direction of, the army to the northward under Gates, that captured Burgoyne; nor of that to the South under [Nathanael] Greene, that recovered the Southern States. The nominal rank, however, of Commander-in-Chief served to throw upon him the lustre of those actions, and to make him appear as the soul and centre of all military operations in America.

He commenced his command June, 1775, during the time the Massachusetts army lay before Boston, and after the affair of Bunker Hill. The commencement of his command was the commencement of inactivity. Nothing was afterwards done, or attempted to be done, during the nine months he remained before Boston.

If we may judge from the resistance made at Concord, and after-wards at Bunker Hill, there was a spirit of enterprise at that time, which the presence of Mr Washington chilled into cold defence. By the advantage of a good exterior he attracts respect, which his habitual silence tends to preserve; but he has not the talent of inspiring ardour in an army. The enemy removed from Boston in March, 1776, to wait for reinforcements from Europe, and to take a more advan-tageous position at New York.

The inactivity of the campaign of 1775, on the part of General Washington, when the enemy had a less force than in any other future period of the war, and the injudicious choice of positions taken by him in the campaign of 1776, when the enemy had its greatest force, necessarily produced the losses and misfortunes that marked that gloomy campaign. The positions taken were either islands or necks of land. In the former, the enemy, by the aid of their ships, could bring their whole force against a part of General Washington's, as in the affair of Long Island; and in the latter, he might be shut up as in the bottom of a bag.

This had nearly been the case at New York, and it was so in part; it was actually the case at Fort Washington; and it would have been the case at Fort Lee, if General Greene had not moved precipitately off, leaving everything behind, and by gaining Hackensack bridge, got out of the bag of Bergen Neck.

How far Mr Washington, as general, is blameable for these matters, I am not undertaking to determine; but they are evidently defects in military geography. The successful skirmishes at the close of that campaign (matters that would scarcely be noticed in a better state of things) make the brilliant exploits of General Washington's seven campaigns. No wonder we see so much pusillanimity in the *President*, when we see so little enterprise in the *General*!

The campaign of 1777 became famous, not by anything on the part of General Washington, but by the capture of General Burgoyne, and the army under his command, by the Northern Army at Saratoga, under General Gates. So totally distinct and unconnected were the two armies of Washington and Gates, and so independent was the latter of the authority of the nominal Commander-in-Chief, that the two generals did not so much as correspond, and it was only by a letter of General (since Governor) Clinton, that General Washington was informed of that event. The British took possession of Philadelphia this year, which they evacuated the next, just time enough to save their heavy baggage and fleet of transports from capture by the French Admiral d'Estaing, who arrived at the mouth of the Delaware soon after.

The capture of Burgoyne gave an éclat in Europe to the American arms, and facilitated the alliance with France. The éclat, however, was not kept up by anything on the part of General Washington. The same unfortunate languor that marked his entrance into the field, continued always. Discontent began to prevail strongly against him, and a party was formed in Congress, while sitting at York Town, in Pennsylvania, for removing him from the command of the army. The hope, however, of better times, the news of the alliance with France, and the unwillingness of showing discontent, dissipated the matter.

Nothing was done in the campaigns of 1778, 1779, 1780, in the part where General Washington commanded, except the taking of Stony Point by General Wayne. The Southern States in the meantime were over-run by the enemy. They were afterwards recovered by General Greene, who had in a very great measure created the army that accomplished that recovery.

In all this General Washington had no share. The Fabian system of war, followed by him, began now to unfold itself with all its evils; but what is Fabian war without Fabian means to support it? The finances of Congress, depending wholly on emissions of paper money, were exhausted. Its credit was gone. The Continental Treasury was not able to pay the expense of a brigade of wagons to transport the necessary stores to the army, and yet the sole object, the establishment of the Revolution, was a thing of remote distance. The time I am now speaking of is in the latter end of the year 1780.

In this situation of things it was found not only expedient, but absolutely necessary, for Congress to state the whole case to its ally. I knew more of this matter (before it came into Congress or was known to General Washington), of its progress, and its issue, than I choose to state in this letter. Colonel John Laurens was sent to France as an envoy extraordinary on this occasion, and by a private agreement between him and me I accompanied him. We sailed from Boston in the *Alliance* frigate, February 11, 1781. France had already done much in accepting and paying bills drawn by Congress. She was now called upon to do more.

The event of Colonel Lauren's mission, with the aid of the venerable Minister, Franklin, was that France gave in money, as a present, six millions of livres, and ten millions more as a loan, and agreed to send a fleet of not less than thirty sail of the line, at her own expense, as an aid to America. Colonel Laurens and myself returned from Brest the first of June following, taking with us two millions and a half of livres (upwards of one hundred thousand pounds sterling) of the money given, and convoying two ships with stores.

We arrived at Boston the twenty-fifth of August following. De Grasse arrived with the French fleet in the Chesapeake at the same time, and was afterwards joined by that of Barras, making thirty-one sail of the line. The money was transported in wagons from Boston to the bank at Philadelphia, of which Mr Thomas Willing, who has since put himself at the head of the list of petitioners in favour of the British treaty, was then president. And it was by the aid of this money, and this fleet, and Rochambeau's army, that Cornwallis was taken; the laurels of which have been unjustly given to Mr Washington. His merit in that affair was no more than that of any other American officer.

I have had, and still have, as much pride in the American Revolution as any man, or as Mr Washington has a right to have; but that pride has never made me forgetful whence the great aid came that completed the business. Foreign aid (that of France) was calculated upon at the commencement of the Revolution. It is one of the subjects treated of in the pamphlet *Common Sense*, but as a matter that could not be hoped for, unless independence was declared. The aid, however, was greater than could have been expected.

It is as well the ingratitude as the pusillanimity of Mr Washington, and the Washington faction, that has brought upon America the loss of character she now suffers in the world, and the numerous evils her commerce has undergone, and to which it is yet exposed. The British Ministry soon found out what sort of men they had to deal with, and they dealt with them accordingly; and if further explanation was wanting, it has been fully given since, in the snivelling address of the New York Chamber of Commerce to the President, and in that of sundry merchants of Philadelphia which was not much better.

When the Revolution of America was finally established by the termination of the war, the world gave her credit for great character; and she had nothing to do but to stand firm upon that ground. The British Ministry had their hands too full of trouble to have provoked a rupture with her, had she shown a proper resolution to defend her rights. But encouraged as they were by the submissive character of the American Administration, they proceeded from insult to insult, till none more were left to be offered. The proposals made by Sweden and Denmark to the American Administration were disregarded. I know not if so much as an answer has been returned to them.

The Minister *penitentiary* (as some of the British prints called him), Mr Jay, was sent on a pilgrimage to London to make up all by penance and petition. In the meantime the lengthy and drowsy writer of the pieces signed CAMILLUS held himself in reserve to vindicate everything; and to sound in America the tocsin of terror upon the inexhaustible resources of England. Her resources, says he, are greater than those of all the other powers. This man is so intoxicated with fear and finance that he knows not the difference between *plus* and *minus* – between a hundred pounds in hand and a hundred pounds worse than nothing.

The commerce of America, so far as it had been established by all the treaties that had been formed prior to that by Jay, was free, and the principles upon which it was established were good. That ground ought never to have been departed from. It was the justifiable ground of right, and no temporary difficulties ought to have induced an abandonment of it. The case is now otherwise. The ground, the scene, the pretensions, the everything, are changed. The commerce of America is, by Jay's Treaty, put under foreign dominion. The sea is not free for her. Her right to navigate it is reduced to the right of escaping; that is, until some ship of England or France stops her vessels, and carries them into port. Every article of American produce, whether from the sea or the sand, fish, flesh, vegetable, or manufacture, is, by Jay's Treaty, made either contraband or seizable. Nothing is exempt.

In all other treaties of commerce, the article which enumerates the contraband articles, such as firearms, gunpowder, etc., is followed by another article which enumerates the articles not contraband: but it is not so in Jay's Treaty. There is no exempting article. Its place is supplied by the article for seizing and carrying into port; and the sweeping phrase of 'provisions and *other articles*' includes everything. There never was such a base and servile treaty of surrender since treaties began to exist.

This is the ground upon which America now stands. All her rights of commerce and navigation are to begin anew, and that with loss of character to begin with. If there is sense enough left in the heart to call a blush into the cheek, the Washington Administration must be ashamed to appear. And as to you, Sir, treacherous in private friendship (for so you have been to me, and that in the day of danger) and a hypocrite in public life, the world will be puzzled to decide whether you are an apostate or an impostor; whether you have abandoned good principles, or whether you ever had any.

[19] TO THE CITIZENS OF
THE UNITED STATES

(1802–3)

Paine returned to America in 1802 and, as was his wont, plunged himself immediately into political controversy. He published seven letters To the Citizens of the United States in the Jeffersonian press between November 1802 and April 1803. An eighth letter appeared in 1805. In the three letters included here it is clear that joining Washington in the villainous Federalist camp is John Adams, who is described by Paine as hypocritical, arrogant and contemptuous.

After an absence of almost fifteen years, I am again returned to the country in whose dangers I bore my share, and to whose greatness I contributed my part.

When I sailed for Europe, in the spring of 1787, it was my intention to return to America the next year, and enjoy in retirement the esteem of my friends, and the repose I was entitled to. I had stood out the storm of one revolution, and had no wish to embark in another. But other scenes and other circumstances than those of contemplated ease were allotted to me.

The French Revolution was beginning to germinate when I arrived in France. The principles of it were good, they were copied from America, and the men who conducted it were honest. But the fury of faction soon extinguished the one and sent the other to the scaffold. Of those who began that Revolution, I am almost the only survivor, and that through a thousand dangers. I owe this not to the prayers of priests, nor to the piety of hypocrites, but to the continued protection of Providence.

But while I beheld with pleasure the dawn of liberty rising in Europe, I saw with regret the lustre of it fading in America. In less than two years from the time of my departure some distant symptoms painfully suggested the idea that the principles of the Revolution were expiring on the soil that produced them. I received at that time a letter from a female literary correspondent, and in my answer to her, I expressed my fears on that head.

I now know from the information I obtain upon the spot, that the impressions that then distressed me, for I was proud of America, were but too well founded. She was turning her back on her own glory, and making hasty strides in the retrograde path of oblivion. But a spark from the altar of *Seventy-six*, unextinguished and un-extinguishable through the long night of error, is again lighting up, in every part of the Union, the genuine name of rational liberty.

As the French Revolution advanced it fixed the attention of the world, and drew from the pensioned pen of Edmund Burke a furious attack. This brought me once more on the public theatre of politics, and occasioned the pamphlet *Rights of Man*. It had the greatest run of any work ever published in the English language. The number of copies circulated in England, Scotland and Ireland, besides translations into foreign languages, was between four and five hundred thousand.

The principles of that work were the same as those in *Common Sense*, and the effects would have been the same in England as that had produced in America, could the vote of the nation been quietly taken, or had equal opportunities of consulting or acting existed. The only difference between the two works was that the one was adapted to the local circumstances of England, and the other to those of America.

As to myself, I acted in both cases alike; I relinquished to the people of England, as I had done to those of America, all profits from the work. My reward existed in the ambition to do good, and the independent happiness of my own mind.

But a faction, acting in disguise, was rising in America; they had lost sight of first principles. They were beginning to contemplate government as a profitable monopoly, and the people as hereditary property. It is, therefore, no wonder that the *Rights of Man* was attacked by that faction, and its author continually abused. But let them go on; give them rope enough and they will put an end to their own insignificance. There is too much common sense and independence in America to be long the dupe of any faction, foreign or domestic.

But, in the midst of the freedom we enjoy, the licentiousness of the papers called Federal (and I know not why they are called so, for they are in their principles anti-federal and despotic), is a dishonour to the character of the country, and an injury to its reputation and importance abroad. They represent the whole people of America as destitute of public principle and private manners.

As to any injury they can do at home to those whom they abuse, or service they can render to those who employ them, it is to be set down to the account of noisy nothingness. It is on themselves the disgrace recoils, for the reflection easily presents itself to every thinking mind, that *those who abuse liberty when they possess it would abuse power could they obtain it*; and, therefore, they may as well take as a general motto, for all such papers, *We and our patrons are not fit to be trusted with power.*

There is in America, more than in any other country, a large body of people who attend quietly to their farms, or follow their several occupations; who pay no regard to the clamours of anonymous scribblers, who think for themselves, and judge of government, not by the fury of newspaper writers, but by the prudent frugality of its measures, and the encouragement it gives to the improvement and prosperity of the country; and who, acting on their own judgement, never come forward in an election but on some important occasion.

When this body moves, all the little barkings of scribbling and witless curs pass for nothing. To say to this independent description of men, 'You must turn out such and such persons at the next election, for they have taken off a great many taxes, and lessened the expenses of government, they have dismissed my son, or my brother, or myself, from a lucrative office, in which there was nothing to do' – is to show the cloven foot of faction, and preach the language of ill-disguised mortification.

In every part of the Union, this faction is in the agonies of death, and in proportion as its fate approaches, gnashes its teeth and struggles. My arrival has struck it as with an hydrophobia, it is like the sight of water to canine madness.

As this letter is intended to announce my arrival to my friends, and to my enemies if I have any, for I ought to have none in America, and as introductory to others that will occasionally follow, I shall close it by detailing the line of conduct I shall pursue.

I have no occasion to ask, and do not intend to accept, any place or office in the Government. There is none it could give me that would be any ways equal to the profits I could make as an author, for I have an established fame in the literary world, could I reconcile it to my principles to make money by my politics or religion. I must be in everything what I have ever been, a disinterested volunteer; my proper sphere of action is on the common floor of citizenship, and to honest men I give my hand and my heart freely.

I have some manuscript works to publish, of which I shall give proper notice, and some mechanical affairs to bring forward, that will employ all my leisure time. I shall continue these letters as I see occasion, and as to the low party prints that choose to abuse me, they are welcome; I shall not descend to answer them. I have been too much used to such common stuff to take any notice of it.

The Government of England honoured me with a thousand martyrdoms, by burning me in effigy in every town in that country, and their hirelings in America may do the same. . . .

As the affairs of the country to which I am returned are of more importance to the world, and to me, than of that I have lately left (for it is through the New World the Old must be regenerated, if regenerated at all), I shall not take up the time of the reader with an account of scenes that have passed in France, many of which are painful to remember and horrid to relate, but come at once to the circumstances in which I find America on my arrival.

Fourteen years, and something more, have produced a change, at least among a part of the people, and I ask myself what it is? I meet or hear of thousands of my former connections, who are men of the same principles and friendships as when I left them. But a nondescript race, and of equivocal generation, assuming the name of *Federalist* – a name that describes no character of principle good or bad, and may equally be applied to either – has since started up with the rapidity of a mushroom, and like a mushroom is withering on its rootless stalk.

Are those men *federalized* to support the liberties of their country or to overturn them? To add to its fair fame or riot on its spoils? The name contains no defined idea. It is like John Adams's definition of a republic, in his letter to Mr Wythe of Virginia. *It is*, says he, *an empire of laws and not of men*. But as laws may be bad as well as good, an empire of laws may be the best of all governments or the worst of all tyrannies.

But John Adams is a man of paradoxical heresies, and consequently of a bewildered mind. He wrote a book entitled, *A Defence of the American Constitutions*, and the principles of it are an attack upon them. But the book is descended to the tomb of forgetfulness, and the best fortune that can attend its author is quietly to follow its fate. John was not born for immortality. But, to return to Federalism.

In the history of parties and the names they assume, it often happens that they finish by the direct contrary principles with which they profess to begin, and thus it has happened with Federalism.

During the time of the old Congress, and prior to the establishment of the Federal Government, the Continental belt was too loosely buckled. The several States were united in name but not in fact, and that nominal union had neither centre nor circle. The laws of one State frequently interfered with, and sometimes opposed, those of another. Commerce between State and State was without protection, and confidence without a point to rest on. The condition the country was then in was aptly described by Pelatiah Webster, when he said, 'thirteen staves and ne're a hoop will not make a barrel'.

If, then, by *Federalist* is to be understood one who was for cementing the Union by a general government operating equally over all the States, in all matters that embraced the common interest, and to which the authority of the States severally was not adequate, for no one State can make laws to bind another; if, I say, by a *Federalist* is meant a person of this description (and this is the origin of the name), *I ought to stand first on the list of Federalists*, for the proposition for establishing a general government over the Union, came originally from me in 1783, in a written memorial to Chancellor Livingston, then Secretary for Foreign Affairs to Congress, Robert Morris, Minister of Finance, and his associate, Gouverneur Morris, all of whom are now living; and we had a dinner and conference at Robert Morris's on the subject. The occasion was as follows:

Congress had proposed a duty of five per cent on imported articles, the money to be applied as a fund towards paying the interest of loans to be borrowed in Holland. The resolve was sent to the several States to be enacted into law. Rhode Island absolutely refused. I was at the trouble of a journey to Rhode Island to reason with them on the subject. Some other of the States enacted it with alterations, each one as it pleased. Virginia adopted it, and afterwards repealed it, and the affair came to nothing.

It was then visible, at least to me, that either Congress must frame the laws necessary for the Union, and send them to the several States to be enregistered without any alteration, which would in itself appear like usurpation on one part and passive obedience on the other, or some method must be devised to accomplish the same end by constitutional principles; and the proposition I made in the memorial was, to *add a Continental legislature to Congress, to be elected by the several States.*

The proposition met the full approbation of the gentlemen to whom it was addressed, and the conversation turned on the manner of bringing it forward. Gouverneur Morris, in talking with me after dinner, wished me to throw out the idea in the newspaper; I replied, that I did not like to be always the proposer of new things, that it would have too assuming an appearance; and besides, that *I did not think the country was quite wrong enough to be put right.*

I remember giving the same reason to Dr Rush, at Philadelphia, and to General Gates, at whose quarters I spent a day on my return from Rhode Island; and I suppose they will remember it because the observation seemed to strike them.

But the embarrassments increasing, as they necessarily must from the want of a better cemented union, the State of Virginia proposed holding a commercial convention, and that convention, which was not sufficiently numerous, proposed that another convention, with more extensive and better defined powers, should be held at Philadelphia, May 10, 1787.

When the plan of the Federal Government, formed by this convention, was proposed and submitted to the consideration of the several States, it was strongly objected to in each of them. But the objections were not on anti-Federal grounds, but on constitutional points. Many were shocked at the idea of placing what is called executive power in the hands of a single individual. To them it had too much the form and appearance of a military government, or a despotic one.

Others objected that the powers given to a President were too great, and that in the hands of an ambitious and designing man it might grow into tyranny as it did in England under Oliver Cromwell, and as it has since done in France. A republic must not only be so in its principles, but in its forms.

The executive part of the Federal Government was made for a man, and those who consented, against their judgement, to place executive power in the hands of a single individual, reposed more on the supposed moderation of the person they had in view, than on the wisdom of the measure itself.

Two considerations, however, overcame all objections. The one was the absolute necessity of a Federal Government. The other, the rational reflections, that as government in America is founded on the representative system any error in the first essay could be reformed by the same quiet and rational process by which the Constitution was formed, and that either by the generation then living, or by those who were to succeed.

If ever America lose sight of this principle, she will no longer be the *land of liberty*. The father will become the assassin of the rights of the son, and his descendants be a race of slaves.

As many thousands who were minors are grown up to manhood since the name of *Federalist* began, it became necessary, for their information, to go back and show the origin of the name, which is now no longer what it originally was; but it was the more necessary to do this, in order to bring forward, in the open face of day, the apostasy of those who first called themselves Federalists.

To them it served as a cloak for treason, a mask for tyranny. Scarcely were they placed in the seat of power and office, than federalism was to be destroyed, and the representative system of government, the pride and glory of America, and the palladium of her liberties, was to be overthrown and abolished. The next generation was not to be free. The son was to bend his neck beneath the father's foot, and live, deprived of his rights, under hereditary control.

Among the men of this apostate description, is to be ranked the ex-President *John Adams*. It has been the political career of this man to begin with hypocrisy, proceed with arrogance, and finish in contempt. May such be the fate of all such characters.

I have had doubts of John Adams ever since the year 1776. In a conversation with me at that time, concerning the pamphlet *Common Sense*, he censured it because it attacked the English form of government. John was for independence because he expected to be made great by it; but it was not difficult to perceive, for the surliness of his temper makes him an awkward hypocrite, that his head was as full of kings, queens and knaves, as a pack of cards. But John has lost deal.

When a man has a concealed project in his brain that he wants to bring forward, and fears will not succeed, he begins with it as physicians do by suspected poison, try it first on an animal; if it agree with the stomach of the animal he makes further experiments, and this was the way John took. His brain was teeming with projects to overturn the liberties of America and the representative system of government, and he began by hinting it in little companies.

The secretary of John Jay, an excellent painter and a poor politician, told me, in presence of another American, Daniel Parker, that in a company where himself was present, John Adams talked of making the government hereditary, and that as Mr Washington had no children, it should be made hereditary in the family of Lund Washington.

John had not impudence enough to propose himself in the first instance, as the old French Normandy baron did, who offered to come over to be king of America, and if Congress did not accept his offer, that they would give him thirty thousand pounds for the generosity of it; but John, like a mole, was grubbing his way to it under ground. He knew that Lund Washington was unknown, for nobody had heard of him, and that as the President had no children to succeed him, the Vice-President had, and if the treason had succeeded, and the hint with it, the goldsmith might be sent for to take measure of the head of John or of his son for a golden wig.

In this case, the good people of Boston might have for a king the man they have rejected as a delegate. The representative system is fatal to ambition.

Knowing, as I do, the consummate vanity of John Adams, and the shallowness of his judgement, I can easily picture to myself that when he arrived at the Federal City he was strutting in the pomp of his imagination before the presidential house, or in the audience hall, and exulting in the language of Nebuchadnezzar, 'Is not this great Babylon, that I have built for the honour of my Majesty!' But in that unfortunate hour, or soon after, John, like Nebuchadnezzar, was driven from among men, and fled with the speed of a post-horse.

Some of John Adams's loyal subjects, I see, have been to present him with an address on his birthday; but the language they use is too tame for the occasion. Birthday addresses, like birthday odes, should not creep along like mildrops down a cabbage leaf, but roll in a torrent of poetical metaphor. I will give them a specimen for the next year. Here it is:

When an ant, in travelling over the globe, lifts up its foot, and puts it again on the ground, it shakes the earth to its centre: but when

YOU, the mighty Ant of the East, was born, etc., etc., etc., the centre jumped upon the surface.

This, gentlemen, is the proper style of addresses from *well-bred* ants to the monarch of the ant hills; and as I never take pay for preaching, praying, politics or poetry, I make you a present of it. Some people talk of impeaching John Adams; but I am for softer measures. I would keep him to make fun of. He will then answer one of the ends for which he was born, and he ought to be thankful that I am arrived to take his part.

I voted in earnest to save the life of one unfortunate king, and I now vote in jest to save another. It is my fate to be always plagued with fools. But to return to Federalism and apostasy.

The plan of the leaders of the faction was to overthrow the liberties of the New World, and place government on the corrupt system of the Old. They wanted to hold their power by a more lasting tenure than the choice of their constituents. It is impossible to account for their conduct and the measures they adopted on any other ground.

But to accomplish that object, a standing army and a prodigal revenue must be raised; and to obtain these pretenses must be invented to deceive. Alarms of dangers that did not exist even in imagination, but in the direst spirit of lying, were spread abroad. Apostasy stalked through the land in the garb of patriotism, and the torch of treason blinded for a while the flame of liberty.

For what purpose could an army of twenty-five thousand men be wanted? A single reflection might have taught the most credulous that while the war raged between France and England, neither could spare a man to invade America. For what purpose, then, could it be wanted? The case carries its own explanation. It was wanted for the purpose of destroying the representative system, for it could be employed for no other. Are these men Federalists? If they are, they are federalized to deceive and to destroy.

The rage against Dr Logan's patriotic and voluntary mission to France was excited by the shame they felt at the detection of the false alarms they had circulated. As to the opposition given by the remnant of the faction to the repeal of the taxes laid on during the former Administration, it is easily accounted for. The repeal of those taxes was a sentence of condemnation on those who laid them on, and in the opposition they gave in that repeal they are to be considered in the light of criminals standing on their defence and the country has passed judgement upon them. . . .

To ELECT, and to REJECT, is the prerogative of a free people.

Since the establishment of independence, no period has arrived that so decidedly proves the excellence of the representative system of government, and its superiority over every other, as the time we now live in. Had America been cursed with John Adams's *hereditary Monarchy,* or Alexander Hamilton's *Senate for life,* she must have sought, in the doubtful contest of civil war, what she now obtains by the expression of public will. An appeal to elections decides better than an appeal to the sword.

The Reign of Terror that raged in America during the latter end of the Washington Administration, and the whole of that of Adams, is enveloped in mystery to me. That there were men in the Government hostile to the representative system, was once their boast, though it is now their overthrow, and therefore the fact is established against them.

But that so large a mass of the people should become the dupes of those who were loading them with taxes in order to load them with chains, and deprive them of the right of election, can be ascribed only to that species of wildfire rage, lighted up by falsehood that not only acts without reflection, but is too impetuous to make any.

There is a general and striking difference between the genuine effects of truth, and the effects of falsehood believed to be truth. Truth is naturally benign; but falsehood believed to be truth is always furious. The former delights in serenity, is mild and persuasive, and seeks not the auxiliary aid of invention. The latter sticks at nothing.

It has naturally no morals. Every lie is welcome that suits its purpose. It is the innate character of the thing to act in this manner, and the criterion by which it may be known, whether in politics or religion. When anything is attempted to be supported by lying it is presumptive evidence that the thing so supported is a lie also. The stock on which a lie can be grafted must be of the same species as the graft.

What is become of the mighty clamour of French invasion, and the cry that our country is in danger, and taxes and armies must be raised to defend it? The danger is fled with the faction that created it, and what is worst of all, the money is fled too. It is I only that have committed the hostility of invasion, and all the artillery of pop-guns are prepared for action.

Poor fellows, how they foam! They set half their own partisans in laughter; for among ridiculous things nothing is more ridiculous than ridiculous rage. But I hope they will not leave off. I shall lose half my greatness when they cease to lie.

So far as respects myself, I have reason to believe and a right to say that the leaders of the Reign of Terror in America and the leaders of the Reign of Terror in France, during the time of Robespierre, were in character the same sort of men; or how is it to be accounted for, that I was persecuted by both at the same time? When I was voted out of the French Convention, the reason assigned for it was, that I was a foreigner.

When Robespierre had me seized in the night, and imprisoned in the Luxembourg (where I remained eleven months), he assigned no reason for it. But when he proposed bringing me to the tribunal, which was like sending me at once to the scaffold, he then assigned a reason, and the reason was, *for the interests of America as well as of* France. '*Pour les interêts de l'Amérique autant que de la France.*'

The words are in his own hand-writing, and reported to the Convention by the committee appointed to examine his papers, and are printed in their report, with this reflection added to them, '*Why Thomas Paine more than another? Because he contributed to the liberty of both worlds.*'

There must have been a coalition in sentiment, if not in fact, between the Terrorists of America and the Terrorists of France, and Robespierre must have known it, or he could not have had the idea of putting America into the bill of accusation against me.

Yet these men, these Terrorists of the New World, who were waiting in the devotion of their hearts for the joyful news of my destruction, are the same banditti who are now bellowing in all the hackneyed language of hackneyed hypocrisy about humanity and piety, and often about something they call infidelity, and they finish with the chorus of *Crucify him, crucify him.* I am become so famous among them, they cannot eat or drink without me. I serve them as a standing dish, and they cannot make up a bill of fare if I am not in it.

But there is one dish, and that the choicest of all, that they have not presented on the table, and it is time they should. They have not yet *accused Providence of Infidelity*. Yet according to their outrageous piety, she must be as bad as Thomas Paine; she has protected him in all his dangers, patronized him in all his undertaking, encouraged him in all his ways, and rewarded him at last by bringing him in safety and in health to the Promised Land.

This is more than she did by the Jews, the chosen people, that they tell us she brought out of the land of Egypt, and out of the house of bondage; for they all died in the wilderness, and Moses too.

I was one of the nine members that composed the first Committee of Constitution. Six of them have been destroyed. Sieyès and myself have survived – he by bending with the times, and I by not bending. The other survivor joined Robespierre; he was seized and imprisoned in his turn, and sentenced to transportation. He has since apologized to me for having signed the warrant, by saying he felt himself in danger and was obliged to do it.

Herault Sechelles, an acquaintance of Mr Jefferson, and a good patriot, was my *suppléant* as member of the Committee of Constitution, that is, he was to supply my place, if I had not accepted or had resigned, being next in number of votes to me. He was imprisoned in the Luxembourg with me, was taken to the tribunal and the guillotine, and I, his principal, was left.

There were two foreigners in the Convention, Anarcharsis Clootz and myself. We were both put out of the Convention by the same vote, arrested by the same order, and carried to prison together the same night. He was taken to the guillotine, and I was again left. Joel Barlow was with us when we went to prison.

Joseph Lebon, one of the vilest characters that ever existed, and who made the streets of Arras run with blood, was my *suppléant,* as member of the Convention for the department of the Pas de Calais. When I was put out of the Convention he came and took my place. When I was liberated from prison and voted again into the Convention, he was sent to the same prison and took my place there, and he was sent to the guillotine instead of me. He supplied my place all the way through.

One hundred and sixty-eight persons were taken out of the Luxembourg in one night, and a hundred and sixty of them guillotined next day, of which I now know I was to have been one; and the manner I escaped that fate is curious, and has all the appearance of accident.

The room in which I was lodged was on the ground floor, and one of a long range of rooms under a gallery, and the door of it opened outward and flat against the wall; so that when it was open the inside of the door appeared outward, and the contrary when it was shut. I had three comrades, fellow prisoners with me, Joseph Vanhuele, of Bruges, since president of the municipality of that town, Michael Rubyns, and Charles Bastini of Louvain.

When persons by scores and by hundreds were to be taken out of the prison for the guillotine it was always done in the night, and those who performed that office had a private mark or signal, by which they knew what rooms to go to, and what number to take. We, as I have stated, were four, and the door of our room was marked, unobserved by us, with that number in chalk; but it happened, if happening is a proper word, that the mark was put on when the door was open, and flat against the wall, and thereby came on the inside when we shut it at night, and the destroying angel passed by it. A few days after this, Robespierre fell, and Mr Monroe arrived and reclaimed me, and invited me to his house.

During the whole of my imprisonment, prior to the fall of Robespierre, there was no time when I could think my life worth twenty-four hours, and my mind was made up to meet its fate. The Americans in Paris went in a body to the Convention to reclaim me, but without success. There was no party among them with respect to me.

My only hope then rested on the Government of America, that it would *remember me*. But the icy heart of ingratitude, in whatever man it be placed, has neither feeling nor sense of honour. The letter of Mr Jefferson has served to wipe away the reproach, and done justice to the mass of the people of America.

When a party was forming, in the latter end of 1777, and beginning of 1778, of which John Adams was one, to remove Mr Washington from the command of the army on the complaint that *he did nothing,* I wrote the fifth number of the *Crisis,* and published it at Lancaster (Congress than being at York Town, in Pennsylvania), to ward off that meditated blow; for though I well knew that the black times of '76 were the natural consequence of his want of military judgement in the choice of positions into which the army was put about New York and New Jersey, I could see no possible advantage, and nothing but mischief, that could arise by

THOMAS PAINE READER

distracting the army into parties, which would have been the case had the intended motion gone on.

General Lee, who with a sarcastic genius joined [to] a great fund of military knowledge, was perfectly right when he said, '*We have no business on islands, and in the bottom of bogs, where the enemy, by the aid of its ships, can bring its whole force against a part of ours and shut it up.*' This had like to have been the case at New York, and it was the case at Fort Washington, and would have been the case at Fort Lee if General Greene had not moved instantly off on the first news of the enemy's approach. I was with Greene through the whole of that affair and know it perfectly.

But though I came forward in defence of Mr Washington when he was attacked, and made the best that could be made of a series of blunders that had nearly ruined the country, he left me to perish when I was in prison. But as I told him of it in his life-time, I should not now bring it up if the ignorant impertinence of some of the Federal papers, who are pushing Mr Washington forward as their stalking horse, did not make it necessary.

That gentleman did not perform his part in the Revolution better, nor with more honour, that I did mine, and the one part was as necessary as the other. He accepted as a present (though he was already rich), a hundred thousand acres of land in America, and left me to occupy six foot of earth in France.

I wish, for his own reputation, he had acted with more justice. But it was always known of Mr Washington, by those who best knew him, that he was of such an icy and death-like constitution that he neither loved his friends nor hated his enemies. But, be this as it may, I see no reason that a difference between Mr Washington and me should be made a theme of discord with other people. There are those who may see merit in both without making themselves partisans of either, and with this reflection I close the subject.

As to the hypocritical abuse thrown out by the Federalists on other subjects, I recommend to them the observance of a commandment that existed before either Christian or Jew existed:

> Thou shalt make a covenant with thy senses:
> With thine eye, that it behold no evil,
> With thine ear, that it hear no evil,

> With thy tongue, that it speak no evil,
> With thy hands, that they commit no evil.

If the Federalists will follow this commandment, they will leave off lying.

[20] THE CONSTRUCTION OF
IRON BRIDGES
———◆◆◆———

(1803)

Next to politics and religion the subject that most preoccupied Paine was en-
gineering. In the 1780s, in fact, politics seemed secondary to Paine's passionate
interest in iron bridges. The first cast-iron bridge in the world spanned the river
Severn, near Telford in England, in 1779, but Paine is still credited with being a
pioneer in this area. Included here is a memorandum originally prepared for the
United States Congress in 1803. Even here Paine could not resist political pol-
emics.

TO THE CONGRESS OF THE UNITED STATES

I have deposited in the office of the Secretary of State, and under the
care of the Patent Office, two models of iron bridges; the one in
paste-board, the other cast in metal. As they will show by inspection
the manner of constructing iron bridges, I shall not take up the time
of Congress with a description of them.

My intention in presenting this memoir to Congress is to put the
country in possession of the means and of the right of making use of
the construction freely; as I do not intend to take any patent right for
it.

As America abounds in rivers that interrupt the land communication, and as by violence of floods and the breaking up of
the ice in the spring, the bridges depending for support from the
bottom of the river are frequently carried away, I turned my attention, after the Revolutionary War was over, to find a method of
constructing an arch that might, without rendering the height inconvenient or the ascent difficult, extend at once from shore to
shore, over rivers of three, four or five hundred feet and probably
more.

The principle I took to begin with and work upon was that the
small segment of a large circle was preferable to the great segment of
a small circle. The appearance of such arches, and the manner of
forming and putting the parts together, admit of many varieties, but

the principle will be the same in all. The bridge architects that I conversed with in England denied the principle, but it was generally supported by mathematicians, and experiment has now established the fact.

In 1786, I made three models, partly at Philadelphia, but mostly at Bordentown in the State of New Jersey. One model was in wood, one in cast iron, and one in wrought iron connected with blocks of wood, representing cast iron blocks, but all on the same principle, that of the small segment of a large circle.

I took the last mentioned one with me to France in 1787 and presented it to the Academy of Sciences at Paris for their opinion of it. The Academy appointed a committee of three of their own body – Mons. Le Roy, the Abbé Bossou, and Mons. Borda. The first was an acquaintance of Dr Franklin, and of Mr Jefferson, then minister at Paris. The two others were celebrated as mathematicians. I presented it as a model for a bridge of a single arch of four hundred feet span over the river Schuylkill at Philadelphia. The committee brought in a report which the Academy adopted – that an arch on the principle and construction of the model, in their opinion, might be extended four hundred feet, the extent proposed.

In September of the same year, I sent the model to Sir Joseph Banks, president of the Royal Society in England, and soon after went there myself.

In order to ascertain the truth of the principle on a larger scale than could be shown by a portable model five or six feet in length, I went to the iron-foundry of Messrs Walker, at Rotherham, County of Yorkshire, in England, and had a complete rib of 90 feet span, and 5 feet of height from the chord line to the centre of the arch, manufactured and erected. It was a segment of a circle of 410 feet diameter; and until this was done no experiment on a circle of such an extensive diameter had ever been made in architecture, or the practicability of it supposed.

The rib was erected between a wall of a furnace belonging to the iron-works and the gable end of a brick building, which served as butments. The weight of iron in the rib was three tons, and we loaded it with double its weight in pig-iron. I wrote to Mr Jefferson who was then at Paris, an account of this experiment, and also to Sir Joseph Banks in London, who in his answer to me says – 'I look for many other bold improvements from your countrymen, the Americans, who think with vigour, and are not fettered with the trammels of science before they are capable of exerting their mental faculties to advantage.'

On the success of this experiment, I entered into an agreement with the iron-founders at Rotherham to cast and manufacture a complete bridge, to be composed of five ribs of 210 feet span, and 5 feet of height from the chord line, being a segment of a circle 610 feet diameter, and sent it to London to be erected as a specimen for establishing a manufactory of iron bridges to be sent to any part of the world.

The bridge was erected at the village of Paddington, near London, but being in a plain field, where no advantage could be taken of butments without the expense of building them, as in the former case, it served only as a specimen of the practicability of a manufactory of iron bridges. It was brought by sea, packed in the hold of a vessel, from the place where it was made; and after standing a year was taken down without injury to any of its parts, and might be erected anywhere else.

At this time my bridge operations became suspended. Mr Edmund Burke published his attack on the French Revolution and the system of representative government, and in defence of government by hereditary succession, a thing which is in its nature an absurdity, because it is impossible to make wisdom hereditary; and therefore, so far as wisdom is necessary in a government, it must be looked for where it can be found, sometimes in one family, sometimes in another. History informs us that the son of Solomon was a fool. He lost ten tribes out of twelve (2 Chron. ch. x). There are those in later times who lost thirteen.

The publication of this work by Mr Burke, absurd in its principles and outrageous in its manner, drew me, as I have said, from my bridge operations, and my time became employed in defending a system then established and operating in America, and which I wished to see peaceably adopted in Europe. I therefore ceased my work on the bridge to employ myself on the more necessary work, *Rights of Man*, in answer to Mr Burke.

In 1792, a convention was elected in France for the express purpose of forming a Constitution on the authority of the people, as had been done in America, of which convention I was elected a member. I was at this time in England and knew nothing of my being elected till the arrival of the person who was sent officially to inform me of it.

During my residence in France, which was from 1792 to 1802, an iron bridge of 236 feet span, and 34 of height from the chord line, was erected over the river Wear near the town of Sunderland, in the County of Durham, England. It was done chiefly at the expense of the two members of Parliament for that county, Milbanke and Burdon.

It happened that a very intimate friend of mine, Sir Robert Smyth (who was also an acquaintance of Mr Monroe, the American Minister, and since of Mr Livingston), was then at Paris. He had been a colleague in Parliament with Milbanke, and supposing that the persons who constructed the iron bridge at Sunderland had made free with my model, which was at the iron-works where the Sunderland bridge was cast, he wrote to Milbanke on the subject, and the following is that gentleman's answer.

'With respect to the iron bridge over the river Wear at Sunderland, it certainly is a work well deserving admiration, both for its structure and utility, and I have good grounds for saying that the first idea was suggested by Mr Paine's bridge exhibited at Paddington. What difference there may be in some part of the structure, or in the proportion of wrought and cast iron, I cannot pretend to say, Burdon having undertaken to build the bridge, in consequence of his having taken upon himself whatever the expense might be beyond between three and four thousand pounds sterling, subscribed by myself and some other gentlemen.

'But whatever the mechanism might be, it did not supersede the necessity of a centre.'[1] (The writer has here confounded a centre with a scaffolding.) 'Which centre (continues the writer) was esteemed a very ingenious piece of workmanship, and taken from a plan sketched out by Mr Nash, an architect of great merit, who had been consulted in the outset of the business when a bridge of stone was in contemplation.

'With respect therefore to any gratuity to Mr Paine, though ever so desirous of rewarding the labour of an ingenious man, I do

---

1 It is the technical term, meaning the boards and numbers which form the arch upon which the permanent materials are laid; when a bridge is finished the workmen say they are ready to strike centre, that is to take down the scaffolding. – Paine.

not feel how, under the cirumstances already described, I have it in my power, having had nothing to do with the bridge after the payment of my subscription, Mr Burdon then becoming accountable for the whole. But if you can point out any mode according to which it would be in my power to be instrumental in procuring him any compensation for the advantages the public may have derived from his ingenious model, from which certainly the outline of the bridge at Sunderland was taken, be assured it will afford me very great satisfaction. – RA. MILBANKE.'[2]

The year before I left France, the Government of that country had it in contemplation to erect an iron bridge over the river Seine, at Paris. As all edifices of public construction came under the cognizance of the Minister of the Interior (and as their plan was to erect a bridge of five iron arches of 100 feet span each, instead of passing the river with a single arch, and which was going backward in practice, instead of forward, as there was already an iron arch of 230 feet in existence) I wrote the Minister of the Interior, the citizen Chaptal, a memoir on the construction of iron bridges. The following is his answer:

'*The Minister of the Interior to the citizen Thomas Paine.* – I have received, citizen, the observations that you have been so good as to address to me upon the construction of iron bridges. They will be of the greatest utility to us when the new kind of construction goes to be executed for the first time. With pleasure, I assure you, citizen, that you have rights of more than one kind to the thankfulness of nations, and I give you, cordially, the particular expression of my esteem. – CHAPTAL.'[3]

A short time before I left France, a person came to me from London with plans and drawings for an iron bridge of one arch over the river Thames at London, of 600 feet span, and 60 feet of height from the chord line. The subject was then before a committee of the House of Commons, but I know not the proceedings thereon.

As this new construction of an arch for bridges, and the principles on which it is founded, originated in America, as the documents I have produced sufficiently prove, and is becoming an object of importance to the world, and to no part of it more than to our own country, on account of its numerous rivers, and as no experiment has

2 The original is in my possession. – Paine.
3 The original, in French, is in my possession. – Paine.

been made in America to bring it into practice further than on the model I have executed myself and at my own expense, I beg leave to submit a proposal to Congress on the subject, which is:

To erect an experiment rib of about 400 feet span, to be the segment of a circle of at least 1,000 feet diameter, and to let it remain exposed to public view, so that the method of constructing such arches may be generally known.

It is an advantage peculiar to the construction of iron bridges that the success of an arch of a given extent and height can be ascertained without being at the expense of building the bridge; which is, by the method I propose, that of erecting an experiment rib on the ground where advantage can be taken of two hills for butments.

I began in this manner with the rib of 90 feet span and 5 feet of height, being a segment of a circle of 410 feet diameter. The undertakers of the Sunderland bridge began in the same manner. They contracted with the iron-founder for a single rib, and, finding it to answer, had five more manufactured like it and erected into a bridge consisting of six ribs, the experiment rib being one.

But the Sunderland bridge does not carry the principle much further into practice than had been done by the rib of 90 feet span and 5 feet in height, being, as before said, a segment of a circle of 410 feet diameter; the Sunderland bridge being 206 feet span and 34 feet of height, gives the diameter of the circle of which it is a segment to be 444 feet, within a few inches, which is but a larger segment of a circle 30 feet more diameter.

The construction of those bridges does not come within the line of any established practice of business. The stone architect can derive but little from the theory of practice of his art that enters into his construction of an iron bridge; and the iron-founder, though he may be expert in moulding and casting the parts, when the models are given him, would be at a loss to proportion them, unless he was acquainted with all the lines and properties belonging to a circle.

If it should appear to Congress that the construction of iron bridges will be of utility to the country, and they should direct that an experiment rib be made for that purpose, I will furnish the proportions for the several parts of the work and give my attendance to superintend the erection of it.

But, in any case, I have to request that this memoir may be put on the journals of Congress, as an evidence hereafter that this new method of constructing bridges originated in America.

[21] CONSTITUTIONAL REFORM

(1805)

In 1805 Paine at the age of sixty-eight wrote his last political pamphlet. Fittingly enough, it was on a topic which brought him full circle back to his earliest years in America: Pennsylvania politics. The radical Constitution of 1776 had been revised in more conservative terms in 1790. Fifteen years later the citizens of Pennsylvania were once again contemplating constitutional reform. Paine sent his advice from his farm in New Rochelle, New York, 'on the ground of principle and in remembrance of former times and friendships'. The text here is an edited version of the 'collection of thoughts and historical references' offered by Paine in his last pamphlet to those 'in the place of my political and literary birth'.

TO THE CITIZENS OF PENNSYLVANIA ON THE PROPOSAL FOR CALLING A CONVENTION

As I resided in the capital of your State, Philadelphia, in the *time that tried men's souls,* and all my political writings, during the Revolutionary War, were written in that city, it seems natural for me to look back to the place of my political and literary birth, and feel an interest for its happiness. Removed as I now am from the place, and detached from everything of personal party, I address this token to you on the ground of principle and in remembrance of former times and friendships.

The subject now before you is the call of a Convention to examine and, if necessary, to reform the Constitution of the State; or to speak in the correct language of constitutional order, to propose written articles of reform to be accepted or rejected by the people by vote, in the room of those now existing that shall be judged improper or defective.

There cannot be, on the ground of reason, any objection to this; because if no reform or alteration is necessary the sense of the country will permit none to be made; and, *if necessary,* it *will* be made because it *ought* to be made. Until, therefore, the sense of the country can be collected and made known by a convention elected for that purpose, all opposition to the call of a convention not only passes for nothing, but serves to create a suspicion that the opposers are conscious that the Constitution will not bear an examination.

The Constitution formed by the Convention of 1776, of which Benjamin Franklin (the greatest and most useful man America has yet produced), was president, had many good points in it which were overthrown by the Convention of 1790, under the pretence of making the Constitution conformable to that of the United States; as if the forms and periods of election for a territory extensive as that of the United States is could become a rule for a single state.

The principal defect in the Constitution of 1776 was that it was subject, in practice, to too much precipitancy; but the groundwork of that Constitution was good. The present Constitution appears to me to be clogged with inconsistencies of a hazardous tendency, as a supposed remedy against a precipitancy that might not happen. Investing any individual, by whatever name or official title he may be called, with a negative over the formation of the laws, is copied from the English Government, without ever perceiving the inconsistency and absurdity of it, when applied to the representative system, or understanding the origin of it in England.

The present form of government in England and all those things called prerogatives of the Crown, of which this negative power is one, was established by conquest, not by compact. Their origin was the conquest of England by the Normans, under William of Normandy, surnamed the Conqueror, in 1066, and the genealogy of its kings takes its date from him. He is the first of the list.

There is no historical certainty of the time when parliaments began; but be the time when it may, they began by what are called grants or charters from the Norman Conqueror, or his successors, to certain towns, and to countries, to elect members to meet and serve in Parliament[1] subject to his control; and the custom still continues with the King of England calling the Parliament *my Parliament*; that is, a Parliament originating from his authority, and over which he holds control in right of himself, derived from that conquest.

It is from this assumed right, derived from conquest, and not from any constitutional right by compact, that kings of England hold a negative over the formation of the laws; and they hold this for the purpose of preventing any being enacted that might abridge, invade,

1 *Parliament* is a French word, brought into England by the Normans. It comes from the French verb *parler* – to speak. – Paine.

or in any way affect or diminish what they claim to be their hereditary or family rights and prerogatives, derived originally from the
conquest of the country.[2] This is the origin of the King of England's
negative. It is a badge of disgrace which *his* Parliaments are obliged
to wear, and to which they are abject enough to submit.

But what has this case to do with a legislature chosen by freemen,
on their own authority, in right of themselves? Or in what manner
does a person styled Governor or Chief Magistrate resemble a
conqueror subjugating a country, as William of Normandy sub-
jugated England, and saying to it, *you shall have no laws but what I
please*?

The negativing power in a country like America is of that kind,
that a wise man would not choose to be embarrassed with it, and a
man fond of using it will be overthrown by it. It is not difficult to see
that when Mr M'Kean negatived the Arbitration Act, he was induced
to it as a *lawyer,* for the benefit of the profession, and not as a
magistrate, for the benefit of the people; for it is the office of a chief
magistrate to compose differences and *prevent* lawsuits.

If the people choose to have arbitrations instead of lawsuits why
should they not have them? It is a matter that concerns them as
individuals, and not as a state or community, and is not a proper case
for a governor to interfere in, for it is not a state or government
concern: nor does it concern the peace thereof, otherwise than to
make it more peaceable by making it less contentious.

This negativing power in the hands of an individual ought to be
constitutionally abolished. It is a dangerous power. There is no pre-
scribing rules for the use of it. It is discretionary and arbitrary; and
the will and temper of the person at any time possessing it, is its only
rule. There must have been great want of reflection in the Convention
that admitted it into the Constitution. Would that Convention have
put the Constitution it had formed (whether good or bad) in the
power of any individual to negative? It would not. It would have
treated such a proposal with disdain. Why then did it put the legislatures thereafter to be chosen, and all the laws, in that predicament?

Had that Convention, or the law members thereof, known the

2 When a king of England (for they are not an English race of kings) negatives an
act passed by the Parliament, he does it in the Norman or French language, which was
the language of the Conquest, the literal translation of which is, *the king will advise
himself of it*. It is the only instance of a king of England speaking French in Parliament;
and shows the origin of the negative. – Paine.

origin of the negativing power used by kings of England, from whence they copied it, they must have seen the inconsistency of introducing it into an American Constitution. We are not a conquered people; we know no conqueror; and the negativing power used by kings in England is for the defence of the personal and family prerogatives of the successors of the conqueror against the Parliament and the people. What is all this to us? We know no prerogatives but what belong to the sovereignty of ourselves.

At the time this Constitution was formed, there was a great departure from the principles of the Revolution, among those who then assumed the lead, and the country was grossly imposed upon. This accounts for some inconsistencies that are to be found in the present Constitution, among which is the negativing power inconsistently copied from England. While the exercise of the power over the state remained dormant it remained unnoticed; but the instant it began to be active it began to alarm; and the exercise of it against the rights of the people to settle their private pecuniary differences by the peaceable mode of arbitration, without the interference of lawyers, and the expense of tediousness of courts of law, has brought its existence to a crisis.

Arbitration is of more importance to society than courts of law, and ought to have precedence of them in all cases of pecuniary concerns between individuals or parties of them. Who are better qualified than merchants to settle disputes between merchants, or who better than farmers to settle disputes between farmers? And the same for every other description of men. What do lawyers or courts of law know of these matters? They devote themselves to forms rather than to principles, and the merits of the case become obscure and lost in a labyrinth of verbal perplexities. We do not hear of lawyers going to law with each other, though they could do it cheaper than other people, which shows they have no opinion of it for themselves.

The principle and rule of arbitration ought to be constitutionally established. The honest sense of a country collected in convention will find out how to do this without the interference of lawyers, who may be hired to advocate any side of any cause; for the case is the practice of the bar is become a species of prostitution that ought to be controlled. It lives by encouraging the injustice it pretends to redress.

Courts in which law is practised are of two kinds. The one for criminal cases, the other for civil cases, or cases between individuals respecting property of any kind or the value thereof. I know not what may be the numerical proportion of these two classes of cases to each other; but that the civil cases are far more numerous than the criminal cases, I make no doubt of. Whether they be ten, twenty, thirty or forty to one, or more, I leave to those who live in the state, or in the several counties thereof, to determine.

But be the proportion what it may, the expense to the public of supporting a judiciary for both will be, in some relative degree, according to the number of cases the one bears to the other; yet it is only of them that the public, as a public, have any concern with. The criminal cases, being breaches of the peace, are consequently under the cognizance of the government of the state, and the expense of supporting the courts thereof belongs to the public, because the preservation of the peace is a public concern.

But civil cases, that is, cases of private property between individuals, belong wholly to the individuals themselves; and all that government has consistently to do in the matter is to establish the process by which the parties concerned shall proceed and bring the matter to decision themselves, by referring it to impartial and judicious men of the neighbourhood, of their own choosing. This is by far the most convenient, as to time and place, and the cheapest method to them; for it is bringing *justice home to their own doors,* without the chicanery of law and lawyers.

Every case ought to be determined on its own merits, without the farce of what are called precedents, or reports of cases; because, in the first place, it often happens that the decision upon the case brought as a precedent is bad, and ought to be shunned instead of imitated; and, in the second place, because there are no two cases perfectly alike in all their circumstances, and therefore, the one cannot become a rule of decision for the other. It is justice and good judgement that preside by right in a court of arbitration. It is forms, quoted precedents and contrivances for delay and expense to the parties, that govern the proceedings of a court of law.

By establishing arbitrations in the room of courts of law for the adjustment of private cases, the public will be eased of a great part of the expense of the present judiciary establishment; for certainly such a host of judges, associate judges, presidents of circuits, clerks and criers of courts, as are at present supported at the public expense, will not then be necessary. There are, perhaps, more of them than there are criminals to try in the space of a year.

Arbitration will lessen the sphere of patronage, and it is not improbable that this was one of the private reasons for negativing the arbitration act; but public economy, and the convenience and ease of the individuals, ought to have outweighed all such considerations. The present Administration of the United States has struck off a long list of useless officers, and economized the public expenditure, and it is better to make a precedent of this, than to imitate its forms and long periods of election, which require reform themselves.

A great part of the people of Pennsylvania make a principle of not going to law, and others avoid it from prudential reasons; yet all those people are taxed to support a judiciary to which they never resort, which is as inconsistent and unjust as it is in England to make the Quakers pay tithes to support the Episcopal Church. Arbitration will put an end to this imposition.

Another complaint against the Constitution of Pennsylvania is the great quantity of patronage annexed to the office of governor.

Patronage has a natural tendency to increase the public expense by the temptation it leads to (unless in the hands of a wise man like Franklin) to multiply offices within the gift or appointment of that patronage. John Adams, in his Administration, went upon the plan of increasing offices and officers. He expected by thus increasing his patronage, and making numerous appointments, that he should attach a numerous train of adherents to him who would support his measures and his future election.

He copied this from the corrupt system of England; and he closed his midnight labours by appointing sixteen new unnecessary judges, at an expense to the public of $32,000 annually. John counted only on one side of the case. He forgot that where there was *one* man to be benefited by an appointment, all the rest had to pay the cost of it; and that by attaching *the one* to him by patronage, he ran the risk of losing *the many* by disgust. And such was the consequence; and such will ever be the consequence in a free country, where men reason *for* themselves and *from* themselves, and not from the dictates of others.

The less quantity of patronage a man is *incumbered* with the safer he stands. He cannot please everybody by the use of it; and he will have to refuse, and consequently to displease, a greater number than he can please. Mr Jefferson gained more friends by dismissing a long train of officers than John Adams did by appointing them. Like a wise man, Mr Jefferson dismantled himself of patronage.

The Constitution of New York, though like all the rest it has its defects, arising from want of experience in the representative system of government at the time it was formed, has provided much better in this case than the Constitution of Pennsylvania has done.

The appointments in New York are made by a *Council of Appointment*, composed of the Governor and a certain number of members of the Senate taken from different parts of the State. By this means they have among them a personal knowledge of whomsoever they appoint. The Governor has one vote, but no negative. I do not hear complaints of the abuse of this kind of patronage.

The Constitution of Pennsylvania, instead of being an improvement in the representative system of government, is a departure from the principles of it. It is a copy in miniature of the Government of England, established at the conquest of that country by William of Normandy. I have shown this in part in the case of the king's negative, and I shall show it more fully as I go on. This brings me to speak of the Senate.

The complaint respecting the Senate is the length of its duration, being four years. The sage Franklin has said, 'Where annual election ends, tyranny begins'; and no man was a better judge of human nature than Franklin, nor has any man in our time exceeded him in the principles of honour and honesty.

When a man ceases to be accountable to those who elected him, and with whose public affairs he is entrusted, he ceases to be their representative, and is put in a condition of being their despot. He becomes the representative of nobody but himself. *I am elected*, says he, *for four years; you cannot turn me out, neither am I responsible to you in the meantime. All that you have to do with me is to pay me.*

The conduct of the Pennsylvania Senate in 1800, respecting the choice of electors for the Presidency of the United States, shows the impropriety and danger of such an establishment. The manner of choosing electors ought to be fixed in the Constitution, and not be left to the caprice of contention. It is a matter equally as important, and concerns the rights and interests of the people as much as the election of members for the State Legislature, and in some instances much more.

By the conduct of the Senate at that time, the people were deprived of their right of suffrage, and the State lost its consequence in the Union. It had but one vote. The other fourteen were paired off by compromise – seven and seven. If the people had chosen the electors, which they had a right to do, for the electors were to represent *them* and not to represent the Senate, the State would have had fifteen votes which would have counted.

The Senate is an imitation of what is called the House of Lords in England, and which Chesterfield, who was a member of it, and therefore knew it, calls *'the Hospital of Incurables'*. The Senate in Pennsylvania is not quite a hospital of incurables, but it took almost four years to bring it to a *state of convalescence*.

Before we imitate anything, we ought to examine whether it be worth imitating, and had this been done by the Convention at that time, they would have seen that the model from which their mimic imitation was made, was no better than unprofitable and disgraceful lumber.

There was no such thing in England as what is called the House of Lords until the conquest of that country by the Normans, under William the Conqueror, and like the king's negative over the laws, it is a badge of disgrace upon the country; for it is the effect and evidence of its having been reduced to unconditional submission.

William, having made the conquest, dispossessed the owners of their lands, and divided those lands among the chiefs of the plundering army he brought with him, and from hence arose what is called the *House of Lords*. Daniel de Foe, in his historical satire entitled *The True-born Englishman*, has very concisely given the origin and character of this House, as follows:

> The great invading Norman let them know
> What conquerors, in after times, might do;
> To every musketeer he brought to town,
> He gave the lands that never were his own. –
> He cantoned out the country to his men,
> And every soldier was a denizen;
> No parliament his army could disband.
> He raised no money, for he paid in land;

The rascals, thus enriched, he called them *Lords*.
To please their upstart pride with new made words,
And Domesday Book his tyranny records;
Some show the sword, the bow, and some the spear,
Which their great ancestor, forsooth, did wear;
But who the hero was, no man can tell,
Whether a colonel or a corporal;
The silent record blushes to reveal
Their undescended dark original;
Great ancestors of yesterday they show,
And Lords whose fathers were – *the Lord knows who*?

This is the disgraceful origin of what is called the House of Lords in England, and it still retains some tokens of the plundering baseness of its origin. The swindler Dundas was lately made a lord, and is now called *noble lord*! Why do they not give him his proper title, and call him *noble swindler*, for he swindled by wholesale? But it is probable he will escape punishment; for Blackstone, in his commentary on the laws, recites an act of Parliament, passed in 1550, and not since repealed, that extends what is called the benefit of clergy, that is, exemption from punishment for all clerical offences, to all lords and peers of the realm who could not read, as well as those who could, and also for 'the crimes of *house-breaking, highway-robbing, horse-stealing and robbing of churches*'.

This is consistent with the original establishment of the House of Lords, for it was originally composed of robbers. This is aristocracy. This is one of the pillars of John Adams's 'stupendous fabric of human invention'. A privilege for house-breaking, highway-robbing, horse-stealing and robbing of churches! John Adams knew but little of the origin and practice of the Government of England. As to constitution, it has none.

The Pennsylvania Convention of 1776 copied nothing from the English Government. It formed a Constitution on the basis of honesty. The defect, as I have already said, of that Constitution was the precipitancy to which the legislatures might be subject in enacting laws. All the members of the Legislature established by that Constitution sat in one chamber and debated in one body, and this subjected them to precipitancy. This precipitancy was provided against, but not effectually.

The Constitution ordered that the laws, before being finally enacted, should be published for public consideration. But as no given time was fixed for that consideration, nor any means for collecting its effects, nor were there then any public newspapers in the State but what were printed in Philadelphia, the provision did not reach the intention of it, and thus a good and wise intention sank into mere form, which is generally the case when the means are not adequate to the end.

The ground-work, however, of that Constitution was good, and deserves to be resorted to. Everything that Franklin was concerned in producing merits attention. He was the wise and benevolent friend of man. Riches and honours made no alteration in his principles or his manners.

The Constitution of 1776 was conformable to the Declaration of Independence and the Declaration of Rights, which the present Constitution is not; for it makes artificial distinctions among men in the right of suffrage, which the principles of equity know nothing of; neither is it consistent with sound policy. We every day see the rich becoming poor, and those who were poor before, becoming rich. Riches, therefore, having no stability, cannot and ought not to be made a criterion of right. Man is man in every condition of life, and the varieties of fortune and misfortune are open to all.

Had the number of representatives in the Legislature established by that Constitution been increased, and instead of their sitting together in one chamber, and debating and voting all at one time, been divided by lot into two equal parts, and sat in separate chambers, the advantage would have been, that one-half, by not being entangled in the first debate, nor having committed itself by voting, would be silently possessed of the arguments, for and against, of the former part, and be in a calm condition to review the whole.

And instead of one chamber, or one house, or by whatever name they may be called, negativing the vote of the other, which is now the case, and which admits of inconsistencies even to absurdities, to have added the votes of both chambers together, and the majority of the whole to be the final decision – there would be reason in this, but there is none in the present mode. The instance that occurred in the Pennsylvania Senate, in the year 1800, on the bill for choosing electors, where a small majority in that House controlled and negatived a large majority in the other House, shows the absurdity of such a division of legislative power.

To know if any theory or position be true or rational in practice, the method is to carry it to its greatest extent; if it be not true upon the whole, or be absurd, it is so in all parts, however small. For instance, if one house consists of 200 members and the other 50, which is about the proportion they are in some of the States, and if a proposed law be carried on the affirmative in the larger house with only one dissenting voice, and be negatived in the smaller house by a majority of 1, the event will be that 27 control and govern 223, which is too absurd even for argument, and totally inconsistent with the principles of representative government, which know no difference in the value and importance of its members but what arises from their virtues and talents, and not at all from the name of the house or chamber they sit in.

As the practice of a smaller number negativing a greater is not founded in reason, we must look for its origin in some other cause.

The Americans have copied it from England, and it was brought into England by the Norman Conqueror, and is derived from the ancient French practice of voting by ORDERS, of which they counted three; *the Clergy* (that is, Roman Catholic clergy), the *Noblesse* (those who had titles), and the *Tiers État,* or Third Estate [3] which included all who were not of the two former orders, and which in England are called the *Commons* or *common people,* and the house in which they are represented is from thence called the *House of Commons.*

The case with the Conqueror was, in order to complete and secure the conquest he had made, and hold the country in subjection, he cantoned it out among the chiefs of his army, to whom he gave castles and whom he dubbed with the title of *Lords,* as is before shown. These being dependent on the Conqueror, and having a united interest with him became the defenders of his measures, and the guardians of his assumed prerogative against the people; and when the house called the *Common House of Parliament* began by grants and charters from the Conqueror and his successors, these lords, claiming to be a distinct ORDER from the Commons, though

3 The practice of voting by *orders* in France, whenever the States-General met, continued until the late Revolution. It was the present Abbé Sieyès who made the motion, in what was afterwards called the National Assembly, for abolishing the vote by *orders,* and established the rational practise of deciding by a majority of numbers. – Paine.

smaller in number, held a controlling or negative vote over them, and from hence arose the irrational practice of a smaller number negativing a greater.

But what are these things to us, or why should we imitate them? We have but one ORDER in America, and that of the highest degree, the ORDER OF SOVEREIGNTY, and of this ORDER every citizen is a member of his own personal right. Why then have we descended to the base imitation of inferior things? By the event of the Revolution we were put in a condition of thinking originally. The history of past ages shows scarcely anything to us but instances of tyranny and antiquated absurdities. We have copied some of them and experienced the folly of them. . . .

America has the high honour and happiness of being the first nation that gave to the world the example of forming written constitutions by conventions elected expressly for the purpose, and of improving them by the same procedure, as time and experience shall show necessary. Government in other nations, vainly calling themselves civilized, has been established by bloodshed. Not a drop of blood has been shed in the United States in consequence of establishing constitutions and governments by her own peaceful system. The silent vote, or the simple *yea* or *nay*, is more powerful than the bayonet, and decides the strength of numbers without a blow.

I have now, citizens of Pennsylvania, presented you, in good will, with a collection of thoughts and historical references, condensed into a small compass that they may circulate the more conveniently. They are applicable to the subject before you, that of calling a convention, in the progress and completion of which I wish you success and happiness, and the honour of showing a profitable example to the States around you and to the world.

Yours, in friendship,

NEW ROCHELLE, NY, August, 1805.   THOMAS PAINE.

FOR THE BEST IN PAPERBACKS, LOOK FOR THE

In every corner of the world, on every subject under the sun, Penguins represent quality and variety – the very best in publishing today.

For complete information about books available from Penguin and how to order them, write to us at the appropriate address below. Please note that for copyright reasons the selection of books varies from country to country.

In the United Kingdom: For a complete list of books available from Penguin in the U.K., please write to *Dept EP, Penguin Books Ltd, Harmondsworth, Middlesex, UB7 0DA*

In the United States: For a complete list of books available from Penguin in the U.S., please write to *Dept BA, Viking Penguin, 299 Murray Hill Parkway, East Rutherford, New Jersey 07073*

In Canada: For a complete list of books available from Penguin in Canada, please write to *Penguin Books Canada Limited, 2801 John Street, Markham, Ontario L3R 1B4*

In Australia: For a complete list of books available from Penguin in Australia, please write to the *Marketing Department, Penguin Books Australia Ltd, P.O. Box 257, Ringwood, Victoria 3134*

In New Zealand: For a complete list of books available from Penguin in New Zealand, please write to the *Marketing Department, Penguin Books (N.Z.) Ltd, Private Bag, Takapuna, Auckland 9*

In India: For a complete list of books available from Penguin in India, please write to *Penguin Overseas Ltd, 706 Eros Apartments, 56 Nehru Place, New Delhi 110019*

A CHOICE OF PENGUINS AND PELICANS

The Second World War (6 volumes)   Winston S. Churchill

The definitive history of the cataclysm which swept the world for the second time in thirty years.

1917: The Russian Revolutions and the Origins of Present-Day Communism
Leonard Schapiro

A superb narrative history of one of the greatest episodes in modern history by one of our greatest historians.

Imperial Spain 1496–1716   J. H. Elliot

A brilliant modern study of the sudden rise of a barren and isolated country to be the greatest power on earth, and of its equally sudden decline. 'Outstandingly good' – *Daily Telegraph*

Joan of Arc: The Image of Female Heroism   Marina Warner

'A profound book, about human history in general and the place of women in it' – Christopher Hill

Man and the Natural World: Changing Attitudes in England 1500–1800
Keith Thomas

'A delight to read and a pleasure to own' – Auberon Waugh in the *Sunday Telegraph*

The Making of the English Working Class   E. P. Thompson

Probably the most imaginative – and the most famous – post-war work of English social history.

A CHOICE OF PENGUINS AND PELICANS

The French Revolution   Christopher Hibbert

'One of the best accounts of the Revolution that I know . . . Mr Hibbert is outstanding' – J. H. Plumb in the *Sunday Telegraph*

The Germans   Gordon A. Craig

An intimate study of a complex and fascinating nation by 'one of the ablest and most distinguished American historians of modern Germany' – Hugh Trevor-Roper

Ireland: A Positive Proposal   Kevin Boyle and Tom Hadden

A timely and realistic book on Northern Ireland which explains the historical context – and offers a practical and coherent set of proposals which could actually work.

A History of Venice   John Julius Norwich

'Lord Norwich has loved and understood Venice as well as any other Englishman has ever done' – Peter Levi in the *Sunday Times*

Montaillou: Cathars and Catholics in a French Village 1294–1324   Emmanuel Le Roy Ladurie

'A classic adventure in eavesdropping across time' – Michael Ratcliffe in *The Times*

Star Wars   E. P. Thompson and others

Is Star Wars a serious defence strategy or just a science fiction fantasy? This major book sets out all the arguments and makes an unanswerable case *against* Star Wars.

The Apartheid Handbook Roger Omond

This book provides the essential hard information about how apartheid actually works from day to day and fills in the details behind the headlines.

The World Turned Upside Down Christopher Hill

This classic study of radical ideas during the English Revolution 'will stand as a notable monument to . . . one of the finest historians of the present age' – *The Times Literary Supplement*

Islam in the World Malise Ruthven

'His exposition of "the Qurenic world view" is the most convincing, and the most appealing, that I have read' – Edward Mortimer in *The Times*

The Knight, the Lady and the Priest Georges Duby

'A very fine book' (Philippe Aries) that traces back to its medieval origin one of our most important institutions, modern marriage.

A Social History of England New Edition Asa Briggs

'A treasure house of scholarly knowledge . . . beautifully written and full of the author's love of his country, its people and its landscape' – John Keegan in the *Sunday Times*, Books of the Year

The Second World War A. J. P. Taylor

A brilliant and detailed illustrated history, enlivened by all Professor Taylor's customary iconoclasm and wit.

A CHOICE OF PENGUINS AND PELICANS

Adieux Simone de Beauvoir

This 'farewell to Sartre' by his life-long companion is a 'true labour of love' (the *Listener*) and 'an extraordinary achievement' (*New Statesman*).

British Society 1914–45 John Stevenson

A major contribution to the Pelican Social History of Britain, which 'will undoubtedly be the standard work for students of modern Britain for many years to come' – *The Times Educational Supplement*

The Pelican History of Greek Literature Peter Levi

A remarkable survey covering all the major writers from Homer to Plutarch, with brilliant translations by the author, one of the leading poets of today.

Art and Literature Sigmund Freud

Volume 14 of the Pelican Freud Library contains Freud's major essays on Leonardo, Michelangelo and Dostoevsky, plus shorter pieces on Shakespeare, the nature of creativity and much more.

A History of the Crusades Sir Steven Runciman

This three-volume history of the events which transferred world power to Western Europe – and founded Modern History – has been universally acclaimed as a masterpiece.

A Night to Remember Walter Lord

The classic account of the sinking of the *Titanic*. 'A stunning book, incomparably the best on its subject and one of the most exciting books of this or any year' – *The New York Times*

PENGUIN CLASSICS

Netochka Nezvanova Fyodor Dostoyevsky

Dostoyevsky's first book tells the story of 'Nameless Nobody' and introduces many of the themes and issues which will dominate his great masterpieces.

Selections from the Carmina Burana A verse translation by David Parlett

The famous songs from the *Carmina Burana* (made into an oratorio by Carl Orff) tell of lecherous monks and corrupt clerics, drinkers and gamblers, and the fleeting pleasures of youth.

Fear and Trembling Søren Kierkegaard

A profound meditation on the nature of faith and submission to God's will which examines with startling originality the story of Abraham and Isaac.

Selected Prose Charles Lamb

Lamb's famous essays (under the strange pseudonym of Elia) on anything and everything have long been celebrated for their apparently innocent charm; this major new edition allows readers to discover the darker and more interesting aspects of Lamb.

The Picture of Dorian Gray Oscar Wilde

Wilde's superb and macabre novella, one of his supreme works, is reprinted here with a masterly Introduction and valuable Notes by Peter Ackroyd.

A Treatise of Human Nature David Hume

A universally acknowledged masterpiece by 'the greatest of all British Philosophers' – A. J. Ayer

PENGUIN CLASSICS

A Passage to India   E. M. Forster

Centred on the unresolved mystery in the Marabar Caves, Forster's great work provides the definitive evocation of the British Raj.

The Republic   Plato

The best-known of Plato's dialogues, *The Republic* is also one of the supreme masterpieces of Western philosophy whose influence cannot be overestimated.

The Life of Johnson   James Boswell

Perhaps the finest 'life' ever written, Boswell's *Johnson* captures for all time one of the most colourful and talented figures in English literary history.

Remembrance of Things Past (3 volumes)   Marcel Proust

This revised version by Terence Kilmartin of C. K. Scott Moncrieff's original translation has been universally acclaimed – available for the first time in paperback.

Metamorphoses   Ovid

A golden treasury of myths and legends which has proved a major influence on Western literature.

A Nietzsche Reader   Friedrich Nietzsche

A superb selection from all the major works of one of the greatest thinkers and writers in world literature, translated into clear, modern English.

PENGUIN CLASSICS

Horatio Alger, Jr.	**Ragged Dick** and **Struggling Upward**
Phineas T. Barnum	**Struggles and Triumphs**
Ambrose Bierce	**The Enlarged Devil's Dictionary**
Kate Chopin	**The Awakening and Selected Stories**
Stephen Crane	**The Red Badge of Courage**
Richard Henry Dana, Jr.	**Two Years Before the Mast**
Frederick Douglass	**Narrative of the Life of Frederick Douglass, An American Slave**
Theodore Dreiser	**Sister Carrie**
Ralph Waldo Emerson	**Selected Essays**
Joel Chandler Harris	**Uncle Remus**
Nathaniel Hawthorne	**Blithedale Romance**
	The House of the Seven Gables
	The Scarlet Letter and Selected Tales
William Dean Howells	**The Rise of Silas Lapham**
Alice James	**The Diary of Alice James**
William James	**Varieties of Religious Experience**
Jack London	**The Call of the Wild and Other Stories**
	Martin Eden
Herman Melville	**Billy Budd, Sailor and Other Stories**
	Moby-Dick
	Redburn
	Typee
Frank Norris	**McTeague**
Thomas Paine	**Common Sense**
Edgar Allan Poe	**The Narrative of Arthur Gordon Pym of Nantucket**
	The Other Poe
	The Science Fiction of Edgar Allan Poe
	Selected Writings
Harriet Beecher Stowe	**Uncle Tom's Cabin**
Henry David Thoreau	**Walden** and **Civil Disobedience**
Mark Twain	**The Adventures of Huckleberry Finn**
	A Connecticut Yankee at King Arthur's Court
	Life on the Mississippi
	Pudd'nhead Wilson
	Roughing It
Edith Wharton	**The House of Mirth**